Administration in the
Public Interest

Administration in the Public Interest

Principles, Policies, and Practices

Stephen M. King

Bradley S. Chilton

CAROLINA ACADEMIC PRESS
Durham, North Carolina

Library of Congress Cataloging-in-Publication Data

King, Stephen M. Ph. D.
  Administration in the public interest : principles, policies and practices / Stephen M. King, Bradley S. Chilton.
      p. cm.
  Includes bibliographical references and index.
  ISBN 978-1-59460-667-0 (alk. paper)
  1. Public administration. 2. Public interest. I. Chilton, Bradley Stewart, 1955- II. Title.

  JF1351.K493 2009
  351--dc22

                                    2009002991

CAROLINA ACADEMIC PRESS
700 Kent Street
Durham, North Carolina 27701
Telephone (919) 489-7486
Fax (919) 493-5668
www.cap-press.com

For Debbie, Michelle, Joshua, and "Dakota" (our pet Schnauzer).
SMK

For the Next Christendom.
BSC

Summary Table of Contents

Contents

Part III
Lessons of Administration in the Public Interest

Preface

Welcome to our survey of public administration! Whether you are looking for a basic overview of public administration—or an in-depth analysis of the concept of the public interest—we believe you will find this text useful. We hope you find it a more *readable* examination of public administration. We believe it is also more *teachable* for instructors, too! We have taught public administration for many years. More and more students study public administration for understanding federal, state and local bureaucracy, for their personal career management in public service, as well as for studies in criminal justice, social work, and other closely-related areas. Yet, nearly all public administration texts seem to be written in cryptic, professional jargon—the language of *bureaucratese*. And few include an in-depth look at the reality of non-profit organizations or faith-based initiatives in public administration.

This book includes all the usual concepts, persons, histories, typologies, and chapter topics found in most public administration texts. Instead of civil service preparation; however, we thought you might instead enjoy a current-issues tour of conflicting values in public administration, such as constitutional rights, utilitarianism, and leadership. Our tour includes more specifics and interaction on nonprofits, faith-based initiatives, and private groups in public administration. Further, we weave it all together around a theme of the public interest. We believe in a commonsense understanding of public administration that is all about the public interest, the commons, and so forth—and we promise to be honest and drop the facade of pseudo-scientists in these pages. Each chapter relates concepts of public administration with action steps for things to do in your local setting, boxed inserts on interesting persons and events, exam preparation guide (someone will have to take a test somewhere!), recommended readings, and web sites.

We assume a post-positivist world in which the public interest is ordinary, common, meaningful, and central to any understanding of the activities of public administration. Those on a quest for a "value-free" public administration will find no refuge in these pages. We appreciate a philosophy of science beyond Nietzsche and logical positivism; we instead prefer a commonsense study of how things work, ordinary talk, and the experiences of real people. We prize a century of science history that debunks hypothesis-testing models of science; we favor more radically-empirical models of science such as grounded theory, the trash-can model, and other honest science. We seek a systematic understanding of administration in the public interest, such as described in the actual experiences of bureaucrats, officials, citizens and other real-world people—not by some hidden logic in the towers of academe. Scholars should have some acquaintance with these ideas, but many have not been exposed to the humbling feeling you get when you grasp the history and philosophy of science and realize just how little we know. And others have sold their souls for money or status in a brave new world. We have written this book without assuming your knowledge on these issues, but we will still re-visit and discuss these ideas periodically.

The public interest is just right as a concept for a better understanding of public administration—not too hard, not too soft. We are not like many contemporary secular cynics who discard the public interest as literal nonsense because its existence cannot be proven with any of the five senses—and similarly throw out other valued concepts like God, love, justice, and hope. We believe these cynics throw out the proverbial "baby with the bathwater;" in their hard-nosed pursuit of scientific truth, they betray the very empirical principles of science they supposedly uphold. When we take a radically empirical approach to the public interest, we find it within ordinary experiences, commonly shared meanings, and practical outcomes. But neither are we like scholastics that would prove the existence of the public interest by some elevated logic. Instead, we find the public interest to be written on the heart, a pattern of decision-making by good public administrators which belies the praxis of actions, rules, and being. Our perspective comes out of an appreciation which seems ascendant today—from religion to ethics to politics to science. Like so many of the important meanings of life, we find the public interest to be heartfelt and understood in context. We hope you may share this sense with this book in which we seek to present a more systematic, yet realistic, understanding of administration in the public interest.

We write this book with hope for a new generation of students of public administration. The discipline seems more balkanized than ever before. Our scholarly generation seems to have pushed away perspectives in the field such as the study of public choice, nonprofits, faith-based organizations, criminal justice, education, health policy, and other areas, and embraced positivist, post-modern, and multi-cultural issues and topics, that really hold little if any relevance to the real world of public administration and public administrators engaged in the pursuit of the public interest.

Further, many scholars have left public administration for the attraction of greater freedom and prosperity in schools of business administration or other academic stations. For whatever reasons, we believe public administration is the poorer for it, both in numbers and ideas. But we are encouraged by many young scholars who seek to reintegrate these disparate perspectives and policy topics with traditional public administration approaches—often assembled around a broader conception of the public interest as we present in this book. To this future hope, we offer *ADMINISTRATION IN THE PUBLIC INTEREST: PRINCIPLES, POLICIES, AND PRACTICES.*

The text is divided into three parts. PART ONE introduces the conceptual, historical, constitutional, legal, and local framework, or the **foundations** of administration in the public interest. We discuss the public interest within contemporary and historical public administration and three perspectives on the nature of the public interest: practices, principles, and policies. The practices approach to the public interest focuses on life-world and leadership experiences in public administration and attends to the ethical theory of virtue. The principles approach to the public interest focuses on duties and rules, such as the Constitution and laws within public administration, and attends to the ethical theory of deontology. The policies approach to the public interest focuses on the calculation of happiness, individual preferences, or benefits/costs within public administration, attending to the ethical theory of utilitarianism. A highlight is our focus on state and local levels of public administration and a stand-alone chapter on federalism, states and communities, as well as the usual national level examples.

PART TWO is an examination of the core functions of public administration and the role of the public interest with each, or the **applications** of administration in the public interest. The core functions include getting organized, in theory and in-fact, and pursuit of the public interest through closed and open systems, in public and in private organizations. The core function of public management focuses on the entrepreneurial approaches and strategies of the New Public Service, and pursuit of the public interest through strategic planning and various leadership styles. Public personnel management attends to historical and current recruitment and human resources development in the public workplace, and pursuit of the public interest in issues such as whistle-blowing and loyalty, unions/collective bargaining, and affirmative action. Public budgeting and finance focuses on a pursuit of the public interest by the utilitarian calculations of economic benefit/costs analyses in these historical and current tax-finance and budgetary politics at the local, state, and federal levels. Our examination of public policy processes and analysis include a variety of public interest approaches in the study of policy-makers, policy-influencers, and the action procedures and investigative and evaluative methods of assessing public policies. And we include the core function of nonprofits and faith-based organizations, examining the history, public interest applications, and ascendance of the voluntary sector.

PART THREE brings together our findings on the public interest theme throughout the chapters with a future hope for public administration, or the **lessons** of administration in the public interest. Our analysis of administrative ethics applies public interest findings throughout the book to basic definitions and systems of philosophical ethics, including utilitarianism, deontology, and virtue ethics. We critique four dominant approaches to administrative ethics, including Terry Cooper's rational-comprehensive model, John Rawls' justice as fairness model, John Rohr's constitutional regime values, and the approach of religion and spirituality in the workplace. We apply lessons of the public interest to current concerns with administrative accountability, professionalism, ethics codes, and efforts to control or elicit ethical administrative behavior. Finally, we conclude with a future hope, embedded in trends such as information technology and administrative ethics, to anticipate a truly public aspiration of administration in the public interest.

Acknowledgments

It is not possible to name all the persons—our faculty and mentors, colleagues, students, friends, and family—who have directly or indirectly contributed to the development of this book. It would require many more pages, and even then we may miss someone. Please know that you are all dearly appreciated—and you know who you are! We give special thanks to the support of chairpersons and administrators at our various academic stations that have supported this project, including Appalachian State University, Campbell University, Patrick Henry College, Regent University, and the University of North Texas. We appreciate this publication birthing by Keith Sipe, Publisher at Carolina Academic Press. We also give thanks to folks at Wadsworth Publishing Company, such as Editor-in-chief Michael Rosenberg, Editor Laurie Runion, and others who solicited this book, encouraged us with its potential, and sent us with good graces to Carolina Academic Press. And we are especially appreciative to the many anonymous outside reviewers who carefully read, gave insightful constructive criticism, and followed through with directions needed.

The intellectual and spiritual heart of this book came from the decades of dialog and friendship since we were young newbie junior faculty together in the Department of Political Science/Criminal Justice at Washington State University-Pullman. It was a time of intense debate over ideas, earnest aspirations for our shared discipline of public administration, and often laughter—at ourselves and our limitations, as well as at the comedy of our times. We sought to articulate a new perspective on life, spirituality, and even public administration that reflected the ascendance of the next global Christendom that we felt a part of—in which we remember the pools of transcendence. After the decades and many explorations of diverse academic stations, we now come together to express some small portion of that vision. We may not have written it all down in these pages, but we stand in responsibility for this book.

Part I

Foundations of Administration in the Public Interest

PART ONE introduces the conceptual, historical, constitutional, legal, and local framework, or the **foundations** of administration in the public interest. We discuss the public interest within contemporary and historical public administration and three perspectives on the nature of the public interest: practices, principles, and policies. The practices approach to the public interest focuses on life-world and leadership experiences in public administration and attends to the ethical theory of virtue. The principles approach to the public interest focuses on duties and rules, such as the Constitution and laws within public administration, and attends to the ethical theory of deontology. The policies approach to the public interest focuses on the calculation of happiness, individual preferences, or benefits/costs within public administration, attending to the ethical theory of utilitarianism. A highlight is our focus on state and local levels of public administration and a stand-alone chapter on federalism, states and communities, as well as the usual national level examples.

Chapter 1

Administration in the Public Interest

"Let each of you look not to your own interests, but to the interests of others."

Philippians 2:4 (NRSV)

"Public administrators are often put in ethically compromising situations where they must consider several questions about dutifully carrying out their jobs. Whom do I serve? Must I uphold the Constitution and the law of the land at all times? Will this action serve the public good? What is the public good? Can I carry out this duty even if it is against my moral beliefs?"

Brian Fabian, "A Public Administration Perspective on Physician Assisted Suicide," *PA Times* (February 2005): 15–16.

Chapter Objectives

Upon completion of this chapter you should be able to:

1. Overview the concept of "bureaupathology" and the basic critique of public administration in Franz Kafka's, *The Trial*;
2. Grasp the importance and application of the concept of the public interest as a ethical response to "bureaupathology" and the critique of public administration;
3. Distinguish between Principles, Policies, and Practices approaches to the public interest, that attend to Deontological, Utilitarian, and Virtue ethical theories, respectively;
4. Understand the nature of public administration and the value of promoting the public interest.

Do you remember what it was like in America in the weeks after the tragic terrorism events of September 11, 2001? Do you remember how everyone came to one another and tried to work together, Republican and Democrat, liberal and conservative, right and left? Do you remember your feelings in seeing people working together in unity who were former bickering political enemies? Or perhaps you remember better the efforts of police, firefighters, and many others who rescued flooded families in New Orleans after Hurricane Katrina. Or the helicopter pilots who searched for, dropped food and blankets, and retrieved stranded cars of people after the 2006 snow blizzards of Colorado? Or maybe you've seen these united, exhausted but heroic public servants on the streets where you live after that tornado, flood, earthquake, or other massive tragedy? Do you remember how people tried to see the other person as a fellow American rather than a competitor in the game of life, or someone who is different in race or ethnicity, or an obstruction to their will to power?

If you remember these moments, the moments of public service after a crisis or tragedy, you remembered **administration in the public interest**. For it is in such moments that good people escape the overwhelming emphasis of contemporary American culture that focuses on looking out for number one. It is after times of great tragedy that we remember other lessons of our youth—lessons of empathy, goodwill toward others, and caring for one another. It is in these moments that we often witness the best in ourselves and within one another. Why can't we have administration in the public interest the whole year around?

We seek to understand what it would be like if public servants in America made everyday an event into which they poured their best, like so may did in those weeks after 9/11. And like so many others who picked up the pieces and got things back together after tragedies near and far. What would it be like to have administration in the public interest the whole year around?

So, What's Wrong with Real Bureaucracy?

However, most of us don't see such a beautiful bureaucracy in our day-to-day world. So, what's the deal with the real bureaucracy we see today on the television, down at city hall, or at the university? Why do we wring our hands at the very thought of going down to the state DMV office? Why do we cringe at the mention of "bureaucracy?" So, what's wrong with "real" bureaucracy?

Some scholars have thought long and hard about what's wrong with bureaucracy. You know scholars, always thinking it out; the wringing of hands isn't enough! Over the years, scholars have developed a list of things that are wrong with bureaucracy; they call them **bureaupathologies**.[1] They are often tongue-in-cheek and describe in jest those things that are too much to deal with in complete seriousness. After all, most of us (including you the reader) are doomed to spend the rest of our lives in a bureaucracy somewhere, living out the story line in some *Dilbert* comic strip. So, what are some examples of bureaupathologies?

- **Gresham's Law**: bureaucratic routines drive out creativity and fill all available time, e.g., the patrol beat designed for Officer Sue requires specific streets and miles to be covered in one shift so that she doesn't have the time to use her experience to better patrol crime hot spots or usual criminal targets;
- **Mile's Law**: bureaucrats tend to adopt the organization's norms as their personal norms, e.g., First-grade teacher Dan spends so much time on lesson plans and creating new activities for his students that his own kids and wife complain he no longer has time for them;
- **Parkinson's Law**: bureaucracies grow 5–6 percent per year regardless of their [in]efficiency, e.g., the city building inspection department continues to request an annual budget increase at city hall even though new housing and building starts have been down for years;
- **The Peter Principle**: bureaucrats are eventually promoted up to their level of incompetence, e.g., Warden Les is promoted to Director of the computer records division of the state corrections department even though she is computer-phobic and knows little about computers or software designs for collecting data;
- **Authority Leakage (Anthony Downs)**: orders lose their authority and "distort" as they filter down; e.g., Mayor Fred's budget-cutting ban on all long-distance calls by city agencies is taken to mean "no more personal long-distance calls on the city" by prosecutors in the municipal court;

- **Centralized policymaking**: organizations tend to decentralize the work and blame, while centralizing policymaking, e.g., professor Dave at Struggling College must now help process student admissions and financial aid applications, but President Jane determines all policies on who gets admitted and who gets financial aid;
- **Goal Displacement (Richard Merton)**: as organizations mature, the main goal(s) will be marginalized, e.g., Big State Reformatory was established for the rehabilitation and restoration of juvenile offenders, but is now overcrowded, all jobs-training programs cut, with new medium-security fencing and guard towers in place;
- **Iron Law of Oligarchy (Robert Michaels)**: all organizations tend to evolve into oligarchies over time, e.g., the county Information Technology Office confiscates Department of Streets Director Rock's APPLE computer and mandates that he must use a computer exclusively built and maintained by their office;
- **Quantification & Value Reduction**: bureaucrats tend to reduce the tragedy by quantifying it, e.g., in the first year after Hurricane Katrina, FEMA spends more manhours determining the costs, pollution counts, and contracting with providers for temporary housing than in the delivery of mobile homes to victims.

We think you get the picture!

The Trial is a much more hilarious, yet systematic and highly acclaimed novel on the pathology of bureaucracy written by **Franz Kafka** (1883–1924). His comical depictions of administrative failings in the contemporary world are so popular that we label as "Kafkaesque" the bureaucratic bungling by FEMA after Hurricane Katrina, or our vandalized criminal justice system.[2]

Kafka was born on July 3, 1883, in Prague, Czechoslovakia, the eldest son to Herman and Julie (Lowry) Kafka, who owned a lucrative haberdashery business. His mother was from a wealthy Orthodox Jewish family in Germany, his father of a-religious German Jews, who had worked his way up from butcher's delivery boy to independent businessman. Franz was his mother's boy and resented his strong-willed father as a tyrant, yet always sought his father's approval. Raised by a governess in a lonely, privileged childhood in Prague, Franz was not accepted by Czechs (as a German), nor by other Germans (as a Jew), nor by Jewish society (his father was an atheist). Franz graduated from German University in 1906 with a Juris Doctor (JD) degree and completed a legal internship. Franz fell in love with Felice Bauer from Berlin, the relative of his long-time friend Max Brod, and they were engaged twice but never married. He worked in the Worker's Accident Insurance Institute in Prague from 1908 until 1922, when his tuberculosis became too painful and he spent the remainder of his life in a sanatorium. Diagnosed with tuberculosis in 1917, he died on June 3, 1924, just shy of 41.[3]

Like his alienated and disenfranchised life, Franz's writings were comically original and profoundly moral in tone, centrally concerned with the essential loneliness of modern life within large-scale organizations in the struggle to comprehend an incomprehensible world. *The Trial* was published posthumously by Franz's long-term and best friend, Max Brod. As the literary executor to Kafka's will, Max Brod was instructed to destroy this unfinished manuscript. But Brod was completely taken by *The Trial*; when Kafka had first read the first unfinished chapter of *The Trial* to a group of friends; they had all laughed riotously (including Kafka). So, Brod assembled the manuscript and had it published—to become a literary classic.

The Trial is a surreal, nightmarish story of alienation featuring Joseph K., a respectable banker accused of an unnamed crime who must spend the remainder of his life fighting an incomprehensible justice system. The Trial features other bureaupathologies, such as the punishment seeks the offense (the accused must find their offense), culpabilization (incomprehensibility leads to acceptance of the blame), boundless labyrinths (talking without ever getting anywhere), power deifies itself (bureaucrats aren't real but merely shadows of the bureau file), and comic conclusions in which everything is destroyed in the end.[4]

Basically, if we were to sum up the bureaupathologies, it may boil down to one common gripe: bureaucrats just don't LISTEN! Oh, sure, maybe they did when they were young and bright-eyed and bushy-tailed newbies, but one or another of these bureaupathologies has infected them and the ability to listen was ground out of them the way a millstone grinds flour-dust out of wheat-stalks. Medical pathologists suggest that this may be true of all pathologies; for example, Alzheimers disease causes what we call senility when, over the decades, brain cells excessively insulate themselves with thicker and thicker cell walls and get cut off from neurochemical messages and nutrients.[5] They just stop listening! And so it will be (or already has been?) with all of us. What tragedy! If only there were some ways of shaking off these bureaupathologies! If only we could make bureaucrats listen!

The bureaupathologies of public life may be due to a modern cynical attitude in which we have reduced all value statements to nonsense and alienated ourselves from one another. We stop listening to one another when we believe all normative statements are merely the will to power and that there is no common ground on which to discourse. This attends to **ethical egoism** which argues that the only valid moral standard is the obligation to promote your own well-being above all others. It is the morality of always looking out for number one. Ethical egoism as a normative theory advocates selfishness in all moral activity, and cynically asserts that all other moral talk is merely the will to power.

Ethical egoism asserts that no matter what people may argue, they are really acting for the sake of their personal well-being only. For example, radicals in the 1960s, such Huey Newton and Bobby Seale of the Black Panthers or Bill Ayers of the Weather Underground claimed that even when interest groups brought new voices and ideas to the public forum, the decisions and actions by policy makers continued to reflect old status quo notions, thus shutting out the minority voices. Further, critics argued, policy makers duped the American public by depicting their decisions as the operation of a market place exchange of private interests.[6]

Behind the facade of pseudo-science was the operation of a will to power and rhetorical ploys to advance the status quo or private interests of political elites.[7] Critics argued this was no different than Nazi Germany of WWII, who made the **will-to-power** philosophy and Friedrich Nietzsche the official philosopher of the Third Reich. It is argued the Nazis employed a façade of pseudo-science and a depiction of laws as the operation of a market place exchange of private interests to advocate and justify holocaust of the Jews. If all the value statements in public life were mere rhetoric and will to power, what would stop this horrible scenario from happening again? It was of Friedrich Nietzsche's will-to-power theories of ethical egoism, and the influence on leaders such as Hitler, Freud, and many others, that John Maynard Keynes wrote: "The ideas of economists and political philosophers, both when they are right and when they are wrong, are more powerful than is commonly understood. Indeed the world is ruled by little else. Madmen in authority, who hear voices in the air, are distilling their frenzy from some academic scribbler of a few years back."[8]

Even more despairing may be bureaupathologies triggered by the related attitude of **moral relativism**, the perspective that all normative values and moral beliefs are relative to an individual or culture. We stop listening when we believe that basic value judgments of different individuals (Osama bin Laden) or cultures (radical Islam) are so different and conflicting that no one's values apply to the conduct of others. In its extreme and most cynical form, moral relativism casts aside all value statements, including ethics, the public interest, even ethical egoism, as complete nonsense—and closes the mind to the possibility of dialog and meaningful exchange of ideas.[9] However, even if moral standards are not 100 percent absolute across all cultures all the time does not mean there are no moral standards at all; moral standards do not have to be absolute in human reality in order to exist.[10] They only have to be perceived as such.

However, close study reveals empirical patterns of **moral development** in all individuals, genders, and across cultures throughout the world—even among public administrators.[11] Building on the pragmatism of John Dewey and cognitive development theory of Jean Piaget, **Lawrence Kohlberg** (1927–1987), who taught at both the University of Chicago and Harvard, found that we learn basic approaches to moral judgment through patterns of cognitive structure, debunking the cynicism of moral relativists and ethical egoists. Kohlberg and many others empirically verified how people learn these basic moral development stages in tens of thousands of case studies of individuals across over 50 countries, females and males, and by other differences. Echoing the ancient account of ethical theories by **Plato** (424–357 BCE), Kohlberg found that people learn by stages of Pre-conventional moral judgment (based on obedience, punishment, and self-interest), Conventional moral judgment (based on interpersonal accord, conformity, and law), and Post-conventional moral judgment (based on a social contract and universal ethical principles).[12]

While most people progressed through these moral development stages from childhood through adulthood, Kohlberg found there was **moral stage regression** among many adults due to inadequate integration of a stage or other in their cognitive development.[13] Bureaupathologies may be attributed to the regression of individuals to a moral stage focus on authoritarianism, moral relativism, or a law and order orientation. Thus, bureaupathologies may crop out after a time of individual tragedy, physical or mental struggle, or intense narcissism and self-focused behavior. When bad things happen to people in public service—such as with some New Orleans police officers, who either vacated their duty, or beat innocent citizens senseless during what should have been routine stops, during the mayhem that followed devastation of Hurricane Katrina—individuals may regress and act-out with behaviors that are NOT in the public interest.[14] Can we help these individuals and avoid the cycle of scandal that often accompanies these melt-downs at the workplace?

The Cycle of Scandal

Public scandals have been the fodder for the sale of newspapers, TV time, even webspace for so long that we have come to call it "yellow journalism." Corruption, sex, abuse of power and other vices of individuals in the public service are regularly paraded on display by the media to excite, titillate, and outrage the consumer. And destroy careers. You've seen it, for example, the public school teacher who had sex with a student, the cop who took a bribe to ignore the drug dealer, the city manager who had a street crew blacktop his driveway for free, or even the Senator from up north who was convicted on seven counts of corruption charges. We talk about the "cycle of scandal" because it never seems to go away. A scandal seems to keep dredging up over and over again to brand individuals, groups, or organizations who can never escape a mark of shame.[15]

The real reason public administrators may have for paying attention to the public interest and administrative ethics may be to avoid the cycle of scandal. For if one can predict and control the patterns of moral judgment within individuals—and moral stage regression and melt-downs—then one may avoid the cycle of public scandal. And from the research by Kohlberg and others, we have begun to see that a tendency to ethical egoism and relativism may predict the likelihood of moral stage regression. The more aggressive a public servant advocates their personal career above the public interest, the more likely and more often they may be accused or convicted in a public scandal. So, we may study the pathology of ethical egoism and relativism to root out the individual who is a likely candidate for moral stage regression to authoritarianism and so forth. We can become "pathologists" of bureaupathology to predict and control these dysfunctions.

But is there a more pro-active approach to avoid bureaupathologies and help individuals to avoid moral stage regression? Rather than simply getting by from day-to-day, hoping to avoid a public scandal, can we take a more positive approach to public service and aspire to greatness? We certainly can: and that approach is "the public interest" response!

The Public Interest Response

Taylor Branch, a Pulitzer Prize winning author (and M.P.A. student), once observed that public service can be divided into two categories: "deliver the mail" and **Holy Grail**." Public service at times involves performing neutral, mechanical, logistical duties (i.e., deliver the mail). However, Branch argued, even these activities are part of a larger context that always begs the big question and pursuit of the mandate to realize some "grand, moral civilizing goal" (i.e., the "Holy Grail"), such as the civil duty forthcoming of President-Elect Obama's economic team to counter the negative effects of the financial meltdown and economic recession.[16] The introductory quote at the very beginning of the chapter helps introduce our public interest response to bureaupathology and modern public failures. The public interest response is the return to aspiration in public service by asking the big "Holy Grail" question of public administrators at every point in the process: what is the public interest? For example, what is the public interest of pursuing and administering a "New New Deal?" Of course, there may be several roles and functions of public administrators in aspiration of the Holy Grail precept of the public interest, e.g., upholding the law, following a society-wide benefit-cost analysis, pursuing the common-weal, achieving excellence, and so forth.

The public interest is an age-old and accessible way to conceptualize the knotty problems of ethics and values in public life. **Ethics** is the highly developed philosophical study of morals touching upon all aspects of human values, not just public affairs. The academic discipline of ethics has highly nuanced theories from over 2400 years, at least 300 canonical names in ethical philosophy, and parry and thrust arguments that are not so simple to master and cannot be easily summarized in a paragraph or even an entire book. It would be disingenuous of us to pretend to survey and adequately discuss all the myriad aspects of ethics in this single survey textbook, even if we limited ourselves to public administration issues alone. However, the public interest has been a useful concept of **applied ethics** for millenniums in a more focused dialog about the morality of public life. The public interest concept does not require that we unpack all of ethics for our discussion. So, instead of engaging in an ethical academic marathon of sorts, we present this critique of bureaupathology and of public administration from the familiar, applied ethics concept of the public interest.

We disagree with contemporary cynics who discard the public interest as literal nonsense because its existence cannot be proven with any of the five senses—just as they throw out other valued concepts like God, love, justice, and hope. These cynics throw out the baby with the bathwater; in their hard-nosed pursuit of scientific truth, they betray the very scientific principles of empiricism they suppose. We argue that when you get radically empirical and follow people around, you find the public interest within ordinary experiences, commonly shared meanings, and practical outcomes. No, we're not trying to prove the existence of the public interest by some elevated logic or scholasticism. Instead, we find the public interest to be written on the heart, a pattern of intuitive deci-sion-making by good public administrators which belies the praxis of actions, rules, and being. Like so many of the important meanings in our lives, we find the public interest is heart-felt and understood in context.

We contend the most basic responsibility, moral duty, and aspiration of the public ad-ministrator is to pursue fulfillment of the **public interest**.[17] So—what is the public interest? Is there even such a thing as the public interest? Philosophically and normatively, of course, this would beg the additional question: Is there a public? If we have to ask this ques-tion—is there such a thing as the public interest?—then we are essentially questioning the framework of democracy that there may not even be such a thing as public; at least not the public interest. Oh, there might be many publics, such as clientele groups (the poor, the wealthy, and so forth), bureaucratic organizations and departments (Department of Homeland Security and the North Carolina Department of Revenue), interest groups (National Right to Life and Sierra Club, respectively), institutions (Congress, Presidency, Supreme Court), public officials (mayors, city councilpersons, city managers), neigh-borhood councils, citizen groups that may be categorized by race, ethnicity, gender, re-ligion, sexual orientation, disability, and so forth.

Is each of these entities a specific public, each with individual agendas, plans, and pur-poses? Or are they all part of one large public, unified by common values and characteris-tics? And even if the second question is answered affirmatively, then, legitimately, one might ask an additional question: what common values and characteristics exist? Do these values and characteristics apply to everyone at all times in the same way? And if this is true, then doesn't this mean that public administrators simply become automatons, not drawing upon discretion or intuition, but simply facilitators of sorts, lining up all of these values and characteristics according to some pre-defined measure of importance, such as utilitarian ben-efit-cost analysis or performance measurement, and then make the required decision?

This seems all rather complicated, and thus to make some sense out of these ques-tions—and perhaps even provide an answer or two ourselves—it is necessary for us to provide a brief historical and philosophical background of the concept the public inter-est, including accepted working definitions, characteristics, and typologies of the public interest, and then provide analysis of the phrase, including characteristics, definition, ex-planation, and application to public administration.

Box 1.1   Norton E. Long's 1991 John Gaus Lecture: Addressing the Importance of the "Public Interest"

In his 1991 John Gaus Lecture: "Politics, Political Science and the Public Inter-est," Norton E. Long assessed the influence of the public interest, particularly as it was reflected in politics, and, unlike many of his political science and public administration contemporaries, such as Pendleton Herring, Glendon Schubert and Frank Sorauf, Long did find normative meaning in the term, even high-lighting the work of philosopher Richard Flathman. We quote at some length a portion of Long's lecture, which raises several interesting questions regarding the importance of the "public interest."

"It is now over fifty years since Pendleton Herring wrote his *Public Administra-tion and the Public Interest* and the subject remains largely where he left it. In the post war years Glendon Schubert examined the various theories of the pub-lic interest and found them empty. Frank Sorauf conceded some value to the notion as a "kind of hair shirt." More recently Richard Flathman has attempted to rehabilitate the concept ... as an evaluatory expression whose justification can be argued by giving persuasive reasons for its use. However Flathman's efforts seem to have provoked but a modest response. This is a pity since a normative structure for the study and practice of politics would seem to be of the greatest importance to direct inquiry and to evaluate performance ... Colleagues refer to the public interest as the Holy Grail for which one might search as if it were the abominable snowman.

"If however one sees the public interest as a humanly created tool for human purposes, an evaluatory instrument much as Flathman suggests one might devise for judging the worth of motor cars or fountain pens one is in better if less exalted shape. The public interest thus conceived is a standard for appraising the polices and performance of some jurisdiction as it affects the lives of the population of the jurisdiction ... Developing a clearly articulated standard of the public interest and a process for its actualization in policy and public recognition and debate should be a high priority of students of political science and public administration."

Source: *PS: Political Science and Politics 24*, no. 4 (December 1991): pp. 670–675.

What Is This Thing Called "The Public Interest"?

Walter Lippmann (1889–1974), the renowned public philosophical pundit of fifty years ago, described the public interest as something that is obtainable when men think rationally and logically, while acting in a disinterested and benevolent way. Others claim it is when society maximizes the values of life, health, and freedom, or when members of society work together to accomplish common goals or purpose.[18] For example, even though the national government reportedly acts on the behalf of the public's interest, such as in the re-licensing of local radio and television stations through the authority of the **Federal Communications Commission** (FCC), the public interest is not directly nor necessarily tied to the will of the government, but instead to each person in society. The FCC is the focus of a case study we present at the end of this chapter that we believe conveys a greater sense of what is the public interest and how it operates in sync with various economic and political interests. More on that later!

Context and Characteristics of the Public Interest

The concept of the public interest is as old as written political thought. Socrates, Plato, and **Aristotle** (384 BC–322 BC) wrote it about in various forms and iterations. Seeking the public interest can be many things. It may be partial fulfillment of the **social contract** written of by Thomas Hobbes, John Locke, David Hume and others. It may be the embodiment of Jean Jacques Rousseau's **General Will**. It may tap into Jeremy Bentham's principle of utility. The Founding Fathers addressed it by noting the **Constitution** was partly established to protect the interests of the majority from the infringement of the minority and vice versa. Alexis de Tocqueville examined it under the priority of customs and manners above the laws. And John Stuart Mill sought it in the protection of individual rights. The public interest has been traditionally used over the centuries in political philosophy to denote the **common good** or common-weal between and among citizens. For example, the Founding Fathers routinely discussed and defended the protection of individual rights, property, constitutional heritage, and other civic, social, economic, and religious values. And rightly so these values are or have been at one time at the heart of civic community and the public interest. Of course, the public interest cannot be understood, nor certainly applied, without conception of political power to make it so. This concept of power, whether administrative or political, is the fulcrum for balancing the interests of the state with the common interests, group interests, and the like.[19] Clearly, then, the student of public administration *should* be concerned with the public interest.

One of the first notable academic discussions of the public interest was by political scientist **E. Pendleton Herring** (1903–2004)[20] in the mid-1930s.[21] In his attempt to unearth the pursuit of the public interest in the work and practice of government agencies, such as the Interstate Commerce Commission, Tariff Commission, Federal Trade Commission, Herring found no common or even definite understanding of the public interest among the agencies. Rather, he determined that in order to "resist the onslaught of particularistic groups" it was necessary to pursue the "autonomy of the state," specifically the administrative state. Some even believe that Herring's work might be considered "a bible for the contemporary state autonomy movement."[22] Herring's conclusions inspired other scholars to continue grappling with this elusive concept. Some embraced it as normatively understandable and even plausible. However, few saw it as empirically operational. Many dismissed it altogether. We will examine a few of their ideas below.

By the 1950s, with the advent of the behavioral revolution in the social sciences and especially political science, the public interest was found to be too normative and theoretical for these skeptical empirical scholars. The public interest had no meaning because it did not refer to anything that one could detect with any of the five senses; it was literal non-sense. Of course, this damning critique also applied to many of our most cherished concepts in life, such as love, justice, and happiness. For example, political scientist **Frank Sorauf** provided one of the first structured categorizations of the term, finding five basic meanings for the term: 1) rhetorical, 2) elitist, 3) morally pure, 4) balance between individual and social interests, and 5) no meaning at all. The only meaning Sorauf could accept for the public interest was not substantive, but only methodological, similar to the concept of due process within the law. Following in his footsteps, political scientist Glendon Schubert systematically categorized the term and declared it effectively dead on arrival. Using typological language, where the goal is to provide a working definition and to try and link theory to practice, Schubert analyzed administrative decision making in the public interest in one three groups: 1) Rationalists, who traced the public interest within the rational, logical positivist framework of the decision making process, depending upon the work of Herbert Simon and others for justification; 2) Platonists, who viewed the public interest in a highly moral world, such as Emmette Redford who argued that administrative decisions are based on the common interests of society, and Paul Appleby who contended that the public interest was greater than the sum of private interests, administrative, political, economic, or even social; and 3) the Realists, who argued that the public administrator is merely a catalyst through which conflict, criticism, and compromise among various interest groups is examined, analyzed, and transmitted into framing the public interest. In the end, Schubert sided with the Realists; what is logical and real in public interest talk is that which was given to the parties involved, the question at hand, and the outcomes sought.[23]

The Commons

However, economists, philosophers, and **policy analysts** observe the public interest in day-to-day decisions in the interplay of markets, morality, and policy making. The public interest is not just some challenging and obtuse philosophical cacophony of ideas! This realistic, everyday interplay of ideas was often described as **the commons**. First, economists such as Anthony Downs—one of the leading proponents of **public choice theory**—argued that the public interest functions or serves: 1) as a barometer for citizens to judge public decisions; and 2) to placate individuals not otherwise open to the concept. In this way the public interest was largely a rhetorical and symbolic device, such as when the FCC seeks to meet the public interest by limiting what types and how much profanity and nudity can be viewed on network television; and 3) as a check or balance on politicians and public administrators.[24]

However, the primary contribution of the economists has been to focus our attention on the diversity of interests the public interest, or the commons. Economists have referred to the public interest as the commons, but many now use the phrase 'the public interest.' The commons are based on the distinction between private goods and public goods. The commons are goods and services that benefit the larger public, such as parks, streets, and schools. The commons provide rational benefits to a large number of people, and are paid for by the taxes and efforts of many people. In contrast, private goods such as real estate, cars and refrigerators, have a particular material benefit (but not always rational benefit, e.g., a 54" HDTV screen!) for the person who obtains the item.

By recognizing the existence of the commons, the economists also establish a **fiduciary trust** or **duty** where the government as a whole or individual public servant must specifically act primarily for the benefit of others.[25] For example, regulatory agencies, like the FCC, are established and instructed to form and implement regulations that provide a good to the public, such as regulating the content of network shows. But today's government agencies, such as the Department of Education or Homeland Security, unlike in the world of E. Pendleton Herring of past decades, now have a clear expectation of public accountability to *all* interests, citizens, and groups, even if that interest is not easily or readily and operationally defined. Bear in mind that not all public administrators are immune or isolated from behavior that profits them personally and is in direct conflict with the pursuit of the public interest (e.g. bribery or embezzlement).

Richard Flathman and the Universalizability Principle

The 1960s and '70s saw a breakthrough, both normatively and empirically, in thinking about the public interest. Political philosopher **Richard E. Flathman** broke faith with interest group liberalism because, he argued, it did not actually work empirically in the life-world of the **public administrator** or other public sector decision making and behavior. Instead, Flathman found that public actors routinely worked with the concept of the public interest, which he defined as "public values, such as justice and freedom, that are used to evaluate decisions or politics." He empirically found that public administrators ordinarily used the phrase the public interest to describe decisions or policies, such as affirmative action, that are directed to work on behalf of the entire class of affected individuals (i.e.

ethnicities, gender, etc.) and not simply a select few. Thus, if a city manager only talked with their next-door neighbors to develop a city-wide strategy to rank-order the needed street maintenance of potholes, then this would not be considered a decision in the public interest.

Flathman called this decision habit of good public administrators the **Universalizability Principle**, which required public servants to take into account a decision or policy on all affected persons, not just select groups or self-interests. It is best understood when one compares public administrators as professionals with those who practice the law or medicine. As professionals they share normative values in assessing how effective their peers are in delivery services. Under the universalizability principle, the practice of a public administrator from street sweeper to city manager is not strictly a science or an art, but it is a professionally based and understood craft that requires the practitioner embrace and balance—if at all possible—subjective interests (e.g., justice for all) and objective benefits (e.g., performance based outcomes of local budgeting practices). The universalizability principle describes the professional craft or good habit of public administrators to look beyond their self-interests, the interests of those like themselves, or a small sub-section of the public. More than any other descriptor, the decision-making habit of thinking about others and seeking out the interests of all who are affected, characterizes the good public administrator who acts in the public interest.[26]

Other scholars, like Virginia Held, continued Flathman's groundbreaking work. Held studied the Federal Communications Commission (FCC) and found that the public interest meant more than a mere compilation of individual preferences. It was more than a sum of its parts. It also included significant normative content that was based on constitutional values, such as the need for openness of public discourse regarding regulation of TV and/or radio content.[27] Still others continued to develop the role of public administrators and policy analysts in normative policy analysis on behalf of others or in regulatory behavior.[28]

Richard E. Flathman

Richard E. Flathman was born on August 6, 1934, in St. Paul, Minnesota, married, with three kids. He is currently the George Armstrong Kelly Professor Political Science at Johns Hopkins University. Along with Brian Barry, David Braybrooke, and Abraham Kaplan he is best known for pioneering the application of analytic philosophy to key concepts in political science.

A graduate of Macalester College, he received his Ph.D. from the University of California-Berkeley in 1962 and taught at the Universities of Washington and Chicago and later at Reed College. He joined Johns Hopkins' political science department in 1975 as a Professor.

Flathman embraces the philosophy of liberalism and sees himself as a champion of greater social freedom and a more vigorous individuality in contemporary life. But his acclaimed works are known for lending clarity to important concepts in politics and public life. For example, his highly-acclaimed first book, *The Public Interest: An Essay Concerning the Normative Discourse of Politics* (1966), presented an empirical application of contemporary phenomenology, ordinary language philosophy and pragmatism to analyze how public servants used the phrase, the public interest.

Various Interpretations

The Blacksburg Gang. The 1980s and '90s witnessed contrasting understandings of the public interest and the role of normative values that support the study and practice of public administration. For example, the **Blacksburg Gang** (several professors who teach Public Administration at Virginia Tech University in Blacksburg, Virginia), led by scholars such as Gary Wamsley Charles Goodsell, and John Rohr, helped to re-direct public administration students and scholars to the philosophical roots of public administration. The Blacksburg Gang believed the study of these roots had been pushed aside in favor of trendy contemporary dilemmas in public administration. Although defining the public interest was not the Blacksburg Gang's primary aim, to do so would require a philosophy of the public interest.

PI as Politics. On the other hand, this is hardly what Michael Harmon contended, when he defined the public interest as nothing less than "… the continually changing outcome of political activity among individuals and groups within a democratic political system." He asserted that the public interest is individualistic, descriptive, procedural, and dynamic. In other words, the public interest is only what the proverbial political winds say that it is: during good economic times, tax cuts are in the public interest (if you are fiscal conservative that is); or during challenging times of civil liberties and rights, such as during the 1950s and '60s, passage of federal laws banning discrimination (e.g. Civil Rights Act of 1964) is in the public interest. For Harmon there is no moral, ethical, or constitutional base underpinning the concept itself. It is, well, it is only what we want it to be! That does not sound very encouraging.

Constitutional School of Public Administration. More recent understandings of the public interest have combined with the study of constitutional law and diverse historical and contemporary moral traditions of American constitutionalism. The **Constitutional School of Public Administration** is now emerging within the discipline, combining elements of traditional doctrinal study of constitutional law with contemporary law and economics approaches. The study of constitutionalism is found in some public administration textbooks, but in very few! Thus, scholars are beginning to systematically study public administration by looking at court interpretations, federal statutes, international treaties, and important individuals that have had an impact on public administration in pursuance of the Constitution. In such an inclusive approach, constitutionalism is not merely about the adherence to legal doctrines or deontological principles, but also includes the calculation of society-wide needs or utilitarian polices.[29] Thus, the practice of the public interest must include the diversity of ethical approaches, both deontological (rule-based) and utilitarian (such as economic reasoning). Taking this inclusive approach to the public interest gives new attention to a merger of constitutionalism and ethics, something we look at in chapters 3 and 11, and something we believe has largely been lost in contemporary public administration.[30]

Information Transparency & Public Interest. The most significant and visible change in public administration is the increased use of information **technology**. With the rise of e-government have come changing regulatory patterns at the federal, state and local levels over areas such as the environment, education, transportation, criminal justice, homeland security, and so forth. For example, there are new patterns of regulation, public-private co-production of public order, and e-governance, such as Wikinomics—the use of mass collaboration in regulation—which works like Wikipedia.[31]

The transparency of public administration in such a diffusion of innovative information technology has shifted our focus from ideological oppression in governance (as in previous generations), to questions of **values** we hold in common at a deeper, philosophical level.[32] For example, Congress is greatly expanding the regulation of all digital communications (not just radio and TV) under the "public interest standard" in the Digital Age Communications Act. In this new transparent world of e-governance, dated images of ideological bureaucrats are false-to-life (e.g., conserving what? liberal to whom?). Instead, a new politic of public administration is open to all and focuses attention to values questions such as, what is the public interest?

The ideological bent of the past generation of political scientists perhaps moved too far to a behavioral, skeptical perspective of reality, reducing these administrative decisions to mere ideological preferences. Transparency, e-governance, Wikinomics, and other new information technology have opened up these bureaucratic processes to a far more values-oriented, indeed, even philosophical level of discourse in administrative life.[33]

Summary. Thus, we define **administration in the public interest** as the normative role of public administrators based in fiduciary duties to the commons, which are constrained by criteria of principles of the Constitution, policies that are congruent with our democratic values and the practice of moral administrative leadership and decision-making. This normative, fiduciary role of the public administrator, constrained by principles, policies and practices, is the day-to-day reality of public administration and public administrators. The concept of the public interest is a criterion for public administrators that are designed to keep their focus on the interests of the people — to keep their "eye on the ball." This is the Holy Grail of what it means to do public administration!

Yet, contemporary cynics continue to argue that the public interest is nothing more than assertions by administrators of their own personal individual preferences. There are no referents of the public interest to any thing that can be seen, heard, touched, smelled, or tasted. In other words, the public interest is nothing more than the will-to-power of administrators and remains a literal nonsense. A question is raised: Can administration in the public interest be re-founded to overcome the nihilism of cynical scholars and critics? We argue "Yes!"

From a contemporary literature that observes ordinary reality in public administration, we seek to rebuild an administration in the public interest that is more than just the policy preference of bureaucrats or cynical scholars. This rebuilding begins with the meaning given to values by public administrators through the Constitution. Founded in the three foundational theories of philosophical ethics (deontology, utilitarianism, and virtue),[34] scholars suggest there are three theories of the nature of administration in the public interest: (1) decisions that conform to pre-existing **principles,** such as the U.S. Constitution; (2) decisions by legislating and executing **policies** that are congruent with our democratic values, and (3) **practices** of moral administrative decision-making and leadership that are non-idiosyncratic and universalized. Let's examine each.

While often criticized, the role of the public administrator as a neutral, objective, and rational interpreter of pre-existing principles is part of the accepted ideology of constitutionalism in public administration. Contemporary public administration studies in the U.S. Constitution attend to a **deontological model** of applied ethics of rule-bound reasoning in which bureaucrats learn the rules and make their decisions as the living repositories of such legal rules, intuitions, or principles, declaring the appropriate principle to make their decision in each case. Scholars, such as John Rohr, posit that the proper role of public administrators is to conform to pre-existing constitutional principles and to not legislate.[35] And his "ideal" public administrator seems to be one who can find one-right-answer in every case, even with competing principles. For example, the F.B.I. officer is to rigidly adhere to Fifth Amendment limits and can only interrogate a suspect only after giving *Miranda* warnings; under this rule-bound approach, the officer cannot simply blurt out the question, "Where did you drop the gun?" However, a more dynamic ethical approach would allow the officer to consider the public safety concerns and ask about where the gun was dropped, to keep this dangerous weapon, dropped somewhere near a school playground, away from the kids. The principles approach to constitutionalism seems too much like pat-answers in which you take pre-existing constitutional principle and, voila, simply apply it to the decision, and the parties are rationally obligated to comply. Sounds simple, but the reality is far different, far more dynamic. Yet, while constitutional principles seem too much like pat answers, we generally agree that constitutional principles may serve as markers improving when a decision is clearly NOT in the public interest.

There are many problems and decisions where public administrators do NOT (and, really, CAN NOT) simply discover and apply pre-existing constitutional principles. Some argue that public administrators often make policy through their decision making authority—something that is part of the "administrative state." What delimits, or what we say constrains these policy decisions, is their congruence—or agreement—within our democratic political system and/or democratic values. In other words, the public interest is only what the proverbial political winds say that it is.

The policy focus within the public interest attends to an ethical theory of **utilitarianism** where good and bad are defined by balancing or calculating benefits and costs, pleasure and pain, or needs versus needs. It is a skeptical ethical theory in asserting that there are no pre-existing principles of the public interest beyond this balancing or calculating of individual interests or needs. John Locke, for example, argued that there is no meaning with the concept of the public interest beyond simply the aggregation of multiple personal interests.[36] In other words, the whole is merely the sum of its parts; rights are merely individual needs combined. In this way, economics scholars such as **James Buchanan** and Elinor and Vincent Ostrom, refer to the commons in discussions of the public interest as the collective needs of society, such as owning public property (e.g., electric cooperatives). Much of the academic work devoted to this line of thinking comes under the rubric of public choice theory or other related labels, such as positive theory, rational choice, law & economics analysis, and so forth. For example, from positive theory, scholars argue that interest group liberalism helps explain how individual public policy decisions may conflict with the public interest. Many special interests projects, like the "Basketball at Midnight" programs of the 1990s, may not be the desire of the public at large, but it may be rational for individual politicians or public administrators to support these projects when the program funding benefits their constituents. The benefits may be psychological in making them feel powerful or important (the mayor and city manager strongly favored it and pushed it to the top of the legislative agenda), constituent or client support in their current position (downtown street vendors, neighborhood businesses, and families with small children) or financial benefits (what is saved in city outlays for overtime pay for police officers).

These special interest groups are also behaving rationally with huge government pork barrel funding with little outlay and getting the edge on competitors who don't seek government favors. Even the taxpayers find it rational not to squeal in protest, as each government give-away only costs them pennies and they may expect similar benefits to themselves that may cost the other guy only pennies. Everyone has a rational incentive to do exactly the same, even if the desires of the general public are against it.[37] For some critics, this means that the public interest has become an unwieldy, cumbersome, and—really—meaningless jumble of individual desires. Everyone seeks what is in their rational interest, and thus it has become the governments' responsibility and public servants' authority to ensure these individual and often times conflicting interests are some-how met.[38]

James M. Buchanan

James M. Buchanan, winner of the Nobel Prize in Economics in 1986, was born October 3, 1919, in Murfreesboro, Tennessee, received his B.A. from Middle Tennessee Sate College in 1940 and his Ph.D. in political science from the University of Chicago in 1948. He holds the Distinguished Professor Emeritus of Economics at George Mason University in Fairfax, Virginia, and Distinguished Professor Emeritus of Economics and Philosophy at Virginia Tech in Blacksburg, VA. He is best known for developing the "public choice theory" of economics, which changed the way economists analyze economic and political decision making. Buchanan's work opened the door for the examination of how politicians' self-interest and non-economic forces affect government economic policy. Along with co-author Gordon Tullock, his highly-acclaimed book, *The Calculus of Consent: Logical Foundations of Constitutional Democracy* (1962), blended the fields of economics and political science to help create the "public choice" approach.

Source: James M. Buchanan, "What is Public Choice Theory?" *Imprimis* (March 2003), http://www.hillsdale.edu/news/imprimis/archive/issue.asp?year=2003&month=03.

Public administrators may seek out these individual and group personal preferences by direct means (e.g., city managers sending out community or client surveys, public opinion polls, or interviews regarding the public's opinion of a community interest) or by deferring to the processes within their agency designed to elicit input from clients, the market, or interest groups. For example, should a city manager alter the zoning ordinances for downtown construction to allow for a big-box retailer? It will certainly be a revenue-generator, but its very appearance and position may very likely detract from the environmental ambience of rustic antique shops, coffee houses, old furniture-makers and so forth. The public administrator takes a role in this process to facilitate the input of various clients or interest groups and supply the demands or execute the mandates produced. This may be politically popular, but by itself this is not in the public interest. In fact, this policy skepticism has led to what Robert Putnam refers to as "bowling alone," (we will examine some of Putnam's ideas in future chapters) which is a breakdown in community relations and participation, something he calls a loss of **social capital**.[39] Community is no longer; there are no more truly common values. Such a community is merely what individuals define as their individual desires. Social life—from meeting at the local Elks Club to participating in neighborhood watch groups—loses any sense of commonality or ethical meaning.

Political philosophers, such as Richard E. Flathman (see above), present a theory of the public interest as practices, or social practices of moral administrative leadership and decision-making.[40] It shifts our attention in a radical empirical focus on the lived-world of ordinary public servants, their day-to-day concerns and decision. This attention to the "lived-in world" of public administrators attends to the age-old ethical theory of **virtue**, the good moral character and being of the person who deals with the ordinary issues, decisions, and actions of public service. As a framework for analysis, it promises a means of understanding these complex organizational behaviors, and accommodates both the individual and social dimensions of the public interest in a theory based on people's actions. From the observations of researchers,[41] the criterion of in the public interest may be tested against **administrative behavior** by non-idiosyncratic, universalized, social practices of moral decision making.

Beyond the skepticism of economic theory or the advocacy of will-to-power perspectives, came empirical attempts within the social sciences to understand human rights and behavior within a concrete, lived-in world. A social practice, like the practice-of-medicine or the practice-of-law, is often used to describe these various approaches to uncover such a context-based social practice as distinguished from theory or science alone. As a public administrator, you must work in a real world filled with real political, policy, financial, administrative, and other values challenges and conflicts. You may be constantly trying to work out solutions for planning and zoning problems, such as where to build the next high school, or economic development issues, such as how much growth to allow in a predominantly rural county in order to address the demand for affordable housing. You cannot simply theorize, although it would be certainly useful to have a philosophy about your tasks. And in the real world, you do not have unlimited resources to give everyone whatever they want, but as a public administrator you must allocate scarce resources to the public interest—the primary focus or need of all those who are affected. But how is this done—if at all?

Some scholars have traced developments of the philosophical underpinnings that led to this practice approach in the social sciences, including public interest theory. With the end of traditional philosophy and rationality, which seems to have died after **Friederich Nietzsche's** (1844–1900) **will-to-power** philosophy,[42] radical new approaches to philosophy arose in the last century, including American pragmatism, **ordinary language philosophy**,[43] and phenomenology.[44] They emphasized the need to work outside of the ivy tower and closely study everyday work, ordinary talk, and common people. They found a new way of reasoning that was not based on old notions of science or will; it was largely focused on real people and how things worked (e.g., pragmatic success), on shared social meanings (e.g., in communities, families, and social groups), and on various ordinary-life experiences with faith, love, family, coworkers and friends. This is what public administration is all about: real people! Civil servants or public administrators work for people to address and maybe even solve their disputes and problems. This is what administration in the public interest is all about!

Contemporary administration in the public interest illustrates this practice perspective, not as iron-clad conformity to static principles only (e.g., Rohr's constitutional regime principles), but in an inclusive approach that incorporates principles and policies within a larger social and moral practice. While critics may still fault a particular public administrator in a specific decision for imposing their will-to-power or individual preferences only, it is clear that administration in the public interest is comprised of discourse, negotiation, and compromise—not imposition of the imperial will of the public administrator. In this process, public administrators act as catalysts in order to direct individuals, groups, agencies, and organizations in a general direction to resolve social conflicts and concerns and make policies. Changing social forces, politics, legal mandates, human imagination, as well as costs and duration, frustrate any individual public administrator from exercising will-to-power.

The practice approach to the public interest provides a theory of public administration that preserves attention to pre-existing constitutional principles, insures the congruence of administrative policies with our democratic institutions and values, and clarifies the normative fiduciary leadership role of administrators. Administration in the public interest is transformed into a discourse between a large number of key decision-makers in every situation: from top-level administrators and managers, citizens, politicians, street-level personnel, and non-profit and faith-based organizations. In so doing, the central question changes from: what about my interests? To: what about the public interest?

Conclusion

Bureaupathology may describe the "real world" of public administration—the comic, gritty and often tragic condition of life. Attending to bureaupathology are the theories of ethical egoism and moral relativism, which cynically argue that any objections or reforms of the status quo are non-sense; it's just your opinion, your will to power to make things your way or for your benefit. Yet, vast empirical research posits recurring, universal, and meaningful moral development patterns in human cognitive structure that is cross-national, cross-gender, and such. Thus, we object to and reform bureaupathology—by positing a positive aspiration for public administration from the perspective of the dear, old, familiar concept of the public interest.

The public interest has been a useful concept of applied ethics for millenniums to debate the morality of public life. Yet, the public interest is a much maligned and misunderstood concept. While political scientists of the past seemed to show disdain for the use of the concept, economists and political philosophers find common usages for the concept. We contend that there are at least three approaches to the public interest: principles (i.e., pre-existing deontological values), policies (i.e., utilitarian balancing of benefits/costs, etc.), and practices (i.e., virtues of leadership and administrative decisiveness).

We contend the most basic responsibility and moral duty of the public administrator is to uphold and pursue the fulfillment of the public interest. With the chapters to come, we seek to avoid the study and practice of public administration as a disjointed application of the theories and descriptions of management, people, organizations, processes, and policies. Rather than a plain-vanilla or generic textbook jumble of topics, we will survey public administration by the theme of administration in the public interest. So, to conclude our introductory chapter, let us take a closer look at one of the oldest and most respected federal regulatory agencies: the Federal Communications Commission (FCC). This brief overview of the FCC and the role it plays in regulating the airwaves for "pursuit of the public interest" will go a long way toward describing and explaining the role that public administration and public administrators play in the development and continuation of the public interest.

The Public Interest and the Federal Communications Commission

So, what does administration in the public interest look like in reality? As teachers of public administration, we usually get called on the carpet by our students at this point in our introduction to the course. Students are often polite and diplomatic about all the theory presented in this chapter. But they want to know: what can I do with all this theory? Or, What does administration in the public interest really look like at the jobsite? Thus, it is a good time to give a brief case study example of administration in the public interest. The following special case study provides an overview of the administration of the public interest by the Federal Communication Commission (FCC). This is especially timely as the U.S. Congress is now undertaking the greatest expansion of the FCC in history—to apply the public interest standard to regulate all of digital media, not just radio and television. (Instructors: Feel free to use this brief case study in any way you believe will be useful.)

Case Study   The Federal Communications Commission and the Public
              Interest

The Federal Communications Commission. The Federal Communications Commission (FCC) is entrusted with the Holy Grail of ensuring the public interest in all USA radio and television broadcasting. FCC Chairman Kevin Martin, appointed by President George W. Bush, has allied himself with a Democratic Congress and is poised to expand FCC regulation of the public interest in all aspects of the Internet as well! This case study of FCC public interest regulation is made further relevant by the many other agencies entrusted with *the public interest* or *the commons* in policy sectors as diverse as other media, the insurance industry, economic regulation, pharmaceuticals, health care, the environment, gambling, and other arenas. And like these varied policy sectors, FCC regulation has featured distinct styles of administration in the public interest that are both principle-based and market-based.

The Public Interest Standard. The FCC was created by Congress under its Commerce Clause powers, to regulate the spectral scarcity of a finite number of public airwaves. The public interest standard was mandated by Congress in the statute that created the FCC: The Communications Act of 1934, 47 U.S.C. sections 151 and 154. The 1934 Act was based on prior statutes, such as the Radio Act of 1927, and in both the assurance of the public interest was of central concern. The U.S. Supreme Court first upheld the FCC public interest standard in *Nelson Brothers v. FRC* (1933), in which the Federal Radio Commission (FRC) revoked two licenses after evaluating three stations for public interest programming. As stated in the 1934 Act, the public interest, convenience and necessity mandate was never defined by consensus and has been a storm center for debates over the FCC's proper regulatory role ever since. But former FCC Chairman Newton Minow believed the 1934 Act—and the role of the FCC—may have been worthless without it. The U.S. Supreme Court again upheld the public interest standard in *FCC v. Pottsville Broadcasting* (1940), and did not require the FCC to consider economic injury to existing stations when considering applications for a new station in *FCC v. Sanders Brothers Radio* (1940). These cases underscore the one major regulatory weapon of the FCC, revoking licenses.

From the 1940s through the 1960s, the FCC was much more aggressive in promoting broadcasting under the public interest standard. In *NBC v. US* (1943), the U.S. Supreme Court upheld the FCC's chain-broadcasting regulations that allowed local network affiliates free of network constraints in the power to select programming to meet the public interest standard. The FCC issued programming guidelines to broadcasters under its public interest standard in the 1946 "Blue Book" (called for it's blue cover), including non-sponsored programs, local live programs, local public issues programs, and elimination of excessive advertising. The "Blue Book" did not mandate such programs, but merely clarified the FCC's consideration of such public interest programming at renewal time. The 1960 Programming Policy Statement further clarified the public interest standard with an additional mix of programs that were usually necessary to the public interest and considered as evidence that broadcasters were serving the public interest at renewal time. These fourteen programming elements were to be locally determined by broadcasters in a series of interviews conducted with community leaders in nineteen FCC-specified categories ranging from agriculture to religion.

The **Fairness Doctrine** involved a highly principled style of administration introduced by FCC regulation 13 FCC 1246 in 1949, early during the anti-Communist Red Scare. It was a general FCC policy that both sides of a controversial issue ought to be presented by broadcasters. Congress never explicitly authorized the doctrine. And the equal time principles of the Fairness Doctrine were applied only rarely, until a 1967 FCC regulation uniformly required this. In *Red Lion Broadcasting v. FCC* (1969), the U.S. Supreme Court upheld both the public interest standard and the Fairness Doctrine of the FCC. Red Lion Broadcasting refused any reply time to Fred J. Cook after a 15-minute attack by Rev. Billy Jones Hargis on his "Christian Crusade" radio show, in which Hargis said Cook was fired from a newspaper for making false charges against city officials, Cook had worked for a communist-affiliated publication, Cook had defended Alger Hiss and attacked J. Edgar Hoover and the CIA, and now Cook had written a book to smear Barry Goldwater (Cook's book was entitled, *Goldwater: Extremist On the Right*). Although newspapers could not similarly be required to provide equal time, the Court reasoned that radio and broadcasting were unique because of the limited nature of the public airwave spectrum. The Court reasoned that: "It is the right of the viewers, not the right of the broadcasters, which is paramount … There is nothing in the First Amendment which prevents the Government from requiring a licensee to share his frequency with others and to conduct himself as a fiduciary."

Radio and broadcasting are treated differently than the newspapers because "the broadcast media have established a uniquely pervasive presence in the lives of all Americans," the Court similarly reasoned in *FCC v. Pacifica Foundation* (1978), where the Court affirmed the FCC decision that George Carlin's "filthy words" monologue was indecent. Later, the FCC cracked down on indecency after Janet Jackson's wardrobe malfunction in Super Bowl XXXVIII, and President George Bush signed into law the Broadcast Decency Enforcement Act of 2005.

While the Fairness Doctrine was originally enacted to promote pluralism, by the 1970s the FCC and other policy decision-makers were concerned that it had the opposite effect. In *CBS v. Democratic National Committee* (1973), the Court warned of the end of the Fairness Doctrine with changes in technology: "problems of regulation are rendered more difficult because the broadcast industry is dynamic in terms of technological change, solutions adequate a decade ago are not necessarily so now, and those acceptable today may well be outmoded 10 years hence." In *Miami Herald Publishing v. Tornillo* (1974) a unanimous Court decided that "government-enforced right of access inescapably dampens the vigor and limits the variety of public debate." Justice Brennan, writing the Opinion of the Court in *FCC v. League of Women Voters* (1984), wrote that the Fairness Doctrine was "chilling speech." Broadcasters challenged the Fairness Doctrine for promoting censorship instead of diversity, and openly worried that their advertising time would be wasted by individuals invoking the equal time rule.

The FCC & the Commons. Against this background, the FCC developed a new marketplace interpretation of the public interest standard. By this market-failure approach, public interest regulation only enters in when the marketplace clearly has failed to protect the general interest or *the commons*. Then FCC Chairman Mark Fowler, who had been on Ronald Reagan's campaign staff, argued in 1982 that: "Put simply, I believe that we are at the end of regulating broadcasting under the trusteeship model. Whether you call it 'paternalism' or 'nannyism' — it is 'Big Brother,' and it must cease. I believe in a marketplace approach to broadcast regulation … Under the coming marketplace approach, the Commission should as far as possible, defer to a broadcaster's judgment about how best to compete for viewers and listeners, because this services the public interest."

In *FCC v. WNCN Listener's Guild* (1983), the Court upheld the FCC's decision not to involve itself in a change of ownership of WNCN and a resulting format change from classical to rock music, reasoning that "marketplace regulation was a constitutionally protected means of implementing the public interest of the act."

Further, in 1981 the FCC began to deregulate radio by eliminating all requirements for program logs, commercial time limits, required interviews of community leaders, and non-entertainment programming. FCC decision-makers reasoned that: "… Congress established a mandate for the Commission to act in the public interest. We conceive of that interest to require us to regulate where necessary, to deregulate where warranted, and above all, to assure the maximum service to the public at the lowest cost and the least amount of paperwork."

Further, since 1994, the FCC has allocated commercial broadcasting spectrum by competitive auctions to the highest bidder, instead of by the old best-public-use system. Yet, the FCC has thus far given a digital TV channel to each holder of an analog TV station license. But this may change in 2009 as all USA analog broadcast licenses will expire with conversion to digital.

Finally, with the rise of marketplace FCC regulation came also the abolition of the Fairness Doctrine. The U.S. courts noted the chilling effect the doctrine had, but refused to find the Fairness Doctrine unconstitutional without some signal from Congress or the FCC. The FCC found the Fairness Doctrine to be unconstitutional and abolished it by a vote of 4–0 in the *Syracuse Peace Council* decision in August 1987. The FCC no longer found validity in the spectrum scarcity rationale for the doctrine, or in its effectiveness to insure pluralism: "the intrusion by government into the content of programming occasioned by the enforcement of [the Fairness Doctrine] restricts the journalistic freedom of broadcasters … [and] actually inhibits the presentation of controversial issues of public importance to the detriment of the public and the degradation of the editorial prerogative of broadcast journalists."

Congress tried in a last-ditch effort to preserve the Fairness Doctrine in statutory form in 1987, but President Reagan vetoed the bill. The threat of a veto by President George H.W. Bush staved off a 1991 attempt to resurrect the Fairness Doctrine. A 2007 attempt to restore the long-dead Fairness Doctrine was voted down 309–115 by most Democrats and all Republicans in Congress. However, under the Obama Administration, the Fairness Doctrine, under one form or the other, seems to be making a political comeback of sorts.

The FCC marketplace approach to regulation continues to reign ascendant with reforms under both Democrat and Republican presidents, as well as bi-partisan efforts in Congress. For example, the Telecommunication Act of 1996 was highly touted as a bi-partisan effort to create a more competitive communications market by removing many media ownership restrictions, distinguishing between information and communication services, and structuring new cooperation. But critics point out that the 1996 Act promised to deliver a $2 trillion boost to the economy, 1.5 million related jobs, and cost savings to consumers of over $550 million—but instead we received a $2 trillion loss in the value of the U.S. telecommunication industry, a loss of 500,000 U.S. jobs, and a tremendous up-surge in cable and phone rates. What's worse, say the critics, is the intense media consolidation that resulted, i.e., five companies now control 75 percent of all prime-time viewing.

Chellie Pingree, President of Common Cause, argued persuasively in 2005 that, "Those who advocated the Telecommunications Act of 1996 promised more competition and diversity, but the opposite has happened." Congress and the FCC are working on current legislation that promises to remedy the 1996 Act (and other prior issues) with the Digital Age Communications Act (DACA). DACA proposals are praised by academics for greater common sense in federal-state relations and for converging public interest regulation of all information, communication and broadcasting services and discarding out-of-date stovepipe regulations that once separated these media. Critics remain skeptical of what may be produced, given that the big eight media giants have pumped over $400 million into lobby efforts with the Congress on these issues. But should the Congress and FCC continue to move in the direction of administration of *the commons* and a market-oriented, competition-based public interest standard grounded in economic analysis? Is this congruent with U.S. constitutionalism and ordinary understandings of the public interest?

Conclusion. An understanding of *the public interest* is central to an understanding of the day-to-day reality of work at the FCC. But this brief case history of the FCC public interest standard affirms that the current market-oriented focus on utilitarian considerations may be incomplete and must be supplemented by other approaches to the public interest. For earlier FCC policy and regulatory decisions made under the public interest standard continue to have a significant influence on the most current of FCC reforms, such as issues of obscenity and programming diversity, as we have seen in this brief case study. And comparative studies bear this out in other comparative regulatory environments. For example, the promotion of media diversity by regulatory agencies in the United Kingdom and Australia in a climate of deregulation and marketplace approaches is heavily influenced by earlier policy and regulatory decisions that include other approaches to the public interest. It seems that Principles, Policies, and Practices approaches operate in the contemporary day-to-day decision-making of the FCC and many other public agencies.

Action Steps

1. Break the class into several groups of three, with each group focusing on one specific public bureaucracy, e.g., a public high school, university, city hall, driver's licensing agency, etc. What bureaupathologies and public administration failures can you list and describe from observations within this specific bureaucracy? Try your hand at literary (even poetic?) description of life within these bureaucracies.

2. Split the class into several groups of three. Each group will take on one single contemporary public policy problem, one that any ordinary public administrator, such as a city manager or state agency head, might grapple with. What would you think about the issue in light of the Holy Grail question: what is the public interest? For-

mulate a workable solution that meets the various Principles, Policies, and Practices public interest approaches. Try writing down the responses, including all thoughts and strategy as a group that went into a final decision.

3. Interview a civil servant, asking them what they think is the public interest and how their duties and responsibilities fulfill the public interest.

4. After reading the case study of U.S. Supreme Court decisions, legislation, and administration in the public interest by the F.C.C., consider the Holy Grail of the public interest in radio and television broadcasting (and soon all digital media). Divide the class into groups of three or four. Answer the following questions: 1) How would you administer radio or television broadcasting in the public interest? 2) How would you administer regulation of all digital media in the public interest? 3) How would you administer return of the Fairness Doctrine in the public interest?

Exam Review Preparation

1. Explain and apply Richard Flathman's Universizability Principle to the study of administration in the public interest.

2. Define and/or describe the following concepts:
   a. administration in the public interest
   b. policy advocacy
   c. practice
   d. constitutional principles

3. Trace the historical and scholarly work of political scientists on the public interest. Why are political scientists so skeptical about terms like the public interest?

4. How does the economists' perspective of the commons differ from other conceptions of the public interest?

5. List and discuss bureaupathologies and the critique of public administration by Franz Kafka and others you may know.

6. Discuss E. Pendleton Herring's conception and understanding of the public interest.

7. Define and identify the importance of the following terms:
   a. "bowling alone"
   b. social capital
   c. Franz Kafka's *The Trial*
   d. Walter Lippmann's definition of the public interest
   e. The Blacksburg Gang

Key Concepts

Administration in the public interest
Administrative behavior
Aristotle
Blacksburg Gang
Bureaupathology
Constitutional regime principles
E. Pendleton Herring

Federal Communications Commission
Fiduciary trust or duty
Frank Sorauf
Franz Kafka
Friedrich Nietzsche
Gresham's Law
James Buchanan
John Rohr
Ordinary language philosophy
Peter Principle
Plato
Principles, Policies, Practices
Public interest
Richard Flathman
Robert Putnam's "bowling alone" thesis
Social capital
The commons
The Trial
Universalizability Principle
Walter Lippmann
Will-to-power

Recommended Readings

Appleby, Paul. *Morality and Administration in Democratic Government*. Baton Rouge, LA: Louisiana State University Press, 1952.

Flathman, Richard J. *The Public Interest: An Essay Concerning the Normative Discourse of Politics*. New York: John Wilsey and Sons, 1966.

Herring, Pendleton. *Public Administration and the Public* Interest. New York: McGraw-Hill, 1936.

Ostrom, Elinor. *Governing the Commons: The Evolution of Institutions for Collective Action*. London: Cambridge University Press, 1990.

Stillman, Richard, II. *The American Bureaucracy: The Core of Modern Government*. 3d ed. Belmont, CA: Wadsworth, 2004.

Wamsley, Gary, and J. Wolf, eds. *Refounding Democratic Public Administration: Modern Paradoxes, Postmodern Challenges*. Sage, CA: Sage, 1996.

Related Web Sites

American Political Science Association John Gaus Lecture
    http://www.apsanet.org/content_13171.cfm
Aristotle
    http://www.philosophypages.com/ph/aris.htm
Deontology
    http://www.ascensionhealth.org/ethics/public/issues/deontology.asp

Ethics in public affairs
    www.globalethics.org/
    www.ethics.org/
Federal Communications Commission
    http://www.fcc.gov/
Public Choice Theory
    http://people.virginia.edu/~hms2f/pubchoic.html
U. S. Department of Housing list of public interest groups
    http://www.hud.gov/offices/oir/oirpublicinterestgroups.cfm
Virginia Tech University's Center for Public Administration and Policy
    http://www.cpap.vt.edu/

Chapter 2

Public Administration History and Public Interest Practices

"Who should study public administration? … The basic reason is understanding. All people in a civilized society need an appreciation of the role of administration in their culture because, willy-nilly, administration is an important aspect of their lives, from the nearest physical aspect to the remotest spiritual or intellectual aspect. *All* persons in a civilized society are consumers of administration, and they should be *good* consumers, prepared to react intelligently and appreciatively, or with intelligent criticism."

Dwight Waldo, *The Study of Public Administration*

Chapter Objectives

Upon completion of this chapter you should be able to:

1. Understand, define, and apply the term public administration;
2. Recognize the important scholars and practitioners that contribute to the evolution of public administration;
3. Distinguish the important events, people, and ideas of public administration over the last two plus centuries;
4. Understand the practices approach to the public interest and aspects of the attendant virtue ethics theory, with examples from public administration history.

Introduction

Like **Dwight Waldo** (1913–2000), in this chapter we seek a systematic understanding of the lived-world of public administration in the U.S.A. and the variety of human experiences with public goods and services, a-to-z, from the administration of criminal justice to the local zoo. We present this through a brief history of public administration. There is a rich and growing scholarly literature on the history of administration and management in both the private and public realms. Some focus on great men—sometimes on great women—such as George Washington, Thomas Jefferson, Alexander Hamilton, Andrew Jackson, Abraham Lincoln, Franklin Delano Roosevelt, Jane Addams, and others. Other histories focus on ordinary lives of individuals, groups, and their organizations and institutions. Still others place people, whether great or ordinary, within the context of schools of thought as shorthand for the human experiences that give meaning to the lived-world. All seek a big picture of public administration through history that may be more meaningful because it focuses on people and the world they live and work in.

This examination of the lived-world of the history of public administration allows us to focus attention on the practices approach to the public interest and applied ethics of the attending virtue theory. History has always focused on the lived-world of people, about human practices in the meanings, conflicts, and resolutions within an empirical reality. This focus on the actual lived-world of persons fulfills a human need to judge the person and the context of a character, not just some generic disembodied behaviors. Of course, it is a matter of degree, and any good history also includes aspects of the principles approach, such as the laws people live by, and the policies approach, such as the economy and political compromises people create. Further, history has been so much about "his-story" that new feminist perspectives are compelled to posit "her-story" as well. So, what does it mean to be a good public administrator?[1]

The practices approach (and virtue) is a good starting point in our study of administration in the public interest because it is ordinary, common, and practical in its simplicity. TV, movies, novels, the internet, and the stories of family and friends—all ordinarily present narratives of people and assess their character, motives, and judgments. You know, who's the good one or the bad one—who's wearing the white hat or the black hat? Even children's books ordinarily depict the character of public servants, and highly influential authors like Dr. Seuss (Theodore Seuss Geisel) more often depict public servants as less-than-benevolent and less-than-competent (which may explain "real" bureaucrats today?).[2] We commonly judge who is a good person by their virtue or character, defined as a "fixed disposition, habit, or trait to do what is morally commendable."[3] The practices approach answers the question—what ought I do?—with practical simplicity: "be patient" or "be brave" or "be a man" or "be a woman" or "be a good citizen,"[4] rather than some detailed list of actions. This practical simplicity may also be popularly expressed by emulating a person, whether it be the imitation of a hero (e.g., be like Spiderman), a great historical figure (e.g., be like George Washington), or with a W.W.J.D. bracelet (e.g., what would Jesus do?).[5]

In Chapter 2 we do two things. First, we provide a brief historical overview of the lived-world of American public administration, including individuals, political groups, and scholarly schools of thought. Second, we provide concrete examples of the practices approach to the public interest, interjecting discussion of the meanings, criticisms, and defenses of this applied ethics approach to administration in the public interest.

Dwight Waldo

Dwight Waldo, who died on October 27, 2000, was a major figure in the intellectual development of public administration. He was a Midwestern at heart. Born in DeWitt, Nebraska he did not earn his B.A. at a prestigious Ivy League school. Rather he attended and graduated from Nebraska State Teachers College. He did receive his Ph.D. from Yale University, and later worked at the Office of Personnel Administration and the Office of the President in Washington, D.C. He moved into academic circles, beginning with the University of California-Berkeley in 1946 and then moving to the Maxwell School at Syracuse University in 1967, where he stayed until his retirement in 1979. He served as editor-in-chief for the *Public Administration Review* for 11 years. However, his major contribution to the field of public administration was *The Administrative State* (1948).

What Is Public Administration?

Our history of administration in the public interest is founded within the academic discipline of **public administration**. What is public administration? The many textbook definitions of public administration, used at both the graduate and undergraduate levels, are surprisingly diverse. Only a few of these definitions include a normative context or a discussion of the public interest.[6] But it is like the ancient story about six blind men trying to define an elephant. Each touched only a certain part of the elephant, but not the whole. So, the blind man touching the trunk talked of the elephant as a creature with a huge elongated nose. The blind man touching the leg talked of the tree-trunk foot. The blind man touching the tail talked of a snake. So it is with empirical descriptions from an external perspective, no one really sees the big picture and certainly not from the elephant's perspective.

Clearly, scholars of public administration do not agree on what public administration is much less on what are its key themes. But it does make a difference for public administrators and it *should* make a difference for scholars regarding clarifying a definition and highlighting various themes. And the definition of public administration makes a difference in an understanding of what is the public interest. Certainly, American politics and government are linked to the administration of policy, but the administration of policy must be tied to fulfilling the interest of the public over simply the interests of specialized clientele groups or the private market itself. But has the pursuit of market demands, performance management, and clientele group demands overshadowed the need of the common good, or the public interest? We believe it has, and the consequence is an ensnared administrative system, with no clear public interest agenda or focus. The need for reigniting the flame of the public interest is great.

The Evolution of Public Administration

Administration has been with us as long as recorded history. Anytime people, materials, and services were moved or rendered there was a need for administration. Ancient civilizations, such as China, Babylonia, Egypt, and Rome, required the administration of people to build cities, aqueducts, and roads; fight wars, process information, protect their cities from outside invasion, and police themselves; regulate business and civic matters, educate their children, and care for their needy. From communities to nations the need for administration is ever present. It is a natural state and process. People are by nature social creatures, and therefore when we engage and cooperate in various activities the need to plan, organize, staff, direct, coordinate, report, and budget (i.e. alluding to Luther Gulick's acronym POSDCORB) is ever-present.

Management has a more recent origin in human affairs (We will examine public management and leadership in more detail in Chapter 6). The word manage arose from the French word *ménage* involving the care and training of animals, especially horses. The menagerie was a small dog and pony show that traveled across Europe. In the nineteenth century, the term "manage" moved from its rural setting to the newly emerging industrial world, referring in part to the managerial European industries and economies. Management became the modern task of segmenting processes to manipulate the efficiency of human workers and to increase productivity. With this concept also came a more behavioral approach to the oversight and direction of human organizations.[7] But the concept of management was simply added into the much more ancient and larger concept of administration. Administration was a phenomenon long before the late nineteenth or early twentieth centuries, spurred on or stimulated by the **Industrial Revolution**, Progressive reforms, administrative state, and backroom politics. Writings on administration date back to the very beginnings of human society.

It is commonly accepted among scholars that the modern academic discipline of public administration began at the end of the nineteenth century, when an obscure academic at Johns Hopkins University named **Woodrow Wilson** (1856–1924) wrote his now famous article, "The Study of Administration," first published in 1887.[8] Wilson's article delineated what he considered the stark differences between the "science of administration" and the "art of politics," with the latter inferior to the former. Wilson, and those he influenced, such as Frank Goodnow,[9] Leonard White,[10] W. F. Willoughby,[11] Luther Gulick and Lyndall Urwick[12] among others, argued that there is and must be a science of public administration, where there is no influence or confusion between it and politics. Typically, politics is understood to be concerned with the development of policy, while public administration is thought to be concerned with the implementation of policy. As we will see throughout the rest of this text, both encompass much more.

Woodrow Wilson

Woodrow Wilson was born in Staunton, VA to the Reverend Dr. Joseph Ruggles and Janet Woodrow Wilson. Both were of Scottish descent, with his mother immigrating to America from Europe. Raised in a pious and academic household, Wilson had a love of learning and Reformed religious beliefs ingrained in him at an early age.

He received his B.A. in 1879 from Princeton, his J.D. from the University of Virginia in 1883 and his Ph.D. in governmental studies from Johns Hopkins University in 1886. After an early and unsuccessful attempt at pursuing a law career, he turned to intellectual endeavors and eventually landed on the Princeton faculty in 1890, where he spent over a decade lecturing, teaching, and writing on history and government. In 1902 he assumed the presidency of Princeton and imposed "democratic" processes—eliminating the influence of "social clubs" and re-emphasizing academics. His reform tendencies led the Democratic Party machine of New Jersey to seek him out as gubernatorial candidate. He later accepted the Democratic national nomination for president in 1912, leading the country through a series of turbulent economic and social times at home, and, of course, through the end of World War I and the failed attempt at securing his beloved League of Nations through negotiations of the treaty of Versailles. He succumbed to a major stroke in 1919 and later died in 1924.

Sources: See the following websites for biographies of Woodrow Wilson: Nobel Foundation, "Woodrow Wilson: The Nobel Peace Prize 1919," http://nobelprize.org/nobel_prizes/peace/laureates/1919/wilson-bio.html (accessed October 2007); E-Notes, "Woodrow Wilson, 1856–1924," www.enotes.com/twentieth-century-criticism/woodrow-wilson/introduction?print=1 (accessed October 2007); and "The White House: Biography of Woodrow Wilson," at www.whitehouse.gov/history/presidents/ww28.html (accessed October 2007).

Table 2.1 highlights an historical evolution of administration in American history. The remainder of this chapter will briefly chronicle these time periods and major figures and scholars connected to the study and practice of public administration.

Table 2.1   Pre-Modern through Modern Public Administration in the United States

Category	Description	Time Period	Major Figures, Scholars
Founding Period	First American Administrative State	1787–1829	*The Federalist Papers* (1787–1788) by Hamilton, Madison, and Jay
Pre-Civil War Period	Jackson's Democracy to the Radicals' Impact	1829–1876	Andrew Jackson; Major General Montgomery C. Meigs, Lincoln's quartermaster general; Lincoln
Post-Civil War Period	Second American Administrative State	1876–1887	Cleveland; Civil Service Commission (1883);
Pre-Classical Period	The Beginnings of Modern Administration	1887–1900	Dorman B. Eaton (1879); Richard T. Ely's autobiography (1938); Woodrow Wilson (1887)
Classical Period	Intellectualizing the Politics-Administration Dichotomy	1900–1926	Frank Goodnow (1900); Frederick Taylor (1911); Taft Commission on Economy and Efficiency in Government (1912–1913); Bureau of Budget Act (1920) and Charles G. Dawes; Leonard White (1926); Mary Parker Follet (1923; 1940)
The Principles Approach	Principles Approach of Scientific Management	1926–1937	W.F. Willoughby (1927); Luther Gulick and Lyndall Urwick (1937); Henri Fayol (1930)
Behavioral Revolution	Behavioral Challenge to the Principles' Approach	1938–1948	Chester Barnard (1938); Fritz Morstein Marx (1946); Herbert Simon (1947); Dwight Waldo's (1948) exception
Public Administration and Political Science	The effect of political science upon public administration	1950–1969	David Easton (1953); Glendon Schubert (1957; 1960); Frederick Mosher (1968); Dwight Waldo's challenge (1956); Emmette S. Redford (1969)
Administrative Management	Decision-making as theme	1956–1967	March and Simon (1958); McGregor (1960); Katz and Kahn (1966)
Reform Management	*New* public management	1968–1979	Marini (1971); Downs (1967); Wildavsky (1964)
Public choice	Economic theory and public administration	1970s–1980s	Buchanan (1969), Tullock (1970), and Ostrom and Ostrom (1971)
Privatization of Government	Privatization and reinvention	1980s–early 1990s	Savas (1987), Osborne and Gaebler (1992)

| Performance Management | Enhancing performance of public agencies | Mid-to-late 1990s | Ingraham, Joyce, and Donahue (2003) |
| Re-founding of Public Administration | Re-emphasis of normative and philosophical emphasis | 1990s–present | Wamsley (1990; 1996) |

The Founding Period (1787–1829)

When **George Washington** (1732–1799) exited public life in 1796, he left a mark on the presidency: that the office of the president was to play an important role in the development and implementation of public policy. Although it is true that the administrative and management of public affairs was generally in the hands of local elected and patronage positions, statesmen such as Washington and **Alexander Hamilton** (1755–1804) recognized the need for central government direction in the formulation, development, and implementation of public policy initiatives. No formal personnel system was in place, although Washington, for example, advocated selection from the educated elite of men of character (alas, they were gender-specific). This clearly attended to a virtue theory of ethics and a practices approach in which we deferred to these elite gentlemen the determination of the public interest. The office of the presidency was in its infancy, but with the efforts and vision of individuals like Hamilton it was apparent that facets of society such as the economy and public finances should be unusually directed by this elite group of gentlemen within the national government.

Of course, famous others of the founders such as Thomas Jefferson and James Madison, concluded that too much centralized control impeded the life and vision of the citizens of various states. Other less famous and sometimes forgotten founders, such as William Livingston, George Mason, John Hancock, Richard Henry Lee and John Witherspoon were no less passionate about public service and the cause of American liberty than their more famous compatriots.[13] **Lynton Caldwell** (1913–2006) contends that Jefferson's experience in France as ambassador and minister to the court of France only reinforced his disdain for centralized bureaucracy. Caldwell quotes from a letter that Jefferson wrote to Madison: "Never was there a country where the practice of governing too much had taken deeper root and done more mischief."[14] Obviously Jefferson was fearful that such an outcome was close to reality in the new United States under the direction of Hamilton as Treasury Secretary, particularly in the establishment of a central banking system.

Hamilton favored rule by an educated elite and Jefferson argued for greater civic input by the citizenry, yet it was evident that both advocated a virtue theory of government ethics by gentlemen of good character. It was a matter of degree as to how many were to be included; Hamilton tended to be more exclusive, Jefferson favored broader civic input. Hamilton argued that politicians must direct administrators. He also called for the determination of the public interest by the educated elite through greater centralization of authority, respect for constitutional principles, and above all a strong, central leader — the President. In this way, Hamilton's practice approach to the public interest was most like (and perhaps inspired by?) the philosopher-kings of Plato and Aristotle who ruled because they possessed greater knowledge, judgment and skill.[15] By contrast, Jefferson may have promoted more broad-based civic input in virtuous administrative leadership to fulfill his popular political predispositions. This included fostering a culture of decentralization of authority, encouraging harmony among the branches of government, promoting simplicity in governing, being flexible with change, and advocating greater responsiveness of civil servants and government to citizens. Jefferson theoretically disagreed with Hamilton's insistence on strong centralization of authority in the executive branch, but at a practical level, Jefferson also advocated a government by educated elite gentlemen and, as President, embraced a very strong central executive leadership.[16]

Washington, Hamilton, Madison, Jefferson, and other founders understood a vision of public interest practices within the classical Greek school of virtue ethics. Plato and Aristotle posited that people have a moral function and well-being defined by the unique human capacity of reason. Merely pursuing pleasure was a life fit for cattle. Our function was "arête," a Greek word meaning moral excellence, as well as magnificence, dignity, cheerfulness, and in the practical wisdom to make it so. Aristotle's *Nichomachean Ethics* detailed a practical wisdom of learning to avoid two extremes in moral decisions: excess (too much) and defect (too little). For example, the virtue of courage is the mean between foolhardiness (excess) and fear (defect).[17]

However, the founders' classical liberal arts education in Plato and Aristotle also may be faulted for fostering a "gentleman's code" of the public interest with few obligations, duties or limits. The result was an elite polity dominated by white male property owners. Washington, Hamilton, and others were criticized for creating strong national government where the public interest was determined by "guardian kings" who were busy pursuing their excellences, but obligations or limits on their actions were sketchy at best. What about the obligations of public servants to the people? What about the proper limits of government?

Pre-Civil War through Reconstruction (1829–1876)

In the interim before the second American administrative state commenced came a half-century of debating, political wrangling, and administrative spoils. It was mostly initiated by Andrew Jackson's philosophy to emphasize populist political responsiveness. **Jacksonianism** was characterized by a redirected emphasis away from a more centralized executive to a much more free-wheeling democracy. The era of gentlemen passed, as Jackson and his democrats were not of the educated elite of that bygone era, but pursued a policy approach to the public interest that favored populism and the promotion of the people's voice — as evidence in part by Jackson's rejection of a national bank.[18]

During this interim, the Civil War also contributed much to the development and understanding of civil service and the necessary administrative apparatus. Staffs, organization, and procedure were the order of the day. According to Paul Van Riper, Major General **Montgomery C. Meigs** (1816–1892), for example, who was President Lincoln's quartermaster general, established the first unified logistical organization in wartime, which helped contribute to the North's ability to develop a sound and systematic organizational apparatus, leading to the South's defeat.[19] National organizations that were patterned after and promoted administrative detail were formed, including the U.S. Government Printing Office and the National Academy of Sciences. Personnel reform was an issue both before and after the War, and in 1871 Senator Lyman Trumbull of Illinois was successful in getting a rider attached to an appropriations bill that authorized the president to regulate various personnel procedures, with President Grant forming the first civil service organization in 1871.[20] Even though it died in 1875 due to lack of funding, it set the course for what would later become the passage of the Pendleton Act in 1883, which created the first permanent Civil Service Commission.

Jacksonianism and the **State's Rights** perspectives of the Civil War presented a more egalitarian approach to the public interest, including the preferences of those who were not part of the educated elite of the era of gentlemen. This marked a shift from classical virtue theory in which elite guardians determined the public interest, toward more utilitarian attempts to calculate the preferences of a more inclusive list (but still, unfortunately, excluding women, blacks, non-property owners, and others). Yet, virtue in public service was still recognized as dedication beyond obligations and excellence above and beyond the call of duty, e.g., Generals Lee, Grant, and Meigs.[21]

Pre-Classical Period (1876–1900)

Public administration historian Paul Van Riper argues that the four decades after the conclusion of the Civil War marked the beginning of the second American administrative state. However, this transition may not have actually occurred until after the passage and implementation of the Pendleton Act in 1883. This short interlude marked the aftermath of the Civil War, with the period of **Reconstruction** taxing the nation's attention. Reconstruction marked a significant period in our administrative history, one that highlighted the engineering, construction, financing, and coordination of major building projects throughout the war-ravaged South. In addition to the reconstruction efforts, major attempts were made at passing civil rights amendments, including the **Civil Rights Act of 1875**, which was designed to eliminate racial discrimination in public places.[22] It failed, but the attempt nonetheless raised the bar for reigniting the federal government's role in state affairs, a move that was not only political in nature but administrative as well.

The passage of the **Pendleton Act in 1883**, forming the first national-level **Civil Service Commission**, was the administrative highlight of this period. President Arthur signed into law a bill titled, "A Bill to Regulate and Improve the Civil Service of the United States," which included several key provisions toward establishing a modern public administration system, including 1) competitive exams, 2) open civil service, and 3) initially no higher educational requirement, although this was modified by the 1930s, with a move toward professionalizing civil service, and 4) the Pendleton Act did not establish a broad administrative hierarchy, such as existed in England at the time, but left the top positions open to executive choice.[23] Clearly, the Pendleton Act did diverge somewhat from the parallel British model, particularly with regard to the practical aspect of administering competitive exams and, especially, the ability to enter the civil service at a variety of levels, whereas the British model entailed entry-level selection only. In addition, the President was to be de facto head of the civil service, given that the Pendleton Act provided the President power to 1) appoint and remove members of the Civil Service Commission, and 2) to approve the making of the rules of the Civil Service Commission.[24]

Box 2.1   Establishment of the Civil Service Commission

Following the assassination of President James A. Garfield by a disgruntled job seeker, Congress passed the Pendleton Act in January of 1883. The act was steered through Congress by long-time reformer Senator George Hunt Pendleton of Ohio. The act was signed into law by President Chester A. Arthur, who had become an ardent reformer after Garfield's assassination. The Pendleton Act provided that Federal Government jobs are awarded on the basis of merit and those Government employees are selected through competitive exams. The act also made it unlawful to fire or demotes for political reasons employees who were covered by the law. The law further forbids requiring employees to give political service or contributions. The Civil Service Commission was established to enforce this act.

The Pendleton Act transformed the nature of public service. Today many well-educated and well-trained professionals have found a rewarding career in Federal service. When the Pendleton Act went into effect, only 10 percent of the Government's 132,000 employees were covered. Today, more than 90 percent of the 2.7 million Federal employees are covered.

Source: Reprinted from Our Documents, "Pendleton Act (1883)," www.ourdocuments.gov/doc.php?doc=48 (accessed October 2007).

In addition to political action being taken at the national level to make more orderly and equitable civil service policy, there were rumblings at the state and local levels. New York and Massachusetts passed civil service legislation in the mid-1880s, and later, between 1900 and 1920, several other states did as well, including California, New Jersey, Ohio, and Wisconsin. As some scholars title this time period, **"Government by the Good,"** laid the groundwork for what would become the birth of modern public administration.[25] That groundwork, for example, came in the form of Woodrow Wilson's 1887 article titled, "The Study of Administration."

Wilson's primary thesis was that politics and administration are and must remain separate, because politics was grounded in what Wilson called the "devilishness" of partisan persuasion, while administration was rigorous and scientific, guided by principles of administration and management. Interestingly enough, though, the supposed influence of Wilson's groundbreaking article did not take place in the developmental years of the scientific management and principles' approach period. According to Paul Van Riper, "an examination of major political and social science works of the period between 1890 and World War I showed no citation whatever of the essay in any of these volumes."[26] It was not until the 1930s, and really even into the 1950s, before any significant importance was placed upon Wilson's essay. Wilson set the stage for encouraging the systematic and rigorous study of public administration.

This period marked a return to the practices approach and virtue, although not of the classical Greek virtue theory of the era of gentlemen. Virtue in the life of the individual public servant was redefined as 'merit' and attempts were made to measure merit by new sciences of the mind. To be sure, those determined to have merit governed a larger and larger bureaucracy. But merit was defined more equitably, without the founders' emphasis on elite class-background, education, or aspiration. The pre-classical period has been labeled a middle-class reform movement, focusing on middle-class notions of competence in public service while avoiding the excess of elite gentlemen and the defect of populist spoils.[27]

Classical Period (1900–1937)

Scholar Jeff Greene contends that besides the carrying over of Wilson's dichotomy into the rapidly changing political and economic society at the beginning of the twentieth century, this time period was marked by two distinct models of power fighting for supremacy in American democracy. The first was "rule by factions," which highlighted the use of party machines in the control of urban politics, and the second was the ascendance of a public interest model, which reflected the dreams of political and administrative reformers, one that highlighted reforms on the local level.[28] For example, the **New York Bureau of Municipal Research** (1906) established the nation's first school of public administration in 1911. Under the leadership of Charles Beard, the school's mission was to train and educate local administrative personnel. By 1924 the school moved to Syracuse University and became what is now the **Maxwell School of Citizenship and Public Affairs**. These reformers embraced the assumption "that politics should not be mixed with management and that management can be studied scientifically."[29]

Box 2.2   Maxwell School of Citizenship and Public Affairs

George Holmes Maxwell was a successful Boston patent attorney, financier, inventor and shoe manufacturer, and a steadfast defender of democracy, education, and the American Way, as it was defined in New England in 1900. Although distressed with American politics as it was practiced in that era, Maxwell retained his optimism about the nation's future. He helped create a fund of $500,000 for Syracuse to establish a School of American Citizenship. He noted that "The primary object of this school is to teach good citizenship," said Maxwell at the time of the School's founding, "to cull from every source those principles, facts, and elements which, combined, make up our rights and duties and our value and distinctiveness as United States citizens. This involves the diffusion of good citizenship throughout the entire student body." Thus the school would focus on civics.

But Frederick Morgan Davenport, a former educator and politician who had signed on as a consultant to the new college, argued for a school that also would graduate trained practitioners in public affairs—young people who could instantly enter government and immediately effect a change. The name of the school—the Maxwell School of Citizenship and Public Affairs—reflected the coexistence of these two often diverse curricular directions; both of which were represented in the same school, thus making Maxwell a singular experiment in higher education in the United States.

Source: Reproduced from the Maxwell School of Syracuse University, "Maxwell History," www.maxwell.syr.edu/deans/history.asp (accessed October 2007).

Frank Goodnow's Influence. A quarter of a century earlier, with the publication of **Frank Goodnow's** (1859–1939) *Politics and Administration* (1900), the intellectualization of public administration began in earnest. Even though Woodrow Wilson came first, we concur with Paul Van Riper's belief that it is Frank Goodnow who spawned the new era of academic public administration.[30] Goodnow argued that there were two different functions of government: politics and administration. Politics, led by the legislative branch, dealt with the idealisms and values of the public good, while administration, led by the executive branch, dealt with the implementation of that good. Both were necessary to the fulfillment of governmental obligations, such as the public good, but they were not the same. In fact, Goodnow considered administration the superior given its aspiration to be objective and unbiased in the pursuit of the public good.

This scholarly movement and practical application of scientific management was spurred on by the scientific revolution that swept Europe, especially Germany and Great Britain, requiring people to recognize the meaning and merit of machines and the relationship between the two, and the ability to apply this relationship to the administration of organizations. Thus, it was the **scientific management** movement, led by such luminaries as **Frederick Taylor** (1856–1915) and Henri Fayol, which spawned government commissions and reports touting the need for improving governmental economy and efficiency, such as the **Taft Commission on Economy and Efficiency in Government (1912–1913)** and legislative acts, such as the **Bureau of Budget Act of 1920**. The latter, for example, was not only intended to provide the executive branch with much needed input in to the budget-making scenario, but was to show that government was to function more business-like, meaning it should embrace the values of economy and efficiency.[31] Leonard White's 1926 public administration textbook titled *Introduction to the Study of Public Administration*—the first full-length treatise on public administration as a discipline—reflected a belief that public administration was to be a science that should strive to be unbiased.

A second major component of the classical period was the development of **scientific principles** for application in administrative areas. Both private industry and government sought scientific principles of management that could be universally applied. In other words, administration was administration and management was management, regardless of the venue.[32] These were not the pre-existing principles approach to the public interest found in the values of the Constitution or other deeply-rooted sources (which is the focus of later scholars, e.g., the Blacksburg Gang). Rather, these were scientific principles glossed from an overview of military history and the Industrial Revolution—where the primary focus was to produce as many widgets as possible—and other operational similarities in bureaucratic implementation of public policy. The goal of the scientific management process was to discover and apply these operational principles to any number of government functions and operations, with the anticipated result being greater efficiency, effectiveness, and economy of administration. Several questions remained: What were these principles? How did one discover them? How were they applied?

W.F. Willoughby's book, *Principles of Public Administration* (1927), was published as the second major text in the discipline of public administration. Willoughby furthered the argument that public sector organizations, like their private brethren, could achieve the outcomes of efficiency, effectiveness, and economy when properly administered, using techniques gathered from the business world, overseeing such functions as data gathering, personnel, finance, organizational staffing, and others. Along with notables such as Frederick A. Cleveland, Frank Goodnow, historian Charles Beard, and management genius Luther Gulick (see below)—Willoughby was a member of the Taft Commission to reform the national bureaucracy. This experience contributed to his thesis that government was destined to be run like a business.[33]

POSDCORB. It was not until the late 1930s that the use of scientific principles was seriously applied by the national government. Both **Luther Gulick** (1865–1918) and **Lyndall Urwick** (1891–1983), who were friends of President Franklin Roosevelt, were tapped to give scholarly legitimacy to FDR's plan to create what may have been an imperial executive branch. Their *Papers on the Science of Administration* (1937) was part of a broader report to the President's Committee on Administrative Science, whose primary task was to not only accept principles as academically important but as administratively practical. The management principles promoted by Gulick and Urwick were summarized in the form of the acronym, **POSDCORB**:

- Planning: envision and strategize for the future;
- Organizing: plan and systematically align and categorize;
- Staffing: meet all personnel and human resource needs;

- Directing: develop sound leadership and managerial skills;
- COordinating: bring together all resources for fulfillment of organization goals;
- Reporting: develop sound communication means and technology
- Budgeting: control the organization through fiscal planning and accounting.[34]

Whether it was building a bridge, manning a tank, or sweeping city streets, the need for POSDCORB was (and still is!) readily apparent.

The Behavioral Revolution (1937–1960)

By the WWII generation a new "wind" was blowing through the Ivy Tower, and would soon be replicated in the public workplace. The **behavioralists** challenged the doctrines of politics-administration dichotomy and scientific principles of administration. The result was a revolution in public administration—both parts of the classical school's theoretical framework were eventually discarded. First, the politics/administration dichotomy was flawed as illogical. **Fritz Morstein Marx**, for example, argued that no administrative-based decision was ever completely free of politics, simply because by definition an administrative decision involved personal and political aspects.[35] Was it ever possible to discern the difference? Was the underpinning of the politics/administration dichotomy in public administration, at best, naïve?[36] The general answer by academics at the time was yes. If the dichotomy could be challenged; then what was the reality of the nearly sacrosanct scientific principles of administration? Some had stood for millennia and were widely accepted. Could they be challenged as well? The answer, too, was a resounding yes!

The students of the behavioral revolution did not simply accept statements or ideas or even principles without subjecting them to rigorous empirical testing. At the very least they should undergo strict tests of reason and logic. This is what the behavioral revolutionaries did; they subjected the normative values and application of the principles' approach to the rigors of reason and empiricism. From their perspective, the principles were wanting.

Barnard and Simon. The first challenge did not come from the academic community, but from the pen of **Chester I. Barnard** (1886–1961), former president of New Jersey Bell Telephone. Barnard did not look at organizations as functionalist bureaucracies; he saw them as cooperative systems, where the "functions of the executive" were to balance the work of the employers, particular in the area of creating and maintaining more effective forms and types of communication.[37] But it was the work of a brilliant University of Chicago political science Ph.D. named **Herbert Simon** (1916–2001) that revolutionized the study of public administration, and in particular the decision-making process, that formed the second and most formidable challenge.[38]

It is interesting to note that the young, twenties-something Simon, who took a position at the University of California-Berkeley before his dissertation at Chicago was complete, had never held an administrative position in either the private or public sector. So, how could he critique the classical era figures before him who had vast executive experiences? What could he say that they didn't already know? The first question is answered by Simon himself. In his autobiography, *Models of My Life*, Simon indicated that he read with great care Barnard's book, and drew from Barnard many of the ideas that formed the basis for his *Administrative Behavior*, including the "zone of indifference," the "equilibrium of inducements and contributions" and "bounded rationality."[39] As for the second question, he said that pioneers before him did not accomplish a theoretical and systematic approach to explaining decisions and decision making. This was the primary task that Simon assumed.

Simon was convinced that the scientific principles of administration were more contradictory than practical. For example, since the days of Classical Greece, the principle of span of control required a small number (i.e., a span of 6-to-8) who were directly under the control of a superior in order for communication to be effective and to achieve greater efficiency. If the span of control is small under each supervisor (i.e., a span of 6-to-8), then the hierarchy of the larger pyramid-shaped organizations increases in size and height. Yet another principle states that messages within the organization are better communicated or maximized in a flatter hierarchy. Simon argued that both principles could be correct; the principle of a small span of control (thus, a taller hierarchy) is contradictory with the principle of better communication through a flatter organizational structure. It is the contradictory, illogical nature of the principles that revealed them to be unscientific, or as he wrote in 1946, mere "proverbs."[40] Proverbs are fine for poems and songs, Simon argued, but not for administrative decision-making. Instead, he urged more academic attention that required testing, reasoning, and empirical verification.

Simon, like many other scholars in the behavioral revolution of the twentieth century, explicitly applied the radical skepticism of **logical positivism** to the study of public administration. Simon cited the logical positivist A.J. Ayer, who taught that empirical science was the sole source of knowledge. Logical positivists formulated the so-called "verification principle" requiring empirical evidence of the senses for any proposition to be meaningful. Otherwise, it was literally "hot air"—merely the expression of one's own desires or will to power. Simon judged the classical principles of administration wanting by this empirical verification standard and thus, mere proverbs. So, too, was the concept of the public interest discarded by the behavioralists as nonsense. Instead, he sought what he called a "value-free" approach to administration—free from proverbs and the "hot air" of the public interest.[41]

Yet, Simon and most behavioralists did not go to the value-free extreme of ethical egoism and Nietzsche, the Nazis, and others in a world in which the only valid moral standard was the obligation to promote your will to power above all others. Instead, Simon's new scientific approach to administrative behavior applied new formulations of microeconomic concepts such as "satisficing", equilibrium of inducements and contributions, and bounded rationality—for which he won the 1978 Nobel in economics. His utilitarian approach to values and public service did not embrace the cynical will to power of ethical egoism. For Simon, the public interest was the sum of its parts—calculations of individual preferences.[42]

Somehow during this time of intense skepticism by academics, public administration continued on and prospered at the national, state, and local levels; perhaps even in spite of these earlier revelations. Perhaps the trust in public administrators was spurred on by the practical successes of bureaucrats in WWII and the post-war economic boom. Perhaps it was the trust in public servants that people knew personally, like the local cop, city manager, or soldiers who came home. Or perhaps the radical skepticism of academics was assessed by most Americans as false-to-life and a bit hair-brained. Contracts were made, business was conducted, and people usually made things work even without empirical verification of every proposition. The fact that all propositions could not be empirically verified, or that people sometimes disagreed, or perhaps even that they did not care, did not mean that there was a complete lack of meaning or mere will to power. Things continued to work in spite of these damning academic criticisms. But this academic venom seemed to close the door to further study of public administration for Simon, who left the study of public administration to spend most of his life seeking a workable approach to artificial intelligence.[43]

Management Emphasis (1960–1968)

Within academe, the study of public administration became for many an orphan in a brave new world. It had no home it could call its own; it was not wanted in political science departments taken over in the behavioral revolution. It did not fit into other social-science disciplines, e.g., when it took up residence in many colleges of business administration during the 1970s. A teaching and research emphasis placed on case studies and the inauguration of comparative public administration during the 1960s and 1970s helped to dispel some of the poison coming forth from the dominant behavioral approach to political science.[44] In addition, the center of epistemological attention became the government bureaucracy. This led to both normative questions of legitimacy, civic pride, and democratic values, and to a new interest in management. Was public administration up to the challenge of embracing management studies, particularly as management research was coming out of business schools and departments of industrial psychology, sociology, and others?

In the "real" world, the 1960s held a new fascination with management and corporate life, improving the decision-making capabilities of managers, as well as examining the process of making decisions.[45] Popular culture celebrated the rise of American management culture, such as the 1961 Broadway musical, "How to Succeed in Business Without Really Trying" (made into a 1967 film). The movers and shakers for a new "management is management" movement came into academe by way of new colleges of business administration. The curricula for new MBA programs displayed many of the same courses that public administration schools had tried to fit within political science departments without success. Classes such as organization theory, personnel management, and budgeting and finance were all about management, and management was all about people and systems. Both were necessary, and both were affected by management principles and ideas; the majority of individuals who believed that there was no difference, or at least little difference, between public and private management.

But public administration scholars came to ask: if this was case, then why is the term public used in public administration and business used in business administration? Obviously there must be something different between the two. Those who believed that the two disciplines were similar examined the world instrumentally or in parts; they didn't study the organization as a whole or the environment or nature in which it existed. There really was no need. Surely, there must be something different between public and private management, public and private personnel systems, private and public budgeting and finance systems, and so forth?

The so-called participatory approach to decision-making and management change, which was firmly rooted in the behaviorist school, came into vogue with works by **Douglas McGregor** (1906–1964), Robert Blake and Jane Mouton, and Chris Argyris.[46] These and many others contributed to the broad influence of social scientists adapting cybernetic theory from biology and developing theories of open versus closed organizational systems. These influences and others shifted the focus of public administration scholars toward redefining themselves, and often separating themselves from historic roots with political science. One result of this era was that most public administration graduate programs were no longer taught within political science departments.

The New Public Administration (1968–1984)

The 1960s were a radical era in politics and culture—and in public administration, too. Searching for a renewed public administration, an aging Dwight Waldo in 1968 convened a conference made up primarily of younger scholars. The focus and eventual outcome of the conference was known as the New Public Administration. What was new about it? The newness was in the focus. Instead of going over and over the how's and whys of achieving greater efficiency, economy, and effectiveness—often called the Big E's—a fourth E was presented: **social equity**.[47] Public bureaucracies were still the locus of their study, but their focus was entirely redirected toward developing a softer side, one that was more normative and ideological and less behaviorist, more socially activist and less functional, more directed toward meeting the needs of clients, and even creating not only the opportunity for social change but creating social change itself.[48]

New Public Administration scholars criticized the behavioral revolution and Herbert Simon for hidden status quo conservatism. In contrast, the New Public Administration openly promoted normative, ideological, activist, and client-oriented social change. To criticize Simon, New Public Administration scholars turned the positivist assumptions of the behavioral revolution upon itself. Logical positivism, underlying the behavioral revolution, cynically asserted that all non-empirical talk is merely the imposition of the will to power or "hot air." Positivism was closely tied to ethical egoism, which asserted that no matter what people may say, they were really acting for the sake of their personal well-being only. Thus, these 1960s critics claimed that even when the **behavioral revolution** attempted to include new voices and ideas to the public forum, the decisions and actions by policy makers continued to reflect old status quo notions. Further, the behavioral revolution duped the American public by depicting public policy decisions as the operation of empirically verifiable markets and political processes.[49] So, for these 1960s critics, the behavioral revolution was a facade of pseudo-science that disguised the actual operation of a will to power and rhetorical ploys to advance the status quo or private interests of political elites.[50]

While this criticism of the behavioral revolution stuck, the New Public Administration quickly ran out of gas. Their detractors argued that public administration had to accomplish something tangible; it had to focus on outputs, outcomes, and a more concrete public interest. While Dwight Waldo and H. George Frederickson and the **Minnowbrook** I (1968), II (1988), and III (2008) crowds, respectively, argued for social equity and social justice to be dispensed by agency bureaucrats, Vincent and Elinor Ostrom, James Buchanan and **Gordon Tullock**, for example, contended that the theories of microeconomics included in public choice theory should instead be applied to public bureaucracies.[51] Anthony Downs theorized that economics as a whole would go much further toward explaining bureaucratic behavior. Aaron Wildavsky laid the groundwork for budgetary incrementalism. **Peter Drucker** (1909–2005) argued that public administration needed to adopt business principles, strongly suggesting that by adopting them it would enhance the business end of public administration.[52] All of these micro changes sowed the seed for the later 1980s privatization, the 1990s re-engineering and reinvention, and later the 2000s version of performance management. It also balanced with a policies approach to the public interest and utilitarian benefits/costs analysis against excesses of justice, equity and ambiguous philosophical approaches to the public interest by the New Public Administration.

The Re-Founding of Public Administration (1984–Present)

Gary Wamsley and others from The Virginia Polytechnic Institute and State University (or Virginia Tech), located in Blacksburg, Virginia, published what is now referred to as the **Blacksburg Manifesto** and its various iterations.[53] The Manifesto is an inherently normative prescription for the problems of public administration within the current democratic and political environment, largely focusing on the founding principles, specifically those values that framed the Constitution. Conceptually, the Blacksburg scholars desired to re-conceptualize public administration from an organizational concept to "The Public Administration"—the institution of government. The focus is not on whether there should be a government or even how to reduce whatever level of government there is, but on what form of governmental intervention is most effective in the real world. The Blacksburg scholars attended to a principles approach to the public interest as central in defining public administration. But, unlike the ambiguous principle of equity, the Blacksburg scholars focused on exacting pre-existing principles such as freedom of speech, press and religion, property rights, equal protection, and due process of law as written and interpreted by authoritative cases involving the U.S. Constitution and enduring laws.

The Manifesto was a normative statement advocating an enhanced and more complex role for The Public Administration "... to run a Constitution" (a phrase quoted from Woodrow Wilson). The disjuncture between what is good government and good management increases the likelihood of damning the former and praising the latter, without realizing (or wanting to realize anyway) that both are necessary to run a Constitution. The Blacksburg scholars did public administration a great service by redirecting the focus of the public administration practitioner and scholar toward greater awareness and appreciation of the role of the public interest within a constitutional system as envisioned by the founders.[54]

But is virtue more primary or basic to our sense of what is right and wrong than duty—does it have greater moral worth? Philippa Foot has argued, "The man who acts charitably out of a sense of duty is not to be undervalued, but it is the other who most shows virtue and therefore to the other that most moral worth is attributed."[55] While the narrative public interest practices of virtue and character seem deeply rooted in the human experience, they do not seem sufficient to show virtue ethics to be primary or more basic than ethics based on principles of duty or policies of preferences. Instead, both approaches seem to be complementary; for every principle of duty or policy of preferences, there is a corresponding virtue practice. Are the virtue practices merely the mirror image of the principles and policies of the public interest?

The application of constitutional principles to the practices of the public interest in the Blacksburg Manifesto follows the injunction that "traits without principles are blind."[56] Students of the Blacksburg School have greatly enriched our understanding of public interest practices and virtue in the lives of great American administrators, such as Alexander Hamilton, Thomas Jefferson, and others.[57] Yet the Blacksburg scholars went beyond biographies of the virtues and practices of great administrators to analyze their applications of specific constitutional doctrines. Without these specific constitutional principles, how can virtue ethics theory and public interest practices determine the rightness or wrongness of actions? When virtuous founders committed evil, such as the 1804 duel in which Aaron Burr killed Alexander Hamilton, did we simply call it a moment of weakness in an otherwise good life and turn a blind eye? No, even Burr, who initially and without seemingly any remorse for his evil deed, was later indicted and remembered in infamy.[58]

Rather, virtue of the administrator was not distinct from the means or behaviors in public interest activities, but virtue was always focused on the special moral value of these ends of excellence in character. The goal of the public interest practices was to provide the opportunity for, and development of, moral excellence of the person. The law and other public interest principles are not the only model of wisdom on human worth—virtue practices focus on a greater moral value of aspirations beyond mere legal duties.[59] As John Rawls argued in what he called the Aristotelian principle: "The virtues are excellences ... The lack of them will tend to undermine both our self-esteem and the esteem that our associates have for us."[60] The Blacksburg scholars called much-needed attention to the importance of close ties between the practices and the principles of the public interest.

Waves of Change (1992–Present)

Several contemporary approaches to public administration seek greater inclusiveness in defining who is a part of public administration. After all, implementing the public interest involves more than civil service employees. These contemporary approaches give greater attention to the role of private and non-profit organizations, faith-based initiatives, postmodern perspectives, feminist perspectives, and digital information shared by all with individual citizens. With such diversity of perspectives, contemporary waves of change greatly expand who is included as the focus of virtue in the practices of public interest, and more closely tie the principles, policies, and practices approaches to the public interest.

E.S. Savas promulgated the **privatization thesis**, which argued that various aspects and components of public administration or public organizations would be more efficient and economical if they were farmed out to the private sector.[61] The Reagan Revolution spurred this type of thinking, given that Ronald Reagan said that big government was the enemy of the American people and the freedom they love. Instead of government cleaning the streets, guarding the prisoners and picking up the trash, the privatization scholars urged that we turn over these and many other tasks over to the private sector. They argued that the private sector was more efficient and frugal with its funds and the spending of those funds; it was more effective in putting together people, management, and processes that it only seemed right to privatize.

Privatization evolved into **reinvention** by the late 1980s and early 1990s. David Osborne and Ted Gaebler and Osborne and Peter Plastrik argued that it wasn't enough to privatize or re-engineer government; it was necessary to reinvent it.[62] Transform it from the inside out. Changing the focus and the locus of public administration was not even the primary ingredient to success (however one defines success). Osborne and Gaebler studied dozens of local governments, talked to many city, town, and county managers, and interviewed many line and staff personnel, who worked in local organizations that engaged in the process of reinventing themselves, all the while redefining their purpose for even existing. The notion was to assume a risk-taking outlook and sport an entrepreneurial spirit that was to enhance the bottom line of public service.

Performance management blossomed in the mid- to late-1990s and continues to the present. Calling for strict guidelines on spending, financial, and output measures, the clarion call among like-minded public administration scholars is one of performance output and performance enhancement, striving to enhance and improve the bottom line performance of public agencies, without engaging in privatization techniques.[63]

Non-profit organizations and faith-based initiatives play a significantly important and influential role in government service delivery. **Robert B. Denhardt** and Joseph W. Grubbs pointed out that the importance of nongovernmental organizations (NGOs) was multi-fold: "NGOs must be considered not only for their part in implementing public programs, but also their growing influence in raising issues to the public agenda, lobbying for particular policy alternatives, and guiding political and administrative decision making."[64] Non-profit organizations filled roles and functions in society that many governmental organizations, departments, or agencies cannot do as well as non-profit organizations. A non-profit organization is defined as an independent or third-sector of the nation or state's economic, social, political, and religious make-up. The Johns Hopkins University Center for Civil Society Studies found that U.S. nonprofits had 9.4 million paid workers (or 7.6 percent of all paid employment in the U.S.) and another 4.7 million full-time equivalent volunteers, for a total workforce of 14.1 million as of mid-2004. Nonprofits do make a profit—or else they could not stay in business—but they do not transfer those profits to shareholders. Whatever profit is used, which of course is tax-exempt, must, according to their 501(c)3 status return to the organization itself.[65]

What is the purpose of nonprofits in public administration? How do they help deliver public services? **Lester Salamon**, a longtime researcher and advocate of non-profit organizations, argued that nonprofits were a "... special class of entities dedicated to mobilizing private initiative for the common good."[66] Furthermore, nonprofits have a substantial stake in affecting, directing, and ultimately administering public policy. Given the fact, for example, that approximately half of all tax-deductible nonprofits are related to the health and human services' industry; it is easy to agree with Brookings Institution scholar, Jeffrey M. Berry, that, "They (meaning nonprofits) have an enormous stake in what government does ..."[67]

Although scholars are just beginning to examine their impact within traditional public administration, faith-based initiatives are beginning to assume a much more powerful role in the shaping of public policy, especially in the areas of health and human services. Although faith-based solutions to thorny human services problems, such as poverty and homelessness, are not new to the fabric of American caring and compassion; President George W. Bush made them the corner piece of his supposedly "compassionate conservatism" agenda.

Box 2.3   Faith-Based Initiatives

The White House Office of Faith-Based and Community Initiatives (renamed The White House Office of Faith-based and Neighborhood Partnerships), originally headed by Jim Towey (now led by Joshua DuBois), spearheaded a multi-prong federal effort for expanding the "charitable choice" provision of the 1996 Welfare Reform Act. Substantial negative attention was paid to the government's advocacy and use of faith-based initiatives through the federal grants process, largely because of disagreements over the nature and extent of church-state separation.

Source: Ira Lupu and Robert W. Tuttle, "Freedom from Religion Foundation, Inc (and others) v. Jim Towey, Director of White House Office of Faith-Based and Community Initiatives (and others)," www.religionandsocialpolicy.org/legal/legal_ update_display.cfm?id=32 (accessed October 2007).

Other challenges to behaviorism or modernism in public administration come from streams of thought within postmodernism and feminist perspectives. Following one stream of postmodernism within contemporary sociology and philosophy, scholars believe that modern symbols and language in public administration may be deconstructed in order to get at the truth of social and cultural phenomena. For example, to move beyond hierarchical bureaucracy as the dominant form of organization under modernism, scholars Charles Fox and Hugh Miller argue that this concept does not truly represent the reality of organizations; hierarchical bureaucracy is a modernist social construct that we may break down by use of new word construction, puns, etymology and other word play. Similarly, David Farmer believes that, through "reflective interpretation," we can be more sensitive in how use of language alters our understanding of what public administration is and what it can do. Scholars of these **postmodern** streams and feminist perspectives generally posit that our concept and application of public administration are hindered because of cultural and societal constructs that frame our understanding. Once these constructs (e.g., hierarchy) are reduced then will it be possible for all persons to realize our dependency upon each other, and not upon false ideas of organization and order.[68]

A final wave of change comes by way of the high-tech, information-based revolution that aspires to allow every individual to be informed and participate in public administration through transparency reforms, such as "Wiki-governance," or "collaborative administration." Technological innovations in government, especially in the area of enhanced communication between citizen and the state are nothing new, and in fact have a rich history.[69] What is new is the speed and transparency with which these technological innovations are changing—or least requiring recognition and responses to the innovations—the way public administration operates, such as the use of e-government, web portals and the **Internet**. As one scholar notes, "The promise of e-government is not, as some suppose, putting existing paper-based processes of bureaucracy into digital form. Rather, the promise is really nothing less than a profound transformation of the way the government does business."[70]

According to some scholars, building the virtual state[71] is not simply technologically different, but it requires an institutional theoretical framework to help explain the changes that are underway. This theory is important, especially for public administrators, because it questions the way government officials at all levels of government do business *or* can do business within a technologically and virtually enhanced state of affairs. In fact, it is this technological challenge, coupled with understanding and working with and within "multi-organizational arrangements," that spawned the Minnowbrook III (2008) conference.

E-government, e-citizens, and even e-democracy are terms that did not exist ten years ago, but are now becoming ingrained in our language, culture, and consciences. With the use of web portals or web sites, for example, citizens at all levels of government can not only download and print forms, pay tax bills, renew driver license registrations, and see a digital map of their downtown through **Geographical Information Systems** (GIS) technology, but may also engage in an e-forum via streaming video, go online and chat with the city manager, town mayor, or county commissioner, or register their disapproval (or approval) of a specific policy decision. The computer, the Internet, and the various components associated with this technological creation are changing the way citizens and public officials interact and affect the way government actions are made.[72]

What does this revolution mean, especially in terms of bureaucratic responsibility and political accountability? Who becomes the more important figure in agenda setting, for example: the mayor or the CIO (chief information officer)? Does it mean that if a citizen does not have access to or cannot afford a computer or a fast Internet hookup that they have less citizen rights than others who can? Does increased e-government capacity reduce the number of government officials needed, thus having a negative effect upon personnel retention? On a more positive note, we need to ask about the impact of e-government's (even e-governance) upon outsourcing, contracting, performance measurement, and the impact upon the Third Sector of society: non-profits. These and many other questions require thoughtful and critical responses.

Conclusion

This brief overview of public administration presented the lived-world of public administration. Some of our history is focused on great persons, such as Thomas Jefferson and Alexander Hamilton. Other attention was given to more ordinary lives of individuals, organizations and institutions. All were placed within the evolving schools of thought in public administration through history that may be more meaningful because we focused on people, on the lived-world.

Public administration is anything but a static process. It is a lived-world of people in organizations changing with the cultural, political, economic, social, and even psychological winds; winds that come from both the academic halls and the offices of practitioners. It is not so important or concerning that change occurs, but it is somewhat disconcerting to note that the changes were often made in order for academic public administration, especially, to find its place. Was public administration a discipline within political science, business, schools of management, economics, social psychology, or perhaps as the Blacksburg scholars hint, even departments of history and philosophy? Does it make a difference?

This examination of the lived-world of the history of public administration allowed us to focus on the practices approach to the public interest and virtue ethics to ask the fundamental question: what does it mean to be a good public administrator? The practices approach (and virtue ethics) is ordinarily found in TV, movies, books, the web, and in our oral traditions. We commonly make judgments as to who is a good person, and share the practical simplicity of answering moral questions with advice to adopt good traits, imitate heroes, and be virtuous. The practices approach seems to complement other approaches to the public interest, and new waves of change include a greater diversity of perspectives from the private sector, nonprofits, faith-based initiatives, women, and the many through e-governance and transparency.

However, there are criticisms of the practice approach. First, are there no obligations on the philosopher-kings who determine the public interest by pursuing excellence? Aristotle and the founders seemed to live by a "gentlemen's code" which failed to express limits, obligations, or duties. How can you have a public interest theory or ethics without a theory of obligation? How can you claim moral excellence in the public interest, yet have few or no obligations to serve others? In its defense, the public interest practices approach was never so fully divorced from the real-world of legal obligations, legal duties, and service to others. But the practices approach disputes the idea that law and legal obligation constitute the only model of wisdom in valuing human worth. The practices approach and virtue ethics focuses on the higher ends of human aspirations, not just dutiful performance of obligations—and we can all recognize the difference in moral worth between a labor of love and dutiful labor. Second, how can the practices approach and virtue ethics determine the rightness or wrongness of actions? While practices of virtue seem deeply rooted in the narrative of human history, they do not seem to be primary but rather complementary. For every principle of duty or policy of preferences, there is a corresponding virtue practice. We are left with a question for following chapters: are the virtue practices merely the mirror image of the principles and policies of the public interest?

We argue that the lived-world of public administration has always focused, in varying ways, on the public interest. This should be the ultimate goal of public administration and public administrators. But how can this happen, when the discipline is rooted in and tries to draw from so many different disciplines, alters its focus and locus at the slightest hint of political, economic, and social change, cynically discounts the commitment to fulfill common substantive goals, and instead settles for a process-market framework that supposedly allows each one to accomplish their individual preferences? Perhaps this history may mirror the experiences of others to reveal that the public interest has not been found in reinvented techniques, enhanced performance measurement standards, or postmodern postulates of social change. Rather it is found in the concept of public interest practices.

Action Steps

1. Discuss the role of history in administration in the public interest by reading the U.S. Supreme Court case of *Winter v. Natural Resources Defense Council*, 555 U.S. ___ (decided 11/12/2008). This case concerned an injunction to stop the Navy's use of sonar that may have caused serious injuries to marine mammals and their habitats. The Court found that "the balance of equities and the public interest.... tip strongly in favor of the Navy." Do you believe the Supreme Court would have treated the Navy as a bureaucracy any differently in some past era of public administration? Would the public interest have been similar or different in past eras of public administration?

2. Students break into teams of three or four. Instructor assigns a one-to-two sentence statement to each group, one that reflects the importance of any of the historical periods of public administration. Ask each group to take a decidedly value-based position on the statement, discuss it in the group, form a position, and then reassemble to debate the various positions. Each group should assign a secretary and spokesman to record and articulate, respectively, the group's position. For example, in the *Management (1960–1968)* phase provide the following statement: "Business administration principles were expected to be translated into public values, particularly in the fulfillment of agency performance." [The instructor may want to direct them to some of Peter Drucker's works, especially his opus: *Management: Tasks, Responsibilities, and Practices* (1973; 1993).]

3. Have the students read excerpts from Herbert Simon's *Models of My Life* (1991), where he noted he was strongly influenced by the writing of Chester Barnard's work *Functions of the Executive*. Examine Simon's reasoning and how this shaped his own thinking regarding the development of the behavioral revolution in social sciences, particularly political science and later public administration.

4. What is the re-founding movement of public administration as initiated by Gary Wamsley and others at Virginia Tech? Why is it significant to our understanding of the public interest in public administration? Write a short two-page description and critique of the re-founding movement. Bring to class and be prepared to discuss and defend your ideas.

5. Do a *Google* search of the term public interest. What do they find? What is being said about the term, whether negative or positive? In what context is it being written? Write a short two-page summary-analysis.

6. Assemble into groups of three and contact about five to ten public administration officials and ask them what they believe the public interest is. Record their responses and come back to class and discuss the findings.

Exam Review Preparation

1. In a short essay, assess the common characteristics of the various definitions of public administration. What are they? What does this tell us about public administration? Write your own definition of public administration. Defend it.

2. Identify the importance of each public administration personality or time period.

    a. Frank Goodnow's *Politics and Administration* (1900)

    b. Woodrow Wilson's "The Study of Administration," (1887)

    c. Alexander Hamilton and James Madison

    d. Classical Period of Public Administration (1900–1937)

    e. Herbert Simon's critique of the principles approach.

    f. The re-founding period and the Blacksburg Manifesto.

    g. POSDCORB

3. Explain the main impact the behavioral revolution had upon the development of public administration.

4. Discuss the various waves of change that influenced public administration, especially from the 1990s to the present.

5. Assess the differences and similarities between business and public administration.

6. Is the privatization thesis viable to the vast majority of public services? Explain.

7. What role are non-profits and even faith-based organizations playing in the delivery of public, especially social, services? How do they assist and/or detract from traditional means of public service delivery?

Key Concepts

Behavioral revolution
Blacksburg Manifesto
Chester I. Barnard
Dwight Waldo
E-government, e-citizens, and e-democracy
Frank Goodnow
Frederick Taylor
Fritz Morstein Marx
George Washington and Alexander Hamilton
Gordon Tullock
Herbert Simon
Hierarchical bureaucracy
Jacksonianism
Lester Salamon
Luther Gulick and Lyndall Urwick
Lynton Caldwell
Maxwell School of Citizenship and Public Affairs

Montgomery C. Meigs
New Public Administration
New York Bureau of Municipal Research
Pendleton Act
Peter Drucker
POSDCORB
Public administration
Public choice theory and application
Reinvention of government
Robert B. Denhardt
Scientific management movement
Taft Commission on Economy and Efficiency in Government
Woodrow Wilson's famous article "The Study of Administration,"

Recommended Readings

Barnard, Chester I. *Functions of the Executive.* 30th anniversary edition. Cambridge, MA: Harvard University Press, 1968.

Dahl, Robert A. *Modern Political Analysis.* Englewood Cliffs, NJ: Prentice-Hall, 1984.

Downs, Anthony. *Inside Bureaucracy.* Glenview, IL: Scott, Foresman and Company, 1967.

Easton, David. *The Political System: An Inquiry into the State of Political Science.* New York: Alfred A. Knopf, 1953.

Frederickson, H. George. *The Spirit of Public Administration.* San Francisco: Jossey-Bass, 1997.

Fry, Brian R. *Mastering Public Administration: From Max Weber to Dwight Waldo.* New York: Chatham House Publishers, 1998.

Goodsell, Charles T. *The Case for Bureaucracy: A Public Administration Polemic*, 4th ed. Washington, DC: CQ Press, 2004.

McGregor, Douglas. *The Human Side of Enterprise.* New York: McGraw-Hill, 1960.

Mosher, Frederick. *Democracy and the Public Service.* New York: Oxford University Press, 1968.

Simon, Herbert. *Models of My Life.* New York, NY: Basic Books, 1991.

Wildavsky, Aaron. *The New Politics of the Budgetary Process.* Glenview, IL: Scott, Foresman and Company, 1988.

Related Web Sites

Alexander Hamilton
http://xroads.virginia.edu/~CAP/ham/hamilton.html

American Society of Public Administration
http://www.aspanet.org/scriptcontent/index.cfm

Budget and Accounting Act of 1921
http://www.u-s-history.com/pages/h1375.html

Center for Public Administration and Policy—Virginia State University
http://www.cpap.vt.edu/

Chester I. Barnard
http://www.onepine.info/pbarnard.htm

Civil Rights Act of 1875
http://www.arch.ksu.edu/jwkplan/law/Civil%20Rights%20Acts%20of%201866,%
201870,%201871,%201875.htm

Herbert Simon and the Nobel Prize
http://nobelprize.org/nobel_prizes/economics/laureates/1978/simon-autobio.html

Public Choice Theory
http://faculty.chass.ncsu.edu/garson/PA765/publicchoice.htm

Reinvention of Government—Cornell University
http://government.cce.cornell.edu/doc/viewpage_r.asp?ID=Reinventing_
Government

Woodrow Wilson
http://www.whitehouse.gov/history/presidents/ww28.html

Chapter 3

The Constitution, Administrative Law, and Public Interest Principles

"The public interest is the standard that guides the administrator in executing the law. This is the verbal symbol designed to introduce unity, order, and objectivity into administration. This concept is to the bureaucracy what the 'due process' clause is to the judiciary. Its abstract meaning is vague but its application has far-reaching effects."

E. Pendleton Herring, *Public Administration and the Public Interest*

Chapter Objectives

Upon completion of this chapter you should be able to:

1. Summarize the constitutional foundations of public administration;
2. Recognize the importance of the legal foundation of public administration, especially in constitutional case law;
3. Delineate the role and function of administrative case law in the foundation of public administration;
4. Understand the principles approach to the public interest and aspects of the attendant deontological ethics theory, with examples from constitutional and administrative law.

Introduction

E. Pendleton Herring expressed the hope of a past generation of scholars to somehow frame the public interest as the archetype concept of public administration, just as due process of law was for the judiciary. Instead, contemporary scholars and practitioners of public administration have made due process of law (and other core legal concepts) the source of empirical expression to give the public interest the real meaning Herring had hoped for. The Constitution and laws pursuant to the Constitution give us a real world empirical expression of values, problems, and resolutions within public administration. Further, through case law judges give meaning to these dilemmas by converting whatever is submitted to them for decisions into claims of right or accusations of fault.[1] Popular culture depictions of public administration have come to focus on these expressions of values in the Constitution, laws, and cases.[2] Many scholars have come to focus on the Constitution and laws as meaningful empirical expressions of the values, disputes, and issues of public administration, such as Rosemary O'Leary, **David Rosenbloom**, Philip Cooper, the Blacksburg scholars, and many others in the ascendant Constitutional School of Public Administration.[3] The law is a powerful vehicle for these public interest principles and ethical values. It is the nature of legal rights to retain the moral dialogue of the disputes as presented before the law. For over a century, legal scholars have recognized that the operation of legal rights do not mean automatic resolution of these disputes with a mechanical jurisprudence of the judge simply declaring the applicable law and compliance by litigants.[4] Rights illuminate the successful paths taken by judges, administrators, officials, and others to use the law to resolve these disputes over values. Rights in the USA are typically founded in the U.S. Constitution and its amendments, as well as federal and state statutes, local ordinances, case law interpretations, and customary or common law.

Administration in the public interest exists within the larger context of law that impacts the operation of public administration. Public administrators have daily legal concerns that are typical of all enterprises. For example, public administrators daily encounter situations such as graft and corruption that involve **criminal law**, or public wrongs that are subject to criminal sanctions and punishment by the government. Negligence or intentional wrongdoing by public administrators may involve the law of **torts**, also known as private wrongs that may require compensation for damages. Public administrators routinely make promises, either in writing or orally, that may be enforceable under the law of contracts. The law of property not only protects private parties from governmental action against their property interests, but limits the use of properties owned or operated by the government. **Corporate law** not only specifies the relations of persons within a business, but also limits the interaction of government with the corporation, directing government contact to the top executives entrusted with corporate authority. And of course, **constitutional law** provides the underlying basis of all law in the U.S., limiting administrative agencies as well as non-profits and private parties in their behavior toward others.

As detailed in chapters 1 and 2, scholars in the ascendant Constitutional School of Public Administration have renewed the importance of study of the U.S. Constitution and enduring laws as a way of understanding the public interest within public administration. Contemporary waves of change urge the inclusion of new perspectives in public administration, such as feminist perspectives, based on civil rights notions of equality. And all this is founded upon long-standing legal foundations of public administration within constitutional law, administrative law, and other branches of the law.

Our study of the U.S. Constitution and administrative law also gives us the chance to focus on the principles approach to the public interest and the attending deontological theory of ethics. When we think of the Constitution and the laws, we think of principles — duty or conscience of a deontological approach to "do the right act," no matter what the outcome may be. Following the Constitution and laws means dutifully obeying rules or intuitions, rather than abandoning these universal means in order to achieve a particular desired end result[5] Public interest principles attend to deontological ethical theory, which focuses on the "binding duty" (Greek, *deon*) in the study of (Greek, *tology*) human affairs to define what is good and bad. The goal of deontology consists of universal, valid means of behavior or activities that are applied fairly and without bias — even if dutifully following the rules should result in mischief, injustice, or tragic ending for a particular person or group. While reflecting a line of ethical thinking since the time of Plato about the intrinsic good of following one's duties, the term "deontology" may have first been used as a restatement of these ethical theories in 1930.[6] In the applied ethics of the principles approach to the public interest, public administrators are judged by doing the right act, not by good (or bad) consequences of their acts. People ordinarily don't have the capacity to predict or control the consequences of their actions, but they can act with the right intent. The approaches of virtue practices and utilitarian policies distort the reality of public administrators in the false belief they have the capacity and choice to select what they want to be or do in bureaucratic life. The principles approach presents an administrative reality that seems more bounded by rules, law, and duties that you are required to follow —but with a belief that you can act with good intent and achieve greater moral worth. Further, the principles approach doesn't simply look at the benefits-costs of a benefactor-beneficiary role, but includes the diverse roles and corresponding duties of the public administrator, such as fiduciary-entrustor, principle-agent, supervisor-supervisee, bureaucrat-citizen, promisor-promisee, lawyer-client, physician-patient, parent-child, and many other roles. Finally, the principles approach to the public interest gives consideration to the past as an indicator of the good; past precedents may create obligations in the present. For example, what the city manager did to help get water out to Sue's business may create an obligation to help get water out to Fred's business, too.[7]

Of course, the Constitution and administrative law includes perspectives other than just the public interest principles approach. As with all applied ethics concepts, it is a matter of degree and all three public interest approaches may be found within the Constitution and administrative law: principles, policies, and practices. Contemporary legal scholars posit a variety of ethical approaches to law and legal dispute resolution that includes the moral reading of law for pre-existing deontological principles.[8] But many scholarly analyses of the Constitution and administrative law also include the economic analysis of law for utilitarian calculus of benefits/costs,[9] as well as judicial biographies, critical race theory and other virtue analyses of character of legal participants.[10]

This chapter is designed to examine administration in the public interest from its constitutional, administrative law, and legal foundations. First, the chapter will explore the basis of law in the U.S.—the Constitution. We will define **constitutionalism**, examine its roots, and provide the historical and legal basis for the role that a written constitution plays in the governance and administrative structures of public administrators. Second, we examine the three basic legal contexts of freedom, property, and equality—highlighting several policy and administrative issue areas that impact the role of the public administrator in the public interest. Third, we end with an overview of administrative law and due process of law limitations within the U.S. system of governance. Finally, throughout the chapter we discuss meanings, strengths, and weaknesses of the principles approach to the public interest with numerous court cases—most of them from the U.S. Supreme Court—to illustrate our points.

Constitutionalism

While the Constitution forms the basic rules of the game for all law in the U.S., the historical roots of the Constitution help us to understand the nature of law and public administration in American today. Our constitutional rules of the game came out of the colonial charters and activities, the **Declaration of Independence**, the **Articles of Confederation**, and other prior American legal experiences. For example, each of the colonies began with a written charter that specified institutions of governance, as well as a political economy of mercantilism against which we revolted. And the Declaration of

Independence of 1776 declared our human rights and the necessity of revolution. This was the beginning of a principles or deontological approach to governance, rejecting the virtue of King George III of England and instead placing trust in a more universal set of rules. Our first try at a set of rules of the game began with the failed Articles of Confederation. From 1781 to 1789, the thirteen states grew further apart, the national government and defense grew weak, and the public order declined with Shay's Rebellion of 1786 and other usurpations of the law of property by debtors and so forth. From such writings—and grumblings—came the impetus to create a new nation by a new Constitution.[11]

The Constitution as a Process

The 1787 Constitutional Convention brought together fifty-five delegates in Philadelphia, sent by twelve states for the original purpose of reforming the Articles of Confederation. The Framers who attended were mostly lawyers who saw threatened property interests and grumbling populists, a weak national defense and potent invaders. The revolutionaries, such as Thomas Paine, **Patrick Henry** (1736–1799), John Adams, Sam Adams, and Thomas Jefferson, were not there. Neither were there any women, black, or Native American representatives. Even Rhode Island sent no delegates. General George Washington was elected to preside and it soon became clear that most delegates wanted to scrap the Articles and start over, quickly producing an entirely new plan for a strong national government to protect property and national security. And in ratification, the people of the several states also seemed eager to approve the new Constitution and create a strong national government.

The **Constitution of 1789**, followed by its twenty-seven Amendments, is a relatively short, 7000-word outline of governmental institutions, roles and duties. It takes about a half-hour to read—you might want to read it sometime! Australia, Liberia, the former USSR, and other nations have used it as a model for their own constitutions. It's simplicity in what it leaves out is what belies the compromises that went into it—and how it succeeded in creating a strong national government in an individualistic, revolutionary world. It outlines powers and duties of legislative, executive, and judicial branches without spouting political theory (i.e., no talk of Montesquieu's separation of powers, for example). It recognizes the states without specifying the exact limits of the powers of national or state governments. It posits the Constitution as the supreme law without detailing how to deal with conflicts of law. It asserts human rights and processes of governance without itemizing how to administer such rights and processes—instead leaving these details to succeeding generations of Americans.

Without waxing on-and-on with theories, the Constitution clearly produced a social contract of the sort envisioned by canonical figures in deontological ethical theory. The original body of the Constitution created a strong, central government to secure the people, similar to the social contract urged by **Thomas Hobbes** (1588–1679) in the *Leviathan* (1651) where atomistic materialistic individuals were willing to give up everything they have to avoid a return to the state of nature of "every man against every man." The Bill of Rights (Amendments 1–10) amended this strong, secure government with limitations on governmental powers in order to protect individual freedoms and property rights as envisioned by **John Locke** (1632–1704) in *The Second Treatise on Government* (1690).

Box 3.1 "Fast Facts" of the U.S. Constitution

- The U.S. Constitution was written in the same Pennsylvania State House where the Declaration of Independence was signed and where George Washington received his commission as Commander of the Continental Army. Now called Independence Hall, the building still stands today on Independence Mall in Philadelphia, directly across from the National Constitution Center.

- Some of the original framers and many delegates in the state ratifying conventions were very troubled that the original Constitution lacked a description of individual rights. In 1791, Americans added a list of rights to the Constitution. The first ten amendments became known as The Bill of Rights

- Of the 55 delegates attending the Constitutional Convention, 39 signed and 3 delegates dissented.

- Established on November 26, 1789, the first national "Thanksgiving Day" was originally created by George Washington as a way of "giving thanks" for the Constitution.

- Of the written national constitutions, the U.S. Constitution is the oldest and shortest.

- The original Constitution is on display at the National Archives in Washington, D.C. When the Japanese bombed Pearl Harbor, it was moved to Fort Knox for safekeeping.

Source: National Constitution Center, "Constitution Fast Facts," www.constitution center.org/explore/FastFacts/index.shtml (accessed October 2007).

Congress, President, and Court. The Constitution outlines national government powers that are allocated to legislative, executive and judicial branches. Separation of powers is the label often attached to discussions of these concerns, but the reality is inter-branch relations, cooperation, and duplication of power. Separation of powers is never expressly stated in the Constitution. The Framers did not seek to separate or obstruct government, but to improve upon the discredited Articles of Confederation which had only a national legislature. Combinations and overlapping powers, not separations, are featured in the Constitution. For example, the budget is proposed by the President, subject to approval by Congress (although this was modified in some ways with passage of the Budget and Accounting Act of 1921). The President may veto legislation, subject to a two-thirds override vote of Congress. The Senate must confirm appointments by the President, and approve his treaties. Executive and judicial officers may be impeached by the House of Representatives. Over the last two centuries, administrators in the executive branch have increasingly been the focus of combination and overlapping power between branches of the national government.

Some features of administrative governance were not mentioned in the Constitution, but developed over time and by custom. First was the **delegation of authority** by Congress to executive branch agencies that has worked to combine government branches. Except for some instances of excessive delegation by Congress without clear standards in the 1920s and 1930s, the Court has allowed the delegation of congressional powers to create the massive national bureaucracy that exists today—from the U.S. Sentencing Commission, to the U.S. Post Office, and beyond. And after *INS v. Chadha*, 462 U.S. 919 (1983), the Court no longer allows the Congress to take back its delegated powers in piecemeal fashion for some later legislative review of individual agency decisions.[12]

Box 3.2   *INS v. Chadha* (1983)

Docket:	80-1832
Citation:	462 U.S. 919 (1983)
Appellant:	Immigration and Naturalization Service (INS)
Appellee:	Chadha
Consolidated:	*United States House of Representatives v. Immigration and Naturalization Service* (INS), No. 80-2170; *United States Senate v. Immigration and Naturalization Service* (INS), No. 80-2171

Abstract

Oral Argument:	Monday, February 22, 1982
Oral Re-argument:	Tuesday, December 7, 1982
Decision:	Thursday, June 23, 1983
Issues:	Miscellaneous, Legislative Veto
Categories:	aliens, justiciability, political questions, standing

Facts of the Case

In one section of the Immigration and Nationality Act, Congress authorized either House of Congress to invalidate and suspend deportation rulings of the United States Attorney General. Chadha had stayed in the U.S. past his visa deadline and was ordered to leave the country. The House of Representatives suspended the Immigration judge's deportation ruling This case was decided together with *United States House of Representatives v. Chadha* and *United States Senate v. Chadha*.

Question

Did the Immigration and Nationality Act, which allowed a one-House veto of executive actions, violate the separation of powers doctrine?

Conclusion

The Court held that the particular section of the Act in question did violate the Constitution. Recounting the debates of the Constitution Convention over issues of bicameralism and separation of powers, Chief Justice Burger concluded that even though the Act would have enhanced governmental efficiency, it violated the "explicit constitutional standards" regarding lawmaking and congressional authority.

Vote

7–2

Source: The Oyez Project, *INS v. Chadha*, 462 U.S. 919 (1983), www.oyez.org/cases/1980-1989/1981/1981_80_1832/ (accessed September 2007).

Second is the practice of **constitutional judicial review**. The Constitution is not explicit about who is to review the constitutionality of government activities. At least since *Marbury v. Madison*, 5 U.S. 137 (1803), the U.S. Supreme Court has asserted that it is the proper role of the judicial branch to have the final say on the constitutionality of government activities. After all, judicial review has existed as long as recorded human history as the judicial interpretation of the conformity of parties to laws written by public actors. Constitutional judicial review expands on this traditional role of courts to allow judges to also interpret conformity of public actors to the supreme law of the land, the Constitution. Constitutional judicial review has been used by all levels of courts to insure constitutionality by individuals as well as organizations, such as shipping and railroad monopolies in the nineteenth century, and with schools, prisons, jails, police, mental institutions, public housing, and others in recent times. Constitutional judicial review is said to have created a partnership between judges and the public service in the United States.

Constitutional judicial review has also created new legal liability of public administrators in civil suits for money damages for violating the constitutional rights of individuals or groups they serve. Traditionally, a government and its administrators had absolute immunity and could not be sued for monetary damages for the unconstitutional wrongs it committed against a person, e.g., police racial profiling to harass minorities. You could ask for an injunction to change government procedures, but public administrators and officials had immunity. However, since the 1970s the courts have developed a new doctrine of **qualified immunity** in which public administrators may be liable in creating regulations and managing existing laws, e.g., racial discrimination in a hiring decision. Yet, public administrators remain immune from liability for their adjudicatory functions, e.g., deciding not to issue a license after failing the driving test. Nobody likes to be sued or pay monetary damages, so many have sought insurance, some have quit the public service in order to work in the private sector, and others do as little as possible to avoid liability. Such laws force a more ambiguous language of compromise in legislation, decisions, and execution.

The delegation doctrine and constitutional judicial review are accepted today, but illustrate how ambiguous understandings of intuition, faith, and conscience may enter into public interest principles. Judges, officials, administrators, and others may reasonably disagree on the brief and ambiguous constitutional language on delegating legislative power to agencies or the power of courts to review the constitutionality of other spheres of government. But the U.S. Supreme Court cases above illustrate how interpretation of these principles were products of intuition, faith, conscience, or other ways of knowing that did not solely rely on rules or expressed law—causing some scholars to argue that the justices originally CREATE individual constitutional rights in areas such as racial discrimination, the death penalty and sexual freedom.[13] Justice William O. Douglas once stated, "The Supreme Court is really the keeper of the conscience. And the conscience is the Constitution."[14] This attends to **act deontology**, the ethical theory that holds that particular judgments, rather than rules, are basic in morality. Individual intuitions, faith, conscience, love, and existential choice have each been proposed by someone as the standard for act-deontology. With each, a public administrator faced with a decision will take a moment to somehow grasp what should be done, without relying on rules. For example, in his decision to allow litigation to reform the Georgia State Prison, U.S. District Judge Anthony Alaimo found one morning that he couldn't look at himself in the mirror if he didn't allow the case to proceed. It was obedience to conscience, not to rules of civil procedure and jurisdiction, which compelled his decision and ultimately produced the first accredited, "constitutional" prison in the USA.[15]

Yet, the act-deontology approach may be criticized for inherent weaknesses. How would you know if a jailor acted wrongly in disciplining an inmate with a whipping if only intuition, faith, or conscience were relied upon? How would we ever prefer one act over another if there were no proscribed behaviors with rules or duties? Act deontology gives attention to the moral worth of intentions in our actions by focusing on intuition, faith, conscience, love and choice, but we need something more than these ambiguous notions to know what to do in specific situations.

Freedom, Property, and Equality

Constitutionalism shaped the institutions of U.S. public administration, but for most people the law of civil rights and liberties defines ordinary, day-to-day experience with government. **Civil liberties** were traditionally known as individual freedoms that limited government intrusion by law, as found in the **Bill of Rights** (Amendments 1–10 of the Constitution). **Civil rights** were laws of empowerment, as found in the **Fourteenth Amendment** of the Constitution, by which government helped individuals overcome public and private unconstitutional acts against them. Today, when we claim, "I've got my rights!" we usually include both civil liberties AND civil rights as constitutional rights.

Constitutional rights are limited to public actions, and do not extend to wholly private relations. For example, when I'm babysitting my nephew and tell him to go to sleep, it makes no sense for him to refuse and argue, "I've got my constitutional rights!" While the Bill of Rights and other constitutional rights originally applied only to the national government, the courts have incorporated the principles of most of the Bill of Rights into the Fourteenth Amendment due process of law requirements, thus, making them uniformly applicable to states and localities as well.[16] With the changing liability of public servants, constitutional rights are very important limitations on what may be done at the public workplace, as well as with clients, charges, and the public.

This section of the chapter begins to survey a principles approach to the public interest that attends to **rule deontology**. Rule-deontologists, like act-deontologists, deny that the balance of good over evil consequences is the deciding factor in determining what is in the public interest. However, rule-deontologists focus on the conformity of actions with one or more principles or rules to determine if they are right or wrong. Rules are the measure of moral worth and of the public interest. Some rule-deontologists hold that there is only one principle or rule, such as Divine command theory in which conformity to the commands of God are the criterion of right and wrong.[17] **Immanuel Kant** (1724–1804) based rule-deontology on one principle he called the **categorical imperative**: "act only on that maxim which you can at the same time will to be a universal law." Other rule-deontologists hold that there are two or more basic rules in morality, such as W.D. Ross's six **prima facie duties**, or basic moral duties that are apparent "on their face": non-malfeasance, self-improvement, beneficence, justice, gratitude, and duties that rest on previous acts of our own (e.g., duties of reparation and fidelity).[18] Many people believe that there are some things that are just plain wrong, yet not for any single reason. The "ordinary common sense morality" that many public administrators apply to determining what is in the public interest is usually of this sort.

The many rules and duties of the principles approach and deontology may be criticized as non-systematic, too pluralistic, and failing to provide some unified goal. Virtue practices focus on arête or excellence, however differently this may be defined over time and between persons. Utilitarian policies focus on benefits/costs or some other unified measure of value. As a result, deontological principles often seem like an endless list of concerns and issues with differing criteria for right and wrong among items. That is also the strength of deontology principles in its very broad view of the issues, roles, and relations of people, including diverse roles and duties of the public administrators as fiduciary-entrustor, principle-agent, supervisor-supervisee, bureaucrat-citizen, promisor-promisee, lawyer-client, physician-patient, parent-child, and many other roles. To help work such a long list of deontological principles, we will briefly summarize constitutional rights by the protection of freedom, property, equality, and due process.

Box 3.3   Fourteenth Amendment, Section 1 (1868)

All persons born or naturalized in the United States, and subject to the jurisdiction thereof, are citizens of the United States and of the State wherein they reside. No State shall make or enforce any law which shall abridge the privileges or immunities of citizens of the United States; nor shall any State deprive any person of life, liberty, or *property*, without *due process of law*; nor deny to any person within its jurisdiction the *equal protection of the laws*.

Source: U. S. Constitution.

Freedom

The most historic of constitutional rights have been those associated with freedoms of religion, expression, and privacy, i.e., found in the **First Amendment**. First, the freedom of religion was of primary importance to the Founders of the Constitution. While most Americans have sought the free exercise of their religious beliefs, or freedom OF religion, others have pursued freedom FROM religion or prohibitions on the **establishment of religion**. Our Constitution includes both conflicting protections. For example, when you allow an employee to wear a highly visible cross on their person while they work in an area with much contact with the general public, you also make an official place for Christianity at the public workplace.[19] Generally, in such conflicts, the courts have favored the free exercise of religious beliefs because of other protections, e.g., free speech. The courts seem to favor the non-establishment of religion when the religious belief is expressed in a way that is dominating a public space or function with a particular religious perspective not open to other perspectives, e.g., a large Ten Commandments statue in the courthouse foyer.[20] So, too, religious activities are not protected when they excessively interfere with public goods or service provision.

Second, the freedom of expression includes constitutional rights to free speech and press, petition/redress freedoms, and freedom of association. The First Amendment right to free speech and press may include protection of the discussion, teaching, or even advocacy of the revolution against the U.S. government, to commit a crime, or to illegally discriminate against others. Of course, once that person does something in furtherance of this discussion, teaching or advocacy, they may be charged and found guilty of conspiracy to commit an unlawful act. Or if their expression is obscene, defamatory, or would **imminently incite** a reasonable person to respond with a crime or unlawful act, there is no protection of free speech or press. But the right to free speech and press is one of the most protected of all freedoms today. For example, in *Brandenburg v. Ohio*, 395 U.S. 444 (1969), the Supreme Court protected the right of the Ku Klux Klan to march in the state capitol square. *Rankin v. McPherson*, 483 U.S. 378 (1987), ruled that a public employee's right to free speech in a non-public area, regardless of how inflammatory it may seem to others (i.e. after hearing of an attempt on the President's life remarked, "if they go for him again, I hope they get him"), is protected speech. Yet, *Garcetti v. Ceballos*, 547 U.S. 473 (2006), ruled that when a public employee makes a statement, they are not speaking as citizens and thus the Constitution does not protect their speech from employer sanction. A series of high profile right to privacy cases, based in the Fourth Amendment and other provisions of the Bill of Rights, includes, *Stanley v. Georgia* 394 U.S. 557 (1969), which held that private possession of obscene material a crime; *Griswold v. Connecticut* 381 U.S. 479 (1965), which held that married couples have the right to use contraceptives; *Roe v. Wade* 410 U.S. 113 (1973), which held that states' anti-abortion statutes are unconstitutional and violates a woman's right to terminate her pregnancy; and *Cruzan v. Director, Missouri Department of Health* 497 U.S. 261 (1990), where the Supreme Court denied the legal guardians of a patient who is in a vegetative state to stop her from eating and drinking in order to let her die.

Public administrators must tolerate a great deal of free expression by clients, charges, and the public, with exceptions of expressions prohibited by law or regulation that are not overbroad and are narrowly specific on what cannot be expressed and why (i.e., no cross burning, as it imminently incites illegal discrimination toward minorities). Even at the public workplace, the courts have interpreted the First Amendment to give greater freedom of speech to public employees to express ideas in settings away from the public, clients, or their charges. Similarly, the courts have broadly interpreted the right to petition and seek redress of grievances as a highly protected right of the public, clients, charges, and of public employees. **Freedom of association** has been interpreted to allow both inmates and public employees to unionize, and to allow the public to collectively seek answers or satisfaction for their needs from public agencies.

Third, the right of privacy, though not explicit in the Constitution or Amendments, is found in the meanings of the Bill of Rights. Administration in the public interest is most often focused on respect for autonomy and concerned with privacy of information. Clients, charges, the public, and even public employees have a right to keep primarily personal information private, such as their personal medical records. Yet, psychological, polygraph, background checks, and drug testing may be required of public employees. The identification of certain personnel may be kept private to avoid jeopardizing operations, such as with undercover police, CIA field operatives, or the Secret Service. Other privacy rights generally involve bodily matters of sex, reproduction, and end-of-life. For example, administration in the public interest must respect the right of adults to possess pornographic materials in the privacy of their own home, the right of married or single persons to obtain contraceptives, the right of women to obtain abortions in certain circumstances, the right to plan one's family, the right to direct termination of life-maintenance medical devices, and other privacy concerns.

Property

The protection of **property rights** was a major motivation of the Founders, including constitutional provisions limiting the power of government under the commerce power, the taxing and spending clause, the contract clause, the taking clause, and the concept of substantive due process.[21] Continuity of interpretation of these property rights belies the meaningfulness of deontological principles against the criticisms of logical positivists who belittle these concepts as "nonsense." Does the Court merely assert its preferences, its will to power? Many scholars still repeat the myth by 1930s **Progressive historians** who sought to justify the New Deal with a tale of an out-of-control laissez-faire U.S. Supreme Court from the 1870s to 1937.[22] Using examples like *Lochner v. New York*, 198 U.S. 45 (1905), the Progressives argued that the Court of "nine old men" merely asserted their preferences for protection of individual property rights and struck down as unconstitutional any attempt by states or national government to interfere with property rights. But **Revisionist historians** and legal scholars who later counted the cases found that nearly all the hundreds of decisions by the Court during that time upheld and allowed the state or national intrusions upon property rights.[23] The congruence of meaning from these early property rights cases to current interpretation helps to lend validity to the deontology principles approach.

Property rights have never been about freedom FROM government, but rather, WHICH government is supreme in regulating property rights. Indeed, the **commerce clause**, found in Article I, section 8 of the Constitution, has been interpreted since *Cooley v. Board of Wardens*, 53 U.S. 299 (1852), to give the national government supreme power over interstate commerce in any area in which Congress displaces state or local laws. So, too, the power to tax has been vested in the national government as the supreme law of the land under the taxing and spending clause of Article I, Section 8, as well as the Sixteenth Amendment of the Constitution. The Constitution also provides specific limitations on the power of state or national governments from impairing the Obligation of Contracts (the contract clause, Article I, Section 10), from taking property for public use, without just compensation (the taking clause, Amendment V), or from taking property without due process of law (the substantive due process clause, Fifth and Fourteenth Amendments). Yet, the courts have repeatedly allowed state and national governments to impair the obligation of contracts (e.g., requiring a higher standard of coal for industrial smokestacks), to take property for public use with questionable or unfair compensation (e.g., assessing compensation value long after eminent domain proceedings have lowered the land value), and to take property without due process of law (e.g., requiring all pharmacies to be mostly owned by in-state residents to keep out pharmacy chains). Property rights under the Constitution have been about uniformity under national supremacy, not about the freedom FROM government. Like nearly all governments in Western history, property rights in America have been subject to the will of the sovereign and the power to tax or impose this will has also been the power to destroy in whole or in part. Administration in the public interest promises no free lunch!

But disagreement remains over deontology principles and may spur reflection on these principles by a new generation of public administrators. For example, *Kelo v. City of New London*, 545 U.S. 469 (2005), permitted condemnation and use of eminent domain by the city of New London, Connecticut, to take homes from individuals and give the property to corporate developers as permissible "public use" under the Takings Clause of the Fifth Amendment. The broad public outcry against the case and perceived abuse of property rights power by state and local administrators has forced many to rethink these principles. For example, Freeport, TX, city administrators faced overwhelming public opposition and were condemned for greed in their attempt to bulldoze a family-owned shrimping business to make way for corporate ocean-front developers.[24] What about the morality of the common use of long delays in land-use planning and eminent domain procedures to "lock-up" private lands and homes from other resale — and drive down their "fair market value," promote foreclosures by homeowners, and otherwise obtain these lands more cheaply for proposed roadways and public improvements?

Equality

The equal protection of the laws has been guaranteed in the Fourteenth Amendment and many other aspects of the Constitution, national and state laws, and regulations. Deontology principles of equality have focused on respect for persons. Equality in America has been more about an **equality of opportunity** than **equality of distribution** found in socialist or Communist nations. U.S. equal protection laws also distinguish between favored and less-favored categories of persons, or tiers of protection, so that racial minorities receive the highest degree of empowerment, but women and the poor receive lesser levels of protection from arbitrary discrimination. Since the 1970s, the Court has formulated three tiers of equal protection classifications.

The Court started with their traditional **rational basis test** to determine if a law or public action was unconstitutional in its arbitrary discrimination between persons. The law or action was valid if the purpose behind it was a legitimate one and it was rational (or able to be articulated).[25] For example, national and state financial aid programs for college students may discriminate between students on the basis of wealth or income because wealthier students are better able to pay their own way. With *Korematsu v. US*, 323 U.S. 214 (1944), the Court created a new tier of protection and treated racial discrimination with **strict scrutiny**. That is, discrimination by race or ethnicity is lawful only if the classification by race/ethnicity is necessary to achieve a compelling state interest. For example, a national health program for sickle cell anemia that affects only blacks may discriminate to serve only blacks. In the 1970s, with issues of gender discrimination, the Court developed a middle tier, or intermediate scrutiny that applied to discrimination by gender.[26] That is, discrimination between persons was lawful if it substantially related to the achievement of an important state interest. For example, the military service draft could be male-only because men had greater upper body strength and other abilities required to fight at the front lines of battle.

Race. America is known for a racism that is embedded in over 250 years of racist slavery. The only human right provided to slaves as chattel (livestock) was a ban on unseemly cruelty, but slave owners ignored these laws with impunity. The Constitution recognized and protected the continuation of slavery, and explicitly stated the lesser human worth of slaves. *Dred Scot v. Sanford*, 16 U.S. 393 (1857), declared that slaves were not citizens and had no rights. The Civil War marked the defeat of the forces of slavery. Lincoln freed the slaves in 1863 and the 13th, 14th, and 15th Amendments gave human rights, citizenship and the right to vote to the former slaves. Congress passed seven different Civil Rights Acts from 1866–1875 to protect the rights of African Americans, but enforcement of these rights quickly dissipated. Jim Crow laws (named for a minstrel show character) were passed throughout the U.S., enforcing official racial segregation in travel, housing, education, even drinking fountains, parks, and toilets. In *Plessy v. Ferguson*, 163 U.S. 537 (1896), the U.S. Supreme Court legitimized these laws, and we continue to live with the impact of **Jim Crow** to the present day. Official segregation legally ended when the U.S. Supreme Court reversed itself in *Brown v. Board of Education*, 347 U.S. 483 (1954), declaring that "separate is … inherently unequal." Over the past decades, courageous courts, public servants, officials, civil rights activists, and citizens have upended and set out to change the long history of chattel, discrimination, hatred, and non-compliance with equality laws in public life, including housing, jobs, schools, prisons, the family, and in justice and public affairs.[27]

Criminal and civil sanctions exist to end racial discrimination by public administrators and within public organizations. For example, the 1989 movie, "*Mississippi Burning*," presented a racist system of justice and public affairs in 1964 Mississippi. The state wouldn't bring charges against three cops and 15 citizens who killed civil rights workers, so in *United States v. Price*, 383 U.S. 787 (1966), federal criminal sanctions were brought under 18 U.S.C. 241 and 242. Congress later increased the maximum potential sentence to life imprisonment for causing death.[28] Civil lawsuits may be filed under 42 U.S.C 1983, allowing class-actions that group together many similarly-affected parties to sue a public official or agency for civil rights violations.

Affirmative action is yet another remedy to America's long history of racism. First proposed by President Kennedy in 1961 with the issuance of Executive Order 10925, it was not institutionalized until in 1965 President Johnson issued Executive Order 11246, which effectively prohibited "employment discrimination based on race, color, religion, and national origin." Later, it was President Nixon who advocated affirmative action as a remedy to reward upwardly-mobile minorities in competitive jobs and programs. **Affirmative action** remains a valid remedy where disparate-treatment is proven (discrimination by law or policy). For example, in *United States v. Paradise*, 480 U.S. 149 (1987), the Court upheld court-ordered affirmative action quotas in hiring and promoting blacks within the Alabama State Patrol, who had a long history of policies discriminating against blacks.

And more recently in *Grutter v. Bollinger*, 539 U.S. 306 (2003), the Court continued to allow the use of non-numeric, non-quota style affirmative action in agencies that did not have the long history of racist discrimination (or disparate impact).

Religion. Hate toward different religions is often expressed by hate crimes, such as vandalism of mosques, churches or synagogues, as well as discrimination in the public or private workplace. Yet, religious discrimination by public administrators and within public organizations continues in the name of neutrality. *Employment Division v. Smith*, 494 U.S. 872 (1990), is the leading case for the Court's neutrality doctrine, which ruled that states may criminalize peyote use under uniform and evenly-applied drug laws, even if it is part of a sincere religious ritual of the Native American Church. Congress responded to the *Smith* decision with the **Religious Freedom Restoration Act of 1993** (RFRA) and other statutes protecting Native American religions to give greater protections against religious discrimination. But in *City of Boerne v. Flores,* 521 U.S. (1997), the Court struck down portions of the RFRA as unconstitutional and allowed a City Historic Landmark Commission the power to rule against a local Roman Catholic Church which sought to build an addition to their church building. Similarly, the Court in *McCreary County v. ACLU*, 545 U.S. 844 (2005), ruled that courtroom displays of the Ten Commandments were unconstitutional establishment of religion, because Kentucky legislators discussed sectarian purposes for erecting the statutes, not just a proscribed neutral and secular purpose. What was in the public interest?

Case Study   Religious Freedom Restoration Act (RFRA)

In 1993, Congress enacted the Religious Freedom Restoration Act (RFRA) in response to the Supreme Court's 1990 ruling in *Employment Division v. Smith*. In that ruling, the Court upheld an Oregon law used to deny unemployment benefits to two Native American men who lost their jobs because of their religious use of peyote. The Court determined that neutral, generally applicable laws may be applied to religious practices even when not supported by a compelling government interest.

After *Smith,* Congress passed RFRA to prevent the government from substantially burdening a person's free-exercise rights unless the burden furthered a compelling government interest and was the least restrictive means of furthering that interest. Section 2000bb-2(1) declared the law applicable to any form of government — federal, state or otherwise. In applying RFRA to the states, Congress relied on its powers under Section 5 of the Fourteenth Amendment to adopt and enforce laws that protect citizens' due-process and equal-protection rights. It is on this ground that the Supreme Court ruled RFRA unconstitutional as applied to state and local governments.

The Supreme Court's ruling came in 1997 in a case involving a zoning dispute in Texas. In 1995, the Catholic archbishop of San Antonio applied for a building permit to enlarge a church in Boerne (pronounced "Bernie"), Texas. Located in a historic district, the church was no longer large enough for its congregation. The zoning board turned down the archbishop's request, citing historic-preservation laws. The archbishop sued the city, claiming that RFRA required the city to exempt the church from its historic-preservation laws.

The federal district court, however, found that Congress had never had the constitutional authority to enact the law and apply it to the states. The Fifth U.S. Circuit Court of Appeals reversed that decision, finding the act constitutional and declaring that the denial of the permit substantially burdened the Catholic diocese's free exercise of religion. City officials appealed to the Supreme Court.

In *City of Boerne v. Flores,* the Court said RFRA exceeded Congress' authority under the Fourteenth Amendment. The Court ruled RFRA was not a proper exercise of Congress' enforcement power under Section 5 of the amendment because it violated the separation of powers.

Source: Reprinted from article by Greg Groninger, "Religious Freedom Restoration Act Analysis," First Amendment Center, www.firstamendmentcenter.org/ analysis.aspx?id=14383 (accessed September 2007).

Sexual Orientation. Throughout Western history, homosexuality has been persecuted as an abomination to God, as were other sexual orientations that differed from heterosexuality under a marriage covenant. While many homosexuals made great contributions to Western society, heavy stigma attached to homosexual activities. For example, the American Psychiatric Association did not "un-list" homosexuality as a psychiatric disorder until 1974. In the U.S. in 1961, all 50 states and the District of Columbia criminalized homosexual sodomy. But over recent decades the practice of homosexual relations has become more accepted, so that in *Lawrence v. Texas*, 539 U.S. 558 (2003), the Court struck down a Texas statute as unconstitutional for focusing only on male homosexuality in criminalizing sodomy. Further, in *Oncale v. Sundowner Offshore Services*, 523 U.S. 75 (1997), the Court ruled that sexual harassment at the workplace was NOT limited to rights violations of women by men, but may include homosexual harassment between men. The U.S. military and many other public affairs agencies have taken a **"don't ask, don't tell"** policy to avoid sexual orientation discrimination at the workplace. Yet, cases such as *Hurley v. Irish-American GLIB*, 515 U.S. 559 (1995) and *Boy Scouts v. Dale*, 530 U.S. 640 (2000) have ruled that homosexuals and those of various sexual orientations may not violate the Free Speech rights of others who voice their disapproval of their sexual orientation, or force their way into associations or forums by private groups who disapprove of their sexual orientation.

Gender. Women for most of Western history were considered chattel, like slaves and cattle, treated as property and often listed on the property deeds. The common law doctrine of **covertures** did not allow a woman, singularly, to own real property, but her ownership was covered by a husband, father, son, brother, or other male. With the Nineteenth Amendment, ratified in 1920, women gained the right to vote and citizenship, as well as increasing property rights. However, gender discrimination still exists, often as sexual harassment at the workplace. Sexual harassment may be either quid pro quo (trading), sexual favoritism (for favored status at work), or hostile work environment (abusive or sexually-charged workplace). In *Pennsylvania State Police v. Suders*, 542 U.S. 129 (2004), the Court allowed a more streamlined path to the federal courts for a victim of sexual harassment while working with the Pennsylvania State Police. The Court reasoned because Nancy Drew Suders could prove a hostile working environment so intolerable that quitting qualified as a fitting response—that she could proceed directly to federal court and ignore the many administrative hearings required by the agency in sexual harassment complaints.

Mental and Physical Disabilities. Over 43 million Americans today have one or more mental or physical disabilities protected by constitutional rights. Significant congressional legislation has sought to address the injustices and issues of the disabled, including: Age Discrimination in Employment Act of 1967 (ADEA) sought to end age discrimination in employment; Architectural Barriers Act of 1968 required greater access to public buildings; Rehabilitation Act of 1973 prohibits employment discrimination against people with disabilities; Comprehensive Employment and Training Act of 1973 (CETA) created jobs and job training programs for the disabled; Rehabilitation Education Act of 1976 (REA) developed affirmative action for the disabled; **Americans with Disabilities Act of 1990**

(ADA) required the reasonable accommodation of the disabled. Disability law in the administration of the public interest tends to focus on the Age Discrimination in Employment Act (ADEA) and the Americans with Disabilities Act (ADA). Issues of mental disability typically involve either some type of mental illness or mental retardation, while issues of physical disability often focus on bodily challenges and age discrimination. For example, in *Smith v. City of Jackson*, 544 U.S. 228 (2005), the Court ruled that city police officers alleging age discrimination in a new pay scheme had a valid claim, were not limited by state sovereignty, and could proceed in the federal court to prove either disparate treatment (age discrimination by policy) or disparate impact (age discrimination as practiced).

Due Process and Administrative Law

Administrative law is the law governing the powers and processes of administrative agencies. Since the 1940s, law school scholars have distinguished the body of **administrative law** by the rulemaking, adjudication, and informal decision-making issues addressed in the **Administrative Procedure Act of 1946**, and similar state acts. In the USA, federal and state governments are intended to maintain a tripartite balance of powers (legislative, executive, and judiciary). It also deals with the creation, by statute or executive order authorized by statutes, of independent agencies (e.g., Federal Aviation Administration) or executive branch agencies (e.g., the F.B.I. of the U.S. Department of Justice). Thus, American administrative law deals primarily with the grant of power by a legislature to an agency, the assumption of power by executive branch agencies not originally envisioned as exercising them, and with judicial reviews of administrative agency regulations, decisions and actions.[29]

By contrast, regulation or **regulatory law** is the law developed by administrative agencies in the course of their operation. In reaction to the great expansion of agency activity, the Federal Register Act of 1935 required executive agencies to record all rulemaking, actions and procedures in the Federal Register. Thus, since the Code of Federal Regulations began similar collections of state and local agency regulations have also developed. Professor Lief Carter contrasts the definition of regulatory law with administrative law as: "Regulatory law includes such things as antitrust statutes and environmental protection policy ... Administrative law by contrast states procedures for controlling that power. Administrative law regulates the regulators ..."[30]

Due Process

The constitutional foundations of administrative law and regulation in America date back to 1789, with the founding of the Constitution. The Fifth and Fourteenth Amendments prohibited the national government (Fifth) and states (Fourteenth) from taking "life, liberty or property without due process of law." Early legislation by Congress to interpret the meaning of due process by administrative processes included customs laws, regulation of sea-going vessels, and payment of pensions to veterans of the Revolutionary War. But administrative law and regulation grew substantially in the late nineteenth century, with the growth of public transportation (e.g., railroads) and public utilities. Passage of the **Interstate Commerce Act** and establishment of the Interstate Commerce Commission in 1887 mark the start of administrative law and regulation as we know it today.

Commerce Power. The Commerce Power of the U.S. Constitution, Article I, Section 8, Clause 2, provided the U.S. Congress with the power to regulate commerce "between the several states and the Indian tribes." The commerce power has been delegated to create administrative agencies that would undertake these economic regulatory operations of Congress. In *Gibbons v. Ogden*, 22 U.S. 1 (1824), the Supreme Court ruled that Congress had supreme authority to regulate interstate commerce under the Constitution's Commerce Power. Any state or local or private laws that conflicted with Congress' interstate commerce regulations were null and void.

But what is interstate? What is local? The Supreme Court has gone back and forth in defining these limits. Under the Tenth Amendment to the Constitution, local **Police Powers** were reserved to the states and to the people. Since ancient times, Police Powers were granted to local authorities to regulate the health, safety, welfare, morality, and education of the people. Thus, under the Constitution, the states had local Police Powers to regulate misdemeanor and felony crimes, for example, and create law enforcement agencies (later called police) to make it so. So, in *Carter v. Carter Coal*, 298 U.S. 238 (1935), the Court decided that Congress could not regulate the health and working conditions of coal miners because it was not interstate commerce, but local and under the Reserved Powers of the states.

President Franklin Delano Roosevelt was so outraged that he threatened to pack the Court with six additional justices (from 9 to 15) that he would appoint to vote his way against the "nine old men" on the U.S. Supreme Court. Rather than face public humiliation of the Court in this way, two Justices agreed with President Roosevelt to arbitrarily switch their votes to uphold such interstate laws ("the switch in time that saved nine"). But these debates continue, e.g., in *U.S. v. Lopez*, 514 U.S. 549 (1995), the Court decided that Congress could not regulate the sale of guns near schools because it was not interstate commerce, but were reserved to the states. Are there any real limits to the Commerce Power of the national government?

Delegation Doctrine. Under our Constitution, the sovereignty of all government ultimately resides in the people. In ratifying the Constitution and continuing to make it so, the people have delegated to Congress the power to make all laws on their behalf. Since the time of classical Rome, legislators lived by a maxim of law: *delegatus non potest delegare* (Latin, a delegate cannot delegate). Thus, by tradition and under common law, Congress could not delegate the powers that have been delegated to it by the people. And it makes sense, for example, who would want Congress to delegate to the Pentagon its power to declare war? And how could you maintain checks and balances of power if the Congress gave away all its powers?

Yet, we the people have steadily built up an incredible, almost countless, list of daily concerns that we have entrusted to government to take care of our lives, the lives of our family members, even the lives of people we may never know. Congress is simply incapable of making the countless governmental decisions we have entrusted to it, from academic standards for degree programs to zoo standards of care for animals, and so much more.

American administrative law has developed a way of coping with these awesome pressures and respecting the delegation doctrine by having the U.S. Congress set the primary standards and delegating to agencies only the power the fill in the gaps. Authorization is limited to allowing administrative agencies to fill in the details of the general laws of Congress. For example, Congress authorized the Federal Communications Commission (FCC) to regulate the broadcasting industry in the public interest.[31] FCC professionals, who are experienced and expert in the workings of various broadcast media, make rules that govern, for example, the licensing of stations. As the delegated agent of the Congress, these FCC professionals make regulations that are just as binding on broadcasters as if Congress itself had enacted them. Without this system, Congress would have to abandon any attempt to regulate this high-tech and quickly-changing technical industry. For example, in *FCC v. Pacifica Foundation*, 438 U.S. 726 (1978), the Court ruled that the First Amendment does NOT deny the government, in this case the FCC, the power to restrict a public broadcast that contains indecent language. In this example, concerning comedian **George Carlin's** (1937–2008) **monologue, "Filthy Words,"** the Court famously stated: "When the Commission finds that a pig has entered the parlor, the exercise of its regulatory power does not depend on proof that the pig is obscene." This illustrates the discretionary authority of public administrators to fulfill the greater public good.

Are there any real limits of the delegation doctrine today? Of course! First, with the enabling statute that creates an administrative agency, Congress writes the primary standards and delegates that the agency to fill in the gaps. Thus, the agency may be successfully challenged and limited for exceeding its authorization language. Second, the delegation doctrine today limits the excessive delegation of authority by congressional language that is too vague in defining the limits and primary standards of the agency. The enabling statute and all delegations by Congress to agencies must clearly limit the boundaries on delegated authority. Third, the Constitution itself sets important limits on the procedures and substantive areas of agency authority. For example, just as Congress cannot force people to go to church, neither can an agency require church attendance as a condition for receiving public assistance. Finally, some argue that state and local legislatures are largely limited by the traditional delegation doctrine and cannot delegate what has been delegated to them by the people.[32] Since most governance is at the state and local levels, the delegation doctrine is alive and well!

Congress and U.S. Administrative Law. While administrative law developed within the larger context of private and public law, under changing delegation doctrines and interstate commerce powers, the real story is the congressional takeover and continued domination of administrative law today. The year 1946 was a banner year for public administrators governing according to administrative rules and regulations: Congress enacted the Administrative Procedure Act (APA), Employment Act, and Legislative Reorganization Act (LRA) that included the Federal Tort Claims Act and General Bridge Act, among other laws.

After the tremendous growth of the U.S. bureaucracy under President Roosevelt's **New Deal** programs and the international applications of WWII, members of Congress felt themselves antiquated of the horse-and-buggy days of American government. The U.S. civil service bureaucracy had grown to become many large-scale organizations, and the military was assembling new branches and a Pentagon. Administrators were central to government, quoted in the media, lobbied by industry, and held the status once reserved for Senators and Representatives. To keep up with the demands of the New Deal and WWII, Congress had delegated legislative authority to agencies on an unprecedented scale, with little thought to oversight, evaluation, or control. This concerned some in Congress. Representative **Estes Kefauver** (1903–1963) (**D-TN**) was alarmed, "Is Congress Necessary?"[33] And Senator Robert M. LaFollette, Jr. (Progressive-WI) claimed there was "widespread congressional and public belief that a grave constitutional crisis exists."[34]

Congress asserted itself as the source of powers delegated to agencies and made clear that U.S. administrators served as extensions of Congress. For example, Senator **William Fulbright** (1905–1995) (D-AR) warned that old procedures and old rules may not work to control the burgeoning bureaucracy, its regulations, or the budgetary costs. Congress first debated the Walter-Logan Act of 1940, in which they agreed to return to traditional delegation doctrine (i.e., *a delegate cannot delegate*) and condemn the broad delegation of congressional power to executive branch agencies. President Franklin D. Roosevelt vetoed the bill successfully. And then WWII rocked the world and by 1946, Congress came to accept what had been done in the name of delegation during the New Deal and WWII. But was there a way to compel a massive bureaucracy to honor and uphold the values of the people as expressed through their representatives, the U.S. Congress?

Administrative Procedures Act

The Administrative Procedure Act of 1946 (APA) and other laws (see above) passed in the same year proved significant for Congress and the exertion of public administrators over quasi-legislative and judicial powers. First, even though much of the delegation was already done, Congress revisited it all through passage of the APA. With the APA, Congress asserted that the complexity of modern public policy, civil administration, and national security required the use of agencies as extensions of itself to carry out legislative functions. Representative Francis Walter (D-PA) made the point clearly: "Day by day, Congress takes account of the interests and desires of the people in framing legislation; and there is no reason why administrative agencies should not do so when they exercise legislative functions which the Congress has delegated to them." Thus, agency rule-making procedures were made standard and required public hearings, responses, and more representative input. The APA and follow-up statutes required greater transparency of agency information to the public. Excessive intrusion and heavy regulatory burden on business by agency activities was curbed. And procedures were streamlined for agencies to be more responsive to demands and their responsibilities, such as Federal Tort Claims Act of 1946 (FTC) that allowed agencies to settle claims against the government without going through private congressional bills.[35]

Second, Congress re-asserted its role in the oversight, evaluation, and control of agencies. In the Legislative Reorganization Act of 1946 (LRA) Congress re-inserted itself back into the daily life of U.S. bureaucracy by reforming both the House and Senate committee structures to more closely parallel and follows the structure of the U.S. bureaucracy. The number of standing committees was reduced and, for the first time in history, was given responsibility for exercising "continuous watchfulness"[36] over their list of agencies. The LRA authorized hiring of professional specialized experts (not just clerical staff) to assist committees in oversight, including the Legislative Reference Service, Congressional Research Service, Inspector General Act, and the General Accounting Office.[37] But the LRA failed in an attempt to place the budgetary process more squarely within close legislative control; however, this was later accomplished with the 1974 Congressional Budget and Impoundment Control Act. Other later acts further empowered Congress to the original goals of the 1946 LRA, e.g., the Legislative Reorganization Act of 1970 bolstered the power and staff of legislative committees to oversee agencies, and the 1993 Government Performance and Results Act required agencies to consult with Congress in adopting strategic plans and objectives.

Third, Congress re-asserted its interest in public works projects and other benefits to their constituents and district. The Employment Act of 1946 put Congress in control of public works projects — often the **pork-barrel** extras that bring development, jobs, and federal monies to a state or district. Through this control, it was clear that your local member of Congress — not some federal agency administrator — was owed for the largess of the new hydro-electric dam, park-building project, or other public works employment and monies.[38] This helped representatives and senators in retaining their tenure; pork was now controlled by the Congress and those with a longer tenure in office would get the goodies. Thus, the length of tenure of members of Congress went up significantly as both office-holders and their constituents realized the benefits in pork for the district and other expertise in casework to help constituents.[39]

Long-term tenure was most important for the continuous watchfulness of Congress over agencies to work; it took time to learn the agencies and all their complexity and only an experienced Senator or Representative could match the bureaucratic games of long-term civil service employees. The 1946 LRA further helped to develop this long-term expertise by eventually creating high-level assistants to help solve casework issues for constituents, as well as a retirement system for members of Congress. Of course, much of the pork and self-serving benefits did little to control the bureaucracy in the name of the people, but in a totality of the circumstances, the 1946 statutes and lengthened congressional careers helped to foster a more democratic and constitutional control of the U.S. bureaucracy.[40] The original 1946 APA and its many statutory amendments and augmentations over the decades principally focused on three major concerns: (1) public information and the provisions of agency information; (2) adjudication, rulemaking, and other agency operations; and (3) judicial review of administrative agencies.

First, the original 1946 APA did little in defining public information beyond previous statutes that required agencies to publicize information about their organization, opinions, orders, and public records in the *Federal Register* since the 1930s. Since the original 1946 APA, the **Freedom of Information Act of 1966** amended the APA and required agencies to make available their records and documents to any person requesting them, except under certain exemptions of the statute or other laws. For example, you can't request the medical records of a federal employee (unless it's your personal medical record). The **Privacy Act of 1974** protects the right to privacy of individuals, prohibiting agencies from releasing records concerning individuals without their consent, preventing the collection of information that is not relevant and necessary, and allowing individuals to review and seek to correct agency records on themselves. The **Government in the Sunshine Act of 1976** requires open meetings by federal agencies, commissions, and boards under most circumstances.

Second, the original 1946 APA focused most of its sections in dealing with agency operations, including adjudication and rule-making. The concern was with agency abuse in rule-making, adjudication, and other enforcement of their powers:

> "... the Constitution of the United States has divided the powers of our Government into three coordinate branches, the legislative, executive and judicial. These have been swallowed up by some administrators and their staffs who apparently believed that they were omnipotent. These have exercised all of the powers of government, arrogating to themselves more power than ever belonged to any man, or group. This has made necessary the enactment of such legislation as is now in the process of passage."[41]

In rule-making, the APA required notice and comment proceeding by agencies in most instances. Before the APA, cases such as *BiMetallic Investment Co. v. State Board of Equalization*, 239 U.S. 441 (1915), deferred to agencies in rule-making, allowing complete discretion in making law—like the deference given to Congress. But informal rule-making under the APA required agencies to publish a **notice** of the proposed rule in the *Federal Register*, and to receive and consider **comment** from all interested parties. Any agency-proposed procedures to make or interpret rules must similarly be published in the *Federal Register*. In some instances, the APA provided for rule-making on the record, also known as formal rule-making, as specified by the statute that created the agency. But formal rule-making and it's on the record proceedings are very rare under the APA.

In adjudication, the APA required various levels of due process in agency hearings. These due process standards are designed to promote procedural regularity, fairness, and reasoned decisions by agencies. For example, hearings are presided over by administrative law judges (a title adopted by the APA in 1972), who must be independent of the agency hierarchy. Administrative law judges make decisions over policies, benefits, or budgets that may conflict with their agency director. This has been called **judicialization** of the federal administrative process.[42] The high water mark of the judicialization of agency hearings was in the Court's decision in *Goldberg v. Kelly*, 397 U.S. 254 (1970), in which a disabled police officer was cut off public assistance. The "Goldberg Ten" required procedural protections before particular public services were cut off, including: timely adequate notice, right to a hearing, right to an impartial judge, right to a reasoned decision, right to judicial review, right to an attorney, right to cross-exam, right to disclosure, opportunity to obtain witnesses, and right to decision on the record. Formal adjudication under the "Goldberg 10" exists under the APA only when an authorizing statute of Congress required a hearing and decision determined on the record in that situation.

And third, the original 1946 APA provided for a limited scope of judicial review of agencies by the courts. The courts may review the substantive rules or actions of an agency, agency information activity, agency adjudication procedures, agency rule-making procedures, and even alternative dispute resolution processes by agencies. But the intensity of judicial review may vary from zero to 100 percent, depending on the deference to agency decisions required by the law. For example, APA Section 706(2) (E) states judicial review must defer to all-agency fact-finding except if it is unsupported by substantial evidence. On the other hand, if an administrator's decision clashes with the agency's own rules, judicial review will not defer to the factual, legal or discretionary agency decisions because the decision was "… arbitrary, capricious, an abuse of discretion, or otherwise not in accordance with the law."[43] An extensive case-law has interpreted the APA and constitutional law of judicial review of administrative agencies.

Conclusion

While E. Pendleton Herring hoped to design the public interest for public administration as due process had structured the judiciary, contemporary scholars, practitioners and judges have made due process of law and other core legal concepts the source of empirical expression to give the public interest the real meaning Herring had hoped for. The Constitution and laws pursuant to the Constitution give us a real world empirical expression of values, problems, and resolutions within public administration. Administration in the public interest exists within the larger context of law, including the Constitution, constitutional rights to freedom, property and equality, and the provision of due process of law through administrative law. The Constitution has provided a structure for administration in the public interest, such as legislative, executive and judicial branches, the delegation of authority by Congress to public agencies, and judicial review and the legal liability of public administrators. Constitutional limits and protections of the freedoms, property, and equality of persons, continue to expand and define many of the day-to-day ordinary interactions with public administration. Finally, due process of law and administrative law are highly specific in protecting individuals through procedural limitations on government and the public.

This overview of the U.S. Constitution and administrative law also focused on the principles approach to the public interest and the attending deontological theory of ethics. Following the Constitution means dutifully obeying rules or other ways to grasp the meaning of these laws applied fairly and without bias. The deontology principles approach may be criticized, first, for dutiful obedience even though it should result in mischief, injustice, or tragic ending for a particular person or group. Of course, in their defense people who apply deontology principles as the criteria for determining the public interest are affected by the outcomes or end results of their actions and respond accordingly.

Deontology principles approaches argue that while people ordinarily don't have the capacity to predict or control the consequences of their actions, they can act with the right intent. The principles approach presents an administrative reality that seems more bounded by rules, law, and duties that you are required to follow — but with a belief that you can act with good intent and achieve greater moral worth. Second, the deontology principles approach may be criticized for its pluralism, lack of unity, and non-systematic long lists of issues, roles, and topics. In its defense, the principles approach doesn't simply look at arête/excellence or a benefits/costs relation, but includes the diverse roles and corresponding duties of the public administrator, such as fiduciary-entrustor, principle-agent, supervisor-supervisee, bureaucrat-citizen, promisor-promisee, lawyer-client, physician-patient, parent-child, and many other roles. Finally, the principles approach to the public interest gives consideration to the past as an indicator of the good; past precedents may create obligations in the present. Of course, the Constitution and administrative law includes perspectives other than just the public interest principles approach. As with all applied ethics concepts, it is a matter of degree and all three public interest approaches may be found within the Constitution and administrative law: principles, policies, and practices.

The many case examples included in this chapter were included to illustrate more than just the rules of the game of law as applied administration in the public interest. These case examples of ordinary disputes with public administrators also illustrate the variety of applied ethical approaches — deontological principles, utilitarian policies, and virtue practices — in the legal resolution of these disputes. The development of the legal context surrounding administration in the public interest demonstrates how courts, executives, legislatures, administrators, and citizens have come to develop and refine their interpretation of the law in light of their understanding of the public interest. Thus, the cases illustrate how it is not the law that directs the public interest, but rather, the public interest which directs the law.

Action Steps

1. Why are checks and balances and limits on power necessary in the principles approach to administration in the public interest? Articulate your reasoning by reading and applying the U.S. Supreme Court case *INS v. Chadha*, 462 U.S. 919 (1983), in which the Court no longer allows the Congress to take back its delegated powers in piecemeal fashion for legislative review of agency decisions. How does the principle of separation of powers prevent the abuse of administration in the public interest?

2. Reflect on the principles of administration in the public interest by reading U.S. Supreme Court case *Goldberg v. Kelly*, 397 U.S. 254 (1970), in which injured NYPD police officer Kelly was cut off the public welfare assistance given to disabled officers. The "Goldberg 10" requires procedural protections before public assistance can be cut off, including: timely adequate notice, right to a hearing, right to an impartial judge, right to a reasoned decision, right to judicial review, right to an attorney, right to cross-exam, right to disclosure, opportunity to obtain witnesses, and right to decision on the record. Is the principle of public welfare assistance like a "property right" that NYPD officer Kelly possessed?

3. Break into teams of three or four, in which the instructor assigns to each group a one-to-two sentence statement summarizing the rule of law decided in a Supreme

Court decision on administration in the public interest, from the many examples within this chapter. Ask each group to state what is the public interest value expressed within each case decision. Each group should assign a secretary and spokesman to record and articulate any opposing viewpoints that may be possible in expressing the public interest values of the particular case. For example, in the *Brown v. Board of Education*, 347 U.S. 483 (1954), the Court's rule of law conclusion was deontological in that "separate was ... inherently unequal." Opposing public interest perspectives on this rule of law may focus on virtue and the need for equal opportunity in the public interest or, alternatively, for utilitarian distributive justice of public goods and services.

4. How has the contemporary practice of administration in the public interest deviated from the Constitution and laws? How was the administrative state re-directed toward constitutionalism and the law by the Administrative Procedure Act of 1946 and its amendments? Overview an article or book by David Rosenbloom and other administrative law scholars (e.g., Rosemary O'Leary, Richard Green, etc.) to retrofit constitutionalism into the administrative state. Write a short one-to-two page description and critique of these efforts to retrofit constitutionalism into public administration. Why is this effort significant to our understanding of administration in the public interest?

5. Read excerpts from some of the many excellent biographies of U.S. Supreme Court Justice Hugo LaFayette Black, such as Gerald T. Dunne, *Hugo Black and the Judicial Revolution* (1978), Roger K. Newman, *Hugo Black: A Biography* (1997), and Steven Suitt, *Hugo Black of Alabama: How His Roots and Early Career Shaped the Great Champion of the Constitution* (2005). The biographies of Black feature his Baptist background and how a literal interpretation of the Bible also directed his close reading of the Constitution. While many considered Justice Black one of the most liberal members of the Court in the expansion of the rights of blacks, criminal defendants, and the poor, Black felt this was simply a literal reading of the Constitution. Respond to these selections and meanings with a one-to-two page critique of the following questions: (1) How may constitutional interpretation approaches of justices, executives, legislators, administrators, and the public influence the meaning of these laws? (2) How may various constitutional interpretation approaches direct our understanding of the public interest?

6. Contact a federal or state attorney generals' office, or a municipal counsel's office, and inquire about select cases decided in their jurisdiction that deal with the public interest. How is the public interest defined and operationalized by the legal agency? Compare your findings with each level of legal counsel offices (federal, state, and municipal). Is there a difference between how the federal, state, and city officials view the public interest?

Exam Review Preparation

1. In a short essay, summarize and critique constitutionalism within administration in the public interest. What are the components of constitutionalism for public administration, including the structure of governance, federalism, civil liberties & rights, and due process of law? Write your own summary statement of constitutionalism within administration in the public interest. Defend it.

2. Identify the importance of each legal concept or case:

    a.   moral reading of the law

    b.   economic analysis of law

    c.   virtue jurisprudence

    d.   *INS v. Chadha* (1983)

    e.   *McCulloch v. Maryland* (1819)

    f.   *Smith v. Employment Division* (1990)

    g.   *Brown v. Board of Education* (1954)

    h.   The Framework of Equal Protection

    i.   *Red Lion Broadcasting Co. v. FCC* (1969)

    j.   Article IV of the U.S. Constitution (the Federal Article)

    k.   Administrative Procedure Act (APA)

    l.   *Goldberg v. Kelly* (1970)

3.   Explain how we now retrofit constitutionalism into the administrative state.

4.   How have the civil liberties & rights protections of freedoms, property and equality come to define the nature of administration in the public interest today? Do these individual protections go too far — or not nearly far enough — in the administration of the public interest? Why or why not?

5.   Overview and discuss the development of the Administrative Procedure Act of 1946 (APA). What public interest was articulated by the legislative reformers who called for the APA? What public interest was not articulated?

6.   Summarize the procedural protections accorded to public service recipients in the "Goldberg 10" under *Goldberg v. Kelly* (1970). What public interest is expressed by the procedural limitations on the government in *Goldberg v. Kelly* (1970)?

Key Concepts

Act Deontology
Americans with Disabilities Act
Categorical Imperative
Criminal law, corporate law, constitutional law
David Rosenbloom
Declaration of Independence, Articles of Confederation
Deontology
"Don't ask, don't tell"
Economic analysis of law
Estes Kefauver
First Amendment
Fourteenth Amendment
Freedom, property, equality, and due process
George Carlin
INS v. Chadha, 462 U.S. 919 (1983)
Judicialization
Korematsu v. US, 323 U.S. 214 (1944)

Lawrence v. Texas, 539 U.S. 558 (2003)
Legislative Reorganization Act
Marbury v. Madison, 5 U.S. 137 (1803)
McCulloch v. Maryland, 17 U.S. 315 (1819)
Moral reading of the law
Patrick Henry
Plessy v. Ferguson, 163 U.S. 537 (1896)
Prima Facie Duties
Qualified immunity
Rational basis test; strict scrutiny
Red Lion Broadcasting Co. v. FCC 395 U.S. 367 (1969)
Religious Freedom Restoration Act
Revisionist and progressive historians
Rule Deontology
Tenth Amendment
Thomas Hobbes
Virtue jurisprudence
William Fulbright

Recommended Readings

Beckett, Julia, and Heidi Koenig, eds. *Public Administration and Law: An ASPA Classic*. Armonk, NY: M.E. Sharpe, 2005.

Beth, Loren. *The Development of the American Constitution, 1877–1917*. New York: Harper and Row, 1971.

Carter, Lief H. *Administrative Law and Politics: Cases and Comments*. Boston, MA: Little, Brown, 1983.

Davis, Kenneth Culp. *Administrative Law Text*. St. Paul, MN: West, 1972.

Dworkin, Ronald. *Taking Rights Seriously*. Cambridge, MA: Harvard University Press, 1978.

Lee, Yong, David Rosenbloom, and Rosemary O'Leary. *A Reasonable Public Servant: Constitutional Foundations of Administrative Conduct in the United States*. Armonk, NY: M.E. Sharpe, 2005.

Rawls, John. *A Theory of Justice*. Cambridge, MA: Harvard University Press, 1971.

Semonche, John. *Charting the Future: The Supreme Court Responds to a Changing Society, 1890–1920*. Westport, CN: Greenwood, 1978.

Related Web Sites

Administrative Procedures Act, 1946
    http://www.ombwatch.org/article/articleview/176/1/67/

Articles of Confederation
    http://www.usconstitution.net/articles.html

Bill of Rights
   http://www.billofrightsinstitute.org/

Declaration of Independence, 1776
   http://www.ushistory.org/declaration/

Federalist Papers
   www.yale.edu/lawweb/avalon/federal.fed.htm

Senator William Fulbright
   http://exchanges.state.gov/education/fulbright/fulbbio.htm

Chapter 4

Federalism, States, Communities, and Public Interest Policies

"It is a known fact in human nature, that its affections are commonly weak in proportion to the distance or diffusiveness of the object. Upon the same principle that a man is more attached to his family than to his neighborhood, to his neighborhood than to the community at large, the people of each State would be apt to feel a stronger bias towards their local governments than towards the government of the Union; unless the force of that principle should be destroyed by a much better administration of the latter."

Alexander Hamilton, *The Federalist*, no. 17

"There is cause for concern about the future of public higher education. The unease is driven in part by the recent cuts in state funding of most public universities and by the harsh reality that today's strains are merely a continuation of a three decades-long trend driven by systemic tensions in state budgets ... In today's world, open and affordable access to high-quality education is crucial in every state ... Ultimately we must ask: 'What new policies and approaches can reconcile forces now threatening both the public interest and public colleges and universities?' The answers should form the backbone of a new social contract defining the relationship between public higher education and society."

Stanley Ikenberry, "Higher Ed: Dangers of an Unplanned Future."

Chapter Objectives

Upon completion of this chapter you should be able to:

1. Define the concept of federalism and discuss how managerial decentralization permeates the relationship between the national and state governments;

2. Discuss the importance and history of public administration, policymaking, and reform and reorganization at the state and local levels;

3. Distinguish the role, function, and constraints of state and local public administrative officials, especially as they differ from their national government counterparts;

4. Be familiar with several state and local policy issues, including education, planning and zoning, and crisis management;

5. Understand the policies approach to the public interest and the attendant utilitarian theory of ethics, with examples from the public administration of federalism, states, and communities.

Introduction

Federalism, states, and communities present a common challenge to public administration of balancing, compromising, and getting along in close quarters with those who may be next door. A study of administration in the public interest would be incomplete without at least a general overview of administrative and policy process within federalism and at the state and local levels. For example, changes in federalism and intergovernmental relations after events such as 9/11 and Hurricane Katrina provide significant challenges to local and state administrative, political, and non-profit decision making officials—those who we refer to as **first responders**—in the areas of communication, coordination, and especially the dollars! The problems facing citizens of various states and localities are as diverse as preparing and responding to natural disasters, coping with reductions in higher education funding, or dealing with the increasing costs of Medicare and Medicaid. The responses are generally the same: how are state and local administrators and officials suppose to balance, compromise, and get along with dwindling resources while dealing with increasing citizen needs?

This chapter is unique in public administration textbooks. Many public administration textbooks give attention to the nature of federalism and intergovernmental relations between, among, and within state and local governments. Most give particular attention to relations between state and local governments and the national government, and a smattering of examples of state and local issues and problems here-and-there in the textbook. But few, if any, public administration textbooks have a separate chapter on the administrative and policymaking influences of state and local governments and the roles and functions of major state and local public administrators. Public administration in states and communities is different than what we see in Washington, D.C., and the national level. Thus, we believe this chapter is necessary and important.

Our overview of the balancing, compromises and managing of federalism, states, and communities also gives us opportunity to examine the policies approach to the public interest and the attendant utilitarian theory of ethics. Public interest policies are all about these highly local and radically democratic calculations of the needs, preferences, and resources of all who are involved or affected by the decisions of public administration. As a result, public administration within federalism, states, and communities requires an additional level of recognition, respect, and accounting to these nearby people. Public interest policies, as an applied ethics concept, is similar to utilitarian ethical theory in which good and bad are determined by calculation of pleasure-and-pain, benefits-costs, and other measures of human needs or preferences of intrinsic value to produce maximal value. The public interest or moral value is not in the thing of intrinsic value itself (e.g., inmates want to eat delicious food), rather "Actions are right in proportion as they tend to promote happiness, wrong as they tend to produce the reverse of happiness."[1] Utilitarian ethical theory is not based on the discovery of pre-existing or universal rules or duties, but is skeptical of the value of such rules or duties without specific empirical reference to and calculation of the pleasure, happiness, or individual preferences of all who are involved. Utilitarianism emphasizes the ends of life (teleology) and achievement of desires, justice, and avoidance of tragedy and pain, rather than following the rules for their own sake. Utilitarianism may be hedonistic in focusing on pleasure or happiness or pluralistic with the inclusion of values beyond hedonism, but scholars and administrators tend to take a third approach of aggregating individual preferences. Of course, public administration in federalism, states, and communities includes perspectives other than just the public interest policies approach. As with all applied ethics concepts, it is a matter of degree and all three public interest approaches may be found within these localized administrative processes—principles, policies, and practices.[2]

The chapter begins, first, with an overview of the concept of federalism and discussion of how managerial decentralization now permeates the relationship between the national and state governments. We also set the stage for the remainder of the chapter's focus on public administration by states and communities. Second, we discuss the importance and meaning of studying public administration and policymaking in states and communities. Third, we provide a brief historical and conceptual overview of reform and reorganization efforts by state and local governments. Fourth, we explore the roles, functions, and distinctions (as well as constraints) of state and local public administrators and officials, especially as they differ from their national government counterparts. Fifth, we examine various state and local policy issues, including education, planning and zoning, e-government, and crisis management. And throughout the chapter, we illustrate and discuss the meanings, strengths, and weaknesses of the public interest policies approach and attendant utilitarian ethical theory.

Federalism

Nowhere is the ambiguity of compromise more evident in the U.S. Constitution than in the language of **federalism**. The term came from the Latin *foedus*, which means covenant. The concept dates back to the Hebrew Bible — or Old Testament for many Christians — in which a *b'rit* (Hebrew, "contract"), and later *pactum* (Latin, "pact") was made between God and Noah, Abraham, Moses, David, and Jesus. Similarly, a federal form of government was designed as a contract or pact between the government and the citizens. The Framers revolted against the weakness of the **Articles of Confederation** of 1781–1789, but also rejected the British model of a **unitary state**. Under the Articles of Confederation, all power was held by the states, even that granted to the national government. America suffered as the states held back authority to provide for national defense, to coin a national currency, or develop a strong national economy. The unitary state of Great Britain; however, placed oppressive power in the hands of the Crown and Parliament.

Constituting Federalism

The Framers compromised with federalism, a division of powers between states and the national government. Thus, it's technically wrong to call the national government the federal government, although everyone understands what you mean. James Madison declared in *Federalist No. 46* that the states and national government "are in fact but different agents and trustees of the people, constituted with different powers." The **Federal Article,** or Article IV of the Constitution (see below) recognizes the legitimacy and power of the states, requires the states to respect one another, and gives the national government duties in admitting new states to the nation and insuring democratic governance.

Box 4.1   Article IV of the U.S. Constitution

Section 1: Full faith and credit shall be given in each state to the public acts, records, and judicial proceedings of every other state. And the Congress may by general laws prescribe the manner in which such acts, records, and proceedings shall be proved, and the effect thereof.

Section 2: The citizens of each state shall be entitled to all privileges and immunities of citizens in the several states.

A person charged in any state with treason, felony, or other crime, who shall flee from justice, and be found in another state, shall on demand of the executive authority of the state from which he fled, be delivered up, to be removed to the state having jurisdiction of the crime.

No person held to service or labor in one state, under the laws thereof, escaping into another, shall, in consequence of any law or regulation therein, be discharged from such service or labor, but shall be delivered up on claim of the party to whom such service or labor may be due.

Section 3: New states may be admitted by the Congress into this union; but no new states shall be formed or erected within the jurisdiction of any other state; nor any state be formed by the junction of two or more states, or parts of states, without the consent of the legislatures of the states concerned as well as of the Congress.

The Congress shall have power to dispose of and make all needful rules and regulations respecting the territory or other property belonging to the United States; and nothing in this Constitution shall be so construed as to prejudice any claims of the United States, or of any particular state.

Section 4: The United States shall guarantee to every state in this union a republican form of government, and shall protect each of them against invasion; and on application of the legislature, or of the executive (when the legislature cannot be convened) against domestic violence.

Source: Cornell University Law School, LII/ Legal Information Institute, found at www.law.cornell.edu/constitution/constitution.articleiv.html

---

In addition, the Tenth Amendment, ratified in 1791, reserved to the states all powers that were not specifically enumerated in the Constitution. The Tenth Amendment reads, "The powers not delegated to the United States by the Constitution, nor prohibited by it to the states, are reserved to the states respectively, or to the people." But the ambiguity of the Tenth Amendment has confused courts, officials, and administrators for generations; exactly what is reserved to the states and local governments?

The **centralization of federalism** became evident early in American history, even with a later Civil War fought to finally decide these issues.[3] First, Alexander Hamilton proposed creation of a government bank in 1791 to help raise monies and take care of government business. Secretary of State Thomas Jefferson objected that under a **strict construction** interpretation of the Constitution a government bank was not listed as a national power, and the Tenth Amendment reserved all non-listed powers to the states. Hamilton, who was Secretary of Treasury, countered that the Constitution was concerned with ends and not means, and under a **loose construction** interpretation the means of a national bank to achieve ends was not forbidden. President George Washington agreed with Hamilton and a national government bank was created. Jefferson later agreed, as President, that Hamilton was right and used his argument to justify the Louisiana Purchase, the use of military in undeclared war, and so forth.

While the creation of a national government bank by George Washington in 1791 was the first step, the end came in 1819 with the case of *McCulloch v. Maryland*, 17 U.S. 315 (1819). Maryland taxed all out-of-state banks doing business within the state, including the national government bank branch in Baltimore. McCulloch was the clerk of the Baltimore branch who refused to pay the Maryland tax, because he claimed a state could not tax the national government. Maryland sued McCulloch, arguing that the national government had no constitutionally-enumerated power to create a bank, thus, the states reserved that power and Maryland had the power to tax the national bank branch in Baltimore. Luther Martin, lawyer for the state of Maryland, argued that since a bank was not necessary (Constitution: Article I, section 8, clause 18) to carry out any of its powers, Congress had no right to create a bank and it was under the reserved powers of the states (Tenth Amendment) which states may tax. **Daniel Webster** (1782–1852), lawyer for the national government, argued the reverse—since a bank was helpful to Congress to carry out its powers to collect taxes and care for property, it was necessary and proper under the Constitution (Article I, section 8, clause 18). Chief Justice **John Marshall** (1755–1835) agreed with Webster and upheld the power of Congress to create a bank under the Constitution, arguing that the Tenth Amendment did not limit this power of the national government. For Marshall, the necessary and proper clause gave significant *implied powers* to the national government, as he defined:

> "Let the end be legitimate, let it be within the scope of the Constitution, and all means which are appropriate, which are plainly adapted to the end, which are not prohibited, but consist with the letter and spirit of the Constitution, are constitutional."[4]

America continued to struggle with issues of federalism and states' rights, but *McCulloch v. Maryland* (1819) was the beginning of the end for what we refer to as dual federalism with the end not coming until the early 1930s. The Civil War and the ending of slavery, racial discrimination, and so forth with the Thirteenth, Fourteenth, and Fifteenth Amendments brought an end to these struggles, at least institutionally—but politically, economically, and, certainly, culturally and ethically the battle was just beginning. In order to create and ratify the 1789 Constitution, compromises were made to allow states' rights to slavery. But slavery was ended after changes in a common moral consciousness.

Utilitarian policies, like those that legitimated slavery, have often been criticized for the way in which a tyranny of the majority may impose an injustice upon minorities when it is to the advantage of the majority. The definition of public interest policies as merely the calculation of "individual preferences" has been used by American majorities to legitimate morally unacceptable results, such as slavery, torture in prisons and mental institutions, interrogating criminal suspects in the third degree, and other abuses. Under the policies approach to the public interest, calculations of individual preferences and benefits/costs in have been used to justify and mask the evil done by bureaucrats—hidden to the public and to themselves. How can slavery or abuses of minorities ever be in the public interest or moral? In its defense, utilitarian policies today are supplemented by concepts of justice to prevent abuses of minorities, such as from the Fourteenth Amendment and Bill of Rights. And some scholars of utilitarianism argue that these levels of harm are of such disvalue that they far outweigh any benefit or vote, when properly calculated. Yet, the criticisms of the abuses of minorities stick to utilitarian policies and many remain uneasy about the lack of built-in safeguards. Is anything ever intrinsically wrong?[5]

Changing Face of Federalism

What has federalism come to mean today for public administration? In the first theoretical analysis of federalism to date, Malcolm Feeley and Edward Rubin argue that most discussions of federalism are "remarkably mushy" as a "... thinly disguised defense of political conservatism, which is conveniently set aside whenever objectives are better pursued at the national level."[6] Although there is no shortage of scholarly and popular literature about federalism, little to none of it presents a theory of the subject. This may belie the genius of the Framer's use of ambiguous language on federalism to achieve compromise with confederation supporters, while still achieving a strong, central government. Or it may document the pragmatic American as a person who prefers what works. For example, when judges took over the prison systems of 42 states in the 1970s to protect fundamental rights and create constitutional prisons, why was there no intense political opposition?[7] Of course, there was some scholarly resistance, but why didn't the bar, the press, politicians, and the public oppose or slow down what scholars called a "judicial juggernaut"? Feeley and Rubin documented that the public never "bought in"[8] because the cause of rallying around states' rights was empty, that "... federalism is no longer an operative principle in the United States. What passes for federalism, we argue, is merely managerial decentralization."[9]

The current **managerial decentralization** of federalism in the administration of the public interest is characterized by changing models of allocation of authority, a new emphasis on diversity and innovation, and "grantsmanship" (or perhaps gamesmanship?). First, models for allocation of authority between national and state government have evolved toward disengagement of the national government and greater power and responsibility of the states. The early model of **dual federalism** or layer-cake theory, from 1789 to 1933, sought to create separate sovereign spheres of power in national, state and local governments, restricting the national role to powers enumerated in the Constitution. The New Deal of the 1930s and the expansion of national powers to deal with the Great Depression marked the rise of **cooperative federalism** or marble cake theory, from 1933 to 1964, characterized by sharing and mutual interdependence of national, state, and local governments.

The role of states and local governments became delivery of services funded by the national government. The **new federalism** is the model which characterizes relations from 1964 to the present time, focused on restoring power and responsibility to states and localities.[10] But unlike earlier eras, authority within new federalism seems to flow within areas of expertise and not by separate sovereign spheres of national, state and local governments. For example, former North Carolina Governor Terry Sanford characterized new federalism as **picket-fence federalism**, where national, state, local and other specialists within each policy area clustered with one another, rather than separate by level of government.[11] (See the diagram below.) And the power on each picket may be based in states or localities, with the disengagement of the national government and increasing state and local power and responsibility.

Figure 4.1   Picket-Fence Federalism

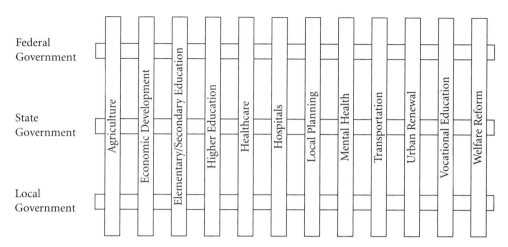

Note: The vertical slats represent the *inter-governmental* connections across the three main levels of government.

Source: Based upon Terry Sanford's description of federal, state, and local relations in his book, *Storm Over the States* (New York, NY: McGraw-Hill, 1967).

Second, diffusion and innovation of policy, rather than uniformity, now characterize the managerial decentralization of contemporary federalism. For much of U.S. history, the national government has sought uniformity among the states and localities in policy. The Congress, President and national courts required uniformity of states and localities in the areas of racial equality, the rights of criminal defendants, interstate commerce, and other policy areas that were brought up to national standards. This is clearly defined in the multitude of civil rights cases, largely dating back to *Plessy v. Ferguson*, 163 U.S. 537 (1896), and progressing toward *Brown v. Board of Education*, 347 U.S. 483 (1954), and the enforced desegregation of public schools. While the Congress, President and national courts have maintained the uniform standards of these prior precedents as a minimum, greater authority has been given to states and localities in developing ways to conform to these and other new needs. Similarly, cities and localities have been freed from the constraints of state control, contrary to the famous **Dillon's Rule**, by which localities possessed only those powers given them by a state. Thus, the unique culture and politics of a state of locality may be expressed within its policies more fully, more creatively, and with variety. For example, clean government in Wisconsin, individualism in Wyoming, traditionalism in Mississippi, or internationalism in N.Y.C. may not be the same for Iowa, Idaho, Alabama, or Boston.

Third, managerial decentralization is also focused on **grantsmanship** and the networking of connections to obtain national, state, and private funds for governance. Since 1964, the national government has simplified grant-giving to the states by allocating money to each state. Most grants are categorical grants, provided to states and localities for specific programs and narrow purposes. For example, the U.S. Department of Housing and Urban Development (HUD) houses the Grants Management Center (GMC) which oversees the grant application process for categorical grants. HUD awards the grants on either a competitive or lottery basis. One example is the Housing

Choice Voucher program, which provides rental assistance for low-income families who want to find a home in the private market that, based upon income, could not otherwise do so.[12]

Box 4.2   Block Grants and Revenue Sharing

Block grants provide for more general purposes and diverse activities, such as health services, education, and law enforcement. For example, Community Services Block Grant (CSBG) provides states and state-recognized Indian Tribes with funds for programs that try and alleviate causes and conditions of poverty. In addition, block grants are found in the policy area of law enforcement, such as the Local Law Enforcement Block Grant (LLEBG), which provides much needed funds to state and local law enforcement agencies to fund programs that try and reduce crime and improve public safety.

Revenue sharing grants, which were effectively outlawed in 1987, allowed states to spend the monies as they like, as long as they do not discriminate by race or other unlawful activities. As you can imagine, conservatives, such as Ronald Reagan, were none too happy to have the national government borrowing money it did not have to provide unchecked to states and local governments for projects that he—and other conservatives—did not believe were necessary (water parks, tennis courts, etc.).

Grants may also be classified by how the national government decides to fund the grant. *Project grants* are funded because a state or locality submitted a proposal that specified the project to be funded. *Formula grants* are funded by simple decision rules based on the state's population, miles of highway, and so forth. *Matching grants* require the state or locality provide some of its own funding which is variously matched by national monies.[13]

Unfunded Federalism

While the managerial decentralization of federalism gives more discretionary power and managerial authority to states and localities, thus state and local public administrators, entitlements, unfunded mandates, and deregulation may limit innovation. **Entitlements** are national programs administered by state or local governments, such as unemployment, public housing, and many health services. While states can redefine eligibility to reduce the number of beneficiaries of entitlements, it is difficult for a state to cut off a person's benefits. **Unfunded mandates** are individual property interests in public goods or services that are protected by legal rights, including adequate public education, prison and jail conditions, etc. For example, state and local governments complain that they are struggling in a competitive global economy. The federal government imposes laws upon them—well-intentioned though they may be—such as the Occupational Safety and Health Act, the Family and Medical Leave Act, and most recently President Bush's first legislative proposal, **No Child Left Behind Act of 2001**. Each piece of legislation requires states and localities to fund large parts of each program, while at the same time being regulated by the federal government. Costs are enormous to state and local governments. Congress responded in 1995 by passing the **Unfunded Mandates Reform Act**, which effectively required Congress to double-check itself before imposing any more requirements upon the states and localities. The results are mixed as to whether or not it really made any difference.[14] Some are simply skeptical from the start, and do not believe Congress did much of anything to check itself.[15]

What has happened to states' rights in this era of **deregulation**? Many have espoused national government deregulation—the process of simplifying, reducing, or removing legal restrictions by national government on businesses and people to support and develop the market economy. Since the 1980s, deregulation was a states' rights mandate designed to give these issues back to the states to regulate how, and if, they saw fit. So, when the national government scaled down enforcement of laws regulating the environment, civil rights, predatory lending, and workplace safety, many states entered into the void. After all, shouldn't states enact laws to protect their people in conformity with their prevailing community standards? Yet, the national government has crushed attempts by states to provide added protections. For example, the national government prohibited heavily-polluted California from setting its own standards on greenhouse emissions, blocked states from regulating bankers who caused a meltdown in mortgage lending, and limited state workplace safety regulations for mines or factories.[16] How did the deregulation of national government come to mean the end of states' rights? Entitlements, unfunded mandates, and state deregulation by the national government take a greater share of state and local budget dollars and limit states and communities from thinking outside the box in the innovation of new governance strategies.

Public Administration at the State and Local Levels

Thomas P. "Tip" O'Neil (1912–1994), former Speaker of the House, once quipped, "All politics is local." Perhaps, too, all public administration is state and local. This is probably not true, however, we do contend that administration in the public interest is best realized at the state and local levels. State and local governments, and especially the state and local public administrators who develop, implement, and evaluate the many programs that provide the public services we as citizens enjoy, impact our daily lives much more than the federal government does. Everyday you travel a street, drink a glass of water, stop at a Stop sign, eat lunch, talk on a cell phone, or pay some kind of state and/or local tax (sales, food, property etc.), all of these activities, either directly or indirectly, is affected, impacted, or regulated in some way by state and local governments. As an example, take a look at a **local economic development** and planning controversy. (See case study for Purcellville, Virginia.)

Case Study   Building a School in Northern Virginia: Can It Really Be This
              Difficult?

The Town of Purcellville, Virginia, and Loudon County, Virginia, entered into a joint planning agreement in 1995 titled, "Purcellville Urban Growth Area Management Plan" (PUGAMP), which was designed to project future growth needs of the rural western town of Purcellville, including a high school. The County of Loudon, however, who was going to be largely affected by this growth, both in terms of additional residents, demand for services, and most importantly tax growth, wanted equal input into the approval of future projects. One such project was the intended development and construction of a high school in Fields Farm, just north and west of Purcellville. That construction has been delayed by court rulings and judgments. Appeal to the Virginia Supreme Court by the Town will cause further delay.

The need for an additional public high school in Loudon County sounds reasonable enough—doesn't it? Perhaps not, though. Purcellville does not want the additional traffic and congestion that will come with the high school, considering it already has a high school—Loudon Valley High. Proponents of the high school argue that the current high school enrollment is beyond its acceptable capacity and therefore impedes the student's ability to learn effectively. Opponents counter that there are plenty of other locations within Loudon County, particularly near the small German settlement of Lovettsville, which is about 10 miles north of Purcellville. But what is really at issue is jurisdictional authority: who—the Town or the County—has the greater control or influence over and in the PUGAMP. At the center of the controversy are a number of local elected and administrative officials including, the Loudon County Commission, Purcellville Mayor (Bob Lazaro) Town Council, Loudon County Administrator (Kirby M. Bowers), Purcellville Town Manager (Rob Lohr) Loudon County's Director of Planning (Julie Pastor) as well as her counterpart, Purcellville's Director of Planning (Martha Semmes).

Source: Shannon Sollinger, "County Ok's Field Farm's School," *Loudon Times Mirror*, 6 June 2007, www.timescommunity.com (accessed June 2007).

The development, implementation, and evaluation of public policy is anything but a federal matter. In fact, public administration is much more prevalent at the state and local levels than at the federal level—at least in terms of direct influence or impact upon residents in a variety of ways and policy areas, including tax burden, regulatory policy, economic pressure, education policy, and a host of others. The impact of state and local governments is vital to the continuation of our American political and administrative systems.

Public administration at the state and local level involves the citizenry, engages the public, private, and non-profit sectors, encompasses a wide range of interests, issues, and policy areas, while at the same time is largely dependent upon the federal government for much of the funding that supports so much of what goes on at the state and local levels. Before we provide some basic historical and conceptual overview of state and local governments relationships and autonomy, let's review five basic reasons why we should study public administration in the public interest at the state and local levels.

Studying Public Administration in State and Local Communities

Why is the study of public administration in states and communities important? First, if "all politics is local," then the democratic administrative state is best realized at the state and local levels for many important issues of everyday life. One author commented in the early part of the twentieth century that "Public administration in the United States, partly because it is federal, partly because it reflects attitudes of democracy and self-government, is deeply rooted in the local communities."[17] The Ninth and Tenth Amendments to the Constitution and common law history recognize the **police powers** granted to state and local governments. Police powers are government powers over objects that are near-and-dear and close to the people, such as their health, welfare, education, morality, and general safety. It is from the concept of police powers that state and local governments created law enforcement forces called police, such as the London Constabulary of Metropolitan Police (first named "bobbies" for founder Robert Peeler) in 1829. The constitutional concept of police powers necessitates that state and local governments fiercely maintain governance that is highly local in order to be immediately responsive to these personal needs and safety.

State legislative control of local municipal charters, for example, was designed to provide significant political input and oversight of local government actions. This action led to less **home rule**, or governing autonomy on the part of the local governments. Even so cities, which had been in existence long before states came about during the Revolutionary era, were largely and sufficiently self-contained governing and economic units, and so the states did not need to keep close tabs on their actions. That changed with the migration of farmers to the cities, but it also included foreign immigration. For example, city dwellers comprised nearly half of the U.S. population (46 percent) in 1910.[18] This influx of people to the cities, instigated in large part by the Industrial (and technological) Revolution, put into motion a whole series of events, including municipal reform movement (which we will discuss in more detail later) that largely impacted not only state and local politics, but also the administration of both old and new policy areas, such as economic development and local planning.[19]

Second, public administration at the state and local levels is closer to the people than public administration at the national level. It is true that about 90 percent of all federal bureaucrats work outside of the **Washington, D.C., beltway** and thus live close to where they work, but they are not as easily accessible to the common citizen living in Mount Pleasant, Iowa, Kootenai County, Idaho, or any number of the thousands of small towns, communities, and counties scattered across the United States as is the town administrator, city manager, parks and recreation director, waste water treatment plant manager, or the town street sweeper (yes, some towns still have one). All of the people who hold these local government positions are generally required to live within the jurisdiction they work in — sometimes because it is law, but most of the time because they want to live in the community they work in. They want to know and serve their neighbor and community. They want to make and have a lasting impact upon their fellow citizens. They want to positively affect the public interest. The downside, of course, is that being too chummy might lead to cronyism and unfair political games based on who you know rather than following legal and administrative guidelines.[20]

Third, an examination of public administration at the state and local levels reveals a greater sense of community and **civic understanding**, awareness, and practice of civic duties, i.e. greater pursuit of the public interest. Local government, for example, attracts some 85 percent (as of 1999) of all volunteers who serve at all three levels of government. Local government managers, both at the county and municipal levels, strongly encourage volunteers and citizen activists.[21] However, this position of civic understanding and community awareness is being challenged. For example, a 2006 study[22] revealed that public and private higher education failed to provide adequate knowledge on American history and government. Since the more a student learns about civics and history the more they will be an active citizen, the study concluded there is a coming crisis in American citizenship. Similarly, it is getting more difficult to attract and keep young people in positions of public administration — at any level — because of the lure of big money in the private sector. As the level of **social capital** declines ("bowling alone," see below), so does our broader sense of community, thus, the less likely that individuals will participate in civic duties, citizen councils, and initiatives.[23] The reversal of these trends is critical to continuing citizen awareness and involvement in civic activities, and thus pursuing the public interest.

Box 4.3   Social Capital on the Decline

Social capital, a termed coined by Robert Putnam, Director of the Saguaro Seminar and professor of public policy at Harvard, in his groundbreaking work, *Bowling Alone*, goes beyond the resources necessary to engage community on a cultural and social level. It suggests that the implications of NOT having social capital means that state and local governments, specifically communities and sub-communities within those jurisdictions, lack the necessary tools capable of a sense of community or togetherness that is vital to the development and continuation of democracy and democratic institutions, and more importantly— or as importantly—deters civic and social *disengagement*. With greater levels of disengagement and a continuing loss of social capital, states and local governments see: a) higher crime rates; b) lower education performance; c) higher rates of teen pregnancy; d) lower low-birth weight babies; and e) higher infant mortality rates. Thus, the consequences of a decrease in "social capital" can impose policy and administrative difficulties upon various state and local officials.

Source: Bowling Alone, "Bowling Alone," Saguaro Seminar, www.bowling alone.com/ (accessed June 2007).

Fourth, state and local governments are major contributors of public services. The number of state (approximately 5 million) and local (approximately 13 million) government employees is nearly 6 times the size of the civilian federal government workforce (about 3 million). [The last number is likely to increase with the national government expansion under President Obama's administration.] Of the nearly 18 million state and local government employees, over 7 million work in elementary and secondary education, with another 3 million in higher education.[24] Demand is high for various services, including education, medical care, criminal justice, judicial and legal, fire and police protection, state liquor stores, and much more. What does all of this cost? And who pays the bill? (This second question is easy to answer: the taxpayer does!). In 1998, for example, total state and local taxes, fees, and other revenue generating means brought in approximately $1.3 trillion dollars; by 2008 that figure increased to $2.4 trillion dollars! This nearly equaled the federal government budget in FY 2008—nearly a whopping $3.0 trillion![25] State and local governments are not only big business, but they are vital to the civic and governmental sustenance of America.

Fifth, the states and communities have interesting policy innovations and reforms of administration. Devolving responsibility to the lower levels of government, such as President Reagan advocated in the 1980s, meant that state, municipal, and county governments, as well as special districts, assumed greater responsibility for funding and implementing basic public services, including Medicare and Medicaid and education. In recent years, because of 9/11 and **Katrina**, more attention is paid to state and local levels to be first responders. In addition to greater financial and human resources and commitment, both professional and volunteer, it means that state and local governments must become innovative in policy experiments.

In 1932, U.S. Supreme Court Justice **Louis Brandeis** (1856–1941) argued that citizens serve as a "laboratory," where they "try novel social and economic experiments without risk to the rest of the country."[26] Justice Brandeis, and many others since, have been fascinated with the new and creative policy innovations of states. For example, Michigan, Missouri and Wisconsin experimented with welfare-to-work policies in the 1980s, which ultimately became the impetus for future national welfare change in the 1990s. Of course, much of the policy innovation in a state may be related to state or local wealth, the presence and impact of interest groups, and general public interest in the topic. U.S. and states laws and constitutions place even more restrictions on cities, counties, and other localities. But even so, communities often have different freedoms to privatize, outsource, and other means to pursue the public interest through policy innovation.[27] For example, *Governing Magazine*, in conjunction with the **Ash Institute for Democratic Governance and Innovation**, produces several winners each year for "Innovations in American Government." For example, 2006 winners included the City of Indianapolis, "Mayor's Charter Schools Initiative," State of Connecticut, "Supportive Housing Pilots Initiative," and Broward County, Florida, "Urban Academies Program" (see below).

Case Study   Charter Schools, Housing Programs, and Urban Academies: Pursuing the Public Interest

Mayor Bart Peterson believes in high educational standards, so much so that in 2001 he petitioned the General Assembly of Indiana to grant him, and all other local chief executives, the authority to grant and revoke school charters. He is the only mayor with that kind of power.

Very few schools are granted charters. (Currently, there are only 12, educating some 3,000 students.) However, seven more schools are slated to open in 2006, and that will bring the statewide total up to 8,400 students.

In order to remain open the schools must meet rigorous standards, including a) high academic achievement levels, b) intense parent and faculty (and staff) feedback, and c) frequent outside site visits.

It must be working; the performance numbers are going up. From 2002–2004 there was an average of 22 percent increase in passage rate on statewide exams; between 2003–2005 it increased to nearly 26 percent. During 2002–2004, for example, Indianapolis' traditional public schools rated an increase of only 1 percent. And these numbers reflect students coming from low-income and or otherwise challenging areas of the city.

Peterson is clear on his purpose for instituting charter schools: to put pressure on traditional public schools, forcing them to respond in kind, and thus raise their performance levels.

Source: "The Innovations in American Government Awards," *Governing Magazine* (August 2006). For more information on the Indianapolis Charter School Project, contact David Harris, the Director for the Indianapolis Charter Schools Project; 2501 City-County Building, 200 E. Washington Street., Indianapolis, IN 46204; 317-327-3601; daharris@indygov.org.

The State of Connecticut's Supportive Housing Pilots Initiative is not only about getting the homeless off of Connecticut's city streets; it is about how to build a network to achieve this goal. What specifically is the goal: "to move homeless individuals wrestling with mental illness and addiction … into 'supportive housing'—that is, housing that is affordable and makes support services available." Independent living is the objective of the Initiative, and various state departments and agencies are working together to meet the goal, including the state's Office of Policy and Management, Mental Health and Addiction Services, Economic and Community Development and the Housing Finance Authority, along with the Corporation for Supportive Housing, a national non-profit.

Supportive housing is not a new idea, but in Connecticut the approach is sweeping and integrative; it tries to involve as many integral organizations and agencies as possible, bringing as many people and resources as possible to weigh in on finding adequate supportive housing for mentally-ill homeless. Some 400 individuals and families in 25 communities have found housing and employment. Even after three years of operation, over 66 percent off the tenants still live in their apartments. As Anne Foley, senior advisor in the Office of Policy and Management, remarked "We're breaking the cycle of homelessness."

Source: "The Innovations in American Government Awards," *Governing Magazine* (August 2006). For more information, contact Anne Foley, Office of Policy and Management, 450 Capitol Ave., Hartford, CT 06106; 860-418-6268; anne.foley@po.state.ct.us.

Broward County, Florida's Urban Academies Program is designed to retain top teachers in difficult school districts—mainly urban areas, where crime, drugs, and gangs are at their worst. A newly minted school teacher is usually like bait for the sharks: chewed up and swallowed. With little cultural training to go along with their academic skills, these "rookies" are not prepared for entering into the urban war zones called public schools. This is particularly true in Broward County, Florida.

Nationwide urban schools have some of the least qualified teachers and the highest teacher attrition rate—50 percent. Couple this with the fact that urban schools are generally under-achievers when it comes to standardized exams, it poses a big problem for administrators and politicians alike. So, what is a county to do?

Broward County School Board decided to begin a series of experiments that were aimed at better preparing teachers in poor and minority K-12 schools, using the resources of two state universities—Broward Community College and Florida Atlantic University, and two private schools—Barry and Nova Southeastern universities.

In a nutshell, the goal is two-fold: find college students interested in teaching and give them actual experience in urban schools—along with full college scholarships. The second component is to nurture these students as early as their freshman year in high school through information, real world experience, and promises of full-scholarships.

What are the results? As of 2004–2005 15 academy schools have a 93 percent retention rate for third-year teachers, compared with 83 and 67 percent district and nationwide, respectively. Further, no academy teachers were fired during probation and 100 percent of participating high school students went on to college.

Source: "The Innovations in American Government Awards," *Governing Magazine* (August 2006). Contact: Sara Rogers, Coordinator, Urban Academies program, 1800 SW 5 Place, Fort Lauderdale, FL 33312; 754-323-2115; sara.rogers@browardschools.com.

State and Local Government Reforms

In addition to policy innovation, state and local public administrative organizations have undergone significant changes of structure and procedures, more than in the national government. These changes have focused on increasing professionalism, enhancing how work is accomplished (i.e., efficiency, effectiveness, and economy), and past attempts to try (unsuccessfully) to separate administration from politics. **Patronage** or spoils system was the preferred state and local personnel system until recent decades. From the time of President Andrew Jackson (1820s) to the end of the nineteenth century, the spoils system dominated state and local government hiring. Government jobs were exchanged for political party support and allowed the influence of political machines, such as **William "Boss" Tweed** (1823–1878) of New York and **Tom Pendergast** (1873–1945) of Kansas City, to thereby rule state and local government public administration machinery and control delivery of social and welfare services. The corruption of the system was interrupted and derailed from time-to-time by progressive reformers. Reformers were often civic-minded, socially-connected, and moral in their tone. They were known for holding strong civic and religious values that under-girded their belief in and practice of reform, and who eventually succeeded in changing the organizational culture of public administration.[28] We examine two broad examples of reform: local government re-structuring and state executive reorganization.

Municipal Reform Efforts. American reform efforts at the local level largely began during the scientific management revolution, where reformers focused on separating administration from politics by emphasizing scientific task analysis and time-and-motion studies. Many reformers were prompted by Woodrow Wilson's 1887 article advocating a separation of administration from politics. For example, reformer George W. Curtis advocated merit-based hiring systems, Emory Upton spoke for greater professionalism, and Richard S. Childs was the most influential individual in establishing the council-manager form of local government.[29] All focused first on breaking down the strongholds of the political machines in local administrations. Independent organizations and institutions, aimed largely at researching, writing, and activism, sprang up and placed considerable pressure on the political machines. These included the National Municipal League (1894) [now the National Civic League], **National League of Cities** and National Civic Federation (1900), National Child Labor Committee (1904), and a host of others.[30]

Box 4.4   National League of Cities and the National Civic Federation

The National League of Cities is the oldest and largest national organization representing municipal governments throughout the United States. Its mission is to strengthen and promote cities as centers of opportunity, leadership, and governance.

Working in partnership with the 49 state municipal leagues, the National League of Cities serves as a resource to and an advocate for the more than 19,000 cities, villages, and towns it represents. More than 1,600 municipalities of all sizes pay dues to NLC and actively participate as leaders and voting members in the organization.

Founded amidst the 1893 economic depression, the Civic Federation of Chicago began as a relief organization but soon addressed a great variety of the city's social and political problems, including political corruption, union-employer disputes, and inefficient public administration. It soon underwent a transition from a broadly oriented reform organization to an agency specializing in taxation.

Led by banker Lyman Gage and journalist Ralph Easley, the Civic Federation became a quintessential Progressive-era reform organization. In 1900, Easley formed the widely acclaimed National Civic Federation, which despite its name functioned independently of the Chicago organization. Departing from the elitist strategies of previous civic groups, the Civic Federation of Chicago sought to gain broad popular support for its nonpartisan reform proposals. During its early years, membership crossed class boundaries and included trade unionists from the Chicago Federation of Labor and social reformers like Jane Addams. The Civic Federation engaged in such innovative strategies as petition campaigns, protests at City Hall, and newspaper publicity. Yet it opposed measures that called for greater direct democracy, such as the initiative and referendum, and instead promoted centralization of government as well as rule by professionally trained experts. Municipal problems, increasingly complex in nature, were to be removed from politics altogether and subjected to rational, fact-based solutions, for which the federation's numerous published investigations would form the basis.

The unions left the Civic Federation soon after the turn of the century, and by 1917 it focused on taxation and efficiency in public administration, leaving other tasks to separate organizations that had grown out of its earlier activities such as the Chicago Bureau of Charities and the Municipal Voters League. As governmental functions widened during the early twentieth century, the federation sought to augment public revenues by streamlining municipal administration, thereby avoiding higher taxes. Since the 1920s, by means of policy statements and research assistance to legislators, it has fought to minimize public spending, serving as a watchdog on government finance and administrative efficiency.

In 1929, as the Civic Federation operated increasingly on the state level, it omitted Chicago from its name. Three years later, it merged with the Chicago Bureau of Public Efficiency, founded in 1910. Temporarily known as the Civic Federation and Bureau of Public Efficiency, it dropped the latter part of that name in 1941. It is considered the oldest taxpayers' research organization in the country.

Source: Reprinted from National League of Cities, "About NLC," http://www. nlc.org/ INSIDE_NLC/aboutnlc.aspx (accessed October 2007). "Civic Federation," Encyclopedia of Chicago, www.encyclopedia.chicagohistory.org/pages/ 291.html (accessed October 2007).

One main reform was to replace the strong mayor form of local government with the commission and council-manager form of government—which emphasized professional management over elected political office. Today, the council-manager form is the most popular form of local government structure. And because the machines were pursuing their own interests rather than the broader public interest, the reformers focused on developing public services such as water and sewer, education, welfare, economic development, and city planning. These were hard-fought reforms in highly fragmented urban societies. American cities included many different races and ethnicities, different cultural values and languages, making it difficult to meet the needs of all. However, reformers seemed able to gather most people around a basic set of needs for clean cities, healthy climates, and the elimination of political corruption.[31]

State Executive Reorganizations

Executive re-organizational efforts made way to the political agendas of state governors and legislators sometime before 1920. As early as 1915 Illinois and New York experimented with constitutional changes,[32] to reduce political influence in regulatory agencies and independent commissions with oversight of railroad rates, barbering, and so forth. The goal of state executive reorganizations was to streamline organizations, departments, and agencies by function and place them under central control of the governor. Reorganizations didn't touch the constitutionally defined state offices, such as secretary of state, treasurer, and attorney general. But all others were viable targets. The primary goals of state executive reorganization were to increase economy and efficiency (and) clarify chains of command. In many instances the changes were as much symbolic and rhetorical as they were substantive. Consolidating agencies by function, such as budgeting or personnel, sounded great but each individual department still had to make their own budgeting and personnel decisions. A guiding presence may have been helpful, but to eliminate these functions from individual departments or agencies was not realistic. In the end, it was more political rhetoric, or symbolism, than helpful.

By the 1930s, state executive reorganization efforts had slowed. Establishment of "The Brownlow Commission" revived the process and continued it for forty years.[33] The Brownlow Commission was also referred to as the Commissions on Organization of the Executive Branch, or **The President's Committee on Administrative Management** (1937). It focused on executive reorganization in both the national and state levels and urged greater efficiency, economy, and effectiveness. Results were often disappointing because the organizations defensively protected their power. Yet, reformers continued to pursue the public interest by eliminating waste and fraud, pursuing more efficient and economical delivery of public services, and separating politics from administration.[34]

State and local governments—especially local communities—are incredibly diverse. The U.S. Constitution contains only sparse details on the states, but no mention of local governments, including municipalities, counties, and special districts. Local governments are constrained by state constitutions and laws. This brief overview of the administration of state and local government outlines their structures, roles, and functions.

State Governments

State government authority and power is given some attention in the Constitution. For example, the bond between the states and the union is clearly laid out. In 1869, **Chief Justice Salmon P. Chase** (1808–1873) wrote that "The Constitution, in all of its provisions, looks to an indestructible union, composed of indestructible states."[35] The Constitution also provides for states' rights and states' sovereignty in Article IV, in which section 4 requires the "guarantee of a republican form of government." And the Tenth Amendment reserves powers to the states (e.g., police powers). The states, unlike local governments, are guaranteed an administrative and political position in the union by the Constitution.

Theories abound that try to explain the role of state governments in the federal system. First, the capacity thesis contends that the states play a central role in the federal system. **Capacity** refers to a state government's "ability to respond effectively to change, make decisions efficiently and responsibly, and manage conflict."[36] How well a state is able to muster fiscal and leadership resources is largely based on how well the administrative agencies perform. So, state governments define good administration by performance management, performance budgeting, and the like. Getting more "bang for the buck," so to speak, is becoming the norm for state governments. This has intensified since the 1980s with states increasing cooperation among and between states and localities. The bottom line: state capacity is tied to administrative performance on various policy issues.

Box 4.5   Utah and Virginia Are at the Top of Their Class!

Utah and Virginia received *"As"* for enhancing performance management. In 2005, *Governing* magazine, the trade periodical for state and local administrative managers and administrators, annually ranks states for performance. Utah and Virginia were the only two states to receive *"As."* The reason: both states had the fiscal, political, administrative, and technological capacity to perform not only the basic functions of state governments, i.e. collect state income and sales taxes through their highly functional Departments of Revenue, but also to deal with a variety of other issues. For example, Utah's Department of Transportation ran a panel truck around the highways and byways of Salt Lake City soliciting specific questions from citizens regarding transportation needs of commuters. When the panel truck stopped, commuters stopped as well, swarming the truck and peppering the driver with questions and comments.

And in Virginia, for example, the Department of Human Resources implemented a Learning Management System, which is essentially a workforce planning tool to gauge how much time, effort, and fiscal resources will be necessary to plan for future state personnel needs, particularly once the Baby Boomer generation of civil servants begins retiring in earnest.

Source: Katherine Barrett, Richard Greene, Zach Patton, and J. Michael Keeling, "Grading the States '05: The Year of Living Dangerously," Governing (February 2005), www.governing.com/gpp/2005/intro.htm (accessed June 2007).

A second framework is the politics in a comparative approach. The approach here is to compare states along a variety of factors (e.g., population growth, income disparity, ideology, religion) and issues (e.g., education, racial and civil rights, economic development), asking the basic question of "What are the differences between and among states?" and "How are the differences explained?" For example, comparative analysis can help understand the key role of state expenditures to prisons to avoid federal district court prison reform litigation and judicial decrees.[37] While less focused on administration, the comparative approach is helpful for studying historical, cultural, constitutional, and political factors associated with states and with roles played by public administrators (see below, comparative approach with regard to education policy).

Case Study   No Child Left Behind: Is It in the Public Interest?

Education policy compared along state lines. For example, most states spend most of their money on education, along with welfare, healthcare, and corrections. With regard to education, states pass enabling legislation that provides local school districts with the authority and finances to operate individual school systems. Even though school districts have their own authoritative jurisdictional boundaries, complete with staff, personnel, and finances to run the district, the state is largely in control, determining the funding formulas (New York ranks highest at just over $12,000 per pupil with, surprisingly, Utah last in per pupil spending at just over $5,000), the number of days a school must stay open, the number of grades to be taught, and a host of other details — most of which should probably be decided at the local level. Nonetheless, despite the state influence in education, the federal government is becoming more involved. A great example is the implementation and impact of the **No Child Left Behind Act of 2001** (NCLB).

NCLB is really an amendment to Title I of the **Elementary and Secondary Education Act of 1965**. According to NCLB, all states were required to meet certain levels of accomplishment in reading and math measured through regular examination in grades 3–8. The test results are to be published and the test scores are to be categorized according to race, ethnicity, gender, and other factors. The argument for mandatory testing is to ensure that no group of students, regardless of race, gender, or ethnic background is "left behind." In fact, upon the urging of the First Lady, Laura Bush, reading scores became the primary focus, encouraging all schools to have all students reading by the third grade. Those schools and districts that do not meet the adequate yearly progress (AYP) levels will be scrutinized and ultimately punished (withholding of federal educational funding). The key public administration officials, i.e. those held accountable for implementing the new federal law included everyone from the Secretary of the federal Department of Education all the way down to school principals. In between are parents and students, who are generally given very little leeway in determining their educational focus and goals.

Source: For a sound overview see Thomas R. Dye and Susan MacManus' state and local textbook titled *Politics in States and Communities,* 12th ed. (Upper Saddle River, NJ: Prentice-Hall, 2007), 580, 582.

Counties

Counties or parishes (as they are referred to in Louisiana) are the legal administrative arm of states. Almost all 3,000 counties (and parishes) in the United States have representation in the **National Association of Counties** through the 53 state associations with 47 states represented (some states have multiple associations, such as Illinois with three). Historically, counties' roots go back to the English shire, or political division, nearly 1,000 years ago.[38] When the framers of the U.S. Constitution did not include local governments, and they left that responsibility to the states, counties (as well as municipalities) became the creatures, so to speak, of the states. In other words, counties and municipalities are formed by the states to serve at the behest of the state government.

Prior to the reform movement of the early twentieth century, counties were limited. Beyond being simply the administrative apparatus of the state, counties held no real power. After the reform movement, however, things changed, particularly with the urbanization and later suburbanization of America. Counties, especially urban counties, began to act more like municipalities, trying to cope with the expanding economic and population growth. For example, urban counties, especially, engage the county population with the same basic types of administrative and governmental functions as rural counties do, including law enforcement, courts, road maintenance, and election oversight, but many, for example, such as Loudon and Arlington County, Virginia, or Wake and Mecklenburg, North Carolina, also provide fire, water and sewer, library, and mass transit. Others, such as Orange County, California, also support tourism, airports, sports stadiums, and even pollution control.

Counties are formed in three ways, with many of the administrative responsibilities vested in elected and constitutionally defined officers (clerk, sheriff, etc.). At the same time, however, more and more counties are employing the services of a professional manager. The three forms are: **commission** (32 percent of all counties), with the primary feature being a single body (commission) performing both the legislative, such as enacting ordinances and establishing budgets, and executive, such as implementation of the budget; **county administrator** (56 percent of all counties), where the county is run by an appointed manager, who oversees the daily operations of the county; and **elected county executive** (12 percent of all counties),[39] where there is a distinct separation of legislative (elected council) and executive (elected county executive) powers. Generally speaking, rural counties embrace the pure commission form, while large urban counties prefer the elected county executive type. Of course, the pressing demands placed upon counties to not only shoulder the typical administrative duties but also to provide input and some oversight with policy issues (such as mentioned above) requires more counties to seriously consider adopting the county administrator/manager model. Harnett County, North Carolina, for example, a semi-typical rural southern county embraces the administrator/county type, where **Neil Emory** was the former county manager. [Scott Sauer is the new manager.] Harnett County is growing and expanding, with Campbell University as the educational corner and hospitalization and medical facilities among other services moving in to meet the growing retirement and elderly community. Counties just don't look or do what their predecessors looked like and did years before!

Neil Emory

Neil Emory, former county manager of Harnett County, North Carolina, was born in Weaverville, North Carolina, just outside of Asheville, Mr. Emory, who had always had an interest in civil service, attended and graduated from Appalachian State University with undergraduate and Master's degrees in political science and public administration, respectively. After spending some time as a county finance director, he landed his first position as county manager with Caswell County. He was only 24. After several county management positions he landed as the top administrator for Harnett County, North Carolina, in 1992. He believes in his role as public servant. As a public servant he sees his role twofold: first, it his objective to measure the priorities of the community, (including) the civic and moral standards of the community, and what the community wants to be and then help; and second, he believes that government must perform basic functions, such as fire, law enforcement, etc.

Source: Neil Emory, interview with Stephen M. King, June 2005.

Municipalities

Cities, towns, and townships make up the bulk of sub-state administrative and political entities, equaling over 25,000 units alone! They are the epicenter of communities. Even though municipalities and towns are workhorses of local governments, there is really no rhyme or reason, as they say, for planning local governments. Instead they come about, or are incorporated, via migration patterns, economic expansion, citizen demand, interest group pressure and a variety of other means. Really, no rational reason exists to explain the growth and development of municipalities—other than to note that the state permits them to be created. Therefore they are what we refer to as creatures of the state.

Municipalities, including cities and towns, are established via state charters, or a legal and uniform grant of power. City charters spell out what a city or town can or cannot do and to a great extent determines how a local government entity can be organized. Even though there are various types of charters, including special, classified, optional, and home rule we will concentrate only on the home rule charter, particularly as it differs from the more traditional limited grant of state power that is derived from **Dillon's Rule.**

Dillon's Rule was established as the result of an 1868 Iowa Supreme Court case opinion written by **Judge John Forrest Dillon** (1831–1914),[40] where he noted that municipalities have only those powers that 1) expressly granted by the state (fiscal power), 2) implied powers (taxing powers), and 3) indispensable powers (water and sewer). Any other power that is not expressly defined in the specific state constitution or granted to the municipal corporation by the state is therefore "expressly prohibited" to the municipal corporation.[41] Dillon's Rule is still the most popular, with 31 states operating under it, 10 states not operating under it, 8 having only certain municipalities under it, and 1 (Florida) that has conflicting authority.[42] By far, then, it is the most popular for states, but the most unpopular among local public administrative types, particularly county, city and town managers. The most popular charter preferred by municipal reformer types is the **home rule charter.** It permits city residents to choose whatever form of government they desire, but again only within the limits of state legislation. Even though home rule provisions are available in most states, communities have to file formal requests or petition with the state legislature to even access these powers. As you can imagine local public administrators see the infringing power of the state legislature as obtrusive to their ability to fulfill the public interest.

Forms of City Government. Municipal governments take on one of three basic forms: council-manager, mayor-council, or commission. The **commission** form developed in the early part of the twentieth century, specifically created in Galveston, Texas, in order to more efficiently deal with the aftermath of a tidal wave that killed thousands of people in 1900. The necessity for moving and setting up emergency manpower and materials was too much for the weak mayoral form of government. It was thought that putting an elected commission in charge of one particular city department, such as police, fire, or water, the level of efficiency would increase. But because there was no chief executive, either in the form of a mayor or manager, the in-fighting took away from meeting the public interest.

A second form of municipal government evolved that emphasized a professional **city manager.** The council-manager form of municipal government was first used in Staunton, Virginia, in 1908. It was born out of both the Industrial Revolution and the later reform movement, first as an attempt to incorporate French and German methods for incorporating greater tools of efficiency and economy, and second as a means to separate politics from administration. The typical city manager, who is a trained professional, and who today has a Masters of Public Administration (MPA) degree, is hired by the city council to implement the policies adopted by the city council. However, as one can guess this form of municipal governing is anything but immune from politics. City managers are required to refrain from engaging in partisan politics, but they are certainly part of the policy development process, largely because they are asked by the council members themselves, interested community parties, such as citizens and interest groups, to provide their professional opinion. When this happens politics is part of the administration process! Generally, the city manager form is found in medium sized cities, anywhere from 10,000 up to 225,000 or so.

Jim Twombly

Jim Twombly, city manager, arrived in Broken Arrow, Oklahoma, a thriving suburb of Tulsa, in July 2004. Previously he served as City Administrator for Pella, Iowa, corporate home of the world famous Pella Windows and the May Tulip Festival. Previously he served as Assistant to the City Manager of Oklahoma City and

Associate Planner. He holds a BA and MA in Urban Affairs from St. Louis University. He also has attended the Public Executive Institute at the LBJ School of Public Affairs at the University of Texas at Austin. He sees his role of City Manager as bringing together all different groups and integrating many variables in order to serve not only the city, but private and non-profit interests as well — in other words to serve all interests for the "betterment of the city." One of the major projects he is tasked with is the complete renewal and updating of the downtown, using his planning background to help develop a long range plan for not only the economic development, but also the beautification of the downtown businesses and infrastructure.

Source: Interview with Stephen M. King, July 2005.

Last is the **mayor-council** form of government. It is most popular in cities over 250,000 in population and in small towns, usually under 2,500. Depending upon the size of the city or town, the mayor is weak, where he is appointed or voted from among the elected council. He serves at the behest of the council and is largely a figure heard. However, in the large cities, such as San Francisco and Chicago, the mayor is a powerful political and administrative figure, setting the budget, appointing committee heads, and overseeing city regulatory bodies. Unlike its weak mayor counterpart it is a job filled with political tension, usually between the mayor and council, but also with the rank-n-file merit employees, many of whom are union-based.[43]

Special Districts

Special districts are specialized local units of government, such as airport and mass transit authorities, such as **New York's Metropolitan Transportation Authority**, and school districts, such as Virginia's Loudon County School District, that do just what their title implies: meets a single need, where other forms of local governments cannot or will not meet them. They are generally managed by special governing boards, usually appointed by governors, legislatures, or even local officials, but they can also be elected. They are created in a number of ways, including by special enabling legislation or referendum. Mass transit and education are not anywhere close to being the largest special district as a percentage of function; that status belongs to natural resources and fire protection.[44]

Special districts have exploded in growth over the last few decades. Currently, there are some 35,000 special districts spread throughout the United States, with Illinois having the largest number (over 3,000, largely because of Chicago) and Alaska having the fewest (less than 10). School districts, on the other hand, have plummeted in number from just over 108,000 in the early 1940s to just over 13,000 in 2002 — the reason, of course, is the large number of mergers and consolidations beginning in the 1950s. In fact by the early 1970s the consolidation of school districts bottomed out with the number of school districts nationwide remaining fairly constant thereafter.[45] Argument in favor of using special districts is that they coordinate and apply funding and attention to specialized areas that do no generally overlap municipal boundaries. A drawback, of course, is the political nature of special districts, such as school boards, and they also tend to lack accountability to the public.

State and local governments have an important influence on the public policy in the United States. For example:

- State constitutions create rights that do not exist at the national level, such rights to public education, to define marriage, to allow marijuana for medicinal use, to require a waiting period before an abortion, and so forth;

- State governments are becoming more dominated by the executive branch;

- Local governments are policy entrepreneurs, in seeking ways around restrictions on raising tax revenue by instead calling it an impact fee;

- Local governments place greater power on managers to act not only as chief administrative officers, but as economic development planners.[46]

What are examples of the nature and influence of state and local governments in the policy process? The following section includes a brief overview of four policy areas that confront the state and local government administrator: education, planning and zoning, e-government, and crisis management. This brief overview cannot begin to cover the details of each area and the many state and local responses. Rather we emphasize aspects of the diversity of issues that face state and local governments, the creativity in responding to these issues, and their policy impact in promoting the public interest.

Education Policy

Education policy is a state and local government priority. As early as the mid-seventeenth century (1640s), when the Massachusetts colonial legislature required towns and villages to provide some form of education for their children using public funds, education was understood to be under the purview of the state government and local community. All state constitutions specifically designate public education as a right for its citizens. For example, North Carolina's constitution states in Article IX that "Religion, morality, and knowledge being necessary to good government and the happiness of mankind, schools, libraries, and the means of education shall forever be encouraged." Like most states, North Carolina, in order to meet this goal requires a uniform system of schools (section 2), a State Board of Education (section 4) that will administer and supervise the free public school system (section 5), and supply much of the funding (section 2).[47] By the late eighteenth century the United States government recognized the importance of public education and through passage of the Northwest Ordinance of 1787 Congress provided for grants of federal land to states to build public schools. But it was not until the mid-nineteenth century that the first state (Connecticut in 1850) mandated free and public education. By the turn of the twentieth century most states had compulsory attendance laws. Today, most state constitutions require the provision of an adequate public education and the issue is not open for a policies approach to the public interest calculation of benefits/costs.

State governments and state boards of education, led by state superintendents of instruction or education, provide much of the funding and regulation of public education. Yet, local governments led by independent school districts oversee the daily operations of education policy. The local school districts, led by **district superintendents**, hire teachers, principals, and staffs, oversee curriculum, and perform basic operational and regulatory functions. As one can imagine the school districts are extremely diverse in curriculum formation. Many of these issues are viewed as too political and socially divisive, such as

teaching about creationism, sex education, and abortion. These and other curricular issues seem to provoke advocates and critics who argue over the proper role of public
schools in teaching controversial topics and criticisms.[48]

Box 4.6   Power of Public School Superintendents

School superintendents are similar to city and county managers: they are hired
by an elected body (school board) and serve at the discretion of the board. They
are hired because of their expertise in educational policy and administration,
and like local managers, school superintendents have substantial oversight and
input into budget formation, operational oversight, and personnel issues. However, because education is a political issue, school superintendents tend to be on
the political hot seat more so than city or county managers overall. Still, their roles
are similar: working between an elected board, citizen and local group interests,
and trying to meet personnel demands.

The job is certainly not easy; it is physically, mentally, and emotionally demanding, requiring 10- to 12-hour days, more during budget season, and living
in a community fish bowl, where the superintendent's life is not his or her own.
In addition, with the onslaught of imposed national government educational
performance measurement standards, the pressure on superintendents to lead their
districts to perform at pre-determined standards or lose accreditation and standing is multiplied. Some states, such as North Carolina, are reportedly failing to
reduce the high-school dropout rate and are not meeting increased testing expectations, even with increases in public funding. Education policy and administration is an extremely hot-topic issue, one that is only increased because of
the pressure to perform. Another hot-button, state and local government policy
issue is planning and zoning.

Source: For detail on the North Carolina see Karen McMahan, "Standard 'Solutions' Not Rem-
edying Ed Problems," *Carolina Journal* (November 2006): 8.

Planning and Zoning

Planning and zoning is almost entirely a local government policy issue area, usually involving a variety of individual interests, including interest groups, citizen councils, state
legislative boards, executive commissions, and others. Planning controversies arise and
are usually settled with compromise, balancing, and calculation of interests.[49] With the
conclusion of World War II, the suburbs exploded in growth, largely because of returning veterans taking out GI loans to subsidize new homes outside their old towns and
cities. Developers sold the new tracts of land with the vision of paradise, hoping that
people, whether they could really afford to or not, would move to the other side of the
tracks, and thus escape the drudgery of urban life. It worked. Suburbs sprang up like unwanted weeds, from California to New York, and with it came the need for greater local
planning than ever before.[50]

Early city planning guidelines, dating back to the late seventeenth century, dictated that
cities take the form of grids, with streets running in straight lines north-south and east-west.
Parks, buildings, homes and other features were carefully laid out to fit into the grid pattern.

This was especially true of most southern, Midwest and West new towns that sprang up through most of the nineteenth century. However, cities in the East, particularly Boston, Philadelphia, and New York, which were founded and grew long before grid patterns, had to absorb much of the new growth from immigration during the late 19th and early 20th centuries. The large cities became a hodge-podge of housing projects, streets that went nowhere, row after row of tenement housing that did not meet any type of code enforcement, and industrial parks and buildings that provided low income jobs, but little of anything else substantive to the community. There was no code enforcement largely because there were few, if any, codes to enforce—and very few willing to enforce the few codes that existed.

Later, **city planners**, most of whom had engineering backgrounds, began to create master plans, where they followed comprehensive planning guidelines. These included factors such as projected growth rates, transportation development, and even cultural patterns. The master plans are developed for cities to consider when they expand. City councils do not usually read or review them. Rather, the councils established committees, commissions, and neighborhood councils to exercise oversight of the planning process.[51] Today, planners are highly professionalized, with undergraduate and graduate degrees in planning and development. Many belong to professional associations, such as the **American Institute of Planners**. The development of planners as professionals spurred the replacement of citizen planning commissions with city and county planners who provided the guidelines and oversight in the planning process of a community.[52]

The Politics of Planning. Today, the professional world of planning is not without its politics. Application of the policies approach to the public interest of calculating benefits/costs or allowing the market to determine individual preferences may sometimes lead to unacceptable conclusions, such as the urban sprawl that chokes many urban areas. State **Smart Growth** programs, which first began in Maryland in the 1990s, have spread across the country. Smart growth is a concept that understands growth is inevitable, but believes it is the responsibility of public officials, at both the state and local level, to ensure that this growth is fair and equitable. Many cities and counties, such as Portland, Oregon, and Loudon County, Virginia, instituted smart growth strategies to control growth, strategies such as "urban growth boundaries, preservation of agricultural lands, historic areas, and sensitive environmental regions."[53] Sun Belt cities, such as Charlotte, North Carolina, incorporate mixed-use development with well-planned mass transit offerings to combat **suburban sprawl**.[54] However, free market advocates contend that smart growth does not prevent many of the problems it claims it does. In fact, because of increased government regulation at the state and local level, smart growth only increases the cost of available land and houses and does not relieve congestion.[55]

Zoning ordinances are passed by the city council or county commissioners at the discretion of the professional planners. Zoning ordinances divide the jurisdiction into specific districts, whether residential, commercial, industrial or other. **Zoning** is an attempt to separate residential growth pattern from commercial and industrial uses; the logic being, of course, that property owners don't want to buy or build a house in an area that might allow a tool and die shop to be built next door. Changes to the zoning ordinances come from citizens, developers, builders and others; anyone who wants to build or buy a piece of property and turn its existing zoning mandate into something else. This requires a variance, or exception, to the zoning ordinance. This is where the professional planners, the party requesting the zoning change, and the elected body can clash. Planners, who are professionals and who only play an advisory role and cannot dictate planning policy, know the laws and regulations. Councilmen and commissioners are elected by the people to meet the public interest. And the individuals requesting the zoning change do so for individual gain. What is best for the community, including town, city, or county?

What is in the public interest? Most recommendations of professional planners are accepted as truth, but there are times when a council or commission must listen to the demands of their local constituents and approve a zoning change that does not benefit the whole but only a narrow interest. For example, the Fields Farm issue described at the beginning of this chapter is a primary example. What is in the public interest: a second high school in western Loudon County, Virginia, in Purcellville? Or a second high school in western Loudon County, Virginia, somewhere else?

E-Government

What is e-government? And what does it mean for state and local governments, citizens, and the public interest? Electronic-government, or e-government, means that various government entities, departments, and agencies have their own portal and pages that allow citizens to search for information and in fewer instances to interact, such as pay bills or even participate in a live electronic town hall. Few state and local governments provide the latter service, but over 80 percent of all states and communities provide web portals to all citizens to search for information.

At the national level, the president sponsors e-government initiatives (*see*, www.whitehouse.gov/omb/egov), encouraging citizens and businesses to access information and use e-tools to participate in governance. For example, in 2002 President Bush launched the e-government initiative, introducing **E-Government Performance Management** and the Federal Enterprise Architecture, which is designed to simplify and unify federal agency work processes. Since then President Obama has directed that the Whitehouse website (www.whitehouse.gov) be updated, and reflect greater access to the ordinary citizen, such as search, blogging capacity, information links, and much more. Since then the citizen who has access to the Internet can gain entrance with three mouse clicks at www.usa.gov and access to all federal, state, and local government websites and multiple government agencies at all levels.[56]

At the state and local level, governments give e-access to citizens to download and fill out forms, such as hunting and fishing licenses, tax forms, vehicle registration, e-bank transfers, pay parking tickets, utility bills and other fees. Studies also show positive citizen participation and involvement in municipal government affairs by and through the use of websites.[57] The only real drawback to providing more services is the legal liability question and the cost of improving the state and local government's portal. More than states and the federal government, local governments are labeled the "nation's e-gov leaders, accounting for some 1,500 different applications, (and) the number of new digital government applications by local governments is projected to surpass by a factor of three the number of new applications introduced by the federal and state governments" over the next ten or so years.[58]

Are there any limits to the public interest value of open information for all in e-governance? Obviously, there must be some limits on information access to protect national security interests, to prevent libelous falsehoods about innocents from being spread, to protect certain digital property rights, and to prohibit morally unacceptable preferences such as obscenity and illegal pornography. And, we saw in chapter 3 on administrative law, certain private information on public employees and others must be protected, e.g., medical records. These limits on information openness seem based in principles of the public interest based in constitutions and laws, rather than a policies calculation approach to the public interest.

From the perspective of the Universalizability Principle, the administrator's decision habit of listening to all affected persons, what does e-government mean for the public interest? Certainly e-government promotes the public interest by allowing citizens, businesses, and government agencies to better communicate, organize, and disagree with one another. Others contend that e-government and open information technology has created institutional change in governance with different venues for working together, creating virtual communities, and promoting values of diversity, common-weal, and, of course, performance[59] Clearly state and local administration in the public interest will not remain the same with increasing e-government technology.[60]

Box 4.7   E-Government's Impact on State and Local Communities

E-government technology boom means that state and local governments are a 24/7 organization. State and local governments are always open thanks to the Worldwide Web. State and local government presence on the Web has exploded. Consider some facts:

- By 2003 over 70 percent of all Americans were online;
- Nearly 200 million people in the United States are online daily;
- Forty-two states allow citizens to pay some form of their taxes online;
- Nearly 100 percent (96 percent) of all U.S. counties and cities are online, with 84 percent of local government websites searchable by citizens for specific types of information.

Source: Nicholas Henry, *Public Administration and Public Affairs*, 9th ed. (Upper Saddle River, NJ: Pearson-Longman, 2004), 164; and David Osborne and Peter Hutchinson, *The Price of Government: Getting the Results We Need in an Age of Permanent Fiscal Crisis*, (New York: Basic Books, 2004), 202.

Crisis Management

Although not restricted to state and local governments, crisis management is rising in importance as a state and local issue, especially after the Oklahoma City bombing, 9/11, and Hurricane Katrina disasters. Average citizens now recognize the important role of first responders, such as fire, police, and other emergency officials, in a crisis. Crisis management illustrates an important limit of the policies approach to the public interest—the calculation of benefits/costs is humanly impossible in an emergency. Is there time to stop and calculate when horrible tragedy is all around? Of course not. In defense of the policies approach to the public interest, people ordinarily rely on common sense, past experiences, and a rule of thumb to guide our actions when a crisis demands immediate response. It is often important that we determine the best possible action, i.e., to save human lives versus saving houses in a flood. But there are times when the tragedy of death and human loss is so great that stopping to calculate benefits and costs is simply not the right thing to do, i.e., just send in all the first responders after the 9/11 terrorism. In times of crisis, the policies approach to the public interest may presuppose greater human capacity to predict and control the future than we can deliver, i.e., the failures of federal agencies to act after Hurricane Katrina. To illustrate state and local policies in crisis management we briefly overview three disasters, the Oklahoma City bombing, 9/11, and Hurricane Katrina, and focus on the role public servants played during and after each incident, with attention to public interest concerns.

Oklahoma City Bombing. At 9:02 a.m. on April 19, 1995, a rented Ryder truck, loaded with 5,000 pounds of ammonium nitrate fertilizer, parked in front of the Murrah Federal Building in downtown Oklahoma City (OKC) detonated. The blast killed 168 people, including 19 children.[61] **Timothy McVeigh** (1968–2001), the primary suspect, and accomplices Terry Nichols and Michael Fortier, were all tried and convicted. Nichols received 161 consecutive life sentences, Fortier received a 12-year prison sentence and a $200,000 fine, and McVeigh was executed by lethal injection June 2001.

Rescue efforts began immediately at the scene of the bombing. The Emergency Medical Services Authority (EMSA) responded to over 1,800 calls to 911. EMSA ambulances, city fire and police, and various civilians immediately responded. Within a half-hour of the bombing the State Emergency Operations Center (SEOC) was set up, with various members of the State of Oklahoma Departments of Public Safety, Human Services, and others. SEOC was assisted in its efforts by federal, state, local, and non-profit agencies, including the Civil Air Patrol and the American Red Cross. Over 12,000 people took part in the next several days and weeks of ongoing rescue operations.

The OKC bombing prompted immediate federal and state legal action, including the Antiterrorism and Effective Death Penalty Act of 1996 and the **Victim Allocution Clarification Act of 1997**, which provided victims of manmade acts of violence the right to observe trials and offer testimony. In addition, the federal government, in conjunction with state and local officials, barricaded all federal buildings in major American cities with what is known as Jersey barriers. Years after the attacks the temporary barriers have been replaced with permanent steel-enforced cement barriers. Deep street setbacks and armed guards are now typical at federal buildings. It cost hundreds of millions of dollars.

September 11, 2001. September 11 (or 9/11) was composed of a series of planned and coordinated attacks by terrorists affiliated with Osama bin Laden and Al-Qaeda.[62] On the morning of 9/11, four large commercial airliners were hijacked, 2 with American Airlines and 2 United Airlines aircraft. Each was fully fueled up. American Airlines Flight 111 crashed into the North Tower of the World Trade Center, while the second American flight 77 struck the Pentagon. The first United plane, Flight 175, crashed into the South Tower of the WTC, while the second United aircraft, Flight 93, crashed over southwest Pennsylvania, the result of passengers trying to gain control of the plane from the hijackers. Total casualties were nearly 3,000.

In New York City (N.Y.C.), rescue and recovery operations began immediately, with city fire, emergency services, police officers at the command centers established in the lobby of the World Trade Center, on Vesey Street, and in a firehouse in Greenwich Village. Poor communication devices caused outages to occur between commanders and firefighters, many of whom were working their way up the stairs of the two towers looking for victims when the towers collapsed. Hundreds of firefighters were killed. Police, EMTs and others quickly arrived at the devastating scene. N.Y.C. police, Port Authority of New York police, and New Jersey police were killed while rescuing people from inside the towers when they collapsed. New York City **Office of Emergency Management (OEM)** was responsible for coordination of the City response. OEM's headquarters had to be moved twice, finally to a pier on the Hudson River. It was here that then-Mayor Rudolph Giuliani provided press conferences and coordinated over 90 different city, state, and federal rescue and recovery agencies working for months after the disaster.[63]

The after effects of 9/11 continue. The **National Commission on Terrorist Attacks** upon the United States (a.k.a. the 9/11 Commission) published its findings.[64] Chaired by former New Jersey governor Thomas Kean, the Commission prepared a complete account of the attacks, both before, during, and after with stern rebukes. The findings also commended many civil servants, especially the local N.Y.C. police and New Jersey fire, po-

lice, and EMS workers, who placed their lives on the line to assist in the rescue and recovery operation. The Inspector General of the Central Intelligence Agency (CIA) completed an internal review of the CIA's involvement in investigating terrorism and specifically
Al Qaeda. Even the United States Department of Commerce's **National Institute of Standards and Technology (NIST)** conducted a thorough investigation of the collapse of the
two towers. This led to improved coding and building standards for future commercial
construction of buildings like the two towers.

From the events of 9/11 and follow-up reports came the term "first responders." It was
local and state emergency crews who were the first to respond to 9/11 tragedies, continued on to resolve the problems, and required new ways of funding and support to meet
these and future emergencies.

Hurricane Katrina was the costliest ($81.2 billion) and one of the deadliest (1,836 lives
lost) natural disasters in United States history. On August 29, 2005, Hurricane Katrina
slammed into New Orleans, Louisiana, with Category 5 sustained winds and flooding, breach-
ing levees around the city. The low lying city was almost completely engulfed in flood
water. The death toll in Louisiana alone was nearly 1,600, with the largest percentage in
New Orleans. On August 28, New Orleans mayor **Ray Nagin** ordered mandatory evacu-
ation. Many of New Orleans' residents who had no means of transportation out of the
city were encouraged to make their way to various refuges of last resort, such as the Su-
perdome. There was a large-scale breakdown of public order, with widespread looting, residents were stranded on rooftops, bodies floating down flooded streets, and entire parishes
destroyed. The aftermath of responses by national, state, and local governments to the Hurricane Katrina disaster were sorely criticized. Did our system of federalism breakdown?
Did political and administrative leadership fail?

Many first responders were sent in to New Orleans by national, state, and local government organizations, as well as non-governmental agencies. But it seems their efforts
were hampered by a number of factors: poor communication and coordination between
and among government organizations, faulty planning process, the very slow response of
the national government, among other problems.[65] Scholars found that administrative
breakdowns were rampant in the response to Katrina: little mobilization of resources,
personnel problems galore, and an unclear mission and lack of focus plagued national
and local agencies.[66] According to recommendations of the **National Response Plan**, disaster planning and response is first and foremost the responsibility of local government.
But when those resources quickly ran out in the face of such a large natural catastrophe,
responsibility went directly to state and national governments, requiring additional assistance.[67]
Yet, at the national level, the **Federal Emergency Management Agency (FEMA)** seemed
bogged down with problem after problem, from logistics to implementation of plans for
getting trucks and supplies to stranded residents. As a result of the poor communication
and coordination of resources at FEMA, the Department of Homeland Security (DHS)
under the leadership of **Michael Chertoff** took over all federal, state, and local operations.[68]

While national, Louisiana, and New Orleans governments seemed to falter, incredible rescue efforts came in from other cities around the country, non-profit and faith-
based organizations, and the private sector. Within days of Hurricane Katrina, local
governments around the country sent police, fire, and other public safety officers to provide assistance, aiding New Orleans police and fire personnel, many of whom were working in 24-hour shifts. The charitable efforts of these outsider non-governmental
organizations provided much of the temporary shelter, clothing, food, and other ne-
cessities for New Orleans evacuees. Nonprofits and faith-based organizations quickly
organized and came to the rescue, including the American Red Cross, Salvation Army,

Service International, and the Southern Baptist Association, raising over $4 billion in contributions to Katrina victims. Private businesses and corporations provided over $400 million in relief aid. Most important, however, is what can be learned from the mistakes in order to prevent the same problems from occurring once again.[69]

Conclusion

Federalism, states, and communities present a common challenge to public administration of balancing, compromising, and managing public policies with people who are local to us, with needs we can see, who are sometimes in-our-face. State and local citizens are people on the streets where we live, not like the seemingly invisible people we do not know who benefit from our tax dollars to the national government. As a result, public administration within federalism, states, and communities requires an additional level of recognition, respect, and accounting to these nearby people. A policies approach to the public interest may describe the reality of these highly localized and radically democratic calculations of the needs, preferences, and resources of all who are involved or affected by the decisions of public administrators.

The constitutional structure of federalism has developed over the decades according to the customs of the people and what worked for administration in the public interest. For example, while the Constitution was ambiguous in outlining a dual federalism with neatly divided national and state power, it has come to authorize the marble cake federalism of today, with a sharing of power and empowerment of states and communities through the reality of managerial decentralization.

In delivery of services under their police powers, states and communities provide much of our safety, welfare, and responsive service to crime, education, health. States and communities must respond to citizen demand for action, interest group complaints, powerful business and corporate lobbies demanding tax credits for possible incoming economic development projects, and every unfilled pothole! From governors to mayors, legislatures to city councils, state bureaucrats to city managers, this is where the buck stops in administration of the public interest. In an age of devolution, transformation, reinvention, and performance management, state and local governments try to change and adapt organizationally to meet the growing need for a wide variety of services.

Two centuries of state and local government reform and reorganization have focused on efficiency, effectiveness, and responsiveness to the public interest. For example, nineteenth century municipal reformers sought to end the incompetence and corruption of the spoils system, restore the moral value of public service, and re-instill the public trust. Citizens still wanted public services and goods, yes, but they also demanded that government be responsive and listen to an additional level. Due to their proximity to the public, state and local governments—especially local governments—are much better at this than is the national government.

Education, planning and zoning, e-government, and crisis management are but four policy issue areas of the many that face state and local public administrators. What these four policy areas demonstrate is a commitment by state and local administrators to deliver the public interest. State and local public servants demonstrate an unending resiliency and Job-like patience when dealing with thorny social policy issues.

These many examples of public administration within federalism, states, and communities throughout this chapter give meaning to the policies approach to the public interest and the attendant utilitarian theory of ethics. Democratic calculations of the needs, desires, and resources of all who are affected seem to characterize state and local public administration. As in utilitarian ethical theory, state and local public administrators determine desirable and undesirable policies by calculation of benefits-costs and other measures of human needs, desires, or resources. Sometimes, however, entitlements, unfunded mandates, and deregulation of states by national policy-makers may impose pre-existing duties upon states and local administrators. But the states and communities seem to respond with skepticism of the long-term value of such principles imposed upon them and ultimately seek more democratically calculated policies, such as referendums, initiatives, and the ballot box.

With aging and retiring Baby Boomers, the current and future generations will be needed to fill many of the vacancies that occur at the state and local levels. For example, the average tenure of a city manager is approximately five years. The average age of a city manager is 56. What does this tell us? Soon there will be a vacuum of empty city manager positions to fill. But with the majority of young people who graduate college moving to the private and non-profit sectors, who will fill these types of positions? What OKC, 9/11, and Katrina taught us among other things, is that committed and hard-working young people are required to continue the pursuit of the public interest—if our democratic republic is to continue.

Action Steps

1. How does the policies approach of calculating the public interest by majority vote relate to the development of a majority and centralization of government power? Articulate your analysis of this tendency to centralize with a reading of the U.S. Supreme Court case of *McCulloch v. Maryland*, 17 U.S. 315 (1819) and the U.S. Bank in Baltimore. How might you check and balance this tendency to centralize government power (hint: by use of the principles approach to the public interest)?

2. Read the "nitty-gritty" about local economic protectionism in the New York trash and recycling industry in the U.S. Supreme Court case of *C&A Carbone v. Town of Clarkstown*, 511 U.S. 387 (1994). The town of Clarkstown, New York, forbade the use of any out-of-state trash services and required use of one particular (local) private trash company at well above the market rates. How may the policies approach to the public interest be faulted for prompting and promoting such local economic protectionism? How may this abuse of power and the public interest be reformed?

3. Divide the into two large groups for a large-scale debate over federalism and the historic "North" and "South" perspectives decline of states' rights (as in the Civil War). Each side must pick a representative President for public debate and a General to develop strategies and oversee responsive actions by group members. How do the "North" and "South" perspectives on federalism and the decline of states' rights reflect differing conceptions of the public interest? What does this say about the meanings of the current debates over the new federalism and the meaning of confederate federalism? [dressing in grey and blue colors and re-enacting Civil War battles is completely optional!]

4. Visit 20 state and local government websites. What is similar? Different? Use the various options available. How easy or difficult was it? Put yourself in the position of a citizen of that state, city, county, or special district. Ask yourself whether or not the e-government opportunities help you be a better citizen, more aware, informed, and active.

5. Interview several state and local public administrators regarding their recent reorganization, reinvention, or otherwise reform-based efforts. What do they think? Does it make their job easier? Does it even affect how they do their job? Is it rhetoric or results?

6. Break up into groups of manageable numbers (no more than five, preferably three). Have your instructor determine your jurisdictional authority, roles, responsibilities, and authority for acting. He/she will choose a crisis (for the entire class), such as the OKC bombing, 9/11, or Katrina and a specific problem to address. Establish various guidelines for action; require the students to do background information (outside class) on their various roles; and then return to either role play (simulation or skit) or simply address the problem in groups. At the end of the exercise address the following questions:

    a. Was the problem solved? Why or why not?

    b. What problems or obstacles existed? How were they overcome?

    c. What additional resources were needed to complete your various assignments?

Exam Review Preparation

1. Define and describe the impact of e-government upon the pursuit of the public interest.

2. Examine the role and state and local governments and government personnel during times of crisis, such as the OKC bombing, 9/11, and Katrina. How did they respond? How could they have responded better? What improvements have been made?

3. Define the following: police powers, Dillon's Rule, city charter, planning and zoning ordinances, first responders, and performance management.

4. Discuss the impact that state and local reform efforts had upon the development of state and local governments.

5. What are the differences between municipalities, counties, and special districts?

6. Contrast home rule with Dillon's Rule. Give examples.

7. Describe the roles that Ray Nagin, mayor of New Orleans, and Michael Chertoff, Director of Homeland Security, played in the Katrina disaster.

8. Identify and discuss the three types of local government governing frameworks.

9. Discuss the impact that e-government is having on the delivery of services at the state and local levels.

10. What is meant by "managerial decentralization?"

Key Concepts

Antiterrorism and Effective Death Penalty Act
Ash Institute for Democratic Governance and Innovation
"Boss" Tweed and Tom Pendergast
Brownlow Committee
Chief Justice John Marshall
Chief Justice Salmon P. Chase

Citizen planning commissions
City manager form of government
Commission form, county administrator form, and elected county executive
Devolution
Dillon's Rule
Economic development
E-government
Federalism
FEMA
Home rule charter
Judge John Dillon
Justice Louis Brandeis
Katrina
Loose verse strict construction
Michael Chertoff
Municipal reform
National League of Cities
New York City Metropolitan Transit Authority
Police powers
Ray Nagin
Smart Growth programs
Special districts
State executive reorganizations
Suburban sprawl
Timothy McVeigh
Title I of the Elementary and Secondary Education Act
Unfunded mandates
Unitary state
Victim Allocation Clarification Act

Recommended Readings

Banfield, Edward C. *Big City Politics: A Comparative Guide to the Political Systems of Atlanta, Boston, Detroit, El Paso, Los Angeles, Miami, Philadelphia, St. Louis, and Seattle.* New York: Random House, 1965.

_____. *Political Influence: A New Theory of Urban Politics.* New York: MacMillan, 1961.

_____. *The Un-heavenly City: The Nature and Future of Our Urban Crisis.* Boston: Little, Brown and Company, 1968.

Berman, David R. *Local Government and the States: Autonomy, Politics, and Policy.* Armonk, NY: ME Sharpe, 2003.

Feeley, Malcolm M. and Edward Rubin. *Federalism: Political Identity and Tragic Compromise.* Ann Arbor: University of Michigan Press, 2008.

Grodzins, Morton. *American System: A New View of Government in the United. States* Edited by Daniel J. Elazar. New Brunswick, NJ: Transaction Publishers, 1984.

ICMA. *The Effective Local Government Manager.* 3d ed. Washington, DC: International City/County Management Association, 2004.

Kettl, Donald F. *System Under Stress: Homeland Security and American Politics.* Washington, DC: CQ Press, 2004.

Meyerson, Martin, and Edward C. Banfield. *Politics, Planning, and the Public Interest.* New York: The Free Press, 1955.

Osborne, David, and Peter Hutchinson. *The Price of Government: Getting the Results We Need in an Age of Permanent Fiscal Crisis.* New York: Basic Books, 2004.

Sanford, Terry Sanford. *Storm over the States.* New York: McGraw-Hill, 1967.

Stillman, Richard J., II. *Creating the American State: The Moral Reformers and the Modern Administrative World They Made.* Tuscaloosa, AL: University of Alabama Press, 1998.

Watson, Douglas J. and Wendy L. Hassett, editors. *Local Government Management: Current Issues and Best Practices.* Armonk, NY: M.E. Sharpe, 2003.

Related Web Sites

American Planning Association
http://www.planning.org/

Ash Institute for Democratic Governance and Innovation
http://ashinsttest.org.ezdeal.no/

Center for Local and State Solutions
www.napawash.org/pc_local_state

Department of Homeland Security
http://www.dhs.gov/index.shtm

Judge John Dillon—U.S. Eighth Circuit Court
http://www.ca8.uscourts.gov/library/coa8_judicial-bibliography.html

National Association of Schools of Public Affairs and Administration (NASPAA)
http://www.naspaa.org/

New York Port Authority
http://www.panynj.gov/

Publius: The Journal of Federalism
http://ww2.lafayette.edu/~publius/

The Federalism Project: The American Enterprise Institute
http://www.federalismproject.org/

The Urban Institute—New Federalism
http://www.urban.org/center/anf/index.cfm

Part II

Applications of Administration in the Public Interest

PART TWO is an examination of the core functions of public administration and the role of the public interest within each, or the **applications** of administration in the public interest. The core functions include getting organized, in theory and in-fact, and pursuit of the public interest through closed and open systems, in public and in private organizations. The core function of public management focuses on the entrepreneurial approaches and strategies of the New Public Service, and pursuit of the public interest through strategic planning and various leadership styles. Public personnel management attends to historical and current recruitment and human resources development in the public workplace, and pursuit of the public interest in issues such as whistle-blowing and loyalty, unions/collective bargaining, and affirmative action. Public budgeting and finance focuses on a pursuit of the public interest by the utilitarian calculations of economic benefit/costs analyses in these historical and current tax-finance and budgetary politics at the local, state, and federal levels. Our examination of public policy processes and analysis include a variety of public interest approaches in the study of policy-makers, policy-influencers, and the action procedures and investigative and evaluative methods of assessing public policies. And we include the core function of nonprofits and faith-based organizations, examining the history, public interest applications, and ascendance of the voluntary sector.

Chapter 5

Organization Theory and the Public Interest

"As public organizations are being asked to do more with fewer resources, greater attention has been focused on better understanding of internal dynamics, leadership, and behavior within organizations."

George J. Gordon and Michael E. Milakovich,
Public Administration in America

Chapter Objectives

Upon completion of this chapter the student will be able to:

1. Understand and recognize the differences between open and closed organizational systems;

2. Distinguish the key terms, concepts, ideas, academics, and practitioners of the open and closed organizational systems;

3. Recognize the importance of studying organizational systems and how they are understood and applied in the public sector;

4. Clarify the differences and similarities between public and private sector organizational systems;

5. Clarify the importance of organization theory in pursuit of the public interest.

Introduction

Organizations are the core of society. Whether public or private, organizations strive to meet the needs of individuals, groups, businesses, governments, communities, and fulfill various goals from efficiency to equity. To meet these needs, organizations employ their finances, time, and especially people in positions of leadership, skills, and other activities. The real challenge today is for traditional Weberian-style organizations with a machine-model emphasizing uniformity and control, to confront new forms of organization that are flatter, more task-driven, technology-emphasizing, and people-friendly in seeking to develop creative energy and potential in all. Whether public, private or non-profit, the twenty-first century organization will seek to better meet the needs and fulfill the demands of not only its workers, but also the citizen and clientele it serves. As many have paraphrased, "This is not your mother's organization!"

This chapter reviews the history, theory and evolution of organizations in the public interest. We examine the various and many major authors, ideas, and philosophies as they have had an impact on the development of organization theory, focusing primarily upon the public organization as a means for addressing the need of fulfilling the public interest. Those who study organizations categorize organizations in a variety of ways—each with assumptions about the public interest—such as closed versus open models, classical models and ideology, managing the dynamics of organizations, and managerial, political and legal approaches to studying organizations. Scholars of administration generally agree that organizations evolve, but do not agree, and in many cases do not even address the issue, of what organizations evolve into, or, what their evolutionary pattern evokes, especially in terms of administrative and policy outcome. We contend that the outcome must benefit the public interest.

The chapter is divided into three sections, largely modeled after the open and closed systems framework. The first section explores the historical development of closed organizations, including discussion of classical theories and their theorists, which delegate responsibility to the public interest to other key decision-makers, such as politicians. The second section provides an overview of open systems, including the human relations, informal group, decision-making, neo-classical, and systems approaches in organization theory. Open systems maintain some level of responsibility to the public interest for all participants. The third section concludes with discussion on the differences between private and public organizations in fulfilling the public interest.

History of Organizations and Organization Theory

Just as we saw there were many definitions and operation for public administration so, too, are there many definitions for organization theory. Organizations are usually defined according to specific contexts and perspectives. Some definitions, for example, revolve around the specialization of task and integration of specialists in order to achieve desired ends,[1] while others define organizations as a system of coordinating informal groups with formal ones in order to accomplish a goal.[2] Most concur that any formal organization, and in many cases informal ones as well, are designed to accomplish a goal, and to do it in a structured way.[3] We agree. For our purposes a **formal organization** is defined as a "group of people coming together for a common purpose, dividing up responsibilities according to tasks, skills, and knowledge, and coordinating and leading these efforts in order to reach the desired goal."[4] Granted, this is a broad definition, and really applies to any formal organizations, such as Microsoft, the Department of Defense, or the Salvation Army, but even in the emergence of informal organizations, there are people, they generally have some consensus on why they are informally organized, and they have common goals and objectives. So, even though **informal organizations**, such as tens of thousands of small nonprofits and faith-based or para-church organizations, are not as large and formalized in terms of structure, rules, lines of communication and the like, they still represent the core of what organizations are all about: bringing people together to achieve a common goal.[5]

Keep in mind there is no single theory of organizations. Instead, there are many theories, each compelling, but each falling short of explaining the totality of organizational structure, behavior, and development. No one theory is able to explain everything about organizations, how they evolve, how people operate within them, what is their purpose, and many other aspects. As one scholar notes organization theory is a "loosely knit community of many approaches to organizational analysis."[6] Even though the scientific study of modern organization theory is a fairly recent phenomenon, the study and practice of organizations is thousands of years old.[7]

Moses and the Bible

Dating back to biblical times the use of tribes, nomads, the formation of Egyptian courts, and Babylonian administrative hierarchies all ascribe to the use and development of organizations to advance common goals—administration in the public interest. For example, during the exodus from Egypt, which is recorded in chapter 18 of *Exodus*, Moses' father-in-law, **Jethro the Midianite**, chastises Moses, God's appointed leader, administrator, and judge, for trying to adjudicate all the cases brought before him. Instead, Jethro wisely advises Moses to establish a hierarchical arrangement of authority—much like nineteenth century's German sociologist Max Weber's ideal type of organization, called a **bureaucracy**—delegating the smaller and less important cases to trusted persons, while Moses heard only the more significant ones. Other biblical accounts of organizational structure and process, which include the descriptions of kings' administrative courts, such as Kings David and Solomon, Nehemiah and the re-building of the temple, and others, reflect the human need to create, build, and organize.

Ancients and Organizations

Sun Tzu's (ca sixth century BCE) *The Art of War* (date unknown) highlighted the need for hierarchy, communication, and planning in successful warfare. Winning a war is not simple; it is costly, administratively nightmarish, and organizationally challenging. Tzu knew that amassing and coordinating large number of troops, munitions, and material was just the start. Winning the campaign took planning and strategy by top officials, who could confidently pass down orders and expect them to be followed. This was achieved through a formal organization.

Sun Tzu

Sun Tzu was a Chinese general who lived in the state of Wu around the sixth century BCE, and one of the earliest realists in international relations theory. His popular book *The Art of War* was a piece on military strategy, suggesting that winning war is not simple, but can be done with planning, strategy, and coordination of effort and resources. Actually, some believe that Tzu did not even exist, and that the book was written by Chinese philosophers somewhere around the fourth century BCE. Nothing is confirmed and so the legend and his ideas live on.

The Greeks also emphasized organizational techniques to win their battles with enemies. Philip of Macedon and his son, **Alexander the Great** (356–323 BCE), used a number of modern organizational techniques, such as line and staff, organization by function (infantry versus cavalry), mobility, intelligence, and support services to achieve a fighting machine unequaled in the known world. In addition to their legions of warfare, which were developed around strict rules, line and staff, delegation of authority, hierarchy, and communication, the Romans built roadways, cities, and aqueducts. All of these achievements were impossible without the formal use of organization.

Aristotle (384–322 BCE), in his *The Politics*, developed a political philosophy that was based on constitutionalism and the rule of law. His philosophy was reflective of organizational principles, such as the specific nature of the chief executive's powers, was not the same for all states or organizations but ultimately reflected the specific environment. Aristotle relied on the basic belief that people are social creatures and are therefore motivated to form an organization (or state) in order to protect themselves, family, and property. The state (organization) is composed of rules (laws), communication, purpose, and objectives and goals. Each variable is representative of the makeup of modern organizations.

Niccolo Machiavelli's *The Prince* reflected the role and posture of the shrewd, practical manager of public goods and services. Machiavelli's description and advocacy of questionable tactics, such as the destruction of enemies when they serve no further purpose, were tempered by practical considerations that any wise administrator in an organization should follow. These included merit as a way of moving up in the ranks of the organization, favoring unity of command, and learning when and how to unseat your foes through cunning (political) craftiness. Although Machiavelli has never been accused of abiding by fundamental principles of moral conduct, he did advocate how the Prince could be effective within limits of political and organizational environments in achieving the public good.

The Americanization of European Designs

The 19th and 20th centuries brought along the integration and organization of the industrial might of American entrepreneurs and their capital, the adoption of European means of scientific management principles, the growth of cities and urban environments and the influx of many immigrant workers, all producing an outflow of products and services never before seen. With this output was the need for sound principles of authority, management, communication, hierarchy, and other basics of organization. As one author noted, organizations changed from "… 'communal' forms based on the bonds of kinship and personal ties … to 'associative' forms based on contractual arrangements among individuals."[8] The modern organization was born.

Late nineteenth century European means of management and personnel in industry contributed to the need for the modern organization. Two phases of industrialism pressed for new forms of organization; the first beginning in the early 1800s, and marked by the emergence of factories, such as the British textile industry; and the second, which began in the mid-1800s, in which the factory system diversified into clothing, food, engineering, iron, and other products. The complexity and precision of industrial organizations made clear the need for new structures and organizations.[9] In order to produce the volume of products and services demanded by the world, the need for rational — meaning efficient, economical, and effective — organizational design grew exponentially. It was during the second major phase that the classical organizational theorists emerged, advocating a bureaucratic structure and process that would maximize output while at the same time minimizing costs. The demand for economic and industrial growth punctuated the private sector, while at the same time resonating with the need for government to regulate and oversee this tremendous increase. Karl Marx and Max Weber, for instance, both from the German school of rational efficiency and technical expertise, believed that bureaucratic structures would contribute to the economic, political, and social development, including new classes of workers, called managers, whose primary responsibilities was directing and coordinating resources within the newly minted modern organization for the purpose of achieving predetermined goals.

Box 5.1 What Did Karl Marx Say?

"The worker becomes all the poorer the more wealth he possesses, the more his production increases in power and range. The worker becomes an ever cheaper commodity the more commodities he creates. With the increasing value of the world of things proceeds in direct proportion to the devaluation of the world of men. Labor possesses not only commodities; it produces itself and the worker as a commodity—and does so in the proportion in which it produces commodities generally."

Marx, *Economic and Philosophic Manuscripts* (1844)

Mary Jo Hatch, an American organization historian at the University of Virginia, has compared the industrialism which laid the foundation for producing the classical theories and theorists of organization, with the post-industrialism which superseded the industrial state in such a way so as to reinvent, even radically transform the means, ends, and purposes of not only doing work but in living and interacting in a technology-infused age. For Hatch, the industrial phase marked by nation states regulating economies, the **routinization** of method, bureaucratic structure, standardization and centralized control and functionalization, stood in contrast with the post-industrialism marked by global competition, **decentralization** of authority, emphasis on speed, timing, and information output, flatter organizational structures, loose boundaries between organizations and functions, diversity and innovation in meeting customer needs, and emphasis on task-based teamwork and organizational learning.[10] Post-industrial societies required new ways of organizing, particularly focused on people and means rather than upon structure and function. This laid the groundwork for developing new contemporary theories of organization, such as neoclassical, human relations, and open systems approaches.

The Americanization of European designs strongly suggests that the seminal works of organization theory, whether from a sociological or management perspective, were adopted to emphasize American industrial might, as well as infuse them into what became the administrative and welfare states. The influence of modern American public administration, from the late nineteenth century, particularly with emphasis on the scientific management approach, through the pre-World War II time period, and the strength of FDR's executive branch co-optation of administrative authority—a la the Brownlow Report—strongly suggests that American influence was directed toward increasing the role and function of government at all levels to address the pressing economic, political, and social needs of society. The following sections examine the various ideas and personalities that shape organization theory and behavior, particularly as they relate to public administration and pursuit of the public interest.

Closed System: The Classical Theories

The academic study of organization is in no way the exclusive province of business management or political science. As a matter of fact, other more diverse disciplines, such as anthropology, sociology, psychology, social psychology, and economics provided much of the information, questions, and knowledge regarding organizations and organizational behavior that we draw upon today.[11] It is safe to assume, we argue, that rigorous and analytical multidisciplinary investigations of organizations, particularly among industrial psychologists and sociologists, prompting theoretical discussions and empirical hypotheses, did not emerge in earnest before the 1940s.[12] Further, the varieties of **organization theory** studies focus largely around what several researchers claim is: (1) subject matter, such as individuals, structure, and processes; (2) type of theory, such as systems, public choice, group politics, and personality; and (3) that the purpose of organization theory is predictive, using empirical research methods and techniques, in order to determine what is knowable and what is not about organizations.[13] Let's begin our investigation of the various theories of organizations with the classical period.

The Classical School

The **classical school** of organization was the first to develop. The classical school derives its name from the pioneer scholars and practitioners who established working theories and models depicting organizations and their behavior. Classical theorists are as diverse as Adam Smith and his economic theories of the firm to sociologist Emile Durkheim and his theory of shifting societies to **Max Weber** (1864–1920) and the definition of bureaucracy. Classical theorists do not emphasize the responsibility of each organizational participant to the public interest; the public interest is of concern only to the elites who set the mandates of the organization. Classical theorists instead emphasize the structural aspects of the organizations, finding that formal organizations are to be almost machine-like, placing preeminence on attaining efficiency, economy, and effectiveness. They contend that there is one best way of doing work in order to achieve the highest rates of productivity, and therefore it is imperative to order the organization's characteristics such as hierarchy, chain of command, communication, authority, and, ultimately, organizational behavior accordingly. Further, a major goal of classical organization theory is to reduce performance variation of both human and capital elements of production. Often the metaphor of a machine is chosen given that the goal to calibrate work process and outcomes is within an acceptable error range.

Early Economic Theories of Organizations. In 1776, Scottish economist **Adam Smith** (1723–1790)[14] theorized that organization of time and personnel was necessary to mass produce manufactured goods, such as the pin factory he discusses in *The Wealth of Nations*. According to Adams it is crucial to organize men and material, using specialization of function as the primary measure, to produce the goods necessary to sell and distribute both home and abroad, but to do it in such a way that the individual contributions of one worker is not as important as the multiplied efforts of many workers in the organization. Each worker is trained to do a specialized task, and when those tasks are combined and monitored for efficiency and economy they produce a sum that is greater than its parts. This thinking led to the development and implementation of the factory system, which ultimately contributed to evolution of the Industrial Era toward the end of the nineteenth century.

By the mid- to late-1840s a brilliant German philosopher and economist named **Karl Marx** (1818–1883) developed his famous theory of capital.[15] Marx believed that labor, or what he termed collective effort, was the social foundation for all societies worldwide. Individual labor was useless unless it is understood within the larger physical environment of organization, or the function of collective labor. Collective labor, when organized under the political and economic oversight of the state, will produce a more rational and humane treatment of workers than afforded by the capitalists (bourgeoisie), whose sole intention is to produce profit based off the forced labor of the worker. Capitalists demand more profit and thus impose more controls upon the worker, forcing workers to work more efficiently, and thus increasing the tension between the two groups. Workers organize collectively, such as in unions, to ward off the pressures of capitalists and managers. This antagonistic relationship precipitates the need for intervention from government, a civil form of organization, with authority and power to control the actions of each.

Adam Smith

Adam Smith was born in Kirkcaldy, Fife, Scotland. In 1751 he was appointed professor of logic at Glasgow University and then transferred to the chair of moral philosophy. He moved to London in 1776 where he published his now famous *The Wealth of Nations*, or as the full citation reads: *An Inquiry into the Nature and Causes of the Wealth of Nations*. His work examined in some detail the various consequences of pursuing economic freedom within a democratic society, engaging in topics such as the role of self-interest, division of labor, functions of the market, and other such ideas. It was Smith's work that effectively laid the intellectual foundation for future theorists and theories on free market.

Source: See Robin Chew, "Adam Smith: Economist and Philosopher," Lucidcafe, www.lucid cafe.com/library/96jun/smith.html (accessed October 2007).

Sociology and Bureaucratic Theory. Even though **Emile Durkheim** (1858–1917), the French sociologist, expanded Adam Smith's notions of the manufacturing organization to one of industrialization by the late nineteenth century, arguing that all aspects of human society work together like parts of a machine, something he referred to as sociological functionalism, and thus contributing greatly to the sociological literature and knowledge of organizations; it was the work of Max Weber, an eminent German sociologist, whose contribution to organizational theory was the formal definition and explanation of the bureaucratic structure.[16] While society and industry expanded during the latter part of the nineteenth century, creating jobs, building cities and towns, and increasing the size and authority of government; there was no formal description and explanation of this organizational phenomenon known as bureaucracy. Weber filled this void by constructing what he termed the "ideal type" of organization, called the bureaucracy. It was not labeled ideal because it was perfect; it was labeled ideal because it was approximation of what Weber believed society and individual organizations could evolve into if there were no outside forces restricting its evolution.

Weber's **theory of bureaucracy** imposed rational constraints upon the social environment, or organization, as evidenced in the prescription of several key values:

- *Division of labor*, where work is divided according to purpose and type, and there are clear lines of jurisdiction or authority;
- *Specialization of function*, where there is no overlap or duplication of functions, providing for greater efficiency of productivity;

- *Hierarchy* is defined as a vertical chain of command, with the orders going down and the responses coming up;
- *Framework* of rules and procedures is designed to enhance greater predictability and stability of routine in the organization;
- *Impersonal relationships*, where no person is viewed more important than any other person, thus ensuring that all are provided the same attention;
- *Professionalization* of workers is promoted, where a person's knowledge, skills, and abilities are elevated over name recognition, societal status, and economic background; and
- *Record-keeping system* provides that actions are current and consistent with previous actions.

Each element or value — and the combination thereof — was designed to promote greater efficiency, control, and growth of the bureaucracy. Conformity to standards was expected; deviance from the standards was not tolerated, because it was expected that any movement away from the elements described above would detract from attaining the goals of bureaucracy. This is what many scholars refer to as a closed system of organization.[17]

A great deal of criticism has been heaped upon Weber and his ideal construct; primary among them is that real world organizations simply do not look like nor run like what Weber said they should look and run like! The criticisms are numerous and include among others that rules are arbitrary, informal organizations are numerous and sometimes even subverts the formal structural apparatus, individuals are often confused about their roles, primarily because they play numerous roles instead of one, and that individuals are motivated for reasons other than rational ones, such as money and promotions, including that they just really like doing their job.[18] We will examine some of these criticisms later; suffice it to say that Weber's contribution to organization theory became the benchmark for future classical theorists.

Engineers, Businessmen and Scientific Management. A second major theme of the classical school of organizational theory is scientific management. It is a rather broad ranging stratum of ideas, but its main thesis is directed toward improving organizational efficiency and economy by analyzing tasks and work flow. The key values of scientific management are 1) maximizing efficiency; 2) striving for rationality in work procedures; 3) maintaining high productivity levels; and 4) achieving a profit.[19] The primary spokesperson for the movement was **Frederick Winslow Taylor** (1856–1915).[20] Taylor and others, like **Frank** (1868–1924) and **Lillian Gilbreth** (1878–1972),[21] emphasized that machine-like efficiency was necessary in order for the organization to achieve full production. This purpose inspired Taylor to advance the idea of **time and motion studies**, a concept that required factory and industry workers to rework their physical motions for carrying out a specific task, such as shoveling coal, hauling pig-iron, or even laying bricks. The belief was that by altering or changing the physical movement necessary to complete a particular task it would be possible to more efficiently and thus effectively and economically accomplished the task in less time. Ultimately, Taylor and the Gilbreths celebrated the industrial zenith of the day by arguing that humans were dignified by joining the machines as its efficiently designed appendage.

Frank Bunker Gilbreth and Lillian Evelyn Moller (Gilbreth)

Frank Bunker Gilbreth and Lillian Evelyn Moller (Gilbreth), who were married in 1904 and the parents of twelve children, formed a management consulting firm of Gilbreth, Inc., based almost entirely on the application of engineering time and motion studies to management situations, both public and private. They

were obsessed with making even the most menial tasks more efficient and effective by the reduction of time and motion to complete the activity. This included everything from improvements in brick-laying to laying out the ideal
kitchen for a person with a heart disease (meaning the person will not be able
to move about as much as someone without the disease, and so the idea was to
construct the kitchen in such a way that all parts of the kitchen, from utensil
holders to the stove, would be easily and efficiently accessible. After Frank's un-
timely death, Lillian carried on the work, raising the children, lecturing, and
consulting until her death in 1972.

Source: The Gilbreth Network, "Frank and Lillian Gilbreth," http://gilbrethnetwork.tripod.
com/bio.html (accessed October 2007).

Although Henry Laurence Gantt, who worked for Taylor and from whom the **Gantt
Chart** is named—a visual display chart for scheduling work based on time rather than
quantity of work achieved—emphasized the human aspect of work, arguing, for example,
that the physical conditions people work in should be respectable; the machine-like dehumanizing effect favored by Taylor and the Gilbreths is what most remember of scientific management studies. This dehumanizing effect would not be tolerated today, of course, and with
good reason, but because the industrial system of the early twentieth century relied on the
piece-work method, the alterations were beneficial for both management and the worker.
The worker could produce more and thus be paid more, and management would get more
out of the worker and thus achieve a higher production rate and profit.[22]

Scientific management would have remained an isolated phenomenon, one relegated
to the business industry had it not been for **Harrington Emerson** (1853–1931). Emerson was born into a wealthy and prominent New Jersey family, received a European education, and then showed his maverick side by embarking on a journey westward that
included stints as a professor in modern languages at the University of Nebraska, banker,
land speculator, and all-around entrepreneur. He is best known for his pioneering work
in industrial engineering and scientific management. He promoted scientific management not so much in the workplace, but to mass audiences. He established a successful
consulting business, labeling himself as an **efficiency engineer,** published books on industrial efficiency that described his Emerson Efficiency System, a system that included
production routing procedures, standard working conditions, Taylor's time and motion
studies, and worker bonus plans.[23] In effect, Emerson disseminated his ideas of scientific
management, promoting not only the theory itself, but by default many of its adherents,
such as Taylor and the Gilbreths, through lectures, articles, and books.

The Principles Approach. The third stream of thought and practice in the classical tradition of organization theory and behavior is broadly known as the principles approach,
and more specifically as **administrative management**. The scientific management adherents attempted to change and rationalize the organization from the bottom up, with
changes in the way work is done; the administrative management proponents argued that
the best way to change the organization is from the top down, emphasizing that managers were the key parts in the organization and therefore various rationalizing principles
should direct their administrative functions.[24] One of the best known proponents of the
principles' approach was a Frenchman named **Henri Fayol** (1841–1925).

Fayol, who was a wealthy French industrialist, wrote in the early part of the twentieth
century, but his work was not translated into English until after World War II.[25] After
turning around a failing mining company he retired and started a center for the study of
administration in order to put into print and practice his ideas.[26] His basic ideas were:

(1) to reorganize the upper management positions, (2) educate everyone in the organization in management theories, (3) eliminate as much red tape as possible, and (4) establish lateral lines of communication within the organization. To accomplish this he argued that every organization should comprise five essential functions: *plan* (or what many refer to today as strategize), *organize, command, co-ordinate,* and *control.* He even went so far as to identify fourteen **principles** common to all organizations (see table below). Fayol's work set the stage for future studies of management.

Table 5.1   Fayol's Fourteen Principles of Management

- Division of labor
- Authority with responsibility
- Discipline
- Unity of command
- Unity of direction

- Subordination of individual interests to organizational interests

- Adequate remuneration

- Centralization of authority
- Chain of command
- Order
- Fairness
- Guarantee of lifetime job for employees with good behavior

- Encourage employee initiative

- Promote *spirit de corps* within rank-n-file of organization

Source: Wendy Clark, "People Whose Ideas Influence Organisational Theory: Henri Fayol," Onepine, www.onepine.info/fayol.htm (accessed October 2007).

Others, like **James D. Mooney** (1884–1957), along with Alan C. Reiley, substantiated Fayol's work. In 1931 Mooney and Reiley published *Onward Industry: The Principles of Organization and their Significance to Modern Industry* (later republished in 1939 as *The Principles of Organization*).[27] They argued there were four main principles of management, including coordination, scalar chain of command, specialization, and line/staff functional differences. Given that both Mooney and Reiley were General Motor executives in the early 1930s the bulk of their observations are from practical experience in the private sector.[28]

Where scientific management placed the emphasis on the workers following simplified and quantified procedures for accomplishing various work tasks, the administrative management theorists argued that management should be the priority item of any organization. Later, others such as **Leonard White** (1891–1958), summarized the previous work of both the scientific management and principles' schools. In 1926, for example, White published the first recognized textbook devoted exclusively to public administration and management,[29] where he discussed at some length the belief that management lends itself to a value-free analysis, the emphasis on the intersection of science and technology, the management of organizational resources, and even basic comparisons between the private and public sectors. White also drew heavily upon the politics/administration dichotomy, which most scholars contend is drawn from Woodrow Wilson's 1887 essay,[30] arguing that administration was a science and politics was a craft, and never shall the twain meet. Most contemporary scholars and practitioners understand that administration and policy are anything but separate; however, in the early part of the twentieth century, when the vestiges of the Reform Movement were still evident, there was the need to justify the rational and empirical world of administrative action in comparison to the non-rational and normative world of politics.

The last major contribution to the principles' approach—*a la* administrative management theory—was through the work of Luther Gulick and Lyndall Urwick.[31] Because of Gulick's ties to President Roosevelt's administration through being a member of the Committee for Administrative Management [a.k.a. the Brownlow Committee, named after committee chairman Louis Brownlow] and consultant to the **National Resource Planning Board** and his close personal friendship with the President, he had actual experience in the government world. He believed that various rules or principles existed to make every organization, particularly government organizations, run more efficiently and be controlled from the manager's perspective. Again, these principles were not much different from the principles first introduced by Fayol. They included: hierarchy, unity of command, specialization of function, span of control, and rational organizational design. Most importantly to Gulick and Urwick they believed that the right structural arrangements of management authority had to be discovered and then fill the available positions with the right people in order for the organization to function properly.[32]

Management was the key. The greater the emphasis on management authority, working from the top down, the better the organization. In order to form a rational construct of management principles, Gulick and Urwick devised an acronym, POSDCORB, which described the basic functions of any management system: Planning, Organizing, Staffing, Directing, Coordinating, and Budgeting. But how would this strictly management oriented and administratively-driven perspective connect to democratic pluralist values? The answer was to require the administrator to be responsible to the elected official, primarily the president.[33]

Summary. Closed systems focused on development of machine-like qualities of efficiency, effectiveness, and economy. The primary goal, whether in the private or public sector, was to achieve the greatest output for the least input, while doing so at the least possible cost. Surely there is not much inherent in this philosophy of organization that speaks to fulfilling the public interest. If you said this you would be mistaken. Fulfilling the public interest is indeed a normative concept, and as such it focuses on meeting the values of fiscal, organizational, and policy economy. Granted, human well-being and fostering inter-personal and organizational relations was not a priority in the closed system, but the common good of recognizing the strengths and weaknesses of large-scale hierarchical organizations was achieved.

Bureaucratic Politics:
The Influence of Dwight Waldo

Before we continue with our discussion of the various open systems' approaches to organization theory and behavior, it is necessary to examine the post-war critique of Wilson's politics-administration dichotomy—what we typically refer to as **bureaucratic politics**—particularly through the seminal thinking and work of Dwight Waldo.

Dwight Waldo was keenly aware of the relationship that existed between politics and administration; in fact, he considered it a false dichotomy. As he famously stated, "Administration is politics." He understood better than most that the underpinnings of public administration was philosophical and historical—one that had a more direct impact upon the pursuit of the public interest—and that the true aim of the early reformers, and what should be the aim of reformers even today, was moral rather than economic. To this end, Waldo emphasized the importance of public morality and argued that government should be administered "not only with knowledge but with integrity."[34] Further, and what is critical for us to understand, is that politics and administration are not separate entities, but that public administration draws from various elements of public management and leadership in order to carry out simple service delivery functions, which is partly the fulfillment of the public interest.

Administration is by nature political; one cannot escape the other. Waldo was troubled by the claims of some students of administration who on the one hand argued that politics was largely distant to administrative pursuits, while at the same time they examined administration within a strong political and historical framework. In other words, administrative theory and political theory are not separate; the one (political theory) informs the other (administrative theory), while administrative theory lends substance and practical application to political theory. Those early scholars, like Frank Goodnow, Frederick Taylor, and Woodrow Wilson, wanted as we say "to have their cake and eat it too."

They believed that the best administration was the most efficient, not the most equitable, but as they accepted this principle they did so by recognizing the democratic pluralist framework. This makes it difficult to frame a sound and separate administrative theory, whose primary values of efficiency, economy, and effectiveness are opposite of democratic values of justice, freedom, and equity, which are commonly understood to be central to the public interest. The key, argued Waldo, was not to abandon democracy — which, by the way, the early administrative reformers did not attest to — but to accept the fact that administrators or bureaucrats operated politically AND administratively, which demonstrated that both were central to pursuit of the public interest. They pushed their own programs, with managers acting like power brokers among various interest groups. Thus, Waldo noted, "... the concept of democracy and all its messy implications had to be brought back into administrative theory."[35]

Waldo's critically important piece was the launching pad, so to speak, for a great deal of literature that critically and analytically examined the role of what became widely known as bureaucratic politics. This genre of literature explores the murky relationship between bureaucracy and politics, whether it was presidential, international relations, personality studies, organizational behavior, executive reorganization, representative bureaucracy, or street-level bureaucracy.[36] The primary point is this: Waldo exposed to the academic world the commonsensical reality that there is an inescapable relationship that exists between and among bureaucrats and appointed or elected officials, or organizationally between administrative hierarchies and appointed or elected political bodies.

Waldo's influence was critical to understanding the central role that administrative theory had in developing a well-orbed or fuller understanding and depiction of the role that public administration played in the development of the public interest. Separating the two was not possible nor even desirable; it was inevitable that the one (politics) influenced the other (administration) and that in turn administration began to come into its own, developing theoretical constructs of organization, administration, hierarchy, and especially political-administration, or what Waldo referred to as bureaucratic politics. Pluralism and diversity were terms no longer reserved for the political world; they were shaped by and were shaping the rich administrative universe they were part of.

Open Systems: Modern Theories

Differing dramatically from the closed systems as well as the more diffuse bureaucratic politics is the **open systems** approach. The human relations approach is a subset or group of a broader open, natural, informal and even organic model. The basic argument is that unlike the classical approach, which views organizations in a rational and mechanistic fashion, with workers and managers operating largely based on economic means; the open systems model, particularly the human relations sub-component, contends that workers worked and contributed to the overall organization for non-economic reasons.[37] These reasons may include a sense of responsibility to the public interest shared by each participant within the organization. In addition to the human relations perspective found under the open systems' umbrella we will also look at decision-making, neo-classical, systems approach, and organizational learning. Clearly, the human dimension of organizational morality was beginning to take shape, delineating more clearly the focus on pursuit of the public interest.

Informal Organizations

A step or two ahead of her time was **Mary Parker Follet** (1868–1933). As a social psychologist, she balked against the time-honored traditions of the classical school, believing instead that worker satisfaction was a key factor in the development of productive social organizations. Individuals and informal social groups within the larger organization must reconcile their differences and goals. One way was through effective administration, sound communication, and promotion of differences among and between workers. Due to her insistence on these less than formal traits of traditional classical organization theory, her ideas of power with the employees rather than power over the employees ushered in the ideas behind the human relations approach, including the famous Hawthorne Studies.[38]

Case Study   The Hawthrone Experiments

The Hawthorne experiments were conducted during the late 1920s and early 1930s at Hawthorne Western Electric Plant, located just outside of Chicago. Elton Mayo (1880–1949), who was with the Harvard Business School, and his research associate, Fritz J. Roethlisberger, conducted experiments on worker productivity. Mayo believed that such factors as worker fatigue affected organizational productivity. In order to test this thesis, they conducted several on-site controlled experiments. One such experiment was to divide plant workers into multiple groups, isolating one set of workers from other groups of workers, and controlling or manipulating certain variables, such as the intensity of lighting illumination. In the experiment group the level of illumination was changed frequently, while the control group's level of illumination remained unchanged. The researchers expected to find that the level of productivity would decrease in the experiment group, while remaining the same or even increasing in the control group. To their surprise, the productivity levels of both groups actually increased.

Unsure of why the results turned out the way they did, the researchers actually went to the workers for explanation, and the workers admitted that despite the varying levels of illumination they worked just as hard because they were the center of attention. In other words, worker productivity changed not necessarily because of changes in the physical environment but because of changes in the social group environment. Workers encouraged each other to keep up the pace, and continue to work hard despite the physical conditions. This was especially true of female workers. They responded well to the attention given them by the researchers. This became known as the *Hawthorne effect*.

A second important contribution of the Hawthorne experiments was the informal group. Where the formal organization is the organization that is outlined on paper, with boxes, titles, and arrows pointing down; the informal group "is the group formed by employees that exists over and above the formal organization ... [with] a leadership structure quite apart from the formal organization, and that the group had its own norms with respect to production." In many respects what Mayo and his associates found was that productivity was more the result of worker-to-worker motivation to produce within the informal group than it was a result of management. Thus it struck a blow against the classical approach which stressed there was one right way to manage and organize.

Source: F.J. Roethlisberger, *Man-in-Organization: Essays of F.J. Roethlisberger* (Cambridge, MA: Belknap, 1968). For Mayo's own analysis see Elton Mayo, *The Human Problems of an Industrial Civilization* (New York: Viking, 1933; reprint, 1960). Also, for more extensive overview of the experiments see Scott, *Organizations*, 61–62; Vasu, Stewart and Garson, *Organizational Behavior*, 36–38; and LeMay, *Public Administration*, 120.

Decision-Making Approach

Others, including Chester Barnard, were also influential in promoting the informal group concept. Barnard, who was not a scholar but a successful businessman and leader with the New Jersey Bell Telephone Company in the 1930s, wrote *Functions of the Executive* in 1938.[39] His book was somewhat of a bridge between the classical and human relations schools, because he saw the organization in human rather than simply structural terms. Still, he recognized that decision making was a key variable to working through the minefield of equilibrium changes or exchanges between workers and management. The manager's job was to "... allocate satisfactions or rewards in exchange for the employees' acquiescence to the prescribed behavior; behavior that the organization required to meet its goals and survive."[40] Barnard contended that there were differences between the informal and formal organizations, especially with regard to measuring behavior. He believed "... that workers had a social-psychological zone of acceptance, referring to their relative willingness to obey the leader's directives."[41] The best workers, then, were workers who were compatible with management on a variety of factors, including education and personality, not just skill level.

Herbert Simon's work in the science of administrative decision-making expanded upon and went beyond Barnard's work to include a portrayal of "... organizational decision-making as a kind of compromise between rational, goal oriented behavior and non-rational behavior."[42] Simon distinguished between facts and values, where administrators give validity to values, weighing means and ends, and ultimately assessing the consequences of action within the parameters of these values.[43] It is the organization that defines what values determine rational over non-rational behavior. Administrators or other decision-makers ultimately make decisions regarding these various values, including the laws, rules, and regulations commonly implemented in society. But no decision is based on pure rational thought or behavior; the best the administrator can hope for is to both satisfy and suffice, or what Simon coined satisficing. This form of satisficing recognizes that rational behavior is thus bounded by its very administrative environment, including the level and amount of information, skills, and knowledge, both of the administrator, the worker, and the overall organization itself.[44] Simon's work was critical in learning more about how administrative decisions are made.

Neo-Classical Approach

The new **human relations approach** to organization theory focused on methodology: the use of empirical research to determine workers' interpersonal relations affecting the overall organization. Similar to the human relations approach it focuses on the individual and not the organizational structure; however, motivation of the individual, as opposed to informal groups and decision-making, within the organization is critical to explaining decisions and productivity. Two theorists are most prominent: **Abraham Maslow** (1908–1970) and Douglas McGregor.

Maslow, who received his Ph.D. in psychology from the University of Wisconsin in 1934, focused his attention on the theoretical development of humanistic psychology, particularly in the development of the concept of self-actualization and human motivation. Maslow is most well known for his needs hierarchy, where he believed that humans have five basic needs ordered in a hierarchy of needs: physiological, safety, love or affiliation, esteem, and self-actualization.[45] Each lower need must be met before higher needs emerge in the person's life. A person, for example, must have food for physical nourishment, but once his physical need for food is met he has additional and higher needs, which in turn when they are met he advances up the hierarchy, ultimately trying to reach the nirvana of needs: self-actualization. From an administrative point of view, Maslow's theory was not easily adaptable; not until the organizational humanists, such as Douglas McGregor and others came along to apply Maslow's theory of human needs and motivation into an administrative and organizational setting.

McGregor, who earned his Ph.D. from Harvard, argued in his classic *The Human Side of Enterprise* (1960),[46] that workers could be self-motivated (Theory Y) as opposed to externally motivated by management (Theory X). Both theories make assumptions about human motivation and behavior. **Theory X** assumptions are that:

- Work is generally not desired, but is done only out of economic necessity;
- Workers like to be closely supervised;
- Workers do not generally assume new responsibilities without having to be told;
- Workers are strictly motivated by money and threat of punishment.

Obviously, these same assumptions of human motivation were the foundation of scientific management theory. McGregor; however, believed that post-World War II research in industrial psychology, for example, validated another set of assumptions about human need and motivation. He labeled this **Theory Y**. The assumptions included:

- People enjoy work;
- People are self-motivated and controlled;
- People do in fact create and innovate;
- And finally, people's motivation is largely due in response to rewards, not punishment.

McGregor accepted Maslow's theoretical work and adapted it to management/worker behavior, suggesting that the reason why organizations do not meet more goals is because they expect too little out of workers; they don't meet the higher end level of needs, such as esteem and self-actualization.[47] Some contend that McGregor actually modeled his two theories after real life organizations: Theory X and the military and Theory Y and professional organizations, such as law and medicine.[48] Whether or not this is true is not as relevant as the fact that McGregor's work legitimated the esoteric work of Maslow and other humanistic psychologists as a means to help explain administrative and management behavior in large scale organizations.

Systems Approach

Systems theory recognizes the importance of both process and outcome within the organization. The systems framework developed after World War II, with an emphasis on interaction and interrelationship between various elements. These elements included: the environment, inputs (resources), the system itself or processes, outputs (product or service of the system or process), and feedback (effects of the outputs on the environment.[49] One advantage of the systems theory is its streamlined and linear approach to decision-making; equally so, one of its disadvantages is found in its linearity, meaning critics believe it is too simple to fully explain the interaction and interrelationship between organizations in society. Two of the more notable systems' theorists are David Easton and Daniel Katz and Robert Kahn.

David Easton, who is a Canadian and came to the United States in 1943, applied the cybernetic or systems model to political science.[50] Easton set forth on an ambitious project: to deal with the empirical and behavioral side of political science, a side that emerged from the institutional cover of bygone days, when the intention of students of politics were focused on the legal and institutional characteristics of government. The **Chicago School**, as it came to be known, argued for a more exacting science of politics, one whose theory and inquiry were to be strictly scrutinized from a position of interdependence with society. Easton's contribution to this strict scrutiny reinstated the notion that political theory was important, particularly as it helped to explain the behavioral aspects made so prominent in the aftermath of the War. Thus he theorized that political and policy issues, such as women's and civil rights, should be examined through the systems' process described above.

Daniel Katz (1903–1998) and Robert Kahn, both psychology scholars, launched into an open systems perspective of organizations, declaring that organizations were more than simply lines and arrows and boxes on a hierarchy chart. Rather organizations were seen as "whole beings, complex and constantly interacting with their environment."[51] Katz and Kahn envisioned the organization as complex, but also as a constantly changing phenomenon; therefore, it is never static, and always changing, depending in large part on the environment it operates within. As some have described, the university setting is a model of the open systems approach as explained by Katz and Kahn.[52]

In addition, the systems theory approach to organizations—at least according to Katz and Kahn—examined the role of smaller groups internal to the larger organization, which to a great extent focuses on what scholars refer to as **Organizational Development (OD)**. OD is defined as "a planned organization-wide attempt directed from the top that is designed to increase organizational effectiveness and viability through calculated interventions in the active workings of the organization using knowledge from the behavioral sciences."[53] In other words, OD is focused on the role and input of the individual and small group within the larger organization, focusing less on structural aspects of organizations and more on what is referred to as organic or natural aspects of organizations. **Kurt Lewin** (1890–1947) is recognized as the leading pioneer/guru of OD, as early as the 1940s.[54] OD made its mark in the private sector, but in addition to Total Quality Circles (TQC) and more broadly, **Total Quality**

Management (TQM), impacted the organizational dynamics of the public organization as well. We turn now to our final topic: examining the differences (and similarities) between public and private organizations, especially as it applies to the public interest.

Organizational Learning

A more recent perspective of the open model approach to organizational behavior is **Organizational Learning (OL)**. The key premise of OL is that: (1) organizations are like organisms—they are constantly (or should be) changing to their respective external environments; and (2) that organizations will not learn unless individuals within the organizations learn. If organizations (or really individuals) stop learning, or adapting to changes in their respective environments, particularly social, economic, administrative, managerial, and even political, then both individuals and organizations stagnate and cannot function as they are designed to.

According to OL, there are two basic types of learning: **adaptive**, where there are changes made in reaction to the environment, and **proactive**, where changes are made on a more deliberate basis. Adaptive learning is more or less lower-level learning, i.e. learning by reacting, whereas proactive learning is higher-level learning, i.e. learning by doing, so to speak. Pioneers of OL, such as **Richard Cyert** (1921–1998) and **James G. March**, argued that OL is mainly an adaptive process; one where goals, Standard Operating Procedures, or what they referred to as attention rules, and search rules are all essentially made to fit the organization, or at least with each other within the organization. Essentially, Cyert and March argue from a behavior approach of the market: the organization, in order to act rationally, focuses on its rules of order and operation in order to perform more efficiently. Reacting positively or initially to changes in the external environment, such as to inflation, recessions, ups and downs in the stock market, were not a part of their thinking as to what an organizational learning environment is all about.[55] Later, March along with **Johan Olsen**, who is currently the Research Director of Advanced Research on the Europeanization of the Nation State (ARENA), make a similar argument for institutional learning cycle, which "involves the selective recollection and interpretation of experiences (the usable history), understandings of the rules and identities derived from these experiences, interpretations of the nature of previous institutional actions and their consequences, and the adaptation of rules and identities based on these interpretations."[56]

More recently, scholars and researchers have contributed to a better understanding of OL; none probably more influential than **Chris Argyis**, Donald Schon, and Peter Senge (1947–). Argyris builds upon systems theory by developing an organizational learning model that sees an organization as a system, where learning involves the detection and correction of error. He outlines two types of learning that occurs in organizations: **single-loop** and **double-loop** learning. The first, single-loop, occurs without asking questions, either about the reason for the issue or how to correct consequences that result because of the issue. For example, President George W. Bush sought to partially privatize Social Security, by making it possible through tax changes and other means for younger payers to hold back a certain percentage of their paycheck and privately invest it. If no questioning occurs, which, of course, it has, but if none did occur, then this would be a form of single-loop or adaptive learning. On the other hand, double-loop learning provides alternative responses to the very issue itself. With the Social Security example, critics would challenge the basic assumption of privatization itself, while criticizing the President's initial plan for implementing privatization. The first form of learning simply reacts to changes in the environment, but the second not only reacts but actually modifies the organization (or in this case institution's) basic norms and philosophy. Obviously, for Argyris double-loop learning is superior, particularly during times of radical change.

Building on Argyris' work is **Donald Schon** (1930–1997) and his concept of the **learning society**. Not only did he concur with Argyris' initial assumption that double-loop learning was superior for organizations, but he took it step further. He contended that organizations should be in a constant state of learning (double-loop learning), given the changing nature of society and societal institutions, including economic, political, and social. In his key work, *Beyond the Stable State* (1973), Schon argued that "We must … become adept at learning. We must become able not only to transform our institutions, in response to changing situations and requirements; we must invent and develop institutions which are 'learning systems', that is to say, systems capable of bringing about their own continuing transformation."[57] So for Schon, learning is not simply something that is individual; it is also institutional or social. This is critical when public or private organizations are trying to exist, for example, in an ever-changing high-technology world.

Third, **Peter Senge**, who was strongly influenced by both Argyris and Schon, and credits much of what he understands about modern organizations and institutions from both, nevertheless, established himself as a seminal thinker. He contended that organizations must be constantly learning and enhancing their capabilities to learn, primarily through development of five disciplines Senge regards as the centerpiece of learning organizations. The five disciplines are systems thinking, personal mastery, mental models, building shared vision, and team learning. The key discipline, which he explores in *The Fifth Discipline* (1990), is the discipline "that integrates the others, fusing them into a coherent body of theory and practice." Each of the five disciplines is interwoven along three dimensions: practices, or what a person does, principles, a person's guiding ideas and insights, and essences, a high-level of being. So, the learning organization is an organization that incorporates all individuals, led by leaders who are designers and teachers and stewards.[58] Developing **learning organizations** should be the motivation of all managers and administrators, given that learning organizations, as opposed to non-learning organizations, will thrive and change, and thus be higher performing.

Summary. Whether described and explained through the development of informal organizations, through various means of learning how administrative and organizational decisions are made (satisficing), the neo-classical or human relations school, behavioralism as evidenced through the output driven systems approach to decision making, or the more recent organizational learning concepts; the point is clear: fulfilling the public interest is morally justified and sought after through better understanding and clarity of the human dimension of organizations. Organizations are composed of people; people who create informal groups within the larger organization in order to make sense out of their work life and to try and find meaning through the production of widgets and delivery of services that they perform on a daily basis. They are pursuing the public interest, not only for themselves but for their co-workers, families, and secondary relationships (those who buy their goods, take advantage of the services etc.)

We conclude our discussion of organizations, theory, and behavior with a brief description of the differences between public and private organizations. Questions abound: Is there a difference? Does it matter if there is or is not a difference? Clearly in our thinking there is and MUST be a distinguishable difference between what Microsoft is and does as compared to what the Department of Defense (or some similar and comparable public sector organization) is and does. Why? Because even though many private sector companies have strong social consciousnesses, that is they are concerned about the impact, both negative and positive, that their business, industry, product and/or services have upon the greater public good; public organizations are bound by statute or regulation to meet the greater good, not for profit but because there is demand or need to be met. Electric energy companies, for example, surely must be cognizant of where they plan on stringing new wires and setting new 100 foot tall power poles. However, when all the political dust and environmental groups' complaints settle, unless there is a law or regulation that forbids the company from providing new wires and poles—which of course is based upon public demand and use—or the public outcry is so great that the state legislature cannot close their political ears tight enough, then the electric company organization continues its job, which it believes is in the public interest.

So, the following discussion helps us better understand 1) the differences between public and private organizations, but 2) to recognize that public organizations have the inherent, legal, and perhaps even constitutional responsibility to fulfill the public interest. We then conclude the chapter with a few closing remarks.

Public-Private Differences

Are there any differences between Exxon and the Department of Energy, between General Motors and the Department of Transportation, or between Steve Ballmer, CEO of Microsoft, and Barak Obama as President of the United States? On the surface the answer seems an easy "Yes." But critics contend that there is such a blurring effect between what is private and public that, perhaps, the obvious answer is not an unequivocal "Yes." For both traditional public actors, such as police, and private actors, such as law firms, work to enforce the criminal law and achieve the public interest. If a blurring effect does occur, does this mean we should privatize all government departments and agencies, and nationalize all private firms?[59] We don't think this would be prudent or politically acceptable.

One way to help explain the difference between private and public organizations is according to differences between politics and markets, or between government and economics. **Robert Dahl** and **Charles Lindblom**[60] argued that the primary reason for the existence of public organizations was due to how governments were formed and why economic market mechanisms worked in the first place. Dahl and Lindblom originally contended in the 1953 edition that the complex pluralistic and multi-headed beast that is government, departments, and agencies, which they termed "polyarchy," controlled the economics of a society. In their 1976 edition, however, they conceded that various changes over the interim period, both institutionally and procedurally, contributed not so much to a change in the original thesis, but in the dynamic of that relationship; for example, a shift from legislative control over the economy to an imperial presidential control over the economy directly influenced the growth of the public sector, particularly in terms of regulatory nature.

Politics of society regulates human behavior; behavior that is often displayed through economic markets, which is the voluntary buying and selling of goods and services in an open market system, such as in a capitalist state like the United States.[61] It is the responsibility of the government to oversee or correct any problems that arise in the free market system, such as collusion, illegal mergers, depressions and recessions, monopolies and the like. In addition, government uses its taxing power to distribute and redistribute goods and services from those who have to those who have not; a practice that is politically and ideologically divisive. Liberals, for example, call for a greater involvement of the government in the market itself, whereas conservatives generally disfavor unwanted advances by government into the private market.[62] However, after the financial meltdown of the lending, mortgage, and financial institutions in the fall of 2008, future reforms and reformers, including the Obama administration, may seriously rethink how and to what extent governments should and will allow the free-market, well, "free reign" in a democratic society.

Some say that public means people and private means being "deprived of public office or set apart from government as a personal matter."[63] Public derives from two Greek words: the first is *pubes*, antecedent to our word maturity. The Greeks understood that maturity was a moving away from oneself toward an understanding of others. The second word is **koinon**, meaning common. Koinon is also derived from another Greek word, *kom-is*, meaning to care with.[64] Thus, both terms imply some kind of relationship, presumably between those who govern and those who are governed. That relationship is not one of self-directedness, but one of public directedness; directed outward, not inward. Public organizations, then, are designed to administer to needs and demands of the public as a whole, not to a select few, thus fulfilling the public interest.

H. George Frederickson and others contend however, that the original meaning of public has been lost, and is replaced with terms like politics and government. Frederickson even argues that the word public is now considered frivolous, inadequate, and even meaningless, especially when attached to other words, such as public good or public interest. He argues that this transformation is a philosophical one: moving from the original Greek influence to a utilitarian one, where, as he notes, "We are to determine well-being, pleasure, or utility by consequences or results—preferably by bureaucratic, technological, or scientific means. There is no public, only the sum of atomistic individuals. And there is no public interest, except in summing up the aggregate of individual interests."[65] It is utilitarianism that Frederickson claims is behind the development of Dahl and Lindblom's politics and markets explanation, thus "judg(ing) consequences or results by the technology of the market ..." and by implication "... contribut(ing) to the loss of an ennobling concept of the public."[66] By default, then, this lays at least a partial foundation for addressing the broader concern of the public interest.

Differences between Public and Private Organizations and Officials

By definition public officials (President Barak Obama), as opposed to private officials (Steve Ballmer), hold an office that is bound by legal authority, usually via a constitution or written contract of some form. Public officials are then bound by oath and affirmation to uphold this legally binding document. They are then empowered to legislate, execute, adjudicate, and administer decisions, such as laws, executive orders, court decisions, and regulations, to the greater public. Public officials are publicly accountable for their decisions, both in terms of legal authority and at the ballot box. Finally, public officials are empowered to consider the interests of the whole body or constituency and not just the interests of a few.

According to the atomistic notion of our free-market system, private sector officials and companies are only required to make a profit. Private sector officials, such as Steve Ballmer, the CEO of **Microsoft**, are not bound by a constitution or other legally binding document. Rather they are bound by a pledge to their company's shareholders to make a profit and return some of that profit to them in the form of stock dividends. Further, Microsoft, for example, is not publicly accountable, not at least in the political sense; they are accountable to the buying public of their product and services. And last, Steve Ballmer's sole concern is to make sure Microsoft's buying public is satisfied with the product and service(s) he produces; not with someone who buys an Apple. That is Steve Jobs' responsibility.

However, more and more companies do recognize that they have a larger, more systemic place and purpose in society today, such as promoting the public good or the commons, and not one of simply making a profit for themselves. Wal-Mart and Target stores, for example, work with and in the local communities they reside in, sponsoring events and movements from environmental protection to educational progressivism. There is growing public pressure upon the private sector, especially with mega-retail companies like Wal-Mart, or power companies like AES, to contribute back to the community rather than simply taking from it. Wal-Mart, for example, markets itself as being committed to building community relationships and partnerships through such programs as Kids Recycling Challenge and Community Grant Programs;[67] while the relatively new power company, AES, provides not only electrical power to many customers in the United States and in 27 nations worldwide, but it also helps establish infrastructure in China, Venezuela, and Qatar, as well as donates funds for habitable parkland in Indiana.[68] This pursuit of the public good by many in the private sector lends credence to the development of the public interest. So, even though the terms public and private do have differences in meaning, especially with regard to philosophical, legal, political, economic, and even ethically, there are indeed practical similarities.

Conclusion

The role and function of organizational theory is critical to the development of a sound public administration practice. Our framework for organization theory, by open and closed systems, is a means to categorize and explain how public organizations function independently and *inter*-dependently, along with private and non-profit sectors, in pursuit of the public interest. For both open and closed systems of organization are designed to achieve the public interest.

Closed systems emphasized structure, rules, and regulations, with the organizations focused on accomplishing efficiency, economy, and effectiveness. Born during a period of economic, technological, political, and social change the closed models, such as Weberian, principles and administrative management, focused on directing and administering physical resources toward accomplishing an end task. Human effort and need was acknowledged as a means toward an ends, not an end of itself. Administrative and political values, such as the public interest, were not the focus of these closed systems of organization. Instead, the focus was upon operational administrative principles, manipulated to accomplish the predetermined goals as efficiently and economically as possible.

Open systems suggested something quite different. Theories such as organizational humanism and organizational learning, for example, do not focus only on the structure and operational process of the organization. Instead, open systems theories include the input and responsibility of each organizational participant in working toward the public interest. Individuals are what make up the organization. Individuals give organizations their character, whether in groups—informal or formal—or working independently. From the early work at the Hawthrone Electric plant outside of Chicago to Maslow's hierarchy of needs to McGregor's Theory Y explanation of human behavior, the open models of organization theory and behavior strongly emphasizes the need for human input into the organizational process.

Waldo's challenge of the empirical uprising in the social sciences in the late 1940s, particularly in political science and public administration, summoned the courage to state unequivocally that individual, group, and institutional morality, fixed within normative philosophy of administration and management, should not be so readily dismissed in the wake of logical positivism and the behavioral outcomes it produces. In his famous written tug-of-war with Herbert Simon in 1952 published in the *American Political Science Review*, Waldo rejected Simon's claim that administrative decisions focused solely on facts as opposed to values was scientifically valid and moved ever closer to the overall goal of administrative efficiency. Why? Because as Waldo so succinctly yet forcefully put it: the administrative world is not the same as the political world. Efficiency by itself is a claim of values, one that is determined by the decision-maker himself.

Making claims of administrative efficiency or democratic justice is *de facto* a claim for the public interest, for the root of the public interest is not only constitutional, historical, and philosophical, but it is naturally political. Political values require decision opportunities and decision opportunities require the selection of choices; choices are what make the public interest, whether those choices are administrative or political or both.

Action Steps

1. Does formal organizational structure dictate a particular approach to the public interest? Consider how the U.S. Supreme Court has deferred so completely on the nature and structure of bureaucratic organization in the case of *Wilson v. Seiter*, 501 U.S. 294 (1991), involving prison bureaucracy. In this case, the Court prohibited judicial review of prison organizations, procedures or conditions unless there was proof prison administrators acted with "deliberate indifference" to inmate injuries or constitutional rights violations. Does the Constitution suggest a particular organizational structure as within the public interest?

2. What do the ancients and classical thinkers of organizational theory have in common (Moses, Sun Tzu, Alexander the Great, Aristotle, and Machiavelli)? Break into groups of three or four. Have each group isolate their top three factors of commonality; after fifteen minutes of discussion bring them back together.

3. In a three-page essay, discuss the impact that the Germans Karl Marx and Max Weber had upon the formation of modern organizations. If both were alive today, what would be their reactions to the development of the modern bureaucracy?

4. Analyze each of Weber's key values that are commonly associated with his theory of bureaucracy (division of labor, specialization of function, hierarchy, framework of rules and procedures, impersonal relationships, professionalization, and record-keeping system). Provide actual examples, both in the private and public sectors, of where these values are still very much prominent in the organization. How (if at all) have they changed from Weber's conceptualization?

5. Prepare a Gantt Chart of how you anticipate scheduling you time for the remainder of the semester. Include their time in class, studying, social activities, work schedules, breaks, etc. Write a three-page analysis on their findings. What do you learn about yourself, your time management skills, or other related factors?

6. Do a short biographical sketch of the following: Frederick Taylor, Frank and Lillian Gilbreth, Henry Gantt, and Harrington Emerson. What are the similarities and differences in these individuals thinking regarding scientific management?

7. Go on site to a town, county, or city's street, water, sewer, or parks' department. Using personal observation, informal or formal interviewing, and document analysis learn how the department uses (or does not use) James D. Mooney and Alan C. Reiley's four main principles of management: *coordination, scalar chain of command, specialization,* and *line/staff functional differences.* Write a short three to four-page summary and report it back to the class. What did you learn?

8. Role play Mary Parker Follet as a social psychologist, who is confronted with two employees who simply do not like each other, but are required to work with each other. Insisting that the classical school's approach was antiquated, she believed that worker satisfaction (and, perhaps, worker relationships) could be achieved through *effective administration, sound communication,* and *promotion of worker differences.* Research and practice the role play in a small group of three, concentrating on trying to use non-coercive means of getting workers to get along with each other. What is successful? What is not?

Exam Review Preparation

1. In a short essay, assess the scientific management approach to organizations.

2. Identify the importance of each public administration personality or time period.

    a. Elton Mayo

    b. Chester Barnard and *Functions of the Executive* (1938)

    c. Mary Parker Follet

    d. Abraham Maslow and Douglas McGregor

    e. Closed versus open systems of organization theory

    f. David Easton, Daniel Katz and Robert Kahn

    g. Henri Fayol and James Mooney and Alan Reiley

3. Explain Follet's informal organization thesis. Why was she ahead of her time?

4. Compare Theory X and Theory Y. What do both approaches say about human nature, especially with regard to worker motivation?

5. Discuss Robert Dahl and Charles Lindblom's thesis on politics and markets. How did their thesis change between the early 1950s and the mid 1970s? What do you believe contributed to this change?

6. What does public mean in Greek? Why is this important to know? Is it easy to tell a public organization from a private one? What are the tell-tale signs? Or, is it difficult? If so, why?

7. Identify and discuss the key components of the administrative state.

8. Discuss why there are many theories of bureaucracy, and not just one theory.

9. Explain Sun Tzu's *The Art of War.* What relevance does it have for explaining theories of organization?

10. Contrast centralization and decentralization of authority.

Key Concepts

Abraham Maslow
Administrative state
Alexander the Great
Bureaucracy
Chris Argyris
Classical school of organization
Decentralization of authority
Formal and informal organizations
Frank and Lillian Gilbreth
Gantt Chart
Harrington Emerson
Henri Fayol's Fourteen Principles of Management
Human relations approach
Invisible hand theory
Jethro the Midianite
Learning society
Leonard White
Machiavelli's *The Prince*
Mary Parker Follet
Organizational Development
Organizational Learning
Richard Cyert and James March
Robert Dahl and Charles Lindblom
Routinization
Schools of organization theory: classical versus modern
Scientific management principles
Sun Tzu's *The Art of War*
Theory of bureaucracy
Theory X and Y
Total Quality Management

Recommended Readings

Denhardt, Robert B. *Theories of Public Organization*, 4th ed. Belmont, CA: Thomson-Wadsworth, 2004.

Frederickson, H. George, and Kevin B. Smith. *The Public Administration Theory Primer*. Boulder, CO: Westview, 2003.

Gawthrop, Louis C. *Administrative Politics and Social Change*. New York: St. Martin's Press, 1971.

Harmon, Michael M. *Action Theory for Public Administration*. New York: Longman, 1981.

Janis, Irving L., and Leon Mann. *Decision-Making: A Psychological Analysis of Conflict, Choice, and Commitment.* New York: The Free Press, 1977.

Kaufman, Herbert. *Time, Chance, and Organizations: Natural Selection in a Perilous Environment.* Chatham, NJ: Chatham House Publishers, 1985.

Morgan, Gareth. *Images of Organization.* Newbury Park, CA: Sage, 1986.

Ott, J. Steven. *The Organizational Culture Perspective.* Pacific Grove, CA: Brooks/Cole, 1989.

Presthus, Robert. *The Organizational Society*, revised edition. New York: St. Martin's Press, 1978.

Richardson, William D. *Democracy, Bureaucracy, and Character: Founding Thought.* Lawrence, KS: University Press of Kansas, 1997.

Simon, Herbert A. *Administrative Behavior: A Study of Decision-Making Processes in Administrative Organization*, 3d ed. New York: The Free Press, 1976.

Thompson, Victor A. *Bureaucracy and the Modern World.* Morristown, NJ: General Learning, 1976.

_____. *Modern Organization*, 2d ed. University, AL: University of Alabama Press, 1977.

Von Mises, Ludwig. *Bureaucracy*, revised edition. Indianapolis, IN: Liberty Fund, 2007.

Related Web Sites

Abraham Maslow
www.nidus.org/

American Society for Quality (Total Quality Management)
http://www.asq.org/learn-about-quality/total-quality-management/overview/overview.html

Chicago School
http://cepa.newschool.edu/~het/schools/chicago.htm

Jackson Productivity Research, Inc. (time and motion studies)
http://jacksonproductivity.com/timestudy.htm

Mary Parker Follet Foundation
http://www.follettfoundation.org/mpf.htm

Max Weber
http://www.faculty.rsu.edu/~felwell/Theorists/Weber/Whome.htm

Peter Senge
http://www.infed.org/thinkers/senge.htm

Society for Industrial and Organizational Psychology
www.siop.org/

University of Kansas, Department of Public Administration
http://www2.ku.edu/~kupa/

Chapter 6

Public Management and the Public Interest

"Government shouldn't be run like a business; it should be run like a democracy."

Janet V. Denhardt and Robert B. Denhardt,
The New Public Service: Serving, Not Steering

Chapter Objectives

Upon completion of this chapter the student will be able to:

1. Define and distinguish the basic characteristics of public management;
2. Distinguish between three foundational paradigms of public administration generally and public management specifically: Old Public Administration, New Public Management, and the New Public Service;
3. Determine why the New Public Service paradigm better serves the normative foundation of the public interest and public management;
4. Distinguish between public management and leadership;
5. Explain the various theories of leadership.

Public Management

Over the past thirty years, and especially over the past ten, much has been written about managing the public sector at all three levels more like a business and less like a government. The argument is supposed to be simple: running a government like a government leads to waste, abuse, inefficiency, unaccountability, and a host of other problems associated with the organizational malaise that typically inhibits large bureaucratic organizations generally and government agencies particularly. So, the critics contend, institute business thinking, business principles, and especially market incentives into the public sector, and one will discover that as civil servants become principal agents and citizens become customers, the process of governing somehow becomes more, well, business-like.

Like **Janet and Robert Denhardt**, professors of public administration at Arizona State University, we contend that this is not what government is or was designed to do. Government is not just another business—contrary to popular thinking. Certainly there are some similarities in organization, management and process between business and government, and we will examine these. Government, however, is fundamentally different from business. The purpose of government is to govern; the work of government is to serve; the outcome of government is pursuit of the public interest. How that is accomplished is certainly within the domain of the process and technique of general management principles and practices. Further, how public management is done, how it is carried out is also critical to the success of accomplishing the public interest. But the end of public management is not — or it should not be — the means of public management. The degree of efficiency, effectiveness, and economy of implementing public decisions is certainly important, but the end is pursuit and accomplishment of the public interest. Or, as the Denhardts put it, "What is most significant, and most valuable, about public administration is that we serve citizens to advance the common good."[1]

This chapter introduces the definitions of public management, theories and approaches to the study of public management, including the **New Public Service**, of recent developments of public management philosophy and techniques, and concludes with a discussion on how good public managers can also be good leaders. We begin our discussion of public management in the context of the Denhardts' *The New Public Service*. Contrasting what they term the "new public service" with the "old public administration" and the "new public management" approaches to public administration, the Denhardts reignite the age-old debate of the public interest. We believe it is a debate that is well worthy of re-ignition. Let's light the fire!

Defining Public Management

Before considering three approaches to studying public management, we need to ask a more basic question: what is management? Those who run things may be called management, as well as running the process itself. But **management** also is a basic part of human relationships, in being and in activity. It occurs in all spheres of life: family, education, business, religion, and government. For our purposes, though, we will confine our discussion to the areas of business and government.

Ironically enough, much of what we know about public management has derived from the business and/or public administration research. Management is generally viewed as an internal organizational mechanism, working toward the pursuit of certain objectives in order to meet specific goals. The only way to do that efficiently and effectively is to "develop plans, build organizations, create systems of information in order to gauge success, institute a system of measurement and compensation, one that retains the interests of the individual rather than the interests of the organization, develop individual relationships" as well as other similar procedural and systemic functions.[2] More specifically, some, like George Gordon and Michael Milakovich, distinguish between public administration and public management where "... the latter emphasizes methods of organizing for internal control and direction for maximum effectiveness, whereas the former addresses a broader range of civic and social concerns."[3]

Others, such as David Rosenbloom, take a much more positive view of the role and relationship of public administration in the administration of the public interest. Public administration is defined as "the use of managerial, political, and legal theories and processes to fulfill legislative, executive, and judicial governmental mandates for the provision of regulatory and service functions for the society as a whole or for some segments of it."[4] Hence, public management is simply one aspect or *subset* of the broader concept of public administration. According to Rosenbloom, like many others,[5] public administration is distinguished according to various approaches, including traditional managerial, the New Public Management, political, and legal. Each approach perceives management differently. The first is rooted in the old Wilsonian politics and administration dichotomy; the second views administration from a market-based incentive perspective; the third concerns the emphasis of democratic-representation values; and the fourth adopts a procedural and legal-administrative perspective.[6] Regardless, though, as someone once wrote, "Management matters."[7]

David Rosenbloom

David Rosenbloom, Distinguished Professor of Public Administration, American University, and main author of *Public Administration: Understanding Management, Politics, and Law in the Public Sector,* 6th edition (2004), takes a positive view of the role and relationship of public administration in the public interest, arguing that public management specifically and public administration more generally serve normative as well as practical purposes: upholding the constitutional principles of freedom, justice, and order as well as striving to develop sound, practical governing principles that require government to work as efficiently and effectively as possible.

Source: School of Public Affairs, "Dr. David H. Rosenbloom," American University, http://spa.american.edu/listings.php?ID=105 (accessed October 2007).

Another more recent claim is that public management is specifically defined by policy analytical techniques and economics, thus infusing management with a strong analytical and empirical emphasis into the study and practice of public management.[8] From this perspective public management is essentially the same as **program management**, which requires the use of five basic management functions, all of which have roots in the traditional model of public administration: "planning, decision making, organizing, leading, and controlling."[9] An even older and more complex argument holds that public management is rooted in the organizational behavioral theories of general management, but as it is ultimately caught in the vortex of the public sphere it must adapt to changing constitutional, administrative, and legal changes.[10]

So, where does this leave us? Somewhat confused, we contend. Public management appears to be many things to many people, mostly depending upon the context in which the need for management occurs (political, legal, administrative, economic, organizational, etc.). What is needed is a fairly clear but concise historical and theoretical overview of public management within the larger sphere of public administration in the public interest. Although some authors attempt to discuss this subject, largely their efforts are weak and non-substantive at best. We believe the Denhardts provide a much needed discussion (and theoretical framework) of public administration and the public interest generally and public management more specifically: a phenomenon they refer to as the New Public Service.

Explaining Public Management

What is new about the **New Public Service** (NPS)? It is not that it is so much new as it is a return to understanding and appreciating public service for what is its foundation and source: public and service. It is contrasted with the **New Public Management** (NPM) and **Old Public Administration** (OPA). The NPS is less empirical and more normative, asking such questions as "How can we define the essential character of what we do ... ? What is the motivating force that propels our actions? What gives us strength and capacity when the trials and turmoil of our work get us down? How can we face problems that are complex and intractable with extremely limited resources and a public that often resents and criticizes what we do?" The answer for the Denhardts and for us is commitment to public service and pursuit of the public interest.[11]

New Public Service. NPS is not easily defined or even readily definable. It is not something that can be earmarked. It is as we noted above much more normative and subjective, yet it contains several key characteristics that help to distinguish what it is—and perhaps what it is not. Each of these characteristics (serving citizens, seeking the public interest, valuing citizenship, thinking strategically, assessing accountability, serving rather than steering, and valuing people not just productivity) are contrasted with two other historical and theoretical approaches: the Old Public Administration (hereinafter referred to as OPA) and the New Public Management (hereinafter referred to as NPM). In this section we will briefly describe and explain the three approaches, showing how each marks the wider parameters of public administration generally and public management specifically. We intend to use the Denhardts' thesis as a means to convey the differences between the three approaches, and to show how the NPS is a better model or approach for 1) explaining the practice of public management, and 2) placing it within the context of the wider public interest.

Old Public Administration. As we showed in chapters one and two, the history of public administration is much older than the end of the nineteenth century and into the turn of the twentieth century, but from a modern standpoint this is a good place to begin. OPA reflects the values associated with the advent of the Industrial Revolution and the Progressive Movement—greater efficiency and economy of service delivery, improved mechanization, increasingly effective communications technology, organizational and administrative enhancements, municipal reform, and a growing tendency toward adopting business approaches to non-business ventures, such as government and government reorganization and reform efforts. At the heart of OPA was the belief that politics, which was defined as the initiation of policy development, and administration, which was understood to be the implementation of policy, were two separate entities. As we learned earlier this belief was rooted in the early writings of Woodrow Wilson, which emphasized two key themes: 1) the distinction between politics and administration, and 2) that organizations, whether private or public, are to seek the "greatest possible efficiency ... through hierarchical structures of administrative management."[12]

New Public Management. Whereas OPA sought to create greater efficiency and economy through organizational hierarchy, NPM takes a more drastic turn toward not only incorporation and application of business techniques to government practices and application, which is not really new, but NPM is "a normative model, one signaling a profound shift in how we think about the role of public administrators, the nature of the profession, and how and why we do what we do."[13] NPM's basic purpose is to banish OPM; what its proponents, such as **David Osborne** and **Ted Gaebler**,[14] Osborne and Peter Plastrik,[15] Donald Kettl[16] and others, claim is an outdated, antiquated, and ill-equipped closed organizational system, unprepared to adapt to the management and organizational changes of the twenty-first century. The use of market mechanisms, such as supply and demand, enhanced communication and information technology, outsourcing and privatization, are regarded to be much better for purposes of guiding and leading the public sector.[17] Each of these factors is designed to improve output productivity and thus enhance policy outcomes, through greater accountability to customers and clients, redefinition of agency and department missions, and above all in decentralizing the decision making process in order to include greater input. Although some claim that democratic accountability is missing in the NPM model,[18] the NPM crowd is undeterred in its efforts to create a streamlined, market-based, entrepreneurial public sector. Responsiveness, accountability, measurability, adaptability, results-oriented, customers, clients, revenue generation and others are not only the buzzwords of the NPM, but what NPM proponents believe is the transformed purpose of public management.

NPM first gained an American audience with the publication of Osborne and Gaebler's *Reinventing Government* (1992). The authors, one a former city manager and the other a journalist and consultant, spent several years interviewing and researching government officials, primarily at the local and state levels, that adopted NPM techniques, and examined them for similarities. What they discovered unleashed a wave of change throughout all three levels of government, but especially at the federal level.

Reinvention Principles. The **reinvention principles** that Osborne and Gaebler found during their extensive research and interviewing of government officials regarding their approach to governance were straight out of a business management text, something that might have been penned by Tom Peters and Peter Drucker. Business thought, strategy, and procedures encompassed the work of many government officials, assisting them to deliver government services in a much more efficient, economic, and effective way. Osborne and Gaebler were clear in their pro-government affirmation: "Our purpose is not to criticize government, as so many have, but to renew it. We are as bullish on the future of government as we are bearish on the current condition of government."[19]

Box 6.1   Reinvention Principles from Osborne and Gaebler

1) *"Steering rather than rowing"*: where public officials act more like business entrepreneurs, seeking out a wide range of policy possibilities to choose from, "steering" the community toward a variety of options;

2) *"Empowering rather than serving"*: where public entrepreneurs shift ownership of public policies and policy initiatives to the community as a whole, "empowering" citizens and neighborhoods;

3) *"Injecting competition in service delivery"*: with public entrepreneurs recognizing that governments cannot provide every service at optimal satisfaction levels, and thus increases the use of privatization and contracting-out as two means of achieving higher levels of service quality and policy effectiveness;

4) *"Transforming rule-driven organizations"*: into mission-seeking, purpose-driven organizations that do not stifle human creativity and ingenuity;

5) *"Funding outcomes, not inputs"*: becomes the policy thrust of public officials, who believe that government should be directed toward accomplishing policy goals and outcomes as opposed to simply overseeing budget outlays;

6) *"Meeting the needs of the customer, not the bureaucracy"*: where the public entrepreneur learns from his private-sector counterpart "that unless one focuses on the customer, the citizen will never be happy;"

7) *"Earning rather than spending"*: where the public official responds to fiscal constraints by finding innovative ways to deal with impending budget shortfalls, rather than simply cutting programs;

8) *"Prevention rather than cure"*: where public entrepreneurs believe that preventing public policy problems is better than always trying to deal with the after effects of policy problems, even disasters (both natural and political);

9) *"From hierarchy to participation and teamwork"*: is the key phrase organizationally, where the public official sidesteps the old hierarchical organizations of the early twentieth century, to embrace a technologically savvy information-based age, one that governments and public managers must embrace in order to meet the current political, administrative, and social problems;

10) *"Leveraging change through the market"*: which is probably the crux of the NPM approach; it strongly argues that market forces, not politics, should govern each government jurisdiction, with the public manager creating the right environment so the market can operate efficiently and effectively.

Source: Janet V. Denhardt and Robert B. Denhardt, *The New Public Service: Serving, Not Steering* (Armonk, NY: M.E. Sharpe, 2003), 18–19.

Osborne and Gaebler's principles were quickly put into practice at the federal level. President Clinton appointed Vice President Gore to head the **National Performance Review** (NPR), an ad hoc organization with the mission to implement various elements of NPM into the federal bureaucracy, in order to achieve reduction of waste and overlapping functions. For example, within one year of implementation the NPR federal movement resulted in over 300,000 FTE reductions, regulatory reductions, and other cost-saving measures. In addition, Congress passed the **Government Performance and Results Act (1993)**, which required federal managers to establish specific performance standards and to manage for results. The law sought to reduce the level of waste and inefficiency found in federal government programs. (See the boxed insert below that provides Congress' findings and the purposes of the Act itself.) And just ten years later, during President Bush's first administration, the Office of Management and Budget (OMB) instituted the **Program Assessment Rating Tool (2001)**, which was an attempt "to link executive branch budget recommendations to the performance of specific federal programs."[20] One way to achieve this kind and level of performance in government at all levels was to forge a strong relationship between the forces of strategic planning (not a new thing to government) and performance management (somewhat of a new thing to government). The results were to prove beneficial, but with some concerns. In order to better understand, let's take a brief look at two tools used by performance managers: strategic planning and performance measurement.

Strategic Planning

While strategic planning is common occurrence in the private and non-profit sectors — and although a major element of any public manager's job is to plan — the systematized approach of strategic planning, particularly when connected with NPM principles, including performance measurement and ultimately leading to performance management, was somewhat different for public managers. Planning is simple; we all do it. However, when organizations, programs, and even institutions plan the process must be more formal and guided by not only principles but procedures and processes that will connect the goals and mission of the organization to fulfillment by the organization of those goals and objectives. However, in order to determine if and how well it accomplished various goals (from filling potholes in the city streets to achieving racial equality), organizations must tie their strategic planning to performance-based measures. Let's begin with some definitions.

Strategic planning is a comprehensive and continuous process that looks toward organization-specific goals and defines the performance to be measured. These organization-specific goals include the public interest, as stated in the enabling statute or incorporation mission by which the organization was created. Strategic planning is not the same as long-range planning in several ways. For example, long range planning is only interested in setting goals, not on how to achieve those goals; long range planning does not take into consideration the specific organizational environment, such as federal, state, or local governments; and third, long range planning is often a document that is put together by one or two individuals, usually top-level managers, whereas strategic planning is bottom-up process that involves several layers of the organization and many people, each contributing their skills and talents to the process of drawing up a strategic plan.[21]

There are several generally accepted steps in strategic planning.[22] First, the organization must establish its mission. A good place for a public agency to begin is to look at the **enabling statute** by which a legislature first created the agency. Private and non-profit organizations often are required to include such a mission statement in their articles of incorporation. A proper enabling statute includes some reference to the specific powers that were delegated from the legislature to the public agency, sometimes on all four corners (in the 1930s, this often meant four examples of what the agency could do). For example, Missouri's Office of Administration (OA) established a four-year (2005–2009) Strategic Plan based on the statute by which the Missouri state legislature first created their organization, and re-articulated by stating its Vision, Mission, and Values. OA's Vision is to "Ensure initiatives, policies, and services are implemented in a uniform and consistent manner throughout state government." Its Mission is to "provide guidance and assistance to state government entities through the implementation of executive office initiatives, the establishment of uniform procedures and rules as well as providing services to them in a cost-effective manner." The Missouri Office of Administration's four key values through which it hopes to accomplish its Vision and Mission are leadership, responsiveness, accountability, and partnership.

Second, the organization must assess the environment in which the strategic plan will be implemented, particularly looking for political, economic, or cultural factors that may affect, negatively or positively, the implementation and impact of the strategic plan. For example, before the city of Vancouver, Washington, initiated its recent Strategic Plan, it assessed the following environmental variables, noting that each was critical to the success of the Strategic Plan. To do so it conducted a citizen survey in 2004. The variables included 1) dealing with population growth; 2) traffic congestion, quality of road systems, and availability of public transportation; 3) fostering a small town feel; and 4) ensuring an environment of livability.[23]

Third, the organization must assess its own strengths and weaknesses—not an easy thing to do. Using the information derived from the Citizen Survey in 2004, for example, the City of Vancouver convened many public hearings, listening to the needs of its residents, and heard from its city employees through focus groups to understand how to deal with these various challenges. Fourth, according to Denhardt and Grubbs and others, the fourth step in the strategic planning process is to listen to the leaders of the organization who will be required to implement the plan and direct the organization. For example, the State of Oregon developed a collaborative effort "to enhance watershed health and restore native fish to Oregon waters." To accomplish this goal required the commitment, direction, and leadership of not only the planning organizers, but of the directors and their staffs of key state regulatory agencies which were charged with implementing the plan, such as the Oregon Water Resources Department and the Oregon Fish and Wildlife Department.[24] Planning by itself—even strategic planning—that is not tied to a performance system that provides accountability measures is simply an event or worse, "just a document. Therefore, it must be tied to performance measurement standards.[25] Some even go so far as to label this integrated process as **managing for results.**[26]

Performance Measurement

Performance measurement is a performance management tool that aims to quantitatively measure the inputs, outputs, and, especially, outcomes of public programs, thus providing public managers with more information regarding the efficiency and effectiveness of those programs. Another way to define it is that "performance measurement is government's way of determining whether it is providing a quality product or service at a reasonable cost." Basically, a good performance measurement system should be able to provide answers to questions such as 1) what was achieved? 2) how efficiently and effective was the work completed? and 3) how were the citizens aided by the effort?[27]

In 1980 the federal **Government Accounting Standards Board (GASB)**, based on authority granted it from the Civil Service Reform Act of 1978, defined performance measurement "as an assessment of an organization's performance, including measures of productivity (quantifying the outputs and inputs of an organization and expressing the two as a ratio—output to input, such as inspections per personnel per day); effectiveness, which determines the relationship of an organization's outputs to the organization's prescribed goals; quality, which examines the accuracy, thoroughness, and complexity of an output; and timeliness, which measures the time involved to accomplish the output."[28] Today, the categorization of performance measures is fairly routine and accepted. The various categories include:

- *Input measure* (agency level and indicates the quantity and quality of various organizational resources, such as personnel and funding);
- *Process measure* (agency level and indicates how well goods and services are delivered, i.e. the effectiveness measure, such as percentage of tax refunds mailed within 30 days);
- *Output measure* (agency level and indicates the quantity and quality of goods and services produced, such as number of potholes filled, percentage of city households participating in citywide voluntary recycling program, number of foster care homes, etc.);
- *Outcome measure* (agency level and indicates the societal effect of these goods and services, i.e. the output measures, such as impact of voluntary recycling program upon citizen's civic involvement or percentage of training school residents taking the GED test who pass it).[29]

Generally speaking, a sound and working performance measurement system should be, among other things, a) results-oriented, b) reliable, c) valid, d) quantitative, e) cost-effective, f) easy to read, and g) comparable. In addition, **benchmarks**, or baseline data provided for comparative purposes, must be established in order to provide direction and guidance to the organization's performance measurement system. North Carolina's Benchmarking Project, which began in 1995 as an initiative by University of North Carolina's School of Government, is a good example of how local governments can assess and compare service delivery and costs associated with that service delivery in a variety of areas (residential refuse collection, policy patrols, street maintenance and repair, building inspections, jail operations, and foster care to name a few) to other localities and municipalities.[30] Before we conclude our discussion on the use of strategic planning and performance measurement systems, let's look at a state government example.

Minnesota Pollution Control Agency (MPCA). The MPCA has developed and carried out strategic plans since the early 1990s, with the primary goal of facilitating quality agency operation and enhancing controls for more effective environmental protection.

Originally organized according to air, land, and water categorization, the MPCA realized that by the end of 1999 its organizational structure was not well-suited for an outcome-based performance measurement system. Thus the MPCA instituted a three-phase operation: 1) developing program performance measures, 2) adding environmental outcome measures to the program performance measures to enhance organizational and program effectiveness, and 3) finally adding cost efficiency to program effectiveness and environmental outcome measures to provide a well-balanced **performance measurement system**.

As to be expected there is a wrinkle in the system. The MPCA operates within the context of the National Environmental Performance Partnership System (NEPPS), which is in agreement with the national government Environmental Performance Agency (EPA). The NEPPS has a contractual relationship with the MPCA to report performance measurement data. The wrinkle is that NEPPS is based largely on outputs, but the MPCA prefers to deal with outcomes. In order to fulfill its contractual obligations with the EPA through the NEPPS the MPCA is "institutionalizing periodic reporting as an aid to executive-level decision-making." Now the MPCA's upper level management team is beginning to focus on outcome-based measures, something that is more difficult to quantify; yet is politically more desirable. Accomplishing this goal requires a sophisticated data management system, one that is costing MPCA approximately $8 million—one that will focus on outcome-based, geographically-based (natural ecosystem and river basin components) systems.

The results: the MPCA is now up-to-date with a performance management system; one that has redesigned business processes, a fully integrated strategic planning performance measurement system, and a fully revamped public personnel system that will enable the MPCA to meet future performance measurement and strategic planning needs. For example, in order to accomplish these goals the MPCA will institute five-year strategic plans rather than one-year plans. This will provide a larger performance data base of information to draw from, thus enhancing the MPCA's goal of environmental protection and agency effectiveness.[31]

Summary. Performance-based measurement coupled with strategic planning tools, has taken the public sector by storm. We have seen that strategic planning is not a new phenomenon in the public sector. All levels of government have engaged in some form of strategic planning, particularly in the area of budgeting,[32] for the last four decades. The problem lies in implementation. Development of a strategic plan is one thing, but implementing it requires some type of accountability system, something that ties goals with results; hence, the need for a performance based measurement system. But more important than simply a performance based measurement system is the movement to performance management. Robert J. O'Neill Jr., executive director of the **International City/County Management Association (ICMA)**, for example, writes that "When used in conjunction with (strategic planning), performance data become (s) part of a larger performance management system to improve quality, productivity, and customer satisfaction."[33] A large and steadily growing literature base strongly advocates the use and effectiveness of performance measurement systems, particularly when coupled with strategic planning tools, in order to accomplish a variety of goals, including the use of better marketing techniques, to promote public service delivery. In fact, some even claim that performance management is one of six trends that are transforming government.[34] Performance management is transforming the public sector.

However, is the transformation all for the better? Some disagree for several reasons. One, the managing for results idea, which as we noted earlier is a subset of the larger NPM movement, embraced not only an increased emphasis on results but on the managerial authority to achieve such results. After a decade of results reform there is a gap between achieving results and increased managerial authority to oversee and govern those results.[35] Two, the application of private sector performance measurement variables, based largely on meeting the profit motive, to a public sector system raises various tensions between the competing administrative and political goals and means to accomplish those goals.[36]

Does the performance measurement theology adequately attend to the public interest? At an empirical level, the performance measurement approach seems to neglect or ignore the reality that public servants who attend to the public interest are more productive.[37] Yet, performance measurement practices continue to ignore the importance of ethical behavior in the public interest. In a recent national survey, only 43 percent of human resources professionals said their organizations include ethical conduct as part of employees' performance appraisals.[38] Many critics argue that the pursuit of performance-based measurements for public organizations comes at the expense of democratic values and social justice values, such as social equity, which are not easily quantifiable, but nevertheless essential to democracy.[39] Similarly, the performance measurement movement subordinates "core aspects of democratic constitutionalism to simply achieving results."[40] Finally, there are many who challenge the performance movement and argue that the one-size-fits-all mentality, a panacea to perceived inefficiency, is not the only answer to correcting performance-based ills in a democratic society.[41]

Performance-based measurement is more than likely here to stay, particularly since it plays well to politicians and a citizenry that is demanding wasteful spending, for example, be curtailed. (See Case Study on Iowa Charter Agencies.) One of the main questions and ultimately hurdles to overcome for both the proponents and opponents, however, is to learn how to adapt a highly sterile, quantitative and results-oriented movement to a dynamic, qualitative, and public interest motivated democratic system. Not many argue against program inefficiency and ineffectiveness; not many contend that accountability is passé. It is clear, though, that at least some make valid arguments against the one-size-fits-all mentality that pervades the results-oriented or outcomes-based organizational and program mindset, precisely because it adequately fails to account for non-measurable administrative and policy outcomes, or that seemingly circumvent constitutional values.

Case Study   Refocusing Government on Results: Iowa's Charter Agencies

The princely sum of $212 doesn't sound like much for a state facing a $300-million budget shortfall, but what it represents is priceless in the eyes of some Iowa officials. That's how much one agency saved by buying a round-trip plane ticket itself instead of through the state's travel contractor. It's just one example, says (former) Iowa Governor Tom Vilsack, of a new way of doing the state's business that "throws rules and regulations out the window in return for a focus on results."

While the notion of trading freedom for results isn't new, government struggles to capitalize on such a notion. Iowa's answer: Charter Agencies. Under legislation worked out between Vilsack, a Democrat, and a Republican-controlled legislature, all of the state's major departments were offered a deal: be cut loose from a whole range of rules governing everything from procurement to personnel, and be spared across-the-board budget cuts, if they would commit to produce measurable results and collectively come up with $15 million in savings, new revenues or some combination of the two.

While money triggered the deal, the heart of the matter was freedom. Six agencies signed up: social services, corrections, veterans affairs, natural resources and the department of revenue, along with the state alcoholic beverage division. These Charter Agencies represent 30 percent of the executive budget and 50 percent of executive branch employees. The state lottery, which operates independently, also signed on.

The five-year pilot program has produced some intriguing early results. First, Charter Agencies were indeed spared the across-the-board cuts. Second, they did come up with $22 million—$2.2 million in cuts and $20 million in increased revenues.

More valuable than the savings may be the changes in how the Charter Agencies conduct business. Charter Agencies can quickly staff up (and down) according to need. They can purchase information technology systems expeditiously. For example, the alcohol control board has been able to quickly and effectively revamp its systems for tracking licenses, collecting taxes and handling inventory. Corrections are working more actively to get inmates work experience. Natural resources have streamlined permitting. Social services have streamlined eligibility screening. Revenue has pushed its tax e-filing effort to the highest rate of any state.

Not every change was a direct result of this new freedom, but it has clearly inspired a new way of thinking.

Source: Ash Institute for Democratic Governance and Education, "State of Iowa Wins Award from Harvard," Harvard University, John F. Kennedy School of Government, http://www.ash institute.harvard.edu/Ash/pr_2005w_casi.htm (accessed October 2007).

New Managerialism. NPM was not limited to the practicalities of government management. As the Denhardts note NPM was rooted in sound academic and intellectual foundations, including public choice theory (and its companion theory principal agent theory)[42] and the **new managerialism** that swept across Australia and New Zealand in the late 1980s and early 1990s.[43] Both intellectual foundations argued that public managers require incentives to manage; incentives that are founded in market mechanisms, such as supply and demand and privatization. Interestingly, while NPM sought to make public management and the public sector more like private management and the private sector, some like H. George Frederickson, Louis Gawthrop, Gary Wamsley and the Blacksburg scholars, **Charles Goodsell** and many others[44] argued that the characteristics associated with NPM, such as those emphasized by Osborne and Gaebler in their groundbreaking work,[45] were not representative of government service and government employees. Challenging the notion that NPM can only be compared with OPA, the Denhardts argue that the NPS is a viable democratic alternative to NPM, focusing on "public service, democratic governance, and civic engagement."[46]

Theoretical Foundations of the New Public Service

First, at its core NPS is a normative model for public agency purpose and public management work. Whereas OPA called for a closed model of organization, NPS called for an open model; whereas NPM argued for a market-based system oriented toward customer satisfaction, NPS countered with a return to democratic pluralism and greater citizen input into the decision-making process. Early critics of the OPA model, such as Dwight Waldo and Robert Dahl, sought to highlight the need for competing values to efficiency and economy, such as administrative responsibility and democratic pluralism,[47] but their prophetic voices were too early and faint at the time, and the rational man model spawned by Herbert Simon drowned out all others.[48] With questions regarding the exclusive viability of NPM for bringing about greater organizational and individual productivity,[49] and more importantly the wealth of literature and public attention to the need for greater community and citizen involvement in the democratic process,[50] and coupling that with the enhanced community role of public managers;[51] it is clear that neither OPA or NPM approaches to public administration and public management are sufficient to explain or describe the contemporary changes and current demands placed upon public officials, or more importantly, to explain the importance of the public interest. The NPS model described by the Denhardts is such an attempt.

Box 6.2   Democracy and the Public Interest

Michael Sandel, a democratic philosopher, argues that individual interest and choice should be protected by government through enactment of various legal and political procedures, but that in order to pursue the greater good or the **public interest**, citizens must look beyond or even set aside their self-interests, which requires a more knowledgeable and active citizenry. Others, such as H. George Frederickson and Jane Mansbridge, claim that there is a need for a "spirit of public administration" and a "public spirit." Frederickson's intent is directed more toward the enhancement of social equity, whereas Mansbridge's emphasis is on political and managerial altruism.

Sourcses: See Denhardt and Denhardt, 27. Denhardt and Denhardt cite Michael Sandel, *Democracy's Discontent* (Cambridge, MA: Belknap, 1996), 30, 5–6; H. George Frederickson, *The Spirit of Public Administration* (San Francisco, CA: Jossey-Bass, 1997); Jane Mansbridge, ed., *Beyond Self-Interest* (Chicago, IL: University of Chicago Press, 1990); Jane Mansbridge, "Public Spirit in Political Systems," in *Values and Public Policy*, ed. Henry J. Aaron, Thomas Mann, and Timothy Taylor (Washington, D.C.: Brookings Institution, 1994), 146–72.

Second, over the past decade plus there is a renewed interest in community and civil society. The Denhardts claim that several reasons surface as to why individuals, and especially Americans, are interested in renewing community, including increased alienation in a technological society, social and political dislocations in response to the **Vietnam War** and the civil rights movement of the 1960s, and even the fear associated with the existence of and threat to use weapons of mass destruction.[52] Whatever the reason, people are searching, and the search runs the gamut of society, including education,[53] religion,[54] moral order,[55] and politics.[56]

Putnam's analysis, for example, suggests a decrease in the number of Americans who engage in voluntary associations, including bowling leagues, churches, neighborhood groups, and various civic associations. Because these institutions and organizations are the heartbeat of society, with their decreasing emphasis in the development and order of society the unencumbered pursuit of individual rights takes precedent. The role that public administrators and managers play is critical to facilitating and directing the discussion of good public policy based on sound administrative and managerial principles, while at the same time listening to and interacting with various interests and the community as a whole.[57]

A third theoretical strand in the development of the NPS is **organizational humanism**. Having covered this perspective in our chapter on organizational theory and behavior, it is our intention to simply highlight a couple of points that figure prominently in the foundation of NPS. First, organizational humanism is not new. It dates back to the 1920s and the work by Harvard organizational theorists Roethlisberger and Dickson at the Hawthorne plant of the **Western Electric Company**, where they discovered that human beings are important components in the workplace.[58] Social psychology and group dynamics was the centerpiece of Kurt Lewin's work in the 1930s, where among many other findings he showed that group commitment was critical to decision making.[59]

Probably the most crucial to the development of organizational humanism was the work of psychologist Abraham Maslow, management theorist Douglas McGregor, and organizational behavioralist Chris Argyris.[60] Each was committed to fostering growth in what was becoming known as the human relations school of thought; the stream of research and thought that emphasized the role of the individual *in* the organization rather than the adaptation of the individual's needs *to* the organization. Argyris and **Robert Golembiewski** took this research to another level, labeling it organizational development, which was contrary to the popular research and thinking of the rational model of administration. Other aspects of organizational humanism were captured in the movement labeled the New Public Administration (not to be confused with NPM), led by such luminaries as H. George Frederickson and Robert Denhardt,[61] where among other critiques they argued against the traditional hierarchical model of bureaucratic organization and some, like Frederickson, argued for even greater administrative discretion on the part of the public manager in order to facilitate social equity in the implementation of public policy.

The fourth theoretical root of the NPS is **postmodern public administration**. Adherents of postmodern public administration contend several things. One, we have lost the capacity to determine what is real and what is not. Using world views and scientific theories to describe and explain reality is simply not good enough; there are too many unexplained phenomena. Two, individuals are human, not robots, and they have feelings and emotions. It is difficult to describe such reality in terms of the rationalist model of behavior, and thus the postmodernists advocated interpretive and value-critical approaches or examinations of human behavior and reality. And three, communication in the traditional hierarchical organizational pattern is devoid of what postmodernists refer to as discourse, or "the notion that public problems are more likely resolved through discourse than through 'objective' measurements or rational analysis."[62] Human beings want to talk, including public managers, and they want to talk in a non-rational, goal-oriented way; they simply want to discuss problems, hoping that continued discussion will develop into "negotiation and consensus building."[63]

Summary. These four theoretical foundations discussed by the Denhardts and highlighted here largely account for the primary theoretical differences between NPS and OPA and, especially, NPM. Next, we introduce the student to seven practical public management differences between the NPS and the other two approaches. The Denhardts readily acknowledge "that differences, even substantial differences, exist in these various viewpoints,"[64] but that these seven capture the heart of the NPS, which is fulfilling public service in the public interest.

The Practice of New Public Service

The NPS is not simply a theoretical construct, but it is a management reality. It is where the city and county manager live and work; it is the crux of the state personnel director's job focus; it is where the non-profit agent interacts with public sector agencies on a daily basis, working for better social service delivery to people in need; and most importantly it is where the citizens interact with public officials on a variety of policy and management issues. The NPS is about public service. Elmer Staats, retired Comptroller General of the United States, probably said it best when he paraphrased the British scholar Harold Laski on what is public service: "It is the discovery that people serve themselves only as they serve others."[65] To truly have this understanding of public service requires a different mindset than either the OPM or NPM represents.

Serve Citizens, Not Customers. First, the NPS stresses that the focal point of public service is the citizenry, not customers or clients. Certainly, the recipient of a direct transaction of government, such as public daycare for latchkey children, is a customer; or the parent who sends their child to the public school system is a client of that agency (education), but each one is first a citizen. David Osborne and Ted Gaebler even use the terms customer and citizen interchangeably. "... rather than government managers choosing service providers in a competitive bidding process, it lets each citizen choose his or her service provider. It establishes accountability to customers."[66] But even Osborne and Gaebler acknowledge that citizens are not always the focus of government service; it is the recipient of government contracts, or the beneficiary of government program funding. For example, who is the real customer of the Department of Defense: the citizenry or Boeing? Who are the primary clients or customers of the **Department of Education**: parents or principals?

Our point is that the concepts of citizenry and customers are different. Customers seek to maximize their self-interests and individual benefits, while the citizenry are described as individuals within the common contractual arrangement of a democratic-republic who, because of giving up certain private rights to government and government's authorities, gain protection and security from each other and outsiders. Citizens remain citizens even though they reasonably expect the government to deliver services in a convenient, secure, reliable, personal, fair, and fiscally responsible fashion.[67]

Seek the Public Interest. Second, the NPS argues that public managers "have a central and important role in helping ... citizens to articulate the public interest, and conversely, that shared values and collective citizen interests should guide the behavior and decision making of public administrators." The Denhardts, and others who promote the NPS (or variations thereof),[68] do not necessarily reject the need for performance outcomes of the political process, or that public managers should use substantial discretionary authority to substitute their beliefs for the will of the people, but they do contend that public managers "have a unique and vitally important responsibility to engage with citizens and create forums for public dialogue."[69]

Box 6.3   Public Interest in the NPS

The search for **public interest** is found in citizens' search for the needs of the larger community, to look beyond their individual short-term interests, which are often economic and politically-based, to a broader public interest that encompasses what Sandel refers to as "a sense of belonging, a concern for the whole, and a moral bond with the community." Of course the naysayer and cynic is ever present, arguing that there is no such thing as the public interest; that the public interest is simply a procedural or process oriented concept, one that avails itself to furthering the political and administrative rights of all citizens; or that it is the collection of broad and shared individual and group interests. We contend that the public interest is not simply a procedural concept, but a normative concept, even an ethical idea, that denotes a standard "for evaluating specific public policies and a goal which the political order should pursue." It is THIS that the public manager should strive to fulfill.

Sourcses: Denhardt and Denhardt cite Sandel, 79. Denhardt and Denhardt also cite early eminent public administration statesmen, such as Paul Appleby (early work) and Emmette Redford, as examples of public interest voices crying out in a world of pluralism and negativism toward the normative and moral meaning of the public interest.

Value Citizenship over Entrepreneurship. The third principle of public management stressed by the Denhardts as being a crucial part of the NPS is citizenship over entrepreneurship. The first of these seven principles stressed the value of citizen over customer; that it is critically important to recognize that governments govern in a political environment, and as such the focus of government programs and service delivery are citizens, not merely customers. Citizen is a political concept; customer is a business concept. Citizens are the heart of a democracy; customers and those who serve the customers (entrepreneurs) are the center of a market. Thus, it behooves us to briefly explore this third principle, because it is at the heart of what is truly the goal of the NPS: the public interest.

Recall that Osborne and Gaebler stressed that government should be steering rather than rowing, meaning that government generally and public managers (or public entrepreneurs) specifically are to guide or steer the apparatus and delivery of services to the specific client and/or customer, using, among other means, the market-based system of supply and demand to provide these services in the most efficient and economic way. The NPM manager is not so much a manager as he/she is an **entrepreneur**, or a risk-taker. This view sees the public entrepreneur with considerable more discretionary authority than the public manager in the OPA approach. Of course, along with risks for success come risks resulting in failure: leveraging the county employees' retirement funds in high risk stocks and bonds, and in the end losing everything.

The NPS approach envisions the public manager not as a policy or administrative entrepreneur, but as an enabler, guide, and **facilitator**. Government is not the end all; governance, or the "exercise of public authority,"[70] is the key factor in public management today. Governance is the cooperation between government, non-profit, and private sources in order to develop and implement public policy.[71] The public manager, thus, becomes a conduit or facilitator in matching resources, infrastructure, citizen groups, and policy objectives in order to meet a desired end. Simply basing one's public management decision on the vagaries of the market is short-sighted at best and detrimental to the democratic governance process at worst. Whereas OPA is bound by laws and regulations, and the public administrator is simply the implementer of political defined objectives; and where the NPM bases managerial decision making on the externalities of economic and market considerations; it is the NPS that focuses the role of government (or governance) on democracy and social criteria, where the voice of the citizen is necessary and desirable in the public decision making process, whether it is where to put the new soccer field in Anywhere, USA, to whether and/or how Social Security should be changed.[72]

Think Strategically, Act Democratically. This fourth principle embodied in the NPS argues that establishing the vision of a new policy (e.g. the federal No Child Left Behind Act) and implementing that new policy is not merely the role of government officials located in Washington D.C., Raleigh, North Carolina, or Polk County, Iowa, but the focus "is to join together all parties in the process of both designing and carrying out programs that will move (the policy, our words) in the desired direction."[73] Enjoining greater involvement in the policy making process, as well in the development of the policy, is the focus of the NPS. Among other factors, the desire is to encourage greater civic knowledge and participation. Obviously, not all citizens are interested in participating in policy matters. In fact, most Americans are both unaware of and uninterested in political and policy matters. And when Americans do participate, it is usually when they have a vested political or economic self-interest, not because they want to become more aware of the civic and political—to say nothing of the administrative. So, how is this a realistic means to thinking strategically, while acting democratically?

Government (and/or the **governance process**) is indeed not the only answer, but the answer, or at least part of the answer, lies in the fact that government must create opportunities for igniting citizen action and building community. And this means that government must be perceived as being open and accessible, or being responsive to citizen demands. If the citizens do not believe this, do not perceive this to be true, then regardless of whether or not the government is open, accessible and responsive, the citizens will not respond.

One tool to enhance citizen involvement in the twenty-first century is to enhance civic knowledge. And one way to do that is to increase awareness and knowledge of information technology and its application to simple government service delivery as well as the governance process. Congress passed the *E-Government Act* in 2002 in order to "enhance the management and promotion of electronic government services and processes …" and to "promote the use of the Internet and other information technologies to provide increased opportunities for citizen participation in government." The Act was designed to expand e-government initiatives, such as e-rulemaking, e-records management, e-authentication, such as e-signatures, and other such enhancements. Many of these goals have been reached. Check out any federal government web site and see what you can do as a citizen!

But e-service delivery is only part, and a small part at that. What about e-town halls or e-citizen complaints and e-government response and/or action to those complaints, all within a much shorter time period than in a non-e-government environment? Virtual town halls are a reality, and much of the success of e-government is taking place outside of the United States. For example, the Barcelona City Council (Spain) has a program that facilitates exchange of information between citizens of Barcelona and its city council members. The city council holds an e-town hall meeting, with different topics covered each month. Also, much work is being done in England to enhance the "potential of e-democracy to empower grassroots civic networks …"[74] Here in the United States, the Office of E-Government facilitates upgrading all federal agency sites, and initiating greater use of e-democracy techniques. States and local governments are also moving into e-government. For example, former Minnesota governor Jesse Ventura received up to 13,000 emails a week from citizens, giving him their opinions of a range of state and local issues.[75]

Recognize That Accountability Isn't Simple. Citizen involvement in democratic accountability takes us to the fifth principle of NPS: that all need to recognize and understand that democratic accountability is not as simple as the proponents of the NPM wish us to believe. In fact, as researcher **Robert Behn** advocates, the OPM approach is actually more dedicated, at least indirectly, to **democratic accountability** than is the NPM, primarily because the OPM sees accountability in an indirect relationship between citizens and public managers through the check and balance system.[76] Democratic accountability is not an ancient concept, but it is certainly a key variable in the clash between the democratic and administrative states, and between elected officials and public managers.

The question arises: to whom are the public officials accountable, and for what? According to the NPS approach, as opposed to either of the other approaches, accountability is both a legal and moral issue. It requires that public managers respond not only to their personal conscience, but the citizenry conscience and predispositions toward right and wrong as well as the organizational framework, including rules, regulations, and culture in which they work. OPM contends that public managers are accountable to the organization in which they work, while the NPM contends that managers are responsible to the entrepreneurial influence of the market. Second, what are unelected civil servants accountable to? Behn answers this: both process and results.[77]

Answering this question; however, only raises additional ones, such as "Who decides what results government should be accountable for producing? How are the results determined? How and who determines whether or not the results have been met?

Who is responsible for implementing the accountability process? How will this process work?"[78] The NPS response: the public manager is accountable to more than just the organization and hierarchy, more than just the market; the public manager is responsible to a myriad of institutions, laws, groups, norms, values, and processes. Why? Because the NPS contends that at the center of accountability is citizenship and the public interest.[79]

Serve Rather Than Steer. The sixth principle of the NPS approach to public management is the emphasis on using value-based, shared leadership. Under the OPA approach, for example, leadership was concentrated in the hands of top-level officials of the hierarchy, while in the NPM style decision making and leadership is decentralized.

The NPS approach to leadership is threefold: values-based, shared, and servant-oriented. First, values-based leadership is *transformational*, not simply transactional.[80] James MacGregor Burns describes **transformational leadership** as leadership that unites leaders and followers, rather than envisioning leadership as something that leaders do to followers. Burns' view of leadership is one of purpose and power, where effective transformational leaders are able to successfully use the power of their office for the benefit of the follower, rather than to force the follower into some type of submission. On the other hand, **transactional leadership** is an exchange of values between a leader and a follower, or between what Burns identifies as "initiator and respondent."[81] The transactional leader is one who provides the follower with a reward for meeting the expectations of the leader (the toddler receives cheers and claps from the parent when she goes to the restroom on her own), whereas transformational leadership is based more on the enduring values of morality, ethics, and the like. Ethical leadership causes both the leader and the follower to respond differently, both toward each other and toward the accomplishment of the goal.[82]

Second, the NPS approach advocates **shared leadership**. Shared leadership engages the citizenry; it empowers them to be part of the decision-making process. Obviously, not every public management venue is open to shared leadership (I don't think we expected President Bush to take a vote of the citizens and residents of New York City to determine whether or not the United States should respond militarily to Osama bin Laden after it was learned he was the mastermind of 9/11.) However, the decision by the city council to decide whether or not to use a vacant lot for an expansion of the town recreation center or to build one Little League regulation baseball field and two soccer fields is an issue that the town's citizens can and should be involved in making. The theory and developing concept of shared leadership has a growing literature base, focusing on networks of involved diverse stakeholders.[83]

Third, the NPS approach promotes serving rather than owning. The NPM approach sees public managers as entrepreneurs, seeking out the best buy for various public services, their delivery and implementation, and evaluation. The Denhardts are quick to point out that results, whether good or bad, of entrepreneurial decision-making in the private sector falls squarely on the shoulders of the business owners and investors—a limited group. **Entrepreneurial decision-making** in the public sector has a much broader effect upon the citizens and not just the recipients of the services provided. Thus when the decision to privatize jails, for example, does not work, primarily because of poor or no levels of accountability, then the effect is not felt in simply the penal environment, but to the citizenry and taxpayers at large.

Value People, Not Just Productivity. The seventh principle associated with the NPS approach is the emphasis on people. People are the center-piece of the NPS's approach to public administration broadly and public management narrowly. Slightly modifying the Denhardts' language we might say that the OPA used control to achieve efficiency, the NPM used incentives to achieve productivity, and the NPS used people to respect the ideal of the public interest. It boils down to this: What is most important? In the OPA approach the focus was solely on achieving efficiency, and the role of people was simply that of an automaton, one that according to theorists like Frederick Taylor, were simply cogs in the wheel of efficiency. Management could basically do what it wanted to with the people in order to get them to produce the most number of goods and/or services with the least number of inputs of resources. Under the NPM approach public managers, or rather public entrepreneurs, use people to meet objectives, reach desired results, using among other means contracts to set and enforce the level of results desired. Thus, if you want the person to perform differently or better then you must entice them with market-based incentives. The NPS approach; however, does not see people as simply cogs in the wheel of commerce, or agents in a principal-agent theory, but as human beings who display values and norms, such as trust, dignity, and service.[84] Of course for this to happen, argue the Denhardts, government must advance the notion of citizen participation and empowerment, which in turn "build(s) citizenship, responsibility, and trust, and advance(s) the values of service in the public interest."[85]

Contrasting Management and Leadership in the Public Interest

When we think of leadership we conjure up images of General George Patton riding high in the turret of a tank, commanding the respect of his troops. Or we see Bill Gates, the quiet billionaire technocrat-entrepreneur of Microsoft, musing and mulling over other ideas about how to make computer software better, specifically Microsoft software. And we see President George Bush surveying the damage at Ground Zero following the deadliest attack on American soil since Pearl Harbor, and later issuing the order to hunt down the mastermind, Osama bin Laden. But we guarantee that the average person, student or not, does not see a mid-level federal manager in the Department of Transportation, or envision the Broken Arrow, Oklahoma, city manager (Jim Twombley), or the Harnett County, North Carolina, Director of Planning (formerly George Jackson), or even the State of North Carolina's Director of Budget (David McKoy) as leaders. We contend that each of these civil servants is and should be considered leaders; perhaps we should refer to them as leader-managers.

What Is Leadership?

Leadership is many things to many people—trite, but true. Justice Stewart of the U.S. Supreme Court once defined obscenity as, "I know it when I see it." The same holds true for leadership. Popular images of leaders focus on individual talent and the "self-made man." Closer examination of leadership reveals that talent may be over-rated compared the luck of riding a tide of advantages of location, timing and background. Was Bill Gates a leader due to his talent and genius alone, or was his success due to being born in 1955 —just old enough for the PC, but too young to have taken the IBM junior executive track? Of course Bill Gates had a unique talent, but was his leadership genius born—or was it made by his family, society, schools and the uncanny timing and location of success (luck?)[86]. There are theories of leadership, but there are very few solid definitions of leadership. What is public leadership all about? And are there any similarities with public management?

Box 6.4   Definitions of 'Leadership'

"A leader is one who attempts to exert influence through some form of power that results in gaining compliance from those being led" (Vasu, Stewart, and Garson).

"Leadership is the process of influencing the activities of a group in efforts toward goal attainment in a given situation" (Starling).

"Leadership is the capacity of someone to direct and energize people to achieve goals" (Rainey).

"Public leadership may thus be defined as an inter-human process of identifying, defining, and carrying out goals using democratically sanctioned norms and behaviors" (Rusaw).

"The new leader ... is one who commits people to action, who converts followers into leaders, and who may convert leaders into agents of change" (Bennis).

"Leadership is a concept of owing certain things to the institution. It is a way of thinking about institutional heirs, a way of thinking about stewardship as contrasted with ownership." (De Pree).

Sources: Michael L. Vasu, Debra W. Stewart, and G. David Garson, Organizational Behavior and Public Management, 3d ed. (New York: Marcel Dekker, 1998), 90; Grover Starling, Managing the Public Sector, 5th ed. (Fort Worth, TX: Harcourt Brace, 1998), 358; Hal G. Rainey, Understanding and Managing Public Organizations (San Francisco, CA: Jossey-Bass, 2003), 290; A. Carol Rusaw, Leading Public Organizations: An Integrative Approach (Fort Worth, TX: Harcourt, 2001), 3–4; Warren Bennis and Burt Nanus, Leaders: The Strategies for Taking Charge (New York: Harper and Row, 1985), 3; and Max De Pree, Leadership is an Art (New York: Dell, 1989), 12, 148.

Similarities with Management

First, leadership is about people—the people who are leaders, the people who the leaders lead (followers), and the people who are the recipients, clients, customers, citizens, etc. of the goods or services that are produced and/or delivered by the organizations, both private and public, that the leaders lead in order to produce the good and/or deliver the service. Second, leadership is about relationship—the relationship between the leaders and the followers. Third, leadership is about use of authority to influence—influencing others in the organization in order to achieve a desired goal. Fourth, leadership is about achievement of goals—goals that are set for the purposes of furthering the mission of the organization. Fifth, leadership is about change—change of the processes, goals, people, relationship, influence, and even the means of achievement in order to accomplish the mission of the organization. People, relationship, influence, achievement, and change: Isn't this what public managers do as well as what generals, presidents, and business icons do? They may do them in different organizational settings and cultures, under different written and unwritten rules, in closer or more distance quarters with the front line workers, but there are enough similarities to warrant that managers do leadership things and leaders do manager things.

Warren Bennis and Ben Nanus wrote that there is a major difference between leaders and managers (whether private or public). Bennis said that, "Managers are people who do things right and leaders are people who do the right thing." He clarified this by noting that, "The difference may be summarized as activities of vision and judgment—effectiveness versus activities of mastering routines—efficiency."[87] For Bennis the leaders he interviewed viewed themselves as leaders and not managers. Their perspective of leadership was to concern themselves with basic purposes, general direction, vision, and transformation, not only of the organization they led, but of the culture or environment in which they found themselves and their organization. Managers, however, did not do the same thing as leaders, and thus were not considered leaders. Managers "... spend their time on the 'how tos,' the proverbial 'nuts and bolts' of the organization, not with the larger picture."[88] Rainey takes umbrage with Bennis' unfair assessment of the lack of substance in the volumes of recent management and leadership literature. In addition, he notes that the authors' own research on ninety leaders in the public, private, and non-profit sectors, "... lack[ed] clarity and convincing validation."[89] This may be true as well, but in broader terms we simply disagree with Bennis' assessment of the supposed differences between what (or who) is a leader and what (or who) is a manager, and more importantly what each do.

Box 6.5   City Managers Are Leaders, Too

In a recent study of city managers the author found that all of the city managers examined exemplified leadership qualities, whether in terms of leading the charge to dedicate a downtown park, to push for increasing the number of businesses and business start-ups in a downtown economic development enterprise zone, or demonstrating willingness to lead the community by hammering nails in a Habitat for Humanity home on a Saturday morning.

City managers lead by example; city managers lead by displaying administrative discipline in a sometimes volatile political environment; and city managers lead by displaying character.

Leadership is not just about getting the job done or even getting it done right; it is about caring for people and projects enough that the public manager does things right so that he or she gets the right things done.

Source: Stephen M. King, "The Moral Manager: Vignettes of Virtue in Virginia," Public Integrity 8, no. 2 (Spring 2006).

Further, McGill University management expert Henry Mintzberg sees similarities between what leaders and managers do. He categorized the similarities into four distinct roles, including interpersonal, informational, decisional, and negotiation.[90] Interpersonal roles are largely figurehead, liaison, ceremonial, or symbolic, such as when the city manager welcomes dignitaries to the city. Informational roles are when managers act in a broad-sweeping fashion to collect, use, and disseminates information, such as when state department directors of budgeting or even the director of the federal **Office of Management Budget** gathers, uses, and distributes that information for the purpose of putting together the government's budget. Decisional roles are entrepreneurial based, such as when a county manager or county economic development director searches out prospective business and industry owners for possible relocation. And fourth, managers act as negotiators, such as when personnel directors act as a go-between with employees and the state regulatory board investigating personnel issues.

Conclusion: Management, Leadership, and the Public Interest

This chapter establishes public management within the New Public Service (NPS) approach to public administration; an approach that, when contrasted with the Old Public Administration (OPA) and New Public Management (NPM) approaches, emphasizes the roles of citizenship and community as well as organizational humanism and aspects of postmodern public administration, as opposed to strictly defining and attaining efficiency and economy and, whether within the formal organizational structure and rules or within the market orientation. Public management is more than just about rules and hierarchy; it is more ideal than simply setting and establishing performance goals; it is about people. It is about fulfilling the public interest.

Public management differs from private management in several ways. First, public management incorporates the concept of the public interest. We recognize and acknowledge the diversity of opinion regarding the meaning and application of this normative and somewhat subjective concept, but we also understand that the public interest is what public servants talk about when they are asked what it means to them to serve the public, or to do the job they job. Second, public management is situated somewhere in the middle of a continuum ranging from government ownership to private enterprise, depending upon agencies and enterprises that do the serving, to the public that receives the direct and indirect benefit of the services delivered, to the political and administrative influence of public agencies.[91] Third, public management's purpose is simply different from that of private management. Whereas private management is designed to reach the highest performance level in order to make the most profit on the number of widgets sold, public management not only strives for high performance, it also operates under stricter scrutiny, including democratic accountability.

Finally, managers are leaders because they are empowered to establish and reach goals, use resources, set agendas, strategize visions, empower employees and citizens alike, and effectively move the community forward. Public management is not for the weak at heart. It is tough work, but it is deeply gratifying. It is for those who wish to see beyond the account balance ledger, who desire to get more out of life than a bonus check at the end of the year for selling the most widgets, and who have a deep rooted commitment to pursuing and, hopefully, fulfilling the public interest.

Action Steps

1. Do public management approaches give up too much to the bureaucracy to decide what the public interest is and is not? Consider the excesses and abuses of the various tools of public management recited in this chapter against your reading of the U.S. Supreme Court case of *Massachusetts v. Environmental Protection Agency*, 549 U.S. 497 (2007). The Court chastised the EPA for NOT going against the President's orders against the enforcement of environmental regulations in the face of global warming. Is this about putting public management to work for citizens, or placing citizens at the mercy of public management?

2. Is the public interest about particular structures, organizations and procedures—or about effective public service in meeting needs? Consider the privatization of edu-

cation to church-owned schools in a reading of the U.S. Supreme Court case of *Zelman v. Simmons-Harris*, 536 U.S. 639 (2002), where the Court upheld the Cleveland school vouchers allowing poor families to choose public or private schools for their children, including church-owned schools. Is this about putting public management to work for students, or putting students at the mercy of public management?

3. Set up two panels of three students each, with one side representing the Old Public Administration (OPA) and the second representing the New Public Management (NPM). Give them one week outside of class to prepare a scholarly presentation and defense of their particular means of operation so to speak. Set aside 30 minutes for each panel to make its presentation. Ensure that each member speaks in defense of his/her position. And then allow the remaining time for class questions and discussion. The point of the action step is to contrast two different perspectives of management, and how each perspective is both similar and different.

4. Send the students into governmental community—everything from emergency services (police, fire, EMS) to the city manager's office to the state Department of Environmental Services (or whatever the title is)—via the department's, agency's, or government's web site to discover any signs of *reinvention* of management principles and/or techniques. Using Osborne and Gaebler's *Reinventing Government* (1992) as a baseline, see whether or not the government agencies are instituting any or all of the various principles, such as, "steering rather than rowing," or "empowering rather than serving," or "funding outcomes, not inputs" and the like. Encourage them to contact the organization for follow up questions. Submit a three to five-page summary and analysis of their findings.

5. How was NPM implemented in Australia and New Zealand? How is it different (or similar) to reinvention techniques in the United States? Do a brief literature search, summarize the findings, and report to the class.

6. Describe the New Public Service (NPS) as articulated by the Denhardts. What is its theoretical and/or philosophical foundation? How is it implemented? What does it look like inside a city or state government? According to the Denhardts, why is it better than OPM? Write a five-page summary and critique of NPS.

7. Summarize the Carl Friedrich and Herbert Finer debate. How did (and does) this debate set the table so to speak for understanding and applying the concept of bureaucratic accountability?

8. What is a leader? What is a public manager? Are they the same? If not, what are the differences? Refer to Max De Pree, Warren Bennis and Burt Nanus, Malcolm Gladwell, and Henry Mintzberg helping you respond to the questions. Interview several federal, state, and local managers and leaders. How did you determine who was who? Explain your differences and the way you approached the assignment.

Exam Review Preparation

1. Identify the various definitions of public management.

2. In a short-answer explain the importance of each concept as it relates to NPS:

    a. Contrast with OPM

 b. Compare with NPM

 c. Reinvention

3. Describe each of the following principles of reinvention:

 a. "steering rather than rowing"

 b. "empowering rather than serving"

 c. "injecting competition into service delivery"

 d. "transforming rule-driven organizations"

 e. "funding outcomes, not inputs"

 f. "meeting the needs of the customer, not the bureaucracy"

 g. "earning rather spending"

 h. "prevention rather than cure"

 i. "from hierarchy to participation and teamwork"

 j. "leveraging change through the market"

4. According to NPS, community and civil society are key ingredients. Why? What do these variables have to do with public management? Explain.

5. What does postmodern public administration contribute to our understanding of public management?

6. How do public managers serve citizens and not customers as do private sector managers? Explain.

7. Overview and summarize the steps of strategic planning. How does the public interest enter into this process?

8. Discuss the importance of the threefold character of leadership according to NPS: values-based, shared, and servant-oriented.

9. Compare the leadership responsibilities of Steve Bullmer, the CEO of Microsoft, and George W. Bush, former President of the United States. How do they differ? How are they similar? Which leadership responsibility is more important to the fulfillment of the public interest: the President of the United States or the CEO of Microsoft? Explain.

10. Contrast transformational with transactional leadership. Provide examples of each. Explain how each theory contributes to our understanding of leadership in the public service.

Key Concepts

Bill Gates
Charles Goodsell
David Osborne's *Reinventing Government*
Democratic accountability
E-Government Act
Enabling statute
Government Performance and Results Act

International City/County Management Association
National Performance Review
New managerialism
New Public Management
New Public Service
Old Public Administration
Organizational humanism
Outputs and outcomes
Performance-based measurement
Policy entrepreneur model
Postmodern public administration
Public management
Robert Behn
Steve Ballmer, CEO of Microsoft
Strategic planning
Ted Gaebler
Transformational versus transactional leadership
Value citizenship versus entrepreneurship
Vietnam War
Warren Bennis
Western Electric Company

Recommended Readings

Bennis, Warren, and Burt Nanus. *Leaders: The Strategies for Taking Charge.* New York: Harper and Row, 1985.

Bertelli, Anthony, and Laurence E. Lynn, Jr. *Madison's Managers: Public Administration and the Constitution.* Baltimore, MD: Johns Hopkins University Press, 2006.

Carnevale, David G. *Trustworthy Government: Leadership and Management Strategies for Building Trust and High Performance.* San Francisco, CA: Jossey-Bass, 1995.

Cook, Brian J. *Bureaucracy and Self-Government: Reconsidering the Role of Public Administration in American Politics.* Baltimore, MD: Johns Hopkins University Press, 1996.

Dahl, Robert A. and Charles E. Lindblom. *Politics, Economics, and Welfare.* New York: HarperCollins, 1953.

Drucker, Peter F. *Managing for the Future: The 1990s and Beyond.* New York: Penguin, 1992.

Ford, Leighton. *Transforming Leadership: Jesus' Way of Creating Vision, Shaping Values and Empowering Change.* Downers Grove, IL: InterVarsity, 1991.

Gladwell, Malcolm. *Outliers: The Story of Success.* Boston: Little, Brown & Co., 2008.

Hill, Larry B., ed. *The State of Public Bureaucracy.* Armonk, NY: M.E. Sharpe, 1992.

Kettl, Donald F., and H. Brinton Milward, eds. *The State of Public Management.* Baltimore, MD: Johns Hopkins University Press, 1996.

King, Cheryl Simrell and Camilla Stivers. *Government is Us: Public Administration in an Anti-Government Era.* Thousand Oaks, CA: Sage, 1998.

Maccoby, Michael. *The Gamesman: The New Corporate Leaders*. New York: Simon and Schuster, 1976.

Osborne, David, and Peter Plastrik. *Banishing Bureaucracy*. Reading, MA: Addison-Wesley, 1997.

Osborne, David, and Ted Gaebler. *Reinventing Government: How the Entrepreneurial Spirit is Transforming the Public Sector*. Reading, MA: Addison-Wesley, 1992.

Presthus, Robert. *Men at the Top: A Study in Community Power*. New York: Oxford University Press, 1964.

Smith, Howard. *Democracy and the Public Interest*. Athens, GA: University of Georgia Press, 1960.

Stanton, Thomas H., and Benjamin Ginsberg, eds. *Making Government Manageable: Executive Organization and Management in the Twenty-First Century*. Baltimore, MD: Johns Hopkins University Press, 2004.

Waldo, Dwight. *The Administrative State*. New York: John Wiley and Sons, 1948.

Related Web Sites

Government Accounting Standards Board
http://www.gasb.org/

Hawthorne Effect (from the Hawthorne Experiments at the Western Electric Plant outside of Chicago, IL, in the 1920s and 1930s)
http://www.12manage.com/methods_mayo_hawthorne_effect.html

International City/County Management Association
http://www.icma.org/main/sc.asp?t=0

National Center for Public Productivity
www.nccp.us

National Partnership for Reinventing Government
http://govinfo.library.unt.edu/npr/index.htm

New Public Management—Academe Online
http://www.aaup.org/AAUP/pubsres/academe/2007/MJ/Feat/beso1.htm

Peter F. Drucker's Web Site
www.peter-drucker.com

Robert K. Greenleaf Center for Servant Leadership
http://www.greenleaf.org/

Strategic Planning Institute
http://pimsonline.com/

Transformational Leadership (Changing Minds)
http://changingminds.org/disciplines/leadership/styles/transformational_leadership.htm

W. Edwards Deming Institute
www.deming.org

Chapter 7

Public Personnel Management and the Public Interest

"Many elements combine to make good administration: leadership, organization, finance, morale, methods and procedures, but greater than any of these is manpower. To find and to hold capable men and women and to help create and maintain working conditions under which they can do their best are the great tasks of personnel management."

Leonard. D. White,
Introduction to the Study of Public Administration

Chapter Objectives

Upon completion of this chapter the student will be able to:

1. Identify and define public personnel management and the important influence that public servants play in the development of public administration;

2. Identify the major periods of history associated with developments in public personnel;

3. Recognize the importance that people play in the development of public administration in the public interest;

4. Understand the various technical components and stages of public personnel management.

Introduction

For Leonard White, the crux of public administration is the people who serve. We think his point would still deserve an "A" on an essay today, some 50 years later. And of the people who focus on this task, whether we call them public personnel manager or human resource manager or personnel director, the purpose is the same: directing and managing people given their personal skills, knowledge, and abilities, coupled with the resource and capital to do the best job possible. But what is the goal of the public-service personnel manager: efficiency, economy or effectiveness? Is it equity and social justice?

Research assistance provided by Nathaniel Yellis, MBA Student, Acton School of Business, Austin, Texas.

Is it performance appraisal and accountability? Or, is it some combination thereof? We contend, of course, it is pursuit of the public interest. Most importantly, who is the proper recipient of the stewardship exercised by the public-service employee: interest groups, agency clientele, program recipients, or the public interest? Again, we contend it is the public interest.

The greatest resource public-service organizations have is people. It is people who implement laws, people oversee the finances, and people manage programs and other people. Even though in human resource terminology, the terms and concepts, such as human capital or human resource are used in a positive sense to denote public-service employees and, further, to describe their importance to the organization overall, we believe is that this is **philosophical reductionism** (reducing a human being to something akin to a tool or file cabinet). Employees are not just resources in this manner.

We discuss public personnel from a philosophical, historical, and contemporary approach, examining not only the major ideas and trends, but also the many details of people who serve the public interest today. For each of the major systems of personnel selection and steps of personnel management is designed to help achieve the public interest. Most of what we will say is directed toward the public sector, including the state and local as well as the federal branches of government. However, we also discuss the impact of personnel issues in the non-profit and faith-based sectors as well.

The early period of the nation represented the wealthy and politically astute holding governmental positions, usually by virtue of their position rather than their performance, while the end of the nineteenth and beginning of the twentieth century saw the implementation of what is known as the **merit system**. The Constitution did not mention how to appoint individuals to various and sensitive political positions, but only that the president had the power to appoint various officials, ambassadors, and other consuls, including judges and justices. The early appointments, especially during the beginning of the new nation, represented the president's preference for what made a good civil servant.

Various scholars[1] provide different typologies depicting historical phases of public personnel management, changes to personnel development, laws, and regulations, and other aspects of public personnel management. Without a doubt, however, each draw their understanding of civil service and our democratic processes and institutions from **Frederick Mosher's** (1914–1990) landmark work.[2] For clarity, conciseness, and historical accuracy we will draw from several scholars, although we will most closely follow Henry's description of Mosher's typology, while making two changes.[3] Thus we examine five historical eras of public personnel management and show the development of each as it pertains to the public interest.

The Guardians
(1787–1829)

George Washington's presidency (1789–1797) actually marked the rudimentary beginnings of the merit system, but this was never to be because of the intense clash of party warfare between the **Federalists** and the **Jeffersonian-Republicans** partisan and the ideological loyalty that ruled the day. Washington was frustrated by the factions and his problems in making appointments to sensitive administrative posts, such as his first four executive office positions: Thomas Jefferson as Secretary of State, Alexander Hamilton as Secretary of Treasury, Henry Knox as Secretary of War, and Edmund Randolph as Attorney General.[4] Washington wanted men of stature, character, intelligence, and above all loyalty. He also appointed men who had in mind the best interest of the new nation, and who were moral and ethical in their outlook on civic and public affairs. Even though this federal personnel phase was highly elitist and ideologically determined, it contained at its core pursuit of the public interest. In addition to demanding tremendous loyalty and character, a strong united executive was a defining criterion of Washington,[5] and later, too, for John Adams in 1797–1801 and Thomas Jefferson in 1801–1809.[6]

The Spoils Period
(1829–1883)

The term **spoils** is attributed to Senator **William L. Marcy** (1786–1857)of New York who in 1832 said "American politicians see nothing wrong in the rule that to the victor belong the spoils of the enemy."[7] With the presidency of Andrew Jackson in 1829–1837 and the advent of a new, more populist democracy came the increased involvement of the common man rather than the wealthy elite who had dominated the public service in the previous phase. Certainly it is true that Jackson appointed top officials in the manner laid down by George Washington and others, including integrity, honesty, and propriety, but he also advocated the common man.[8]

William L. Marcy

Senator William L. Marcy, was born in Southbridge, Massachusetts, He graduated from Brown University in 1808, and was admitted to the bar in New York where he began to practice law in 1810. Throughout his military and civil service career he held many positions, including as a lieutenant in the War of 1812; a recorder of Troy, New York, in 1816; adjutant-general of the New York militia in 1821; comptroller of the state of New York from 1823–129; associate justice of the New York Supreme Court from 1829–1831; United States senator from December 1831 to July 1832; governor of New York from 1833–1838; Secretary of War under President Polk from 1845–1849; and later Secretary of State under Franklin Pierce from 1853–1857.

Throughout his long career he made no bones about his Democratic loyalties and believed that everyone who supported the winning candidate should be rewarded for their loyalty. Therefore, it is no surprise that Senator Marcy is the author of the famous phrase: "To the victor, go the spoils." This included, of course, all of the perks surrounding civil service positions, regardless of one's knowledge, skills, and abilities for the particular position.

Source: "William L. Marcy," NNDB, www.nndb.com/people/987/000051834/ (accessed October 2007).

Jackson himself rued the idea of engaging in administrative detail and appointments. He enjoyed the game of politics, but the necessity for executive administration forced his hand to apply his populist philosophy to the filling of executive posts as well as shaping domestic and foreign policy. Jackson's supporters actually saw this as a reform away from the elitism of the past. But the advent and continuation of political patronage was taken to mean that since an individual supported a particular presidential candidate, when that candidate won office his patrons should reap the spoils of victory, including "jobs for the boys" in federal service.

Historians posit that Jackson never actually reached out to the common man as much as we are led to believe; it was more symbolic and linguistic than tangible during his presidency. The spoils system truly came into its own with the John Tyler's presidency in 1841–1845, to Abraham Lincoln's administration in 1861–1865, and onward through the latter part of the nineteenth century.[9] Office seekers were rampant. Undue and unmerciful political pressure was put upon presidents and other lesser political appointees to make way for the untold numbers of individuals seeking political patronage payback. President Garfield, for example, wrote to his wife in 1877: "I had hardly arrived [in Washington] before the door-bell began to ring and the old stream of office-seekers began to pour in. They had scented my coming and were lying in wait for me like vultures for a wounded bison." Others, like 1885–1888 Secretary of Interior **Lucius Q.C. Lamar** (1875–1893) noted: "I eat my breakfast and dinner and supper always in the company of some two or three eager and hungry applicants for office … I have no time to say my prayers."[10]

The Reform Period
(1883–1906)

The post-Civil War Period saw an increase in the number of patronage positions, and greater graft and corruption, particularly at the state and local levels. Reforms were more out of the desire for a restoration of "wholesome democracy," i.e., the public interest, than for administrative efficiency. The emergence of the party system, complete with its moral decline in political and administrative standards, led to a number of instances involving various financial kickbacks from contractors, skimming of receipts, and other abuses. However, the nation was growing, the economy, especially in the western states, was booming, and the country was not involved in major foreign disputes.[11] Thus even to the most hardened reformer the need for civil service reform was not really apparent until the assassination of **President James A. Garfield** in 1881 by a psychopathic federal government office seeker named **Charles Guiteau** (1841–1882). This critical incident was the tragic spark that brought attention to the excesses of the spoils system inherent in the corruption of the political parties. Changes were required, and the reformers at all three levels of government were there to see that the changes took place.

Box 7.1   Assassination that Rocked the Personnel World

On July 2, 1881, President Garfield was feeling good about himself, his short term in office as President of the United States (he had been since March), and although he knew the country was still trying to put the Civil War behind them, he earnestly believed that his own Republican party was trying to heal the wounds from the 1880 presidential campaign, which saw division within the Republican ranks. He prepared to set off on a vacation before gearing up for what he expected to be difficult political battles ahead. He and his entourage arrived at the Baltimore and Potomac Railroad station and amid the flurry and hustle of holiday travelers Charles Guiteau, a disgruntled federal office-seeker, appeared out of the crowd, pushed close to President Garfield and fired two shots, one that delivered the fatal blow of shattering bones and puncturing vital internal organs. He tried escaping but an alert guard stopped him. The president was whisked away to a hospital and Guiteau off to a local jail. President Garfield later died as a result of complications from the gunshot wound—only the second president to be assassinated while in office. And Charles Guiteau was tried, convicted, and executed for his part in the assassination.

Source: Douglas MacGowan, "July 2, 1881," Crime Library, http://www.crimelibrary.com/ terrorists_spies/assassins/charles_guiteau/ (accessed October 2007); and "Charles Guiteau," NNDB, www.nndb.com/people/210/000044078 (accessed October 2007).

The Pendleton Act. Thus, it was in 1883 that the **Pendleton Act** was signed into law, and with it came administrative oversight of civil servants by the newly formed Civil Service Commission, and the inclusion of merit examinations. Initiated by **Senator George Pendleton** (1825–1889), an Ohio Democrat, the intention was to end the spoils system. The primary changes of this legislation included:

- Influence of British civil service action, including competitive examinations and a neutral civil service that was free from political influence;
- Establishment of the U.S. Civil Service Commission, which was to establish and carry out personnel rules and laws;
- Lateral entry rather than only bottom level entry—meaning a person could enter public service at a higher level than the bottom level;
- No special administrative class was established as in Britain. Rather, the president was encouraged to appoint high level officials based on political loyalty rather than administrative competence per se.
- Position classification, standard pay schedules, and objective performance appraisals were also developed.
- Personnel selection based on practical job related knowledge, skills and abilities rather than general academic ability.
- Due process protections: dismissal for cause and protection from patronage.

However, with each successive administration, the number of merit positions did not automatically increase exponentially. Each president wanted to leave his mark of loyalty-bearing positions, and so he extended coverage to more employees who were brought into public service by patronage practices. Many of these individuals were European immigrants and the poor who lived in urban America toward the end of the nineteenth century and into early part of the twentieth century.

Administrative and personnel reform took place at both the state and local levels as well as at the federal level. Led by such reform-minded stalwarts as **George William Curtis** (1824–1892) and **Dorman B. Eaton** (1823–1899) the movement for reform was precipitous, particularly in states such as New York, Massachusetts, Pennsylvania, Wisconsin, and California.[12] In fact, it was this very reform-minded thinking that led Woodrow Wilson to pen his famous "The Study of Administration" article in 1887, advocating the separation of politics from administration, and thus prompting the growth of state and local civil service commissions and the thrust for such local administrative changes as the institution of city management as a profession.

With the reformers on one side, largely consisting of the progressive-minded politicians and middle-classes, and the immigrants and lower-classes on the other, the stage was set for a clash of interests, values, and goals. And it did not take long before we began to see a winner of this clash emerge. The reformers, led by such luminaries as George William Curtis, **Emory Upton** (1839–1881), Frederick W. Taylor, Richard S. Childs and many others, who believed in promotion of the public interest more than raw and unbridled partisan politics, relished the fact that their middle-class, often times Midwestern and Western backgrounds, coupled with their strong family and religious training and value indoctrination, would help establish the fact that corruption and graft should not win out over moral and efficient government and governing processes.[13] The reformers moved for changes in how government officials were selected to serve in a government position, from one of spoils to merit. The reformers sought to depoliticize the public interest, in particular through the establishment of civil service commissions, including the federal, state, and local levels.[14]

The Management Period
(1906–1955)

In 1906 the **New York Bureau of Municipal Research** was established and sought to study and apply scientific methods of administration to public administration overall and specifically to personnel management. Bureaus such as this—which were supported by private philanthropy—were established because the reformers did not see a difference between public and private organizations; only that people worked in both and management of people was the same in either. Efficiency was manifested through position classification and overall control of public personnel system. By 1930, for example, over 80 percent of the federal government's nonmilitary personnel were covered by a civil service/merit system. Today, the figure is over 90 percent.

FDR and Eisenhower had an overriding influence in personnel management. FDR, for example, wanted greater authority over his New Deal programs, and the way to do this was to centralize responsibilities and functions. The **Committee on Administrative Management** (a.k.a. Brownlow Committee, 1937) found several key factors that were necessary to meet FDR's goals: 1) challenge the need for specialized and technical employees; 2) blur the distinction between politics and administration; 3) passage of the **Hatch Act of 1939** and publication of the results of the First Hoover Commission, 1949, and various "little Hoover commissions" at the state level, which emphasized greater dependence upon management, including close integration of personnel management with general presidential management, establishment of an executive office of president—the core which was the White House staff and the budget office, and consolidation of all line agencies, including all regulatory commissions, into twelve cabinet agencies, with the idea being greater centralization of authority and oversight by the president.[15]

Second, President Eisenhower, who sought to place greater numbers of Republicans into sensitive and powerful administrative positions long held by Democrats ordered a **Second Hoover Commission** formed in 1953, and its **Second Report** in **1955** reinvigorated the politics-administration dichotomy by its recommendation for 800 more presidential-appointees adding another 3,000 upper-echelon administrative class of civil servants, which was to be called the Senior Civil Service.[16] This followed the already established practice in Britain. It did not last, however, and died by the late 1950s, but was resurrected in the 1978 civil service reform legislation, with the advent of the **Senior Executive Service**, prompting more centralized management of agencies and their personnel.[17]

The Professional Career Period
(1955–Present)

Specialized professionalism established itself creating a civil service system based on the person rather than the position. More lawyers, scientists, etc. became a part of the federal government, but their dislike for politics and political bureaucratic relationships was evident. In the early periods, clerkships and clerical position dominated, where the need for standards of efficiency and effectiveness were warranted, but during the post-WWII period, with the advent of technological and communication advances, came the professionals.[18] The impact of scientists, especially in the aerospace (NASA) and environmental (EPA) areas, was predominant, but large numbers of lawyers, accountants, educators, management specialists and others filled numerous positions at both the federal and state levels. Local governments were at first slower to respond to the professional changes, but by the 1970s greater numbers of local officials acquired management degrees (MPAs) and more individuals with technical degrees, such as in communications and computers, especially in the larger cities and counties, were working in local government.[19]

The Civil Service Reform Act of 1978. The defining point in the final historical phase of public personnel management is the passage of the **1978 Civil Service Reform Act** and the inauguration of a new commitment to civil service.[20] For approximately 100 years the Pendleton Act was the key piece of civil service legislation. However, it became increasingly clear that substantial reform was necessary. One of the main problems was lack of direction between the president and the Civil Service Commission over personnel policy at the federal level. President Carter made it clear that change was necessary and he targeted five problem areas that needed change, including rewriting and discarding the overly technical rules and regulations that detailed every action for recruiting, testing, selecting, and classifying federal civil service employees; over protection of employees who deserved to be fired, but could not be because of the excessive number of rules that protected them from political action; great need for management flexibility; more compensation given due to longevity rather than performance; and trying to reduce the discrimination of women and racial minorities. The Civil Service Reform Act corrected these problems through a series of personnel, organizational, and management changes, bringing about several positive results.[21]

Box 7.2 1978 Civil Service Reform Act

President Jimmy Carter's 1978 statement on signing the Civil Service Reform Act:

"History will regard the Civil Service Reform Act of 1978 as one of the most important laws enacted by this Congress. Congress has done an extraordinary job in shaping this landmark legislation and enacting it in just over 7 months ... In March, when I sent my proposals to Congress, I said that civil service reform and reorganization would be the centerpiece of my efforts to bring efficiency and accountability to the Federal Government. It will be the key to better performance in all Federal agencies. In August, Congress approved Reorganization Plan No. 2 of 1978. ... This Civil Service Reform Act of 1978 ... adds muscle to that structure. This legislation will bring fundamental improvements to the Federal personnel system. It puts merit principles into statute and defines prohibited personnel practices. It establishes a Senior Executive Service and bases the pay of executives and senior managers on the quality of performance. It provides a more sensible method for evaluating individual performance ... The act

assures that whistleblowers will be heard, and that they will be protected from
reprisal ... Our aim is to build a new system of excellence and accountability. ...
The changes we expect will not happen all at once. But I pledge to you today
this administration will implement the civil service reforms with efficiency and
dispatch ..."

Source: Jimmy Carter, "Civil Service Reform Act of 1978 Statement on Signing S. 2640 Into
Law, October 13, 1978," American Presidency Project, www.presidency.ucsb.edu/ws/index.php?
pid=29975 (accessed October 2007).

The Reagan Revolution and Its Impact
(1980–1989)

With the election of Ronald Reagan in 1980, a "devolutionary mindset" took hold;
this means that the Reagan administration's federalism philosophy was to devolve or
hand down responsibility to lower units of government. For example, in his first administration President Reagan appointed good friend and business mogul J. Peter Grace
to examine where regulatory waste was located in the national government, and offer
recommendations for eliminating it. By 1984 the **Grace Commission**—or the **Private
Sector Survey on Cost Control**—produced nearly 2,800 recommendations that it said
would save nearly $425 billion over three years.[22] The effect of such a report led many
to believe that big government was "bad" government, and thus, unfortunately, individuals who worked for the national government were also negatively labeled. It entailed a devaluing of the contributions of government employees and a more formal
embracing of the stereotype that the private sector is more efficient and effective.

Box 7.3   Grace Commission

In 1982, President Reagan directed the Grace Commission, named after its executive director, J. Peter Grace, the late industrialist, to "work like tireless blood-
hounds to root out government inefficiency and waste of tax dollars." For two years,
161 corporate executives and community leaders led an army of 2,000 volunteers on a waste hunt throughout the federal government. Funded entirely by
voluntary contributions of $76 million from the private sector, the search cost
taxpayers nothing. The Grace Commission made 2,478 recommendations which,
if implemented, would save $424.4 billion over three years, an average of $141.5
billion a year—all without eliminating essential services. The 47 volumes and 21,000
pages of the Grace Commission Report constitute a vision of an efficient, well-
managed government that is accountable to taxpayers.

Source: Reprinted in part from J. Peter Grace, "President's Private Sector Survey on Cost Control," A Report to the President, vol. 1, www.uhuh.com/taxstuff/ gracecom.htm (accessed
October 2007).

Before long privatization, contracting out or outsourcing, became the rave. The argument was that the private sector could implement public services at a lower cost and
in a more productive way than could government. This mindset is not new, dating at
least as far back as post-World War II, when the federally chartered government corpo-

ration came into vogue. However, the 1980s' style of contracting out set the stage for a nationwide movement for privatizing many aspects of the public sector, with the belief that it would improve service delivery, enhancement of service provision, and ultimately cost the taxpayer less.

Based on actual requests for FY 2008, the national government spent nearly $530 billion in contractual services with the private, non-profit, and non-governmental sectors.[23] The biggest winners in these contracts were in supplies and equipment (around 35 percent) and with general services (at nearly 45 percent). Observers of this phenomenon posited that costs of contracting out generally were more expensive than the federal civilian payroll, and the number of indirect employees, or what some refer to as shadow employees, had grown to over 5.5 million, nearly triple the number of federal civilian employees.[24] In addition, privatization or outsourcing had given rise to an entirely new brand of elite employee: the Washington lobbyist. This was not your ordinary lobbyist. Often he was a former federal official who resigned from government, and who ended up as a high-paid executive or consultant to a company within the same industry that he once regulated or oversaw as a public employee. One study by the **General Accountability Office**— an independent, nonpartisan agency that works for Congress—found that nearly one-third of 5,000 former mid-and high-level employees, including military officers, had gone to work for private contractors.[25] This revolving door syndrome as some refer to it was certainly impacting the public's negative perception of the greedy former public servant, who gave up their civil service position for a run at the big bucks!

Reinvention
(1990s)

By the 1990s the reinvention of government movement had taken hold, particularly at the local and state levels, and its effects are still felt by personnel experts.[26] Not to be outdone, the Clinton administration initiated the **National Performance Review (NPR)** project, designed by Vice President Al Gore, Jr.[27] The primary emphasis of NPR was to streamline government processes in order to achieve more effective outcomes, including deregulating the public personnel process.[28] This was particularly necessary at the federal level, where close to 200,000 jobs and over nearly 2,000 federal field offices were closed—all in the name of making government more accountable.[29] Although NPR is no longer an active organization in Washington its effects were long-lasting. For example, the recent hue and cry for greater accountability through performance accountability measures seems to be the next generation of NPR. What is troubling is that in government's marked determination to focus on numbers, accountability, and a return to greater efficiency we may have lost sight of the greater call for the civil servant: to serve the public interest. The very emphasis of civil service is people serving people, not programs.

Box 7.4   Outsourcing

What is outsourcing? Today, we have seen even more emphasis on outsourcing. In 1998, Congress passed legislation that required federal agencies to inventory all personnel positions that could possibly be outsourced. This yielded a number of nearly 800,000 positions! President George W. Bush has been a proponent of government outsourcing. Is this good for government? Is it effective for the administration of public services? Is it the best for the public interest? In a fascinating new book, *New York Times* columnist Thomas Friedman has argued that in the new "flat world," outsourcing in and to the private sector has been a must, both nationally and internationally. In other words, the pragmatic aspect of outsourcing may outweigh its potentially negative and harmful public effects. As they say, only time will tell.

Sources: Stephen W. Hays and Richard C. Kearney, *Public Personnel Administration: Problems and Prospects*, 4th ed. (Upper Saddle River, NJ: Prentice-Hall, 2003), 334; and Thomas L. Friedman, *The World is Flat: A Brief History of the Twenty-First Century* (New York, NY: Farrar, Straus, and Giroux, 2005).

Given all this history, especially at the national government level, what are the basic laws, functions, processes and policies of public personnel management? We survey it all, describing relevant key terms, phrases, and laws, discussing basic functions of personnel management, describing basic overall process of labor-management relations in the government arena, and concluding by highlighting two policy areas directly affected by changes in personnel management that impact the public interest.

Basics of Public Personnel Management

Public personnel management is all about serving others! Regardless of the organization, whether it is the Post Office, the city manager's office, the state Department of Transportation (DOT), or the local Salvation Army, or the people they serve, everyone, civilians to military, citizens within the city's jurisdiction, the state road system and those who travel on it, and the self-declared needy—it really just boils down to public servants doing what their title indicates: serving others. And the hope is that by serving others, we may serve the public interest. It is important then to distinguish between personnel administration, which is much more functional, and human resource or personnel management, which is more oriented to the needs of people.

Personnel administration identifies the basic administration of line and staff functions and the system those functions operate in, such as recruitment, selection, compensation, etc. The early period of administrative reform sought to change the corrupt and unethical personnel systems of patronage and spoils, such as the urban political machines of Chicago and New York, to one of merit, and to do so meant a wholesale change in the way government was looked at (organizational and institutional) as well as the way various government functions operated. This change was directed at the entire system, focusing on prioritizing work efficiency and effectiveness, primarily through administrative principles of change and work techniques.

Human resource or personnel management, on the other hand, has come to mean something more—at least symbolically, if not substantively as well. Some believe that public personnel has simply expanded its intellectual boundaries by referring to people in public service as resources, implying more than rote knowledge of personnel systems and functions; others contend that human resource or personnel management is more closely aligned with a sensitivity to values; while others simply mean the term places emphasis where emphasis is due: on people. Whereas traditional personnel administration systems emphasized planning, employee acquisition, employee development, and sanction, personnel management is the broader focus of partnering with line agencies to achieve the organization's mission, such as improving the quality of work life for the civil servant, helping to support the change process in the organization, and even contracting out various personnel functions, such as payroll and benefits, if the need arises. In other words, personnel management over personnel administration seems to imply greater interest in the whole of the person, not just as a number or statistic.

In addition to focusing on the common public administration values of economy, efficiency, and effectiveness, personnel management focuses on how managers, elected officials, and even citizens and citizen groups might influence more traditional political values, such as promoting social equity, enhancing administrative representativeness, fostering employee rights, and promoting the overall well-being of public employees. The latter values, for example, are illustrated in a variety of hot button political issues associated with employee rights in collective bargaining, affirmative action and sexual harassment cases, as well as issues of diversity, such as gender equality and sexual orientation. Given the basic differences between public personnel management and human resources management, what are the elements of these administrative operations and how do they affect the public interest?

Personnel. Personnel are defined as both the employees and the functional and administrative unit responsible for hiring, firing, promoting, and redirecting.[30] Government is often measured by the size of the number of full-time and part-time employees, with the former referred to as **full-time equivalent (FTE) employees**. The numbers are large. Total local and state FTEs were 16.4 million in 2007.[31] Total federal non-military personnel was approximately 1.8 million in 2008, while military personnel (including reserves) was 3 million.[32] If we count shadow employees, the total number of individuals who work directly or indirectly for the government is close to 30 million.

Unfortunately, survey research indicates that the number of top high school and college graduates are thinking less of joining the soon-to-be depleted ranks of government employees,[33] especially at the federal level, where the **Office of Personnel Management** (OPM) predicts up to a 40 percent attrition rate of current federal employees within the next ten years based on retirement eligibility.[34] This results from the sizable number of aging baby-boomers who are retiring or moving in the later stages of their working life to the private or non-profit sectors. Attitudes toward the public service are contradictory, for example, where over two-thirds of Americans trust their bureaucrats to do the right thing, yet fewer and fewer young people want to work for the government. Instead, they are moving to the more short-term lucrative private sector positions.

Merit System. The merit system is based on knowledge and tenure. As we mentioned earlier, George Washington's guardian class may have de facto been the wealthy and elite of their day, but they were also the most knowledgeable, educated, civic-minded, and career-oriented. So in one sense George Washington and his immediate presidential successors actually preferred an early form of merit or civil service system. On the downside, of course, many point out the overemphasis on partisan and social-class loyalty, something that was around for decades later.

The non-civil service system, or **spoils system**, was based on **patronage**, where employees are selected on basis of partisan and/or personal loyalty rather than "knowledge, skills, and abilities" (KSA). Today, some 3,000 political executives are appointed by the president to hold a high level political position with substantial policymaking powers. Some argue that we have exceeded the saturation point for political executives; that when compared with other democracies, such as Great Britain which has about 100, our national bureaucratic system, for example, is top-heavy with too many non-merit based policymakers who are unaccountable except to the president alone. So, what are the basic steps and/or functions of hiring a qualified candidate to be represented by the civil service system?

The Process of Personnel Administration

There are several steps or components for dealing with managing people in the public and non-profit organization. First, **position classification** "organizes jobs under civil service system into classes based on job descriptions denoting similarity of duty and responsibility, separates authority, sets up chain of command, and details pay scales."[35] **General Schedule (GS)** and **Senior Executive Service (SES)** are at the federal level. GS, for example, is a federal system of various levels or grades of pay and job classifications from 1–15, established in 1949 by the Classification Act, which was a continuation and enhancement of a 1923 law called the Classification Act that "established the Classification Programs Division of the Office of Personnel Management" in order to group positions into classes on basis of duties and responsibilities.[36] GS 1–4 are lower level positions; typically secretarial and clerical. GS 5–11 are middle-level positions divided into two subschedules. The first are GS 6, 8, and 10, which are technical, skilled craft, and senior clerical. The second are GS 5, 7, 9, and 11, which are professional career grades, with 5 and 7 entry level positions for college graduates. Finally, GS 12–15 are senior level positions, just below the SES. The SES replaced the "super-grades" of GS 16–18, providing the paygrade link between presidential appointees and normal civilian workers.[37] It was established by the **Civil Service Reform Act of 1978**.[38]

States are not covered by the GS or SES classifications, but the Intergovernmental Personnel Act (IPA) of 1970 reinforced the requirement that states have merit features built into their personnel systems.[39] Local governments are less regulated. As of this writing, all states and most local governments have some type of classification system. Several problems still exist despite the reinvention efforts of the 1990s. First, classification systems have grown more complicated (average number of job classifications in state government is around 2,000!). Second, there is an overemphasis of reviews and audits by the OPM or corresponding state/local agency. And third, job classification is quickly becoming outdated as result of changing technology, particularly with the advent and use of the Internet and website technology. Some changes have occurred to assist in the reclassification of many government positions. One change is the use of **broad banding**, where managers are "urged to consolidate existing classifications into a few smaller numbers, thus reducing complexity and also increasing flexibility and mobility for employees."[40] Another set of recommendations for changes come from National Performance Review (NPR) and the **National Commission on the State and Local Public Service** (a.k.a. the Winter Commission), which called for the reduction in complexity of classification systems.[41]

Second, **recruitment** is the process of advertising job openings and soliciting candidates to apply.[42] There are many challenges in recruiting new applicants to national government. For one there is a shrinking pool of possible candidates, both in terms of "knowledge, skills, and abilities" (KSA) and more importantly the desire to work in government at all. For example, only 1 in 3 Americans even want to work for government. Further, of the best students, such as *Phi Beta Kappa* college graduates, only five percent rank government as their first career choice, while 34 percent rank the private sector as their first choice.[43] Nonetheless, recruiting individuals to the public sector is more or less largely influenced by who is interested in working in the public sector. More minorities, young people, and Democrats are attracted as opposed to non-minorities, older individuals, and Republicans.

The third step in hiring is **examination**. It is a complex process, where the use of written and oral tests are used to determine the level of KSA of potential employees. Open and competitive examinations are at the heart of a solid and competitive civil service system. Exams are the generally the fairest way of determining who is eligible to fill a spot. In order to be fair, exams must be valid.[44] That is, do they measure what they are designed to measure, such as general intelligence (IQ tests), and are they unbiased, the exams neither directly nor indirectly discriminatory against age, race, ethnicity, or other variables? **Race-norming**, where the test givers simply add points to lower scores, especially where the test taker is a minority, began in the late 1980s but was later declared unconstitutional in 1991.[45]

The fourth step in hiring is **selection**. Choosing the best candidate for an open position is critical to maintaining a strong civil service system. Although state and local examination processes are generally in place, there is no systematic process for selecting the best candidate at the sub-national level. Selecting the best candidate is not always easy, especially not in the policy areas of affirmative action, environmental regulations, and veterans' preference. Women and minorities are high on the select list for government positions, but even minority candidates must achieve minimum levels on standardized exams.[46] The certification process means that only a select number of the highest ranking candidates are deemed eligible for possible selection.[47]

The fifth step in hiring is **compensation**. How much is a government employee paid? How much *should* a government employee be paid? The first question is answered dependent upon whether it is a national or sub-national position. The second question is largely dependent upon not only normative values, but also pragmatic concerns, such as economic necessity and geographical location. As we have mentioned state and local government employees' compensation varies as widely as California is distant from Vermont. Municipalities and counties base their compensation levels on state legislative mandates to local economic conditions, such as budget restraints or increases. Federal positions are preset according to the General Schedule mentioned above. GS-1 to GS-15 rankings are determined by Congress and published through the Office of Personnel Management. (See Table 7.1.)

Table 7.1   Salary Table 2008-GS, Incorporating a 2.50 Percent General Increase, Effective January 2008

Grade	Step 1	Step 2	Step 3	Step 4	Step 5	Step 6	Step 7	Step 8	Step 9	Step 10	Within-Grade Amounts
GS-1	$17,046	$17,615	$18,182	$18,746	$19,313	$19,646	$20,206	$20,771	$20,793	$21,324	VARIES
2	19,165	19,621	20,255	20,793	21,025	21,643	22,261	22,879	23,497	24,115	VARIES
3	20,911	21,608	22,305	23,002	23,699	24,396	25,093	25,790	26,487	27,184	697
4	23,475	24,258	25,041	25,824	26,607	27,390	28,173	28,956	29,739	30,522	783
5	26,264	27,139	28,014	28,889	29,764	30,639	31,514	32,389	33,264	34,139	875
6	29,276	30,252	31,228	32,204	33,180	34,156	35,132	36,108	37,084	38,060	976
7	32,534	33,618	34,702	35,786	36,870	37,954	39,038	40,122	41,206	42,290	1084
8	36,030	37,231	38,432	39,633	40,834	42,035	43,236	44,437	45,638	46,839	1201
9	39,795	41,122	42,449	43,776	45,103	46,430	47,757	49,084	50,411	51,738	1327
10	43,824	45,285	46,746	48,207	49,668	51,129	52,590	54,051	55,512	56,973	1461
11	48,148	49,753	51,358	52,963	54,568	56,173	57,778	59,383	60,988	62,593	1605
12	57,709	59,633	61,557	63,481	65,405	67,329	69,253	71,177	73,101	75,025	1924
13	68,625	70,913	73,201	75,489	77,777	80,065	82,353	84,641	86,929	89,217	2288
14	81,093	83,796	86,499	89,202	91,905	94,608	97,311	100,014	102,717	105,420	2703
15	95,390	98,570	101,750	104,930	108,110	111,290	114,470	117,650	120,830	124,010	3180

Table taken from U. S. Office of Personnel Management, http://www.opm.gov/oca/08 tables/pdf/gs.pdf (accessed December 2008).

How much should an employee be paid is dependent upon several factors, such as minimum economic needs. For example, is the employee living in St. Louis, Missouri, or

Boston, Massachusette? If the latter, then the salary levels listed above in the GS table are adjusted by 16.99 percent, whereas in St. Louis the levels are adjusted by only 11.27 percent. This is known as **locality pay** adjustments. Locality pay was instituted in 1993 in order to provide employees living in high cost areas relatively higher salaries than individuals living in lower cost areas. Generally speaking, entry level federal employees are paid better than state and local employees, but that is assumed to be the case because of the inclusion of low paid teachers and criminal justice employees.[48] City managers with a large number of years of experience working in large metropolitan areas, however, can expect salaries and benefit packages to exceed $250,000.[49] Municipal and county health administrators and chief law enforcement officials in large metro areas generally have salaries that exceed $150,000.[50]

Another problem facing public sector employees is the **pay gap** between themselves and private sector employees. Private sector managers that are equivalent to the GS-15 federal employees easily make two and perhaps three times the GS-15 employee. At the state level the difference is not as great, but significant nonetheless. For example, a biologist in the private sector earns approximately $70,500 while his public sector counterpart earns just under $42,000. In 2004 state salaried employees grew only 0.45 percent, while 2005 increase was roughly 1.19 percent increase. This kind of increase does not even keep pace with inflation. Certainly the public-private pay gap is real, and it will never be completely narrowed, but great strides by various public organizations are attempting to do so.

However, the competition for top-level public employees is high, and this drives up the salaries. A 2004 report in *Governing* magazine[51] reported that municipal versus state executives are generally better paid. Allen Frank, Chief Information Officer for the City of Philadelphia, earns $190,000, Rhoda Mae Kerr, Fire Chief for the City of Little Rock, Arkansas, takes in $102,000, and Bill Bratton, Chief of Police for the City of Angels (that is, Los Angeles) brings in nearly $260,000! Still, with all of the big bucks earned by these local government chief executives, their salaries and benefit packages do not come close to what they could earn in the private sector. For example, Kevin Baum, who is assistant fire chief in Austin, Texas, makes one-third less what his organizational counterparts at Austin-based Dell Computer makes.[52]

The sixth step in hiring is **training** and **development** (T&D). Once the employee is recruited, examined, selected, and paid he needs to be continually trained and developed. The Government Employees Training Act of 1958 required federal agencies to provide training. Later, in the late 1960s President Johnson instituted the Office of Training and Development and Regional Training Centers, along with the establishment of the Federal Executive Institutive in Charlottesville, Virginia. The institute has graduated hundreds of federal managers, chiefly those of the SES variety. State and local governments benefited from grants allocated for T&D, but this was reduced during the cutbacks of the mid-1980s. Forty-six states have training requirements for local government employees, with the majority for police, fire, and emergency personnel. Much training is done in-house or through universities, such as the **University of North Carolina's Institute** of **Government**. Training and development programs, particularly in state government, are in need of better training programs and practices, developing training programs, and better assessment of the outcomes sought in training.[53]

The seventh step in hiring is **performance appraisal,** or the evaluation of an employee's work performance. It is primarily used for purposes of retention and promotion, as well as to document any disciplinary actions. It is a management technique, used by individual public managers to address the myriad concerns associated with accounting for how well or how poorly an individual in the public sector does his or her job.

The most common methods of performance appraisal include **supervisor ratings,** where the immediate supervisor rates employees performance; **self-ratings,** when employees rate themselves using a standardized form, usually with some type of narrative and documentation to support claims of performance; **peer ratings**, which, of course, is when fellow employees rate each other; **subordinate ratings**, where employees rate their supervisor; and finally, **group ratings**, where an outside person rates performance of entire group, unit, or organization based on random interviews, "on the job" (OTJ) visits, or use of performance documentation.[54]

Quality of work life (QOL) is the eighth step. Governments and public sector organizations are extremely aware of the need to provide a solid quality of work life indicator for their employees. Recent adjustments include family-friendly rules and regulations, particularly in areas of flex-time, part-time, and pregnancy leave; employee wellness programs, and even sponsoring, if not paying for, alcohol abuse treatment centers. The federal legislation Family and Medical Leave Act of 1993 provided up to twelve weeks of unpaid leave per year for a variety of health and personal problems, including childbirth, child-related services, including adoption and childcare, elder-care, and other similar types of situations.[55]

Summary. The eight steps of public personnel management attest to the importance placed on both administration and organization of the management of people, but some also stress concern for the greater public interest, such as performance appraisal and QOL. Clearly the need for effective and holistic personnel management organizational tools and systems in general is evident. Protection of public personnel rights and responsibilities is the focus of the next section: collective bargaining and unionization.

Even though collective bargaining and unionization is done on behalf of the employee, it impacts the public interest through indirect and direct economic, social, and political means. Oftentimes referred to as **labor-management relations**, the centerpiece of such formal relations is to work out economic and work related differences between labor and management. To a greater extent it is the reordering of power relations between management and labor, something that did not occur during the first half of the twentieth century, but after WWII it became much more active. Of course, the primary historical focus was upon the private sector, particularly in the occupational areas of shipyard workers, truck drivers, dock workers, and other blue collar employees; the possibility of public labor-management interaction, unionization, and even striking did not begin in earnest until the 1960s.

Historical Precedents

The early movement of labor-management relations began in late 1800s and early 1900s, with passage of the **Lloyd-LaFollette Act of 1912**. This legislation allowed for unionization of public sector employees, particularly postal workers, but restrictions on how they could organize and bargain largely made this law ineffective. The number of public sector unions grew slowly, largely because of several concerns.[56] First, the idea of public sovereignty was considered sacrosanct; public sector unionization was considered to be a usurpation of this sovereignty. Second, government services are considered either necessary (fire, police etc) or unprofitable (mass transportation) and thus the need for public unions is less than in the private sector. Third, government is too varied in occupations and greater geographic dispersion to make unionization doable.

Passage of the **Wagner Act of 1935** provided the impetus public employees needed to have the right to bargain collectively. Despite the Wagner Act, the right to negotiate was hampered because of the lack of strong public unions; unions that had the same bargaining power and position as did their private sector counterparts. Several executive and congressional acts have occurred since the mid-1930s to promote public sector labor relations.

In 1962 President Kennedy issued Executive Order 10988 affirming the rights of public sector employees to unionize and to discuss labor issues with management. But the order stopped short of permitting negotiating. Then in 1969 another executive order issued by President Nixon called for a more coherent labor policy at the federal level through establishment of **Federal Labor Relations Council**, slightly expanding the ability and right to bargain collectively, except the main issues of salary and benefits remained outside the bargaining parameters.[57] Then in 1978 the Civil Service Reform Act (CSRA) was passed, and it provided the needed push that corrected most of the historical shortfalls regarding the inability of public sector employees to unionize and collectively bargain in good faith. It accomplished the following: 1) combined executive orders into one legislative act, thus providing some sense of uniformity; and 2) it replaced the FLRC with the **Federal Labor Relations Authority (FLRA)**, a body that was separate from the OPM.[58]

Process of Labor-Management Negotiations

What happens when the two sides—labor and management—cannot work out their differences in a timely fashion, specifically when one side has made what it considers a fair offer, but the other side rejects it, and vice versa? Various forms of reconciliation are available, such as mediation, fact-finding, and arbitration. **Mediation** involves a third party to help work out a settlement, but is not allowed to impose his or her own solution. The use of mediation has reached an all time high, with many lawyers and other trained professionals working as full-time independent mediators. This growth is due largely to the fact that mediation is successful in getting through many labor-management impasses. **Fact-finding** uses the third party more as an informal and non-binding judge, examining evidence on both sides, presenting evidence, and in some cases making specific recommendations for both sides to consider. **Arbitration** is the third technique that both sides use to work through impasses. It is the most stringent of the three methods, where in some cases both parties must make their best offer and then the arbitrator will choose one of the offers, or as it is in most cases will make modifications to one or more offers, and then require both parties to accept the modification.[59]

Of course when all else fails strikes can be effective, but also politically hazardous. In 1970 the Postal Workers Union struck. It began in New York City with some 25,000 postal workers but soon spread to include nearly 200,000 workers. Things were so desperate in the mail business that President Nixon ordered 27,000 National Guardsmen to sort mail. Finally, he broke his own precedent never to negotiate with public sector employees. The government and postal workers reached a settlement, but shortly after Congress passed the **Postal Reorganization Act** that set up the Post Office as a government corporation, and provided the postal employees with the opportunity to bargain.

Box 7.5   *Strikes Do Not Always Work*

A very famous public sector strike was the **Professional Air Traffic Controllers Organization (PATCO)** strike in August 1981. Boosting a membership of over 90 percent of all air traffic controllers PATCO had solidarity and political strength—or so it thought until it pushed President Reagan one step too far. After 95 percent of members rejected then Secretary of Transportation's Drew Lewis' offer of $40 million package of pay and benefits increases, the union decided to strike. President Reagan declared it an illegal strike, threatening public safety and security, and directly fired nearly 12,000 striking controllers. Nearly a year later PATCO filed for bankruptcy.

Source: Robert B. Denhardt and Joseph W. Grubbs, *Public Administration: An Action Orientation*, 4th ed. (Belmont, CA: Wadsworth, 2003).

Summary. So, how do we relate public personnel management to the public interest? Public personnel management is not without its problems and difficult issues, particularly issues that are in the public interest. Because of time and space we will confine our discussion to two policy issues: whistle-blowing and affirmative action.

Both whistle-blowing and affirmative action are somewhat representative of all the other problems mentioned that face public personnel managers in at least a couple of ways. One, they represent individuals who have come under some form of discrimination, thus denying them equal opportunity as guaranteed by the Fifth and Fourteenth amendments. And two, they are judicially and politically hot issues, and are not easily, if at all, resolved outside of the political and judicial parameters imposed by Congress and the courts. We examine each issue, providing some measure of its history, scope, and problems as it relates to the public interest.

Whistle-Blowing

Whistle-blowing involves the revelation of some type of ethical, moral, or legal wrongdoing by an employee. Lately, over the last couple of decades or so there has been a marked increase in the number of instances where public employees have disclosed unethical and even illegal actions within the organization the employee works in. The **whistleblower** reveals unusually sensitive information about wrongdoing in a public organization or program; wrongdoing that can include fraud, waste, or some type of employee or financial abuse.[60] According to survey data, the typical whistleblower has been with the particular agency or department for about seven to ten years, is a male, and is around 45 years of age. Many are in upper-level administrative or professional positions — that is, they have pretty good access to sensitive information, and the inner workings of the organization and/or program they work for or in.[61] The whistleblower usually acts because of the person's position in the organization, the length of tenure spent in the organization, and the desire for alternative employment. In addition, whistleblowers do not really rationally calculate what may occur in terms of retaliation; they tend to rely more on doing what they consider right, holding to a strong sense of individual responsibility, a commitment to absolute moral principles, and commitment to pursue the public interest.[62] Consider the example of Bunnatine Greenhouse.

Case Study   Whistling on Uncle Sam

Bunnatine Greenhouse was the principal assistant procurement officer responsible for contracting in the U.S. Army Corps of Engineers. As a civil servant in the sprawling bureaucratic Department of Defense (DOD), she was responsible for awarding multiple billions of dollars to private companies who were hired to assist in the redevelopment of Iraq, including taking care of the homeless and school-less children, building infrastructure, and doing a variety of other social and community type projects.

Some companies, like Halliburton, the large Texas firm that holds more than 50 percent of all private contracts in Iraq, and once was headed by Vice President Dick Cheney, were getting government contracts without doing any bidding. Are there violations of law, ethics, or other regulations with these private sector companies?

Bunnatine raised the issue, and she was under a great deal of scrutiny and pressure for her whistle-blowing. Her boss, Major General Robert Griffin, the Corps' deputy commander, said her performance was poor and as a result she was demoted. She was offered the chance to take another job elsewhere in the Corps or simply retire. She did not accept any of these options, except to do her job as she was hired to do. According to Greenhouse, reliance on her Christian faith was what gave her the courage and strength to press on.

Source: Deborah Hastings, "Faith Sustains Whistle-blower," *The News and Observer*, 7 August 2005, 22A.

What are the consequences of whistle-blowing? Retaliation against the **whistleblower** includes isolation in the organization, character assassination, demotion and even firing.[63] According to recent survey data, almost 60 percent of federal employees reported they lost their jobs. Another 19 percent reported harassment and/or transfer, and still another 15 percent reported that they had their job responsibilities or even their salary reduced as a direct result of their whistle-blowing.[64] What can whistleblowers do to legally protect themselves? Up until the 1980s legal protections were few, and therefore whistleblowers were very careful about blowing the whistle, given the consequences mentioned above. With passage of the False Claims Act of 1986 and the **Whistleblowers Protection Act of 1989**, whistleblowers are now both encouraged to blow the whistle and can expect protection when they do.[65]

Affirmative Action

Affirmative action is one of the more intense areas of controversy in the public personnel management arena. It has decreased in political and legal strength, but as of 2003 and the *Grutter v. Bollinger* case it is still alive and kicking, although in a companion case, *Gratz v. Bollinger*, the Court struck down a rigid numeric quota system used by the University of Michigan in undergraduate admissions.[66] Actually, there is not simply *one* affirmative action policy; there are a myriad of policies. What, then, precisely is affirmative action? And, if at all, does it act in the public interest? It is the term given to represent any number of policies that have at least three common factors, including 1) a statement affirming the organization's commitment to correct discrimination, 2) some type of analysis of existing practices and their consequences, and 3) a set of goals to improve affirmative action practices.[67] These practices might be quotas, set aside programs, or timetables for change. In many instances, the policies are not as direct as quotas, but they include desire and/or willingness on the part of personnel managers, admissions directors, and others in positions of personnel responsibility to strongly consider the race and sex of an applicant before making a decision. Some critics of affirmative action policies argue this is nothing more than reverse discrimination or just plain old discrimination itself. Only this time it is against white males (and increasingly white females).

Affirmative action's history is tied to the United States' civil rights history. Title VII of the **Civil Rights Right Act of 1964** is the most noteworthy example of civil rights legislation that was passed to prohibit discrimination based on "race, color, religion, national origin, or sex [gender]." As early as before WWII, however, the federal government attempted to address the issue of discrimination, particularly as it affected public sector employment, primarily through the issuance of executive orders. President Roosevelt issued Executive Order 8802, which essentially banned discrimination on the basis of race, religion, or national origins. It was limited, however, to businesses and industries with federal government contracts related to defense production. In 1961, President Kennedy issued Executive Order 10925, which called for the employment of racial minorities, but as in FDR's order it did not have enforcement power. In 1965 President Johnson issued Executive Order 11246, which required that all companies and industries that did any kind of business with the federal government must take affirmative action in providing equal opportunity to job employment, regardless of race, religion, or national origin. The enforcement part came when contracts were severed with companies and industries that refused to abide by the affirmative action statement. Subsequent executive orders that impacted government contractors added women[68] and sexual orientation[69] to the list of protected categories of persons.

What is the Supreme Court position? In *Regents of the University of California v. Bakke* (**1978**), the Court declared that rigid numeric quotas by race in medical school admission decisions at the University of California were illegal, but that race could be considered in a non-quota fashion among many other factors. More important, Justice O'Connor convinced her peers that the goal of diversity, rather than redressing past discrimination, was the greater public interest in their decision. Although she conceded that affirmative action schemes are by nature discriminatory, she argued that such a non-numeric, non-quota level of affirmative action was constitutional and was desirable in promoting diversity. But the Court has continued to limit the expansion of affirmative action policies by numeric quotas, for example, forbidding a public sector employer from laying off more senior employees (who were white and male) in favor of retaining less senior employees (who were black).[70] The exception is that quotas may be ordered from the judicial bench when there is evidence of policies of illegal discrimination, in writing or historical practice, such as the refusal of the Alabama State Patrol to hire blacks from 1940 to 1972.[71]

Conclusion: Pursuing the Public Interest

Deciding to blow the whistle on fellow workers and especially supervisors is obviously not an easy decision. Before doing so the whistleblower should recognize the consequences in doing so, and understand the legal protections available. What is most encouraging about the majority of whistleblowers is that they are doing it because of their personal and professional commitment to moral principles, that is, they understand that lying, cheating, defrauding, stealing, and other such acts are not only wrong in and of themselves, but they are wrong because they damage the relationship and trust established between the public agency or department and the public they serve. In other words, the illegal and unethical acts damage the fragility of the public interest. As Joe Carson of the Oak Ridge National Laboratory said, "Whistleblowers are thinking of what's good for others, not just looking out for number one."

Affirmative action policies that are aimed at making the public workplace more diversified have been generally accepted by minorities and by whites.[72] The Court has maintained the constitutional validity of affirmative action in the *Bakke* (1978) case, but has not expanded the application of numeric quotas without proof of past discrimination. Affirmative action programs are here to stay and include all levels of governance.[73] The diversity of the public service now includes greater numbers of include minorities by categories of race/ethnicity, gender, religions, and disabilities.[74] The public interest of affirmative action remains focused on Justice O'Connor's goal of social and organizational diversity rather than reparation.

Public personnel administration and human resource management play critical roles in the formulation, development, and evaluation of a sound system of functions and values for enabling and protecting the worth of civil servants, as well as promoting the political and legal rights of offended groups and citizens as a whole. Sufficient attention is necessary to ensure the future well-being of both the servant and the served.

Action Steps

1. After lecture and discussion of Frederick Mosher's historical typologies of civil service, divide the class into five groups, with no more than four students per group. Assign each group a time period to research, including a major figure or PA personality-type. Have the groups see civil service through the eyes of the PA personality-type. What is significant about this time period? Explain the role of workers in conjunction with their workplace. How is different from today? What did the groups learn about civil service and civil servants through this action step?

2. Research the history of events and persons leading up to the *Pendleton Act*. How did it come about? Who and what was influential in its development and ultimate adoption as law? What impact did it have upon the organization of federal civil service? Write a five-page essay summarizing and analyzing your findings.

3. Research the political developments surrounding passage of the *Civil Service Reform Act of 1978*. Compare it to the Pendleton Act. What was different? What reforms took place? How did these reforms affect the direction and outcome of federal civil service? Write a five-page essay summarizing and analyzing your findings.

4. What impact did the reinvention of government movement have upon civil service reform? Each student should read the 1993 publication titled *From Red Tape to Results: Creating a Government that Works Better and Costs Less*, and respond to the following questions:

   a. What role did the Clinton administration play in reinvention efforts at the federal level?

   b. How effective were the reform recommendations suggested by the Gore Commission?

   c. What could have been done differently?

5. Survey at least ten different local governments (general and special districts). Speak with a top-level public administration official and inquire 1) if and 2) how they apply reinvention of government principles? What have been the results?

6. Summarize and critique the importance of the basic steps and/or functions of hiring a qualified candidate. Choose a state or local government jurisdiction. Inquire of the personnel department how these basic steps are carried out, especially the *compensation* and *training and development* steps. What are the differences between federal and state and local government? What are the similarities? Explain in a five page essay.

7. Divide the class into at least four groups. Assign each group to research a different aspect of the Professional Air Traffic Controllers Organization strike in August 1981. What happened? Why did the air traffic controllers believe that striking was necessary in order to get their demands met? Why didn't the strike work? What can and should public administrators and political officials learn from this contentious debate?

8. Divide the class into groups of three and five and submit to each group for their decision to hire one of three candidates for a public-service agency position. Assume that each applicant is nearly identical in their background, education, experience, and skills. Choose one for the public-service agency position from the applicants that include one black and two whites. Given a public interest of diversity within the public service, would this necessitate choosing the one black applicant? Why or why not?

9. Is affirmative action in the public interest? Consider a recent U.S. Supreme Court decision that upholds affirmative action by non-numeric, non-quota style considerations of race, ethnicity, gender, and other relevant diversity factors in public service decisions in the case of *Grutter v. University of Michigan*, 539 U.S. 306 (2003). Does the Constitution suggest the equality of opportunity of affirmative action?

Exam Review Preparation

1. Define the following terms: performance appraisal, recruitment, FTE, spoils system, patronage, and classification.

2. Identify the importance of each piece of legislation or court case:

   a.   The Pendleton Act of 1888

   b.   *Griggs v. Duke Power Company* (1971)

   c.   Administrative Careers with America (ACWA), 1990

   d.   Civil Service Reform Act of 1978

   e.   Wagner Act of 1935

3. Identify and discuss the importance of the five historical phases of civil service.

4. Identify and define the various stages of hiring a civil servant.

5. Discuss the importance of whistleblowing and affirmative action in public personnel management.

6. Identify and define the various executive orders and what each meant with regard to promoting affirmative action.

7. Identify the importance of each of the following individuals: Emory Upton, William March, and Charles Guiteau.

8. Contrast mediation with arbitration. Provide examples of each. Which is better at helping to resolve labor and management disputes? Explain.

9. Explain the ethics of public servants staging a strike. When is it appropriate and when is it not?

10. What are the differences between personnel administration and human resource management?

Key Concepts

Charles Guiteau
Emory Upton
Federal Labor Relations Authority
Federalists and Jeffersonian-Republicans
Frederick Mosher's six stages
General Accountability Office
General Schedule
Government Employees Training Act
Grace Commission
Lloyd-LaFollette Act
Mediation v. arbitration
Merit system
National Commission on the State and Local Public Service
Pendleton Act
Performance appraisal
Personnel administration versus human resource management
Philosophical reductionism
Professional Air Traffic Controllers Organization
Race-norming
Regents of University of California v. Bakke
Senior Executive Service
Spoils system
"To the victor go the spoils"
Whistle blowing
William L. March

Recommended Readings

Cayer, N. Joseph. *Public Personnel Administration*. 4th ed. Belmont, CA: Thomson-Wadsworth, 2004.

Kettl, Donald F. and James W. Fesler. *The Politics of the Administrative Process*. 3d ed. Washington, DC: CQ Press, 2005.

Mosher, Frederick. *Democracy and the Public Service*. Cambridge: Oxford University Press, 1968.

National Performance Review. *From Red Tape to Results: Creating a Government that Works Better and Costs Less*. Washington, DC: U.S. Government Printing Office, 1993.

White, Leonard D. *The Federalists: A Study in Administrative History*. New York: MacMillan, 1956.

Related Web Sites

American Federation of Government Employees
>   http://www.agfe.org/

American Federation of State, County, and Municipal Employees
>   www.afscme.org/

Civil Service Commission
>   http://www.csc.gov.ph/cscweb/cscweb.html

Federal Government Jobs
>   www.jobsfed.com/

Federal Labor Relations Authority
>   http://www.flra.gov/

Senior Executive Service, U.S. Office of Personnel Management (OPM)
>   http://www.opm.gov/ses/

U.S. Census Bureau (click for public employment statistics)
>   www.census.gov

University of North Carolina School of Government
>   http://www.iog.unc.edu/

William L. Marcy
>   http://www.nndb.com/people/987/000051834/

Chapter 8

Public Budgeting, Finance, and the Public Interest

"Budgets are beyond dollars. They are choices, policies, and philosophies, and the ways in which budgets are made reflect the choices, policies, and philosophies of governments."

Nicholas Henry, *Public Administration and Public Affairs*

"Public budgeting is an aggravating enterprise under all but ideal circumstances. We generally want more than we can afford, and we often don't agree regarding what we want. If we are honest and have a reasonable degree of humility, we are also aware that we often don't understand what we are doing."

David Nice, *Public Budgeting*

Chapter Objectives

Upon completion of this chapter the student will be able to:

1. Define and identify the basic characteristics of public budgeting;
2. Recognize the important events, people, and ideas through a brief overview the history of public budgeting;
3. Understand the basic steps and process of public budgeting, both from an executive and legislative perspective;
4. Consider the basic problem of public deficits and possible solutions;
5. Overview public budgeting's impact upon the public interest.

Introduction

When President Clinton in 1997 signed the bill that documented for the first time in decades a balanced federal budget, the message emblazoned on the table he sat read: "A Balanced Budget That Protects Our Families, Invests in Our People and Cuts Taxes for Middle

---

Research assistance provided by Nathaniel Yellis, MBA Student, Acton School of Business, Austin, Texas.

Class Families." There may be no better symbolic and substantive realization of public budgeting meeting the public interest than the fulfillment of this statement. All the tools, means, and processes of budgeting are simply ways that elected and administrative officials use to achieve policy outcomes, such as depicted above—outcomes that fulfill the public interest.

Public budgeting is not an exact science, neither is it purely politics, where one interest group or agency or department benefits over another simply because of political connections. What is true today—much more so than it was prior to the beginning of the twentieth century—is the increased involvement of mayors, governors, and the president in the formation and development of budgets. The role of **chief executives** in the budgeting process is enhanced largely because of the perceived need for greater executive oversight, management, and political checks and balance with the legislative branch. As public administration scholar Nicholas Henry implies in his opening quotation above, budgets are not simply about credits and debits, capital versus operating expenses, and performance over program budgeting; budgeting is really about making philosophically tough decisions about the disbursement of public funds. But as political scientist **David Nice** intones, oftentimes we don't even know what we want, but we do know we want something and that it costs. As the pseudo political philosopher once said about politics in general (and we think it applies to public budgeting in particular) it is mostly about "who gets what, when, and how."

This chapter discusses not only the proverbial nuts and bolts of public budgeting, but also points out how effective (or ineffective, as it may be) budgeting is and should be in promoting the public interest. Some argue that public budgeting is simply the allocation of goods and resources, based largely upon individual and/or group perspectives; in other words, who is "the public" is simply relational. We contend that this is a short-sighted view of the true purposes of public budgeting, which is to make the best use of public dollars in order to make decisions that try to benefit the greater public interest, and not simply one interest group or organization over another.

The chapter will discuss five areas related to public budgeting and the public interest. First, it will define public budgeting. Second, it will examine a brief history of public budgeting. Third, it will explore and describe the process of budgeting, particularly from both executive and legislative perspectives. Fourth, it will outline the problem and possible solutions for deficits and deficit spending. And fifth, the chapter concludes with a brief overview of budgeting's impact upon the public interest.

What Is Public Budgeting?

Budgets are simply means of tracking or monitoring income and outflow, revenues and expenses, and, hopefully, in the end the two sides balance each other. When they do not, the result is either a deficit (expenses exceed revenues) or a surplus (revenues exceed expenses). Over the last thirty years or so, especially at the federal level, and in particular during the two Reagan administrations, the United States Government ran excessively high budget deficits. By the end of the 1990s and briefly into the first year of the twenty-first century, the federal government actually experienced surpluses: 1999 ($70 billion), 2000 ($127 billion), and 2001 ($236 billion). The **Congressional Budget Office** even projected a stunning $5.6 trillion in surpluses by 2010![1] (This, of course, was before the financial market meltdown in the fall of 2008, and will most likely not hold true.)

Public budgets fulfill several perspectives and roles: politics, where it is a tool for advancing a public policy agenda; economics, where budgeting is a pseudo-scientific process, concerned with establishing guidelines and factors for raising and spending revenues; and public managers, where the concern is on spending these dollars in the most efficient and effective way feasible. We contend, however, that a more intense discussion of the public interest is missing in much of the public administration and specifically public budgeting literature. The need to raise revenues and expend public dollars is critically important to maintaining or even advancing the greater common good or public interest. This is especially true with the police powers of state and local government efforts in dealing with our health, safety, welfare, education and morals. A larger picture of the history of public budgeting will help explain our position.

Public budgeting is not a new practice. It did not begin in some dusty file cabinet in the early part of twentieth century. Budgeting has been practiced whenever and wherever public administrators and political officials have accounted for the raising and expenditure of revenues. Pre-Sumerian clay tablets detail the budgets of ancient kings some 4000 years ago. However, we will begin roughly at the founding period in America, given that much of what transpired then was largely based on earlier British customs and traditions. For example, the very term **budget** itself was used to describe the leather bag carried by the king's treasurer, who was later titled the Chancellor of Exchequer.[2] Needless to say, the early political, economic, and financial struggles between English rulers and various Parliaments had an impact on the colonies in their struggle with the British crown, and after the American Independence, between the President and Congress.[3]

The Colonial Period

British use of the political economy of **mercantilism** largely defined the economic relationship between itself and the colonies, where they were required to provide cash crops, thus earning enough to purchase goods, including slaves. With an infusion of cash and outflow of tobacco, cotton, and other goods the colonies the colonies became a formidable trading partner, not only with Britain, but with France and other countries. But this economic activity did not alleviate them from enduring political intrusion, particularly in the area of greater taxation without representation. In addition, the colonialists assumed strong parliamentary and financial influence over the royal governors, even to the point of setting their salaries. Even though the governors had fairly extensive political and fiscal powers, the colonialists established some semblance of budgetary authority and power in order to audit and control their own finances, but in terms of modern day budgeting practices, it was fairly basic.

After defeat of the British in 1775 the independent colonies did not trust nor respect strong executives, and thus placed most budgetary authority in the hands of a legislative body. Yet, the Articles of Confederation were established in order for the colonies to exercise considerable influence over both the executive and congressional institutions. National taxation levies, for example, were collected from each state as a state (and usually not paid in the waning years under the Articles!) Still, something was needed to be done to control the escalating war debt, estimated by the Founder Thomas Jefferson to be in excess of $140 million. With operating budgets less than $500,000 each year between 1784 and 1788, the question became: where is the revenue coming from? The government took the easy solution: issue bills of credit. The Articles provided that any revenue raised was done in accordance with a property tax levied in proportion to the value of land within the various states, effectively limiting what Congress could raise and spend. As you can imagine, this financial system was rife with waste, fraud, and disorganization.

After the Articles were thrown out in favor of the new Constitution, the founders who were Federalists, led by Alexander Hamilton and George Washington, favored a stronger executive to counter-balance an already strong legislative branch. The new nation looked to the new Constitution as the primary means for determining fiscal balance and solvency. For example, the Constitution was quite clear on which level of government could and could not spend tax revenue, how money was to be withdrawn from the **U.S. Treasury**, and how all expenditures should be directed toward the benefit of the public interest. Article I, Section 8, of the Constitution established the foundation of congressional budgetary authority, among many other powers of Congress. It was Hamilton who was in favor of strengthening the role of the executive branch, believing in and achieving the establishment of a national bank, national credit system, accrual of previous war debts, and imposition of a system of taxation to pay debts.[4] [But even Hamilton did not believe in nor contend that the national government should assume the nearly unitary role and function it occupies today.] Of course, not all of the founders believed as strongly in a centralized government to oversee the fiscal and budgetary needs of the new nation.

Thomas Jefferson and James Madison—the latter being an important architect of the new Constitution—vehemently disagreed over the role of the national government and specifically the President's place in the development and implementation of fiscal powers. Their conflict went to the point of Alexander Hamilton resigning from his post of Secretary of Treasury in 1794. Despite their disagreements, both believed that the new nation and the new government could not survive without a strong fiscal force, particularly in the areas of domestic and foreign policy. What was more problematic was determining the type of relationship that was to be forged between the President and Congress. How was the Secretary of Treasury to interact—if at all—with the Congress, especially the future House Ways and Means Committee? The former was really seen as working for the latter, given the oversight role that the House had in appropriations matters. For all intents and purposes Hamilton acted more as an emissary of the House, given that there was not an executive budgeting system in place. This did not take place until 1921, with the passage of the Budget and Accounting Act of 1921. (See Box 8.2.)

Box 8.1   Role of the United States Treasury

The United States Treasury history began in somewhat difficult times: the beginning of the American Revolution. The financing of a war is no easy task now, but consider trying to do it with no central agency that oversees the budgeting and financial matters related to public revenues and expenditures! Because of the Articles of Confederation, the Congress, of course, had no powers to "lay or collect" taxes. All of this authority lay with the colonies.

In 1775 the Continental Congress gave the authority to oversee and administer the fledging government finances to two men: George Clymer and Michael Hillegas. By 1776 a Treasury Office of Accounts, which consisted of one Auditor General and several clerks, was set up to keep track of public accounts. Finally, after signing the Declaration of Independence in July of 1776, the new nation was able to borrow money from countries abroad.

Between 1778 and 1781 the Treasury Office was reorganized several times and eventually the 'continental dollars' devalued so rapidly that by May of 1781 public outcry was heard and Robert Morris was tabbed the Superintendent of Finance. Morris stayed on through 1784 and then resigned, but not before he brought stability to the devaluing dollar.

Finally, the First Congress of the U.S. met in March of 1789 and by September it had created a 'Department of Treasury.' Alexander Hamilton served as the first Secretary of Treasury from 1789 to 1795. His first order of business was to insist upon a "dollar for dollar" repayment of the nation's nearly $75 million debt. He wrote, "The debt of the United States ... was the price of liberty. The faith of America has been repeatedly pledged for it, and with solemnities that give peculiar force to the obligation." In other words, it is the right and ethical thing to do.

Source: "History of the Treasury: Introduction," United States Department of Treasury, www.treas.gov/education/history (accessed October 2007).

The first appropriations bill was passed in 1789, with personnel items totaling 45 percent, defense 21 percent, and entitlements nearly 15 percent.[5] Jeff McCaffery noted that the sums listed in a 1790 appropriations bill were listed in general terms, not identifying specific items. Later, by 1792, Congress began itemizing the appropriation bills. By the early part of the nineteenth century the size of the House of Representatives grew, and the need for a permanent or standing committee on appropriations became apparent. In addition, the role and function of the Secretary of Treasury became increasingly seen as executive branch and not as a member of the Congress. This contributed to more disagreements and political clashes between the two branches.[6]

The 1800s

The nineteenth century was marked by the continuation of the philosophical clash between Hamilton and Jefferson. Both believed in the ideals of the new nation, but disagreed over how it should be politically constructed. Hamilton believed the nation should follow the prior British mercantile system, while Jefferson believed in the independence of common workers and farmers as the social and economic backbone of America. While Hamilton advocated the use of a stronger executive government, Jefferson insisted on a deeper division and separation of powers, especially between the executive and legislative branches, with Congress playing the dominant role. Jefferson's ideas and ideals won out, at least for approximately the first forty or so years of the nineteenth century. It was not until the continuing controversies between the northern and southern states over the issue of slavery came to a head in the Civil War did Hamilton's beliefs begin to take root. Then a strong national government emerged, led by charismatic and courageous President Lincoln, increasingly necessary for the nation to financially prosper and overcome economic adversity. Still, even with increased federal spending during the major nineteenth century American wars, including the **War of 1812**, the Mexican-American War of the 1840s, and the Civil War (1861–1865),[7] the national government's responsibility was limited, largely because of limited internationalization of goods and services and pre-industrialization of technology and business innovations. Taxes were minimal, fees and charges were cheap, and customs were the law. Thus, government budgets and the commons, including both national and state, were small. But the Industrial Revolution and the corresponding political and economic changes of the late 19th and early 20th centuries changed everything.

The 1900s

The twentieth century identified the beginning of the Progressive Reform Movement and more of the commons. Science and technology advanced business innovations. Agriculture was slowly losing its grip on the economic mainstream of America, while industry was appropriating the use of machines and scientific management principles to build a new economic dynamo that would require the national government to catch up with the changes or be left behind. Progressives[8] pressed for civil and moral changes, including various labor laws. The federal government responded by passing the **Federal Trade Commission Act of 1914**, which regulated working hours and conditions, as well as protected consumers from unfair business practices.[9] Progressives were similar to socialists in that they demanded immediate political changes, but unlike socialists they did not advocate the use of authoritarian government and control of the major means of production. They did, however, advocate strong, influential government leadership, particularly at the local level. One very important way of providing this municipal leadership was through study and evaluation of the budgetary process through organizations such as the National Municipal League (1899) and the New York Bureau of Municipal Research (1906). The New York Bureau is credited for advocating budgetary reform at the local level,[10] such as the use of an object classification budget for the New York City Department of Health. Later efforts emphasized the use of line-item or object budgeting, and by the late 1920s the first scholarly emphasis is directed toward systematically studying budgeting.[11]

Box 8.2   Budget and Accounting Act of 1921

Passage of the Budget and Accounting Act of 1921 had connections back to President Taft's Commission on Economy and Efficiency (1910–1912), which called for an increased role by the President in the development of a federal budget. However, because the Commission's report did not mention the role of the legislature it languished in Congress. By 1919, however, Congress held hearings and made recommendations for presidential involvement in the federal budgetary process. President Wilson actually vetoed the original bill "because of concern with the constitutionality of a provision involving his removal power over the new office of Comptroller General." President Harding signed the bill into law in 1921.

Source: Joint Committee on the Organization of Congress, "The Executive Budget Movement and the Budget and Accounting Act of 1921," *Organization of the Congress*, 103d Cong., 1st sess., 1993, www.rules.house.gov/archives/jcoc2w.htm (accessed October 2007).

Despite all of these advances, prior to 1921, federal government agencies still accepted the Jeffersonian ideals as gospel: preparing their expenditure estimates, passing them on to Treasury, who in turn passed them on to Congress. Congress rarely considered new items of spending. Rather it maintained the status quo, not really looking to use the budget as a policy tool. This all changed with the publication of President Taft's 1910 **Commission on Economy and Efficiency's** report titled "Need for a National Budget." The Commission, which was chaired by Frederick Cleveland, highlighted the need for greater executive administrative power, particularly in the areas of budgetary guidance and direction. Naturally Congress resisted for political and power reasons, but shortly after the conclusion of World War I Congress passed the **Budget and Accounting Act of 1921**.[12] The act, for the first time, centralized the formation of the federal budget in the executive office, specifically in the newly created **Bureau of the Budget** (BOB), which was to report to the treasury secretary. The BOB's first director, Charles G. Dawes, initiated technological creations, including mandating reserves and using scientific management principles to ensure greater efficiency and economy in the budgetary process. The Act also created the **General Accounting Office** (GAO), which was to report to Congress.[13] Thus, the budgetary process had two major changes: strong executive influence and greater use of checks and balances between the executive and legislative branches.

FDR and the Brownlow Committee. FDR's influence was evident when he initiated a variety of changes aimed at centralizing executive power, including in the making of budgets. His 1937 **Committee on Administration Management** (the Brownlow Committee, named after its chairman, Louis Brownlow) recommended increasing BOB's authority. By 1939 Congress passed the Reorganization Act, which established the Executive Office of the President and effectively transferred BOB from the Department of Treasury to this new office—directly under the authority of the president; de facto the BOB became the budgetary right hand of the president,[14] and thus placed not only the power to initiate budgets, but to also guide policy. By the end of the war Congress extended the BOB's function to include government corporations, oversight of agency operations, regulation of travel allowances, adoption of a performance budget—something much different than the traditional line-item budget common to municipalities at the time—and to update agency budgeting and accounting systems.[15]

Planning and Programming. By the 1960s, with war being waged on two fronts—the domestic war on poverty and a foreign war on Communism—and the costs to fight each escalating daily, the need for more sophisticated forms of budgeting seemed apparent. President Lyndon Baines Johnson's Task Force on Governmental Reorganization in 1964 recommended a more scientific approach to policy analysis, applying economic theory and operations research to the linkage of inputs and outputs. The new budgeting system formed out of such an arrangement was called **Planning-Programming-Budgeting System** (PPBS).[16] This new form of budgeting is concerned with inputs, outputs, effects and alternatives. It was the first truly management-based budgeting system, where it was designed to explain management decisions and, ultimately, the spending of hundreds of millions of dollars.

Drawn from the private sector, specifically General Motors and Ford Motor Company, PPBS was both a president's dream and nightmare. It provided extensive information, but it required reams of information and data in order to be successful. To minimize the nightmare aspect, in 1961 President Johnson lured a young, bright, and energetic **Robert McNamara** away from Ford to become secretary of defense, and implement PPBS, thus bringing about a centralized budget and management system, complete with a strong executive focus.

PPBS was a multidisciplinary budgeting concept, designed to incorporate a more rational rather than incremental data-gathering and analysis process. The intention is for the budget analyst to set goals and then determine cost/benefit ratios in order to choose the best decision for allocation of revenues. President Johnson demanded greater financial accountability and program effectiveness, especially in waging the Vietnam War. He sought to enlist the most sophisticated quantitative techniques of budgeting and program management possible, in order to justify the spending of billions of dollars weekly on the war effort. PPBS was such a system. One way to accomplish this monumental task was to centralize the authority and control of military spending; this was done through the PPBS.

Box 8.3   Robert McNamara's Whiz Kids

Robert McNamara and his "Whiz Kids" brought to the Department of Defense in the 1960s sophisticated policy analytical techniques, including program budgeting and policy evaluation tools, and computer information systems technology that was to revolutionize the way government engaged in public management and policy analysis. The "Whiz Kids" were young, bright, and computer-knowledgeable. Many came with McNamara from the private sector, including Ford Motor Company, where McNamara had been company president in 1960. Based upon these modern techniques for system management, McNamara restructured the military, moving from strict reliance on nuclear technology to a combination of nuclear and traditional military strategy. His disdain for military career officials in favor of business and non-military types irritated Pentagon officials, many members of Congress, and, of course, the anti-war protestors. He resigned as Secretary of Defense in 1967 and became president of the World Bank, lasting from 1968–1981. He continues to write and lecture.

Source: "Robert S. McNamara," Answers.com, www.answers.com/topic/robert-s.mcnamara (accessed October 2007).

McNamara hired his "**Whiz Kids,**" who were bright, computer-savvy, and mathematically-oriented types, drawing them largely from the private sector, to enter the brave new world of government bureaucracy and military jargon, specifically to install a budgeting system that would not only count and keep track of guns, bullets, and dead soldiers, but monitor the costs of doing so. President Johnson was so enthralled that in 1965 he ordered all government agencies to conform to such a system. The system was too complicated and complex to be effective in non-military departments, such as Departments of Agriculture and Interior, that upon entering office in 1969, President Nixon ordered an immediate cease and desist, all but effectively declaring the system dead on arrival by the early 1970s. By 1970 the BOB became the **Office of Management and Budget** (**OMB**), with the focus on managing resources, not necessarily quantifying and analyzing the effective use of resources. Although it is no longer used extensively at the federal government level, PPBS is still used somewhat at the state and local levels.

The 1970s Reforms. Before we discuss further iterations of budgeting methods, we need to provide a brief overview of the significant changes that took place in federal budgeting practices during the mid-1970s, specifically as a result of the **Congressional Budget and Impoundment Control Act of 1974** (the Congressional Budget Act). (We will later exam these reforms as they affected deficits and deficit controls.) This act was designed to bring some sense of congressional control and oversight back to the public budgeting process. Birthed out of an anti-executive movement, largely associated with the political fall out of Watergate, the act sought to reestablish congressional influence, including the making and implementation of federal budgets. This was necessary for a number of reasons, including: 1) the fact that neither the House or the Senate had specific permanent committees designated for reviewing and critiquing the president's budget requests; or 2) for implementing a process to follow for determining what effects the executive budget might have on the total economy; or 3) for extending the budgetary review process to a biennial time frame versus an annual one; or 4) for restricting the president from impounding funds that appropriated for policies and programs he did not approve of; and 5) for establishing an adequate staff to analyze the president's budget requests, while developing specific and reliable alternatives. (See Table 8.1, which depicts the budget calendar of the federal budget process.)

Table 8.1   The Budget Calendar

Executive Budget Documents	Timing & Actions	Congressional Budget Documents
	9/14 — Executive branch agencies submit initial budget requests	
	10/15 — Other agencies submit budget requests	
	Nov–Dec — Legislative & judicial branches submit budget requests	
	December — CBO determines if additional cutting of spending necessary	Final Sequestration Report to the President and Congress for Fiscal Year ...: Y 1.1/7:—U.S. Government Documents Microfiche
	December — OMB provides estimates of the status of discretionary spending	
Budget of the United States Government HJ 2051 .Un31— Business, Lehman *Economic Report of the President.* HC 106.5.U5 A121— Lehman	**1st Monday in February —** President transmits budget to Congress	
	2/15 — CBO reports to budget committees	*Budget and Economic Outlook and Updates* Y 10.13:—U.S. Government Documents
	March	*Budget Options* No print version
	April	*Analysis of the President's Budgetary Proposals* Y 10.19:—U.S. Government Documents *Omnibus Budget Reconciliation Act* Y 1.1/8:—MF—U.S. Government Documents *Omnibus Appropriations Bill*, October 19, 1998 *Consolidated Appropriations Act FY 2000*, November 17, 1999
	6/30 — House completes action	*Consolidated Appropriations Act FY 2001*, December 15, 2000

Table 8.1   The Budget Calendar *continued*

Executive Budget Documents	Timing & Actions	Congressional Budget Documents
	on appropriations bills	Status of FY2002 Appropriations Bills
		Status of FY2003 Appropriations Bills
		Status of FY2004 Appropriations Bills
		Status of FY2005 Appropriations Bills
		Status of FY2006 Appropriations Bills
		Status of FY2006 Appropriations Bills
		Status of FY2007 Appropriations Bills
		Status of FY2008 Appropriations Bills
		Status of FY2009 Appropriations Bills
Mid-Session Budget Review PR EX 2.31:— U.S. Government Documents	July 15 — President submits Mid-session Budget Review	
Sequestration Update Report	August 20 — OMB updates sequestration review	
	October 1 — Fiscal year begins	

See U.S. Government Documents: The Budget Process, http://www.columbia.edu/cu/lweb/indiv/usgd/budget.html (Accessed November 30, 2008).

First, the act created **House** and **Senate Budget Committees**, permanent standing committees, whose jurisdiction was responsible for deciding which program requests were legitimate and realistic among the many funding requests made each year. Second, the act required Congress as a whole body to vote twice per year (congressional budget resolutions) on spending priorities. Third, it established a time table requiring Congress to schedule various actions to take place (authorization and appropriate passages, etc.). Fourth, the act created the Congressional Budget Office (CBO) as a counter agency to Office of Management Budget (OMB). Fifth, so-called "backdoor spending" appropriations were eliminated as was the president's unconstitutional power to impound or stop the appropriation of funds to particular areas of political and ideological disagreement between the executive and congressional.

Congress fully intended to slow down the executive federal budget decision making juggernaut without completely doing away with it. For example, the CBO's responsibility was to:

- Establish a concurrent resolution by setting expenditure and revenue targets for the upcoming fiscal year;
- Provide multiple types of costs estimates;
- Establish fiscal, inflation, and mandate criteria for evaluating when and how to spend dollars;
- Place limits on presidential impoundment power through inclusion of deferrals and rescissions. A **deferral** is a temporary technique used by the president to defer spending because of administrative functions that save money. Deferrals run out at the end of the fiscal year, but can be renewed. A **rescission** is a more controver-

sial and permanent presidential method for reducing spending, where the president or Congress can impound funds based upon ideological and political dislike for a program.[17]
   • And provide an annual report on federal budget options.[18]

Of these five significant changes to the federal budgeting process, **impoundment** of funds by the president and the establishment of **concurrent resolutions** by the Congress standout. With regard to the president's power to impound funds, the president could still delay spending using a deferral, unless the Congress overrode the deferral. In the 1983 case of *Immigration and Naturalization Service v. Chadha,* the Supreme Court ruled that a **legislative veto** of executive agency decisions (delegated to them by Congress) by one house was a violation of the separation of powers doctrine. Instead, Congress could only take back the power it delegated to the agency by a law passed by both houses of Congress (or leave the agency alone). Thereafter, Congress reduced presidential deferrals for strictly policy reasons; otherwise, if it did no,t the president would essentially have unlimited veto power.[19]

With Congress in concurrent resolutions, the president submits a budget in February for the fiscal year that begins each October 1st. Congress then has several options, including: 1) adopting the budget resolutions; 2) passing appropriation bills; and 3) passing other budget-related legislation, such as authorization legislation, reconciliation bills, various tax-related changes, modifications of various entitlement programs, and even debt limit adjustments. The resolution is concerned with listing total spending, program allocations, and "reconciliation instructions," or the means by which the House and Senate committees "report legislation conforming spending, revenue, or debt-limit levels under existing law to current budget policies."[20] What this essentially means is that through an elaborate and intricate process of information dissemination and quality control measures, Congress is better able to check the budgetary actions of the president, by inspecting the spending patterns of each of the thirteen executive departments and by passing individual authorization and appropriation bills.

Budgeting Styles and Techniques

The intention of budgeting is to institute better means of control over spending habits, but at the same time not completely restrict executive freedom to provide various expenditure options. In order to take full advantage of many of these reforms, governments, including both federal and state and local, needed to try new means of budgeting public funds.

Management by Objectives. By the beginning of the second Nixon administration, the White House and OMB encouraged a new approach to budgeting: **management by objectives** (MBO). The idea was for agency heads to establish program and funding objectives and then require a process toward accomplishing those objectives. As one public administration scholar notes, MBO "has a managerial orientation that stresses ... common sense."[21] Perhaps this contributed to its undoing: too much discretionary fiscal authority in the hands of mid-level managers! Although it was extensively and generally successfully used in the private sector, it failed to generate much political support. It was similar to performance budgeting in that it was concerned with inputs, outputs, and effects, but unlike performance-based budgeting it did not stress the use of alternatives. For example, the key question for department and agency officials to ask is: How effective are X-dollars for meeting Y-objectives? Intended to be a decentralized approach to budget decision making, the manner in which it was used in the Nixon administration left much to be desired. Instead of having lower-level bureaucratic input into what objectives should be set and how they should be accomplished given the limited allocation of revenues available; the Nixon administration instituted top-down control. Further, agency goals were often displaced because of the overemphasis of measurable quantitative goals over qualitative and non-measurable aspects of a program. Although it is still an effective tool, it is not used at the federal level. Its greatest use is at the state and local levels, where, for example, some 47 percent of all U.S. cities in 1993 and nearly two-thirds of all states use some form of MBO.[22]

Zero-base Budgeting. Zero-base budgeting was originally used by Texas Instruments, under the direction and leadership of **Peter Pyhrr**, who later assisted Jimmy Carter to implement it when Carter was governor of Georgia.[23] President Carter then brought it with him into the federal government during the late 1970s, but that is as far as it went; it left just as quickly as it came. It is based on the theory that incremental decision making is purely political and does not advocate true budgetary reform. Therefore, it features zero-base analysis, where each agency and department must justify its spending from scratch, or the zero-base, using decision packages, with each package of budget proposals ranked in order of priority. The lowest level packages do not get funded. Supposedly this system is designed to place all programs on equal footing at the beginning of each fiscal year, which theoretically happens. But in reality the wheel that squeaks loudest receives the most grease. In addition, it is counter-productive in many ways, because it consumes significant time, effort, and paper on the part of the various agencies to go back and justify why they want the same level of appropriation from last year plus some.

Target-based Budgeting. History tells us that President Reagan was driven to ratchet down federal government's role as no other president had before (and since). He advocated the reduction of government spending, accomplishing this through the reform and reduction of federal taxes and tax re-structuring. In order to accomplish his ideological task, he required a public budgeting system, such as target-based budgeting (TBB) that was aimed at top down control of agency budgets, generally by the director of the OMB, who at the time was **David Stockman**. Although in all fairness to the Reagan proposal, the agency heads had discretion to spend their allocated dollars, but only within the limits imposed by the OMB director. Further they were expected to demonstrate that they had in fact achieved their goals set forth the year prior for the next year's budget request. Thus, the idea was to target certain goals, such as reducing federal education spending and mandating that states and localities pick up more of the educational tab, while at the same time redirecting funds to other targeted areas, such as defense or military spending. So, instead of the agency heads sending their requests to Congress and/or the budget director, the latter forwarded their allotted amounts to the department and agency heads, informing them what was available to them for expenditure purposes. As you can guess there was considerable discretion in the spending habits and patterns of departments and agencies.

Return to Performance Budgeting. Fueled in large part by the New Public Management revolution—which is in stark contrast to the New Public Service paradigm (see Chapter 6, "Public Management and the Public Interest")[24]—it gained its impetus through publication and dissemination of David Osborne and Ted Gaebler's book, *Reinventing Government*,[25] and through President Clinton's charge to Vice President Al Gore, Jr., to establish the National Partnership for Reinventing Government, which was designed to direct government and government action to be results-oriented, including the budgeting system. Several types of budgets were highlighted by Osborne and Gaebler, including **mission-driven budgeting, output budgeting** (a budget system that focuses on the output of services), **outcome budgeting** (budget that focuses on the quality of services produced), and **customer-driven budgeting**.[26] Each of these budgeting types — although differing in particulars somewhat — were similar with regard to the larger picture: to make local government run more efficiently through control of inputs and outputs. This type of budgeting, as you can well imagine, is similar to performance budgeting, in that it is heavily weighted toward management and incremental decision making, but differs in that it is more participatory and decentralized in nature.[27]

Box 8.4   Performance-Based Budgeting Gains Prominence

Performance-based budgeting drew great attention from states and municipalities. The National Governor's Association (NGA) published *An Action Agenda to Redesign State Government* (1993), calling for "performance based state government," complete with measurable goals and outcomes. Not to be outdone, the National Conference of State Legislatures (NCSL) published its own study 1994 titled *The Performance Budget Revisited: A Report on State Budget Reform*. Now states began jumping on the performance-based-budgeting bandwagon, including Oregon, Minnesota, Montana, Iowa, Texas, Idaho, Ohio, Florida, and many others. Despite the fact that there was still a lack of credibility, time and resource constraints, and political hurdles to overcome, performance based budgeting took off. The public demand to validate spending of public tax dollars was great. Even greater was the need to show quantitative evidence that the tax dollars were, first, actually spent on the items indicated, and two, that there were measurable outputs and outcomes to justify the tax revenue and expenditures. Government, public officials, and public administrators were on a short public relations leash!

Source: Reprinted in part from Charlie Tyer and Jennifer Willand, "Public Budgeting in America: A Twentieth Century Retrospective," Journal of Public Budgeting, Accounting and Financial Management 9, no. 2 (Summer 1997). Reprinted at www.ipspr.sc.edu/publication/Budgeting_in_America.htm (accessed October 2007).

Osborne and Gaebler provided hundreds of examples and illustrations of results oriented government, and it was with this impetus for change that President Clinton chose Vice President Gore to head up the new commission whose primary responsibility would be to not only find ways to save taxpayer dollars, but to make government work better by working more efficiently and economically. When Congress passed the Government Performance and Results Act of 1993 it dedicated itself to exploring ways toward "mission-driven, results-oriented budgets."[28] So, how successful is performance based and/or results-oriented budgeting? Although they are not exactly the same, they are similar enough to justify the following statement: performance budgeting has a semi-long track record, one that is somewhat difficult to assess, especially at the federal and local levels, while at the state level 47 of 50 states have some aspect of performance budgeting inherent in their budgeting and financial management systems,[29] but one that is generally positive toward the use of performance based systems.[30]

The driving force, of course, is **results**. What is government getting for its expenditures? All parties involved claim to want to know where, what, and how public funds are being spent: politicians, public administrators, customer-citizens, and clientele groups. This is performance and/or outputs based budgeting; the latest in a long list of historical approaches to itemize, manage, document, and otherwise know where, when, how, and, perhaps, why public funds are being spent in the way they are spent.[31]

Box 8.5   Limits on Performance Budgeting

First it cannot solve or avert a financial crisis. No matter how many benchmarks, performance measures, etc. a city, state, or federal agency set prior to 9/11 it could not have anticipated nor adequately adapted to the financial problems that resulted because of 9/11, the war in Iraq, or the aftermath of Hurricane Katrina.

Second, try as they might some proponents for performance budgeting who think politics can be eliminated from the equation are simply wrong. They even lay out their own multi-point plan on the use of political strategies or principles for igniting the fire for performance based budgeting.

Third, performance budgeting cannot reduce the influence of interest groups, which are trying to get all the benefits they can from the *very* political process of public budgeting.

Fourth, performance budgeting does not make poor managers suddenly good managers. It can offer tools and techniques for tying goals to budget outlays, for example, but it cannot make a square peg fit in a round hole. If local managers believe, for instance, that continual local recycling programs do not work, despite the evidence to the contrary, then there is not much that performance budgeting can do to help.

And fifth, performance budgeting cannot redirect the priorities of citizens. Citizens are not looking at the city manager's detailed performance based report of the exceptional productivity of the city's street sweeping operation, especially not when the police department, for example, is under fire for not handling a youth gang incident. Their eyes are on their neighborhoods, their elected representatives, and in the case of a city upon the political promises of the mayor, not the quantitative criteria offered by performance or outcome budgeting in a department that does not elicit as much political notoriety.

Performance budgeting has its positive benefits, particularly evident in a cultural outcry of doing more with less. But that cry is not new.

Source: Janet M. Kelly and William C. Rivenbark, *Performance Budgeting for State and Local Government* (Armonk, NY: M.E. Sharpe Press, 2003), 10–11; David Osborne and Peter Hutchinson, *The Price of Government: Getting the Results We Need in an Age of Permanent Fiscal Crisis* (New York: Basic Books, 2004), 328–29; and David N. Ammons and William C. Rivenbark, "Using Benchmark Data to Improve Services: Local Impact of a Municipal Performance Comparison Project," conference paper presented at the *Southeastern Conference of Public Administration*, October 5–8, Little Rock, AR.

Summary. The various budgeting types reflect the range of human nature factors: pluralistic, controlling, but always changing. The basic responsibility elected and administrative officials have toward securing and protecting public funds is a tremendous burden, but it is one that identifies the need to fulfill the public interest. Politics of budgeting certainly plays a significant role in the budgeting process, given that Democrats and Republicans want to control the public purse strings so as to push their policy agenda; however, pursuit of the public interest regarding public spending, deficit control, and other matters related to public budgeting should take precedent. Whether it does or not is questionable.

Before we turn to the nuts-and-bolts process of how public budgeting works we need to briefly cover the taxing-and-spending process. The crux of budgeting, of course, is the collection, management, and administration of public funds. This is where the public must trust elected and appointed officials and merit based public administrators.

This is where we must ask: are public officials operating in and promoting the public interest as they assume the role of steward of the public funds and overseers of public expenditures?

Before we can discuss how public budgeting works, we need to overview the taxing and spending power and/or authority that governments have. The commons (and the public interest) are often defined by taxing and tax spending. Taxes are as old as written history. However, let's take just a brief walk through time and examine some of the major changes that took place in the tax history of the U.S. Government.

Brief History of the U.S. Tax System

During the early years of our nation's founding, citizens had little contact with the national government, given that almost all of the national government's revenue came in the form of excise taxes, tariffs on imported goods, and custom duties. After the Articles of Confederation were abandoned in 1789, the Founding Fathers decided to include a taxing provision in the second article (Congress's article) that permitted Congress to "... lay and collect taxes, duties, imposts, and excises, pay the Debts and provide for the common Defense and general Welfare of the United States." However, despite this authority and the need to pay off debts of the Revolutionary War, fund the War of 1812, and other internal and external encounters that required government expenditure, the U.S. Government did not impose taxes on individual's personal income; instead, it continued with imposing higher rates on excise taxes and custom duties.

By the Civil War the U.S. Government finally enacted a personal income tax, but the rate was only about three percent on incomes above $800. A tiered income tax system was instituted by the middle of the war, but by the early 1870s Congress repealed it. Of course that all changed with ratification of the Sixteenth Amendment to the U.S. Constitution in 1913, allowing Congress the leeway necessary to institute a permanent income tax system. Beginning with World War I and continuing through the next decade, Congress passed successive revenue acts that raised the tax rates. In 1916, for example, the lowest rate went from 1 to 2 percent and the top rate increased to 15 percent (but this only applied to incomes above $1.5 million. You can imagine there were very few incomes that high!) By 1918 the bottom rate went to 6 percent and the top rate skyrocketed to 77 percent, which increased federal revenue to nearly 25 percent of the **Gross Domestic Product (GDP)**. Succeeding years saw passage of the Social Security Act of 1935, a new program of unemployment compensation, and two more tax laws in 1940 which reinstated the withholding provision — the same tax method used during the Civil War.

Since WWII the initiation of higher taxes was generally related to national or world crises, such as the Korean War, Vietnam War, President Johnson's War on Poverty, with the ability to tax being used as a political tool. Not until the **Economic Recovery Tax Act** of 1981, i.e., as the Reagan tax cut, was there a substantial alteration in the taxing structure of the U.S. government. With the Reagan tax cut there came a 25 percent reduction in individual tax brackets, which would be instituted over the next three years, and the top tax bracket, which had been as high as 94 percent, was reduced to 50 percent. Subsequent Reagan administrations promoted and generally acquired tax reform acts (1982, 1984, and 1986), until President Clinton called for and received tax increase in the top tax rate. [For FY 2010, the Obama administration is demanding even higher rates on incomes over $250,000 per year, while providing "tax breaks" to the bottom 40 percent of Americans who pay no federal income taxes.] But in the 1997 the **Taxpayer Relief Act** was passed, which provided as its primary component a tax benefit to families with children (but only those families who met income levels). Finally, President G.W. Bush in 2001 pushed through Congress the **Economic Growth and Tax Relief and Reconciliation Act**, a law that among other things reduced the top tax rate to 33 percent and expanded the Per Child Tax and increased the Dependent Child Tax credit.[32]

Why Taxes at All?

Public funds, or **revenue**, are mostly gathered through taxes (or fees), but there are other means as well. Why taxes? Before the government can engage in distributing or providing a service or program, such as highway maintenance, police protection, or Medicare, it has to have funding. So taxes are established and collected. The result is what we call revenue. Government revenue is further categorized in several ways that will help us understand the commons and the extent of government's influence. First, taxes raised are either direct or indirect. **Direct** revenue comes mainly from personal and corporate income tax, whereas **indirect** comes from sales or **value-added** taxes. Second, public revenue can come through transfers, which are grants of money provided from one level of government, usually the national, to other levels of government, usually state and local governments. Third, government revenue is acquired through borrowing on public bonds and loans. And fourth, public revenue is gathered from "profits from government enterprises, franchising and licensing, and even savings and investment earnings.[33] Before we examine the expenditure side of the public ledger, let's look briefly at the type and kinds of taxes.

Kinds of taxes include regressive, progressive, or proportional. **Regressive taxes**, such as sales on goods and services, are taxes that tax individuals with lower incomes at a proportionally higher rate than those with higher incomes. For example, the single parent with multiple children who works three jobs and makes a combined income of $25,000 and the business executive who makes $250,000 both pay the same sales tax on the $250 grocery bill, but in the first scenario the tax is regressive, taking about 1 percent of the family's income while in the second case the impact is one-tenth of that! That is a substantial difference, particularly when many individuals are working to make ends meet. On the other hand a **progressive tax** is weighted to the higher one's income the more tax one will pay (e.g. the executive making $250,000 will pay the top federal income tax rate of nearly 40 percent, while the single parent working three jobs and making $25,000 will be taxed less than half that amount). The liberal moral argument is that the more one makes, the more the individual should be required to be taxed, while the conservative moral argument claims that it is unfair to tax someone at a higher rate simply he makes more money, causing a disincentive to earn more money, something that it is antithetical in a free-market economy. Finally, a **proportional tax** is where all individuals—both the executive and the single parent—are taxed at the same rate. For example, if a proportional tax rate of 20 percent (one of the many levels floating around) is applied to both cases above the amount taken is considerably different ($5,000 versus $50,000), but the rate is the same. Proponents of the proportional rate claim that total revenue will actually go up (simply because fewer deductions are permitted), and the filing process is far simpler. Opponents are largely against such a plan because they contend it is simply ethically wrong to tax all income groups at the same rate.

Types of taxes differ depending upon the level of government. First, at the national or federal level of government there are two primary types of taxes: individual and corporate. As we noted in our historical survey individual taxes were never used but once prior to the turn of the twentieth century (for a short period during and after the Civil War). Based on the progressive nature of personal income taxes, politicians, depending upon political and ideological persuasion, battle over whether and when to raise such taxes, especially when it is connected to the wealthy (of course that depends on how one defines wealthy). For example, the 1986 tax cut "represented the penultimate installment of an extraordinary process of tax rate reductions." Cutting the top rate to only 28 percent actually contributed to an increase in federal government tax burden as a percentage of GDP, but with the Reagan administration spending large amounts on military-related expenditures, for example, Democrats saw an opportunity to seek for an increase in taxes. In 1990, despite President G.H.W. Bush's infamous statement, "Read my lips: no new taxes," Congress passed and President Bush signed into law a significant tax increase, that raised the top rate to 31 percent. Later in 1993 President Clinton was able to get the top rate increased to 36 percent and then again to 39.6 percent. Today, as a result of President Bush's 2001 tax relief the top rate is back down to 33 percent.

Individual income taxes account for the largest percentage of government revenue. Table 8.1 depicts the increasing dependency on individual income taxes compared to other forms of receipts. In 1934 the federal government took in only $420 million in personal income taxes; by 2006 that number had grown to just over $1 trillion, which accounts for just fewer than 50 percent of total receipts. Even though almost all advanced industrial nations use an individual income tax to fund the lion's share of their programs and expenditures, there is still great debate as to equity of a progressive tax system, prompting many politicians (former presidential candidate Steve Forbes) and pundits (conservative radio personality Rush Limbaugh) to seriously consider major revisions in the current tax system, including serious examination of some type of proportional system. The second type of income tax is corporate income taxes.

Corporate taxes are also a progressive tax, but their controversy stems from the fact that it is considered a double tax, meaning corporations pay income taxes on net corporate income, and then the shareholders are taxed again on the dividends.[34] As of 2004 they accounted for only about 10 percent of total receipts. (See Table 8.2.)

State and Local Levels. At the state and local levels of government the primary means of taxation are sales, excise and property taxes. Instead of concentrating on income, **sales taxes** impact consumption; meaning they are based on how much an individual buys. The more one buys and the higher priced item or service one purchases, the greater the tax burden. But as we mentioned above it is also a regressive tax, meaning that regardless of how much or how large one's purchase is, the tax is the same for all individuals—regardless of income level. Only five states do not have a sales tax (Alaska, Delaware, Montana, New Hampshire, and Oregon), with the average rate among the remaining 45 states at 5.8 percent, with the lowest at 2.9 percent (Colorado) and the highest at 7 percent shared by four states (Mississippi, New Jersey, Rhode Island, and Tennessee). **Excise taxes** are taxes placed on items such motor fuel, cigarette and other tobacco products (chewing tobacco), distilled spirits (liquor), wine and beer. Sometimes referred to as sin-taxes, excise taxes could be placed on any legal item that is traded, purchased, or otherwise exchanged between individuals. In addition to taxation or their own source revenue, state and local governments also receive substantial revenue from the federal government. It comes to them in the form of an **intergovernmental transfer**. It can be a loan or a grant. Total intergovernmental revenue for all state and local governments in 2004–2005 equaled over $438 billion. For example, with regard to education some of this federal money is provided directly to citizens of the various states (e.g. student loans), but much of it is transferred to the state and local governments, who in turn distribute it to K-12 and universities and colleges.[35] (See Table 8.3.)

Table 8.2   Comparison of Federal Government Receipts by Source in Select
Ten-Year Increments (in millions of dollars)

Year	Individual Income Tax	Corporate Income Taxes	Social Insurance Receipts	Excise Taxes	Other	Total Receipts
1934	420 (14%)	364 (12.1%)	30 (1%)	1,354 (4.5%)	788 (2.6%)	2,955
1944	19,705 (45%)	14,838 (33.9%)	3,473 (7.9%)	4,759 (10.8%)	972 (2.2%)	43,747
1954	29,542 (42.3%)	21,101 (30.2%)	7,208 (10.3%)	9,945 (14.2%)	1,905 (2.7%)	69,701
1964	48,697 (43.2%)	23,493 (20.8%)	21,963 (19.5%)	13,731 (12.1%)	4,731 (4.2%)	112,613
1974	118,952 (45.1%)	38,620 (14.6%)	75,071 (28.5%)	16,844 (6.3%)	13,737 (5.2%)	263,224
1984	298,415 (44.7%)	56,893 (8.5%)	239,376 (35.9%)	37,361 (5.6%)	34,440 (5.16%)	666,486
1994	543,055 (43.1%)	140,385 (11.1%)	461,475 (36.6%)	55,225 (4.3%)	58,581 (4.6%)	1,258,721
2004	808,959 (43%)	189,371 (10%)	733,047 (38.9%)	69,855 (3.7%)	78,687 (4.1%)	1,880,279
2008e	1,219,661 (48.4%)	345,336 (13.7%)	910,125 (36.1%)	68,835 (2.7%)	-22,782 (-0.9%)	2,521,175

Source: "The Budget for Fiscal Year 2009, Historical Tables: Table 2.1, Receipts by Source: 1934–2013," Office of Management and Budget, http://www.gpoaccess.gov/USbudget/fy09/hist.html (accessed December 2008).

Table 8.3   State and Local Revenue Sources, 2004–2005

Revenue Source	State/Local ($)	S/L (%)	State ($)	State (%)	Local ($)	Local (%)
Total Revenue	2,523,005,780		1,637,791,549		1,307,002,281	
Intergovernmental	438,155,977	17	408,449,375	25	451,494,652	35
Taxes	1,096,384,739	43	648,111,258	40	448,273,481	34
Charges/Misc.	486,385,597	19	225,757,857	14	260,627,740	20
Utility	113,792,118	4	14,627,471	.4	99,164,647	8
Liquor Store	6,082,057	.2	5,212,04	.3	869,993	—
Insurance Trust	382,205,292	15	335,633,524	20	46,571,768	4
		98.2		99.7		101

Source: "Table 1. State and Local Government Finances by Level of Government and by State: 2004–2005," U.S. Census Bureau, http://www.census.gov/govs/estimate/0500ussl_1.html (accessed October 2007).

Where state income and sales taxes is the mainstay of state revenue, **property taxes** are the backbone of local government revenue. Property tax is not very popular—not by citizens or local officials who have to administer it. There are several reasons, including no one can agree completely on how to valuate property, whether it is assessed value or mar-

ket value or some other means. Even the technical means to figure property tax is somewhat complicated. Based on a benchmark measure called **mills**, which is equal to $1 for
$1,000 of assessed value, a $200,000 piece of property assessed at 30 percent of the market value would yield $6,000. [The formula is *market value* x *assessment rate* x *mills* =
yield].[36] However, sometimes the millage rate may change, depending upon action of the
General Assembly. As in the case of the state of Iowa, for example, at the time the millage rate was used property was assessed at 27 percent of its market value, whereas the
millage rate was applied at 100 percent of the market rate. Therefore, the millage rate
had to be adjusted down 27 cents per $1,000 of assessed value. So, for example, this ex-
plains why some Iowa property tax levies are in multiples of 27 cents. In addition, local
governments are given authority by the state to levy property taxes for any number of
policy or functional areas, including counties, cities, education, township and others.[37]
Confusing, huh! No wonder no one really likes the property tax as a means of collecting
local revenue.

Expenditures: Where Is It All Going?

So where does all of this revenue go? At the national level spending is divided into
two broad categories: **mandatory** and **discretionary**. Mandatory items are items legislated
by Congress and thus required or mandated areas where federal revenue must go. The
largest of these areas are entitlement programs, such as Medicare and Medicaid, which
are largely means-tested, indicating that Congress sets eligibility requirements and rules
to enforce those requirements. Then the amount to be appropriated is determined by
the demand for the service. Mandatory spending makes up about two-thirds of federal
spending, with Social Security making up about one-third of mandatory spending. Discretionary items are items that Congress has the option of whether or not to spend in
this area. Congress has the authority to directly set the spending limits on those items it
wants to spend money on or not. It can increase or decrease at its discretion so to speak.
For example, national defense is a discretionary item, given that Congress has the constitutional power and political authority to add or take away from the military's budget
as it deems appropriate. But during time of war, even though Congress has the constitutional power to control military appropriations, Congress will generally not refuse to
appropriate funds. The war in Iraq is a perfect illustration. The Bush administration
asked for and received numerous supplemental appropriations (appropriations over and
beyond DOD's original budget request). The latest in those installments was $93.4 bil-
lion for 2007 and $141.7 billion for 2008. The FY 2008 DOD request was $481.4 billion.
(See Table 8.4.)

At the state and local levels spending is varied, but the primary areas are education,
public welfare, health, prisons/criminal justice, highways and public works, and parks/nat-
ural resources. Education spending is predominant at the local level, with nearly $500
billion spent and less than $200 billion at the state level. Social welfare programs are
predominantly administered and funded by the states; however, here states spend nearly
70 percent more than local governments (e.g. $317 to $44 billion, respectively). Public
health programs and public safety programs both loom large at the local level.[38] Approximately 77 percent of state expenditures are in the following areas: intergovernmental transfers (27 percent), education (13 percent), public welfare (22 percent), utilities
(7 percent), insurance trust (8 percent), and hospitals (3 percent), while 70 percent of
local expenditures are in education (38 percent), utilities (10 percent), police (5 per-

Table 8.4   Federal Discretionary and Mandatory Spending by Sources, FY 2009

Sources	Discretionary	Sources	Mandatory
National Defense	58%	Social Security	35%
Education, training, employment, and social services	7%	Income Security	19%
Other (Energy, agriculture, commerce and housing credit, community and regional development, general government and administration of Medicare and Social Security)	5%	Net interest on debt	14%
Health	5%	Medicare	21%
Income security	5%	Health (Medicaid)	12%
Administration of Justice	4%	Veterans Benefits and Services	3%
Veterans Benefits and Services	4%		
Transportation	2%		
Natural resources and environment	3%		
General science, space, and technology	3%		
International Affairs	4%		

Source: "Proposed Discretionary Budget 2009," National Priorities Project, http://www.na-tionalpriorities.org/node/6916 (accessed December 2008).

cent), general administration (5 percent), hospitals (5 percent), interest on the debt (4 percent), and housing and community development (3 percent). (See Table 8.5.)

Now, we will examine public budgeting at all three levels of government, focusing on the general steps involved in the process. Remember, the public budgeting process is not conceptually difficult, but it is complex, largely because of the need for significant checks and balances—hence, the need to pursue and fulfill the public interest.

The process of public budgeting has become more complex; there is no doubt. More of everything, including people and governments' needs and wants, necessitates a more complex process of accounting for the increased revenue and expenditures to meet these demands. The **National Advisory Council on State and Local Budgeting** contends that "Good budgeting is a broadly defined process that has political, managerial, planning, communication, and financial dimensions." Budgeting at any government level is strategic in nature, with its overall mission to assist political and managerial decision makers make sound, informed decisions about the level and distribution of financial resources in order to accomplish predetermined goals.[39]

Federal Budgeting

Federal budgeting is certainly a political process, but it has much broader implications, including promoting the public interest. **Aaron Wildavsky** (1930–1993), the dean of the classical politics of the budgetary process approach, contends that budgeting has multiple meanings, largely depending upon the context and actors involved.[40] At the most basic level a **budget** is simply a prediction. It is used by decision makers to guess about

Table 8.5   State and Local Expenditures, 2004–2005

Expenditures	State/Local ($)	S/L (%)	State ($)	State (%)	Local ($)	Local (%)
Total Expenditures	2,372,079,901		1,470,456,615		1,313,749,897	
Intergovernmental	4,713,517	.1	403,467,210	27	13,372,918	.9
Education	689,375,633	29	191,948,821	13	497,426,812	38
Public Welfare	362,007,160	15	317,294,573	22	44,712,587	3
Hospitals	103,313,970	4	42,324,183	3	60,989,787	5
Health	66,929,552	3	31,124,945	2	35,804,607	3
Employment Security Admin.	4,383,230	.1	4,377,732	.3	5,498	—
Veterans' Services	1,349,107	.04	1,349,107	.04	—	—
Highways	123,899,974	5	75,787,718	5	48,112,256	4
Police	74,659,052	3	9,996,942	.6	64,662,110	5
Fire	30,738,976	1	—		30,738,976	1
Corrections	59,252,909	3	38,367,706	3	20,885,203	2
Natural Resources	23,914,154	.9	16,473,142	1	7,441,012	.5
Parks and Rec.	31,890,311	1	4,496,815	.2	27,393,496	2
Housing	39,994,594	2	4,957,263	.2	35,037,331	3
Sewage	36,372,359	2	1,118,239	.06	35,254,120	3
Solid Waste Mgt.	21,279,230	.8	3,196,964	.2	18,082,266	1
Governmental Administration	106,600,527	4	45,180,162	3	61,420,365	5
Interest on debt	80,979,644	3	34,362,180	2	46,617,464	4
Utilities	157,295,449	7	22,785,073	2	134,510,376	10
Liquor Store	4,885,238	.16	4,081,755	.2	2,796,868	.15
Insurance Trust	195,541,749	8	167,974,677	11	27,567,072	2

Source: "Table 1. State and Local Government Finances by Level of Government and by State: 2004–2005," U.S. Census Bureau, http://www.census.gov/govs/estimate/0500ussl_1.html (accessed October 2007).

revenue intake, expenditure outflow, and how to balance the difference. How much will it cost to defeat the insurgents in Iraq? In the early stages of the war the president asked for $80 billion to cover the costs of the war for several months. Later he asked for and received $70 billion—to cover the costs of the war through mid 2009, putting the total cost at over $875 billion.[41] But that was a best a guess—an educated guess, but a guess nonetheless. Budgeting, then, is a prediction about what it will cost to defeat the enemy, pay for prescription drugs, defeat crime, keep the bad guys in prison, and so on.

Aaron Wildavsky

Aaron Wildavsky was the son of Ukrainian immigrants. He grew up in Brooklyn and attended Brooklyn College. He served in the U.S. Army and in 1958 received his Ph.D. in political science from Yale. From 1962 to his death in 1993 he was professor of political science at the University of California at Berkeley,

serving as department chair and founding dean of the Graduate School of Public Policy. He was a prolific author, writing over 35 books and hundreds of articles, ranging from presidential politics, politics of the budgeting process, policy
analysis, and regulatory policy. Those who knew him, like Lawrence Chickering, remember his dynamic personality and engaging sense of wit and wisdom.
Chickering wrote about his (Wildavsky's) book on Moses as a political leader
this way, "There is more Wildavsky than Moses in the book; but then, of course,
Wildavsky was more interesting than Moses."

Source: A. Lawrence Chickering, "Aaron Wildavsky, RIP—Tribute to the late conservative author, policy analyst and professor—Editorial," National Review, 4 October 1993,
http://findarticles.com/p/articles/mi_m1282?is_n19_v45/ai_14667419/ (accessed October 2007).

At a planning level budgeting (the process) is all about translating financial resources
into human purposes. This is where we begin to see how budgeting impacts the public
interest. Many states, including North Carolina (see specifics on North Carolina's budgeting
process), ramped up their expenditures to meet the needs of pre-school age children. The
argument was simple: there is a need for pre-kindergarten age children to receive the necessary educational, social, cultural, and physical support, largely because their mothers
were returning en masse to the workforce. So, to meet a human need and to fulfill a cultural and social good, state level decision makers were required to come up with new dollars to put toward the new pre-school programs, or take from existing programs.

From a legal or trust arrangement budgeting is regarded as a contract between the
governed and the government. Presidential and congressional election campaigns are
filled with promises. The public is promised that the elderly will receive prescription drug
assistance; teacher interest groups are promised higher pay and better working conditions; high tech companies are promised millions of dollars in tax incentives and tax
breaks; and local citizen activist groups are promised the new recreation center will be built.
Whether or not the promise is kept is one thing, but when the budget is put into action
the contractual arrangement is under way.

And finally, from a group perspective, budgeting "is a process in which various people express different desires and make different judgments." The American Federation of
Teachers and National Education Association demand changes in the No Child Left Behind Act, changes that will not unduly burden them; the AFL-CIO demands wage and benefit concessions; the environmental, trucking, legal, defense, big business, small business,
religious, and many more groups make demands upon government, and from a budgeting perspective the government decision makers must make decisions as to whose desires
to fund and whose judgments to adhere to.

Budget Actors and Goals

Who are the primary actors and what are their major goals? First is, of course, the
president. As a result of the changes in executive budgeting practices beginning in the
1920s, the president became the chief agenda setter of budget priorities. However, this role
is highly unpredictable, given the propensity for individuality. Former President George
W. Bush, for example, was elected as a Republican and a conservative, but his spending
record is anything but conservative. His fiscal management strategy is directed to lowering taxes even during periods of economic uncertainty, including high budget deficits.

On the other hand former President Bill Clinton reduced dramatically the level of defense spending during a time of peace, and increased domestic spending in areas such as AmeriCorps, welfare reform, and environmental protections from oil and gas firms. However, President Obama is breaking all records. In an effort to stop the recession of 2008–2009 from spinning completely out of control, he proposed and Congress passed a whopping $780 billion "stimulus bill," thus contributing to an already gargantuan budget deficit that many say will exceed $2 trillion. That is for just one year!

Second is **Congress**. Congressmen are largely motivated by re-election; some are noble in their approach, and are thus moved by fulfilling the public interest. For the former the budget process is one of manipulating the appropriations bills to exact as much pork for their constituents as possible. Former Republican **Senator Ted Stevens** of Alaska and convicted felon, was regarded as the "King of Pork," because of his avaricious appetite for securing state and local pet projects. Others, like former Republican Representative Steve Largent of Oklahoma, saw their role as one of impacting their state and their constituency with the goal of securing a better and higher quality of life for all citizens. For example, Largent consistently sought increases in appropriations in social and human services, including greater access to health care for the elderly. These did not register high on the pork scale, but they were more effective in securing a better quality of life for many Oklahomans.[42]

Third are **bureaucratic agencies**. Agencies are really the driving force in the budgeting process. They are the front-line stakeholders who not only implement the laws, but who actively seek to have their personal and agency goals placed on the president's agenda. To do this they must provide accurate and reliable information to the OMB when requested. They must be trustworthy, honest, and responsive to not only their respective clientele groups, but to all of the other actors discussed in this section, especially the president and Congress. The reader should understand that the role of the agency head, deputy director, program coordinator, and other public administrators is not only one of maximizing their budget desires—although that certainly plays a part in their decision making—but that there are many public values that they seek to achieve, all of which might very well weaken their budget maximization claims including agency autonomy, professionalism, program loyalty, and chain of command.[43]

As a first element, the agencies have to know how much to ask Congress for. This requires looking back on what they spent the prior FY, knowing what they want to do, what the president wants to do, and what all 535 congressmen and senators want to do. Not an easy task, obviously. So, how do they decide how much to ask for? Ask for more than you will need, but not more than you want. In other words, be realistic but not overly idealistic. Agency officials understand that other agencies are in the same predicament, and that to ask for too much will take away from others, and this might not be too popular, particularly during future budget negotiations.

A second element the agencies must decide how much to spend. Does an agency spend all that Congress appropriated? Or does it act too conservatively and retain a carry over? The basic thinking is that agencies avoid carry-overs whenever possible and spend right up to their budgeted amount, but spend wisely, knowing that the all seeing eye of Congress and the various committees and subcommittees that oversee agency appropriations will be looking.

A third element is the various budgetary strategies undertaken by agencies, which are generally intended to at least maintain or even increase their budgeted amounts. Wildavsky adroitly pinpointed several strategies, that when adopted during times of fiscal and economic uncertainty, such as during the Dot Com bust, or in the horror and aftermath of 9/11 and the continuing war on terror, including Iraq and Afghanistan, or with the onslaught of natural disasters, such as Hurricane Katrina, or more recently with the

"Wall Street Bailout" and national economic recession of 2008, would mean that "choice among existing strategies must be based on intuition and hunch — on an 'educated guess' — as well as on firm knowledge."[44] The strategies include being a good politician, cultivating your clientele base, and displaying the appropriate skill in maximizing one's opportunities.[45]

A fourth element involves **interest groups**. Interest groups are at the center of public budgeting in a pluralistic democracy like the United States. Whether we are talking about the role of the American Medical Association, the American Bar Association, the National Education Association, or any of the other hundreds of thousands of small, medium, and large interest groups in the United States today, each is interested in achieving some part of the appropriations pie. Significant increases in human and social services needs over the last forty years have led to an institutionalized interest group force in this area. The **Department of Health and Human Services (DHHS)**, for example, has seen a multifold increase in their budget allocations since the mid to late 1960s, primarily in the areas of Aid to Families with Dependent Children (AFDC), now called Temporary Assistance to needy Families (TANF), Medicare, Medicaid, and a host of other expenditure areas. Lobbying is the key vehicle used by interest groups to affect the budgeting process.

The fifth element is the **citizen**. As a single entity individuals rarely have any substantial influence directly upon the budgeting process, but indirectly they do. Although this is not true at the federal level, almost all states have some type of referendum or initiative process that provides the citizens of each state to impose their will upon policy makers. For example, in 1992 Coloradans passed a referendum that severely restricted public officials from raising taxes. This was called the **Taxpayers' Bill of Rights** (or TABOR). In 2005, however, TABOR was repealed by the voters. At the federal level the public's voice is limited to survey results, public opinion polls, and political town hall meetings or national seminars, where the panelists are willing to listen to what the people have to say regarding fiscal matters.

The Federal Budgetary Process

The federal budgetary process was transformed by the impact of the 1974 reforms. The way Congress establishes taxing and spending legislation is guided by specific procedures set out in the **Congressional Budget and Impoundment Control Act of 1974** (see discussion above), where a greater degree of balance is established between the president and Congress.[46] At the center of the Act is the requirement that Congress construct a budget resolution that is aimed at setting spending and tax cut limits. There are four basic steps.

Step 1: Presidential budget request begins in February. This is when the president submits to Congress a detailed budget request for the upcoming fiscal year.[47] Developed by the president's Office of Management and Budget (OMB) it does several things: 1) determines the amount of money the federal government will direct toward various public purposes; 2) estimates the total amount of revenues needed; and 3) anticipates the deficit (or in rare circumstances, a surplus) of the federal government, reserving to itself the right and responsibility to raise the government's debt limit if necessary.

Next, the president's budget request lays out policy priorities. For this purpose the request is specific and lists recommended funding levels for various programs or accounts. For example, for Fiscal Year (FY) 2006 President Bush recommends $35 billion more by 2011 to reorganize the total Army forces, $3.7 billion for one new economic and community development program that consolidates 18 different programs, $500 million for schools and teachers to close the achievement gap and attract top-quality teachers, $125 million for Health Information Technology in order to have electronic health records by 2014, and $144 million increase to upgrade National Park Service facilities.[48]

Third, the president's budget indicates to Congress the spending and tax changes the president seeks. While most of the federal tax code is permanently set in statute, such as nearly two-thirds of all spending programs, including Medicare, Medicaid, and Social Security, the president does need to request funding for annual **discretionary programs** that fall under the authority of the House and Senate Appropriations Committees. This type of funding is not permanent, such as defense. This is why, for example, President Bush came to Congress in 2005, requesting an additional $82 billion for the war in Iraq. Initial funding ran out, and therefore the president was required to ask for more.

Step 2: Congressional budget resolution provides Congress the authority to establish its own budget priorities. Both the House and Senate Budget Committees hold hearings, listening to and asking senior administration officials questions about their various budget requests. After the hearings are complete the two Committees draft a budget resolution; it goes to the respective floors for debate, where it can be amended by majority vote. Finally, it proceeds to both the joint conference committee where a joint or concurrent budget resolution is passed.

The **budget resolution** is not like a normal piece of legislation; it only requires a majority vote, a filibuster cannot be raised in the Senate to stop it, and the president cannot veto it. A budget resolution is composed of various spending categories or functions that list all of the authorized spending levels for all of the programs and functions. The difference between what Congress says it can spend (**authority or authorization**) and what Congress actually spends (**outlay or appropriation**) is usually sizable. It must be noted that the spending totals outlined in the budget resolution are not the same as the authorizing legislation produced by congressional committees. Authorizing legislation only provides a basis for understanding what Congress *might* spend, not what it is required to spend. That is accomplished through a specific appropriations bill. This bill is usually much less than the original authorization legislation.

Step 3: Appropriation stage begins with appropriation bills and their amendments, which must agree with the numbers from a table called the **302(a) allocation**. This table represents the total spending limits laid out by budget function in the corresponding budget resolution, distributing them by respective congressional committees. Any additional tax or entitlement bills must also fit within the budget resolution's overall spending limit for the specific committee. The Congressional Budget Office (CBO), which is the fiscal and budget management arm of Congress, tallies the cost and measures it against a budgetary baseline, which projects revenue. (See Figure 8.1.)[49]

Step 4: Budget reconciliation begins with a single piece of legislation that Congress may use to instruct various committees to produce legislation by a certain date that meets spending and/or tax targets. The budget committees put all of these reconciliation bills together, and present them on their respective floors for a 'yes' or 'no' vote. Reconciliation bills have the advantage of lumping together spending demands, but is usually limited by imposition of the **Byrd Rule**, named after Senator Robert Byrd of West Virginia, which essentially says that any provision to the reconciliation bill that is deemed out of the ordinary to the general purpose of the law is liable to have a point of order thrown at it. Unless 60 senators vote for the amendment in question, then it is stripped from the bill. This is designed to render non-germane amendments ineffective.[50] Finally, the 1974 Act provides for a **scorekeeping** process to play out. This is where the congressional scorekeepers (the House and Senate Budget Committees) essentially measure the effects of current and enacted legislation, while assessing its impact on the overall budget plan, which is the budget resolution. Scorekeeping keeps congressional

Figure 8.1   The Budget Process in Congress

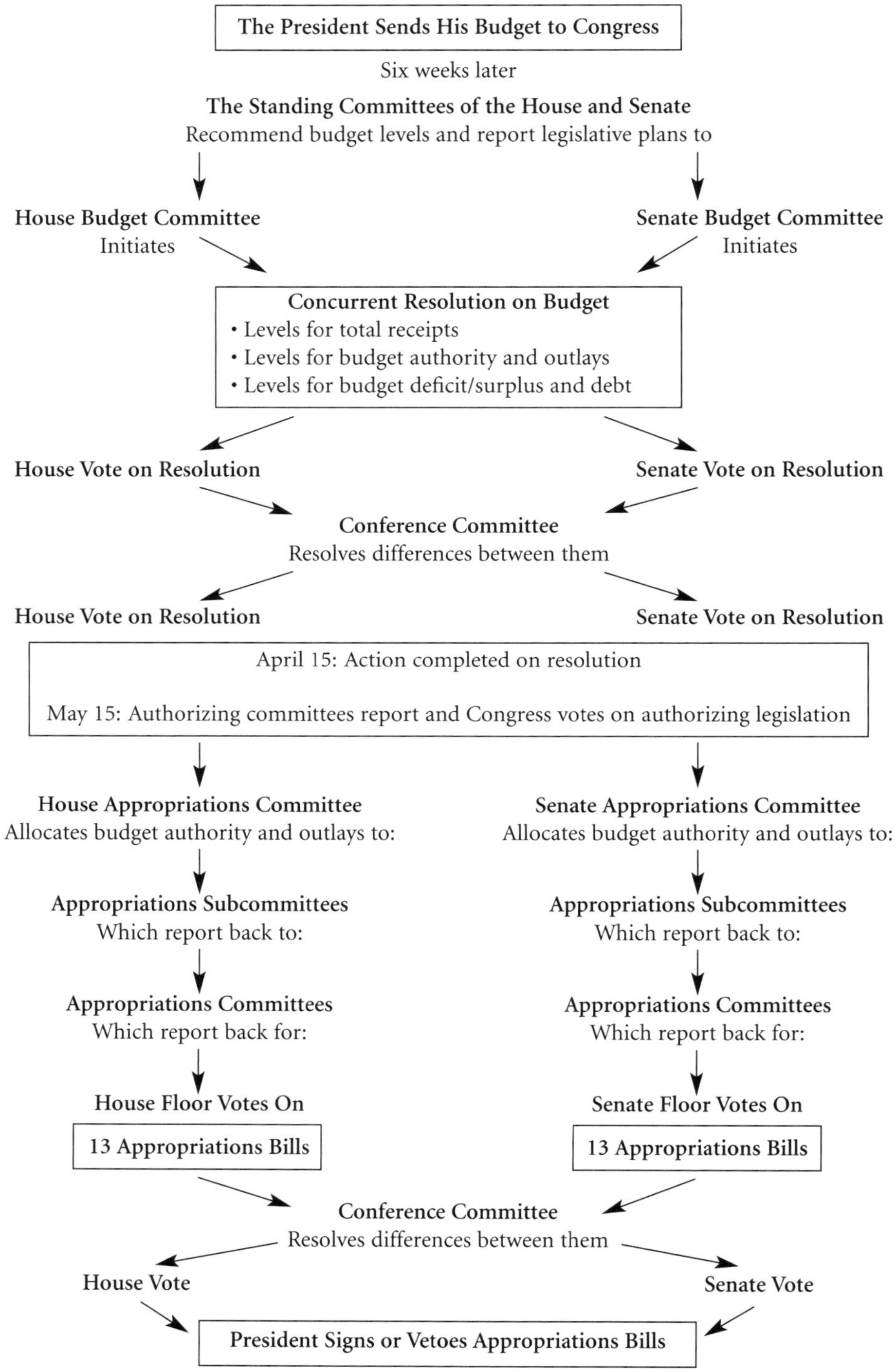

The President Sends His Budget to Congress

Six weeks later

The Standing Committees of the House and Senate
Recommend budget levels and report legislative plans to

House Budget Committee
Initiates

Senate Budget Committee
Initiates

Concurrent Resolution on Budget
• Levels for total receipts
• Levels for budget authority and outlays
• Levels for budget deficit/surplus and debt

House Vote on Resolution

Senate Vote on Resolution

Conference Committee
Resolves differences between them

House Vote on Resolution

Senate Vote on Resolution

April 15: Action completed on resolution

May 15: Authorizing committees report and Congress votes on authorizing legislation

House Appropriations Committee
Allocates budget authority and outlays to:

Senate Appropriations Committee
Allocates budget authority and outlays to:

Appropriations Subcommittees
Which report back to:

Appropriations Subcommittees
Which report back to:

Appropriations Committees
Which report back for:

Appropriations Committees
Which report back for:

House Floor Votes On

Senate Floor Votes On

13 Appropriations Bills

13 Appropriations Bills

Conference Committee
Resolves differences between them

House Vote

Senate Vote

President Signs or Vetoes Appropriations Bills

Source: Aaron Wildavsky and Naomi Caiden, *The New Politics of the Budgetary Process*, 6th ed. (New York: Pearson Longman, 2004), 6.

members informed, but it also makes them accountable to their constituents and to each other.[51]

Before explaining how Congress and the president deal with deficits and deficit spending, we turn to a brief explanation of the state and local budget processes.[52] Both are different and will be dealt with individually.

State Budgeting

State governments face different challenges and problems than the federal government. A similar challenge is to balance budgets; however, that is made easier by the fact that most state constitutions require state and local governments to balance their budgets.[53] Unlike the federal government, most states, including North Carolina, prepare two-year or biennial budgets. The general process entails five steps 1) **Budget instructions** are provided by the governor and his budget office to the various executive departments by asking them for their basic requests, but also placing broad policy limits on those requests; 2) **department requests** are to be submitted some six to twelve months earlier. During this time frame the departments prepare spending priorities, including placing these priorities within their specific departmental plans as well as the broader capital improvement plan of the states; 3) **gubernatorial review** occurs when the governor and his budget office examine and critique these requests and plans for spending, hold public hearings, and then provide instructions to the departments and agencies for revision in requests. It is the job of the governor, then, to determine whether or not which programs to pursue, which are politically viable, where reductions need to be made, and where tax increases or decreases can be made; 4) the **General Assembly** enters the process and converts the submitted gubernatorial budget requests into an appropriation bill, which then follows the normal path of any bill, including committee scrutiny, further public hearings, and legislative tinkering. It must pass in both houses before it can be sent to the governor for his signature; and 5) the governor's *line item* veto power allows the chief executive to change specific aspects of the bill, primarily for political advantage. Let's take a specific look at the process played out in the Tarheel State: North Carolina.

Box 8.6   Budgeting Process in North Carolina

The Governor's Office of State Budget and Management (OSBM) issues instructions to state departments for making their requests known. In February the governor delivers his statewide budget message to a joint legislative assembly in which he releases a detailed balanced budget to the General Assembly and the public.

Between August and October departments submit their requests to OSBM and the governor.

The North Carolina Constitution requires the governor to submit a recommended budget. The General Assembly then makes recommendations for increases, decreases, or other amendments.

The North Carolina Constitution requires the General Assembly to pass a balanced budget through the writing of a appropriations bill. Although the Constitution does not require a two-year budget, the General Assembly has traditionally held to a two-year budget. At this point the General Assembly becomes highly involved in the budget process, particularly through committee and subcommittee work, including debate, amend, and review the specific agency spending request. Once the House and Senate Appropriations Committees have completed their work, the money-raising committees, or the House and Senate Finance Committees take over. Their job is to pass bills that acknowledge the amount requested and to balance the spending with the revenue. Ultimately, these finance bills are incorporated into the appropriations bill so that the General Assembly may vote on one bill. Each chamber debates and makes amendments, votes, and then sends it to the other chamber. This process continues until concurrence is received. Selection of House and Senate conferees is done to negotiate differences between the two chambers and then write what is called a conference report that is based on agreements between the two chambers. Each chamber votes up or down. If not adopted, the conferee process repeats until agreement is reached.

The governor can either sign the budget bill, in which case it is formally enacted. The governor can also veto the bill. The General Assembly can override the governor's veto by a three-fifths vote of those members present in both houses. If veto is overridden, the bill is enacted; if the veto is sustained the process returns to the first legislative stage.

Source: For more specifics on the State of North Carolina's budget process, see North Carolina's Progress Board, *Our State, Our Money: A Citizen's Guide to the North Carolina Budget* (Raleigh, NC: North Carolina Progress Board, 2003), 18–19.

Local Budgeting

Local budgeting is different from both state and federal budgeting. Whereas federal budgeting is a "vast, sprawling enterprise comprised of a variety of organizations," and state budgeting is politically and technically driven, local budgeting is motivated by the public organization, not just political faces and personalities. Local budgets must balance and revenues must equal expenditures; in other words, there is not room for backdoor spending and program-driven policy agendas that so often make up federal and state budget processes.[54] Local budgeting—specifically municipal budgeting—is about solving problems, generally through accepting the reforms that work, and rejecting the reforms that failed, all for the general purpose of promoting the public interest.[55]

The local budgeting process generally begins with what local public administrators refer to as the **chart of accounts**.[56] It is updated annually, and its main function is to classify budget data and other useful information of financial transactions. Each financial activity of the local government entity is recorded in the chart of accounts. Generally, this type of activity is reserved for performance budget measures.

Local governments examine the various fund accounts, trying to determine somewhat precisely where their revenue is coming from, such as **government funds**, which "focus primarily on the sources, uses, and balances of current financial resources," including the general fund, special revenue funds, capital projects funds, debt service funds, and permanent funds; **proprietary funds**, which "focus on the determination of operating income, changes in net assets, financial position, and cash flow, including the two most prominent proprietary funds enterprise and internal service"; and **fiduciary funds**, which "focus on net assets and changes in net assets from assets held in trustee or agency capacity for others, which cannot be used to support general government spending." These include pension funds, investment trust funds, private-purpose trust funds, and agency funds.[57]

A second major similarity among local governments is to establish a **budget calendar** for directing the budget preparation process. One example is the initial revenue forecast. After this forecast is constructed — usually by the city or county manager's office — it is presented to the city council or county commissioners for their review and feedback. If and when the elected officials approve the forecast it is put into operation. A simple illustration is that of Sauk Village, Illinois, where the budget calendar lays out the basic steps and procedures inherent in the local government organization.

Box 8.7   Basic Steps of Local Budgeting for Sauk Village, Illinois

First, find out what the citizens of Sauk Village believe are the important priorities of spending for the next fiscal year;

Second, develop financial trend and forecast revenues and expenditures;

Third, public administrators present the result of citizen information, such as surveys, to the ruling board; in this case it is a village board. In other cases it would be a city council or county commissioners;

Fourth, somewhere near the end of the year budget work sheets are distributed to the various department heads, and by January to no later than February the departments have completed their strategic planning and submitted their requests;

Fifth, public hearings are held;

Sixth, and somewhere between April and June the budget is adopted.

Source: Janet M. Kelly and William C. Rivenbark, *Performance Budgeting for State and Local Government* (Armonk, NY: M.E. Sharpe Press, 2003).

A third similarity for local government budgeting is funding on a cash basis; that is, spend only when the dollars are actually in the coffer, not when revenue is promised (through forecasted revenues, such as in federal grant dollars).[58] Whereas the federal government engages in deficit spending, neither state nor local governments are constitutionally allowed to. This places a major emphasis on solid **revenue forecasting**; that is, trying to determine future revenue, and, most importantly, matching that revenue with anticipated expenditures. Departments and other agencies are required to fill out budget worksheets, where they must anticipate future spending based in large part on itemization and previous budgetary history.[59] Some contend that unless state and local governments stay the course with new performance budgeting, and its emphasis on inputs, outputs, and effectiveness, then the age of the permanent fiscal crisis will be upon us.

Summary. The process of public budgeting is complex — there is no doubt, but the basic premise is simple: prepare a fiscal plan that describes and diagrams how public dollars are to be spent. Inherent in this process is (or should be) the natural inclination of elected, appointed, and merit public officials to care for and protect public dollars. This is primarily how public budgeting influences or pursues the public interest. Whether it the federal government's $ 2.9 trillion 2008–2009 budget,[60] the state of Virginia's $36.9 billion spending plan,[61] or Dunn, North Carolina's $8.7 million local budget,[62] the point is the same: governments prepare plans to spend the citizens' money.

Now we turn to our last section: deficits and deficit spending. What happens when spending outdistances revenue? State and local governments are generally restricted from overspending, either or both by constitutional amendment or statutory guidelines. The national government, however, is not so restricted. Several times throughout history Congress has attempted to deal with spending and overspending. More often than not it becomes a political battle between the president and Congress along with countless private and public interest groups, lobbyists, and many others. We conclude the chapter with some general comments on public budgeting and pursuit of the public interest.

Legislative Controls on
Deficits and Deficit Spending

The 1974 reforms placed fairly strict controls on federal spending; however, it did not stop Congress from spending more than it takes in. Thus, it could still engage in deficit spending, even though the 1974 Act improved spending controls, including reducing the negative effect of **backdoor spending** and nearly eliminating the president's ability to impound funds already appropriated by Congress. Still, probably one of the more important parts of the 1974 Act was implementation of the **reconciliation** procedure; the process "that empowers the budget committees of the House and Senate to direct other committees to recommend actions that will bring policies and their costs within the overall spending limits targeted in budget resolutions; the budget committees may even require the legislative committees to do this, and to change laws, if necessary, to reconcile their recommendations with the budget resolution."[63] Since this time future congresses have battled with how to reign in deficit spending. One way to do this is passing reconciliation acts; acts which force Congress to display the budget in the form of a reconciliation bill. Despite their attempts to reconcile expenditures with revenues, the problems persisted.

A **deficit** is the yearly amount of money it spends beyond what it takes in each year. Accumulated deficits are a large part of the federal **debt**, or the total amount of money the government owes beyond what it has the means to pay. The entire decade of the 1980s, and into the early part of the 1990s, the deficit reached unprecedented heights. According to some figures the deficit increased five times, from roughly $74 billion to nearly $300 billion. By the end of President H.W. Bush's only term the deficit reached nearly $400 billion, which was approaching nearly 8 percent of the nation's Gross Domestic Product (GDP). Critics claim that the major problems began with passage of the **Omnibus Budget Reconciliation Act of 1981** (OBRA-1981). The OBRA-1981 was designed by the first Reagan administration to reform the federal tax system and to cut taxes, thus buying into the supply-side economic theory, which essentially contended that tax reductions would lead to greater spending and investment, and would thus generate a stronger economy.

Congress acted to deal with the increasing federal deficits and overall debt. First, it passed the **Balanced Budget and Emergency Deficit Control Act of 1985**, generally referred to as Gramm-Rudman-Hollings I, named after their legislative sponsors (Senators Phil Gramm, Warren Rudman, and Ernest Hollings). This act was designed to achieve a balanced budget by the early 1990s. The primary tool for accomplishing this was **sequestration**, or the automatic process of enacting a series of spending cuts if the budget did not come within specified targeted deficit figures. Even though the president would have the power to cut all bureaucratic agencies' budgets, he could not touch the two biggest culprits of deficit spending: interest payments and entitlement programs, such as Social Security, Medicare, and Medicaid. By 1987 Congress passed Gramm-Rudman-Hollings II, which simply extended the deadline for achieving a balanced budget to the mid-1990s.[64]

Given the failure of these two pieces of legislation to control deficit spending, Congress passed the Budget Enforcement Act of 1990.[65] It was designed to reduce deficit spending through cuts, by requiring that any increases in one area were offset by equal amounts of reductions in another area. Caps on spending were in effect, but they were to expire in 2002. The idea was to pay-as-you-go, or **PAYGO**, meaning that Congress could not spend more than it took in; effectively garnering a zero-base budgeting mentality. Although it helped to curb some deficit spending, in 1993 Congress, with the House still under Democrat control, passed the Omnibus Budget Reconciliation Act of 1993. It was starkly different from its 1981 counterpart; instead of cutting taxes it raised taxes by some $250 billion, and advocated cutting both domestic and military programs over the next five years. According to its proponents, this combination of increased taxes and reduction in programs supposedly led to a reduction in federal deficits. The opponents claim that the effects of President Reagan's economic policies fueled a strong economy, which aided the cause.

After the House was seized by the Republicans in 1994 for the first time in 40 years, a political tug-of-war ensued between the Republican congressional leadership of Newt Gingrich and President Clinton. One area where they did agree was in passage of the **Line-Item Veto Act of 1996**, where for the first time Congress granted to the President of the United States the unprecedented power of **rescission**, or the authority to strike out wasteful spending on individual lines of appropriations bills. It lasted until 1998 when the U.S. Supreme Court ruled in *Clinton v. City of New York* that the act was unconstitutional.

The tool of spending caps returned to prominence in the Balanced Budget Act of 1997. Despite (or, perhaps, in spite of) the Republican-Democrat feuding over how to correct the problem, Congress decided to clamp down on deficit spending by reducing spending 12 percent and cutting taxes a total of $152 billion. The Act set 2002 as the target date. A balanced budget was achieved sooner than anyone expected. For the first time in nearly three decades the federal government reached a **budget surplus** (taking in more revenue than it expended), even to the tune of $70 billion. By 2000 the surplus was $127 billion and in 2001 it was $236 billion. Sanity seemed to be returning to Capitol Hill and the Whitehouse. But, then, tragedy struck.

On Tuesday morning, September 11, 2001, the United States was attacked by terrorists. Over the next four years the Bush administration pledged to fight a war on terror—globally, in Iraq, and Afghanistan—help the devastated economy, and reorganize the federal government to not only fight terror, but to prevent such horrific events from ever happening again. As a result of these actions, coupled with President Bush's ten year $1.3 trillion tax cuts and increased federal spending, federal deficits skyrocketed. As one pundit notes, only half-way through the current FY 2004 budget, and the federal deficit is at nearly $300 billion, which is only about $10 billion off last year's pace, when the budget deficit grew to over $410 billion.[66] (See Box 8.8 for a brief explanation of the financial crisis and turmoil of 2008, and its negative impact upon the budget process.) Some experts even believe the deficit may reach or even exceed $450 billion.[67] Where and when does it end?

Box 8.8   The Financial and Budget "Mess" of 2008

Beginning in July 2008 and continuing throughout the remainder of the year, a series of financial, market, and general economic events occurred that set the stage for many things: not the least of which was the demise of Senator John McCain's presidential bid. In a nutshell, the housing bubble burst, Fannie Mae and Freddie Mac were seized by the central government (placed in "conservatorship"), the U.S. Treasury Department, led by Secretary Henry Paulson, announced it would provide financial guarantees for money market and mutual funds, and finally the Bush Administration announced an unprecedented $700 billion financial "bailout" or rescue plan; a plan that was designed to relieve various financial and insurance giants, such as AIG, Lehman Brothers, and others, of "bad" debt, while trying to "thaw" the credit markets, both nationally and globally. While this is taking place, President Bush signed a stopgap funding measure that provided for additional funding for the Departments of Defense, Homeland Security, and Veterans Affairs, while continuing previous year funding for many other programs, taking them into the early spring of 2009. In early October, after the first "bailout legislation" bill was rejected by strong-willed Republican representatives of House, the Congress reconstituted the bill into a major pork barrel spending projects bill, including increases in FDIC insurance, "green" energy incentives, tax extenders, and even disaster relief projects. This second bailout legislation passed on October 3. By the end of October, Federal Reserve Chairman Ben Bernanke endorsed a second economic stimulus bill. The incoming Obama administration agreed, and in early 2009 pushed through Congress a $787 billion additional stimulus bill.

How does this affect the budget? Simple: initial estimates placed the $750 billion bailout figure closer to $1 trillion, and perhaps as high as $2 trillion, depending upon how far into the future, and how many more companies, including the Big Three automakers, and even some state and local governments, would be rewarded for extending the "tin cup." Many economists and financial experts predicted the global effects of this crisis and potential **recession** would extend one to two years, piling debt upon debt, with no apparent end in sight. The incoming Obama administration, which stacked its economic team with veteran "insiders" of the Beltway and with bright, young economic, financial, and legal minds, faced unprecedented territory when it assumed office on January 20, 2009. The effect was not just on balancing budgets, raising revenues, or spending tax dollars; it was regaining the confidence and trust of the American people, and restoring hope in pursuing the public interest.

Source: The Concord Coalition: Washington Budget Report, "Washington Budget Report: Budget Effects of the Financial Crisis — October 21, 2008. www.concordcoalition.org/print/1011. (Accessed November 28, 2008.)

Conclusion: Budgeting and the Public Interest

Politicians are supposed to be elected to represent demands of citizens in a democratic process. To do so requires more than simply making a few stump speeches, kissing babies, and promising every interest group to give it what it desires, if it will simply endorse a particular candidacy. It requires prudent decision making, honesty, trustworthiness, respect, fairness, and dedication to pursuing and fulfilling the public interest. These virtues, and others, are seemingly missing from the political agendas of presidents and members of Congress. Why? Because our elected officials simply find it difficult to say one simple two-letter word, "no," particularly when it is in response to further demands placed upon the spending of money that is simply not there. There seem to be many factors involved: the increasing pressure from interest groups; the cyclical nature of politics itself; the changing economic, fiscal, and monetary dynamics of the national economy, such as the increasingly important and influential role the **Federal Reserve Board** has in lowering and/or raising interest rates; and the short-term mindset of elected officials offset with the long-term outlook of merit-based agency officials. It is no wonder that the budgeting process, particularly at the federal level, is complex, complicated, and inter-twined with internal bureaucratic interests and besieged with external political, social, and economic interests. It is really amazing that the government can operate as well as it does!

Students often ask difficult questions on these points, such as "How much longer can government continue to spend more than it takes in?" or "Why doesn't the whole thing just implode?" Unfortunately, it seems that we do not have elected representatives, senators, and a president and vice-president asking these same important questions. Or, if they are asking these questions, they do not seem to want a truthful answer. Budgets (and the budgeting process) is not only a fiscal and monetary resource tool, but it is a political measure of the various and often conflicting components of the public interest.

Yes, budgeting reflects distinct political wants and needs; we recognize this. But it also reflects the greater public interest; which is establishing a firm financial foundation for future generations. This will take our elected leaders and civil servants making difficult and unpopular decisions regarding how to spend our money.

Action Steps

1. Trace the changing role of the president in the budgeting process. Examine how the president influences, impacts, and even steers the policy discussion of budgeting issues in a direction often times opposite of the Congress. In a three-page essay assess how and why this has happened.

2. Hand out a simple line-item municipal budget. Divide the class into groups of four each and have each group respond to the following questions:

    a. What is the total budget allocation amount?

    b. How many different revenue sources are accounted?

    c. Describe what a line-item budget does for the public administrator, elected official, local interest group, and general public.

3. Assess the influence of the federal government in the budgeting process both *before* and *after* passage of the 1921 Budgeting Act.

4. What was the major impact of the PPBS form of budgeting in the 1960s and 1970s? Why was this time period significant? What major changes took place that emphasized planning and programming in the budgeting process? Write a three to five-page essay.

5. Assign each student the task of playing the National Budget Simulation game. (See www.budgetsim.org). Ask them to arrive at a balanced budget using different scenarios—one where the emphasis is placed on military spending, and a second where the emphasis is placed on domestic spending.

6. Research several state and local government agencies. Interview various public administrators and inquire about their use of performance-based budgeting. How are

results measured? In other words, how do local and state governments do performance-based budgeting?

7. Research and discuss the economic and financial "mess" that unraveled in the latter half of 2008. Explain what happened. Then try and project into the future what will be the effects, both of terms of credit availability, the U.S. budget process, and global financial markets.

8. Does the public interest empower judges in the budgetary process? Or limit the intrusion of judges upon these budgetary process? Consider your response in a reading of the case of a federal district court judge who must require a new set of taxes to pay for the desegregation and constitutionality of public schools in your reading of *Missouri v. Jenkins*, 495 U.S. 33 (1990). The U.S. Supreme Court upheld his order for new taxes levied to pay for desegregated, constitutional public schools — even though the voters had rejected the new tax three times in public referendums. However, later the U.S. Supreme Court did limit the remedies of the judge to intrude only within the geographic limits of his district in *Missouri v. Jenkins*, 515 U.S. 70 (1995).

Exam Review Preparation

1. Identify the key elements of the *Congressional Budget Act of 1974*.

2. Compare the state and local government process with that of the federal government. What are the major differences? What factors account for these differences?

3. Explain why the first half of the nineteenth century was marked by the continuing (fiscal) philosophical clash between Hamilton and Jefferson.

4. Explain the general process of planning-programming and budgeting systems.

5. Identify and/or define the following terms, concepts, etc.: concurrent resolution, presidential impoundment, authorization and appropriation of funds, zero-based budgeting, fiscal year, budget outlays, Office of Management Budget, Congressional Budget Office, backdoor spending, reconciliation procedure, deficit, debt, sequestration, PAYGO, recession, and surplus.

6. How does public budgeting affect and/or influence the public interest?

7. Identify the key events, persons, and agencies involved in the financial mess of 2008.

8. What is the role of the Federal Reserve Board, particularly in terms of controlling or directing the U.S. economy?

9. Explain the importance of the Budget and Accounting Act of 1921.

10. Who were Robert McNamara and his "Whiz Kids"?

Key Concepts

Aaron Wildavsky
Ben Bernanke

Budget and Accounting Act of 1921
Budget calendar
Budget surplus
Concurrent resolutions
Congressional Budget and Impoundment Control Act
David Stockman
Deficit and debt
Economic Growth and Tax Relief and Reconciliation Act
Federal Reserve Board
General Accounting Office
Henry Paulson
Intergovernmental transfer
Line-Item Veto Act
Management by objectives
Mills
Omnibus Budget Reconciliation Act
Outcome budgeting
Peter Pyhrr
Public budgeting
Rescission
Robert McNamara's "Whiz Kids"
U.S. Treasury

Recommended Readings

Kelly, Janet M. and William C. Rivenbark. *Performance Budgeting for State and Local Government.* Armonk, NY: M.E. Sharpe, 2003.

Mikesell, John L. *Fiscal Administration: Analysis and Applications for the Public Sector.* 7th ed. Belmont, CA: Thomson-Wadsworth, 2007.

Nice, David. *Public Budgeting.* Belmont, CA: Thomson-Wadsworth, 2002.

Osborne, David and Peter Hutchinson. *The Price of Government: Getting the Results We Need in an Age of Permanent Fiscal Crisis.* New York: Basic Books, 2004.

Rubin, Irene S. *Balancing the Federal Budget: Trimming the Herds or Eating the Seed Corn?* New York: Chatham House, 2003.

_____. *Class, Tax, and Power: Municipal Budgeting in the United States.* Chatham, NJ: Chatham House, 1998.

_____. *The Politics of Public Budgeting: Getting and Spending, Borrowing and Balancing.* 4th ed. New York: Chatham House, 2004.

Schick, Allen. *The Federal Budget: Politics, Policy, Process.* Washington, DC: Brookings Institution, 2000.

Smith, Robert W. and Thomas D. Lynch. *Public Budgeting in America.* 5th ed. Upper Saddle River, NJ: Prentice Hall, 2004.

Wildavsky, Aaron and Naomi Caiden. *The New Politics of the Budgetary Process.* 5th ed. New York: Pearson Longman, 2003.

Related Web Sites

Budget of the U.S. Government: Browse Fiscal Year, 2009
    http://www.gpoaccess.gov/usbudget/fy09/browse.html

Budget Plan State by State: An Interactive Map
    http://www.whitehouse.gov/news/usbudget/states/index.html

Congressional Budget Office
    http://www.cbo.gov/

Economic Recovery Tax Act
    http://www.answers.com/topic/economic-recovery-tax-act?cat=biz-fin

Federal Reserve System
    www.federalreserve.gov

General Accountability Office
    http://www.gao.gov/

General Accountability Office: A Glossary of Terms Used in the Federal Budget Process,
    2005 edition
    http://www.gao.gov/new.items/d05734sp.pdf

National Advisory Council on State and Local Budgeting
    http://www.allbusiness.com/accounting/budget/595085-1.html

National Association of State Budget Officers
    www.nasbo.org

Office of Management Budget
    http://www.whitehouse.gov/omb/

Peter Pyhrr (father of Zero Based Budgeting)
    http://www.swb-inc.com/Zero-Base_Budgeting.htm

U.S. Bureau of Public Debt
    www.publidebt.treas.gov

U.S. Government Documents: The Budget Process
    http://www.columbia.edu/cu/lweb/indiv/usgd/budget.html

U.S. National Debt Clock
    http://www.brillig.com/debt_clock/

Chapter 9

Public Policy, Policy Analysis, and the Public Interest

"There is no area of public administration that is more important than public policy. Public Administration is involved in the entire process and is responsible for implementing public policy."

Jeff Greene, *Public Administration in the New Century: A Concise Introduction*

"Policy analysis (is) the process of researching or analyzing public problems to give policy makers specific information about the range of available policy options and the advantages and disadvantages of various approaches."

Robert B. Denhardt and Joseph W. Grubbs, *Public Administration: An Action Orientation*

Chapter Objectives

Upon completion of this chapter the student will be able to:

1. Define public policy;
2. Understand the importance of studying the policy process;
3. Recognize how public administration affects and is *affected* by the policy process;
4. Distinguish the various stages of the policy process
5. Clarify the distinctive roles of public policy, public administration, and the public interest.

For decades, parents, educators, and policymakers across the country have been concerned about the effectiveness of U.S. schools. In 2001, the U.S. Congress passed the No Child Left Behind Act (NCLB), designed to improve schools through a system of standards-based accountability (SBA). NCLB's accountability provisions require each state to develop content and achievement standards, measure student progress through tests, and intervene in schools and districts that do not meet the targets. Since NCLB went into effect, its accountability provisions have affected every public school and district in the nation.

In 2002, the RAND Corporation launched a project to understand how educators are responding to the new accountability requirements in California, Georgia, and Pennsylvania—three states that represent a range of approaches, regions, and student populations. The researchers aimed to identify the factors that enhance the implementation of SBA systems, encourage positive changes in teaching practices, and improve student achievement through surveys, interviews, and visits to schools in these three states, they found that NCLB is affecting the work of superintendents, principals, and teachers both positively and negatively. Although the three states developed different accountability systems, school and district administrators are engaged in similar school improvement activities.[1]

The **RAND Corporation**, located in Santa Monica, California, has been supporting and performing **policy analysis** projects since World War II. Attention is given to domestic and foreign policy areas, including among other topics economic, education, and intelligence and counterterrorism issues. Since the implementation of NCLB critics challenged its effectiveness, particularly in helping to improve reading and mathematics skills. The key findings in a recent RAND study found:

- School superintendents focused their attention on the use of data for making decisions, making sure school curriculum is in line with state standards, and that low-performing students' needs are met;
- Teachers changed their instruction in both positive and negative ways; and
- Teachers were challenged by the state standards and their implementation.[2]

What does this example of education policy tell us about the role of **public policy** and policy analysis in the public interest? First, it is evident that the NCLB act is controversial. Second, several types and groups of policymakers and other actors (**stakeholders**) are involved in the decision making, research, analysis, and evaluation of education policy, including school personnel, Congress, state lawmakers and bureaucratic officials, school teachers, principals, and superintendents (all government employees), and many others. Third, the focus on education is within the purview of the public interest, and thus the role of the policymaker and public administrator is critical to its development, implementation, and analysis. Too often undergraduate public administration students are introduced only to the implementation and evaluation stages of the policy process—which is generally where the public administrator is most involved, and we will certainly examine those phases within the context of policy analysis. However, as the reader will discover it is imperative that the full-orbed policy process, both in terms of substance and process, is examined and detailed. This will provide the student with a fuller appreciation of the policy depth and breadth that public administrators are subject to and influenced by. Thus we begin our discussion of public policy and policy analysis in the public interest with a discussion of the definition and description of public policy. We draw from the work of James Anderson, among others.

Introduction to the Study of Public Policy

Public policy is the study of the substance of policies implemented by the government, i.e. economic, social, or foreign, and also the process of how these policies are implemented. Public policy is affected by and affects public administration. For example, when we ask "What is the U.S. policy in Iraq?" this raises numerous scenarios regarding substantive policy positions. The official government policy as expressed by President Bush was that the Iraq War, for example, was necessary to stop terrorism on its home turf, and in particular prevent it from further negatively affecting America's national interests, including providing for national security and ensuring freedom, both home and abroad. Another policy position holds that because no Weapons of Mass Destruction (WMD) were ever found the war in Iraq is illegal and unethical. This position holds among other things that the war is about oil or personal revenge, and that it is simply an unnecessary and largely immoral war. Some even go so far as to proclaim the advent of conspiracy theories, directing their anger at President Bush personally, claiming that he and/or his administration knew of the distinct possibility that the 9/11 tragedy could and might happen, but did nothing to prevent it.

Box 9.1   Public Policy Stages

Agenda setting is the stage where individuals and especially interest groups working to get a substantive issue, such as civil rights violations, on the political agenda of the key policy makers.

Policy formulation, or policy adoption, is the second stage. This is where formal laws, such as civil rights legislation like the *Civil Rights Act* of 1964, and other types of executive orders (affirmative action) or judicial decisions (*Brown v. Board of Education*, 1954) are made regarding a specific issue.

Policy implementation, or the administrative or bureaucratic side of policy making, is where the public administrators who work in agencies devoted to specific policy areas, such as the Equal Employment Opportunity Commission, make specific rules and regulations in order to put into operation the laws and decisions passed by the elected officials.

Policy evaluation involves research organizations, universities, think tanks, and even the implementing agencies themselves. Their job is to systematically and critically examine how well the implemented policy met its original goals and objectives.

Source: James E. Anderson, *Public Policymaking*, 6th ed. (Boston, MA: Houghton Mifflin, 2006), 3–5.

Public Policy and Values

Public policy and the political and administrative decisions necessary to formulate public policy involve various values, including social, cultural, political, economic, and even religious. Values are the cornerstone of public policy making; without values there is no policy to articulate or process to explain the policy. Obviously, both at the national and subnational levels of government, there are a plethora of values underscoring a variety of domestic and foreign policies, all of which affect the public interest in one way or the other.

What do Americans value? They value freedom, security, rights, safety law, and many other **democratic values**. In addition, they value efficiency, effectiveness, and economy, especially when it comes to fulfilling their civic and social demands (being kept informed by the city council on the upcoming public school construction project). These are termed **bureaucratic values**. Both sets of normative principles are framed in the public interest. It is the responsibility of government officials, including public administrators, to make decisions that affect, alter, improve, and even challenge our supposition about values. Some Americans are adamantly opposed to increased taxation, believing that increasing the percentage taxation rate of personal income, for example, is damaging to not only personal finances but to the overall state of the economy. And thus these individuals demand fewer and lower taxes. Other Americans, however, do not automatically oppose increasing income tax rates as long as the increased revenue is spent on improving the well being, for example, of the poor, underprivileged children, the elderly, and the infirmed—what they refer to as needs that fulfill the public interest. For these folks increased revenue means increased government support.

But public policy making is not about keeping one group happier over the other. It is not about (or at least it should not be about) enhancing the Republicans over the Democrats (or vice versa); it should not be about benefiting the environmentalists over the oil and timber companies; it should not be about supporting labor over management. It should be about what is important for the public interest. Thus this chapter examines public policy, both in terms of substantive values and procedural steps, and the role and functions that the public administrator plays in meeting the public interest, particularly through policy analysis.

Public Policy and the Public Interest

Important to our consideration of public policy is the affect it has upon the public interest.[3] Although formulating, adopting, implementing, and evaluating public policy is not as simple and linear as it may sound (or even as we will present it later on in this chapter), it also is not a technically or technologically difficult process. What we have found, however, is that public policy making is incredibly diverse, affecting one or many individuals, depending upon the establishment of values, who holds these values, and how elected and administrative officials respond to the distribution, redistribution, and regulation of those values. We contend that public policy making should be made in the public interest. But how is this possible? How, for example, can public policy be made and administered with regard to socially divisive issues, such abortion, euthanasia, or national security interests, such as fighting the war on terror, and still fulfill the public interest? At the very least, doesn't fulfilling the public interest mean that all individuals, groups, and organizations get what they want at the same time? Because this is impossible, this must mean that either there is no such thing as the public interest or the definition is so ambiguous and/or convoluted that it essentially means nothing. We don't believe either extreme is accurate. For a better explanation of public policy influencing the public interest we first turn to a description of various theories of public policy.

Theories of Public Policy

Since post-World War II political scientists have developed (or borrowed) from other social sciences, such as psychology and sociology, various theories for trying to explain how policy makers make policy. **Theory** is needed in any academic endeavor; it is the roadmap, so to speak, for understanding not only how to get to the destination, but what happens along the way. Theory building is all about developing and massaging terms, concepts, and ideas that ostensibly aid both the professional researcher and student in learning and comprehending the depth and nuances of public policymaking. Both the academic and practitioner benefit from this type of inquiry, because for the academic researcher it clarifies concepts and strengthens theory building, and for the practitioner it assists in applying the concepts and variables to professional situations and circumstances. For our discussion we will consider three basic theories that help explain both the substance and process of public policy, including systems, group or pluralism, and elitism.

Systems theory is of the oldest and most reliable theories of public policy. Originally defined and applied in the hard sciences it was made famous and applicable to the social sciences, including political science and public policy.[4] It is largely linear in its projection of policy action and interaction, and because of this, it is probably less helpful to understanding policy reality, given that the policy world is anything but truly linear. However, the systems approach does help explain some of the components within the overall policy world, including environment, institutions, demands and supports, and decisions made. Figure 9.1 is a basic representation of the political systems model.

Figure 9.1   Political Systems Model

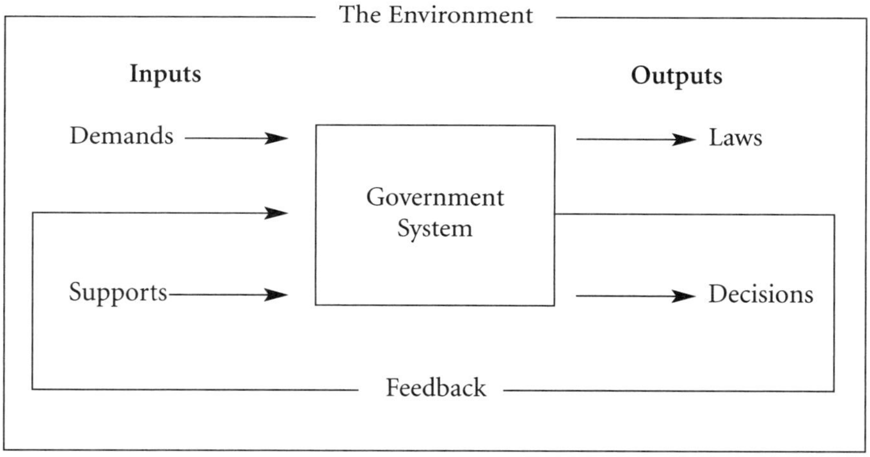

Figure reprinted from James E. Anderson's *Public Policymaking*, 6th ed. (Boston, MA: Houghton Mifflin Company, 2006), 19.

The **policy environment** reflects the political, economic, social, cultural, legal, and even religious context in which policies are framed, adopted, implemented, and to a lesser extent evaluated. Demands and supports represent **inputs** into the political system itself; that is, various indices, such as interest groups, individuals, and other organizations are putting pressure upon the system to respond to a policy problem, such as abortion or the war in Iraq. Second, the political system represents a broad array of institutions, constitutions, laws, rules, and public policies; all of which compose what is termed "the government." It is then the function of "the government," whether at the federal, state, or local level, to utilize the supports, such as taxes, and respond to the demands placed upon it. [One of the drawbacks of this model is that it does not take into account the influence of groups (pluralism) versus the influence of elites (elitism). Rather the model simply lumps all influences together.] Third, the **outputs**, such as the making of laws, passing of rules and regulations, issuing of executive orders, providing judicial decrees, represent official political system reaction to the demands and supports place upon it. In other words, the system, i.e. the government, has to respond and so the response (s) are many and varied, depending upon the institution involved, the issue at hand, and other similar factors. Fourth, there is some type of reaction or **feedback** by and to the system responses, such as protests, letter writing campaigns by interested constituents or groups. These responses provide much needed insight and political reaction to the decisions made; meaning the reaction may be supportive or the reaction may be non-supportive. For example, *Roe v. Wade* was an unfavorable feedback or response by the Supreme Court from the perspective of the pro-life community, but a very supportive response from the perspective of the pro-choice community.

Group theory or pluralist theory "... states that public policy is the product of the group struggle."[5] Philosophers of old have always contended that groups or what the founders referred to as factions have considerable influence in the policymaking or governmental process.[6] The focus is the interaction and struggle between various groups, such as between pro-life and pro-choice. The issue or central value is choosing between life and choice, requiring lawmakers and judicial referees to decide whose value set is more politically viable or (supposedly) constitutionally valid. More and more, however, in the age of media it is also in the news casts, talking head shows, and 24-hour news blitz the American people is subjected to on a daily basis.

Elite theory is somewhat more controversial (and in many people's minds less directed toward pursuit of the public interest) and perhaps even less documented and accepted academically. Some scholars, such as **Thomas Dye**, have made a career out of defining and defending such a model. The basic argument is that based largely upon access and use of political power (as measured by partisan influence, for example), economic authority (as measured by political contributions to campaigns, for example), and even legal force (as measured by the decisions of elite judicial officials, such as Supreme Court justices and federal district and appellate judges, for example) various and few elites, individuals who he says are the "few who have power versus the many who do not,"[7] are the ones who actually influence the making of policy. They do not actually cast the votes, unless one of their elite-fraternity is elected to political office, but they strongly influence the way in which votes are cast. We are not talking about fraud and deception or otherwise illegal activity; no, proponents simply refer to the influence by high powered elite officials, whether in official political capacity or not, who have impact on the making of policy. For example, Iraq war detractors argued that former Vice President Dick Cheney's former position with his company, Haliburton, was a major reason why President Bush chose to go to war.

We now turn our attention from theoretical approaches of defining and explaining public policymaking to a pragmatic discussion of policy-makers to the environments they operate in, such as political culture, socioeconomic factors, ideology, and religion. Even though we are interested primarily in the administrative and bureaucratic environment of public administrators, it is necessary to examine the totality of policy-makers and their environments, given that public administrators, like their political and non-political counterparts, do not operate in a vacuum. Public administrators operate, interact, influence, and are influenced within and between both traditional and non-traditional policy environments in order to make, implement, and evaluate decisions that influence the public interest.

We know that politics and political authority is divided or fragmented, both institutionally (constitutionally) and non-institutionally (administratively and politically), and that opposition to public policies occurs at each stage of the policy process. When we discuss policymakers and influences on them and their environments, especially as they impact policymaking in the public interest, we are talking about a version that reaches far beyond the traditional (constitutional and institutional) bounds of government entities, procedures and processes and incorporates non-traditional (social, cultural, economic and even religious) influence agents in the making and implementation of public policy in the public interest.[8]

Policy Environment(s)

Policy environment(s) affect public policymaking largely through **political culture**. Loosely defined as the transmission of political values, beliefs, and attitudes on what governments should do, political culture influences policymaking by shaping political behavior. Historically the United States moved from a generally national-state bifurcation (pre-Civil War through Reconstruction), with the basic differences of governance taking place between the national and state governments and measured by constitutionally defined spheres of power, to one of greater state political, economic and legal action (beginning with public administration's role in the Industrial Revolution, particularly municipal and state reform movements). Economic conditions resulting in changes in tax policy, for example, have greatly influenced the development, formation, and adoption of public policies. The abandonment of the gold standard in the early part of the twentieth century, the ratification of the Thirteenth Amendment to the Constitution in 1913, which permitted the federal government to tax individual income, and the emergence of the Bureau of the Budget (later called the Office of Management and Budget), which was to play a central role in federal government organizational and fiscal policymaking, set the tone for governmental involvement in manipulating the economy.

Social factors such as increasing in educational levels of workers, continuing improvement in civil rights, including affirmative action among minorities, reducing poverty, decreasing crime, major changes in welfare reform, including welfare delivery systems and the advent of non-profit and faith-based organizations, have also influenced and been influenced by both national and sub-national changes and positions in public policymaking, such as in education [the 1965 Elementary and Secondary Education Act and more recently in the 2001 No Child Left Behind Act (NCLBA).]

Religion plays a significant role in the formation of public policymaking.[9] Religion has always been a major force in the development of American history and civic culture, ever since the founding period and even before, but in recent years it is receiving significant political and administrative attention. Only in the modern era has it come under a firestorm of controversy, primarily beginning with some of the Supreme Court's unfavorable rulings against the role of religion in the public sphere and by extreme left-wing groups, such as Barry Lynn's anti-evangelical Americans for the Separation of Church and State, which largely claim that any tangent or non-tangent involvement by religious organizations, primarily conservative evangelical Christian organizations, have no place in the service delivery function of government. However, President Bush and his faith-based initiatives challenged and even dismissed this anti-religious fervor, claiming that religion, spirituality, and like values do have place in the public square.

Traditional Institutional Policymakers

Constitutionally-defined policymakers are defined by the Constitution: legislative, executive, and judicial. **Legislative bodies**, especially the U.S. Congress, have generally given policy ground, especially at the agenda setting, to the imperial executive or the modern presidency.[10] Over the years, and most importantly since the end of WWII, the Congress exerts less influence over the stage of the policy process where the key issues are defined, discussed, and brought before the people. This has become the key job of the president (and to a great extent the bureaucracy, especially through the use of **administrative discretion**). Second, chief executives have become the center of policymaking attention and thus its impact upon the public interest is substantial. During the early period of the founding and up to and even through the Civil War (although President Lincoln asserted strong executive powers during the administration of the war) the president was really nothing more than a reactive force in national politics. With the beginning of the Industrial Revolution and greater demand for governmental reform, especially on the part of both elected (mayor) and unelected (city managers) executives, the executive branch, including public administrators, asserted itself in the policymaking process.[11] Third, the **judiciary** received scant attention by the founders. According to Hamilton in *Federalist 78*, for example, the role of the judiciary was to simply interpret the Constitution; it was not designed to formulate or make policy. However, with *Marbury v. Madison* (1803) regarding the enhanced power of judicial review, it was soon to become clear, especially by the end of the nineteenth century and the beginning of the twentieth century that the federal judiciary in particular was to become the prominent player in not only judicial interpretation and *re*interpretation, but also with regard to policymaking overall (*Griswold v. Connecticut, Roe v. Wade* and a plethora of other court cases that focused on wresting away from elected officials the authority and responsibility of policymaking). And fourth, although not a constitutional player per se, the **bureaucracy** plays an essential role in the implementation and evaluation of policymaking.[12] Administrative agencies were created by the legislative branch to first oversee public policy, and later to regulate social, political, and economic actions, such as the formation of the Interstate Commerce Commission (ICC) in 1883 to set rates and schedules for interstate transportation (the burgeoning railroad industry). The original goal of bureaucratic agencies was to implement policy through the writing and enforcement of various rules and regulations that were set within the framework of the general legislation. Today, the bureaucracy continues to have a significant impact upon policymaking in the pursuit of the public interest.

Non-Traditional Policymakers

Democracy and the public administrative process are also dependent upon the vigorous involvement of various non-traditional (non-constitutional) policymakers, or influencers. **Citizens** actively influence the policymaking process and pursuit of the public interest. This is especially true at the state and local levels[13] where the use of state initiatives and referendums and the increasingly active local policymaking boards made up of citizens, including school boards, planning commissions, and other special citizen groups point to an active and influential citizenry. **Interest groups** dominate the policy influencing process. Hundreds of thousands of groups influence not only traditional policymakers and public administrators but also individual citizens, mainly through advertising and politicking through the media (pro-life versus pro-choice groups is a good example). **Political parties**, especially at the national level, are a dying breed. Their influence in the national policymaking process is largely non-existent. Campaigns are issue or candidate-based and therefore the role of political parties in educating, involving, and influencing the individual voter has waned over the last few decades. Party politics at the local and state level seem to have much more clout, mobilizing and influencing voters and politicians along a number of important issues, such as education funding, lottery politics, and transportation issues. **National media**, led by cable news coverage on a 24-hour basis, such as CNN and now FOX News, has usurped the big three: ABC, CBS, and NBC. City newspapers are waning in influence as well. National newspapers, such as the *Washington Times, Washington Post, New York Times,* and *Chicago Tribune* still hold a larger number of readers, but even then the advent of on-line newspapers are cutting into the profits of print editions. Talk radio is big and influential, especially conservative talk radio, with the likes of Rush Limbaugh and Sean Hannity. Finally, **non-profit organizations**, including faith-based organizations,[14] have increased, both in terms of administering services but in influencing public policymaking. Non-profit organizations are strongly united with the local community, such as with United Way, Red Cross, Habitat for Humanity or Prison Fellowship. Major research work by organizations such as the Rockefeller Institute of Government at SUNY in Albany, funded in large part by the **Pew Charitable Trust**, as well other organizations such as the Center for Research on Religion and Urban Civil Society, which is part of the University of Pennsylvania's School of Arts and Sciences, conducts and produces ample empirical and qualitative research focusing on the impact of non-profits and faith-based organizations along a variety of issue areas.

Summary. Given these many institutions and elements of public policy, how does public policy come to be? Where do these various actors, organizations, and institutions — both traditional and non-traditional — apply their resources to affect policy change? What and where does the role of public administrators play most prominently? We use James Anderson's **stages model**. Other models, such as the **policy streams metaphor**, which we will discuss in more detail at the agenda setting stage, are also helpful.[15] However, we will focus mainly on the stages model simply because we believe it best conveys the various steps and processes involved in understanding how policy is created and evaluated, and how policy is largely affected and affects the public interest. In addition, it provides a sound conceptual foundation for examining the more detailed policy analysis process.

Policy Process: Focusing on the Stages or Cycles of Public Policy

The stages model directs the policymaking process in a series of steps or events, sometimes referred as the 'policy cycle.'[16] Even though actual policymaking is more complex than discussed here, the stages model is a tremendous pedagogical tool for helping students understand not only how public policy is conceived, but how public administrators examine the administrative and policy effectiveness of a given policy issue, particularly through the policy analysis process. In addition, it aids us in understanding not only how an issue is debated and discussed, but it also explains the roles and functions of various actors involved in policymaking, including public administrators. And as we mentioned, it enables us to incorporate and discuss the 'policy analysis' process — something we will discuss in more detail later. The stages in the policy cycle are briefly outlined and described in Figure 9.2.

Figure 9.2   The Policy Cycle

Figure taken from James E. Anderson's *Public Policymaking*, 6th edition (Boston, MA: Houghton Mifflin Company, 2006): 90.

Stage 1: Problem Identification. A public problem is identified by various actors as one that needs to be addressed. A **policy problem** involves a clash between individuals or groups of individuals over some value in which a government entity is required to settle the dispute. For example, Howard Stern, America's infamous shock jock, disagreed with the Federal Communications Commission (FCC)—a bureaucratic regulatory body—over what kind of language he could utter over the radio airwaves. He wanted to say anything at anytime, but the FCC had rules against such language. The FCC won. Stern left the public radio waves controlled by the FCC and entered into a multi-million dollar agreement with Sirius Radio. What was the problem? One of the primary problems was **public airwaves indecency**, which is defined by the FCC as "language or material that, in context, depicts or describes, in terms patently offensive as measured by contemporary community standards for the broadcast medium, sexual or excretory organs or activities." Even though some indecent material is protected by the First Amendment, there is enough that falls within the parameters of the definition above to eliminate such offenders as Stern. The FCC was responding to federal statute and court rulings that disallowed these actions that were offensive toward the public interest. [See the FCC case study in Chapter 1.]

Stage 2: Agenda Setting. **Agenda setting** is the stage that shows when an issue finally makes it to the government's agenda. No political or administrative action can take place until it is on the government's agenda. How does an issue make it to the government's agenda? [17] One of the more persuasive theories for explaining agenda-setting is John Kingdon's **streams metaphor**.[18] The three streams are the politics stream (political and public opinion), the policy stream (possible solutions to a public problem) and thirdly the problem stream (the defining attributes and characteristics of a problem and whether and how the problem is solvable—usually by public administrators). Once these streams merge they pass through a **window of opportunity**, a point in time in which the effects and resources of all three streams and the presiding governmental entities come together to offer the best possible solution. For example, civil rights action, such as the 1964 Civil Rights Act, came about as the result of favorable politics, such as President Johnson's intention to memorialize President Kennedy's work on civil rights action in 1963 by passing that same act in 1964; favorable policy positions, such as use of the commerce clause instead of the due process clause of the Fourteenth Amendment, to force private businesses from discriminating against blacks; and the use of the problem stream, which was the understanding that unless the federal government acted and acted quickly state and local governments, especially in the south, would continue to discriminate in areas such as education, business, and public accommodations.

Stage 3: Policy Formulation. **Policy formulation** is an incremental process. The U.S. Supreme Court did not arrive at one policy position for determining the outcome of affirmative action policy. Their reasoning was based on several criteria, such as venue (educational admission or job placement), group (racial, ethnic etc.), level of government (federal, state, or local) and even sector of society (public or governmental, private, and non-profit). The proposed solution must be deemed workable. When policymakers are considering technical or scientific questions, they must rely on the latest scientific research, such as the viability of stem cell lines, harmful effects of human cloning, trying to put a man on Mars, etc.), much of what is provided by professional public administrators, such as scientists. The policy formulation stage is therefore an excellent opportunity for incorporating the services of many of the non-traditional policymakers (or policy influencers) discussed earlier. A pertinent illustration is President Clinton's 1993 compromise policy of "don't ask, don't tell" in dealing with homosexuality in the military (see boxed insert below).

Case Study   "Don't Ask, Don't Tell"

A good illustration of policy formulation occurred in 1993 when President Clinton came to office. He demanded that the U.S. military abandon its policy toward homosexuals of not allowing homosexuals into the military and dishonorably discharging them. Democratic presidential candidate Clinton had made a promise in running for office that he would end these policies against homosexuals in the U.S. military. However, opposition to Clinton's reforms came from many sectors, including the military, Republican senators and representatives, conservative interest groups, and the general public. As a compromise, President Clinton issued an executive order and instituted the "Don't Ask, Don't Tell" policy.

The goal of the "Don't Ask, Don't Tell" policy was more pragmatic than idealistic. While on the presidential campaign trail, Clinton had expressed his vision of an ideal world in which there was no bias or discrimination in the U.S. military on the basis of sexual orientation. But when he encountered strong resistance from Congress, interest groups, the American public, and the military itself, he backed off and arrived at what he believed was a reasonable and practical solution with the "Don't Ask, Don't Tell" policy. He believed he put the ideal into a workable or operational policy; the military will not seek to find out the sexual orientation of incoming recruits or other military personnel, but neither would military personnel or recruits reveal their sexual orientation.

Formulating policy in a conflicted political environment is difficult at best and requires ample and diverse political, policy, and knowledge-based resources to bring about some semblance of success. President Clinton found his success with the "Don't Ask, Don't Tell" policy.

Stage 4: Policy Adoption. **Policy adoption** requires some action on the part of the traditional or institutional policymakers, meaning congressmen, presidents, governors, city councilmen, county managers and other public administrators, who will translate a policy issue into a formal governmental action, such as a law, executive order, judicial decree, or administrative rule and regulation. Policymakers are usually confronted with a large number of policy options, such as President Clinton was with regard to the issue of homosexuals in the military: keep the policy the same, eliminate the status quo and institute any range of alternatives, or find some type of compromise. The alternatives bring forth a number of concerns: political, policy, social, economic, religious-oriented, ethical, and moral. The key to the adoption stage is how the policymaker makes a decision, but the decision outcome is also of importance, particularly when the public interest is at stake.

Decision-Making Theories

There are three broad traditional decision-making theories, including rational, incremental, and intuitive. We briefly examine the characteristics and weaknesses of each.

First, **rational decision making** consists of discovering the ends (or outcome) and making an analysis of which means or outcome is most reasonable. For example, a city manager is faced with a male employee who downloaded pornography on his PC at the office and was viewing it when a female employee caught him in the act. The city manager could follow several basic steps to address the issue.

It is evident that the rational approach to decision making, although perhaps best suited to the private sector and its primary concern of profit status, is in no way a viable option for making a difficult, but unfortunately all too common type of public decision, such as the one discussed. The level of information needed, the degree or level of finding consensus on goals, the expense of time needed to engage in a purely rational model are all drawbacks to using the rational model. Certainly, there are quantitative based decisions that can be made in the public sector that might be more appropriate for the application of the rational model, such as reducing a budget deficit or establishing a performance based model for capital outlays (the old PPBS), but even then one can argue that the level of human-based consequences and public interest manifestation supersede the use of the rational model. An even greater argument against the use of rational decision making is the incremental model itself.

Second, **incremental decision making** uses the status quo, not abstract goals, as the key point of reference for decisions. Instead of trying to compute all of the alternatives and consequences, assign numerical values, including financial costs and benefits to each alternative and consequence, the decision maker can begin where he is at, not try and determine where he would like to be.

Let's go back to our city manager. After being informed of the situation, both in oral and written form, the city manager can address the issue with both parties involved and get both stories, and then confront the male employee. The city manager can explain that this type of computer use is unacceptable on city time. The city manager may decide to release the employee immediately, with a thirty-day severance package. In other words, instead of focusing on a maximization of choices the decision maker directs his attention making the best decision with the limited amount of information available.

It is often criticized as being too cautious or conservative, particularly in light of making budgetary decisions that are largely just based upon small incremental changes from the past year. Serious innovative policy changes, particularly in the areas of improving educational delivery, takes decision making that is not status quo, but creative and innovative. Further, a consequence of incremental decision making is that it is often tied to political and policy issues, rather than being more disconnected from the entire process. (Of course in defense of incremental decision making, how objective is rational choice?) Incremental decision making is the standard for public administrators and policymakers, primarily because it is most common and easily adaptable to almost any decision scenario.

The **intuitive model** is a character and personal-based model; it does not easily avail itself to rigid quantification or decision analysis methods, and is not overly popular in public administration scholarly circles. The intuitive model is more about what is right than how the decision is reached. Intuitive decision making is just what it sounds like: policymakers, including public administrators, make public policy decisions based more on how they internally react to a situation (what is their gut reaction) rather than to the more objective, rational, and legal aspects of the decision and its consequences.

Our city manager example may illustrate the intuitive approach. Reacting to the situation from a particular religious background, the city manager may intuit that pornography is not good for the mind or soul. Perhaps it seems demeaning of both men and women and for that reason alone has no place in public, especially in the workplace. But the city manager cannot fire the employee simply on the justification of a gut reaction, and must do what a reasonable person would do in a similar situation. A reasonable person might conclude that what is in the public interest is to release the individual, give him a 30-day severance package to minimally offset the economic consequences of being fired, support him in finding some type of professional counseling to help him address his attraction to pornography, and support the victim, affirming to her that all effort will be made to prevent this type of action from occurring in the future.

Its weakness is also its strength: it is a decision making model that is not quantitatively defined or measured, and for this reason it is realistic because it involves human emotions, conflicts, and interpersonal relationships that can and usually do affect more than just professional, political, and administrative norms, rules and policies; it affects the human psyche and the human condition. It is based in large part upon the make-up of the person, and as such is dependent—right or wrong—upon the human condition: mentally, emotionally, and personally. This is not your cookie-cutter version of decision making; it is about what is right, what is wrong, and how a decision is realistically made to do what is right, or what is in the public interest.

Stage 5: Implementation. **Implementation** is the crux of public policy, because it is here that the law, executive order or judicial decree, for example, is actually put into effect or implemented. It is also the phase that public administrators are mostly involved in, where their professional expertise and knowledge of procedures, techniques, and regulations is most needed to affect and influence the public interest. According to **James Anderson**, implementation requires organization, interpretation and application of statutory, regulatory, and judicial decree.[19] Organization is the role of the administrative agencies, or bureaucracies that actually put the law, executive order or judicial decree into action. Interpretation of law requires public administrators to know the intention (or assume the intention) of the decision making body when it framed its decision. Application of the law is the determination of rules, regulations, procedures and processes necessary to implement public policy and is accomplished through rule-making, adjudication, and bureaucratic precedent. (See below for a more detailed description of the implementation stage as applied to a specific public policy.)

Box 9.2   Steps in the Implementation Stage of the Policy Process: The NCLB Act

Organization: When the U.S. Supreme Court ruled in *Brown v. Board of Education* that public schools would no more be segregated, it required the assistance of various agencies and official organizations to see that its edict was followed, including the U.S. Attorney General's office, various civil rights commissions, and especially state organizations, such as states' attorney generals' offices.

Interpretation: When former President Bush pushed for the No Child Left Behind Act, it seemed clear that the intention of the amending legislation was to hold schools, school districts, and various personnel, including administrators, teachers and students, accountable for their actions in national mandatory standardized testing for reading and writing. Indirect consequences of *mis*-interpretation include: punishing racial minorities, pushing aside civics, history, and economics in favor of reading and writing only, and indirectly forcing teachers and students alike to teach and learn for the exam.

Application: *Rule-making* is governed by the 1946 Administrative Procedures Act, and is intended to provide guidance to bureaucratic agencies. This is accomplished through establishment of guidelines concerning what is a rule, how it should be applied. The Department of Education, in conjunction with state departments or agencies of education, dictate how the mandatory testing is to proceed, what are the guidelines to follow, and what are the consequences.

Adjudication is the use of *pseudo-judicial* powers that allow agencies to hear cases and complaints, such as if a worker or group of workers believe they have been treated unfairly by their employer the case can be heard before the National Labor Relations Board (NLRB), and the NLRB will render a decision and oversee the enforcement of the decision. *Precedent* is a guiding influence toward the implementation of policy. When the Elementary and Secondary Education Act (ESEA) of 1965 was reauthorized as the NCLBA, for example, the social function of the old ESEA was no longer clear. Was the reauthorization designed to assist low-income students, reduce poverty and improve educational facilities? Or was the new NCLB strictly aimed at improving reading and writing scores?

Source: James E. Anderson, *Public Policymaking*, 6th ed. (Boston, MA: Houghton Mifflin, 2006), 202–5; Jeffrey Pressman and Aaron Wildavsky, *Implementation: How Great Expectations in Washington are Dashed in Oakland; Or Why It's Amazing that Federal Programs Work At All, This being a Saga of the Economic Development Administration as Told by Two Sympathetic Observers Who Seek to Build Morals on a Foundation of Ruined Hope* (Berkeley, CA: University of California Press, 1984).

Stage 6: Evaluation. Evaluation determines the effectiveness of a policy program and makes recommendations for alterations to the program itself. Implementation and evaluation are linked.[20] Quite often the bureaucratic agency that implements a program, such as the Department of Education implementing the No Child Left Behind Act (NCLBA), is also the same agency that will evaluate its effectiveness. More specifically, evaluation is dedicated to data collection, interpretation of results, and reporting of those results. In addition, though, evaluation is connected to the political and policy goals and objectives set forth by the original policymakers even during the early stages of the policy formulation stage, which, of course, affects the public interest. Federal educational officials and others associated with successful implementation of the NCLBA, such as the White House Office and the former Bush administration, lobbyists, teacher associations, senators and congressmen and many other individuals and groups, contributed to the dedication of goals and objectives. These goals and objectives, whether in the form of **outcomes** (policy goals) or **outputs** (measurable indices), were considered key variables for study to determine program effectiveness. For example, the level of writing proficiency, an increased percentage of higher standardized test scores and a number of other variables were established early on in the policymaking process as prospective measures for evaluation. How and to what extent these variables would be measured might be determined by the evaluators themselves, but the general goals of evaluation were set early on.

Box 9.3   Policy Evaluation and the NCLB: Does It Work?

Policy evaluation and the evaluators themselves, including the implementing agency itself (internal) and research organizations (external), such as think tanks and research universities, are political. Each has political axes to grind. For example, the White House and Bush administration want to see NCLB to succeed and therefore their evaluation may or may not be as unbiased and complete as possible. On the other hand, outside policy evaluating agencies, even though they purport to be unbiased and nonpartisan, may very well elicit ideological bias toward or against the program under review. For example, the liberal leaning think tank Brookings Institution may be somewhat biased against NCLBA and its purported goal of instituting accountability standards for students, teachers and administrators, given that liberal teachers unions will be more accountable. On the other hand, more conservative leaning think tanks, such as the American Enterprise Institute or libertarian research organizations such as The Cato Institute, may view NCLB more positively, because it provides incentives, economic and otherwise, for all parties involved to reach learning goals.

The Foundation and Technique of Policy Analysis

Policy analysis is not a stage per se in the policy process; it is itself a process through which multi-disciplinary trained and knowledgeable observers of the policy process examine and evaluate the various alternative solutions, policies, and/or programs that may offer some assistance in providing a solution to a public problem. The discussion of policy analysis is varied, but we will highlight the following two points. First, we will introduce two basic types of policy analysis: **theoretical** and **applied**. Second, we will outline the various steps in doing sound policy analysis, steps that are broad in their application but also specific enough for us to describe their importance and applicability to a specific policy area, such as illegal immigration. Here we draw in part upon the work of William Dunn.

Theoretical policy analysis is original in nature; it is designed to improve or add to an existing body of knowledge; it is generally focused on original data collection methods; it is largely quantitative methodologically; and the results are usually for academics and are therefore generally displayed in academic outlets, such as journal articles or books. Applied policy analysis is not original in nature, it is a synthesis and evaluation of existing data sources; it relies on the development of sound policy arguments; it is usually, but not always, methodologically qualitative in nature (literature review, personal observation and interviews, etc.); and the results are for the use of government agencies, citizen groups, non-profit organizations, etc. and is therefore displayed in short policy papers, memos, or issue briefs. (See Table 9.1.)

Table 9.1   Two Kinds of Policy Disciplines

Characteristic	Basic	Applied
ORIGIN OF PROBLEMS	• University colleagues	• Governmental clients and citizens
TYPICAL METHODS	• Quantitative	• Development of sound arguments • Qualitative
TYPE OF RESEARCH	• Original data collection	• Synthesis and evaluation of existing data
PRIMARY AIM	• Improve theory	• Improve practice (policy)
COMMUNICATIONS MEDIA	• Article or book	• Policy memo or issue paper (to public official; online outlet)
SOURCE OF INCENTIVES	• University departments	• Government agencies, citizen groups, non-profit organizations, etc.

Source: Reprinted from William N. Dunn, *Introduction to Policy Analysis*, 3d. ed. (Upper Saddle River, NJ: Prentice Hall, 2004), 437.

Applied type is more conducive to the work of public officials, especially public administrators. Although it does not include a comprehensive scope and in-depth approach to the study of some type of policy problem, it does provide the public administrator with the basic information and tools for understanding the problem, basic alternatives or solutions to the problem, and what are the consequences of those alternatives for future decision making. Busy public administrators and other public officials do not have the time or inclination to read through lengthy academic pieces; they need basic facts, a statement of the problem, possible solutions to the problem, and the consequences and/or implications of one possible solution over another. Thus, whether the problem is how state public educational officials are to deal with the fiscal imbalances regarding the financial needs of special education students[21] or whether elected public officials must decide if and how to implement mandatory government provided preschool programs;[22] the need for solid, well researched and written, and relatively unbiased policy reports is critical to aiding them make sound public decisions.

Steps in Doing Policy Analysis

We now turn to the basic steps in doing policy analysis. Although there are almost as many different models for describing the various steps in doing policy analysis, we will show there are commonalities. As one expert noted the following steps are "common to most of the social sciences and professions, and to human problem solving generally" and therefore are sufficient for our purposes in defining and describing the how-to of policy analysis.[25] In addition, the following steps correspond with the stages in the policy cycle discussed above. (See Table 9.2.) This is not coincidental, given that policy analysis is a process too. In addition, the steps highlight both of the two approaches discussed above: the analycentric and policy process, with the former providing the structure and the latter contributing to the political, policy, and administrative aspects. We introduce each step, briefly define it, and then provide a brief description of its characteristics and how it is understood or applied to a policy issue.

Table 9.2   Policy Stages, Cycle and the Policy Analysis Process

Policy Information	Policy Cycle	Policy Analysis Process
Policy problem: "unrealized value or opportunity for improvement which, however, identified, may be attained through public action."	PROBLEM IDENTIFICATION— Identifying the specific problem; differentiating it from the policy issue	Defining the Problem (**Problem Structuring**)
Expected policy outcome: "probable consequence of a policy designed to solve a problem" (need information about circumstances that gave rise to the problem initially)	AGENDA SETTING (OR Policy Formulation)— Problems that receive serious attention of public officials	Predicting Outcomes (**Policy Forecasting**)
Preferred policy: "potential solution to a problem" (obviously to select a preferred policy analyst needs information about "expected policy outcomes")	ADOPTION—Development of support for a specific proposal so a policy can be legitimized or made authoritative	Prescribing various preferred policies (**Recommendation**)
Observed policy outcome: "past or present consequence of implementing a preferred policy" (consequences are generally not stated or known in advance, nor anticipated, making information both *ex ante* and *ex post*)	IMPLEMENTATION— Application of policy by bureaucratic organization	Describing observed outcomes (**Monitoring**)
Policy performance: "degree to which an observed policy outcome contributes to the attainment of values, goals, or objectives" (in reality problems are rarely solved, instead they are managed)	EVALUATION—To determine whether the policy met its intended goals	Appraising the value of the observed outcomes (**Evaluation**)

Source: See Dunn, 2004.

Step 1: Problem Definition (Problem Structuring). Here the analyst must determine what the problem to solve is. It is critical that the policy analyst correctly define the problem, collect as much information as is possible, particularly within institutional and organizational resource constraints, assess the validity and use of that information, largely by communicating with other analysts and outside organizations, and formulate a statement about the problem. Policy analysts, for example who focus on addressing the problem of **illegal immigration** realize that this a large problem area and it is important to be clear just what part of this broad problem is under investigation (economics, education and social services delivery to illegal immigrants, etc.)

Step 2: Prediction of policy alternatives (Forecasting). This step requires the analyst to assess (or predict) the various possible alternatives or solutions to the stated problem. Choosing possible alternatives is largely an incremental process—meaning the analyst is determining past decisions made and building upon those successes and staying away from past failures. However, a rational process that focuses on resource allocation, such as human and financial in order to achieve the largest possible benefit, is also a possibility. For example, when assessing the illegal immigration problem the analyst must look back over history and learn what worked in various states, such as Texas and Arizona, and what did not work in other states, such as New Mexico and southern California. Or the analyst can assess what type of impact, both negative and positive, the surge of illegal immigration has upon state and local economies, particularly in farming, lawn and nursery, retail, fast food, and other industries that attract large numbers of illegal and legal immigrants. Choosing and tailoring various possible solutions becomes a difficult task, and the analyst is aided by a variety of quantitative methods, such as *time-series analysis,* where the focus is on examining numerical data that reflects statistical time-based trends in illegal immigration, and qualitative methods such as **theoretical forecasting**, that allow the analyst to map and/or model specific elements or trends related to illegal immigration that might prove helpful to the policymaker when selecting policy alternatives.

Step 3: Prescribing the Best Policy Alternative (Recommendation). This third step details the possible alternatives that are BEST able to solve the policy problem. Here the analyst must examine alternatives that are actionable, prospective, value dependent, and ethically complex.[26] First, how **realistic** or **actionable** is the policy alternative? For example, if the United States wishes to stop or slow down the initial flow of illegal immigrants from physically crossing the border the question arises: "Is the construction of a 12-foot high 1,500-mile fence the BEST alternative?" Second, prescriptive claims are **prospective**; that is, they occur BEFORE the time any policy action is taken. The policy analyst prescribes possible actions before they actually are selected. Third, the policy analyst does not eliminate the need for group, individual, or even societal values when prescribing possible policy claims, such as considering how a 12-foot high 1,500-mile fence across multiple borders be considered by a variety of stakeholders. And fourth, analysts must examine the **ethical** component of any prescriptive claim, such as what is the ethical impact of turning away illegal immigrants and forcing them to return to less than desirable economic, social, and living conditions.

Step 4: Describing the Prescribed Alternative (Monitoring). The fourth step in the policy analytic process is **describing** the conditions of the selected solution or "monitoring policy actions after they have occurred."[27] Monitoring is the step that produces information about the causes and consequences of various public policies. Monitoring takes different forms, such as auditing and accounting, but the key component of this step is information gathering at various points in time and is of considerable cost to governments. The primary focus of this stage is to monitor both the **policy outputs**, or the measurable part of the policy solution (the cost of building material for the 12-foot high, 1,500-mile fence), and the **policy outcomes**, or the changes in behavior or attitude toward the policy solution (assessing public reaction to the fence itself).[28] Monitoring depends upon thorough review of facts, statistics, trends, and other measurable and quantifiable indices.

Step 5: Appraising the Worth of Selected Policy Alternative (Evaluation). The fifth stage is assessment of the value of the policy solution chosen. If, for example, we are to examine the worth (or value)—which by the way necessarily implies the ethics of a decision, which we discussed in detail in Chapter 4—of raising a 12-foot high, 1,500-mile fence along our southwestern border with Mexico, then the natural question is: Did this solution work? Whereas the monitoring stage audited and accounted for changes in the recently implemented decision to erect the fence, appraising its action status, so to speak; the evaluation stage now tries to determine whether or not the original goal of restricting illegal immigration was met. How was it met? What are the results, both in terms of policy performance and value (ethical) achievement? To answer these questions the policy analyst must two things: establish a research design and conduct specific types of evaluation studies. Let's look at each.

Evaluation

First, before specific studies can be done the policy analyst must set up evaluative studies using various research designs, such as **experimental** and **quasi-experimental** (see boxed insert below), the policy analyst is concerned with establishing validity, both internal and external.[29] **Internal validity** seeks to determine whether what was intended to be measured was in fact measured. If the analyst wanted to determine whether or not the presence of the wall was significant in deterring would be illegal immigrants from crossing the border, then it would be necessary to develop a research design that met that qualification. **External validity**, however, reaches beyond the immediate policy question and asks whether or not it is applicable to broader and more general situations and circumstances. In other words, does this particular study have merit or worth beyond the current situation? If so, then we contend it is externally valid.

Box 9.4   Experimental and Quasi-Experimental Research Designs

Experimental research designs are most noted for their use in laboratory sciences, such as chemistry, physics, and biological sciences. The key characteristics of an experimental design include 1) control over the experimental treatment (stimuli) to the subject, 2) use of control versus experimental groups, and 3) random assignment of subjects to either the control or experimental groups. Experimental research designs work exceptionally well for controlled environments, such as the inside of a Petri dish or test tube, but they are not extremely reliable for use in a political environment; thus the need for something less rigid, but still reliable.

Quasi-experimental research designs are the ticket for policy analysts. Why? Because they provide the conceptual framework of an experimental design, but are adaptable to the highly charged political environment of the policy world. The use of quasi-experiments extends back to the 1930s. Since then quasi-experiments have been used in a number of policy areas including social welfare policy, micro- and macro-economic policy, highway safety, and a number of other areas. The methodological key to both experimental and quasi-experimental designs is internal validity: the greater the internal validity, the more confident the policy analyst is that the policy outputs are indeed the result of the policy inputs.

Source: See Robert B. Denhardt and Joseph W. Grubbs, *Public Administration: An Action Orientation*. 4th ed. (Belmont, CA: Wadsworth, 2003), 292–3; William N. Dunn, *Introduction to Policy Analysis*, 3d ed. (Upper Saddle River, NJ: Prentice Hall, 2004), 292–93; and for a comprehensive discussion of experimental and quasi-experimental designs, see Donald T. Campbell and Julian C. Stanley. 1966. *Experimental and Quasi-experimental Designs for Research* (Chicago, IL: Rand McNally, 1966).

Second, evaluation studies are of two kinds: **quantitative** and **qualitative**. Quantitative studies include the use of many of the same techniques and methodologies used at the other stages, including cost-benefit analysis, cost-effectiveness analysis, time-series and regression analysis, and many others. Each is designed, as we determined, to quantitatively measure whether or not various numerical and statistical changes occurred and if so to what degree did these changes merit positive or negative association with the desired goals. Qualitative studies are most pertinent and useful for the applied policy analysis report—the type that most public administrators and other policymakers will most likely refer to. These include on-site and indirect observation, personal interviewing, archival research, and extensive reading.[30] The policy analyst takes a much more hands-on approach than is used in most quantitative techniques. He is interested in personal observations by the participants involved in the policy decision—from border patrol agents to state governors to Homeland Security agents to, perhaps, illegal immigrants themselves. What is the impact of the implemented policy? Sometimes simply running regression analysis does not capture the most complete picture of the policy itself and the influence it has or does not have on the policy problem.

Conclusion

So, you think the job of a policy analyst is easy? It is challenging, yes and even rewarding; but easy, no. The public administrator and the policy analyst—sometimes one and the same, although usually policy analysts are specialists who work for public administrators in the various national, state, and local departments and agencies that do policy analysis—operate in the real world of public administration and public policy, administering, managing, and analyzing the effects and outcomes of public policy. The practice of public policy is much more complex than discussed in this chapter. The making of public policy is not left to one traditional or non-traditional actor or sets of actors alone; it is a complex, inter-related network of individuals, groups, organizations, and even institutions that combine to devise and implement public policy. It is the role of the policy analyst to evaluate the implemented policy and determine, either through quantitative or qualitative means (or sometimes through a combination of both), the effectiveness of the policy and whether or not it achieved its stated goals and objectives. Clearly, though, we contend that the study of public policy and the practice of policy analysis are and should be done in full appreciation and acknowledgement of the importance of the public interest in influencing public policy.

Action Steps

1. How may the public interest redirect our thinking of policy analysis, especially economic analysis? Consider the deference the U.S. Supreme Court gives to economic analysis in the case of *Kelo v. City of New London*, 545 U.S. 469 (2005), in which New London, Connecticut, was upheld in taking private property and homes to make way for private economic development. Consider the backlash against the Court's decision in *Kelo* and what this may suggest about the limits the public interest may impose on policy analysis.

2. Students break into teams of three or four. Instructor assigns a one-to-two sentence statement to each group, one that reflects the importance of any of the theories of public policy. Ask each group to take a decidedly value-based position on the statement, discuss it in the group, form a position, and then reassemble to debate the various positions. Each group should assign a secretary and spokesman to record and articulate, respectively, the group's position. For example, under Systems Theory, a value-based position may be: "Public Policy is the logical outcome of a series of inputs (e.g., interest group indices), throughputs (e.g., the decisions of political institutions), and outputs (e.g., the laws passed by political institutions)."

3. Have the students read excerpts from Charles Lindblom, "The Science of Muddling Through" (1959). Examine Lindblom's reasoning and how this shaped thinking regarding the nature and development of the science public policy.

4. Do a brief literature review of journal articles published in any number of scholarly journals on the topic of public policy and the public interest. Determine what the authors have to say about the public interest, and assess whether what is written is generally positive or negative about the worth of pursuing the public interest. Ask the students to record their findings in a two-page paper. Come to class and be prepared to discuss their findings.

5. Contact several public administration officials and question them regarding their 1) understanding of the public policy process, especially as it relates to their job, and 2) how does what they do with regard to the public policy process affect, if at all, the public interest? Report findings back to the class.

Exam Review Preparation

1. In a short essay, assess the various definitions of public policy and the theories that account for its formation and operations. What does this tell us about administration in the public interest? Write your own definition of public policy and defend it.

2. Identify the nature and importance of each stage of the policy process:
    a. Problem Identification
    b. Agenda Setting
    c. Policy Formulation
    d. Policy Adoption
    e. Implementation
    f. Evaluation

3. Define and discuss the three primary approaches to explaining policy decision-making: rational-choice, incremental, and intuitive.

4. What is public policy? Discuss the substantive and process natures of public policy.

5. Overview and critique the three types of policy analyzed by political scientist Theodore Lowi in the 1960s: distributive, redistributive, and regulatory.

6. Overview and critique the four sets or types of interests as analyzes by James Q. Wilson in the 1980s: interest group politics, clientele group politics, entrepreneurial politics, and majoritarian politics.

7. What role(s) do non-profits and faith-based organizations play in the policy process? How do they assist and/or detract from traditional aspects of the policy process?

8. Explain the process of policy evaluation.

9. What are the steps in policy analysis?

10. How can a public administrator operate in both the political world of public policy and the policy process and the more technical world of policy analysis? How are the goals different? And the same? What type of administrator is needed to operate in both worlds effectively?

Key Concepts

Administrative discretion
Agenda setting
Bureaucracy
Internal and external validity
Intuitive model of decision making
James Anderson
John Kingdon's "policy streams" metaphor
Pew Charitable Trust
Policy analysis
Policy evaluation
Policy formulation
Policy implementation
Policy outcomes and outputs
Policy streams metaphor
Political culture
Political systems' model
Problem identification
Public policy
RAND Corporation
William Dunn

Recommended Readings

Dunn, Charles W. *The Seven Laws of Presidential Leadership: An Introduction to the American Presidency.* Upper Saddle River, NJ: Pearson-Prentice Hall, 2007.

Dye, Thomas R. *Top Down Policymaking.* New York: Chatham House, 2001.

Gerston, Larry N. *Public Policymaking in a Democratic Society: A Guide to Civic Engagement.* Armonk, NY: M.E. Sharpe, 2002.

Kingdon, John W. *Agendas, Alternatives, and Public Policies.* 2d ed. New York: Harper Collins, 1995.

Peters, B. Guy. *The Future of Governing: Four Emerging Models.* Lawrence, KS: University Press of Kansas, 1996.

Shafritz, Jay M., Karen S. Layne, and Christopher P. Borick, eds. *Classics of Public Policy.* New York: Pearson-Longman, 2005.

Stone, Deborah. *Policy Paradox: The Art of Political Decision-Making.* Revised edition. New York: W.W. Norton, 2002.

Weimer, David L., and Aidan R. Vining. *Policy Analysis: Concepts and Practice.* 4th ed. Upper Saddle River, NJ: Pearson-Longman, 2005.

Related Web Sites

Association for Public Policy Analysis and Management
http://www.appam.org/home.asp

Charles Lindblom
http://www.yale.edu/polisci/people/clindblom.html

Department of Education (No Child Left Behind Act)
http://www.ed.gov/index.jhtml

National Center for Policy Analysis
http://www.ncpa.org/

National Center for Public Policy Research
www.nationalcenter.org

Pew Charitable Trust
http://www.pewtrusts.org/

Public Policy Forum
www.ppforum.com

RAND Corporation
http://www.rand.org/

State Policy Network
www.spn.org/

Thomas Dye
http://www.thomasrdye.com/

Chapter 10

Nonprofit Organizations, Faith-Based Initiatives, and the Public Interest

"It has been said that the quality of a nation can be seen in the way it treats its least advantaged citizens … the state of nonprofit America is surprisingly robust as we enter the new millennium, with more organizations doing more things more effectively than ever before."

Lester Salamon, *The Resilient Sector:*
The State of Nonprofit America

"The search for meaning and purpose in life begins at the bottom and works its way up. It starts with a call to moral regeneration and personal responsibility in which faith-based organizations (FBOs) can play a crucial role in curtailing the destructive behavior ruining the lives of millions of Americans … To nurture change, federal, state, and local governments, through administrative reforms and legislation, must nurture and encourage FBOs."

Lewis D. Solomon, *In God We Trust? Faith-based*
Organizations and the Quest to Solve America's Social Ills

"Do you know if you are going to Heaven? … [asked my] inquisitor, a television evangelist … He was not asking me, the private citizen. He was asking me, the nation's first 'Faith Czar.' A visible government official. A top presidential appointee. Someone responsible for assisting President George W. Bush in faithfully upholding the Constitution, faithfully executing democratically enacted law, and faithfully acting in the public interest without regard to religious identities."

John J. DiIulio, Jr., *Godly Republic: A Centrist*
Blueprint for America's Faith-Based Future

Chapter Objectives

Upon completion of this chapter the student will be able to:

1. Appreciate the distinctive role that nonprofits and faith-based organizations and initiatives play in the delivery of various public services;

2. Describe the theoretical influences upon which non-profit organizations function;

3. Understand the historical influence and development of the role and impact of
    nonprofits and faith-based organizations in the U.S. today;

4. Recognize that religious faith, as emphasized through faith-based initiatives, has
    increasing influence upon the delivery of various public services today;

5. Clarify the partnership role between government and nonprofits, including faith-
    based initiatives, in the administration of the public interest.

Introduction

There is substantial support for the impact of nongovernmental actors to operate in
policy areas once dominated by government. These actors, including private, non-profit
and faith-based organizations, are increasing in quantity and influence. Many public services are now delivered through nongovernmental organizations, such as nonprofits.[1]
Nonprofits and faith-based organizations are known for the provision of social services,
such as bill payment assistance, food assistance, and job training programs. Within specific public services, such as criminal justice, nonprofits and faith-based organizations
provide crime prevention programs[2] and assist as intermediaries between police and
lower-income communities.[3]

Since 1996, the federal government along with many state and local governments
have worked to meet the public's demand for social and welfare services by coordinating with these nonprofits and faith-based organizations, such as churches and **para-
church ministries**, funded in part through grants made available by the federal
government. The United States has moved from an intergovernmental to an *intersec-
toral*[4] or *interorganizational*[5] administrative and policy system, one where the working
relations between units of government is no longer sufficient to meet increasing societal and citizen demands for service delivery; it requires that government agencies, departments, and organizations work with various private, non-profit, and faith-based
organizations to effect policy changes and deliver vital public services. By sailing more
often and more deeply into the waters of public service, nonprofits and faith-based organizations have become a more significant part of the puzzle of administration in the
public interest. The public interest is no longer—if it ever was—the sole domain of
government; it is frequented by the influence of the private, non-profit, and faith-based
sectors of society.[6]

The purpose of this chapter is to give greater attention and clarity to the place of nonprofits and faith-based organizations in the public sector today. In order to accomplish this task the chapter is divided into five sections. First, it will briefly outline the
purpose, definition, scope, and impact of non-profit organizations. Second, it will describe the theoretical influences upon which non-profit organizations function. Third,
it will provide a brief historical development of the role and impact of nonprofits and,
to a lesser extent, **faith-based organizations**, in the United States. Fourth, it will discuss the influence of faith-based organizations, particularly as they are different from
nonprofits in general. And fifth, it will offer conclusions and implications for explaining
the changing relationships or partnering between government and non-profit and
faith-based organizations over the next few years in the administration of the public
interest.

Non-profit Organizations: Foundation for Civil Society

Non-profit organizations have contributed significantly to the governance process over the past several decades or so. However, depending upon how one defines and examines non-governmental organizations their influence goes back much farther. Theda Skocpol argues that voluntary associations, particularly those with a civic focus, date to the nation's founding.[7] **Marvin Olasky** contends that the use of religious faith—especially Christianity—pre-dated what we term faith-based organizations, extending back to the pilgrims landing at Plymouth. Olasky's argument is that reaching out to others—which is what nonprofits and faith-based organizations are supposed to be all about—is centered not in organizations, per se, but with individual human desires to help others.[8] Lester Salamon, a recognized authority on the role of nonprofits in American society, concurs, "Like the arteries of a living organism, these organizations carry a life force that has long been a centerpiece of American culture—a faith in the capacity of individual action to improve the quality of human life."[9] Suffice it to say that the contributions of people, resources, and ideas, whether voluntarily associated or professionally organized, such as in today's non-profit and faith-based arenas, is significant to governance and administration in the public interest.

Marvin Olasky

Marvin Olasky authored *The Tragedy of American Compassion*, a book that gave impetus to President George W. Bush's emphasis on the use of faith-based organizations for the delivery of social services. He was born into a Jewish family in Boston, became an avowed Atheist and Marxist in high school, and then while attending undergraduate school at the University of Michigan in the 1970s he had a spiritual awakening, dissociating himself from his atheistic and Marxist beliefs, and embraced Christianity. He was baptized into the Presbyterian church in 1976. *The Tragedy of American Compassion* argued that the social ills of today are rooted in the countercultural revolution of the 1960s. Only until churches, para-church organizations, or what has become known as faith-based organizations, become more involved in the delivery of social and welfare services, will there be a lasting effect in society. When Texas Governor George Bush became President G.W. Bush in 2001, Olasky saw his ideas become public policy with the creation of the White House Office of Faith-Based and Community Initiatives.

Source: "Marvin Olasky," NNDB, www.nndb.com/people/325/000058151/ (accessed October 2007).

Defining Our Terms

Before we begin, we need to clarify the use of terminology. The term 'nongovernmental' is generally associated with internationally-based organizations that have global economic and social agendas. However, in this book and specifically this chapter we do not use the term this way. We refer to **nongovernmental organizations** as those organizations that are not particularly authoritative and directly linked or defined by governmental jurisdiction, legal status, or constitutional definition, such as non-profit and faith-based organizations. Over the years various and diverse titles have been used, including the tax-exempt sector, the civil society sector, the commons, the charitable sector, the voluntary sector, the nonproprietary sector, and the non-profit sector.[10] According to Peter Frumkin, it was not until the 1950s and 1960s that the term **non-profit** surfaced and over time replaced the more commonly used and understood term that referred to those organizations that are not directly within the jurisdictional and legal umbrella of national and sub-national governments. But as we will later learn this rather broad distinction includes a hefty number of charitable and voluntary organizations that contribute substantially to the political, social, and economic life of most Americans.[11] For the purposes of this chapter we will use the term nonprofits and faith-based organizations when referring generally to nongovernmental organizations.

Definition of Nonprofits. The basic definition of non-profit organizations is that they consist of private organizations "that are prohibited from distributing any profits they may generate to those who control or support them."[12] Nonprofits are not like their private sector counterparts, which exist for the sole purpose of generating profits for their shareholders, but neither are they like the public sector agency, which is controlled by political, regulatory, and constitutional influences. Instead, nonprofits, including faith-based organizations, straddle both areas. They are private organizations, so it is important that they engage in administrative and management actions promoting efficiency, effectiveness and economy; but they also exist to meet public needs. They must be flexible to meet the challenges of the market, while continuing to focus on the needs of the public clientele and citizenry they were chartered to serve. For the purposes of this chapter we will focus on those nonprofits that serve the public interest.

Purpose of Nonprofits. Why do nonprofits—and as we will later see with faith-based organizations—even exist? What is their purpose (or purposes)? What do they do that government agencies and organizations cannot (or will not) do? They are designed to first and foremost serve the public interest. Gita Gulati-Partee, program director, public policy, at the North Carolina Center for Nonprofits, writes "A nonprofit organization is a private corporation that works for the *public's benefit* (our emphasis) but is separate and independent from government."[13] Further, the **National Council of Nonprofit Associations**, which is a network of nearly 40 state and regional associations representing 22,000 nonprofits, strives to see that nonprofits work "together for the public good."[14] And **Lester Salamon** contends that nonprofits are "dedicated to mobilizing *private initiative for the common good* (his emphasis)."[15]

A second major reason for nonprofits' existence is the motivation inherent in the non-profit workers. They are motivated to pursue goals that benefit society, to help children, elderly, and homeless. As Paul Light notes non-profit workers are "motivated primarily by the chance to do something worthwhile, savoring the chance to make decisions on its own, take risks, and try new things."[16] Where government agencies cannot do the job, where they are unable to reach beyond their regulated boundaries; the non-profit community is able to meet the social, welfare, or economic needs of the public. Nonprofits exist for the good of all, not the select interests of a few. How far-reaching are nonprofits? How expansive is this third sector?

Scope and Growth of Nonprofits

Nonprofits are designated by the Internal Revenue Service (IRS) as an organization that does not distribute profits to shareholders. The National Center for Charitable Statistics, a research subsidiary of The Urban Institute, divides non-profit organizations into three groups: 501(c)(3) public charities, 501(c)(3) private foundations, and "other" non-profit organizations. Public charities, which account for more than 60 percent of all registered nonprofit organizations, include education, health care organizations, and other human services organizations. Private foundations are generally established by the philanthropic endeavors of a family or individual. Their primary purpose, therefore, is to fund other nonprofits. Finally, the "other" category includes everything from trade associations and labor unions to social and recreational clubs. The largest number of nonprofits, over 876,000, falls into the first category, as do the nation's approximately 350,000 religious congregations.[17]

The number and revenue generation of nonprofits is staggering. By most accounts, the total number of nonprofits increased from 1.1 million in 1995 to 1.4 million in 2005, a 27.3 percent change.[18] By 2005, public charities reporting to the IRS declared revenues of over $1 trillion (a 56 percent increase adjusted for inflation since 1995) and assets equaling nearly $2 trillion (an 84 percent increase adjusted for inflation since 1995).[19] Private charitable contributions reached over $295 billion in 2006, an increase of nearly 30 percent in current dollars (but only 10 percent in constant dollars) since 2000. Approximately one-third of private giving in 2006 went to congregations and other religious organizations (what we call "para-church" organizations). Finally, foundation giving exceeded $36 billion in 2005, which was a 142 percent increase since 1995, adjusted by inflation.[20]

The number of volunteers rose dramatically over the next seven years—largely because of the 9/11 effect—to approximately 15 million, with nearly 13 billion volunteer hours logged.[21] Even when broken down by paid and volunteer workers, The Johns Hopkins University Center for Civil Society Studies reports that U.S. nonprofits had 9.4 million paid workers and another 4.7 million "full-time equivalent" volunteers, for a total workforce of 14.1 million as of mid-2004.[22] This equates to over eight percent of the wages and salaries paid in the United States.[23] Thus the growth of the non-profit world is staggering.

Impact upon Society. What is the impact of nonprofits upon society today? Clearly, without the number, size, and growth of nonprofits, including faith-based organizations, which we will examine in more detail later in the chapter, the swath of human services delivered would be negatively affected. Nonprofits arise where government agencies are oftentimes ill-suited to meet the service need. Many nonprofits are locally born and bred, so to speak. Because various cultural factors in society are influential to the initiation and development of nonprofits, including family, church, and school,[24] many nonprofits contribute back and are thus part—if not the heart—of the community they exist in. Habitat for Humanity in Erwin, North Carolina, for example, exists to meet the living needs of many low-income citizens in Harnett County, without which services many would not have suitable living accommodations. Donations to Habitat for Humanity in central Harnett County, as in the many thousands of other locations around the country, come from individuals, educational organizations, church congregations, and para-church ministries.

A second major impact is establishing **partnerships** with public sector organizations to meet public needs. At the University of North Carolina-Chapel Hill's School of Government, for example, much work is being done by researchers to examine the partnering relationship mentioned by national scholars, like Lester Salamon.[25] Margaret Henderson, Gordon P. Whitaker and others make up the project team for the **Project to Strengthen**

Nonprofit-Government Relationships. Much of their work is directed toward to discovering how and why municipal and county governments in North Carolina do interact (or not interact) with nonprofits. Too often collaboration on issues is infrequent or even nonexistent. This is not because the two entities fail to realize the various problems are readily apparent. It is often because of obstacles, such as having different perceptions as to what is the problem, lacking understanding concerning each other's work, dealing with the economic effects and different cultural bases of a county, town, or community, or working with an unbalanced political and organizational power arrangement.[26] Each of these obstacles can be overcome through more frequent and accurate communication, which in turns establishes greater trust by the recipients of services in both the public agency and the non-profit organization.[27]

The extent of partnering increases with the various needs identified, whether it is for a 47 year-old recovering alcoholic to teaching and training former welfare mothers the needed information technology type skills in order for them to land jobs and succeed in the evolving information-driven economy. But in order to further examine this relationship, or partnering, we need to establish and discuss theoretical reasons for the existence of non-profit organizations. For this we turn to the work of Lester M. Salamon.

As an observer of non-profit management noted, non-profit organizations are important for larger reasons than simply issues surrounding "management capacity, fundraising strategies, and public relations campaigns." They are important because they arise "as an institutional response to societal disquiet and need."[28] They are institutional actors in an American pluralistic society; a society that relishes diversity, freedom, and order, but a society that also requires commitment and sacrifice on the part of its citizenry in order to secure these values. Non-profit organizations are a historical part of the fabric of American society.[29] We will briefly examine the historical development of nonprofits in the next section; for now we need to establish a theoretical basis for the existence and importance of nonprofits, particularly in the delivery of social services.

Theories of Nonprofits

Lester M. Salamon, Director for Civil Society Studies, The Johns Hopkins University, asks "What is the role of the non-profit sector and its relationship with government?" Scholars have too often described the role of nonprofits in society, and even detailing their relationship with governments in delivering services; however, they do not do a good job of *explaining* (our emphasis) this relationship.[30] Salamon presents plausible theoretical explanations that we would like to discuss.

We have described that the non-profit sector is immense and contains numerous organizations, particularly in the social service sector, like American Red Cross, **Catholic Relief Services** and many others, that work to meet the avalanche of human needs on a daily basis. Partially as a result of its size, and partially as a result of the sheer need to compete with the private sector for clientele base, the non-profit sector is morphed into something it is not, or at least was not intended to be: a highly professional, organized, revenue-driven institution, competing for customers in an extremely volatile market environment. At the same time, though, when non-profit organization partners with a government entity—such as when New York City and the **American Red Cross** teamed with each other as well as worked in concert with thousands of other non-profit and government agencies in the wake of the September 11th tragedy—the result is generally one of need overshadowed by distrust and uncertainty. Why? Because as Salamon notes the prevailing theories of the welfare state and the voluntary sector are diametrically opposed; proffering different and even disparate explanations for explaining social policymaking.

Theory of the Welfare State. Let's describe these prevailing theories and then offer Salamon's solution—which is only one solution, we acknowledge—to offering a better theory to help explain government and non-profit relations. The first theory is that of the welfare state. It focused on the expansion of government, especially the federal government, particularly since the New Deal (the 1930s), but with some impetus for welfare expansion dating to the Progressive Era, moving through and including the Great Society of the 1960s. It called for the use of government organizations, such as the old **Department of Health, Welfare and Education**, which were hierarchical in structure, governed by reams of rules and regulations that took on the social problems of the day. The problems seemed endless: homelessness; poverty; unwed, uneducated African-American mothers with four children living in Chicago's low-income housing needing food stamps to live on; English language programs for Hispanic immigrants living in south central Los Angeles; and literacy needs for poor whites living in an abject poverty in rural Appalachia. Further, the federal government established Medicare and Medicaid programs for the poor and elderly to receive some basic type of health insurance and healthcare needs; created **Aid to Families with Dependent Children** (AFDC) to supposedly meet monthly living expenses, while all the time requiring state and local governments to assume more responsibility of implementation, administration, and financial co-responsibility of these programs. According to the welfare state model the government was to provide "professionalized public service (in) an integrated state administrative apparatus" with a bent toward currying political favor with the clientele it served.[31] This model did not include the voluntary sector as a direct co-partner in meeting and/or alleviating this human needs and suffering.

Theory of Market Failure/Government Failure. According to Salamon the second prevailing theory of the voluntary sector, which included market/government failure and contract failure, did not provide the necessary linkages between government and the voluntary sector. In fact as Salamon notes, "… the existing theories of the voluntary sector (likewise) leave little room to expect effective cooperation between non-profit organizations and the state." He continues that "… it was to get away from such blurring of the boundaries between the public and private sectors that the concept of the private non-profit sector was invented."[32] So, it was the **voluntary sector**, composed of the non-profit organizations—and more recently the faith-based organizations—that targeted specific areas of need that were either overlooked by government agencies or failed to deliver adequate services, such as in the area of criminal justice and inmate rehabilitation.[33]

Box 10.1   Nonprofits' Real Worth

The basic argument is that neither the market nor the government could produce these goods or services in sufficient quantity to be of worth. The market cannot produce these goods that voluntary associations produce because the market demand is low. Government can tax its citizens to produce the good—called the free rider problem—but even then the government has problems. For example, the government will only produce the goods that receive majority support, which leaves certain groups without goods simply because they cannot convince the majority of the citizenry and/or community to adopt their same views as to what is needed. Therefore, so goes the argument, that in order to meet this demand for collective goods, the voluntary sector was established. It "supplies a range of 'collective goods' desired by one segment of a community but not by a major-

ity. From this it follows that the more diverse the community, the more extensive the nonprofit sector it is likely to have."

Source: Salamon, *Partners in Public Service*, 39; Lester M. Salamon, *America's Nonprofit Sector: A Primer*, 2d ed. (Baltimore, MD: Johns Hopkins University Press, 1999), 12–13.

Contract Failure Theory. A third broad theory or model explaining the existence of the
voluntary sector is contract failure. According to Salamon, the primary focus is that for
goods that services directed toward a certain age or other demographic group, such as
the elderly, "the purchaser is not the same as the consumer," (and thus) "... the normal
mechanisms of the market, which involved consumer choice on the basis of adequate information, do not obtain." Thus some type of proxy has to be created to offer the purchaser a certain level of assurance that the services meet minimum standards of quality.
The non-profit organization provides that assurance, given that they are in business not
to make to a profit, but to meet charitable needs.[34] Thus the argument is that they would
more likely be able to be trusted than would the private sector (because of the profit motive) or government sector (for partisan positioning).

Theory of Third-party Government. This fourth theory capitalizes on the shortcom-
ings of the previous theories. The welfare state theory, for example, fails to account for
the diverse and complex intergovernmental relations, usually called **New Federalism**, and
its various derivations, that sprang to life in the early- to mid-1970s. It advocated devolution (or giving away authority) to lower levels of government—states, counties, and municipalities—for the administration and in many cases increased funding of programs,
such as **Medicare** and **Medicaid**. In addition to governmental agencies and organizations,
it abdicated responsibility to a variety of other entities, such as research and development
(universities), health care administration (hospitals), and social service delivery (faith-based
organizations).[35] In addition, the market-based theories (market and contract theories),
failed to take into account the vast number of individuals with needs that were not adequately being met through a demand and supply relationship; one that measures success
through accumulation of profit and meeting a bottom line. Thus as Salamon notes, "The
result is an elaborate system of 'third-party government' (where) government shares a
substantial degree of its discretion over the spending of public funds and the exercise of
public authority with third-party implementers."[36]

In fact Salamon, like others mentioned above, including contemporaries such as Theda
Skocpol and historical figures, such as Alexis de Tocqueville, contend that voluntary associations exist among other reasons for the benefit of pluralistic freedom and pursuit of
the public good or interest. He refers to this as the **stakeholder theory**, where the "central argument is that a need for non-profit organizations is not sufficient to ensure that
such organizations are created."[37] Rather, people form voluntary associations made up of
others who have a passion for seeing the hurting made well, for the homeless to find shelter, or for weary to find rest. They do not have a political stake as much as a social or
even religious stake, in seeing that community and even national needs are met, in spite
of the failed government and market and contract systems. They recognize they will not
make huge profits; they will not establish bureaucratic agencies in order to lay claim to
sacred turf, but what will happen is that someone's need will be met, all because like-
minded individuals formed a 501(c)(3) or (c)(4) organization, raised funds, instituted
some basic rules for governing, and went about to meet the need.

Voluntary Failure. What happens when the non-profit organizations cannot meet the
need? Was the American Red Cross able to meet every human need on that fateful day in
September 2001? The answer, of course, is no. Can faith-based, or even secular social

service organizations, meet all shelter, medical, job skill development, rehabilitation, alcohol and drug recovery, and a myriad of other human needs without government assistance? The answer, of course, is "no." In other words, there are substantive as well as financial needs that government—not the voluntary sector—has and should provide to fill in the gaps left by the voluntary sector. But we know that governments usually do not act without the problem becoming a formal issue, being placed on the institutional agenda, collecting majorities to support government action, laws are then written, rules are made, and the governmental machinery rumbles into action. It is slow, ponderous, and time-consuming. Voluntary responses, on the other hand, are like Edmund Burke's little platoons, where individuals and community interests realize that they are often the first line of defense (or offense for that matter) to meet the need for addressing, for example, neighborhood crime through the formation of watch groups. Salamon acknowledges that "… government involvement is less a substitute for, than a supplement to, private nonprofit action." Further, he concludes that "… this reformulation of the market failure theory does a far better job of making sense of the fundamental reality of extensive government-nonprofit ties."[38]

Box 10.2   Clara Barton and the American Red Cross

While traveling in Europe during the post Civil War years, Clara Barton learned of the Swiss-inspired International Red Cross Movement and upon her return to the United States struggled to found a Red Cross Society in 1881. She was the head of the American Red Cross for nearly a quarter of a century. The Red Cross has been a symbol of aid and comfort during time of war, natural disasters, and other upheavals that require a healing touch. During both of the world wars it grew at a tremendous rate: with chapters jumping from 107 in 1914 to 3,864 in 1918, and in the Second World War it employed over 100,000 nurses and shipped more than 300,000 tons of supplies overseas. During 9/11 it was at or near Ground Zero, providing much needed assistance, and with the onslaught of Hurricane Katrina it was in the middle of New Orleans assisting those most in need. It is the shining stars of many shining stars in the nonprofit movement, aiding and assisting where government cannot.

Source: American Red Cross Museum, "A Brief History of the American Red Cross," American Red Cross, www.redcross.org/museum/history/brief.asp (accessed October 2007).

Summary. The answer is what Salamon defines and advocates as public-private partnerships, where the public and private entities, such as the non-profit organizations, must not exclude each other. Rather they must partner together to address or manage if not solve many of the social ills we have mentioned. Some critics have questions about these various theories,[39] but the point remains that partnering between government and non-profit organizations is not only at the heart of secular voluntary organizations, but is being pushed politically by President Bush in his own faith-based initiatives program, instituted in early 2001. Next, we briefly describe the history of voluntary organizations, including the development of faith-based organizations.

The bulk (some 90 percent) of non-profit organizations came into existence since the close of World War II.[40] With the millions of GIs returning to civilian life the drain on government resources increased, especially educational services, and by the 1960s under President Johnson's **Great Society** program more and more non-profit activity took place, particularly in the area of social and health services. All of these areas were strongly influenced by the presence of non-profit organizations. However, the history of non-profit or voluntary associations does not begin in 1945, at the turn of the twentieth century, or during or after the Civil War; no, the antecedents of voluntary associations, whether for membership or public service, dates to pre-Colonial days.[41]

Public and Private Merger

Unlike today, where the distinction between public and private is somewhat notable—although some scholars claim a **blurring effect** exists between the two institutions[42]—the distinction between private and public institutions was less noticeable more than three centuries ago. This was particularly true with the institutions of church and state. From Jamestown to Plymouth and forward to the colonization of America from the early- to late-eighteenth century, church, civic government, family, education, philanthropy, and other social capital endeavors moved and merged from the same philosophical and institutional foundation: civic justice and human governance. Instead of voluntary activities and commitments on the part of individuals, civil governments required public service of their citizens, whether in the form of road building, militia training, educational service, or care for family members.[43] As Theda Skocpol argues, the relationship of government with civil society organizations, such as veterans' association, was strong, and thus the idea that civil organizations, or voluntary associations, such as what we label today as non-profit organizations, was strong, too, leading to what she contends was the enhancement of democracy and democratic institutions. As she notes "They [the voluntary associations—authors' words], aimed to gather good men or women ... into vast, encompassing associations that mirrored—and had the power to influence—the democratic republic of which they were a part."[44] But, she argues, this is not the case today, where many of the proponents of voluntary associations are also opponents of any connection with government and politics.[45] The de-emphasis of voluntary associations cripples the complete fulfillment of the public interest.

The Influence of Religion

Beginning in the mid-eighteenth century the United States experienced an unprecedented religious revival called the **Great Awakening** from 1740–1760. It was social and political as well as religious in nature, sweeping evangelicals and other Christians into not only the pews but positions of civic and economic influence. This religious transformation of colonial America laid the foundation for civic freedom organizations, such as the **Sons of Liberty**, which assumed leadership toward resisting British rule.[46] Organizational power became the starting point for civic freedom. Whenever colonists banded together to resist what they perceived was British tyranny, through the formation of such groups as Benjamin Franklin's secret Freemasons, the members realized how much potential there was in a company of many like-minded folks. Other founding fathers, such as Thomas Jefferson, feared that just like unchecked civil government, unchecked voluntary associations held the recipe for abuse of power. Government-sponsored charters of corporations was a partial solution, but it was not until Jefferson supported the government's responsibility for higher education—and thus the establishment of his beloved **University of Virginia**—did the state begin to take a more active role in controlling the burgeoning influence of voluntary associations, especially those affiliated with religious meaning, intention and instruction.

According to Peter Hall, one of the more famous struggles taking place between the Jeffersonians and Federalists at the beginning of the nineteenth century was over the battle for incorporation for Dartmouth College. Instead of the corporation document being recognized as a political tool, where the state could exercise its control over the particular institution, such as a college or university, the Supreme Court argued that the power of incorporation was a "private contract protected from government interference."[47] This ruling, however, did not apply to state restriction of charities.

Alexis de Tocqueville is credited with romantically painting a picture of a free and unencumbered nation filled with private voluntary organizations, separate from state dominance. Although this was true in the Northeast, it was less so in the West and South, where public institutions held sway. It was not until the Civil War did additional opportunities for what Hall refers to as "… further advancing the claims of private eleemosynary enterprise(s)" emerge. The damage caused to the social and civic soul of the United States by the Civil War set the tone for the next half century, with private and voluntary associations of power, especially in the areas of social, religious, and legal leading the way.[48] By the late 1880s a philosophical shift in social thinking took place: the advent of rationalization.

The Scientific Management of Giving

The Industrial Revolution dramatically altered how industry did business, how universities established their curriculum, how governments provided services, and how charities doled out assistance. The age of philanthropy arose with the tycoons of business: **Andrew Carnegie** (1835–1919), J.P. Morgan, and Cornelius Vanderbilt. These three and others, but especially Carnegie, raised the level and attitude of professional giving to new heights. Carnegie believed it was the responsibility of those who engineered the economic and business success of the United States that should contribute in a rational and organized fashion their talents and money to assist those less fortunate. So they developed the foundation and the professional staff to administer the foundation; an institutionalized means for giving financially in the present in order to meet the needs of the future. And while foundation money was set aside for charity, foundations for academic and public policy purposes were also established, foundations such as the **Brookings Institution**, the Social Science Research Council, and the National Bureau of Economic Research.[49] It was believed that research and study by these types of organizations would be beneficial toward finding ways to alleviating the social and economic maladies of the poor.

Government, too, bought into the rationalization philosophy. Efficiency, effectiveness, and economy were the lynchpins of a scientifically managed public administration. The ideal bureaucracy of Weber; the scientific management principles of Fayol and Taylor; and the management philosophy of Gulick all had influence upon the centralization of the federal government and development of the welfare state beginning in 1932, but also in the Progressive Reform movement of municipalities and states as early as the turn of the twentieth century. Each of these philosophical ideas regarding the scientific management of government administration and policy translated into pragmatic concerns for city planning, economic development, housing of homeless and treating the mentally ill.

Historical Overview of Non-Profit Action

Of course, history does not lie. The use of government institutions in the early part of the twentieth century, especially in the care for the homeless and mentally ill, were abysmal failures, resulting in poorhouses and insane asylums that came nowhere close to solving the problems; if anything they only perpetuated the misery. But as Lester Salamon notes, "the task of responding to the poverty and distress created by the massive urbanization and industrialization the late nineteenth and early twentieth centuries was left largely to local governments and private, charitable groups."[50]

New Deal Era. President Roosevelt's New Deal combined a centralization approach to planning and decision-making at the federal level, with "a formalization of the voluntaristic and associational relationship between business, charity, and government that (former Secretary of Commerce) Herbert Hoover had built during the 1920s."[51] According to Peter Hall, Hoover's book *American Individualism* (1922) chronicled the great inequalities and injustices caused by modern industry, and believed that equality of opportunity, combined with an ethos of service and cooperation ... could lead to a new social and economic order.[52] Hoover believed in the concept of **community**, a concept that really never became popular until some 30 to 50 years later. He believed that the thrust of charitable giving, assistance, and respect was to come from voluntary associations, with the role of the national government being something akin to an umpire, encouraging the voluntary organizations through less burdensome rules and laws to apply their knowledge, skills, and abilities to the social ills at hand. Roosevelt supposedly seized on the idea of government sponsorship of voluntary associations, but with the depth of the economic depression created by the stock market crash of 1929 looming, he emphasized central government control of social and economic rebuilding through the alphabet agencies and programs spawned by his vision of New Deal policy. Despite Roosevelt's best intentions, state and local governments continued to dominate the field. State and local welfare spending outdistanced federal government spending clear into the 1960s.[53]

The 1960s–1970s. Voluntary associations, which now take on the title of non-profit organizations, received the lion share of their income from government dollars. For example, beginning in the 1940s government contributions to private universities, especially through grants, the GI Bill, and the **National Defense Education Act** became the single largest source of higher education revenue.[54] After coming out of the 1950s' era of federal government investigation into the tax-exempt status of charitable giving, which tried to determine whether or not large philanthropic organizations such as the Ford, Carnegie, and Rockefeller foundations were fronting communistic alliances and relationships by funneling millions of dollars into anti-American organizations, charities, foundations, and other voluntary associations became more cognizant of their reporting procedures and revenue generating methods, particularly in light of increased federal government oversight and regulation.[55] A softening tone came from **John D. Rockefeller III** (1906–1978). His call "for a public-private partnership in the drafting policies affecting 'private initiative in the public interest' acknowledged the complexities and uncertainties of the relationship between government and the private sectors that had developed since the war,"[56] which included understanding the effects of tax policy upon private giving. It was economist Martin C. Feldstein who, after surveying the field of philanthropy, "found strong connections between tax incentives and giving and suggested a compelling and credible rationale for the tax treatment of nonprofits."[57]

Feldstein's work was accentuated by the results of the blue ribbon commission titled Private Philanthropy and Public Needs, chaired by John Filer, then chairman of Aetna

Life and Casualty. The **Filer Commission**, as it was known, surveyed the role of non-profits, considered the regulatory and tax issues affecting them, urged that private sector financial assistance be expanded, called for a permanent commission on nonprofits. In its 1975 report, then, it concluded that society was indeed composed of a third or independent sector; one that dominated American life in all aspects, and one that could not be overlooked any further.[58] What happened next—the election of Ronald Reagan and the imposition of his ideologically defined devolution of authority—drastically altered the playing field of non-profit organizations.

The Reagan Revolution. There is no doubt that the 1980s saw substantial change directed toward non-profit giving—economically, politically, and socially. Most noticeable was the implementation of the **Economic Recovery Tax Act** of 1981, which among other factors provided an across-the-board tax cut of 25 percent over three years, a reduction in the maximum tax rate from 70 to 50 percent, and increased depreciation expense levels.[59] Because 62 percent of non-profit organizations report that over 41 percent of their revenues come from the federal government in the form of grants and aid, and that fees and service charges (28 percent) and private giving (approximately 20 percent) account for the balance; the end result of the tax cuts was a large reduction of the federal government's involvement in social services, human resource training, and other areas.[60]

Philosophically, the intention of the Reagan administration was to reduce the level and size of federal government through restructuring the tax system, engaging in a major devolutionary transformation of authority and responsibility to state and local governments, particularly in the area of health and social services, and commit to greater voluntary and private action. Politically, Reagan and even George Bush, Sr. tried to encourage private and voluntary giving through non-profit organizations through establishment of Reagan's Task Force on Private Initiatives and Bush's **Thousand Points of Light** initiatives.[61] Realistically, however, according to critics like Lester Salamon and others, Reagan's tax cut and devolutionary federalism transformation proved to be a lost opportunity to develop public and private partnerships, which in turn devastated the non-profit industry by having the reverse effect intended. Using extensive survey data and employing sophisticated statistical methodology, Salamon and his associates at The Johns Hopkins University, concluded that:

- Between 1977 and 1982, inflation-adjusted federal spending in social services dropped by 31 percent;
- Federal levels of education spending were down 36 percent by 1989;[62]
- Private charitable giving was reduced by approximately $10 billion over the period of 1981–1984.[63]

According to the critics, then, what was intended for good turned into disaster for the non-profit industry. The 1990s, however, saw a change.

Box 10.3   **Thousand Points of Light**

The phrase was coined by President G.H.W. Bush in his inaugural address, January 20, 1989. The primary message of the address focused on encouraging the American people to engage their community, to serve their neighbors and friends, and to set a tone for serving that had not been seen in generations. Here is part of that address:

"The old solution, the old way, was to think that public money alone could end these problems. But we have learned that is not so. And in any case, our funds are low. We have a deficit to bring down. We have more will than wallet;

but will is what we need ... We will turn to the only resource we have that in times of need always grows — the goodness and the courage of the American people. I am speaking of a new engagement in the lives of others, a new activism, hands-on and involved, that gets the job done. We must bring in the generations, harnessing the unused talent of the elderly and the unfocused energy of the young ... I have spoken of a thousand points of light, of all the community organizations that are spread like stars throughout the Nation, doing good. We will work hand in hand, encouraging, sometimes leading, sometimes being led, rewarding ..."

Source: Avalon Project, "Inaugural Address of George Bush," Yale Law School, www.yale.edu/lawweb/avalon/presiden/inaug/bush.htm (accessed October 2007).

With the election of Bill Clinton in 1992, Congress moved to restore federal spending in human and social service areas, including Medicaid. Despite a failed attempt in 1993 to overhaul the private insurance industry with a nationalistic model, the Clinton administration believed that greater federal government involvement was needed, and the result was between 1989–1994 areas such as health (5 percent), income assistance (13 percent), and housing (12 percent) all increased.[64] The non-profit sector response is mixed, with overall non-profit revenues up nearly 96 percent compared to similar figures in the late 1970s and early 1980s, but toward the latter part of the 1980s and early part of 1990s that growth slowed, with the greatest slowdown in the health-related services sector. Civic (over 200 percent) and social services (nearly 120 percent) organization revenue was up dramatically between 1977 and 1996, with the largest share of revenue dollars coming from increased fee income (1980s) and revived federal government income (early to mid 1990s). During the same time period, private giving was only up about 4 percent.[65]

Finally, as non-profit organizations began moving into other areas once dominated by the for-profit industry (day care and home health care), they encountered unprecedented competition for services and revenues. What was once viewed as the domain of non-profit or voluntary organizations soon began to be viewed as territory ripe for for-profit picking! Giving and receiving suddenly took on a different dimension — moving from a Mom and Pop corner store mentality to a multi-billion dollar per year Walmart Superstore mentality. The non-profit sector would never be the same.

Next, we examine the burgeoning area of faith-based organizations (FBOs), or as the Bush administration referred to them, faith-based initiatives. What effect have FBOs had upon the voluntary sector and service delivery? What challenges are unique to FBOs? What is the relationship or partnering with governments and public administration, especially at the state and local levels?

God and/in Government: Faith-Based Organizations

The world of **faith-based organizations** (FBOs) is much overlooked by public administration scholars. Even though the role of FBOs has come to the forefront nationally, largely as result of President Bush's White House Office of Faith-Based and Community Initiatives, and where FBOs are at work in every state, cooperating with state and local government organizations to mollify a myriad of social and welfare services problems;

still, very little serious public administration scholarly work is done on the subject. Regardless of the reason why this is the case, the following section explores and describes the role, function, challenges, and future of FBOs as part of the non-profit organizational network.

FBOs are similar to more traditional and largely secular-oriented non-profit organizations in that they are privately organized, governed, and led in order to meet many unmet needs in the areas of social services. They are also dissimilar, because their explicit mission and purpose is to address these individual and social needs through a framework of values centered on religion; hence, the term faith. In fact the term faith is favored over religion, because faith is regarded as less institutional-sounding and rules-defining. **Faith** is broader in context and definition than religion, with the world's three major monotheistic religious institutions, including Christianity, Judaism, and Islam, able to incorporate various and diverse parts of their faith foundations into a working framework supporting service delivery, without necessarily and purposely trying to win over adherents. FBOs are able to retain their basic religious and faith foundational commitments, but they are not allowed to purposely and effectively evangelize their faith doctrines with the use of federal funding.[66]

Box 10.4   Faith-Based Organizations Engage Public Service Delivery

Faith-based organizations are entities tied to the religious community, whether Christian or non-Christian, including congregations, national networks, such as Catholic Charities, and "freestanding religious organizations, that because of their spiritual roots and impact are being called upon to play a greater role in implementing, administering, and managing certain public services." It is clear that faith-based organizations are becoming a larger part of the community development movement, one that tries to build upon the existing social and religious structure that is part of the community.

Source: Office of Policy and Development, "Faith-based Organizations in Community Development," U.S. Department of Housing and Urban Development, www.huduser.org/publications/commdevl/faithbased_execsum.html (accessed October 2007).

In fact, some depict the differences between secular and faith-based non-profit organizations in terms of outputs and values. Peter Frumkin of the **Hauser Center for Nonprofit Organizations at Harvard** distinguishes between instrumental and expressive outputs. The former depicts nonprofits that "focus on operational details as part of the process of becoming an ever more efficient purveyor of programs," while the latter "holds that only by centering its activity on the expression of important private values and commitment (such as religious faith—my emphasis) the non-profit sector remain vibrant and innovative."[67] FBOs are expressive and value-driven, working toward an end that favors the inclusion and even integration of religious faith principles in the development and implementation of service delivery. Lewis D. Solomon, professor of law at George Washington University, ordained rabbi, and author of *In God We Trust* (2003), argues that FBOs are the foundation for moral regeneration in the United States. Solomon claims that "The public interest in FBOs is not a product of heightened religiosity; instead it derives from the public's exasperation with secular social services, whether offered by a governmental unit or a nonprofit provider."[68]

FBOs raise the standard for social service delivery to a new and different level. They not only demarcate the areas in society most ravaged by the lack of governmental attention, but they do so by pointing out that issues ranging from low-income single mothers with several children and no appreciable job skills to the homeless, widowed, and orphaned require attention that perhaps nonprofits will not address. The relationship between FBOs and governments is not new, but the ever increasing attention and influence that is in part given to FBOs through government funding is new. The final section of this chapter will address serious questions over not only the influence of FBOs but government funding as well.

**Case Study   Establishing the Battle Lines over Government Funding:
Is the Public Interest Affected?**

The battle lines are drawn over whether or not government funding is appropriate and constitutional. The opposition, led by such critics as Barry Lynn, executive director of **Americans United for Separation of Church and State**, shock organizations such as **Ethical Atheist** (at ethicalatheist.com) and **Theoc-racyWatch**.org, and research organizations, like the **Cato Institute**, contend for a variety of reasons that government funding of FBOs is clearly unconstitutional and is a deliberate breach of the wall of separation of church and state.

On the other hand, the proponents strongly disagree, led by President Bush and luminaries such as Louis P. Sheldon, founder and chairman of the Traditional Values Coalition, John J. DiIulio, Jr., former assistant to the president and first director of the White House Office of Faith-Based and Community Initiatives, Marvin Olasky, professor of journalism at University of Texas at Austin, founder of *World Magazine*, and author of *The Tragedy of American Compassion* (1992), and the previously mentioned Lewis D. Solomon among many others. They argue that public funding of FBOs—as long as it follows strict federal and state guidelines regarding church-state separation—is not only constitutional, but essential to the amelioration of social and economic decay.

Not all of the proponents agree on what is or is not allowable; however, their basic argument is that FBOs are critical to the moral *re*-transformation of American society through the development and implementation of social service delivery via faith-based values and means.

Sources: Barry W. Lynn, "Pro: Is Bush Violating Separation of Church and State?", *The Wichita Eagle*, 7 January 2003, www.kansas.com/mld/eagle/news/editorial/4886899.htm (accessed February 2005); "Faith-Based Funding," Ethical Atheist, www.ethicalatheist.com/docs/faith_based_funding.html (accessed October 2007); Theocracy Watch, "Faith-Based Initiative," Center for Religion, Ethics, and Social Policy at Cornell University, www.theocracy watch.org/faith_base.htm (accessed October 2007); Michael Tanner, "Corrupting Charity: Why Government Should Not Fund Faith-Based Charities," *Cato Institute: Briefing Papers* 62, no. 22 (March 2001), www.cato.org/pubs/briefs/bp62.pdf (accessed October 2007); President George W. Bush, "Executive Order: Establishment of White House Office of Faith-Based and Community Initiatives," *Press Release*, Office of the Press Secretary, 29 January 2001, www.whitehouse.gov/news/releases/2001/01/print/ 20010129-2.html (accessed October 2007); Louis P. Sheldon, "Con: Is Bush Violating Separation of Church and State?" *The Wichita Eagle*, 7 January 2003, www.kansas.com/mld/eagle/news/editorial/4886897.htm (accessed February 2005); and John J. DiIulio, Jr., "Compassion in Truth and Action: How Sacred and Secular Places Serve Civic Purposes, and What Washington Should and Should No Do To Help," Pew Forum, www.pewforum.org/publications/speeches/diiulio0307.htm (accessed October 2007); Marvin Olasky, *The Tragedy of American Compassion* (Wheaton, IL: Crossway, 1992); and Lewis D. Solomon, *In God We Trust? Faith-Based Organizations and the Quest to Solve America's Social Ills* (Lanham, MD: Lexington Books, 2003), 7.

The Basics of FBOs

Numbers. FBOs are numerous; however, there are no reliable data on their total number, primarily because the National Center for Charitable Statistics does not classify FBOs separately from non-sectarian organizations.[69] Based upon recent survey information, John E. Seley and Julian Wolpert report that, conservatively, that some 37 percent of total non-profit organizations may be religious in nature[70] The ratios in the Bible-belt region of the United States (mainly southern states) may be even higher. However, to be careful the actual percentage of faith-based human service providers may only be in the 18–20 percent range, placing the total number of FBOs, excluding churches that provide human services, between 6,500 to 8,000 such organizations.

Definition of Faith-Based. What is a faith-based human service provider? Robert Wuthnow, Director of the **Center for the Study of Religion at Princeton**, defines an FBO as a private non-profit organization affiliated with faith or religion to provide faith-based social services. Faith-based social services "are a complex array of activities … that often differ little from the activities of nonsectarian organizations … by contributing positively to the functioning of civil society."[71] Lewis D. Solomon characterizes FBOs in several ways: 1) they are often small, parochial groups; 2) while at the same time they defy any specific religious affiliation, given that FBOs are Protestant, Catholic, Jewish, Islamic, and even other faiths; 3) they are found in the inner city and suburbs; 4) they are distinctly ethnically diverse; 5) they provide a wide array of human services; and 6) they present their faith dimension in some way, either directly or indirectly.[72] Notice that FBOs are similar to nonsectarian non-profit organizations in that they attempt to provide human services where and when government can or does not do so, and in doing so they further try and reverse the decline in civil society organizations. However, as we have noted they are strikingly dissimilar because they focus the purpose and goal of service delivery around religious faith.

Differences between FBOs and Secular Nonprofits. FBOs take on a couple of different guises: churches and para-church organizations. Churches, or congregations, provide thousands of opportunities to meet the needs of the widows and orphans, the poor and needy, and individuals in other classes too numerous to mention. Approximately 87 percent of all churches—and some estimates place the number of Christian Protestant congregations around 350,000; this does not include Catholic parishes—engage in human service provision, including recreation, youth camps, meal services, homeless shelters, day care, teenage pregnancy programs, and many more.[73] Para-churches, or faith-affiliated organizations, include large non-profit service organizations such as Catholic Charities, Lutheran Social Services, the Salvation Army, and many smaller organizations that provide shelter to the homeless, food pantries, clothing banks, and even work skills development programs.

Whether the programs are congregation or para-church based, the faith element is extremely important to the development and implementation of the service provision. In an important 2002 study, depicting the faith-based service provision of FBOs in fifteen states, political scientists **John C. Green** and **Amy Sherman** found that faith dimensions range from extremely direct, which they labeled 'Mandatory,' to completely indirect, which they labeled as 'Not Relevant.' Interestingly enough when FBOs were asked, "Which of the following best describes the faith dimension of your organization's social service programs," less than 1 percent said mandatory, while 20 percent said they were no relevant.[74] The largest percentage (45 percent) of both non-congregation FBOs, which Green and Sherman labeled 'nonprofits,' listed their faith dimension as passive, meaning the organizations showed their faith through action rather than invitation to listen to or partake in their religious beliefs. In a 2003 study of five different types of welfare-to-work programs in the urban area of Los Angeles County, the researches found that the FBOs, as opposed to government run, for-profit, and nonsectarian non-profit organizations, were most effective in increasing clients' hope and optimism for the future, based in large part upon the FBOs' message of faith.[75] Therefore, faith is an integral component of FBOs; it is the thing that separates them from their nonsectarian non-profit counterparts.

Brief History of Faith in Human Services Delivery

The role of faith and religion is no stranger to supporting human welfare and social services delivery in the United States. Beginning with Jamestown Colony in 1607 and continuing through the nineteenth century, Americans have responded to the needs of the poor, orphaned, homeless, and others who required some type of financial or other assistance. From ministers such as Cotton Mather, **Charles Chauncey** (1705–1787), to Thomas Bacon and **John Wesley** (1703–1791), to charitable aid societies such as **New York's Society for the Relief of Poor Widows with Small Children**, the Massachusetts Charitable Fire Society, and Richmond, Virginia's Charitable Association of Young Men, the 17th and 18th centuries were filled with thousands of examples of human compassion, reaching out to the needs at hand, and completed largely without government assistance.[76]

The nineteenth century was no less active with human intervention to alleviate and/or mollify human suffering. Irishman Thomas Chalmers' church-based savings banks and work exchanges, were designed to aid the poor and down and out without government involvement. In the early 1800s New York City inhabitants saw the establishment of two organizations: Society for the Prevention of Pauperism and the New York Association for Improving the Condition of the Poor. Both were dedicated to dividing the city into sections, with individual society members assigned to oversee the individuals living in the districts, assess their needs, and minister to them what and when was necessary.[77]

Charles Loring Brace and the Orphan Train. The mid- to late-1800s saw the likes of **Charles Loring Brace** (1826–1890), a Yale graduate, who believed in the worth of children, to seize the opportunity to change the dead-end lives of New York City's orphan population. Combining character development, Bible training, and room and board, he formed the New York Children's Aid Society in 1853. Realizing that this was more short-term than long-term success, he formed what became known as the **Orphan Train**, an attempt to link up orphan children with families living in the West, who were in need of part-time workers. Granted, there were many instances of abuse, but at the same time many children escaped a dreary future in the slums of New York City to live and work on a farm or ranch in a state like Kansas or South Dakota. The program existed through the early 1890s, and over time stipulations were made that host families treat the children right and that they receive Bible and Christian training.[78]

Charles Loring Brace

Charles Loring Brace was born in Connecticut in June of 1826. He was raised and educated for the clergy and later ordained as a Methodist minister. In 1852, however, he became the head of the newly formed Children's Aid Society of New York. It became his life's work and ministry. He did not sit in an office, poring over books or only praying—although he did much of that as well. Mr. Loring walked the streets of New York City, getting to know the people he wanted to help, especially the children. As a knowledgeable critic of society he realized and understood that unless the children were given a chance to make something of their lives, then society itself would tumble into the abyss of social and economic decay.

Taking the children off the street was one thing, but it was not the best. He believed that children needed a family. And so to this end he removed homeless children from New York City and sent them on trains to the far reaches of the western prairies and beyond, where many would be taken into solid family settings, given chances to live a life of hard work and hope. The trains that took the children were known as the orphan trains. He died in 1890 and the orphan trains came to an end in the 1920s, but largely because of changing laws against child labor and because of shifting attitudes toward families staying together. For nearly a half a century Charles Loring Brace and the Children's Aid Society brought aid and comfort where government could not or would not.

Source: Dave Jackson and Neta Jackson, "Charles Loring Brace: The Founder of the Orphan Trains," Trailblazer Books, www.trailblazerbooks.com/books/roundup/ Roundup-bio-html (accessed October 2007).

By the early twentieth century governments worked more closely with private charities. What was believed to be too large for private charities to handle on their own, including church congregations and church organizations, was pinpointed by promoters of government welfare, such as Reverend R.M. Newton, as a means to assist and direct government aid to the most needy. Publications such as *The Christian Century* believed that reformation of the mind was as important as restoration of the soul and spirit, and that reason and rationalism were essential to the building of a new society, one that saw the need for not only philosophical and higher theological changes, but pragmatic and administrative ones as well.[79] Eventually the progress of FDR's New Deal policies became the norm, eclipsing what had been for three centuries the primary domain of families, private charities, including churches, church organizations, and faith-based societies: serving and meeting the needs of the poor and indigent. The welfare state had begun.

Connection with Government and Public Administration

FBOs regained strength with passage of the **1996 Personal Responsibility and Work Opportunity Reconciliation Act** (PRWORA), also known as the 1996 Welfare Reform Act, which included Section 104, or the Charitable Choice (CC) amendment. The CC amendment, which was written by then Senator **John Ashcroft** (R-MO), called for nondiscrimination and equal access of federal funding, primarily with regard to state and federal **Temporary Assistance for Needy Families** (TANF) funds toward religious or religiously-affiliated organizations that provided human welfare or social services. It was expanded to include Welfare-to-Work grants program, the Community Services Block Grant, and some substance abuse and mental health services program.[80] Despite their success, one of the major drawbacks of FBOs is their alleged violation of the church-state principle; particularly prominent is the CC's provision that prohibits gov-

ernment from stopping FBOs to hire employees based on their (the FBOs') religious preference.[81] The argument from the FBOs' perspective is that unless they are able to hire
individuals who hold to their (the FBOs') religious and theological/doctrinal viewpoint, then the organization is ultimately defeating itself by not providing a unified
front in the service delivery. The opponents' position, of course, is that the process is
unconstitutional: government funds should not be spent on unlawful acts of hiring
discrimination.

What acts are constitutional and what are not? This is not the proper place to attempt
to answer this question to the fullest degree it deserves. Suffice it to say; however, the role
of religion and government are not and should not be understood to be diametrically
opposed. John Witte Jr., a constitutional legal scholar, writes in defense of the use of
FBOs: "It is one thing to prevent government officials from delegating their core police
powers to religious bodies, quite another thing to prevent them from facilitating the charitable services of voluntary religious and nonreligious associations alike … To press sep-
arationist logic too deeply into 'unessentials' not only 'trivializes' the place of religion in
public and private life … (It) also trivializes the power of the Constitution, converting it
from a coda of cardinal principles of national law into a codex of petty precepts of local
life."[82]

What is an essential versus an unessential act—the display of the Ten Commandments
on a courthouse lawn? Is government funding of a homeless shelter that displays on its
walls biblical scriptures and provides a Gideon New Testament Bible free-of-charge to
the clients unconstitutional? Is one or both a violation of the church state separation? Is
either an endorsement of religion and/or religious dogma, especially Christianity or Judaism? Which, if any, promotes the public interest? These and many other questions
hound the typical faith-based organization (FBOs).

What is legal and what is not? A 2002 comprehensive legal survey of government partnerships with faith-based organizations reported several major findings: 1) direct financial support to FBOs is now permitted by federal constitutional law, but that such support
must be limited to secular activity; 2) indirect financial support of FBOs, such as education vouchers, is also permitted, as long as recipients have choices between FBOs and
secular counterparts; 3) many state constitutions restrict financial support of FBOs; 4) FBOs
are generally exempt from federal prohibition on religious discrimination in employment; 5) FBOs may retain their religious identity while receiving federal funds; and 6) with
very few exceptions, contracts between states and FBOs are silent on the subject of rights
and responsibilities to FBOs.[83]

The Politics and Administration of
Faith-Based Organizations

President George W. Bush promised to see that faith-based organizations could compete on level ground and for equal opportunity to federal funding as with any other non-
profit organizations servicing clientele. So, in January 2001, in an executive order, he
noted that "Faith-based and other community organizations are indispensable in meeting the needs of poor Americans and distressed neighborhoods. Government cannot be
replaced by such organizations, but it can and should welcome them as partners. The
paramount goal is compassionate results …"[84] With this executive order the **White House
Office of Faith-Based and Community Initiatives** was formed. Before Jim Towey assumed

the directorship, President Bush turned to an academic who had experience and knowledge of the role of faith in affecting human problems: John DiIulio.

John J. DiIulio, Jr, professor of political science at University of Pennsylvania, accepted President Bush's offer to be the first Director, "Faith Czar," and special assistant to the president. DiIulio intended to serve six months, but actually stayed nine. DiIulio's charge was threefold: first, to boost charitable giving, both in terms of human and financial; second, to form centers and conduct program audits in several cabinet agencies; and third, to create a higher octane approach to civic society awareness through "greater government solicitude for faith-based and community organizations."[85] DiIulio's real purpose was to give speeches and promote the faith-based centers. He was an academic, not a politician or administrator. The president understood this, but DiIulio's academic background and scholarly work, especially in the area of prison and prisoner-reform methods and programs, and his commitment to evangelical-Catholic observance, provided legitimacy to the argument that faith was invaluable to addressing many of the human service problems plaguing America.

At the federal level, cabinet level agencies that have faith-based centers include: education, justice, labor, health and human services, housing and urban development, and labor. How is faith initiated in programs located in these various departments? The Department of Education, using the No Child Left Behind Act of 2001 as its poster child, is motivated to encourage greater awareness of opportunities that can assist in strengthening the children and youth's education. Opportunities include FBOs offering mentoring services to children to help lower the drop out rate, partnering with local schools in various programs such as Even Start Family Literacy Program, and integrating literacy training for low-income students and parents. The Department of Housing and Urban Development's Office of Community Planning and Development has a long history of working with FBOs in such areas as Housing for the Elderly or supportive services such as HUD's HOPE VI program, which is geared toward revitalizing rundown low-income housing projects. And, of course, the Department of Justice's Office of Justice Program houses many of the FBOs that provide services in the areas of prisoners and families, victims, and drug-related issues.

State and local governments are prime breeding grounds for FBOs to exist. In our modern federal system of government (more like managerial decentralization), state and local governments are the lynchpins between federal programs and federally *funded* programs. State governments administer the funds, qualify federal rules or make rule of their own, and the local governments, including municipalities and counties, administer the programs. It is at the state and local levels where the proverbial rubber meets the road. As most officials and policy advocates understand, collaboration is the key to success for FBOs. As we have seen federal government, and more and more state governments, is and more than likely always will be the primary factor in the funding and delivering of human social services. However, without the input of state and local governments and, as we have noted, an increasingly important role of FBOs; the much needed services would not be distributed. Study after study has consistently shown the overwhelming use, efficacy, and extent of FBOs throughout the fifty states and in thousands of communities across America.[86]

Conclusion: Nonprofits, FBOs, and the Public Interest

With collaboration or partnering come challenges to successful partnerships between government and the non-profit sector, including FBOs. There is a need to strengthen these relationships, primarily because of the nature of a secular society and government that has not, until recently, recognized and embraced the role of private values, including religion and faith, in the mix of effecting change, especially in the social and health care services network. How long must we despise ourselves and ignore these enduring and very real aspects of life? Shouldn't the public interest include the reality of all of life? In response, many have called for reform,[87] some have argued for a resilient non-profit sector,[88] and some have called for a stronger lobbying voice for the non-profit sector.[89] Salamon, for example, argues that the challenges include fiscal, greater competition with the for-profit sector, need for greater effectiveness, increasing use of technology, enhanced need for policy legitimacy, and human resource development. At the same time, however, he believes that increased opportunities for the non-profit sector (and to some extent FBOs) await as well, including changing demographic and social shifts, new pools of money for private philanthropy, greater visibility and salience in the eyes of government officials and the restless public, and, of course, increased government social welfare spending.[90]

The time for greater awareness and for public administrators to think outside of the governmental box regarding how to address the policy issues revolving around social and human services is not for the future—it is for now. As Donald Kettl has so aptly stated, we live in a transformed society, one in which the old engines of the past will no longer drive the vehicles of the present and future. Government alone is not, nor ever was the sole answer. It must work in tandem or partnership as many declare, with the nexus of private non-profit and faith-based organizations in order to meet the challenges surrounding many of society's perplexing problems.

Action Steps

1. Suppose you are the new "Faith Czar" for the President, governor, mayor or agency—detail would you answer the question put to the first U.S. "Faith Czar," John DiIulio, in the opening quote to the chapter, "Do you know if you are going to Heaven?" How would you answer this and faithfully act in the public interest without regard to religious identity? How did John DiIulio answer this? (see *Godly Republic*, 2007)

2. Does the public interest impose a limit on faith-initiatives in the provision of public services? Consider your response in a reading of the U.S. Supreme Court case of *Lemon v. Kurtzman*, 403 U.S. 602 (1971), in which the Court upheld the privatization of public education in state tax dollars to church-owned schools under laws that had a secular purpose, a secular effect, and no excessive entanglement of the state into church business. Consider also the case of *Santa Fe School District v. Doe*, 530 U.S. 290 (2000), in which the Court used the same test to declare unconstitutional a student-led, student-initiated prayer at football games.

3. Trace the meaning of the different terms and concepts under review: nongovernmental, non-profit, and faith-based. What is their lineage? What are the distinctions between each? How have the latter two (non-profit and faith-based) come to such prominence in social service delivery, especially over the last ten years?

4. Have the students visit a local non-profit or faith-based organization. Talk to the workers, volunteers, and clientele. For the workers and volunteers, ask how they like doing what they do. Why do they do it? What benefits do they personally derive from their work or volunteering? For the clientele, inquire as to when they first started

coming, why they still come, what benefits they derive from the non-profit or faith-based organization? Be prepared to present their students in class.

5. Do a literature search of the four types of non-profit organizations: *funding agencies, member-serving, public-benefit,* and *faith-based,* and acquire some basic empirical information, such as total number, types, membership, location throughout the United States, type of services provided, etc. Put into a spreadsheet or Word table format with brief explanatory narrative for each section.

6. Contact several local nonprofits and inquire about their mission, vision and purpose, and how they perform their duties? In a three to five-page essay respond to these questions: How do we explain the work of nonprofits? What do theories suggest? Identify, discuss, and assess the relevance of the various theories of non-profits.

Exam Review Preparation

1. Identify and define the various theories of non-profit organizations.

2. Explain what happens when non-profit organizations cannot meet the various and diverse needs of society.

3. Discuss what it means for public and private organizations (non-profit and/or faith-based organizations) to merge.

4. Explain the role that Andrew Carnegie, J.P. Morgan, and Cornelius Vanderbilt played in the scientific management of giving.

5. Assess the work and results of the Filer Commission (a.k.a. Commission on Private Philanthropy and Public Needs, chaired by John Filer).

6. What impact did the Reagan economic policies have upon the giving ability of non-profit organizations? Explain.

7. What factors contribute to the role of faith-based organizations being overlooked by public administration scholars? How can this oversight be averted? Explain.

8. Discuss the basics of faith-based organizations: number, definition, and differences between FBOs and nonprofits.

Key Concepts

American Red Cross
Americans United for Separation of Church and State
Blurring effect
Brookings Institution
Catholic Relief
Center for the Study of Religion at Princeton
Commission on Private Philanthropy and Public Needs
Faith-based organizations
Filer Commission

Great Awakening
Great Society
Hauser Center for Nonprofit Organizations at Harvard
John D. Rockefeller, III
Marvin Olasky's *Tragedy of American Compassion*
Medicare and Medicaid
National Council of Nonprofit Associations
National Defense Education Act
New Federalism
New York's Society for the Relief of Poor Widows and Small Children
Orphan train
Para-church ministries
Personal Responsibility and Work Opportunity Reconciliation Act
Social civic organizations
The Christian Century
Thousand Points of Light
University of Virginia
Voluntary Sector

Recommended Readings

Berry, Jeffrey M. and David F. Arons. *A Voice for Nonprofits*. Washington, DC: Brookings Institution, 2003.

Colson, Charles. *Justice That Restores*. Washington, DC: Prison Fellowship Ministries, 2001.

DiIulio, John J., Jr. *Godly Republic: A Centrist Blueprint for America's Faith-Based Future*. Berkeley: University of California Press, 2007.

Frumkin, Peter. *On Being Nonprofit: A Conceptual and Policy Primer*. Cambridge, MA: Harvard University Press, 2002.

Light, Paul C. *Making Nonprofits Work: A Report on the Tides of Nonprofit Management Reform*. Washington, DC: Brookings Institution, 2000.

Monsma, Stephen V. and J. Christopher Soper. *What Works: Comparing the Effectiveness of Welfare-to-Work Programs in Los Angeles*. Philadelphia: University of Pennsylvania, Center for Research on Religion and Urban Civil Society, 2003.

Olasky, Marvin. *The Tragedy of American Compassion*. Wheaton, IL: Crossway, 1992.

Putnam, Robert D. *Bowling Alone: The Collapse and Revival of American Community*. New York: Simon and Schuster, 2000.

Rainey, Hal G. *Understanding and Managing Public Organizations*. 3d ed. San Francisco, CA: Jossey-Bass, 2003.

Salamon, Lester M. *The Resilient Factor: The State of Nonprofit America*. Washington, DC: Brookings Institution, 2003.

Sandel, Michael. *Democracy's Discontent: American in Search of a Public Philosophy*. Cambridge, MA: Harvard University Press, 1996.

Skocpol, Theda. *Diminished Democracy: From Membership to Management in American Civic Life*. Norman, OK: University of Oklahoma Press, 2003.

Wuthnow, Robert. *Saving America? Faith-Based Services and the Future of Civil Society.* Princeton, NJ: Princeton University Press, 2004.

Related Web Sites

American Red Cross
    http://www.redcross.org/

Hauser Center for Nonprofits at Harvard University
    http://www.ksghauser.harvard.edu/

John DiIulio, Jr.
    http://www.polisci.upenn.edu/index.php?option=com_content&task=view&id=14
    &Itemid=73

National Council of Nonprofit Associations
    http://www.ncna.org/

The Bookings Institution
    http://www.brookings.edu/

The Christian Century
    http://www.christiancentury.org/

White House Office of Faith-based and Community Initiatives
    http://www.whitehouse.gov/government/fbci/

Part III

Lessons of Administration in the Public Interest

PART THREE brings together our findings on the public interest theme throughout the chapters with a future hope for public administration, or the **lessons** of administration in the public interest. Our analysis of administrative ethics applies public interest findings throughout the book to basic definitions and systems of philosophical ethics, including utilitarianism, deontology, and virtue ethics. We critique four dominant approaches to administrative ethics, including Terry Cooper's rational-comprehensive model, John Rawls' justice as fairness model, John Rohr's constitutional regime values, and the approach of religion and spirituality in the workplace. We apply lessons of the public interest to current concerns with administrative accountability, professionalism, ethics codes, and efforts to control or elicit ethical administrative behavior. Finally, we conclude with a future hope, embedded in trends such as information technology and administrative ethics, to anticipate a truly public aspiration of administration in the public interest.

Chapter 11

Administrative Ethics and the Public Interest

"Government plays a significant role in creating feelings of mutual obligation and respect in society. People must have confidence that it will protect the public interest, since representative democracy rests on officials and the trust they engender. Career civil servants, accordingly, continually face such questions as 'What constitutes proper behavior in exercising the public trust?' An understanding of ethics, the way values are practiced, is therefore pivotal in democracy."

James S. Bowman, "Ethics in Government: A National Survey of Public Administrators"

Chapter Objectives

Upon completion of this chapter the student will be able to:

1. Understand that public officials are to act and behave in a moral and ethical fashion;
2. Distinguish several ethical streams of thought and how they might apply to administrative situations;
3. Recognize that public officials are accountable for their actions;
4. Administrative accountability is both internally and externally established;
5. Appreciate the role that ethics and public administration play in the fulfillment of the public interest.

After enduring the deaths of his friend John and of the country's former chief executive, Saul, David became the nation's new leader. Even though David was friendly in personality, he was politically shrewd, being able to adapt and change to meet the avalanche of political, economic, and, especially, military problems that besieged the nation. He had reached the pinnacle of public leadership success, yet in just one night—a night he should have been working hard on military plans to defeat the enemy abroad—he sacrificed everything for one sexual tryst with the wife of one of his top field commanders. As one can imagine the situation only grew worse and more complicated, given the propensity by most individuals to cover up their immoral and unethical actions, including pregnancy, murder, cover-up, and finally public exposure.

Imagine this exposé in today's news—or at any political time and with any set of characters! Change the homicides and pregnancy to other shocking stories and it might well be Watergate or Clintongate. It was neither. It occurred over 5,000 years ago in ancient Israel. It was the story of the sexual dalliances of King David and Bathsheba, the wife of one of David's field commanders, Uriah the Hittite. It was **Bathshebagate**!

Box 11.1   Bathshebagate

"And it came to pass, after the year was expired, at the time when kings go forth *to battle*, that David sent Joab, and his servants with him, and all Israel; and they destroyed the children of Ammon, and besieged Rabbah. But David tarried still at Jerusalem. And it came to pass in an evening tide that David arose from off his bed, and walked upon the roof of the king's house: and from the roof he saw a woman washing herself; and the woman was very beautiful to look upon. And David sent and enquired after the woman ... And David sent messengers, and took her; and she came in unto him, and he lay with her ... And the woman conceived" (2 Samuel 11:1–5).

Regardless of the time, situation and circumstances, public officials, including both elected and administrative, are vulnerable to the avarice and temptation that come with the trappings of political and administrative power. David's lack of moral judgment resulted in personal sin and public disgrace, with the latter leading to a series of personal, family and professional tragedies. Yet, good did come of the situation. After David's death, his son Solomon's wisdom was due in large part to the acknowledgment and understanding of the failings of his political predecessor and father.[1]

No one is immune; the temptation to do wrong is always there, whether it is one's personal, family, or professional life. When an immoral or unethical act is committed by an elected public official the trust that is given by the people and/or the Constitution is damaged. The same is true with the public administrator. Although she or he is not elected by the people, they are nonetheless accountable for their actions, whether personal or professional, and particularly as those actions impinge upon their ability to carry out their public duties. Living in the glass bowl of public scrutiny is not easy, but it is a responsibility that goes with the job. Personal character, moral judgment, and ethical behavior are required of political and civil servants for carrying out their duties in the public interest.[2]

Introduction

What are the lessons of administration in the public interest? This last section is a final round-up of the many lessons on the public interest found throughout the book. We believe the developments of public administration recounted throughout the chapters point to the ascendance of the public interest as an applied ethics concept that points toward administrative ethics. After decades of pushing these issues aside and trying to wear the white lab coats of a "real science," we see the center stage is once again focused on the public interest through the public discussion of public administration and morality, ethics, character, regime values, and so forth.

This chapter broadly examines the role of ethics and administration in the public interest. First, the chapter discusses the function and role of moral character and judgment required of the public administrator. We point out that public opinion polls clearly show the importance of good moral judgment and that the public wants those who carry out the duties of public office, whether elected or bureaucratic, to be moral and act ethical. However, there will always be the need for checks and balances of personal and professional character and actions. Second, the chapter explores philosophical frameworks for the study of administrative ethics including virtue ethics, justice as fairness, and constitutional regime values—as well as the foundations of metaphysics in administrative ethics, such as religion and spirituality. Each contributes a different perspective toward a systematic understanding of the importance of ethics and moral behavior and administration in the public interest. Third, we describe the role of ethics and administrative accountability, focusing on several paradigms of accountability. Finally, we conclude by making observations regarding the state of ethics in public administration, what the future holds, and the impact upon the public interest.

Public decisions are not made outside of a value critical framework, whether moral, ethical, legal or some combination thereof. Whether you are a city manager trying to decide how to discipline a male employee who was caught by a female employee watching pornographic images on his desktop PC while on the job or a state lottery board on the hiring and then subsequent dismissal of a member with conflict of interest, these decisions require not only information, but judgment based upon something other than rational analysis techniques: it requires individual character and professional discernment about how to choose between competing values and what value is best to choose for the benefit of the greater public interest.

Politically Correct

Unfortunately, in today's political and bureaucratic environment we often face trying to achieve conflicting goals, which places great pressure on public officials' ability to make sound and ethical decisions. On the one hand, we are to be outcome based (performance based management and performance budgeting), whether it is for federal agencies (Government Performance and Results Act of 1993) or public school students (No Child Left Behind Act of 2002). The goal is to achieve some objectively-defined result that is supposedly fair for all individuals involved. On the flip side we are also bombarded by the demand for justice, usually in some broad policy area, such as racial integration or economic redistribution of a public good, such as in welfare or food stamps, or in assuring equality among the races and ethnicities, such as through affirmative action programs. The focus then is on the process, ensuring that some level of fairness or justice is achieved for all involved.

Our concern with both of these approaches is twofold: 1) the decision maker, whether political or administrative, often makes a decision that simply tries to fit the middle ground, where the end result is supposedly beneficial for all parties involved, but in reality is generally detrimental to the greater public interest; and 2) if and when our first concern is fulfilled, then moral character and ethical judgment can be compromised for the sake of political and bureaucratic correctness. In many cases the decision maker forfeits making the right decision in lieu of making the best decision—if by right decision it means there is only *one* decision that is right. We do believe there is such a thing as a right decision as well as a best decision—the decision based on the display of moral character, influence of moral judgment, and resulting in fulfillment of the public interest.

Moral Character

What is largely lacking in society today, and, perhaps, in many of today's political and public administration officials, is the advocacy and display of moral character.[3] **James Q. Wilson** argues that what is missing in public debate and decision making is not the application of macro or microeconomic analysis to taxation, welfare, education, and criminal justice policies, or the discussion and application of performance based measures of outcome. What is missing is the lack of character. Wilson contends that there are two elements of character: **empathy**, which is the willingness to take into account the thoughts and feelings of others, and **self-control**, which is the willingness to take into account the future consequences of current decisions.[4] Both aspects are necessary elements in the personality and character of public administrators, especially when confronting ethical situations.

James Q. Wilson

James Q. Wilson is the Ronald Reagan Professor of Public Policy at Pepperdine University. Previously he taught political science at Harvard from 1961–1987, where he was the Shattuck Professor of Government. He also served as the James Collins Professor of Management and Public Policy at UCLA from 1985–1997. He is the author or co-author of fourteen major works, including *The Marriage Problem: How Our Culture Has Weakened Families* (2002), *American Government*, and *Bureaucracy*. He has served on many national commissions, including the White House Task Force on Crime in 1966, National Advisory Commission on Drug Abuse prevention in 1972–1973, Attorney General's Task Force on Violent Crime in 1981, and the Police Foundation board of directors from 1971–1993. He received his education at the University of Redlands (B.A., 1952) and the University of Chicago (Ph.D. 1959). The American Political Science Association, of which he was president, presented him with a Lifetime Achievement Award in 2001.

Source: Pepperdine University School of Public Policy, "James Q. Wilson, Ph.D.," http:// publicpolicy.pepperdine.edu/academics/faculty/default.htm?faculty=james_wilson (accessed September 2007).

Os Guiness, cultural philosopher, contends that character is distinct, even separate, from concepts such as personality and image. It implies deeper meaning. Character is the essential stuff a person is made of, "the inner reality and quality in which thoughts, speech, decision, behavior, and relations are rooted."[5] What happens when a decision maker, such as a public administrator, faces an ethical dilemma of sorts? How will or should the administrator respond? Are we just to hope that the administrator has good character and he will, based upon his good character, make the right decision? What if he or she does not? Are there any guidelines to follow in order to make sound ethically correct and morally-based decisions? We argue that there are guidelines to follow, especially when making any decision that involves a moral problem. A moral problem is when a decision maker is faced with competing values that on the surface appear to both respond to the problem.

Consider the case of the city manager confronted by a female employee complaining about internet porn use by fellow employees. She is aghast and offended that her fellow city employee would even think about, much less act upon and display pornographic images on a PC at work. The city manager confronts the male employee. He confesses that he did in fact look at some pornographic images, but that it has not happened in a long time, and he promises the city manager that it will not happen again. The city manager has various options for dealing with behavior unbecoming a city employee, including suspension without pay, especially for first time offenders, thirty-day notice, or in egregious situations immediate dismissal, with or without severance pay. What should the city manager do?

The city manager knows that there is more than one thing that can be done. Is there one right thing to do? Or can we say there are two more courses of actions that are equally correct? What if the city manager chose to fire the employee on the spot? This decision opportunity may be within the city manager's legal range of options, and also their moral range. It may be better to preserve a working atmosphere that was conducive to the betterment of all employees (pursuit of the public interest) than to acknowledge the right of one employee to do something that would disrupt the public interest. The city manager made a value-based decision—an ethical decision—one that had personal and professional consequences, not just an outcomes-based decision; one that was under girded by moral judgment.

Case Study   An Ethics Moment: A Late Night Surprise

Dennis, the city manager of a financially strapped municipality, is working ... late at night. The offices are empty and quiet and as he is leaving, he notices a sliver of light coming from the door of the new budget director, Susan. He decides to stop in and praise her for her excellent report in which she discovered errors that will save the city millions of dollars, projecting for the first time in many years a budget surplus. As he approaches her office he can see through the few inches the door is open that she is in a passionate embrace with Gary, the assistant city manager. Employment policy strictly forbids dating between employees, threatening dismissal to those who do.

Dennis' code of ethics requires him to enforce this policy, yet at the same time he does not want to lose either or both of his valuable employees. It would be difficult if not impossible to bring in someone else with their experience and credentials for the amount of money the city is able to pay.

Discussion Questions: What should Dennis do? Should he report Susan and Steve, in accordance with policy? Should he overlook the situation believing the city will be best served in the long run? Should he speak to each of them and threaten to tell if they don't end the relationship?

Source: Based on a real case submitted by Professor Carole L. Jurkiewicz, University of North Carolina at Charlotte. From Donald Menzel, ed., "Ethics Moment" column, *PA Times*, April 1998.

Moral Judgment

Some contend we live in a world bereft of the ability to comprehend morality, that our politics (and consequently public administration) and culture lack morality (measured by universal principles of right and wrong), and that this lack of morality impedes our ability to make sound decisions. Public administrators are expected to make decisions between competing alternatives that carry moral weight. However, if they only make decisions based largely, if not solely, upon the best process—which might mean the fairest or most equitable means available to all parties affected — rather than making a decision upon the best principles coupled with sound moral character and judgment, doing what they believe is best for the public interest, and not for the interests of a few, then decisions will be mechanical and rational rather than fluid and intuitive. Fluidity and intuition are not the end result anymore than a technical and rational process is or should be the end result. Making decisions that benefit the public interest is the goal. Doing so requires more than just applying the rudiments of rational or judicious decision making; it requires doing what is right, and avoiding what is wrong. Consider the case of "Politics and Gambling in North Carolina."

Case Study   "Politics and Gambling in North Carolina"

North Carolina's former Speaker of the House, Jim Black (D-Mecklenburg), appointed Kevin Geddings as a member of the state's newly established lottery commission. Geddings, a former chief of staff to South Carolina Governor Jim Hodges and the owner of radio stations and a public relations firm in Charlotte, was the only commissioner with some lottery experience. While in South Carolina he led the pro-lottery campaign charge that predated a statewide referendum in 2000 that eventually provided for the state's lottery. However, it was not long before ethical considerations, primarily conflict of interest concerns, began to creep into the picture.

In October of 2005, Geddings disclosed he was a close acquaintance with Alan Middleton, vice president for government relations at Scientific Games Corporation, a leading company that provides instant-win tickets and lottery computer software. Scientific Games is one of the leading bidders to be North Carolina's gambling vendor. Even after this public revelation Geddings said he would distant himself from any potential problems, primarily by recusing himself as a voting commissioner during the process of hiring North Carolina's lottery contractor. However, as statewide media reports brought these facts to light Geddings eventually resigned.

Just days later it was revealed that Geddings resigned from the lottery commission just a few hours before Scientific Games was to have paid him nearly $25,000, including $9,000 the day after he was named to the board. This bit of information was not revealed by Geddings or Scientific Games. As a result of this and other information North Carolina Attorney General Roy Cooper ordered an investigation into apparent violations of state lobbying laws.[6]

Discussion Questions: Should Black have been more careful before appointing Geddings? Should Geddings have even accepted the appointment knowing his background with Scientific Games? What should be the end result?

Source: Jim Morrill and Mark Johnson, "Three Face Inquiry over N.C. Lottery," *Charlotte Observer,* 3 November 2005, http://www.charlotte.com/mld/charlotte/news (accessed November 2005).

Betrayal of trust by a public servant denotes a lack of judgment and character. We expect and believe (perhaps hope?) that our appointed public servants will behave and make decisions with the utmost conscience toward doing what is right, not slipping into doing what is wrong.

Impact of Ethics

Administrative ethics has taken the center stage in today's bureaucratic and political climate. We live in an era dominated by the increasing demands, influences, and criticisms of political and governmental decision making upon the lives of people. Doing what is right is demanded, not simply hoped for, and administrators and officials are often criticized for perceived failures to do what is right. For example, according to a 2000 survey of the federal executive branch, there were significant relationships between program awareness (familiarity with the ethics program and the Rules of Ethical Conduct), program usefulness (in making employees more aware of issues, and in guiding decisions and conduct), and ethics outcomes.[7] State and municipal ethics studies and surveys show similar findings, for example, with the advent of **ethics codes**, there has been a greater ethical awareness by citizens and greater degree of compliance by public officials.[8] And overall public administration scholars find that ethics and the study and teaching of ethics is on the rise.[9] What does all this attention to ethics mean for administration in the public interest?

Ethics is the systematic and theoretical study of morals touching upon all aspects of human values, not just public affairs. The term ethics is derived from the Greek, *ethikos*, meaning virtue or moral custom. Ethics has become a systematic philosophical understanding of the nature of morality, with methodical and holistic theory about what is right and wrong behavior or being.[10] The academic discipline of ethics has highly nuanced theories from over 2400 years, at least 300 canonical names in ethical philosophy, and parry and thrust arguments that are not so simple to master and cannot be easily summarized in a paragraph or even an entire book. It would not be honest of us to pretend we could survey and adequately discuss all the myriad issues of ethics in one chapter, even if we limited ourselves to administrative ethics. However, the public interest has been a useful concept of **applied ethics** for millenniums in a more focused dialog about the morality of public life. The public interest concept does not require that we unpack all of ethics for our discussion.

Administrative Ethics

So, how are public administrators influenced by ethics? We do not review all of the many volumes of literature seeking an answer to these questions, but cull the lessons of administrative ethics for administration in the public interest. **Administrative ethics** is a branch of applied ethics with a focus on the study of morality and normative values in administrative life, organizations, and culture, including but not limited to public administration.[11] We begin this with an overview of the foundational ethical philosophies of virtue, deontology, and utilitarianism, recounting the criticisms and defenses of each from preceding chapters. Next, we examine four highly influential contemporary approaches to administrative ethics within public administration, including Terry Cooper's **rational-comprehensive model**, John Rawls' **justice as fairness** social contract approach, John Rohr's **constitutional regime values** approach, and the **religion and spirituality** approach within public administration. The frameworks were chosen because they represent a broad cross-section of the administrative ethics literature, differ in philosophical perspectives on administrative ethics, and each give a distinct lesson on administration in the public interest. Finally, we apply the diverse administrative ethics literature to the current issue of administrative accountability.

Philosophical Ethics

Administrative ethics is founded upon basic ethical philosophies, including: virtue, deontology, and utilitarianism. We briefly define and describe each of these, with contrast to the "anti-ethics" of ethical egoism/relativism. (See Table 11.1.)

Table 11.1   Summary of Ethical Philosophies, Philosophers, Ideas, and Critiques

Virtue (teleology of character)	Deontology (moral objectivism)	Ethical Egoism/ Relativism (subjectivism, situationalism, or looking out for number 1)	Utilitarianism (teleology of pleasure/pain, happiness, or preferences)
Plato, Aristotle, Alasdair MacIntyre	Immanuel Kant, John Rawls, John Rohr	Friedrich Nietzsche, Joseph Fletcher, Kai Nielsen	Jeremy Bentham, John Stuart Mill, Richard Posner
E.g., Plato & Aristotle's virtue ethics of character; Christian virtues of love, hope, and faith.	*E.g., Rawls' social contract; Rohr's 'constitutional regime' values*	*E.g., Nietzsche's will-to-power ethics and the Übermench; popular subjectivist ethics*	*E.g., Bentham and Mill's utilitarian calculation of pleasure-pain, happiness, or benefit-cost analysis*
Right and wrong are defined by moral character; being, long-term traits, and personhood	Right and wrong are defined by proscribed behaviors; duties and rightful acts	Right and wrong defined as merely personal-cultural preferences or will-to-power	Right and wrong defined by pain-pleasure calculus of each act (Act Utilitarianism) or a predictive rule-of-thumb (Rule Utilitarianism)
Guided by character traits or examples of good persons and beings, e.g., leaders of religions, states, or other institutions	Guided by universal moral rules or principles, e.g., behaviors proscribed by family, legal, or religious sources	Guided by one's own egoism or preferences & cultural mores, e.g., what you prefer based on what you desire or were taught to desire	Guided by the greatest good for greatest number, e.g., cost-benefit analysis of pain and pleasure
Difficult to apply or measure in ordinary life and being	Not generally concerned with consequences of behaviors	Dismisses universal moral truth; cannot be taught	Neglects the value of intent and aspiration by actors
Extensively urged by our greatest ethical leaders, from Christ to Abraham to Muhammed	Firmly rooted in specific proscribed behavior; does not give moral ground due to ambiguity	Scapegoat for explaining the negative side of other views	Recognition of others and precise measures of good and harm/costs

Source: Taken from John R. Walton, James M. Stearns, and Charles T. Crespy, "Integrating Ethics into the Public Administration Curriculum: A Three-Step Process," Journal of Policy Analysis and Management 16, no. 3 (1997): 470–483; Stanley J. Grenz, The Moral Quest: Foundations of Christian Ethics (Downers Grove, IL: InterVarsity, 1997), 177; and Bob Sherman, "Basic Ethics and Morals," http://home.flash.net/~bob001/BasicEthics.html.

Virtue has been featured throughout this book as an attending ethical theory to the practices approach to the public interest. Although it is difficult to precisely know and measure in day-to-day public administration, we commonly judge who is a good person by their **virtue** or good moral character, defined as a "fixed disposition, habit, or trait to do what is morally commendable."[12] TV, movies, novels, the internet, and the stories of family and friends—all ordinarily present narratives of people and assess their character, motives, and judgments. Even children's books and media ordinarily depict public servants, and authors like Dr. Seuss often depict public servants as less-than-benevolent and less-than-competent.[13] Rather than some list of detailed behaviors, virtue ethics gives answers to ethical questions with practical simplicity: "be patient" or "be brave" or "be a man" or "be a woman" or "be a good citizen"[14] This practical simplicity may also be exercised by emulating a person or hero.[15]

Washington, Hamilton, Madison, Jefferson, and other founders understood a vision of public interest practices within virtue ethics. Plato and Aristotle posited that we have a moral function and well-being defined by our unique reason capacity and the mere pursuit of pleasure was a life fit for cattle. Our function was arête, a Greek word meaning moral excellence, as well as magnificence, dignity, cheerfulness, and reason gave us the practical wisdom to make it so. Aristotle's *Nichomachean Ethics* detailed a practical wisdom of learning to avoid two extremes in moral decisions: excess (too much) and defect (too little). For example, the virtue of courage is the mean between foolhardiness (excess) and fear (defect). Yet the virtue ethics of the founders were criticized for the lack of obligations and specific legal duties owed by these "philosopher kings" to the people they served. The Blacksburg scholars brought the remedy of dovetailing the biographical study of the virtue ethics of the founders and others with the specific details of constitutional laws and cases. Contemporary virtue philosophers, such as **Alasdair MacIntyre** and others have had great success in their argument for a return to virtue ethics in public affairs.[16]

Deontology has been featured throughout this book as an attending ethical theory for the principles approach to the public interest. While reflecting a line of ethical thinking since the time of Plato about the intrinsic good of following one's duties, the term "deontology" may have first been used as a restatement of these ethical theories in 1930.[17] The term deontology is derived from two Greek words: *deon*, binding duty; and *ology*, the study of—to focus on the ethics of following duties, promises, and other obligations to define what is good and bad. Deontologists deny that the balance of good over evil consequences (*teleology*) is the deciding factor in determining what is right or wrong. The goal of deontology consists of universal, valid means of behavior or activities that are applied fairly and without bias— even if dutifully following the rules should result in mischief, injustice, or tragic ending for a particular person or group. In deontology, one is judged by doing the right act, not by good (or bad) consequences of their acts. Deontology is critical of other virtue and utilitarian ethics theories because we don't ordinarily have the capacity to predict or control the consequences of our actions, but we can perform our duty with the right intent. Further, the principles approach doesn't simply look at the roles of benefactor-beneficiary, but includes the diverse roles and corresponding duties, such as fiduciary-entrustor, principle-agent, supervisor-supervisee, bureaucrat-citizen, promisor-promisee, lawyer-client, physician-patient, parent-child, and many other roles. Deontology gives consideration to the past as an indicator of the good; past precedents may create obligations in the present.[18]

Act deontology holds that particular judgments, rather than rules, are basic in morality. Individual intuitions, faith, conscience, love, and existential choice have each been proposed as standards for act-deontology. With each, a person faced with a decision will take a moment to somehow grasp what should be done, without relying on rules. Yet, the act-deontology approach may be criticized for inherent weaknesses: how would we ever prefer one act over another if there were no proscribed behaviors with rules or duties? Act deontology gives attention to the moral worth of intentions in our actions by focusing on intuition, faith, conscience, love and choice, but we need something more than these ambiguous notions to know what to do in specific situations.

Rule deontology focuses on the conformity of behavior with one or more principles or rules to determine if they are right or wrong. Rules are the measure of moral worth. Some rule-deontologists hold that there is only one principle or rule, such as Divine command theory in which conformity to the commands of God are the criterion of right and wrong.[19] Immanuel Kant based rule-deontology on one principle he called **The Categorical Imperative**: "act only on that maxim which you can at the same time will to be a universal law." Other rule-deontologists hold that there are two or more basic rules in morality, such as W.D. Ross's six **Prima Facie Duties**, or basic moral duties that are apparent "on their face": non-malfeasance, self-improvement, beneficence, justice, gratitude, and duties that rest on previous acts of our own (e.g., duties of reparation and fidelity).[20]

The many rules, duties, or intuitions of deontology have been criticized as non-systematic, too pluralistic, and failing to provide some unified goal for morality. By contrast, virtue ethics focus on arête or excellence, and utilitarian ethics focus on benefits/costs or some other unified measure for calculation. As a result, deontological principles may seem like a very long list of concerns and issues, each with differing criteria for right and wrong. That is also the strength of deontology principles in its very inclusive listing of many issues, roles, and relations of people.

Utilitarianism has been featured throughout this book as an attending ethical theory to the policies approach to the public interest. It was promoted by Jeremy Bentham, John Stuart Mill, and federal judge Richard Posner, and is associated with the identification of the single act (Act-Utilitarianism) or rule-of-thumb (Rule-Utilitarianism) that will produce the greatest good for the greatest number. It mandates an additional level of recognition, respect, and accounting to the preferences of each and every person affected by a moral decision. In utilitarianism, good and bad are determined by calculation of pleasure-and-pain, happiness, individual preferences, benefits-costs, and other measures of human needs of intrinsic value to produce a maximal value. The thing of intrinsic value itself is not the thing of moral value, rather "Actions are right in proportion as they tend to promote happiness, wrong as they tend to produce the reverse of happiness."[21] Utilitarianism is not based on the discovery of pre-existing or universal rules or duties, but is skeptical of the value of such rules or duties without specific empirical reference to and calculation of the pleasure, happiness, or individual preferences of all who are involved. Utilitarianism emphasizes the ends or consequences of moral decisions (teleology) and the actual production of things of intrinsic value, rather than following the rules for their own sake. Utilitarianism may be hedonistic in focusing on pleasure or happiness or pluralistic with the inclusion of values beyond hedonism, but the trend is to take a third approach of aggregating individual preferences into benefits/costs, especially in the applied ethics world of administrative ethics.[22]

Utilitarianism has been criticized for promoting majoritarianism; the tyranny of the majority imposed upon minorities, such as 250 years of American racist slavery. Defining right and wrong by the calculation of individual preferences has been used to mask the evil done by bureaucrats—hidden to the public and to themselves. In its defense, utilitarianism today supplements its theory with concepts of justice to prevent abuses of minorities, such as found in the Fourteenth Amendment and Bill of Rights. Yet, the criticism of the abuses of minorities sticks to utilitarianism and many remain uneasy about the lack of built-in safeguards. Is anything ever intrinsically wrong?[23]

As we have recounted in previous chapters, public administrators sometimes neglect administrative ethics to their detriment out of a personal cynicism and trashing of ethics in general. This attends to a theory of **ethical egoism**, which argues that the only valid moral standard is the obligation to promote your own well-being above all others. It is the popular morality of always looking out for number one. Ethical egoism as a normative theory advocates selfishness in all moral activity, and cynically asserts that all other moral talk is merely the will to power. Ethical egoism asserts that no matter what people may argue, they are really acting for the sake of their personal well-being only. For example, 1960s radicals claimed that even when new attempts were made to represent minorities and women in public affairs, the decisions and actions continued to reflect old status quo notions, duping the American public by depicting their decisions as the operation of a market place exchange of private interests.[24] Behind the facade of pseudo-science was the operation of a will to power and rhetorical ploys to advance the status quo or private interests of political elites.[25] Critics argued this was no different than Nazi Germany of WWII, who made the will-to-power philosophy and Friedrich Nietzsche the official philosopher and depicted laws as the operation of an exchange of private interests—to advocate and justify the holocaust of the Jews. Even more despairing may be the related attitude of **moral relativism**, the perspective that all normative values and moral beliefs are relative to an individual or culture; the belief that all basic value judgments of individuals or cultures are so different and conflicting that no one's values may apply to the conduct of others. In its extreme and most cynical form, moral relativism casts aside all value statements, including ethics, the public interest, even ethical egoism, as complete non-sense—and closes the mind to the possibility of dialog and meaningful exchange of ideas.[26]

However, even if moral standards are not 100 percent absolute across all cultures all the time does not mean there are no moral standards at all; moral standards do not have to be absolute in human reality in order to exist.[27] Further, close study reveals empirical patterns of moral development in all individuals, genders, and across cultures throughout the world—even among public administrators.[28] Rushworth Kidder, the founder of the Institute for Global Ethics, believes there is evidence of universal ethics that all people everywhere, including public administrators, should strive to achieve including love, truthfulness, fairness, freedom, unity, tolerance, responsibility, respect for life, as well as courage, wisdom, hospitality, obedience, peace, and stability.[29]

We disagree with this dying breed of cynics who discard the public interest as literal nonsense because its existence cannot be proven with any of the five senses—just as they throw out other valued concepts like God, love, justice, and hope. These cynics throw out the baby with the bathwater; in their hard-nosed pursuit of scientific truth, they betray the very scientific principles of empiricism they purport to defend. We believe the reality of public administration recounted in foregoing chapters, suggests that when you get radically empirical and follow people around you find the public interest within ordinary experiences, commonly shared meanings, and practical outcomes. Like so many of the important meanings in our lives, we find the public interest is heart-felt and understood in context.

Terry Cooper's Rational-Comprehensive Model

According to **Terry Cooper**, the Marie B. Crutcher Professor in Citizenship and Democratic Values at the University of Southern California, the best means for making ethical decisions is to frame them in a rational and comprehensive means—meaning the public administrator will examine as much of the problem as possible, formulate various alternatives, and then make his decision. Of course, Cooper recognizes that public administrators are human and thus they will respond to ethical dilemmas in various ways:

emotionally, creatively, and, perhaps, philosophically. First, the administrator simply reacts to a given problem, usually without taking time to critically evaluate the situation, assess the alternative courses of actions, acknowledge the consequences involved with each action, and arrive at an acceptable level of confidence to make the decision. For example, our city manager would not think about the situation in any great detail; he would just react to the charge by firing the offending employee on the spot.[30]

Second, after exploring the vast and rich history of moral values the city manager, for example, would use his own creative imagination for establishing a host of alternative sanctions against the offending party, including, perhaps, firing him, reprimanding him in some way, such as 30 days leave without pay, physically moving him (reassigning him) to another location where he would not come in contact with the offended party (the woman who saw him looking at the pornographic photos), or any number of possibilities. The public administrator should use his creative talents in combination with some basic and guiding moral principles to make a decision. Third, Cooper argues the public administrator might examine broad philosophical and perhaps even religious issues before making his decision on how to act.

Terry Cooper

Terry Cooper is the Maria B. Crutcher Professor in Citizenship and Democratic Values, and Professor in the Department of Policy, Planning and Development at the University of Southern California. His research focuses on citizen participation and administrative and governmental ethics. He is one of the co-principal investigators in the USC Neighborhood Participation Project that is researching the role of neighborhood organizations in the governance process of the City of Los Angeles. He was been a member of the National Academy of Public Administration during the early to mid-1990s where he assisted in the development of a decision-making process to encourage intergenerational equity in the management of hazardous wastes by the U.S. Department of Energy. He serves on the Los Angeles Police Department's Professional Advisory Committee and is President of the International Institute for Public Ethics. His primary work is a textbook on administrative ethics titled *The Responsible Administrator: An Approach to Ethics for the Administrative Role* (2001, 4th edition).

Source: See USC College of Letters, Arts and Sciences, Faculty, "Terry Cooper," www.usc.edu/schools/college/faculty/faculty1003181.html (accessed September 2007).

However the public administrator may respond to the ethical dilemma, Cooper believes these levels must be fluid, that is they must naturally work together to form a basis for ethical decision making, and they should be done within a rationalist-comprehensive framework. In other words, the public administrator assesses a variety of variables, situations, and dilemmas and makes a conscious yet critical decision. So, in the case of our city manager he might very well draw upon his own religious (or non-religious or philosophical) training, consider what is best not only for the victim (the offended party), but also for the offending party (a personal rights mentality), and carefully and consciously (and perhaps intuitively) examine as much of the information received as possible before making his decision. The fluidity, so to speak, comes from the city manager working through and between each of these levels of ethical decision making, while doing it in as much of a rational process as possible. The following case describes the rational process of ethical decision making.

**Case Study   "An Ethics Moment: When the County Knows Best—
Or Does It?"**

West Nile virus, an illness transmitted from wildlife to humans by mosquitoes, has made its second appearance in two years in Phoenix, Arizona, resulting in a number of confirmed fatal cases among birds and a growing number of positive cases in humans, reported by hospitals and doctors to the Maricopa county health department's vector control program. In response, the county has tracked the locations of most intense activity, has ramped up its public education program to ask people to be vigilant in draining any stagnant water sources where mosquitoes breed, and advised the public to wear repellent, particularly in the evenings, at night, and early morning when the insects are most active.

After plotting the outbreaks, the county identified a large 'hot zone' of cases and determined that this area—mostly residential neighborhoods—should be fogged with insecticide to reduce the mosquito population. The insecticide of choice is a synthetic pyrethroid called Anvil. According to the EPA "pyrethroids can be used … without posing unreasonable risks to human health when applied according to the label. Pyrethroids are considered to pose slight risks of acute toxicity to humans, but at high doses, pyrethroids can affect the nervous system."

Maricopa County proceeded with a program to fog an area of about eight square miles in the early morning hours of a Friday; a time when mosquitoes are active, winds are calm, and most people are in their homes asleep. Maricopa county also made the decision to not notify residents in the affected area in advance that their neighborhood would be fogged.

Many of those homes, however, use evaporative cooling, a process that draws outdoor air into the home. The pesticide fog was also drawn into the homes, and the residents exposed while they slept. Some symptoms of pyrethroid exposure include rash and breathing difficulties. Persons with lung ailments and small children are susceptible at a lower dosage than the 'average' person. Persistent exposure or exposure to large concentrations can cause other health problems. Pyrethroids are a carcinogen.

While it is unknown how many residents of Phoenix were affected by the insecticide, none knew they may have been exposed. Therefore none knew whether, if they did show symptoms, they should seek medical treatment. I am one who came down with a rash after sleeping with an evaporative cooler running on a night when the county fogged my neighborhood. Evaporative coolers bring in outside air, cooling the air with water. In this case, the water was off, so it was ambient outdoor air being drawn in. I woke up to the smell of it, but had no idea as to the source. I learned a few days later that one of my neighbors saw the trucks on our street at 3 a.m. (This was the day I came down with the rash.)

Discussion Questions: The ethics question—aside from any legal exposure notification or informed consent requirements—is: "why did the county health department proceed with this application of pesticides without notifying the residents in the target area that they could be exposed, what the pesticide was, and what actions they should take if they wished to limit their exposure?" Is it possible that county officials believed they knew what was in the best interest of the citizens? Or was this just an act of insensitivity or incompetence?

Source: Submitted by Thomas Babcock. From Donald Menzel, ed., "Ethics Moment" column, *PA Times*, December 2004.

John Rawls' Justice as Fairness Model

Political philosopher **John Rawls** (1921–2002), of Harvard University, sought to develop universal rules for ethical decision-making based on equality or justice as fairness. Rawls believes that we can achieve justice by imaging ourselves in a position of radical equality with all other persons behind a **veil of ignorance**. You can imagine such a veil of ignorance if all souls were gathered together before they were each born—a reality in which no one would know their position, status, ability, race, ethnicity, gender, sexual orientation, or other demographics. In such a veil of ignorance, each individual could make unbiased, fair, and rational decisions for the betterment of all, because each would not yet know their specific situation in life.[31] According to Rawls, in such a veil of ignorance we would logically form a social contract for the betterment of all, based on two universal principles of justice: 1) the **liberty principle**: "each person is to have an equal right to the most extensive basic liberty compatible with a similar liberty for others," and 2) the **opportunity principle**: "social and economic inequalities are to be arranged so that they are both a) reasonably expected to be to everyone's advantage, and b) attached to positions and offices open to all." If they come into conflict, the second yields to the first, and thus, respect of human dignity trumps all other considerations.[32] A major criticism of Rawls' theory is that it is better applied to broad social issues, like affirmative action policy, and less so to narrow public administrative positions, such as deciding a budget or personnel concern[33]

Affirmative Action Policy. For example, what about the administrative ethics of hiring a less qualified applicants from a disadvantaged group in society? If Rawls' justice as fairness theory is accurate, then it might be applied in four ways when hiring less qualified applicants and promoting affirmative action policy: (1) not hiring them would further deprive them; (2) hiring them would bring about their realization of basic liberty without harming others of their basic liberty; (3) hiring them ensures them they are not shut out from any open position; and (4) hiring them assures them that privileges that are innate to various offices and positions will continue to work toward the advantage of all in society not only a select few.[34] Consider, if you will, of each of these four possibilities:

First, by not hiring the person, is this person deprived further of freedom or some other value? If I hire an individual who is not qualified to do the job, then I am disadvantaging all individuals: those who would be his co-workers, the management, and the public? This may deprive the individual hired of a certain measure of self-respect and self-esteem. What if the applicant is instead directed to a job-skill development center, with the promise of a possible future interview and hiring based on the development of specific skills in the job description? If there is a later re-interview, I have not deprived the applicant. Instead, the applicant is now is a better position with improved skills and knowledge for better employment opportunities.

Second, hiring someone less skilled over someone more skilled does in fact harm the more highly skilled worker. It denies them of their liberty or freedom to pursue a job with the government or even the private sector, giving them the false impression that they have as equal a chance at landing a position as a less-skilled minority candidate does. And it directly and negatively affects the more highly skilled worker by taking away their opportunity for landing a position that they, unlike the affirmative action hire, are qualified and skilled to assume.

Third, consider the damage of a false sense of self-respect. Hiring a person for a job they are not qualified for only encourages them to believe that they can advance in society where the demand for education, skill, and technical knowledge increases. In today's fast-moving and highly technologically oriented workplace, it is imperative that all workers, affirmative action hires and others are as well-prepared to enter the job market as possible.

And fourth, consider the damage to self-esteem. The offer of a job may inform the applicant that they did not achieve a position based upon merit, but upon some artificial standard set by the government (i.e., affirmative action) that dictates to employers that politics is more important than personal dignity and worth, or of merit. This privilege is not extended toward all in society, but only toward those select few who are deemed the recipients of special government consideration. How does Rawls' theory play out in the following case study?

Case Study   "An Ethics Moment: Should Ethics Exams Be Used to Screen Job Applicants?"

Some local governments, particularly police departments are requiring job applicants to take an ethics examination as part of their application process. The city council of Monroeville, Pennsylvania, for example, approved in 1997 that an ethics evaluation be conducted of all persons seeking to join the Monroeville Policy Department. The Monroeville Police Department also uses ethics testing in the process for promotion to corporal, sergeant, and lieutenant.

According to City Manager Mary Ann Nau, "A couple of local incidents that reflected unethical thinking impressed me with the idea we needed to know that our officers were ethically thinking people from the start. It is too late to wait until an officer comes up for promotion to wonder about their standards for dealing with the situations they encounter."

Monroeville's test is called the Defining Issues Test and is administered by the Center for the Study of Ethical Development and the University of Minnesota. The test consists of six stories, each describing a moral dilemma. Respondents must decide what the major actor in each story should do.

Discussion Questions: So, should ethics exam be used to screen job applicants? If so, how does this agree or disagree with Rawls' theory?

Source: Based on a story published in the February 13, 1997, issue of the *Pittsburgh Post Gazette* and submitted by Gary Zajac of the University of Pittsburg. (From Donald Menzel, ed., "Ethics Moment" column, *PA Times*, May 1998.)

John Rohr's Constitutional Regime Values

The third dominant administrative ethics model is John Rohr's Constitution-based **regime values**.[35] Rohr critiques two common approaches to administrative ethics as wanting: formal codes of ethics, which he calls the low road, and ethical philosophy, which he terms the high road. The low road to ethical and moral behavior is marked by adherence to **formal rules** of order, usually in the guise of codes of conduct, professional statements of ethics (e.g. ASPA's Code of Ethics), legal regulations and the like.[36] They are written with the intention of keeping people from doing wrong behavior, rather than encouraging good behavior. An example is state regulatory board and commissions that enforce ethical ordinances and laws. In our state lottery example, it is the

North Carolina Board of Ethics that is overseeing the legal paperwork regarding the attorney general's investigation into Kevin Geddings failure to disclose $24,500 in payments from Scientific Games.

On the flip side is the high road of ethics: **philosophical ethics**. Of course, John Rohr pursues and is concerned with ethical philosophy in his writings on public administration ethics. However, he is concerned that this profoundly complex literature from humanistic psychology, political theory, and philosophy may be too broad and deep to discuss in any single course—or book—on administrative ethics. He appears to claim the same about religious-spiritual values. He does not dismiss the positive impact that each of these disciplines can have upon administrative ethics' decision making, but practically students of administrative ethics must have a tighter and leaner framework for discussing ethical and moral actions; one that is manageable for the public administration classroom. For Rohr that framework is the Constitution and what he calls regime values.

Regime values are "values of that political entity that was brought into being by the ratification of the Constitution that created the present American republic." Administrative ethics should derive from regime values for several reasons.[37] First, regime values discuss a process that explains professional education for administrators or bureaucrats. Professional education is narrowly tailored to meet the needs of the lawyer, doctor, accountant, or public administrator. Professionals do not require great treatises of religion and spirituality, political philosophy and theory, or humanistic psychology to establish the boundaries of their professional conduct and ethical norms. Public administrators are to be imbued with a desire to serve the public interest; it is not necessary to explain or defend the need for a democratic republic or that the responsibility of the public administrator is to serve the greater good of the people, and not cater to special interests.

Second, regime values are the starting point for ethical considerations. Public administrators took a solemn oath to uphold the values espoused by the Constitution, and therefore the beginning point for determining honesty, truthfulness, and integrity in a public administrator, for instance, is found in the administrator's desire to uphold the same values found in the Constitution.[38] Of course, we know that statesmanship and wealth does not necessarily make a virtuous person; many of the founders were indeed selfish and self-interested. However, as some argue "... remaining within the founders' framework requires that any effort to elevate administrative character above the minimal level needed to sustain the republic be balanced fully by a concern with 'effectual precautions for keeping them administrators virtuous while they continue to hold their public trust,' and the most effectual precaution, of course, is to assume that people are self-interested and moved by a variety of motives, only some of which are likely to be realized through serving the public good."[39]

Third, there must be an educational platform to teach these values.[40] Platforms range from the undergraduate and graduate classrooms to leadership and management training centers (**Federal Executive Institute**, located in Charlottesville, Virginia). Further, regime values should be stressed, rather than more narrowly defined policy issues. For example, Rohr contends that discussing and learning about a regime value such as equality as opposed to bantering back and forth the legal and technical merits or barriers of a policy that supposedly promotes equality, such as affirmative action, is far better in the long run. As a regime value, equality will be around much longer, and be applied in many more policy areas, than will the narrow policy issue of affirmative action.

Fourth, regime values must be discovered through public law, and specifically through careful study of the Constitution and resulting court cases. For example, the Supreme Court case of *Cooper v. Aaron* (1958) dealt with the forced integration of Little Rock High School in the mid-1950s. Justice Felix Frankfurter denotes the importance of America's moral heritage as a way to overcome difficulties, such as experienced in Little Rock. **Moral heritage** is an example of what Rohr argues is a regime value; one that is vague, but not without meaning. It is a term, a value that Rohr believes what Frankfurter meant: "a standard to which it (the United States) can rally in a period of unrest."[41] In other words, it is a value that promotes and pursues the public interest. Consider the North Carolina lottery case.

North Carolina Lottery Case. Rohr's regime values are not so much applied as they are embodied. Far more precise than Rawls' justice theory of ethics, more defined than the religion and spirituality framework, and less complex in understanding and application than virtue ethics, for example, Rohr's regime values framework provides a basic political and legal basis and even administrative justification for how public administrators should embrace ethical decisions. Coupled with a 'what' (regime values) and a 'how' (administrative discretion) for making ethical decisions, Rohr contends that bureaucratic education and understanding of regime values is at the heart of administrative ethical decision making. For example, in the North Carolina lottery case, court cases and legal statutes forbidding impropriety and conflict of interest should have been sufficient cause for warning Geddings to have never accepted the appointment by former Speaker Black.

Religion and Spirituality

Though widely practiced, the dominant approach to administrative ethics from religion and spirituality is the most misunderstood and oftentimes most vilified deontological approach by public administration scholars and ethicists. This is especially true in treatment of the **Abrahamic-tradition** of Judeo-Christian-Islamic believers.[42] Yet, many have shown there is an "empirical connection between individual spirituality and participation in public service."[43] Why the phobia toward religion and spirituality in public administration? It seems that something that has been so successful for so many millennia in the area of ethics and morality would be of help in our public administrative problems, especially as it affects the public interest. But the primary purpose, definitions, descriptions, and moral values of such a religious tradition, being both absolutist and monotheistic, seems to prompt most administrative scholars and ethicists to distance themselves from overt displays of religion and its application to public issues, organizations, and institutions. Yet, public administration scholar Jeff Greene notes that, "Public administrators can look back over several thousand years of philosophical and religious discussion about ethics. The literature contains a rich source of ethical principles."[44] The dean of public administration theorists, Dwight Waldo, argued that religion had much to offer and could be made relevant to formal organizations through "extrapolation and application."[45] Even former ASPA President **Don Menzel** believes that spiritual values should receive greater treatment in graduate level ethics courses.[46] So, how can we apply religion and religious principles or ideas to public administration and administrative ethics? Consider the case study below:

Case Study   "An Ethics Moment: Should Spirituality Be Taught?"

Public administration professionals, both practitioners and educators, have long taken pride in their ability to be objective, analytical, fair, and competent in carrying out their duties. Values, especially those associated with religious or spiritual belief systems, are widely regarded as taboo in the context of the work and mission of one's public agency or employer. Moreover, the historical church-state separation upon which America was founded reinforces this outlook.

After all, public administrators serve a collective clientele, not individuals with specific needs of body and soul. Or do they? Are social agencies and social workers, for example, committed to serving those whose needs are objectively defined and measured (e.g., food, shelter, abuse)? Or, should they serve the needy in a more holistic, even spiritualistic way?

Some observers contend that professional social workers can and should treat only the afflictions of the body, not the mind or soul. Others are not so pure and even suggest that social workers in practice have no choice but to treat the afflictions of mind and body. This is particularly so, says Professor Edward R. Canada of the University of Kansas, when there is "a crisis or occasion of grief and loss."

The challenge of treating mind and body in a professional social work has reached the stage where there are now 50 accredited university social-work programs that offer courses on spirituality and social work. This educational need is driven by what many believe is the reality of practicing spirituality in one's work. For example, a 1999 survey of members of the National Association of Social Workers found that 71 percent of the respondents said they "help clients consider the spiritual meaning and purpose" of their current life situation and 63 percent said they help clients develop spiritual or religious rituals as part of their treatment. Surveys also show that many social workers pray for their clients, often without their permission.

Discussion Questions: Is there a place for teaching spirituality in public administration programs that prepare men and women for public service careers? Or, does this cross over the line of acceptable professional education?

Source: D. W. Miller, "Programs in Social Work Embrace the Teaching of Spirituality," *The Chronicle of Higher Education*, 18 May 2001. From Donald Menzel, ed., "Ethics Moment" column, *PA Times*, September 2001.

Of course, as Jeff Greene writes, there is no doubt that ethical philosophies were greatly influenced by theologians, including St. Augustine, **Thomas Aquinas** (1225–1274) and others, who argued that a right relationship with God was necessary to make behavior ethical —and for entrance into the heavenly kingdom.[47] The question before us is not how Christian ethics monitors individual Christians' lives, or even establishes a Christian ethic through a renewed interest in ethics and a "community ethic of being,"[48] but how religion in general, whether Judaism, Christianity, or Islam—these three being the three largest monotheistic world religions—or spirituality in particular, has an impact upon social and organizational ethical dimensions as well as individual decisional patterns. Obviously, each monotheistic religion perceives itself in a battle for God against forces of evil and oppression around the world, both from a communal (organizational to institutional) to an individual perspective, spirituality. The three monotheistic religions offer what each believes to be necessary and fundamental to meet the spiritual needs of individuals and organizations, without falling prey to various modern or post-modern challenges to their core values.[49]

Separating Religious and Secular Ethics

Can we simply separate religious ethics from secular ethics? In the broadest meaning of the terms, yes we can, and should. But what are we to do about the conflicting views of such closely-tied Abrahamic faiths as Christianity, Islam, and Judaism? A

Christian, for example, firmly believes that knowledge and teachings of Jesus Christ as the incarnate Son of God is paramount for advocating and promoting an authoritative position on matters ethical and moral.[50] However, Muslims do not elevate Jesus Christ to the status of God. Rather, they follow Muhammad the prophet as one who was divinely inspired to write the *Qur'an*, the moral and spiritual guidebook of Islamic teaching. To further complicate matters, many Jews accept Jesus Christ as a good rabbi (teacher) and prophet, but they reject the claim by organized Christianity that Jesus is (or was) the Son of God. To require or even suggest that Christian ethics—ethical and moral guidelines that are framed according to explicitly defined New Testament doctrine—should be the primary moral guidebook for all individuals and organizations is simply not appropriate in a diverse and pluralistic society. However, many ethical philosophers find in Christian ethics a set of moral concepts that are widely accept by those in Abrahamic traditions and society in general—broad enough in scope that Christian New Testament scripture can be used to define and frame an ethics for all.[51]

Some mainstream public administration scholars even recognize that the teachings of Jesus, but not his claim to divinity, are appropriate for normative discussions in public administration, including administrative ethics. Lance deHaven-Smith argues "Public administration is not just a subfield of administration in general, or of the study of bureaucratic organizations. Public administration includes the study of ethics, politics, political theory, and public policy. It is more than mere managerial effectiveness; it is also a search, in theory and practice, for good government in the broadest sense of the term."[52] In other words, we would argue, it is a search for the pursuit of the public interest.

Other public administration writers specifically contend that "The Judeo-Christian tradition establishes the moral barometer of right and wrong behavior, and to exclude its functional as well as ethical utility is to do a philosophical injustice to the study of administrative ethics."[53] **Willa Bruce** argues that religion and spirituality, which she defines as "an individual search for meaning, purpose and values which may or may not include God," are one of the core elements of defining and shaping moral action. Morality and administrative action, whether examined in an individual administrator's decision making or through an agency's position on a policy issue, are influenced by the role of religion and spirituality.[54] Still, others argue that biblical proverbs should be used as guiding principles of public decision-making.[55] Suffice it to say, religion and religious and spiritual values have some type of influence upon ethical issues and ethical decision making. The case study below provides some insight.

Case Study   "An Ethics Moment: Religious Expression in the Workplace"

You are the Chief of the State Division of Vehicular Licensing with 1,250 employees located at six district offices. The Director of District 2 approaches you about a thorny problem: what to do about providing employees who are Muslims a suitable time of the day to worship. The problem began on October 30th when the state shifted from Central Daylight Savings Time to Central Standard Time. As it turns out, the fall back of the clock pulled the Muslim sunset prayer back into the work hours.

A group of Muslim co-workers requested that the District office allow them to conduct their sunset prayer at 5 p.m. The District office closes at 6 p.m. The group said that they would be willing to work from 6:00 p.m. to 7:00 p.m. to make up for the time lost.

The Director is unsure of what other Districts have done and does not know if state law does or does not require public agencies to accommodate employees' religious beliefs. It is, of course, clear to all that public agencies cannot promote religious beliefs and practices but this is not quite the same thing.

As the Division Chief, you inform the Director that other District offices have not faced this issue before. Moreover, state law is reasonably clear: employers (public and private) must accommodate employees' religious beliefs as long as the requests are reasonable and do not create a hardship for the agency.

Discussion Questions: Is the request by the workers reasonable? Would shifting the sunset prayer hour to 5 p.m. create a hardship for the District Office of Vehicular Licensing? (Remember that the primary work of the District Office is to issue licenses to the public on a first come, first serve basis.) Would agreeing to the request be viewed as favoritism toward one group of employees? If so, would this create morale problems? What recommendation should I make to the District Director?

Source: Donald Menzel, ed., "Ethics Moment" column, *PA Times*, February 2006.

North Carolina Lottery Case. In any one of two ethical policy illustrations above religion and spirituality are not specifically applied; meaning that a particular passage from the Old or New Testament, the Quoran, or the Torah would not necessarily be sufficient by itself to determine whether or not, for example, Kevin Geddings should have stepped down from the North Carolina Lottery Commission. What is appropriate, we believe, is that these rich and diverse normative moral depositories of ethical illumination provide just that: a vast wealth of moral information and tradition that the public officials and administrators intuitively draw upon when making decisions (this would be akin to Cooper's philosophical view). But that is also their primary weakness.

There is no guiding light or prescribed direction, per se, that indicates where to tread in any given administrative or policy situation — at least that is applicable for all individuals, believers and non-believers alike. Proverbs and principles aside it would still be necessary for public administrators to use their discretion and intuition for how to apply various religious and spiritual values that positively and genuinely impact the greater public interest. Regardless, we do contend, though, that believers of Jesus, Mohammad, and Jehovah should not be forced to leave their belief and core value system at the door of their responsibilities. But if religion and spirituality does not clearly specify the rules in administrative ethics questions, then perhaps these details may be provided by the more deontological approach or John Rawls' justice as fairness theory or Rohr's constitutional regime values.

Summary. Each of these four ethical frameworks is conducive at one level or dimension or another to apply to the public administrator's job of making decisions within the context of ethical principles and moral values. Certainly, Cooper's rationalist framework is necessary to provide balance and objectivity. Rawls' two universal rules of justice as fairness give us the *sine qua non* of procedural objectivity; that is, applying the same method to the same or similar situations and being able to exact judicial fairness, regardless of the issue or parties involved, is the key to ethicalness. Rohr's regime values places administrative ethical decision making within the parameters of democratic-constitutional system and the values supporting such a system: justice, freedom, equality, equity, etc. The religion and spiritual values context supports the understanding that non-rational and subjective belief systems contribute to the richness, fullness, and diversity of ethical attitudes. Public administrators are and must be accountable for the consequences of their ethical-based decisions.

Finally, we turn to a brief overview of administrative accountability before we close out this chapter on administrative ethics. Accountability is a central component in the fight against a seemingly unruly and unyielding bureaucratic apparatus. The cries of the public against the supposed evils of big government are compounded when the media reports one bureaucratic crisis after another, seemingly showing there is no organizational accountability or individual responsibility. We want to show that there are checks and balances in our system of governing and administration. For the most part they do thwart attempts at bureaucratic irresponsibility while largely promoting the public interest.

Administrative Accountability

One of the most discussed topics related to administrative ethics is **accountability** and its sibling **responsibility**; the first referring to hierarchical linkages and checks in the organization, and the latter focusing primarily upon individual action.[56] Both terms are related. Accountability focuses on an individual's stewardship of some financial or other trust, while responsibility refers to the general law or right, encompassing both accountability and answerability. Ethics in administration was not really considered necessary by the founders, given that they established a government of checks and balances, separation of powers, and federalism, all designed to prevent illegal and unethical actions. *Federalist 51*, for example, calls for the division of powers, and a deliberate measure for checking and balance the multitude of executive, legislative, and judicial powers. With the addition of external groups and organizations, such as interest groups, political parties, and popular elections the need for ethics in public administration seemed essentially absurd. And, of course, internal checks and balances were established through the Weberian invention of bureaucracy—the hierarchical measure of organizational and professional accountability.[57] Hierarchy was meant to dissuade any type of unethical conduct, given the numerous checks available to it. So, why is there so much modern attention to administrative accountability?

Defining Accountability. Accountability is defined as "those methods and relationships that determine which expectations will be reflected in the work of public administration."[58] This is vague to say the least. Others argue that "the premise of bureaucratic accountability holds that public administrators in a democracy are safely constrained by a welter of restraints (just what those restraints are depends on the writer) from making decisions and policies that are anti-democratic, unfair, or unethical."[59] So, if this is case (i.e., there are a welter of restraints in place), then what is the purpose of these four ethical frameworks we just defined, described, discussed, and critiqued? Other public administration theorists claim that accountability is a "primary concept in public sector performance measurement and performance management reforms."[60] For example, the Administration on Aging, which is located in the Department of Health and Human Services, is approximately 67 percent accountable through a Program Assessment Rating Tool (PART), a methodological tool for empirically measuring agency accountability found in the 1993 Government Performance and Results Act. Bureaucratic accountability—keeping public administrators duty bound—is a critical task of government. How is accountability accomplished? And how does it affect the public interest? For one response, let's go back a few decades to revisit the Friedrich-Finer debate.

Understanding Accountability. In the 1930s and 1940s, a seemingly innocuous debate ensued between two scholars: **Carl Friedrich** (1901–1984) and **Herman Finer**. In the vernacular of Notre Dame football Friedrich is "Mr. Inside" and Finer is "Mr. Outside." Friedrich argued that bureaucratic accountability is best achieved through enhanced means of administrative professionalism (internal means), where bureaucrats with high levels of professional expertise and technical knowledge govern each other. Finer on the other hand was more dubious of such a self-directing system of professional codes and mores and argued that bureaucratic accountability was only truly attained through political means (outside means), i.e. bureaucrats are answerable to their political overseers.[61] In other words, bureaucrats should not be allowed to exercise greater amounts of administrative discretion than is profitable or acceptable in a pluralistic democracy. Although some contend that Friedrich won the debate because more political scientists, for example, find that reality in the modern bureaucratic state better matches Friedrich's position, there are others who believe that administrative discretion should be limited. Instead of mindlessly debating who was right and who was wrong, which of these two positions best promotes the pursuit of public interest when it comes to ethical decision making?

Carl J. Friedrich

Carl Joachim Friedrich was a political scientist, political advisor, and educator. For many years he was Eaton Professor of the Science of Government at Harvard (1955–1971); however, his association with Harvard began in 1926 when he became lecturer in the Government Department. He was educated at the Universities of Marburg, Frankfurt and Vienna and eventually received his Ph.D. in history and economics from the University of Heidelberg in 1925. His main areas of interest before WWII were the history of modern political thought, problems of leadership and bureaucracy in government, and public administration, where his early works included *Responsible Bureaucracy* (1932) and *Constitutional Government and Politics* (1937). He also engaged in advisory work where, for instance, he assisted in the reconstruction of post WWII Germany by serving as Constitutional and Governmental Affairs Advisor to the Military Governor of German, Lucius D. Clay (1947–1948). He also served as constitutional advisor to Puerto Rico, the Virgin Islands, and the European Ad Hoc Assembly, which established a draft constitution for the European Political Community in the early 1950s.

Source: See Harvard University Library, "Biographical Note," LINK"http://oasis.lib. harvard.edu/oasis/deliver/1hua27003"http://oasis.lib.harvard.edu/oasis/deliver/1hua27003 (accessed September 2007).

Using the Friedrich-Finer debate as a starting point, we can describe four basic typologies of bureaucratic control mechanisms, including: a) high degree of internal control (Bureaucratic or Weberian); b) high degree of external control (Legal or Statutory); c) low degree of internal control (Professional or Administrative); and d) low degree of external control (Political or Pluralistic).[62] Each typology represents some combination of bureaucratic relationships and controls. The point of the four typologies is not to emphasize one type over the other, but to demonstrate that depending upon the issue, circumstances, and actors involved, public administrators may emphasize one type over the other. We don't disagree, but in reality whatever decision is rendered (Geddings and the North Carolina lottery or the city manager's dilemma) the ultimate outcome should address the needs of the public interest, not simply one narrowly defined set of interests.

Accountability Typologies. First, **bureaucratic controls** elicit a high degree of internal control and structure. They are based upon the hierarchical aspects of any organization, including rules, jurisdictional authority, communication, etc. This type of system is successful because of the working relationship between superior and subordinate, which is highlighted through oversight and supervision. For example, the executive director of a county social service agency oversees various associate executive directors, program managers, and social workers. In order to disburse various social services, such as family and child services, each individual employee works in close cooperation with each other and the clients, under the close supervision of the managers and directors. Following what are termed standard operating procedures (SOPs), or the enforcement of strict rules governing the disbursement of social services, each individual actor in the system is accountable to someone or something, thus mitigating the chances for unethical and/or illegal conduct.

Second, **legal** or **statutory** controls are established outside the bureaucratic framework, usually by the legislative body, but it can also be by executive order or judicial degree, and provide a high degree of external control. When a law is passed, for example, such as the Welfare Reform Act of 1996 and it requires substantial reform within the current bureaucratic system, such as how long and to what degree individual welfare recipients can receive welfare assistance, then this is a form of external legal control. It is not imposed by the organization upon itself; it is imposed by an outside agency or institution, in this case Congress. A further example is when former President Bush signed an executive order in 2001 that established the White House Office of Community and Faith-Based Initiatives. This Executive Office organization was established by written decree of the president, and provided guidance and information for churches and para-church organizations that desired to apply for federal grants under the Charitable Choice provision of the Welfare Reform Act of 1996. The Department of Health and Human Services (DHHS) and specific agencies within DHHS were required to acknowledge the presence and legal right of faith-based organizations to apply for and receive federal money in the area of charitable choice. Federal agencies, such as the General Accountability Office (GAO)—formerly named the General Accounting Office— are available to conduct investigations, collect data and information, and present the data in various written forms, including reports, white papers, and financial audits.

The third type of accountability system is **administrative** and **professionally-focused**. It originates from or within the agency or organization, but its degree of control is much less authoritarian. In highly specialized agencies, such as environmental, space exploration, gas and oil regulation, banking and securities regulation, or budgeting and financial management, the organization, and *defacto*, the head of the organization, rely upon a number of technically skilled and trained specialists to perform the necessary tasks. For example, when the Environmental Protection Agency (EPA) needs highly detailed pollution-related data gathered, analyzed, and interpreted it depends upon Ph.D.s in various science fields to accomplish the task. Each of these highly educated, trained, and skilled EPA employees is able to self-govern, and does not need to be told what or how to do his job. If a mistake occurs, the Ph.D. will correct the mistake and move on. Their professional standards of conduct, which are both internal and organizational, require the utmost in ethical propriety; additional legal and outside regulations are not necessary.

The fourth and final type of accountability system is **political** or **pluralistic**. It is similar to the relationship that exists between a representative and a constituent. It is based upon mutual trust and integrity, where the only check so to speak is through the ballot box. In public administration as opposed to politics the main check is the merit system. Under the merit system what is anticipated is that the public administrator is demographically and culturally representative of the clientele, and thus, hopefully, will make decisions that are generally in line with the social, cultural, political, and economic patterns of the people as a whole. For example, it is likely, but not necessary one would find black social workers working with black clients. But does this type of arrangement mean that the clients will receive better treatment? Not necessarily. However, since the goal is political accountability it is important that a political arrangement, i.e. demographic or racial representation, is established. Does this meet the public interest? Good question.

Summary. So, what did we learn? First, the typology does not, of course, apply equally well to all ethical scenarios. For example, with our city manager the degree of internal control governing his decision making is far greater than any external control that could be imposed (city council, political interest groups, or citizen advocacy groups). Second, as we mentioned earlier each typology is not conclusive or independent in its application. Third, each of these types simply provides support to the argument that all administrative decision have ethical consequences, and thus public administrators constantly place themselves on the altar of accountability.

Conclusion: Ethics and the Public Interest

There are several things this chapter did NOT intend to do. First, the purpose of this chapter is not to develop a specific one, two, three-step process for explaining how public administrators can or should make are ethical decisions; meaning that all decisions have ethical and/or moral consequences. Thus, the inserts from PA Times "Ethics Moments" column provide the reader opportunities to wrestle with difficult choices, while recognizing there is larger public interest that public administrators strive to meet. Second, neither is this chapter an attempt to promote one ethical philosophy over another: we do not specifically and directly argue, for example, that Rawlsian justice theory is superior to Rohr's regime values argument or vice versa. Neither do we contend that Cooper's rational Aristotelian rational framework is inferior to the religion and spirituality context that public decisions can be made in. What we do contend, however, is that public administrators must truly be open to not only recognizing various ethical/philosophical frameworks, but to operating within them when appropriate.

On the other hand, there are several things this chapter DOES directly say about ethics in public administration. First, that ethics and ethical decision-making in the public sector has received and will continue to receive more and well-deserved attention, both academically and practically. Second, we do argue that decisions—ethical decisions—require sound moral sense, judgment, and character. Third, ethical decisions are directed toward an outcome, and should be guided by a set of principles. The outcome we suggest is worth achieving is the public interest, and the set of principles used to guide ethical decision making are normative, traditional, and constitutional in nature.[63] Public administrators are first and foremost *public* servants, and as such their most important responsibility is to uphold the public trust through pursuit of the public interest. Inherent within the concept of public trust is a covenant relationship between the servant and the served, and that relationship is to be clothed in a moral relationship dictated by ethical behavior played out in a democratic-republic.[64]

The area of ethics in administration is substantially important to the proper functioning of any public sector and non-public sector organization. Ethical decision-making is at the heart of public administration, especially in a time of conflicting and postmodern values. Development and application of ethical frameworks in both the classroom and the city manager's office, or with the state or federal program director, is essential for assistance in training and educating public administrators for understanding and combating ethical problems, which are too often cloaked in political dressing. It is the wise, benevolent, and ethical administrator who can discern the truth, and pursue the public interest.

As for students in an introductory course in public administration who are completing the chapter on administrative ethics, we challenge you to take the ethics test listed below. The answers are at the end of the chapter. Don't peek!

Case Study   "An Ethics Moment: Ethics Test for Local Government Employees"

How are your ethics? Take the following test to find out. Test results are located at the end of the chapter. Don't look until you are finished! Discuss in class.

1. An inspector is asked to ok construction work that does not comply with the city's building codes. In exchange, the contractor offers tickets to an upcoming concert. Should you accept the tickets? Yes/No

2. Your relative wants to set up a snow removal business and in addition to other contracts, they want to have a contract with the city. You work for the department that issues this type of contract, but not in the contract section. Should you declare a conflict of interest? Yes/No

3. You have a business in addition to your job with the city. You spend time on the telephone arranging business deals, contacting suppliers and potential clients. Your work for the city suffers because of the amount of time spent on your private business. Is this ethical? Yes/No

4. You have learned several specialized skills working for the city. Another local government learns of your talent and wants you to work for them, moonlighting on the weekends, if you are not called in by your employer to work on an emergency problem. Should you moonlight —that is, work part-time for the other city? Yes/No

5. A department head or city council member contacts you for information about how a city service is handled. You provide the information to the department head or the city council member who made the request. You then send additional information directly to the citizen who had contacted the director or city council member. Should you have sent the additional information? Yes/No

6. You spend several hours during the week using the city supplied computer to download information on a relative's medical condition. Is this ethical? Yes/No

7. A health inspector arrives at a restaurant during the start of the lunch hour. Several violations are noted during the inspection. The manager offers the employee lunch in exchange for waiting to write up the inspection, asking for time to make the needed corrections after the lunch hour. Should the employee accept the free lunch? Yes/No

8. You have inspected a building and find items that do not meet the city's building codes. You write up your inspection and then leave. The contractor contacts you, does not like your answer, and asks to speak to your supervisor. They discuss the situation and find another option that will meet the building codes and not cost the contractor a whole lot of money. Is the supervisor's action ethical? Yes/No

9. You inspect a restaurant just after they have had a spill of grease in the kitchen. It has contaminated surfaces and food. The kitchen staff is busy throwing out food and sanitizing surfaces. You tell the manager you will wait until the kitchen order is restored before conducting your inspection. Is this ethical? Yes/No

10. You are asked to provide a special service to someone, e.g., to just let him or her ride with you, in your city vehicle for a private (not city related) purpose. Is this ethical? Yes/No

11. A manager in another department comes to you and asks that you handle a matter outside of the normal process and it is a service that not everyone in the city would get. The manager states that the person needing help is a very important person and the normal rules and procedures don't apply to their request. Should you handle the matter as requested? Yes/No

Source: From Donald Menzel, ed., "Ethics Moment" column, *PA Times*, January 2000.

Action Steps

1. Do ethical considerations impose a real limitation upon the public interest that transcend the law or political power? Consider your response by a reading of the U.S. Supreme Court case of *Moran v. Burbine*, 475 U.S. 412 (1986), in which the Court decided without considering the lies of police officers to the defendant, Brian Burbine, that his lawyer had not called or asked for him (he did), or the lie to the lawyer that there was no interrogation of Burbine at that time (the police were interrogating at that moment). The Court ruled that police had followed all *Miranda* warning requirements such as his right to a lawyer and his right to remain silent—and Burbine's waiver of his rights and subsequent confession was valid. Should the ethics of lying impinge on the public interest of these bureaucratic behaviors?

2. Ethics is all about making decisions. Break into groups of three or four, propose an administrative or policy problem, and ask the groups to formulate consensus on the steps necessary to solve the problem—not to solve it, just how to solve it. Give them 10 minutes maximum. Re-assemble and have them discuss. What are the obstacles to reach consensus? What were the reasons for not wanting to compromise? How did this affect the decision-making process?

3. Assign the students to research and interact with a public administrator. Interview the public administrator about the problems and obstacles they have in conducting an ethical organizational environment. How does this conflict, if at all, with their own personal ethics? What are the differences between an organizational ethic and an individual ethic?

4. Have them re-read the city manager and the pornography vignette. Would they reach a different outcome? If so, what is it? How did they reach it? What aspects of the various philosophical ethical frameworks presented did they use to reach their conclusion?

5. Break into groups of three. Research an actual ethical administrative problem at the local and/or state level. Assess it. Evaluate it. How is it explained by any or all of the ethical frameworks? Report findings back to the class.

6. Write a short three to four page paper on one of the frameworks, answering the following questions regarding the various ethical philosophical frameworks: a) What does each mean? What is at the heart of each framework? How, if at all, can or does it apply to administrative ethics questions and/or issues?

Exam Review Preparation

1. Discuss the basic elements of the four philosophical frameworks. What are the differences and similarities?

2. What is the importance of Rawls' approach to ethical clarification?

3. Identify the key aspects of Rohr's constitutional regime value approach. Comb through the U.S. Constitution and your state constitution and highlight several of the regime values that Rohr talks about. Once you have identified the values examine how the public administrator uses his/her administrative discretion for making ethical decisions.

4. What are some problems with trying to apply religious-spiritual values to administrative ethical dilemmas? What are some benefits of trying to do so?

5. Define administrative accountability. How does it differ from responsibility? If there is no difference, why do we use both terms?

6. Summarize the four accountability typologies. Describe the 'internal' versus 'external' measures or checks on administrative decision-making.

7. Explain Terry Cooper's rational-comprehensive model of administrative ethics.

Key Concepts

Administrative accountability
Aquinas' application of Aristotelian ethical principles
Augustinianism
Bureaucratic responsibility
Carl Friedrich
Christian ethic
Don Menzel
Ethical relativism
Ethics
Federal Executive Institute
Herman Finer
James Q. Wilson
John Rawls' justice as fairness concept
Moral character
Moral objectivism
Os Guiness
Qur'an (Koran)
Religion and spirituality, specifically the Abrahamic tradition

Terry Cooper's rational-comprehensive model
Utilitarianism
Virtue ethics
Willa Bruce

Recommended Readings

Beauchamp, Tom L. *Philosophical Ethics: An Introduction to Moral Philosophy*, 3rd ed. New York: McGraw-Hill, 2001.

Bonhoeffer, Dietrich. *Ethics.* Edited by Eberhard Bethge. New York: MacMillan, 1962.

Cooper, Terry L., ed., *Handbook of Administrative Ethics*, 2nd ed. New York: Marcel Dekker, 2000.

Frederickson, H. George. and Richard K. Ghere, editors. *Ethics in Public Management.* Armonk, NY: M.E. Sharpe, 2005.

Garofalo, Charles and Dean Geuras. *Ethics in the Public Service: The Moral Mind at Work.* Washington, DC: Georgetown University Press, 1999.

Gawthrop, Louis C. *Public Service and Democracy: Ethical Imperatives for the 21st Century.* New York, NY: Chatham House, 1998.

Gortner, Harold F. *Ethics for Public Managers.* New York: Greenwood, 1991.

Grenz, Stanley J. *The Moral Quest: Foundations of Christian Ethics.* Downers Grove, IL: InterVarsity, 1997.

Holmes, Arthur F. *Ethics: Approaching Moral Decisions.* Downers Grove, IL: InterVarsity, 1984.

Menzel, Donald C. *Ethics Management for Public Administrators: building Organizations of Integrity.* Armonk, NY: M.E. Sharpe, 2007.

Waldo, Dwight. *The Enterprise of Public Administration.* Novato, CA: Chandler and Sharp, 1980.

White, John Kenneth. *The Values Divide: American Politics and Culture in Transition.* New York: Chatham House Publishers, 2003.

Related Web Sites

American Society of Public Administration—Code of Ethics
http://www.aspanet.org/scriptcontent/index_codeofethics.cfm

American Society of Public Administration—*Public Integrity*
http://www.aspanet.org/scriptcontent/index_publicintegrity.cfm

Center for the Study of Ethics
www.iit.edu/departments/csep

Ethics and Public Policy Center
www.eppc.org/

Ethics in public affairs
    www.globalethics.org/
    www.ethics.org/

John Rawls
    http://www.iep.utm.edu/r/rawls.htm

Josephson Institute of Ethics
    http://www.josephsoninstitute.org/seminars/etw_public-administration.php

Santa Clara University-Markkula Center for Applied Ethics
    http://www.scu.edu/ethics/

Thomas Aquinas
    http://www.iep.utm.edu/a/aquinas.htm

U.S. Office of Government Ethics
    www.usoge.gov/index.html

Case Study   "An Ethics Moment: Answers to the Ethics Test:
              How Did You Do"?

1. An inspector is asked to OK construction work that does not comply with the city's building codes. in exchange, the contractor offers tickets to an upcoming concert. Should you accept the tickets? Yes/No. **The answer is a resounding NO by both Kansas City and Ethics Section members.**

2. Your relative wants to set up a snow removal business and in addition to other contracts, they want to have a contract with the city. You work for the department that issues this type of contract, but not in the contract section. Should you declare a conflict of interest? Yes/No. **The KCH contends that there is no reason to declare a conflict of interest while ESM contend otherwise. 72 percent of ESM responded yes.**

3. You have a business in addition to your job with the city. You spend time on the telephone arranging business deals, contacting suppliers and potential clients. Your work for the city suffers because of the amount of time spend on your private business. Is this ethical? Yes/No. **Both the KCH and ESM declare this behavior as unethical.**

4. You have learned several specialized skills working for the city. Another local government learns of your talent and wants you to work for them, moonlighting on the weekends, if you are not called in by your employer to work on an emergency problem. Should you moonlight—that is, work part-time for the other city? Yes/No. **A split opinion is recorded here with the KCH declaring that the answer is yes while 70 percent of the ESM said no-that one should not moonlight.**

5. A department head or city council member contacts you for information about how a city service is handled. You provide the information to the department head or the city council member who made the request. You then send additional information directly to the citizen who had contacted the director or city council member. Should you have sent the additional information? Yes/No. **The KCH declares yes, that it was okay to send additional information. ESM disagree, with 64 percent asserting that it was incorrect to send additional information.**

6. You spend several hours during the week using the city supplied computer to download information on a relative's medical condition. Is this ethical? Yes/No. **No disagreement here. Both the KCH and ESM agree that this is unethical.**

7. A health inspector arrives at a restaurant during the start of the lunch hour. Several violations are noted during the inspection. The manager offers the employee lunch in exchange for waiting to write up the inspection, asking for time to make the needed corrections after the lunch hour. Should the employee accept the free lunch? Yes/No. **Don't accept a free lunch advises both the KCH and ESM.**

8. You have inspected a building and find items that do not meet the city's building codes. You write up your inspection and then leave. The contractor contacts you, does not like your answer, and asks to speak to your supervisor. They discuss the situation and find another option that will meet the building codes and not cause the contractor a whole lot of money. Is the supervisor's action ethical? Yes/No. **The supervisor's action is ethical according to the KCH. ESM largely agree, although one in four do not.**

9. You inspect a restaurant just after they have had a spill of grease in the kitchen. It has contaminated surfaces and food. The kitchen staff is busy throwing out food and sanitizing surfaces. You tell the manager you will wait until the kitchen order is restored before conducting your inspection. Is this ethical? Yes/No. **Yes, this is ethical according to both the KCH and ESM.**

10. You are asked to provide a special service to someone, e.g., to just let him or her ride with you, in your city vehicle for a private (not city related) purpose. Is this ethical? Yes/No. **No, no, no states the KCH. ESM mostly disagree with 4 of every 5 stating it is ethical.**

11. A manager in another department comes to you and asks that you handle a matter outside of the normal process and it is a service that not everyone in the city would get. The manager states that the person needing help is a very important person and the normal rules and procedures don't apply to their request. Should you handle the matter as requested? Yes/No. **The answer is no, according to the KCH and ESM.**

Source: Kansas City, Missouri, Education & Development Office. Ninety-members of the Ethics Section of the American Society of Public Administration responded to the questions. These are the results as interpreted by the Kansas City Handbook (KCH) and Ethics Section Members (ESM). From Donald Menzel, ed., "Ethics Moment" column, *PA Times*, March 2000.

Chapter 12

The Future and Hope of Administration in the Public Interest

"The greatest mistake citizens can make when they complain of 'the bureaucracy' is to suppose that their frustrations arise simply out of management problems; they do not—they arise out of governance problems."

James Q. Wilson, *Bureaucracy: What Government Agencies Do and Why They Do It*

Chapter Objectives

Upon completion of this chapter the student will be able to:

1. Summarize the meaning of administration in the public interest;
2. Forecast various trends that will shape the future direction of public administration;
3. Recognize and appreciate the importance of pursuing public administration in the public interest.

Introduction

Thomas Friedman, the celebrated *New York Times* columnist and author of the best-selling *The World is Flat,*[1] has argued that the world is flattening. Due to technological and telecommunication advances, the business and economic world is shrinking, enabling more and more countries worldwide to enter the global market. His message is essentially one of economic materialism, where the economic forces of the world combine to determine our destinies; those who recognize this fact will jump on board and prosper and those that do not recognize or recognize it but fail to act will suffer the consequences. However tantalizing Friedman's image of a flat world is, the metaphor is empty, for it fails to recognize the human side of it all. As one reviewer wrote:

"In the last few years—really ever since the Internet bubble burst and terror struck—most Americans have become well aware of what Friedman does not recognize: that no matter how beneficial or fascinating the IT revolution may be, the history of the twenty-first century will not begin and end with Global Cross-

307

ing and Geek Squads. Peace and politics, war and friendship, democracy and tyranny, poetry and song, love and commitment, parenting and virtue, morals and devotion and God himself—all these have yet to be digitized. For the most important things, our world, like a vintage record album, is still analog, still round."[2]

Thomas Friedman

Thomas Friedman, a world-renowned author and journalist, joined *The New York Times* in 1981 as a financial reporter specializing in OPEC- and oil-related news and later served as the chief diplomatic, chief White House, and international economics correspondents. A three-time Pulitzer Prize winner, he has traveled hundreds of thousands of miles reporting the Middle East conflict, the end of the cold war, U.S. domestic politics and foreign policy, international economics, and the worldwide impact of the terrorist threat.

Source: "About Thomas L. Friedman," *New York Times*, www.thomaslfriedman.com/thomas friedman.htm (accessed October 2007).

The same is true with administration in the public interest. There is, as Douglas McGregor once wrote, "a human side of (the) enterprise." The pursuit of public administration in America is not all about economic changes, globalization, cultural and demographic shifts, revolution in telecommunications, performance management in a world of permanent fiscal crisis, disaggregated, and fragmented and disarticulated among other academic jargon. It is mainly about values, policies, and people. It is about promoting and fulfilling the public interest. The remainder of this concluding chapter: 1) summarizes several trends forecast for American public administration; and 2) prescribes what forces should and must shape administration in the public interest if it is to remain a viable professional force in our democratic-republic and administrative state.

Trends for the Future

The public administrator in America is part of a relatively recent profession, dating back to the turn of the twentieth century, and perhaps back to **Woodrow Wilson's famous 1887 essay** that describes the now-infamous politics and administration dichotomy. Public administrators were not mentioned in the Constitution nor in many of the founding documents, probably because there was no need for an advanced, permanent, and bureaucratic administrative system, given that the goal of the founders was a national government of limited federal powers.[3] Government was a community of values, policies, and people, not an administrative and bureaucratic machine. Of course, by the time of the Civil War and afterwards all of this changed. We needed organization, administration, management, and efficiency to continue on as a united America. Still, the growth of the administrative state, which is generally lauded by modern scholars, can challenge our democratic notions of citizen input, legal protections, citizen governance, community relations, and the common good.[4] Some scholars even claim that the future of public administration (bureaucracy) "is fundamentally a normative value problem, one rooted in a unique, changing triad of historic national values."[5] What does the future of American public administration look like?[6] First, let us look at a brief overview of four categories of trends; trends that will influence and, perhaps, even direct the future of public administration, both as a discipline and a profession, in the public interest.

Trend One: Explosion in Communication, Economics, and Technology

Advances in communication technology, for example, are some of the key elements mentioned by many.[7] The future of public administration will be dictated in large part by the changing technological and telecommunication advances, such as the Internet, cell phones, GPS monitors, computer programming, satellite uplinks, and a host of other electronic and digital devices and innovations. The conveyance of information across computers the size of coins and subsequently linked to the **Internet** will do to administrative and bureaucratic organizations what Friedman said has happened to the digitized economy: flatten it, breaking down social, cultural, even nationalistic barriers for, presumably, the betterment of society and the governance process.

Box 12.1   Internet's Influence upon Society and Government

The Internet is many things to many individuals. Take a look at the following definitions:

- The Internet is a worldwide, publicly accessible network of interconnected computer networks that transmit data using the standard Internet ... (www.stiltonstudios.net/glossary.htm)

- The globally interconnected collection of IP protocol based networks (www.att.com/gen/general)

- The Internet ... is a worldwide system of computer networks that allows users to send and receive information from other computers (www.aishealth.com/ EHealthBusiness/EHealthTerms.html)

- A worldwide network of computers that can be accessed via the campus computer network. The Internet allows local computer users to find and use information resources on computers of other academic institutions, research institutes, private companies and government agencies (elinks.ecc.edu/library/STAFFINF/ glossary.html)

Source: Google Search, "Definitions of Internet on the Web," found at www.google.com/ search?hl=en&defl=en&q=define:Internet&sa=X&oi=gloassary_de (accessed October 2007).

The changing patterns of political economy, such as brought about by globalization,[8] impact not only the federal government, but states and communities as well. Outsourcing, privatization, and other means of more directly incorporating the business world into the development and delivery of public services is not something waiting for the future: it is here! From county jails to city waste management companies, public services are being loaned out to the private sector in growing numbers. Questions of accountability arise, but the push for saving dollars through enhanced performance management and budgeting systems, for example, particularly in the age of what some call a "permanent fiscal crisis,"[9] trumps other considerations, such as pursuit of the public interest.

Trend Two: Institutional and Organizational Change

Institutional and organizational changes may prompt the greatest number of foreseen trends in public administration.[10] Moving from an industrial economy into an information age based economy requires different ways of organizing and managing financial and human resources, particularly within a democratic-republican state.[11] The Weberian model of hierarchy, with its rules and regulations, jurisdictional patterns of organization, means of efficiency and economy, scalar dimensions of command, and the rest is being replaced by flatter and more customer friendly models of organization. As a result, even though the complexity of issues and problems has and will not diminish (stem cell research, same-sex couple benefits, and global warming) and there is no unifying public administration system to coordinate, plan, and manage these problems, as is present in other Western democracies, such as Great Britain, there is nonetheless a movement toward performance management, greater employee responsibility, and the recognition that today's administrative culture is constantly changing and that the only way to adapt to and flow with this change is streamlined, market-driven organizations and economies, with central government oversight and regulation. It is a far cry from Henri Fayol's conception of the modern organization!

Trend Three: Citizen-Participation and Public Influence

Citizen influence and participation is critical to what most refer to as the need for greater public involvement in the decision-governance process of **administrative-democracy**. What does this mean? Simply put: many scholars argue that one goal of an administrative state—at least one that is democratic in its orientation—is the incorporation of citizen and public influence, especially in the decision making process.[12] Couple this with enhanced technological, economic, and communication advances operating in a flat organizational administrative and democratic world, and you have the makings of a New England town meeting on steroids! Socio-cultural patterns and dimensions of race, ethnicity, religion, gender, sexual orientation, and disabilities are increasing; this means greater sensitivity, interaction, and networking on the parts of public decision-makers.

The challenge, of course, is to incorporate all of these various voices into the administrative decision making process, looking to increase citizen participation and enhancing public confidence in the administrative-democratic process and institutions against the entrenched onslaught of performance-based tools of public administration, and thus influence the promotion of the public interest.[13] How is this done? Can it be done? Can the **public administrator** fashion and shape an administrative and policy-making world that represent the various hues and colors of the quilt that makes America? Is it even necessary to do so? Is it the responsibility of public administrators to meet the demands of every citizen, every group, and every neighborhood council? Or is it (should it?) the responsibility of every public administrator to recognize the differences, but direct his attention to building coalitions of agreement around common normative values? In other words, should instead the public administrator pursue the public interest?

Box 12.2   Public Administrator of Tomorrow

The public administrator of tomorrow works in a revamping field and discipline of public administration today. Here is what Don Kettl, one of the leading public administration scholars in the United States today, has to say about the changing role of public administration, particularly as it appeals to and impacts (or is impacted by) the public interest:

"Public administration … does have important things to say to public officials. Public administration has a rich theory and an even richer tradition analyzing what is truly *public* about government management, and this is the piece most prominently missing from the public reform debate. It has a deep understanding of the tensions between policy making and administration. It has a sense of the subtle influences that shape a public organization's environment. It understands that organizational structure and administrative process matter. In short, public administration is at its bet at explaining (and shaping) the management of public programs, in a direction determined by public organizations, in the *public interest* (our emphasis)"

Source: Excerpted from Donald F. Kettl, "The Future of Public Administration," Humanities and Social Sciences Online: 5–6. http://www.h-net.org/~pub admin/tfreport/kettl.pdf (accessed October 2007).

Trend Four: Ethical, Legal, and Political Challenges

The challenges for exemplifying ethical behavior are rampant in today's administrative and policy-making society.[14] What are the guidelines directing each area? How is the public administrator supposed to know when an action is ethical, legal, or politically motivated? The second two are, probably, fairly evident: if it is legal it should follow jurisdictional and statutory regulations; if it is politically motivated it will be devoted to moving forward in a partisan-political or organizational-political fashion: benefiting the interests of a few over the **public interest**. But what is ethical? What is a moral action? Is it simply following procedure and protocol, making sure the decision abides by rational means, incorporating as many viewpoints as possible, before rendering a decision? Is it abiding by universal values, such as justice and equality? Is it doing what is right and avoiding what is wrong? Or is it following one's conscience and intuition? The latter three questions are subjective rather than objective, drawing upon opinion and value rather than information and fact. So, because we want our public administrators to be fair to all, then it is imperative that an agreed to procedural mechanism be in place that governs his actions and decision-making. This is what is termed not only ethical, but follows formats of legal and political standards, acceptable to the greater number. We question the value of this robotic, automaton aspect of public administration, and believe that the human value and dimension of decision-making is critical to honoring a healthy and whole ethical and legal environment in which to make difficult decisions. That environment is, we believe, the pursuit of the public interest.

The Future and Hope of Public Administration

The intention of this text was to demonstrate that public administration operates (*should* operate) in pursuit of the public interest. Of course, the questions are several: How is public administration defined? How is the public interest defined? Is there even such a thing as the public interest? How do public administrators operate in something that may not even exist? The list goes on. As the reader can now discern we strongly believe that there is such a thing as the public interest and that it is understood within the framework of principles, policies, and practices. As a result of this understanding of the role and benefit of the public interest, the remainder of this conclusion offers ideas for better understanding the future and hope of public administration in the public interest.

The Role of Government

Government's role is a critical topic and it begs the question we must all ask: What do I want my government to do? Until communities, cities, towns, counties, states, and the central government ask this question, grapple with it, and come up with some type of response the critical problems examined throughout this text will continue unchecked. We realize, of course, this question has kept political theorists and philosophers busy for the last several thousand years. Reams of paper and gallons of ink have been spilled trying in vain to address the question. To what end? Dozens of theories, models, systems, and ideologies have been presented, some have even been put into practice, and the results are mixed. Marxism, socialism, capitalism, and a myriad of hybrids, influenced by cultures, languages, peoples, geography, religions and many other factors contribute to establishing institutions, fostering political behaviors, and implementing bureaucratic organizations and systems—all to address this one question. Although the question is well beyond the scope of this text, the study of public administration in the public interest is a critical element in addressing this question.

Defining the Public

The meaning of 'public' is also imperative to the evaluation and study of public administration in the public interest. **Public** means much more than 'government.'[15] Public schools, public transportation, and public restrooms does not necessarily mean that the government (by the way what do we mean when we say the government?) owns schools, transportation systems, and restrooms in the city park. It means by definition that more than one group of individuals or group, such as a family or private party, has access to these societal elements. By implication, then, does it mean that if only public dollars support schools, transportation systems, and restrooms that all who partake of the good that comes from the schools, transportation systems, and restrooms must abide by and follow all laws, rules, regulations established by the government? It would appear the answer is yes, if the results of thousands of court cases that equate the spending of public dollars with obedience to public laws, rules, and regulations is any indication. But as we have demonstrated, for example, the influence of non-profit and faith-based organizations is substantial upon the delivery of goods and services. Further, the flattening of the economic and business world and the blurring of public and private spheres of society demonstrates that what might have been considered public 100 or even 50 years ago can no longer be considered as such today. Therefore, as the literature demonstrates the role and function of public administrators can no longer be solely confined to the procedures and structure of Weberian bureaucracies.

Box 12.3   Public Means What?

One of the areas under considerable debate today is the role of community in shaping our understanding of what public means. Robert Putnam, the Peter and Isabel Malkin Professor of Public Policy, John F. Kennedy School of Government, Harvard University, argues for greater attention on what he calls social capital, which he "refers to (as) features of social organization, such as networks, norms, and trust that facilitate coordination and cooperation for mutual benefit." Public is enhanced when society invests in the various forms of capital: physical, financial, human, and, of course, social, that provide the basis for greater civic and social engagement.

We let Putnam finish: "Students of social capital have only begun to address some of the most important questions that this approach to public affairs suggests. What are the actual trends in different forms of civic engagement? Why communities differ in the stocks of social capital? What *kinds* (Putnam's emphasis) of civic engagement seem most likely to foster economic growth or community effectiveness? Must specific types of social capital be matched to different public problems? Most important of all, how is social capital created and destroyed? What strategies for building (or rebuilding) social capital are most promising? How can we balance the twin strategies of exploiting existing social capital and creating it afresh … ?"

Source: Robert D. Putnam, "The Prosperous Community: Social Capital and Public Life"*The American Prospect*, no. 13 (Spring 1993), http://epn.org/prospect/ 13/13putn.html (accessed October 2007).

Normative and Empirical

Normative versus empirical is an age-old academic dichotomy. Sometimes it surfaces as the fact-value dichotomy. However it is pictured, the bottom line is that when it applies to public administrators the question that is invariably raised is: What goal should the public administrator pursue? Should he pursue performance, reinvention, reorganization, reform or a host of other organizational fads? Or should he follow values, such as those that are rooted in America's historical, constitutional, and traditional fabric, such as pursuit of the public interest? Today, the task of performance management is played out at every level of government. Whether it is called performance management or New Public Management the goal is the same: public administrators are required by either/or legislative act and/or executive mandate to establish and implement rigid performance measurements in a variety of policy areas, from education to budgets to street sweeping to garbage pickup. The goal is to 1) address the pressing public demands and needs within an empirical and quantitative framework, and 2) to do so with the purpose of saving tax dollars. What does this mean for pursuit of the public interest?

We acknowledge that public administrators at all levels of government and within the non-profit and faith-based sectors are inundated with the demand for performance, particularly during difficult economic and budgetary times, and that performance standards and measurements are not themselves inherently wrong in some way. However, we, like many others, contend that the primary focus of public administrators must be on the values that govern our nation, principles found not only in the Constitution, but also in history, theory, and tradition, and not solely on procedural and performance standards.[16] We understand that history, theory, and tradition, nor even the Constitution itself, directly assists the city manager in balancing the budget—there are budgetary and managerial tools and methods that assist in those areas. Beyond even political considerations, such as which interest group or neighborhood coalition or citizen network alliance makes it case for inclusion of budgetary items, there are deeper and more profound values that directly and indirectly motivate the city manager when he puts together the city budget. Questions such as: What is best for the **community** as a whole? How can I balance this budget and still meet the major goals and objectives agreed to during deliberations with the city council? Or, if the budget cannot be balanced while meeting the major goals and objectives set forth, then what items are to be cut, defending both the how and why issues? These are administrative questions, but they are also questions of principles and values; questions that elicit meaning beyond an Excel spreadsheet or performance measurement guidelines. They are questions that influence the public interest.

The Future of American Public Administration

American public administration may well rest on the fulcrum that balances the three values: administration, political efficacy, and common interests.[17] Perhaps this is another way of describing what we mean by **pursuit of the public interest**. Americans demand efficiency and economy in the administration of public goods and services; they expect equity, equality, and justice when a wrong is committed, when they are defrauded, or when the good or service promised or delivered fails to meet their legal or even ethical expectations; and finally, Americans assemble in political interest groups, battling each other in order gain the government's attention to administer the goods and services they believe they deserve. The point that scholars like **Richard Stillman** and others make is that these three values cannot be fulfilled to their maximum. What kind of world would we live in if life was centered on perfect efficiency, political efficacy, or interest group demands? And, further, would we even want this? The answer to the second question is a resounding No! Thus, argue the scholars, there is the need for political and administrative discretion; there is the need for public officials, including public administrators, to make decisions that do not necessarily (or ever) balance all three values. It is simply necessary to have a public administration system (and thus by implication public administrators) that somehow, someway address the demands of all three values, considers the implications and consequences of not meeting each, and finally comes to a decision, whether it regards the making of budgets, the establishing of regulations for air or water quality, and a myriad of other difficult choices.

What type of leadership is required? What type of public administrator is needed to balance these values? What kind of skills, knowledge, character, and other qualities are required to exist in such an environment? What kind of person does it take to make critical decisions in highly charged political environments? We discussed such a public administrator in the chapter on public management, where we introduced the student to principles of the New Public Service notion espoused by Robert and Janet Denhardt. They include:

- To help citizens articulate and meet needs rather than dictate to them;
- To make the public interest value paramount in public administration;
- Meeting public needs is best accomplished through collective efforts and collaborative processes;
- Convincing others that the public interest is the result of a dialogue about shared values rather than the aggregation of self-interests;
- Attend to the public interest and not just the market;
- To work in organizations that are based on collaboration and shared leadership;

- And that the public interest is advanced by public administrators and citizens who believe that making meaningful contributions to society if more important than simply meeting set performance standards.[18]

Each of these principles focus on broader constitutional, historical, traditional, and even normatively theoretical principles, policies, and practice that are tied to the pursuit of the public interest.

In the years to come, when future generations face seemingly unprecedented crises, such as the Oklahoma City bombing, 9/11 terrorist attacks, Hurricane Katrina, or the financial meltdown of 2008; they must draw upon the resources found in all of society: from families to businesses to interest groups to places of worship and governments. Each is necessary to address the various problems that confront Americans. Each is a critical stone in building the foundation of human society. Each stone is cemented into our administration in the public interest.

Action Steps

1. Have the students read portions of Thomas Friedman's *The World is Flat*. Discuss the thesis. Explore it by examining and visiting various businesses around town. How are they plugged into the new world economy? What does it mean to their development and existence in the new global age of telecommunication and technology? Discuss comparisons and/or analogies with the public sector.

2. Discuss the Denhardts' rendering of the public interest compared with Stillman's description of the three sets of normative values governing bureaucracy and government. Have the students investigate several public and non-profit agencies' web sites and/or visit them in person. Develop an operational matrix for the Denhardts' ideas and explore if and how the seven principles are evident in the agencies. Show evidence of how Stillman's three normative values are displayed.

3. Form into small discussion groups. Develop a FUTURE legal conflict in public administration that may arise in the courts — or the U.S. Supreme Court — and write-up the facts of the administrative policy and/or behavior at the heart of the controversy. It can be any combination of variables, including ethical, political, economic, organizational and so forth — that conflict with a basic legal right such as the right to property, equality, liberty and due process. Do some SCIENCE FICTION by setting your scenario far into the future, involving technology and other issues well beyond our current imagination! The purpose of the exercise is to have each member of the group grapple with the scenario's main theme as it underscores how public administrators fulfill the public interest. Re-assemble and report to the class. What future do you envision for administration in the public interest?

Exam Review Preparation

1. Outline the Denhardts' seven principles of the New Public Service.

2. What are the consequences of trying to fulfill all of Stillman's three values simultaneously? Is it even possible?

3.   Explore the trends of public administration. What are they? How are they being played out in the various venues of society: organizationally, administratively, politically, and economically?

4.   What is the future of public administration? What will it look like in 10 years? 20 years?

5.   Apply Friedman's thesis to the public and non-profit sector. What does it look like? How is it different from its private sector counterpart? How is similar?

Key Concepts

Community
E-government
Internet
Internet and public administration
Public administration and the public interest
Richard Stillman
Social capital and pursuit of the public interest
The World is Flat thesis
Thomas Friedman
Weberian model of hierarchy
What does public mean?

Recommended Readings

Box, Richard C. *Citizen Governance: Leading American Communities into the 21st Century*. Thousand Oaks, CA: Sage, 1998.

_____. Editor. *Democracy and Public Administration*. Armonk, NY: M.E. Sharpe, 2007.

Crosby, Barbara C. and John M. Bryson. *Leadership for the Common Good: Tackling Public Problems in a Shared-Power World*. 2d ed. San Francisco, CA: Jossey-Bass, 2005.

Friedman, Thomas L. *The World is Flat: A Brief History of the 21st Century*. New York: Farrar, Straus and Giroux, 2005.

Kettl, Donald F. *The Transformation of Governance: Public Administration for Twenty-First Century America*. Baltimore, MD: Johns Hopkins University Press, 2002.

Peters, B. Guy. *The Future of Governing: Four Emerging Models*. Lawrence, KS: University Press of Kansas, 1996.

Radin, Beryl A. *Challenging the Performance Movement: Accountability, Complexity, and Democratic Values*. Washington, DC: Georgetown University Press, 2006.

Wilson, James Q. *Bureaucracy: What Government Agencies Do and Why They Do It*. New York: Basic Books, 1989.

Related Web Sites

Donald Kettl
 http://www.fels.upenn.edu/faculty/kettl.htm

Internet — The Internet Society
 http://www.isoc.org/internet/history/

Thomas Friedman
 http://www.thomaslfriedman.com/

Whitman Center for Public Service, University of West Florida
 http://www.uwf.edu/whitcntr/Contents.htm

Notes

Chapter 1

1. Ruth Hoogland DeHoog, "Bureaupathology," in Jay M. Shafritz, ed., *Defining Public Administration: Selections from the International Encyclopedia of Public Policy and Administration* (Boulder, CO: Westview Press, 2000): 132–136; H. George Frederickson, *Up the Bureaucracy: A True and Faultless Guide to Organizational Success and the Further Adventures of Knute and Thor* (Lawrence, KS: Better Bureaucracy Press, 2007).

2. E.g., Editorial, "Kafka and Katrina," *The New York Times* (December 2, 2006); Steven T. Wax, *Kafka Comes to America: Fighting for Justice in the War on Terror* (New York: Other Press, 2008).

3. Max Brod, *Franz Kafka: A Biography*, 2nd rev. ed., G. Humphrey Roberts, trans. (New York: Schocken Books, 1963); Sander L. Gilman, *Franz Kafka* (New York: Recktion Books, 2005).

4. For further applications, *see*, Steven T. Wax, *Kafka Comes to America: Fighting for Justice in the War on Terror* (New York: Other Press, 2008); Brendan Seaton, "We're All Kafka Bureaucrats: Reflections on the Writings of Franz Kafka," (2006) available on-line at www.brendonseaton.com/_upload/musings/kafka.pdf; "Editorial: Kafka and Katrina," *New York Times* (12/2/2006).

5. E.g., Y. Liu, Benjamin R. Brooks, Naoyuki Taniguchi, and Henrik A. Hartmann, "CuZnSOD and MnSOD Immunoreactivity in Brain Stem Motor Neurons From Amyotropic Lateral Sclerosis Patients," *Acta Neurpathologica* 95 (1997): 63–70.

6. Eugene P. Dvorin and Robert H. Simmons, *From Amoral to Humane Bureaucracy* (San Francisco, CA: Canfield Press, 1972).

7. Eugene P. Dvorin and Robert H. Simmons, *From Amoral to Humane Bureaucracy* (San Francisco, CA: Canfield Press, 1972): 19–26; Theodore J. Lowi, *The End of Liberalism: Ideology, Policy, and the Crisis of Public Authority* (New York: W.W. Norton, 1969): 85–92.

8. John Maynard Keynes, *The General Theory of Employment, Interest, and Money*, 2007 reprint ed. (New York: Macmillan, 1936): 383–384.

9. E.g., Allan Bloom, *The Closing of the American Mind: How Higher Education Has Failed Democracy and Impoverished the souls of Today's Students* (New York: Simon & Schuster, 1987); Richard B. Brandt, *Ethical Theory* (Englewood Cliffs, NJ: Prentice-Hall, 1959): chapter 11, "Ethical Relativism"; John Ladd, ed., *Ethical Relativism* (Belmont, CA: Wadsworth, 1973).

10. E.g., Walter T. Stace, *The Concept of Morals* (New York: Macmillan, 1965): chapter 1, "Ethical Relativity and Ethical Absolutism."

11. Debra W. Stewart, Norman W. Sprinthall, and David M. Shafer, "Moral Development in Public Administration," in Terry L. Cooper, ed., *Handbook of Administrative Ethics* (New York: Marcel Dekker, 2000): 457–480.

12. W.C. Crain, *Theories of Development* (Englewood Cliffs, NJ: Prentice-Hall, 1985): 118–136.

13. Melanie Killen and Judith Smetana, eds., *Handbook of Moral Development* (Mahwah, NJ: Lawrence Erlbaum Associates, Inc., Publishers, 2006).

14. E.g., Do Lim Choi, "Determinants of Moral Reasoning in Public Service," *International Review of Public Administration* 12 (2007): 81–92; John J. Ryan, "Moral Reasoning as a Determinant of Organizational Citizenship Behaviors: A Study in the Public Accounting Profession," *Journal of Business Ethics* 33 (2001): 233–244.

15. E.g., Jeffrey D. Schultz, *Presidential Scandals* (Washington, DC: CQ Press, 1999); John Garrard and James L. Newell, eds., *Scandals In Past and Contemporary Politics* (Manchester, Eng.: Man-

chester University Press, 2006); John P. Crank and Michael A. Caldero, *Police Ethics: the Corruption of Noble Cause* (Cincinnati, OH: Anderson Publishing, 2000).

16. Taylor Branch, "The Culture of Bureaucracy: We're All Working for the Penn Central," *Washington Monthly* (November 1970): 8.

17. Norton E. Long, "Public Administration, Cognitive Competence, and the Public Interest," *Administration and Society* 20, no. 3, (November 1988): 334–43.

18. Ibid., 341. Long argues that a "commonsense list" of values or dimensions of life would be an appropriate point to begin to define and operationalize the public interest, including life, health, security, self-respect and a host of others.

19. Norton E. Long, "Power and Administration," *Public Administration Review* 9, no. 4 (Autumn 1949): 257–64. See especially Long's discussion of the public interest on pp. 260–61.

20. For an excellent biographical sketch of Pendleton Herring, his life, and contributions, see Fred I. Greenstein and Austin Ranney, "Pendleton Herring: Biographical Memoirs," *Proceedings of the American Philosophical Society* 150, no. 3 (September 2006): 488–92.

21. See Marshall E. Dimock's review of Herring's book, *Public Administration and the Public Interest* (New York: McGraw-Hill, 1936), in *Public Opinion Quarterly* 1, no. 2 (April 1937): 153–57.

22. Gabriel A. Almond, "The Return to the State," *American Political Science Review* 82, no. 3 (September 1988): 853–74; Pendleton Herring, *Public Administration and the Public Interest* (New York, NY: McGraw-Hill, 1936); Norton E. Long, "Bureaucracy and Constitutionalism," *American Political Science Review* 46, no. 3 (September 1952): 808–18; Norton E. Long, "The 1991 John Gaus Lecture: Politics, Political Science and the Public Interest," *PS: Political Science and Politics* 24, no. 4 (December 1991): 670–75; Emmette S. Redford, "The Protection of the Public Interest with Special Reference to Administrative Regulation," *American Political Science Review* 48, no. 4 (December 1954): 1103–13.

23. Paul Appleby, *Morality and Administration in Democratic Government* (Baton Rouge, LA: Louisiana State University Press, 1952); Emmette S. Redford, "Protection of the Public Interest," 1103–13; Glendon Schubert, *The Public Interest: A Critique of the Theory of a Political Concept* (Glencoe, IL: The Free Press, 1960); Herbert Simon, *Administrative Behavior*, 3d ed. (New York, NY: The Free Press, 1976); and Frank J. Sorauf, "The Public Interest Reconsidered," *The Journal of Politics* 19, no. 4 (1957): 616–39.

24. Anthony Downs, "The Public Interest: Its Meaning in a Democracy," *Social Research* 29, no. 1 (1962): 1–36.

25. For more on the theory of "the commons" see: Terry L. Anderson and Randy T. Simmons, eds., *The Political Economy of Customs and Culture: Information Solutions to the Commons Problem*, 2d ed. (Lanham, MD: Rowman and Littlefield, 1998); John A. Baden and Douglas Noonan, eds., *Managing the Commons* (Bloomington, IN: Indiana University Press, 1992); and Elinor Ostrom, *Governing the Commons: The Evolution of Institutions for Collective Action* (London, England: Cambridge University Press, 1990).

26. Richard J. Flathman, *The Public Interest: An Essay Concerning the Normative Discourse of Politics* (New York, NY: John Wiley and Sons, 1966).

27. Virginia Held, *The Public Interest and Individual Interests* (Oxford, England: Oxford University Press, 1970).

28. E.g., Charles W. Anderson, *Statecraft: An Introduction to Political Choice and Judgment* (New York: John Wiley & Sons, 1977); Michael Feintuck, *The Public Interest in Regulation* (New York, NY: Basic Books, 2004).

29. E.g., Bradley S. Chilton and James A. Woods, "Moral Justifications on the Rehnquist Court: Hercules, Herbert, and Druggies under the Fourth Amendment," *Criminal Justice Policy Review* 17 (2006): 343–61.

30. David H. Rosenbloom and Robert S. Kravchuk, *Public Administration: Understanding Management, Politics, and Law in the Public Sector*, 6th ed. (Boston, MA: McGraw-Hill Company, 2005); Richard Green, "A Constitutional Jurisprudence: Reviving Praxis in Public Administration," *Administration and Society* 24, no. 1 (1992): 3–21; John Rohr, *To Run a Constitution: The Legitimacy of the Administrative State* (Lawrence, KS: University Press of Kansas, 1986); John Rohr, *Public Service, Ethics and Constitutional Practice* (Lawrence, KS: University Press of Kansas, 1999); Wamsley and Wolf, 1996; H. Jefferson Powell, *The Moral Tradition of American Constitutionalism: A Theological Interpretation* (Durham, NC: Duke University Press, 1993); Brian J. Cook, "The Representative Function of Bureaucracy: Public Administration in Constitutive Perspective," *Administration and Society* 23, no. 4 (1992): 403–29.

31. Don Tapscott and Anthony Williams, *Wikinomics: How Mass Collaboration Changes Everything* (New York: Portfolio/Penguin Publishers, 2008); Ellen Perlman and Melissa Maynard, "Working In Wiki," *Governing* (May 2008 cover article), available on-line at www.governing.com/articles/ 0805wiki.htm.

32. E.g., Cass Sunstein, *Republic.com* (Princeton, NJ: Princeton University Press, 2001).

33. E.g., Lawrence Lessig, *Code and Other Laws of Cyberspace, Version 2.0* (New York: Basic Books, 2007), also available on-line and in Wiki-versions; Andrew Shapiro, *The Control Revolution: How the Internet is Putting Individuals in charge and Changing the World* (New York: Public Affairs Press, 1999).

34. E.g., Tom L. Beauchamp, *Philosophical Ethics: An Introduction to Moral Philosophy* (New York: McGraw-Hill, 2001); Lee C. McDonald, "Three Forms of Political Ethics," *Western Political Quarterly* 31 (1978): 7–18.

35. John A. Rohr, *Public Service, Ethics and Constitutional Practice* (Lawrence, KS: University Press of Kansas, 1999); John A. Rohr, *Civil Servants and their Constitutions* (Lawrence, KS: University Press of Kansas, 2002).

36. Nicholas Jolley, *Locke: His Philosophical Thought* (Cambridge: Oxford University Press, 1999); Michael Ayers, *Locke: Epistemology and Ontology* (New York, NY: Routledge Press, 1994); Patrick Riley, *Will and Political Legitimacy: A Critical Exposition of Social Contract Theory in Hobbes, Locke, Rousseau, Kant, and Hegel* (Cambridge, MA: Harvard University Press, 1982).

37. William H. Riker, *The Theory of Political Coalitions* (New Haven, CN: Yale University Press, 1962).

38. E.g., Vincent Ostrom, *The Intellectual Crisis In Public Administration* (University, AL: University of Alabama Press, 1973).

39. Robert Putnam, *Bowling Alone: The Collapse and Revival of American Community* (New York, NY: Simon and Schuster, 2000).

40. Flathman, 1966. For an excellent discussion and defense of Flathman's "ordinary language philosophy," particularly as it applies to public administration and policy analysis, see Norton E. Long's "Conceptual Notes on the Public Interest for Public Administration and Policy Analysts," *Administration and Society* 22, no. 2 (August 1990): 170–81.

41. E.g., Charles W. Anderson, *Statecraft: An Introduction to Political Choice and Judgment* (New York: John Wiley & Sons, 1977): chapter 2, "Role and Responsibility"; Michael Feintuck, *The Public Interest in Regulation* (New York, NY: Basic Books, 2004).

42. Friederich Nietzsche, *The Will to Power,* ed. and trans. Walter Kaufman (New York, NY: Vintage Press, 1968).

43. "Analysis of Ordinary Language," http://www.philosophypages.com/hy/6u.htm. (Accessed November 26, 2008.)

44. Center for Advanced Research in Phenomenology. "What is Phenomenology?" http://www.phenomenologycenter.org/phenom.htm. (Accessed November 26, 2008.)

Chapter 2

1. David K. Hart, "Administration and the Ethics of Virtue: In All Things Choose First for Good Character and Then for Technical Expertise," in Terry L. Cooper, ed., *Handbook of Administrative Ethics,* 2nd ed. (New York: Marcel Dekker, 2000): 131–150.

2. Bradley S. Chilton and Lisa M. Chilton, "Rebuilding the Public Service: Research the Origins of Public Perceptions of the Public Service in Children's Literature," *Review of Public Personnel Administration* 12 (1993): 72–78.

3. Tom L. Beauchamp, *Philosophical Ethics: An Introduction to Moral Philosophy,* 3rd ed. (New York: McGraw-Hill, 2001): 150.

4. Terry L. Cooper, *An Ethic of Citizenship for Public Administration* (Englewood Cliffs, NJ: Prentice-Hall, 1991); Camilla Stivers, "Citizenship Ethics In Public Administration," in Terry L. Cooper, *Handbook of Administrative Ethics* (New York: Marcel Dekker, 2000): 583–602.

5. E.g., Richard T. Green, "Character Ethics and Public Administration," *International Journal of Public Administration* 17 (1994): 2137–2164; Larry Hubbell, "The Relevance of Heroic Myths to Public Servants," *American Review of Public Administration* 20 (1990): 139–154.

6. Michael C. Lemay, in *Public Administration: Clashing Values in the Administration of Public Policy* (Belmont, CA: Wadsworth, 2002), defines public administration as "Whatever governments do to develop and implement public policy" (p. 28); Nicholas Henry, in *Public Administration and Public Affairs,* 9th ed. (Upper Saddle River, NJ: Prentice-Hall, 2004), declares that public administration is a "... broad-ranging and amorphous combination of theory and practice; its purpose is to promote a superior understanding of government and its relationship with the society it governs, as well as to encourage public policies more responsive to social needs and to institute managerial practices attuned to effectiveness, efficiency, and the deeper human requisites of the citizenry" (p. 2); Richard Still-

man, II, in his text *The American Bureaucracy: The Core of Modern Government*, 3d ed. (Belmont, CA: Wadsworth, 2004), describes public bureaucracy as "The structure and personnel of organizations, rooted in formal laws and informal processes, that collectively function as the core system of U.S. government and that both determine and carry out public policies using a high degree of specialized expertise and technologies" (p. 3); Melvin J. Dubnick and Barbara S. Romzek, in their *American Public Administration: Politics and the Management of Expectations* (New York, NY: Macmillan, 1991), define public administration as the "Systematic examination and analysis of the institutions, agents, and processes used in government's efforts to manage the pursuit of publicly defined societal values" (p. 12); Jay M. Shafritz and E.W. Russell, in their text *Introducing Public Administration*, 2d ed. (Reading, MA: Addison Wesley Longman, Inc., 2000), provide eighteen different definitions of public administration, each one an iteration of their four primary values associated with public administration and affairs: political, managerial, legal, and occupation; George J. Gordon and Michael E. Milakovich, in their *Public Administration in America*, 6th ed. (New York, NY: St. Martin's Press, 1998), define public administration as "All processes, organizations, individuals … associated with carrying out laws and other rules adopted or issued by legislatures, executives, and courts" (p. 7); George Berkley and John Rouse, in *The Craft of Public Administration*, 6th ed. (Madison, WI: WCB Brown and Benchmark, 1984), define public administration as "The process of implementing those diverse values in our complex and ever changing society and therefore plays a vital role in the daily lives of all citizens" (p. 2); David H. Rosenbloom, in his *Understanding Management, Politics, and Law in the Public Sector*, 4th ed. (New York, NY: McGraw-Hill, 1998), describes public administration as "the use of managerial, political, and legal theories and processes to fulfill legislative, executive, and judicial governmental mandates for the provision of regulatory and service functions for the society as a whole or for some segments of it" (p. 6); Robert B. Denhardt, in his *Public Administration: An Action Orientation*, 3d ed. (Fort Worth, TX: Harcourt Brace, 1999), defines public administration as simply "the management of public programs;" Carl E. Lutrin and Allen K. Settle, in their text *American Public Administration: Concepts and Cases*, 3d ed. (Englewood Cliffs, NJ: Prentice-Hall, 1985), define public administration as "the study of people in organizations, of how these people interact within the organization, and of how the organization relates to the larger political environment, or to that part of the public domain that is primarily concerned with resolving public issues" (p. 19); David Schuman and Dick W. Olufs III, in their *Public Administration in the United States*, 2d ed. (Lexington, MA: D.C. Heath and Company, 1993), provides no definition; and William C. Johnson, in his *Public Administration: Policy, Politics, and Practice* (Guilford, CT: Dishkin Publishing, 1992), defines public administration as "… simply the activities of government that supply goods and services to the public" (p. 4).

7. John L. Anderson and Craig Curtis, "A Developmental Analysis of the Term "Management" and Its Role in Public Administration Thinking," *Administrative Theory & Praxis* 17, no. 2 (1995): 62–73.

8. Woodrow Wilson, "The Study of Administration," *Political Science Quarterly* 56, no. 4 (1887): 481–506.

9. Frank J. Goodnow, *Politics and Administration* (New York, NY: Macmillan, 1900).

10. Leonard D. White, *Introduction to the Study of Public Administration,* 4th ed. (New York, NY: Macmillan, 1955).

11. William F. Willoughby, *Principles of Public Administration* (Baltimore, MD: Johns Hopkins, 1927).

12. Luther H. Gulick and Lyndall F. Urwick, *Papers on the Science of Administration,* (New York, NY: Institute of Public Administration, 1937).

13. Daniel L. Dreisbach, "Founders Famous and Forgotten," *The Intercollegiate Review*, Vol. 42, No. 2 (Fall 2007), 6.

14. Lynton K. Caldwell, "Alexander Hamilton: Advocate of Executive Leadership," in *Administrative Questions and Political Answers*, ed. Claude E. Hawley and Ruth G. Weintraub (Princeton, NY: D. Van Nostrand, 1966).

15. Richard T. Green, "Alexander Hamilton: Founder of the American Public Administration," *Administration & Society* 34 (2002): 541–562; Richard T. Green, "Oracle at Weehawken: Alexander Hamilton and the Development of the Administrative State," doctoral dissertation, Virginia Polytechnic Institute & State University, Blacksburg, VA, 1987.

16. Leonard D. White, *The Jeffersonians: A Study in Administrative History, 1801–1829* (New York, NY: Macmillan, 1959).

17. Henry T. Edmondson, "Teaching Administrative Ethics with Help from Jefferson," *PS: Political Science and Politics* 28 (1995): 226–229; David K. Hart, "A Dream of What We Could Be: The Founding Values, the Oath, and *Homo virtutis americanus*," in Terry L. Cooper, ed., *Handbook of Administrative Ethics* (New York: Marcel Dekker, 2000): 207–225.

18. Leonard D. White, *The Jacksonians: A Study in Administrative History, 1829–1861* (New York, NY: Macmillan Company, 1954).

19. Paul Van Riper, "The American Administrative State: Wilson and the Founders," in *A Centennial History of the American Administrative State*, ed. Ralph C. Chandler (New York, NY: The Free Press, 1987), 13.

20. Ibid., 14.

21. Jeffrey S. Luke and David W. Hart, "Character and Conducting the Public Service: A Review of Historical Perspectives," in Terry L. Cooper, ed., *Handbook of Administrative Ethics,* 2nd ed. (New York: Marcel Dekker, 2000): 529–553.

22. David M. O'Brien, *Constitutional Law and Politics: Civil Rights and Civil Liberties,* 2d ed. (New York, NY: W.W. Norton, 1995).

23. Nicholas Henry, in *Public Administration and Public Affairs*, 9th ed. (Upper Saddle River, NJ: Prentice-Hall, 2004), 251–52.

24. Paul Van Riper, *History of the United States Civil Service* (Evanston, IL: Row, Peterson and Company, 1958), 110.

25. Frederick Mosher, *Democracy and the Public Service* (New York, NY: Oxford University Press, 1968); *see also,* Daniel P. Carpenter, *Forging of Bureaucratic Autonomy: Reputations, Networks,* and *Policy Innovation in Executive Agencies, 1862–1928* (Princeton, NJ: Princeton University Press, 2001).

26. Paul Van Riper, "The American Administrative State: Wilson and the Founders," in *A Centennial History of the American Administrative State*, ed. Ralph C. Chandler (New York, NY: The Free Press, 1987), 9.

27. Frederick Mosher, *Democracy and the Public Service* (New York, NY: Oxford University Press, 1968).

28. Jeffrey D. Greene, *Public Administration in the New Century: A Concise Introduction* (Belmont, CA: Thomson-Wadsworth, 2005), 51.

29. Ibid., 52.

30. Paul Van Riper, "The American Administrative State: Wilson and the Founders," in *A Centennial History of the American Administrative State*, ed. Ralph C. Chandler (New York, NY: The Free Press, 1987), 21.

31. Ibid., 17.

32. Jeffrey D. Greene, *Public Administration in the New Century: A Concise Introduction* (Belmont, CA: Thomson-Wadsworth, 2005), 53.

33. Nicholas Henry, in *Public Administration and Public Affairs*, 9th ed. (Upper Saddle River, NJ: Prentice-Hall, 2004), 32–33.

34. Ibid., 33.

35. Fritz Morstein Marx, ed., *Elements of Public Administration* (New York, NY: Prentice Hall, 1949).

36. Ibid., 34.

37. Chester I. Barnard, *Functions of the Executive*, 30th anniversary edition (Cambridge, MA: Harvard University Press, 1968), 10.

38. Gary S. Marshall, "Public Administration in a Time of Fractured Meaning: Beyond the Legacy of Herbert Simon," doctoral dissertation, Virginia Polytechnic Institute & State University, Blacksburg, VA, 1993.

39. Herbert Simon, *Models of My Life* (Cambridge, MA: MIT Press, 1996).

40. Jay M. Shafritz, Albert C. Hyde, and Sandra J. Parkes, *Classics of Public Administration* (Belmont, CA: Wadsworth, 2004), 136.

41. Herbert Simon, *Administrative Behavior: A Study of Decision Making Processes in Administrative Organization*, 3rd ed. (New York, NY: The Free Press, 1976 [org., 1947]).

42. Herbert Simon, *Models of My Life* (Cambridge, MA: MIT Press, 1996).

43. E.g., Herbert Simon, "Designing Organizations for an Information-Rich World," in Martin Greenberger, ed., *Computers, Communications, and the Public Interest* (Baltimore, MD: Johns Hopkins University Press, 1971): 37–72.

44. Jay M. Shafritz, Albert C. Hyde, and Sandra J. Parkes, *Classics of Public Administration* (Belmont, CA: Wadsworth, 2004), 38.

45. Peter F. Drucker, *Management: Tasks, Responsibilities, Practices* (New York, NY: HarperBusiness, originally published 1973; HarperBusiness edition published 1993).

46. Chris Argyris, *Organization and Innovation* (Homewood, IL: Richard D. Irwin Publishers, 1965); Robert R. Blake and Jane S. Mouton, *The Managerial Grid* (Houston, TX: Gulf Publishing, 1964); and Douglas McGregor, *The Human Side of Enterprise* (New York, NY: McGraw-Hill, 1960).

47. Frank Marini, ed., *Toward a New Public Administration: The Minnowbrook Perspective* (New York, NY: Chandler Publishing, 1971).

48. H. George Frederickson, *New Public Administration* (University, AL: University of Alabama Press, 1980).

49. Dvorin, E. & R. Simmons, From Amoral to Humane Bureaucracy (San Francisco, CA: , 1972).

50. Dvorin, E. & R. Simmons, From Amoral to Humane Bureaucracy (San Francisco, CA: , 1972).

51. James M. Buchanan, *Cost and Choice: An Inquiry in Economic Theory.* (Chicago, IL: Markaham, 1969); Vincent Ostrom and Elinor Ostrom, "Public Choice: A Different Approach to the Study of Public Administration," *Public Administration Review* 31 (1969): 203–216; and Gordon Tullock, *Private Wants, Public Means: An Economic Analysis of the Desirable Scope of Government* (New York, NY: Basic Books, 1970).

52. Anthony Downs, *Inside Bureaucracy* (Glenview, IL: Scott, Foresman and Company, 1967); Peter Drucker, *Concept of the Corporation*, rev. ed. (New York, NY: John Day, 1972); Aaron Wildavsky, *The New Politics of the Budgetary Process* (Glenview, IL: Scott, Foresman and Company, 1988).

53. Robert M. Backer, Charles T. Goodsell, John A. Rohr, Philip S. Kronenberg, and James F. Wolf. *Refounding Public Administration.* Sage Publications, 1990; and Gary Wamsley and James Wolf, eds., *Re-founding Democratic Public Administration: Modern Paradoxes, Postmodern Challenges* (Thousand Oaks, CA: Sage Publications, 1996).

54. Charles T. Goodsell, "Public Administration and the Public Interest," in Gary Wamsley, et al., *Refounding Public Administration* (Newbury Park, NJ: Sage Publications, 1990).

55. Philippa Foot, *Virtues and Vices* (Oxford, Eng.: Basil Blackwell, 1978): 12.

56. William E. Frankena, *Ethics*, 3rd ed. (Englewood Cliffs, NJ: Prentice-Hall, 1973): 65.

57. E.g., Richard Green, "Alexander Hamilton: Founder of the American Public Administration," *Administration & Society* 34 (2002): 541–562; Stephanie Newbold, "Statesmanship and Ethics: The Case of Thomas Jefferson's Dirty Hands," *Public Administration Review* 65 (2005): 669–677.

58. Ron Chernow, *Alexander Hamilton* (New York, NY: The Penguin Press, 2004): 716–720.

59. Lon Fuller, *The Morality of Law*, revised ed. (New Haven, CN: Yale University Press, 1969).

60. John Rawls, *A Theory of Justice* (Cambridge, MA: Harvard University Press, 1971): 443, 445.

61. E. S. Savas, *Privatization: The Key to Better Government* (New York, NY: Chandler Publishing, 1987).

62. David Osborne and Ted Gaebler, *Reinventing Government: How the Entrepreneurial Spirit is Transforming the Public Sector.* (Reading, MA: Addison-Wesley, 1992); David Osborne and Peter Plastrik, *Banishing of Bureaucracy: The Five Strategies for Reinventing Government* (Reading, MA: Addison-Wesley, 1997).

63. National Partnership for Reinventing Government, *Performance-Based Organizations* (Washington, DC: National Partnership for Reinventing Government, 1998).

64. Robert B. Denhardt and Joseph W. Grubbs, *Public Administration: An Action Orientation*, 4th ed. (Belmont, CA: Thomson-Wadsworth, 2004), 106.

65. Ibid., 46.

66. Lester M. Salamon, *The Resilient Sector: the State of Nonprofit America* (Washington, DC: Brookings Institution, 2003), 2.

67. Jeffrey M. Berry with David F. Arons, *A Voice for Nonprofits* (Washington, D.C: Brookings Institution, 2003), 6.

68. H. George Frederickson and Kevin B. Smith, *The Public Administration Theory Primer* (Boulder, CO: Westview, 2003), 168–170.

69. Harold C. Relyea and Henry B. Hogue, "A Brief History of the Emergence of Digital Government in the United States," in *Digital Government: Principles and Best Practices*, ed. Alexei Pavlichev and G. David Garson (Hershey, PA: Idea Group Publishing, 2004), 16–33.

70. G. David Garson, "The Promise of Digital Government" in *Digital Government: Principles and Best Practices*, ed. Alexei Pavlichev and G. David Garson (Hershey, PA: Idea Group Publishing, 2004), 2.

71. Jane E. Fountain, *Building the Virtual State: Information Technology and Institutional Change* (Washington, D.C.: Brookings Institution, 2001).

72. Mark A. Abramson and Therese L. Morin, *E-Government 2003* (Lanham, MA: Rowman and Littlefield, 2003); Gregory G. Curtain, Michael H. Sommer, and Veronika Vis-Sommer, eds., *The World of E-Government* (New York, NY: Haworth, 2003); and R. W. Greene, *Open Access: GIS in E-Government* (Redlands, CA: ESRI Press, 2001).

Chapter 3

1. Lon Fuller, "The Forms and Limits of Adjudication," *Harvard Law Review* 92 (1978): 1–33.

2. Robert H. Chaires and Bradley S. Chilton, ed.s, *Star Trek Visions of Law & Justice* (Dallas, TX: Adios Press/University of North Texas Press, 2003).

3. E.g., John Rohr, *Ethics For Bureaucrats: An Essay in Law and Values*, 2nd edition (New York: Marcel Dekker, 1989); Richard Green, "A Constitutional Jurisprudence: Reviving Praxis in Public Administration," *Administration and Society* 24, no. 1 (1992): 3–21; Yong Lee, David Rosenbloom, and Rosemary O'Leary, *A Reasonable Public Servant: Constitutional Foundations of Administrative Conduct in the United States* (M.E. Sharpe, 2005); David Rosenbloom and Robert Kravchuk, *Public Administration: Understanding Management, Politics, and Law in the Public Sector*, 6th ed. (Boston, MA: McGraw-Hill Company, 2005); Philip Cooper, *Public Law and Public Administration*, 4th ed. (St. Paul, MN: Wadsworth, 2006); NOTE: at the 2008 American Political Science Association meetings, the "Constitutional School of Public Administration" debuted as an ascendant approach to the study of public administration.

4. E.g., Walter F. Murphy, C. Herman Pritchett and Lee Epstein, *Courts, Judges, & Politics: An Introduction to the Judicial Process*, 5th ed. (Boston, MA: McGraw-Hill Company, 2002); Ronald Dworkin, *Taking Rights Seriously* (Cambridge, MA: Harvard University Press, 1978); Lief H. Carter and Thomas F. Burke, *Reason In Law*, 7th edition (New York: Longman's, 2004).

5. Charles W. Anderson, *Statecraft: An Introduction to Political Choice and Judgment* (New York: John Wiley & Sons, 1977): chapter 3, "Rights and Regulations" and chapter 4, "Freedom and Control".

6. Charlie D. Broad, *Five Types of Ethical Theory* (London: Routledge & Kegan, 1930): chapter 5; Tom L. Beauchamp, *Philosophical Ethics: An Introduction to Moral Philosophy*, 3rd ed. (New York: McGraw-Hill, 2001): 109.

7. Ralph Clark Chandler, "Deontological Dimensions of Administrative Ethics," in Terry L. Cooper, ed., *Handbook of Administrative Ethics*, 2nd ed. (New York: Marcel Dekker, 2000): 179–194.

8. E.g., Ronald Dworkin, *Freedom's Law: The Moral Reading of the American Constitution* (Cambridge, MA: Harvard University Press, 1996).

9. E.g., Richard A. Posner, *Economic Analysis of Law*, 7th edition (New York: Aspen Publishers, 2007); Francesco Parisi, ed., *The Economic Structure of Law: The Collected Economic Essays of Richard A. Posner*, 3 volumes (Northhampton, MA: Edward Elgar Publishing, Inc., 2001).

10. E.g., "Symposium: National Conference on Judicial Biography," *New York University Law Review* 70 (1995): 485; J. Woodward Howard, Jr, "Alpheus T. Mason and the Art of Judicial Biography," *Constitutional Commentary* 8 (1991): 41; Kimberlé Crenshaw, ed., *Critical Race Theory: The Key Writings that Formed the Movement* (New York: New Press, 1995); Richard Delgado, *Critical Race Theory: The Cutting Edge* (Philadelphia: Temple University Press, 1995); Colin Farrely and Lawrence B. Solum, ed.s, *Virtue Jurisprudence* (Hampshire, Eng.: Palgrave MacMillan, 2007).

11. David Schuman, *American Government: The Rules of the Game*, (New York: Random House, 1984), 1–33.

12. For various critiques of the case, both liberal and conservative, see Elizabeth A. Martin, "Informational Theory of the Legislative Veto," *Journal of Law, Economics, and Organization* 13, no. 2 (October 1997): 319–43; Louis Fisher, "Judicial Misjudgments About the Lawmaking process: The Legislative Veto Case," *Public Administration Review* 45 (November 1985): 705–11; John C. Fortier, "Executive Branch Overhaul Due," *Washington Times*, 11 February 2002, www.aei.org/include/pub_print.asp?pubID=13600 (accessed October 2007).

13. E.g., Larry Yackle, *Regulatory Rights: Supreme Court Activism, The Public Interest, and the Making of Constitutional Law* (Chicago: University of Chicago Press, 2007).

14. This 1972 interview comment is quoted in John Arthur, *The Unfinished Constitution: Philosophy and Constitutional Practice* (Belmont, CA: Wadsworth, 1989): 1.

15. Bradley Chilton, *Prisons Under the Gavel: The Federal Court Takeover of Georgia Prisons* (Columbus: Ohio State University Press, 1991).

16. Some of the more important "incorporation" cases in the first ten amendments are *Gitlow v. People of New York*, 268 U.S. 652 (1925) ["free speech" of the First Amendment], *Cantwell v. Connecticut*, 310 U.S. 296 (1940) ["religious freedom," specifically the Free Exercise clause of the First Amendment], *Everson v. Board of Education*, 330 U.S. 1 (1947) ["religious freedom," specifically the Establishment clause of the First Amendment], and *Powell v. Alabama*, 287 U.S. 45 (1932) ["right to counsel" in the Fifth Amendment].

17. A classic Judeo-Christian example of such "Natural Law" theories may be found in Russell Kirk, *The Roots of American Order* (Malibu, CA: Pepperdine University Press, 1974). An Islamic ex-

ample may be found in Noel J. Coulson, *Conflicts and Tensions in Islamic Jurisprudence* (Chicago: University of Chicago Press, 1969).

18. W.D. Ross, *The Right and the Good* (Oxford, Eng.: Clarendon Press, 1930).

19. *Draper v. Logan County Public Library,* 403 F. Supp. 2d, 608 (W.D.KY. 2003).

20. *McCreary County, Kentucky, et al. v. American Civil Liberties Union of Kentucky et al,* 545 U.S. 844 (2005).

21. *Charles River Bridge v. Warren Bridge* 36 U.S. 420 (1837) and *US v. Carolene Products Company,* 304 U.S. 144 (1938) [property rights in general]; *Heart of Atlanta Motel, Inc. v. US*, 379 U.S. 241 (1964) and *United States v. Morrison,* 529 U.S. 598 (2000) [commerce clause]; *United States v. Butler,* 297 U.S. 1 (1936) [taxing and spending clause]; *Home Building and Loan Assn. v. Blaisdell,* 290 U.S. 398 (1934) [contract clause]; *Lucas v. South Carolina Coastal Council* 505 U.S. 1003 (1992) and *Kelo et al. v. City of New London et al.,* 545 U.S. 469 (2005) [takings clause]; and *Lochner v. New York*, 198 U.S. 45 (1905) [substantive due process].

22. See Paul A. Freund, *The Supreme Court of the United States: Its Business, Purposes, and Performance* (Cleveland, OH: World, 1961); and Alpheus Mason and Donald Stephenson, *American Constitutional Law: Introductory Essays and Selected Cases*, 14th ed. (Englewood Cliffs, NJ: Prentice Hall, 2004).

23. See, for example, John Semonche, *Charting the Future: The Supreme Court Responds to a Changing Society, 1890–1920* (Westport, CN: Greenwood, 1978); and Loren Beth, *The Development of the American Constitution, 1877–1917* (New York: Harper and Row, 1971).

24. Carla T. Main, *Bulldozed: "Kelo," Eminent Domain, and the American Lust For Land* (New York: Encounter Books, 2007).

25. *McCulloch v. Maryland*, 17 U.S. 316 (1819).

26. *Rostker v. Goldberg*, 453 U.S. 57 affirmed a male-only draft, but in *United States v. Virginia*, 518 U.S. 515 (1996) the Court ruled that the Virginia Military Academy's (VMI) ban of female students, and the provision of a "comparable" institution called the Virginia Women's Institute for Leadership (VWIL), did not provide equal or comparable facilities and educational opportunities as did VMI, and thus ordered VMI to accept female students. And in *Craig v. Boren*, 429 U.S. 190 (1976) the Court upheld Oklahoma's drinking age laws that discriminated by allowing a lower drinking age for women.

27. Gloria J. Browne-Marshall, *Race, Law and American Society: 1607 to Present* (New York: Routledge, 2007); Timothy Davis, Kevin Johnson and George Martinez, *A Reader on Race, Civil Rights, and American Law: A Multiracial Approach* (Durham, NC: Carolina Academic Press, 2001).

28. Such was the lawsuit for wrongful death in *Tennessee v. Garner*, 471 U.S. 1 (1985), to penalize Memphis Police Department with monetary damages in their use of deadly force to apprehend a fleeing felon and death of a 15-year-old black youth.

29. Kenneth Culp Davis, *Administrative Law Text* (St. Paul, MN: West, 1972), 1; *see also*, Julia Beckett and Heidi Koenig, eds., *Public Administration and Law: An ASPA Classic* (Armonk, NY: M.E. Sharpe, 2005).

30. Lief H. Carter, *Administrative Law and Politics: Cases and Comments* (Boston, MA: Little, Brown, 1983), 34.

31. The "classic" case review and upholding the "public interest" standard is *Red Lion Broadcasting Co. v. FCC*, 395 U.S. 367 (1969).

32. Kenneth Culp Davis, *Administrative Law Text* (St. Paul, MN: West,1972).

33. Estes Kefauver and Jack Levin, *A Twentieth-Century Congress* (New York: Essential Books, 1947).

34. Robert LaFollette, "Congress Wins a Victory over Congress," *The New York Times Magazine* (August 1946): 4.

35. David H. Rosenbloom, "'Whose Bureaucracy Is This, Anyway?' Congress' 1946 Answer," *PS: Political Science and Politics* 34, no. 4 (December 2001): 773–77.

36. Joel Aberbach, *Keeping a Watchful Eye* (Washington, DC: Brookings Institution, 1990).

37. Harrison Fox and Susan Hammond, *Congressional Staffs* (New York: Free Press, 1977).

38. Stephen Bailey, *Congress Makes A Law: The Story Behind the Employment Act of 1946* (New York: Columbia University Press, 1950).

39. Charles Bullock, "House Careerists: Changing Patterns of Longevity and Attrition," *American Political Science Review* 66 (December 1972): 1295–1300; Morris Fiorina, *Congress: Keystone of the Washington Establishment*, 2d ed. (New Haven, CT: Yale University Press, 1989); John Hibbing, *Congressional Careers* (Chapel Hill: University of North Carolina Press, 1991).

40. David Rosenbloom, *Building A Legislative-Centered Public Administration: Congress and the Administrative State, 1946–1999* (Tuscaloosa: University of Alabama Press, 2000).

41. *United States Congressional Record: May 24, 1946* (Washington, DC: U.S. Government Printing Office, 1946), 5659.

42. Marshall Dimock, *Law and Dynamic Administration* (New York: Praeger, 1980); David H. Rosenbloom and Rosemary O'Leary, *Public Administration and Law,* 2d ed. (New York: Marcel Dekker, 1997).

43. *Administrative Procedure Act*, Section 706(2) (A).

Chapter 4

1. John Stuart Mill, *Utilitarianism* (London: Longmans, Green & Co., 1863): chapter 2.

2. Gerald M. Pops, "A Teleological Approach to Administrative Ethics," in Terry L. Cooper, ed., *Handbook of Administrative Ethics*, 2nd ed. (New York: Marcel Dekker, 2000), 195–206.

3. For an excellent historical discussion, see Sidney M. Milkis and Michael Nelson, *The American Presidency: Origins and Development, 1776–2002*, 4th ed. (Washington, DC: CQ Press, 2003).

4. *McCulloch v. Maryland*, 17 U.S. (4 Wheat.) 316 (1819).

5. Guy B. Adams and Danny L. Balfour, *Unmasking Administrative Evil*, revised ed. (Armonk, NY: M.E. Sharpe, 2004).

6. Malcolm M. Feeley and Edward L. Rubin, *Federalism: Political Identity and Tragic Compromise* (Ann Arbor: University of Michigan Press, 2008): preface, p 2.

7. E.g., Bradley S. Chilton, *Prisons Under the Gavel: The Federal Court Takeover of Georgia Prisons* (Columbus: Ohio State University Press, 1991).

8. Malcolm Feeley and Edward L. Rubin, *Judicial Policy Making and the Modern State* (New York: Cambridge University Press, 1999).

9. Malcolm M. Feeley and Edward L. Rubin, *Federalism: Political Identity and Tragic Compromise* (Ann Arbor: University of Michigan Press, 2008), 4.

10. For an excellent overview, even though it is dated, see Morton Grodzins, *American System: A New View of Government in the United States*, ed. Daniel J. Elazar (New Brunswick, NJ: Transaction Publishers, 1984). Also, for a chronological review of federalism and intergovernmental relations see Kala Ladenheim, "History of U.S. Federalism," University of South Carolina (1999), www.cas.sc.edu/poli/courses/scgov/History_of_Federalism.htm (accessed October 2007).

11. See Terry Sanford, *Storm over the States* (New York: McGraw-Hill, 1967); and Deil S. Wright, "Revenue Sharing and Structural Features of American Federalism," *Annals of the American Academy of Political Social Science* 49 (May 1975): 100–19.

12. Homes and Communities, U.S. Department of Housing and Urban Development, "Categorical Grants," www.hud.gov/offices/pih/centers/gmc/categorical/index.cfm (accessed October 2007).

13. Peter J. Ferrara, a former Reagan staff member, wrote an attack on revenue sharing. See Peter J. Ferrara, "For Revenue Sharing, Time Has Run Out," *Backgrounder*, no. 417 (13 March 1985), www.heritage.org/Research/Budget/bg417.cfm (accessed October 2007).

14. United States General Accounting Office, "Unfunded Mandates: Analysis of Reform Act Coverage" (Washington, D.C.: U.S. Government Printing Office, 2004), www.gao.gov/new.items/d04637.pdf (accessed October 2007).

15. David S. Broder, "Those Unfunded Mandates," *Washington Post* (3/16/2005): 42.

16. E.g., David Cohen, "What Ever Happened to (the Good Kind of) States' Rights?" *New York Times* (5/23/2008): 4.

17. Leonard D. White, *Introduction to the Study of Public Administration,* 4th ed. (New York, NY: MacMillan, 1955), 25.

18. David R. Berman, *Local Government and the States: Autonomy, Politics, and Policy* (Armonk, NY: ME Sharpe, 2003), 55.

19. John Locke Foundation, "Smart Growth," www.johnlocke.org/agenda2006/smartgrowth.html (accessed June 2007); and Samuel R. Staley, "Outsmarting Growth's Impacts in Virginia," *Virginia Viewpoint*, Virginia Institute of Public Policy, www.virginiainstitute.org/viewpoint/2002_8.html (accessed June 2007).

20. Dennis L. Dresang and James J. Gosling, *Politics and Policy in American States and Communities,* 5th ed. (New York: Pearson-Longman, 2006), 307, 308.

21. Beth Gazley and Jeffrey L. Brudney, "Volunteer Involvement in Local Government after September 11: The Continuing Question of Capacity," *Public Administration Review* 65, no. 2 (March/April 2005): 131–42.

22. Intercollegiate Studies Institute, *The Coming Crisis in Citizenship: Higher Education's Failure to Teach America's History and Institutions* (Wilmington, DE: Intercollegiate Studies Institute, 2006).

23. Terry Christensen and Tom Hogen-Esch, *Local Politics: A Practical Guide to Governing at the Grassroots*, 2d ed. (Armonk, NY: ME Sharpe Publishers, 2006), 216–217; and Rosalynn Silva, "Taking Pulse of Neighborhood Councils," *PA Times* (February 2007): 6.

24. Kevin B. Smith, Alan Greenblatt, and John Buntin, *Governing States and Localities* (Washington, D.C.: Congressional Quarterly Press, 2005), 300.

25. U.S. Federal, State, and Local Government Revenue, FY 1998, 2008. See www.usgovernmentrevenue.com/yearrev2008_0.html#usgs302. (Accessed November 27, 2008).

26. G. Alan Tarr, "Laboratories of Democracy? Brandeis, Federalism, and Scientific Management," *Publius* 31, no. 1 (Winter 2001): 38.

27. Smith, Greenblatt, and Buntin, 20, 21.

28. Ibid., 316–18. See also Richard J. Stillman II, *Creating the American State: The Moral Reformers and the Modern Administrative World They Made* (Tuscaloosa, AL: University of Alabama Press, 1998).

29. Stillman, 1998.

30. Berman, 62.

31. Christensen and Hogen-Esch, 126–27. See also Dennis R. Judd and Todd Swanstrom, *City Politics: Private Power and Public Policy*, 4th ed. (New York: Pearson-Longman, 2004), 70–74.

32. White, 175.

33. James W. Fesler, and Donald F. Kettl, *The Politics of the Administrative Process* (Chatham, NJ: Chatham House, 1991), 101.

34. For a thorough overview of state executive reorganization, especially looking at empirical data that supports their efforts, see James l. Garnett and Charles H. Levine's "State Executive Branch Reorganization," *Administration and Society* 12, no. 3 (1980): 227–76. For a trend-based review of state executive see Stanley B. Botner's, "Recent Trends in State Executive Reorganization in the Midwest," *The American Review of Public Administration* 7, no. 1 (1973): 25–26.

35. Thomas R. Dye and Susan A. MacManus, *Politics in States and Communities*, 12th ed. (Upper Saddle River, NJ: Pearson-Prentice Hall, 2006), 68.

36. Ann O'M Bowman and Richard C. Kearney, *State and Local Government*, 6th ed. (Boston, MA: Houghton Mifflin, 2005), 4.

37. E.g., Bradley Chilton and David Nice, "Triggering Federal Court Intervention in State Prison Reform," *The Prison Journal* 73 (1993): 30–45.

38. For an excellent historical and functional overview of counties, go to the National Association of Counties (www.naco.org) website.

39. Bowman and Kearney, 279.

40. *City of Clinton v. Cedar Rapids and Missouri River Railroad Co.*, 24 Iowa 455 (IA, 1868).

41. *Dillion's Rule: Good or Bad for Local Governments?* by Sally Ormsby, chair, (Fairfax County, VA: League of Women Voters of the Fairfax Area Education Fund, 2004), S-1. www.lwv-fairfax.org/LWV-Dillion-DTP-99041.pdf (accessed April 2007).

42. *Dillion's Rule*, S-4.

43. John J. Harrigan and David C. Nice, *Politics and Policy in States and Communities*, 9th ed. (New York: Pearson-Longman, 2006), 129–33.

44. Dye and MacManus, 461.

45. Harrigan and Nice, 125; see also Bowman and Kearney, 275.

46. See David H. Rosenbloom and Robert S. Kravchuk, *Public Administration: Understanding Management, Politics, and Law in the Public Sector*, 6th ed. (Boston: McGraw-Hill, 2005), 89–90; Dye and MacManus, 51.

47. North Carolina State Constitution, http://www.ncga.state.nc.us/Legislation/constitution/nc-constitution_whole.html (accessed October 2007).

48. David C. Saffell and Harry Basehart, *State and Local Government: Politics and Public Policies*, 8th ed. (New York: McGraw-Hill, 2005), 325–26.

49. For a good case study account of the development and planning of Chicago's public housing in the late 1940s and 1950s, read Martin Meyerson and Edward C. Banfield, *Politics, Planning, and the Public Interest* (New York: The Free Press, 1955).

50. Judd and Swanstrom, 268, 272, 277.

51. Saffell and Basehart, 312, 314.

52. Dye and McManus, 483.

53. Saffell and Basehart, 314, 315; Smith, Greenblatt, and Buntin, 356.

54. Zach Patton, "Back on Track: Sprawling Sun Belt Cities Discover a New Way to Grow." *Governing* (June 2007): 32–38.

55. Randal O'Toole, "The Planning Penalty: How Smart Growth Makes Housing Unaffordable," Public Interest Institute, *Policy Study No. 06-02* (March 2006), 1–48; "The Folly of 'Smart Growth,'" *Regulation* (Fall 2001): 20–25; Robert H. Nelson, "If At First You Don't Succeed, Rename Your Program," *Virginia Viewpoint*, no. 2002-5 (February 2002), www.virginiainstitute.org/viewpoint/2002_5.html (accessed October 2007).

56. David Osborne and Peter Hutchinson, *The Price of Government: Getting the Results We Need in an Age of Permanent Fiscal Crisis*, (New York: Basic Books, 2004), 203.

57. James K. Scott, "'E' the People: Do U.S. Municipal Government Web Sites Support Public Involvement?", *Public Administration Review* (May/June 2006): 349.

58. Henry, 164–65.

59. Jane E. Fountain, *Building the Virtual State: Information Technology and Institutional Change* (Washington, DC: Brookings Institution Press, 2001).

60. Robert B. Denhardt and Joseph W. Grubbs, *Public Administration: An Action Orientation*, 4th ed. (Belmont, CA: Thomson-Wadsworth, 2003) 435.

61. E.g., City of Oklahoma City, *Alfred P. Murrah Federal Building Bombing, April 19, 1995: Final Report* (Stillwater, OK: Fire Protection Publications, Oklahoma State University, 1996); Clive Irving, *In Their Name: Oklahoma City: The Official Commemorative Volume* (New York: Random House, 1995). More in-depth detail on the plot, actors, and first hand accounts, including rescue and government agencies involvement can be found in Edward T. Linenthal's *The Unfinished Bombing: Oklahoma City in American Memory* (New York: Oxford University Press, 2001). For an up-close look at the investigation of Timothy McVeigh and other perpetrators see Richard A. Serrano's *One of Ours: Timothy McVeigh and the Oklahoma City Bombing* (New York: W.W. Norton, 1998).

62. For a brief overview of the details of the coordinated attacks on the Twin Towers, the Pentagon, and crash of Flight 93 in western Pennsylvania see National Commission on Terrorist Attacks Upon the United States, *The 9/11 Commission Report*. (New York, NY: W.W. Norton, 2004).

63. For a critical review of Rudy Giuliani's mayoral leadership read Wayne Barrett and Dan Collins' *Grand Illusion: The Untold Story of Rudy Giuliani and 9/11* (New York: Harper Collins, 2006).

64. Ibid.

65. Jonathan Walters and Donald Kettl, "The Katrina Breakdown," *Governing* (December 2005): 20–22.

66. Saundra K. Schneider, "Administrative Breakdown in the Governmental Response to Hurricane Katrina," Special Report, *Public Administration Review* 65, no. 5 (September/October 2005): 515–16.

67. Walters and Kettl, 22.

68. For a critique of the inter-related roles of local, state, and federal governments in a disaster situation, such as Katrina, see Donald F. Kettl, *The States and Homeland Security: Building the Missing Link* (New York: Century Foundation, 2003); and Anne M. Khademian, "Strengthening State and Local Terrorism Prevention and Response," The Century Foundation, http://www.tcf.org/Publications/HomelandSecurity/4.stateandlocal.pdf (accessed October 2007).

69. Donald F. Kettl, "The Worst is yet to Come: Lessons from September 11 and Hurricane Katrina," *Fels Government Research Service Report 05-01* (Philadelphia: Penn Arts and Sciences, Fels Institute of Government, 2005): 1–17.

Chapter 5

1. Victor A. Thompson, *Modern Organization* (New York: Knopf, 1961).

2. Chester I. Barnard, *Functions of the Executive,* 30th anniversary edition (Cambridge, MA: Harvard University Press, 1968).

3. Harold F. Gortner, Julianne Mahler, and Jeanne Bell Nicholson, *Organization Theory: A Public Perspective,* 2d ed. (Fort Worth, TX: Harcourt Brace, 1997), 2.

4. See Robert C. Ford, Barry R. Armandi, and Cherrill P. Heaton, *Organization Theory: An Integrative Approach* (New York: Harper and Row, 1988), 3.

5. Ibid., 19.

6. Gortner, Mahler, and Nicholson, 5.

7. The discussion of organization theory history is drawn from Jay M. Shafritz and J. Steven Ott, *Classics of Organization Theory,* 5th ed. (Belmont, CA: Wadsworth, 2001), 8–9; Robert C. Ford, Barry R. Armandi, and Cherrill P. Heaton, *Organization Theory: An Integrative Approach* (New York: Harper

and Row, 1988); M. Judd Harmon, *Political Thought: From Plato to the Present* (New York: McGraw-Hill, 1964); and Michael L. Vasu, Debra W. Stewart, and G. David Garson, *Organizational Behavior and Public Management,* 3d ed. (New York: Marcel Dekker, 1998), 27–30.

8. W. Richard Scott, *Organizations: Rational, Natural, and Open Systems*, 5th ed. (Upper Saddle River, NJ: Prentice-Hall, 2003), 4–5.

9. See Mary Jo Hatch, *Organization Theory: Modern, Symbolic, and Postmodern Perspectives* (New York: Oxford University Press, 1997), 22, 23.

10. Ibid., 25–26.

11. Gortner, Mahler, and Nicholson, 7.

12. Scott, 9, 10.

13. Gortner, Mahler, and Nicholson, 9, 10.

14. See Adam Smith, *An Inquiry into the Nature and Causes of the Wealth of Nations* (New York: Random House, 1937).

15. The discussion of Marx is drawn from two sources, including Michael Novak, *The Spirit of Democratic Capitalism* (Lanham, MA: Madison Books, 1991); and Hatch, 28–29.

16. See H.H. Gerth and C. Wright Mills, *From Max Weber: Essays in Sociology* (New York: Oxford University Press, 1946); and Max Weber, *The Theory of Social and Economic Organization* (New York: The Free Press, 1947).

17. See Nicholas Henry, *Public Administration and Public Affairs*, 9th ed. (Upper Saddle River, NJ: Pearson-Longman, 2004), 58.

18. David H. Rosenbloom, and Deborah D. Rosenbloom, *Public Administration: Understanding Management, Politics, and Law in the Public Sector*, 4th ed. (New York: McGraw-Hill, 1998), 148.

19. George J. Gordon and Michael E. Milakovich, *Public Administration in America,* 6th ed. (New York: St. Martin's Press, 1998), 121.

20. See Frederick W. Taylor, "Scientific Management," in *Classics of Public Administration,* 5th ed., ed. Jay M. Shafritz, Albert C. Hyde, and Sandra J. Parkes (Belmont, CA: Thomson-Wadsworth, 2004), 43–46. For a more complete description of Taylor's ideas see Frederick W. Taylor, *Principles of Scientific Management* (New York: Norton, 1911).

21. See Frank G. Gilbreth, *Primer of Scientific Management* (New York: Van Nostrand, 1912).

22. Henry, 61.

23. See "Biographical Note," Pennsylvania State University Library, www.libraries.psu.edu/speccolls/FindingAids/emerson4.html (accessed October 2007). For a more complete description of Emerson see Harrington Emerson Papers, 1848–1931, Accession 1964-0002H, Historical Collections and Labor Archives, Special Collections Library, University Libraries, Pennsylvania State University.

24. Scott, 41–43.

25. See Henri Fayol, *General and Industrial Management* (London: Pittman, 1949).

26. Hatch, 32.

27. James D. Mooney and Alan C. Reiley, *The Principles of Organization* (New York: Harper and Row, 1939).

28. Ford, Armandi, and Heaton, 33.

29. Leonard D. White, *Introduction to the Study of Public Administration*, 5th ed. (New York: MacMillan, 1955).

30. See Woodrow Wilson, "The Study of Administration," in *Classics of Public Administration*, 5th ed., ed. Jay M. Shafritz, Albert C. Hyde, and Sandra J. Parkes (Belmont, CA: Thomson-Wadsworth, 2004), 22–35.

31. See Luther Gulick, "Notes on the Theory of Organization," in *Classics of Public Administration*, 5th ed., ed. Jay M. Shafritz, Albert C. Hyde, and Sandra J. Parkes (Belmont, CA: Thomson-Wadsworth, 2004), 90–98. For a fuller discussion see Luther Gulick and L. Urwick, *Papers on the Science of Administration* (New York: Institute of Public Administration, 1937).

32. Vasu, Stewart, and Garson, 34.

33. Ibid., 35.

34. Ibid., 138.

35. H. George Frederickson and Kevin B. Smith, *The Public Administration Theory Primer* (Boulder, CO: Westview, 2003), 46.

36. Ibid., 48–65.

37. Henry, 63.

38. Michael C. LeMay, *Public Administration: Clashing Values in the Administration of Public Policy* (Belmont, CA: Thomson-Wadsworth, 2004), 119.

39. Barnard.

40. Vasu, Stewart, and Garson, 39.

41. LeMay, 119.

42. Vasu, Stewart, and Garson, 39.

43. LeMay, 126.

44. Ibid., 126.

45. Ibid., 122.

46. Douglas McGregor, *The Human Side of Enterprise* (New York: McGraw-Hill, 1960).

47. Vasu, Stewart, and Garson, 44.

48. LeMay, 122.

49. Ibid., 127.

50. David Easton, *The Political System: An Inquiry into the State of Political Science* (New York: Alfred A. Knopf, 1953).

51. See LeMay, 128; Daniel Katz and Robert L. Kahn, *The Social Psychology of Organizations,* 2d ed. (New York: John Wiley and Sons, 1978).

52. Vasu, Stewart, and Garson, 46, 47.

53. Henry, 66–67.

54. Wendell L. French and Cecil H. Bell, Jr., *Organization Development: Behavioral Science Interventions for Organization Improvement* (Englewood Cliffs, NJ: Prentice-Hall, 1973).

55. "Organizational Learning," SFB 504 Glossary, http://www.sfb504.uni-mannheim.de/glossary/orglearn.htm (accessed October 2007); and Robert B. Denhardt, *Theories of Public Organization,* 4th ed. (Belmont, CA: Wadsworth Publishing, 2004), 94–97, 193–95.

56. Frederickson and Smith, 175.

57. Mark K. Smith, "Donald Schon: Learning, Reflection, and Change," *Encyclopedia of Informal Education* (2001), http://www.infed.org/thinkers/et-schon.htm (accessed October 2007).

58. Mark K. Smith, "Peter Senge and the Learning Organization," *Encyclopedia of Informal Education* (2001), www.infed.org/thinkers/senge.htm (accessed October 2007).

59. Hal G. Rainey, *Managing Public Organizations,* 3d ed. (San Francisco: Jossey-Bass, 2003), 62.

60. Robert A. Dahl and Charles E. Lindblom, *Politics, Economics, and Welfare* (Chicago: University of Chicago Press, 1953; reprint, 1976).

61. Rainey, 63.

62. Dahl and Lindblom.

63. Rainey, 65.

64. The following discussion of the Greek words for "public" and their interpretation is taken from H. George Frederickson, *The Spirit of Public Administration* (San Francisco: Jossey-Bass, 1997), 20.

65. Ibid., 22. Frederickson also cites W.A.R. Leys, *Ethics for Policy Decisions* (New York: Prentice Hall, 1952), 13–32.

66. Frederickson, 22.

67. Wal-Mart Stores, "Community," http://walmartstores.com/GlobalWMStoresWeb/navigate.do?catg=216 (accessed October 2005).

68. AES Corporation, http://www.aes.com (accessed October 2005).

Chapter 6

1. Janet V. Denhardt and Robert B. Denhardt, *The New Public Service: Serving, Not Steering* (Armonk, NY: M.E. Sharpe, 2003), 4.

2. George G. Gordon and Michael E. Milakovich, *Public Administration in America,* 6th ed. (New York: St. Martins Press, 1998), 8.

3. Ibid., 8.

4. David H. Rosenbloom, *Public Administration: Understanding Management, Politics, and Law in the Public Sector,* 4th ed. (New York: McGraw-Hill, 1998), 6.

5. Donald J. Savoie, "What is Wrong with the New Public Management?", *Canadian Public Administration* 38, no. 11 (1995): 112–21.

6. Rosenbloom, 16, 20, 27, 33.

7. Donald F. Kettl and H. Brinton Milward, eds., *The State of Public Management* (Baltimore, MD: Johns Hopkins University Press, 1996), 10.

8. Grover Starling, *Managing the Public Sector,* 5th ed. (Fort Worth, TX: Harcourt Brace, 1998), 23.

9. Starling, 23.

10. Hal G. Rainey, *Understanding and Managing Public Organizations*, 3d ed. (San Francisco, CA: Jossey-Bass, 2003), 8–9.

11. Denhardt and Denhardt, 3–4.

12. Ibid., 6, 7.

13. Ibid., 13.

14. David Osborne and Ted Gaebler, *Reinventing Government: How the Entrepreneurial Spirit is Transforming the Public Sector* (Reading, MA: Addison-Wesley, 1992).

15. David Osborne and Peter Plastrik, *Banishing Bureaucracy* (Reading, MA: Addison-Wesley, 1997).

16. Donald F. Kettl, *Reinventing Government: A Fifth-Year Report Card* (Washington, DC: Brookings Institute, 1998); and Donald F. Kettl, "The Transformation of Governance," *Public Administration Review* 60, no. 6 (2000): 488–97.

17. An adequate description NPM is presented in Christopher Hood, "A Public Management for All Seasons?" *Public Administration* 69 (Spring 1991), 3–19. See also Michael Barzelay, *The New Public Management: Improving Research and Policy Dialogue* (Berkeley, CA: University of California Press, 2001); and Michael Barzelay, *Breaking Through Bureaucracy: A New Vision for Managing in Government* (Berkeley, CA: University of California Press, 1992).

18. Robert D. Behn, "The New Public Management Paradigm and the Search for Democratic Accountability," *International Public Management Journal* 1, no. 2 (1998): 131–64.

19. Osborne and Gaebler, xxii.

20. Beryl A. Radin, *Challenging the Performance Movement: Accountability, Complexity and Democratic Values* (Washington, DC: Georgetown University Press, 2006), 7.

21. Robert B. Denhardt and Joseph W. Grubbs, *Public Administration: An Action Orientation*, 4th ed. (Belmont, CA: Wadsworth, 2003), 256–57.

22. Denhardt and Grubbs, 259. These are identified with Denhardt and Grubbs; however, these particular steps are generally representative of the basic steps for most strategic plans.

23. City of Vancouver, "Strategic Plan: The Importance of Strategic Planning," City of Vancouver, WA, http://www.cityofvancouver.us/StrategicPlan.asp?menuid=10462&submenuid=10480&itemID=11418 (accessed October 2007).

24. Pat Dusenbury, "Governing for Results and Accountability," no. 4 in the series *Strategic Planning and Performance Measurement*, Urban Institute, www.urban.org/url.cfm?ID=310259 (accessed October 2007).

25. Ibid.

26. Performance Measurement Team, Department of Management and Budget, Fairfax County, VA, "A Manual for Performance Measurement: Fairfax County Measures Up," 11th ed. (2007), 11.

27. Ibid., 4.

28. Citizen-Driven Government Performance, "A Brief Guide for Performance Measurement: Local Government," National Center for Public Productivity, http://andromeda.rutgers.edu/~ncpp/cdgp/teaching/brief-manual.html (accessed October 2007).

29. Division of Planning, Department of Administration, RI, www.planning.ri.gov/ (accessed October 2007).

30. School of Government, "North Carolina Benchmarking Project," University of North Carolina, www.iog.unc.edu/programs/perfmeas/index.html (accessed October 2007). For a more detailed overview of the benchmarking project, specifically when compared to other benchmarking projects, see Charles Coe, "Local Government Benchmarking: Lessons from Two Major Multigovernment Efforts," *Public Administration Review* 59, no. 2 (March/April 1999): 110–15.

31. Dusenbury, "Minnesota Pollution Control Agency."

32. Charlie Tyer and Jennifer Willand, "Public Budgeting in America: A Twentieth Century Retrospective," *Journal of Public Budgeting, Accounting and Financial Management* 9, no. 2 (Summer 1997): www.ipspr.sc.edu/publication/Budgeting_in_America.htm (accessed October 2007).

33. Robert J. O'Neill, Jr., "Moving from Performance Measurement to Performance Management," *Public Management* 88, no. 3 (April 2006): 29–30.

34. For a thin slice of the literature, see Mark Abramson, Jonathan Breul, and John Kamensky, "Six Trends Transforming Government," *Public Manager* 36, no. 1 (Spring 2007): 3–11; Theodore H. Poister and Gregory Streib, "Elements of Strategic Planning and Management in Municipal Government: Status after Two Decades," *Public Administration Review* 65, no. 1 (January/February 2005): 45–56; and Philip Kotler and Nancy R. Lee, "Marketing in the Public Sector: The Final Frontier," *Public Manager* 36, no. 1 (Spring 2007): 12–17.

35. Donald P. Moynihan, "Managing for Results in State Government: Evaluating a Decade of Reform," *Public Administration Review* 66, no. 1 (January/February 2006): 77–89.

36. Ronald Simeone, John Carnevale, and Annie Millar, "A Systems Approach to Performance-Based Management: The National Drug Control Strategy," *Public Administration Review* 65, no. 2 (March/April 2005): 191–202.

37. E.g., Willa A. Bruce, "Ethical People Are Productive People," *Public Productivity and Management Review* 17 (1994): 241–252.

38. Ethics Resource Center, "Performance Reviews Often Skip Ethics, HR Professionals Say," available on-line at http://ethics.org/about-erc/press-releases.asp?aid-1150 (accessed June 2008).

39. H. George Frederickson, "Comparing the Reinventing Government Movement with the New Public Administration," *Public Administration Review* 56, no. 3 (May/June 1996): 263–70.

40. Suzanne J. Piotrowski and David H. Rosenbloom, "Nonmission-Based Values in Results-Oriented Public Management: The Case of Freedom of Information," *Public Administration Review* 62, no. 6 (November/December 2002): 643–57.

41. See especially Beryl A. Radin, "The Government Performance and Results Act (GPRA): Hydra-Headed Monster or Flexible Management Tool?" *Public Administration Review* 58, no. 4 (July/August 1998): 307–16; and her book *Challenging the Performance Movement: Accountability, Complexity and Democratic Values* (Washington, DC: Georgetown University Press, 2006).

42. Vincent Ostrom and Elinor Ostrom, "Public Choice: A Different Approach to the Study of Public Administration," *Public Administration Review* 31 (March/April 1971): 203–16; and Laurence E. Lynn, *Public Management as Art, Science, and Profession* (Chatham, NJ: Chatham House, 1996).

43. Christopher Pollitt, *Managerialism and the Public Service*, 2d ed. (Cambridge, UK: Basil Blackwell, 1993); and Larry D. Terry, "Administrative Leadership, Neo-Managerialism, and the Public Management Movement," *Public Administration Review* 58, no. 3 (1998): 194–200; and Christopher Hood, "The 'New Public Management' in the 1980s: Variations on a Theme," *Accounting Organizations and Society* 20, no. 2/3 (1995): 93–104.

44. See Denhardt and Denhardt, 22, 23; literature critical of NPM.

45. Osborne and Gaebler highlighted ten characteristics. For closer examination of each see their book, or read Denhardt and Denhardt's summary on pp. 16–19.

46. Denhardt and Denhardt, 24. Robert Denhardt and Janet Denhardt, "The New Public Service: Serving Rather than Steering," *Public Administration Review* 60, no. 6 (2000): 549–59.

47. Dwight Waldo, *The Administrative State* (New York: John Wiley and Sons, 1948); and Robert A. Dahl, "The Science of Public Administration," *Public Administration Review* 7 (Winter 1947): 1–11; and Robert A. Dahl, *A Preface to Democratic Theory* (Chicago: University of Chicago Press, 1956).

48. Herbert A. Simon, *Administrative Behavior*, 2d ed. (New York: The Free Press, 1957).

49. See Hood, "Public Management for All Seasons?", 1991.

50. Michael Sandel, *Democracy's Discontent* (Cambridge, MA: Belknap, 1996).

51. John Nalbandian, "Facilitating Community, Enabling Democracy: New Roles for Local Government Managers," *Public Administration Review* 59, no. 3 (1999): 187–97.

52. Denhardt and Denhardt, 2003, 32, 33.

53. Hillary Rodham Clinton, *It Takes a Village to Raise a Child* (New York: Simon and Schuster, 1996).

54. Marva Mitchell, *It Takes a Church to Raise a Village* (Orlando, FL: Destiny Image Publishers, 2001).

55. Richard John Neuhaus, *America against Itself* (Notre Dame, IN: University of Notre Dame Press, 1992).

56. Robert Putnam, *Bowling Alone* (New York: Simon and Schuster, 2000).

57. Nalbandian.

58. Rainey, 32.

59. Rainey, 36, 37.

60. Ibid., 38, 39.

61. H. George Frederickson, *The New Public Administration* (Tuscaloosa, AL: University of Alabama Press, 1980); and Robert B. Denhardt, *In the Shadow of Organization* (Lawrence, KS: Regents Press of Kansas, 1981).

62. Denhardt and Denhardt, *New Public Service*, cite O.C. McSwite, *Legitimacy in Public Administration* (Thousand Oaks, CA: Sage, 1997), 41.

63. Ibid., 42.

64. Ibid., 42.

65. Elmer B. Staats, "Public Service and the Public Interest," *Public Administration Review* 48, no. 2 (March/April 1988): 605.

66. Osborne and Gaebler, 169.
67. Denhardt and Denhardt, *New Public Service*, 61.
68. Although a variation of Denhardt and Denhardt's approach to articulation and application of the NPS, Patricia Ingraham and David Rosenbloom's overview of the macro developments in public personnel policy since 1968 warrant attention. See Patricia Wallace Ingraham and David H. Rosenbloom, "The New Public Personnel and the New Public Service." *Public Administration Review* 48, no. 2(March/April 1989): 116–125.
69. Ibid., 78.
70. Denhardt and Denhardt, *New Public Service*, 86.
71. For an excellent discussion of governance in the 21st century see Donald Kettl, *Transformation of Governance in the 21st Century* (Baltimore, MD: Johns Hopkins University Press, 2002).
72. Denhardt and Denhardt, *New Public Service*, 88.
73. Ibid., 103.
74. Stephen Coleman, "The Network-empowered Citizen: How People Share Civic Knowledge Online," Institute for Public Policy Research, http://www.ippr.org.uk/uploadedFiles/research/projects/Digital_Society/the_networkempowered_citizen_coleman.pdf (accessed October 2007).
75. Douglas Holmes, *e.gov: e-business Strategies for Government* (London: Nicholas Brealey, 2001), 274, 285.
76. Ibid., 144.
77. Behn, 142.
78. Ibid., 142, 144, 145, 146.
79. Ibid., 131.
80. Ibid., 145.
81. Ibid., 146.
82. Raymond W. Cox III, "The Profession of Local Government Manager: Evolution and Leadership Styles," in *The Effective Local Government Manager*, 3d ed., ed. Charldean Newell (Washington, DC: International City/County Management Association, 2004), 12.
83. Denhardt and Denhardt draw upon two primary sources. See John Bryson and Barbara Crosby, *Leadership for the Common Good* (San Francisco: CA: Jossey-Bass, 1992); and Jeffrey Luke, *Catalytic Leadership* (San Francisco, CA: Jossey-Bass, 1998).
84. Denhardt and Denhardt, *New Public Service*, 164. For the value of trust see David G. Carnevale, *Trustworthy Government: Leadership and Management Strategies for Building Trust and High Performance* (San Francisco, CA: Jossey-Bass, 1995).
85. Denhardt and Denhardt, *New Public Service*, 166.
86. E.g., Malcolm Gladwell. *Outliers: The Story of Success* (Boston: Little, Brown & Co., 2008).
87. Bennis and Nanus, 21.
88. Ibid., 23.
89. Rainey, 302.
90. Mintzberg is cited in Michael L. Vasu, Debra W. Stewart, and G. David Garson, Organizational Behavior and Public Management, 3d ed. (New York: Marcel Dekker, 1998), 92.
91. Robert A. Dahl and Charles E. Lindblom, *Politics, Economics, and Welfare* (New York: Harper-Collins, 1953); Gary Wamsley and M. N. Zald, *The Political Economy of Public Organizations* (Lexington, MA: Heath, 1973); and Barry Bozeman, *All Organizations are Public: Bridging Public and Private Organizational Theories* (San Francisco, CA: Jossey-Bass, 1987).

Chapter 7

1. N. Joseph Cayer, *Public Personnel Administration*, 4th ed. (Belmont, CA: Thomson-Wadsworth, 2004): 17–41; Grover Starling, *Managing the Public Sector*, 7th ed. (Belmont, CA: Thomson-Wadsworth, 2005), 454–63; Nicholas Henry, *Public Administration and Public Affairs*, 9th ed. (Upper Saddle River, NJ: Prentice-Hall, 2004), 250–55; and George J. Gordon and Michael E. Milakovich, *Public Administration in America*, 6th ed. (New York: St. Martin's Press, 1998), 254–58.
2. Frederick Mosher, *Democracy and the Public Service* (Cambridge: Oxford University Press, 1968), 53–98.
3. According to Henry, Starling attributes the first five periods to Mosher, and the sixth period to Dennis L. Dresang, *Public Personnel Management and Public Policy* (New York: Addison Wesley

Longman, 2003). See Grover Starling, *Managing the Public Sector*, 7th ed. (Belmont, CA: Thomson-Wadsworth, 2005), 458–59. The seventh phase is attributable to Henry.

4. See Leonard D. White, *The Federalists: A Study in Administrative History* (New York: MacMillan, 1956), 517–18.

5. Ibid., 3.

6. Ibid., 29. See also Leonard D. White, *The Jeffersonians: A Study in Administrative History: 1801–1829* (New York: MacMillan, 1959), 5.

7. Henry, 251.

8. Leonard D. White, *The Jacksonians: A Study in Administrative History* (New York: MacMillan, 1954), 5.

9. Ibid., 310.

10. Leonard D. White, *The Republican Era: A Study in Administrative History, 1869–1901* (New York: The Free Press, 1958), 6.

11. White, *The Republican Era*, 8–14.

12. Ibid., 297.

13. See Richard J. Stillman II, *Creating the American State: The Moral Reformers and the Modern Administrative World They Made* (Tuscaloosa, AL: The University of Alabama Press, 1998).

14. David H. Rosenbloom and Robert S. Kravchuk, *Public Administration: Understanding Management, Politics, and Law in the Public Sector*, 6th ed. (Boston: McGraw-Hill, 2005), 209–10.

15. See Starling, 461.

16. Henry, 254.

17. Ibid.

18. Robert B. Denhardt and Joseph W. Grubbs, *Public Administration: An Action Orientation*, 4th ed. (Belmont, CA: Wadsworth, 2003), 213.

19. Henry, 255.

20. Alan K. Campbell, "Civil Service Reform: A New Commitment," *Public Administration Review* 38, no. 2 (March/April 1978): 99–103.

21. The major changes included 1) creation of the **Office of Personnel Management** (OPM), which was designed to provide policy leadership, and the **Merit Systems Protection Board** (MSPB), which was responsible for investigations and appeals. Whereas previously the Civil Service Commission held both responsibilities, the workload would be divided and the old CSC would be abolished; 2) the **Senior Executive Service** (SES) was formed, and it was created as a separate personnel system for high ranking civil service officials; 3) more flexibility within each agency to deal with their own personnel problems and issues; 5) establish federal based performance appraisal system; 6) create a merit pay system for managers below SES; 7) provide better protection for whistle blowers; 8) combine the work of the Equal Employment Opportunity program within the **Equal Employment Opportunity Commission**; and 9) and finally to create a more independent **Federal Labor Relations Authority**, which was designed to oversee changes in labor-management relations at the federal government level. (See Denhardt and Grubbs, 214–17; and Gordon and Milakovich, 1998, 281.)

22. Donald F. Kettl and James W. Fesler, *The Politics of the Administrative Process*, 3d ed. (Washington, DC: CQ Press, 2005), 86.

23. "Agencies Submitting Data to FPDS-NG as of December 11, 2008," The Project on Government Oversite. http://www.fpdsng.com/downloads/agency_data_submit_list.htm. Accessed December 18, 2008.

24. Henry, 334.

25. Ibid., 337.

26. Steven W. Hays and Richard C. Kearney, "Anticipated Changes in Human Resource Management: Views from the Field," *Public Administration Review* 61, no. 5 (September/October 2001): 585–97.

27. National Performance Review, *From Red Tape to Results: Creating a Government that Works Better and Costs Less* (Washington, DC: U.S. Government Printing Office, 1993).

28. Ibid., 20–26.

29. Hays and Kearney, 217.

30. Michael C. LeMay, *U. S. Immigration: A Reference Handbook* (Santa Barbara, CA: ABC-CLIO, 2004), 186.

31. United States Census Bureau, "2007 Census of Governments," http://www.census.gov/PressRelease/www/releases/archives/employment_occupations/012797.html, Accessed December 18, 2008.

32. Bureau of Labor Statistics, "Federal Government Excluding Postal Service," Updated March 12, 2008, Accessed December 18, 2008.

33. Henry, 257. Henry also cites the following: U.S. Merit Systems Protection Board, "Are New College Grads Landing Government Jobs?", *Issues of Merit* (September 2002): 4–5; Philip E. Crewson,

"Are the Best and the Brightest Fleeing Public Sector Employment? Evidence from the National Longitudinal Survey of Youth," *Public Productivity and Management Review* 20, no. 4 (1997): 363–371.

34. Office of Personnel Management, "An Analysis of Federal Employee Retirement Data," March 2008: http://www.opm.gov/feddata/RetirementPaperFinal_v4.pdf: Page 4. Accessed December 18, 2008.

35. LeMay, 189.

36. Henry, 256.

37. Office of Personnel Management. "About the SES," http://www.opm.gov/ses/about_ses/history.asp. Accessed: December 18, 2008.

38. See "Salary Table 2004-ES: Rates of Basic Pay for Members of the Senior Executive Service, Effective January 2004," U. S. Office of Personnel Management, www.opm.gov/oca/04tables/pdf/es.pdf (accessed October 2007).

39. For a summary of the law, see "SL 60001.675 *Intergovernmental Personnel Act of 1970*," Social Security Administration, www.ssa.gov/policy/poms.nsf/lnx/1960001675?opendocument (accessed July 2005).

40. Gordon and Milakovich, 1998, 262. For an extensive survey of results on the use of broad-banding, see Human Resources Management Panel, "Broadband Pay Experience in the Public Sector," National Academy of Public Administration (August 2003): 1–39. http://71.4.192.38/NAPA/NAPAPubs.nsf/17bc036fe939efd685256951004e37f4/0e93d959629dffd385256d9d004dbe30/$FILE/BroadbandPay Public-03-07.pdf (accessed October 2007).

41. National Commission on the State and Local Public Service, *Hard Truths/Tough Choices: An Agenda for State and Local Reform* (Albany, NY: Nelson A. Rockefeller Institute of Government, 1993).

42. LeMay, 191.

43. Henry, 257, 258. See also Lewis and Frank, 2002, 395–404.

44. John Nalbandian, "The U.S. Supreme Court's "Consensus" on Affirmative Action," *Public Administration Review* 49, no. 1 (January/February 1989): 38–45. Nalbandian examines how the Court analyzed *Griggs* and other affirmative action cases in order that it might justify the public employer to consider race in personnel actions and decisions.

45. Henry, 280.

46. Gordon and Milakovich, 265.

47. Most merit systems, whether at the national or sub-national levels, requires the top three candidates. (Note: In many instances this rule has expanded to include more than just the top three candidates). As you can imagine, this *rule of three* is controversial because it can be used to discriminate against women and ethnic minorities. Veterans also are able to receive additional points in the overall ranking system—simply because they are veterans. Other methods are becoming more acceptable, including web-based advertising and recruiting.

48. Gordon and Milakovich, 257–58.

49. Starling, 489.

50. See Evelina R. Moulder, "Salaries of Municipal Officials, 2000," in *The Municipal Yearbook 2001*, ed. International City/County Management Association (Washington, DC: ICMA, 2001), 91–114; and Evelina R. Moulder, "Salaries of County Officials, 2000" in *The Municipal Yearbook 2001*, ed. International City/County Management Association (Washington, DC: ICMA, 2001), 115–35.

51. Jonathan Walters, "Worth the Money?", *Governing* (July 2004): 34–37.

52. Even within public sector employees there are gaps. Consider the State of North Carolina's pay system for its top officials in the UNC system compared with counterparts in similar or the same non-educational based positions. According to the *Raleigh News and Observer*'s reporting of a 2004 study the average salary for lawyers at the three largest universities and the UNC system was $165,594, well above the norm for the state. UNC-Chapel Hill's top attorney, Leslie Strohm, for example, makes $230,000 which is more than double that of State Attorney General Roy Cooper. David McCoy, the state budget director, makes about $125,000, while Charles Leffler, the vice chancellor for finance and business at North Carolina State University, makes $203,000. In addition, the average salary for UNC chancellors was nearly $191,000, while cabinet members and Council of State secretaries drew a paltry $102, 264. "Something is wrong in Denmark," paraphrasing a famous saying. Some discussion has been made by states and localities at offering merit pay—and some in fact do offer some type of performance pay—but the amount of extra dollars to award the best employees is usually limited, given that it is dictated by tight budgets, compounded by lean revenues and high expenditures. Beyond these complications, the question of pay tied to performance is problematic. How does a state agency or municipal department award performance pay? How is the performance measured? And how is the performance pay apportioned? As we noted performance appraisal systems, which were established by the **Civil Service Reform Act of 1978**, tried to establish some fair method for evaluating how an employee's work performance was measured, but there was less emphasis on how to tie additional

pay to that enhanced performance. One way was through comparability to the private sector, with federal legislation (i.e. **Pay Comparability Act of 1990**) requiring federal agencies to close the pay gaps between the public and private sectors by up to 20 percent. Changing economic times, fluctuating budgets, and increasing budget deficits (except for a brief interlude during the second Clinton administration) have essentially prevented such reductions in pay gaps.

53. George R. Gray and others, "Training Practices in State Government Agencies," *Public Personnel Management* 26, no. 2 (Summer 1997): 187–202.

54. LeMay, 196–97.

55. Starling, 234.

56. The following ideas are drawn from Denhardt and Grubbs, 229–31.

57. Ibid., 231.

58. Some of the important public unions are the American Federation of State, County, and Municipal Employees (AFSCME), National Education Association (NEA), American Federation of Teachers (AFT), National Federation of Federal Employees, National Treasury Employees Union, Postal Workers Union, and the National Association of Letter Carriers. Each union is designed to promote and defend its members' positions, both economically and professionally. In addition, public labor unions are becoming more of a political force to be reckoned with, particularly at the state level, where some forty-three states have comprehensive labor-relations laws, most of which are favorable toward unions than similar federal laws.

59. Denhardt and Grubbs, 233.

60. Ibid., 143.

61. Henry, 263.

62. Philip H. Jos, Mark E. Tompkins, and Steven W. Hays, "In Praise of Difficult People: A Portrait of the Committed Whistleblower," *Public Administration Review* 49, no. 6 (November/December 1989): 555, 556, 558.

63. Ibid., 553.

64. Ibid., 554. See Table 1 for more results.

65. Henry cites several the results of surveys that point to not only successful allegations of whistleblowing, but that more individuals (approximately 50%) are willing to blow the whistle than were before the 1989 protection act was passed. See Henry, 264.

66. Starling, 472.

67. Denhardt and Grubbs, 240.

68. Henry, 277.

69. Ibid., 278.

70. *Firefighters Local Union #1784 v. Stotts* (1984).

71. *U.S. v. Paradise*, 480 U.S. 149 (1987).

72. Henry, 288 cites a survey done by Charlotte Steeh and Maria Krysan, "The Polls—Trends: Affirmative Action and the Public, 1970–1995," *Public Opinion Quarterly* 60 (Spring 1996): 144–45.

73. Nelson C. Dometrius and Lee Sigelman, "Assessing Progress Toward Affirmative Action Goals in State and Local Government: A New Benchmark," *Public Administration Review* 44, no. 3 (1984): 241–46.

74. Sylvester Murray and others, "The Role Demands and Dilemmas of Minority Public Administrators: The Herbert Thesis Revisited," *Public Administration Review* 54, no. 5 (September/October 1994): 409–17; James D. Slack, "Affirmative Action and City Managers: Attitudes Toward Recruitment of Women," *Public Administration Review* 47, no. 2 (March/April 1987): 199–206; and Pan Suk Kim and Gregory B. Lewis, "Asian Americans in the Public Service: Success, Diversity, and Discrimination," *Public Administration Review* 54, no. 3 (May/June 1994): 285–90.

Chapter 8

1. Nicholas Henry, *Public Administration and Public Affairs*, 9th ed. (Upper Saddle River, NJ: Prentice Hall, 2004), 243.

2. Robert W. Smith and Thomas D. Lynch, *Public Budgeting in America*, 5th ed. (Upper Saddle River, NJ: Prentice Hall, 2004), 71.

3. See Leonard D. White, *Introduction to the Study of Public Administration*, 4th ed. (New York: MacMillan, 1954), 239, 240; Leonard D. White, *The Federalist: A Study in Administrative History* (New York: MacMillan, 1956), 323; and Jerry L. McCaffery, "The Development of Public Budgeting

in the United States," in *A Centennial History of the American Administrative State,* ed. Ralph Clark Chandler (New York: The Free Press), 349–53.

4. McCaffery, 355.

5. Ibid., 357.

6. Ibid., 358, 359.

7. Allen Schick, *The Federal Budget: Politics, Policy, Process* (Washington, DC: Brookings Institution, 2000), 12.

8. Richard J. Stillman II, *Creating the American State: The Moral Reformers and the Modern Administrative World They Made* (Tuscaloosa, AL: The University of Alabama Press, 1998). See discussion of Frederick Cleveland, Frank J. Goodnow, and W.F. Willoughby in Aaron Wildavsky and Naomi Caiden, *The New Politics of the Budgetary Process,* 5th ed. (New York: Pearson Longman, 2004), 37.

9. Janet M. Kelly and William C. Rivenbark, *Performance Budgeting for State and Local Government* (Armonk, NY: M.E. Sharpe, 2003), 22.

10. For an extensive historical overview of municipal budgeting see Irene S. Rubin, *Class, Tax, and Power: Municipal Budgeting in the United States* (Chatham, NJ: Chatham House, 1998), 31–60.

11. Smith and Lynch claim that in 1929, A.E. Buck, staff personnel of the New York Bureau, was the first to document and write the first text on budgeting (p. 76).

12. Kelly and Rivenbark, 27.

13. Henry, 216.

14. Smith and Lynch, 78.

15. Ibid., 78, 79.

16. Kelly and Rivenbark, 31.

17. David Nice, *Public Budgeting* (Belmont, CA: Thomson-Wadsworth, 2002), 108, 110.

18. Smith and Lynch, 95, 96.

19. Aaron Wildavsky and Naomi Caiden, *The New Politics of the Budgetary Process,* 5th ed. (New York: Pearson Longman, 2003), 90.

20. Ibid., 96, 97.

21. Henry, 221.

22. Ibid., 222.

23. George J. Gordon and Michael E. Milakovich, *Public Administration in America,* 6th ed. (New York: St. Martin's Press, 1998), 316.

24. Janet V. Denhardt and Robert B. Denhardt, *The New Public Service: Serving, Not Steering* (Armonk, NY: M.E. Sharpe, 2003).

25. David Osborne and Ted Gaebler, *Reinventing Government: How the Entrepreneurial Spirit is Transforming the Public Sector* (Reading, MA: Addison-Wesley, 1992).

26. Ibid., 162–63.

27. For a more extensive analysis of "budgeting outcomes" and performance budgeting see David Osborne and Peter Hutchinson, *The Price of Government: Getting the Results We Need in an Age of Permanent Crisis* (New York: Basic Books, 2004), 65–93.

28. Henry, 236.

29. Kelly and Rivenbark, 36–41.

30. Osborne and Hutchinson, 84–87.

31. Charlie Tyer and Jennifer Willand, "Public Budgeting in America: A Twentieth Century Retrospective," Journal of Public Budgeting, Accounting and Financial Management 9, no. 2 (Summer 1997). Reprinted at www.ipspr.sc.edu/publication/Budgeting_in_America.htm (accessed October 2007).

32. This brief historical overview of the U.S. tax system was drawn from Fact Sheets, "History of the U. S. Tax System," U.S. Department of the Treasury, www.treas.gov/education/fact-sheets/taxes/ustax.shtml (accessed October 2007). For additional information see Alan O. Dixler, "Direct Taxes Under the Constitution: A Review of the Precedents," Tax Analysts, 20 November 2006, http://www.taxhistory.org/thp/readings.nsf/ArtWeb/2B34C7FBDA41D9DA8525730800067017?OpenDocument (accessed October 2007); and "A Brief History of U.S. Law on the Taxation of Americans Abroad," American Citizens Abroad, www.aca.ch/hisustax.htm (accessed October 2007).

33. Michael C. Lemay, *Public Administration: Clashing Values in the Administration of Public Policy* (Belmont, CA: Wadsworth, 2002), 269.

34. Jeffrey D. Greene, *Public Administration in the New Century: A Concise Introduction* (Belmont, CA: Wadsworth), 259.

35. Robert B. Denhardt and Joseph W. Grubbs, *Public Administration: An Action Orientation,* 4th ed. (Belmont, CA: Wadsworth, 2003), 167–68.

36. Ibid., 261.

37. Susan Crowley, "Legislative Guide to Local Property Tax," Iowa Legislative Service Agency, Legal Services Division (December 2007): 1, 2.

38. "Table 1. State and Local Government Finances by Level of Government and by State: 2004–2005," U.S. Census Bureau, http://www.census.gov/govs/estimate/0500ussl_1.html (accessed October 2007).

39. National Advisory Council on State and Local Budgeting, *Recommended Budget Practices: A Framework for Improved State and Local Government Budgeting* (Chicago, IL: Government Finance Officers Association, 1998), 3.

40. Wildavsky and Caiden, 2–3.

41. CNN, "Bush spells out $70 billion war-funding request," http://www.cnn.com/2008/POLITICS/05//02/war.funding/index.html. Accessed December 18, 2008.

42. For an interesting overview of both the positive and negative sides of congressional spending see the series of articles in *Extensions: A Journal of the Carl Albert Congressional Research and Studies Center* (Spring 2007), titled "Congress and Money."

43. Irene S. Rubin, *The Politics of Public Budgeting: Getting and Spending, Borrowing and Balancing*, 5th ed. (Washington, DC: CQ Press, 2006), 13.

44. Wildavsky and Caiden, 58.

45. Ibid., 58.

46. The following discussion is drawn from Martha Coven and Richard Kogan, "Introduction to the Federal Budget Process," Center on Budget and Policy Priorities (2004), www.allhealth.org/recent/audio_02-11-05/3-7-03.cbpp.budget-process.pdf; Robert Keith, "A Brief Introduction to the Federal Budget Process," *Congressional Research Service Report for Congress* (1996), www.house.gov/rules/96-912.htm (accessed October 2007); and Schick.

47. Keith.

48. "Overview of the President's 2006 Budget," White House, available from http://www.whitehouse.gov/omb/budget/fy2006/pdf/budget/overview.pdf (accessed October 2007).

49. Coven and Kogan, 5.

50. For a more complete coverage of the federal budget process see Schick, 2000, chapters five and six.

51. Keith.

52. Much of the information presented is drawn from Kelly and Rivenbark's excellent in-depth account of the state and local government budgeting process. Other sources include Osborne and Hutchinson's scathing account of the current fiscal crisis and methods for addressing this crisis in state and local governments and Thomas R. Dye and Susan A. MacManus's *Politics in States and Communities*, 11th ed. (Upper Saddle River, NJ: Prentice Hall, 2003) for an excellent overall perspective of the state and local budgeting process.

53. Dye and MacManus, 279.

54. Gerasimos A. Gianakis and Clifford P. McCue, *Local Government Budgeting: A Managerial Approach* (Westport, CT: Quorum, 1999), 3, 4.

55. Irene S. Rubin, *Class, Tax, and Power: Municipal Budgeting in the United States* (Chatham, NJ: Chatham House, 1998), 2.

56. Kelly and Rivenbark, 48. The majority of the discussion is taken from Kelly and Rivenbark's account of local budgeting process. Although no local government's budgeting process is the same as every other local government's process, there are similarities.

57. Ibid., 50.

58. Kelly and Rivenbark cite Robert J. Freeman and Craig D. Shoulders, *Governmental and Nonprofit Accounting,* 5th ed. (Upper Saddle River, NJ: Prentice-Hall, 1996).

59. Kelly and Rivenbark, 58.

60. Office of Management and Budget, "FY 2009 Summary Tables," http://www.whitehouse.gov/omb/budget/fy2009/summary table.html Accessed December 18, 2008.

61. Virginia Department of Planning & Budget, "2009 Executive Budget Document: Part B: Executive Budget 2008–2010 biennium: Total FY 2009," http://www.dpb.state.va.us/budget/buddoc09/index.cfm Accessed December 19, 2008.

62. City of Dunn, North Carolina, "Budget Adopted June 5 2008," http://www.dunn-nc.org/finance/downloads/Budget%20FY%202008-2009.PDF Accessed December 19 2008.

63. Henry, 241.

64. Ibid., 241.

65. For a general overview of the following discussion see Smith and Lynch, 2004, 105–7, and Henry, 241–42.

66. Jonathan Weisman, "Congress's Willingness to Tackle Deficit in Doubt," *Washington Post*, 16 April 2005, p. A06, www.washingtonpost.com/ac2/wp-dyn/A57535-2005Apr15 (accessed October 2007).

67. Ibid.

Chapter 9

1. Quoted directly from RAND Education, "How Educators in Three States Are Responding to Standards-Based Accountability Under No Child Left Behind," *Research Brief*, RAND Corporation, http://www.rand.org/pubs/research_briefs/RB9259/index1.html (accessed October 2007).

2. Ibid., 1.

3. Anderson is a political scientist who believes that the public interest exists, and second that it has some meaning relative to public policymaking. For example, he writes that "The task of government, it is often proclaimed, is to serve or promote the public interest. Statutes sometimes include the public interest as a guide for agency action, as when the Federal Communication Commission is directed license broadcasters for the "public interest, convenience, and necessity. In this section, this rather elusive normative concept and its usefulness as a criterion for decision-making will be discussed," James E. Anderson, *Public Policymaking*, 6th ed. (Boston, MA: Houghton Mifflin, 2006), 137.

4. David Easton, *The Political System: An Inquiry into the State of Political Science* (New York: Alfred A. Knopf, 1953).

5. Anderson, p. 20.

6. See David Truman's magnum opus *The Governmental Process: Political Interests and Public Opinion* (New York: Alfred A. Knopf, 1951).

7. Anderson quotes from Thomas Dye and Harmon Zeigler's conceptualization of elitist theory, p. 22. See Dye and Zeigler's *The Irony of Democracy*, 10th ed. (Belmont, CA: Wadsworth, 1996), 4–5.

8. See, for example, B. Guy Peters' *The Future of Governing: Four Emerging Models* (Lawrence, KS: University Press of Kansas, 1996).

9. The rate of growth of texts and trade books focusing on the relationship between religion and politics is nearly exponential. A popular text that is replete with examples, illustrations, and additional references is Robert Booth Fowler, Allen D. Hertzke, and Laura R. Olson's *Religion and Politics in America: Faith, Culture, and Strategic Choices*, 2d ed. (Boulder, CO: Westview, 1999). An excellent reader on the topic is Hugh Heclo and Wilfred M. McClay, eds. *Religion Returns to the Public Square* (Washington, DC: Woodrow Wilson Center Press, 2003).

10. An excellent historical overview of Arthur Schlesinger's concept is found in Sidney M. Milikis and Michael Nelson's *The American Presidency: Origins and Development 1776–2002*, 4th ed. (Washington, DC: CQ Press, 2003).

11. See Neustadt and Charles W. Dunn, *The Seven Laws of Presidential Leadership: An Introduction to the American Presidency* (Upper Saddle River, NJ: Pearson-Prentice Hall, 2007).

12. Kenneth J. Meier and John Bohte, *Politics and the Bureaucracy: Policymaking in the Fourth Branch of Government*, 5th ed. (Belmont, CA: Wadsworth, 2007).

13. Larry N. Gerston, Public Policymaking in a Democratic Society: A Guide to Civic Engagement (Armonk, NY: M.E. Sharpe, 2002).

14. See Lester M. Salamon, *Partners in Public Service: Government-Nonprofit Relations in the Modern Welfare State* (Baltimore, MD: The John Hopkins University Press, 1995).

15. See Anderson, pp. 88–90; 210, respectively.

16. Ibid., 86–89.

17. Roger W. Cobb and Charles D. Elder, *Participation in American Politics: The Dynamics of Agenda-Building*, 2d ed. (Baltimore, MD: The Johns Hopkins University Press, 1983).

18. John W. Kingdon, *Agendas, Alternatives, and Public Policies*, 2d ed. (New York: Harper Collins, 1995).

19. Ibid., 200–202.

20. Ibid., xv.

21. Susan L. Aud, "The Fiscal Impact of a Tuition Assistance Grant for Virginia's Special Education Students," *Issues in the State* (April 2007): 1–21.

22. Amy K. Frantz, "For the Children? No, for the Politicians!" *Policy Study*, no. 07-1 PUBLIC INTEREST INSTITUTE (August 2007): 1–18.

23. William N. Dunn, *Introduction to Policy Analysis*, 3d ed. (Upper Saddle River, NJ: Prentice Hall, 2004), 41–43.

24. Ibid., 41.

25. Ibid.; David Weimer and Aidan Vining, *Policy Analysis: Concepts and Practice* 4th ed. (Upper Saddle River, NJ: Prentice-Hall, 2005), 23–38.

26. Dunn, 216–17.

27. Ibid., 276.

28. Ibid., 280.

29. Robert B. Denhardt and Joseph W. Grubbs, *Public Administration: An Action Orientation*. 4th ed. (Belmont, CA: Wadsworth, 2003), 286.

30. Ibid., 287.

Chapter 10

1. Donald F. Kettl, *The Transformation of Governance: Public Administration for Twenty-First Century America* (Baltimore, MD: John Hopkins University Press, 2002), 127–29.

2. Edmund F. McGarrell, G. Brinker & D. Etindi, *The Role of Faith-Based Organizations in Crime Prevention and Justice* (Indianapolis, IN: Welfare Policy Center, Hudson Institute, 1999).

3. John J. DiIulio, Jr., *Living Faith: The Black Church Outreach Tradition* (New York: Manhattan Institute for Policy Research, 1998, No. 98-3); C. Winship & J. Berrien, "Boston Cops and Black Churches," *The Public Interest* 136 (1999): 52–68.

4. Nicholas Henry, *Public Administration and Public Affairs*, 9th ed. (Upper Saddle River, NJ, 2004), 331, 360.

5. Robert B. Denhardt and Joseph W. Grubbs, *Public Administration: An Action Orientation*, 4th ed. (Belmont, CA: Thomson-Wadsworth, 2004), 106.

6. Kettl writes, "Over the last several decades, the federal government's work has increasingly been carried out through an elaborate network of contracting, intergovernmental grants, loans and loan guarantees, regulations, and other indirect administrative approaches" (p. 129).

7. Theda Skocpol, *Diminished Democracy: From Membership to Management in American Civic Life* (Norman, OK: University of Oklahoma Press, 2003), 12.

8. Marvin Olasky, *The Tragedy of American Compassion* (Wheaton, IL: Crossway, 1992), 6.

9. Lester M. Salamon, *The Resilient Factor: The State of Nonprofit America* (Washington, DC: Brookings Institution, 2003), 1–2.

10. Peter Frumkin, *On Being Nonprofit: A Conceptual and Policy Primer* (Cambridge, MA: Harvard University Press, 2002), 10.

11. Ibid., 15.

12. Salamon, *Resilient Factor*, 7–8.

13. Gita Gulati-Partee., "A Primer on Nonprofit Organizations," *Popular Government* 66 no. 4 (Summer 2001): 31, http://www.publicintersection.unc.edu/pdf/aprimer-gita.pdf (accessed October 2007).

14. "Nonprofit Agenda: A Blueprint for Action," National Council of Nonprofit Associations, 1 July 2004, http://www.ncna.org/_uploads/documents/live/bluprint_pdf.pdf (accessed February 2005).

15. Salamon, *Resilient Factor*, 2.

16. Paul C. Light, "The Content of their Character: The State of the Nonprofit Workforce," *The Nonprofit Quarterly* 9, no. 3 (Fall 2002): 6.

17. Amy Blackwood, Kennard T. Wing, and Thomas H. Pollak. The Nonprofit Sector in Brief, Urban Institute Press, Washington, D.C., 2008, p. 1.

18. Ibid. p. 2.

19. Ibid. p. 2.

20. Ibid. pp. 3, 4, 5–6.

21. Blackwood, p. 6.

22. Charles Storch, "Illinois Has the Fifth-Largest Non-Profit Workforce in U.S.," Chicago Tribune, December 28, 2006, sec. 5, p. 4.

23. The Urban Institute, National Center for Charitable Statistics, "Quick Facts About Nonprofits," www.ncces.urban.org/statistics/quickfacts.cfm (October 13, 2008).

24. Jon Van Til, "Nonprofit Organizations and Social Institutions," in *The Jossey-Bass Handbook of Nonprofit Leadership and Management*, ed. Robert D. Herman (San Francisco, CA: Jossey-Bass, 1994), 47.

25. Lester M. Salamon, *Partners in Public Service: Government-nonprofit Relations in the Modern Welfare Estate* (Baltimore, MD: John Hopkins University Press, 1995).

26. Lydian Altman-Sauer, Margaret Henderson, and Gordon P. Whitaker, "Strengthening Relationships between Local Governments and Nonprofits," *Popular Government* 66, no. 2 (Winter 2001): 33–39, http://www.iog.unc.edu/pubs/electronicversions/pg/pgwin01/article4.pdf (accessed October 2007). Also, see Gordon P. Whitaker and Rosalind Day, "How Local Governments Work with Nonprofit Organizations in North Carolina," *Popular Government* 66, no. 2 (Winter 2001): 25–32, http://www.sog.unc.edu/pubs/electronicversions/pg/pgwin01/article3.pdf (accessed October 2007); and Margaret Henderson, Gordon P. Whitaker, and Lydian Altman-Sauer, "Establishing Mutual Accountability in Nonprofit-Government Relationships." *Popular Government* 69, no. 1 (Fall 2003): http://www.sog.unc.edu/pubs/electronicversions/pg/pgfal03/article3.pdf (accessed October 2007).

27. Altman-Sauer, Henderson, and Whitaker, 2001, 38.

28. Van Til, 62.

29. Skocpol.

30. See Denhardt and Grubbs, and Henry. Salamon notes the real problem is "a weakness in theory." He further notes "Both students of the voluntary sector and students of the welfare state have failed to appreciate or come to terms with the reality of extensive government-nonprofit relationships until relatively recently because of faults in the conceptual lenses through which they have been examining this reality" (*Partners in Public Service*, 35).

31. Salamon, *Partners in Public Service*, 37.

32. Ibid., 38.

33. See Charles Colson, *Justice That Restores* (Washington, DC: Prison Fellowship Ministries, 2001).

34. Ibid., 40.

35. Ibid., 41.

36. Ibid., 41.

37. Ibid., 14.

38. Salamon, *Partners in Public Service*, 44.

39. See Estelle James, "Commentary," in *Who Benefits from the Nonprofit Sector?*, ed. Charles T. Clotfelter (Chicago, IL: University of Chicago Press, 1992), 250–55.

40. Peter Dobkin Hall, "Historical Perspectives on Nonprofit Organizations," in *The Jossey-Bass Handbook of Nonprofit leadership and Management*, ed. Robert D. Herman (San Francisco, CA: Jossey-Bass, 1994), 3.

41. Ibid., 4.

42. See Hal G. Rainey, *Understanding and Managing Public Organizations,* 3d ed. (San Francisco, CA: Jossey-Bass, 2003), 59.

43. Hall, 5.

44. Skocpol, 6, 7.

45. She cites several prominent sociologists and other intellectuals that voluntary associations are best defined and developed separate from government. See Robert D. Putnam, *Bowling Alone: The Collapse and Revival of American Community* (New York: Simon and Schuster, 2000); and Michael Sandel, *Democracy's Discontent: American in Search of a Public Philosophy* (Cambridge, MA: Harvard University Press, 1996).

46. Hall, 6.

47. Ibid., 10.

48. Ibid., 12, 13.

49. Ibid., 15, 17.

50. Salamon, *America's Nonprofit Sector*, 56–57.

51. Hall, 18.

52. Ibid., 17.

53. Salamon, *America's Nonprofit Sector*, 59.

54. Hall, 21.

55. Ibid., 22–24.

56. Ibid., 24–25.

57. Ibid., 26.

58. Ibid., 26. See also Salamon, *Partners in Public Service*, 150.

59. Salamon, *Partners in Public Service*, 167.

60. Ibid., 161.

61. Hall, 27.

62. Salamon, *America's Nonprofit Sector*, 64, 65.

63. Salamon, *Partners in Public Service*, 155.

64. Salamon, *America's Nonprofit Sector*, 67.

65. Ibid., 67–70.

66. Ira C. Lupu and Robert W. Tuttle, *Government Partnerships with Faith-Based Service Providers: State of the Law* (Albany, NY: The Roundtable on Religion and Social Welfare Policy, 2002), 1.

67. Ibid., 124, 125.

68. Lewis D. Solomon, *In God We Trust? Faith-Based Organizations and the Quest to Solve America's Social Ills* (Lanham, MD: Lexington Books, 2003), 7.

69. Robert Wuthnow, *Saving America? Faith-Based Services and the Future of Civil Society* (Princeton, NJ: Princeton University Press, 2004), 140.

70. Ibid., 141.

71. Ibid., 6–7.

72. Solomon, 73.

73. Wuthnow, 28; and Solomon, 74.

74. John C. Green and Amy L. Sherman, *Fruitful Collaborations: A Survey of Government-Funded Faith-Based Programs in 15 States* (Charlottesville, VA: Hudson Institute, 2002), 18.

75. Stephen V. Monsma and J. Christopher Soper, *What Works: Comparing the Effectiveness of Welfare-to-Work Programs in Los Angeles* (Philadelphia: University of Pennsylvania, Center for Research on Religion and Urban Civil Society, 2003), 5.

76. Olasky, 10–16.

77. Ibid., 25–27.

78. Solomon, 50.

79. Olasky,136.

80. Rachel M. Haberkern, "Implementing Charitable Choice at the State and Local Levels," *Welfare Information Network: Issue Notes,* 6, no. 5 (July 2002), www.welfareinfo.org/implementingcharitablechoiceIN.htm (accessed October 2007).

81. Gretchen M. Griener. "Charitable Choice and Welfare Reform: Collaboration between State and Local Governments and Faith-Based Organizations," *Welfare Information Network: Issue Notes* 4, no. 12 (September 2000), www.financeprojectinfo.org/Publications/issuenotecharitablechoice.htm (accessed October 2007).

82. John Witte, Jr, *Religion and the American Constitutional Experiment: Essential Rights and Liberties* (Oxford: Westview Press, 2000), 183–84.

83. Lupu and Tuttle, 1–2.

84. President Bush, "Executive Order: Establishment of White House Office of Faith-Based and Community Initiatives," *Press Release*, Office of the Press Secretary, 29 January 2001, www.whitehouse.gov/news/releases/2001/01.htm (accessed October 2007).

85. James Q. Wilson and John J. DiIulio, *American Government*, 8th ed. (Boston: Houghton Mifflin, 2001), 5–6.

86. Byron R. Johnson with Ralph Brett Tompkins and Derek Webb, "Objective Hope: Assessing the Effectiveness of Faith-Based organizations: A Review of the Literature" (Philadelphia: University of Pennsylvania Center for Research on Religion and Urban Civil Society, 2002); Mark Ragan, Lisa M. Montiel, and Daniel J. Wright, "Scanning the Policy Environment for Faith-Based Social Services in the United States: Results of a 50-State Study," State University of New York, Rockefeller Institute of Government, http://www.rockinst.org/WorkArea/showcontent.aspx?id=8894 (accessed October 2007); and John L. Saxon, "Faith-Based Social Services: What Are They? Do They Work? Are They Legal? What's Happening in North Carolina?", *Popular Government* 70, no. 1 (Fall 2004), http://ncinfo.iog.unc.edu/pubs/electronicversions/pg/pgfal04/article1.pdf (accessed October 2007).

87. Light, *Making Nonprofits Work*; and Light, "The Content of their Character."

88. Salamon, *Resilient Factor.*

89. Berry and Arons.

90. Salamon, *Resilient Factor*, 15–34; 35–47.

Chapter 11

1. J. Claude Evans, "'. . . and Nathan Said to David': A Watergate Parallel," *The Christian Century* (27 June 1973): 706.

2. American Society for Public Administration, "Code of Ethics," http://www.aspanet.org/script content/index_codeofethics.cfm (accessed October 2007).

3. James Q. Wilson, *On Character* (Washington, D.C.: The AEI Press, 1991).

4. Ibid., 5.

5. Os Guinness, *Character Counts* (Grand Rapids, MI: Baker Books, 1999): 12.

6. Jim Morrill and Mark Johnson, "Three Face Inquiry Over N.C. Lottery," *Charlotte Observer*, 3 November 2005, http://www.charlotte.com/mld/charlotte/news (accessed November 2005).

7. U.S. Office of Government Ethics, *Executive Branch Employee Ethics Survey 2000: Final Report,* prepared by Arthur Anderson (Washington, DC, 2000), 7.

8. Connecticut Common Cause, "2004 Municipal Ethics Survey" (2005); Charlene Wear Simmons, Helen Roland, and Jennifer Kelly-DeWitt, California Research Bureau, "Local Government Ethics Ordinances in California" (Sacramento, CA: California State Library, 1998).

9. Nicholas Henry, *Public Administration and Public Affairs*, 9th ed. (Upper Saddle River, NJ: Pearson, 2004), 427.

10. Tom L. Beauchamp, Philosophical Ethics: An Introduction to Moral Philosophy, 3rd ed. (New York: McGraw-Hill, 2001): chapter 1.

11. Terry L. Cooper, ed., *Handbook of Administrative Ethics*, 2nd ed. (New York: Marcel Dekker, 2001).

12. Tom L. Beauchamp, *Philosophical Ethics: An Introduction to Moral Philosophy,* 3rd ed. (New York: McGraw-Hill, 2001): 150.

13. Bradley S. Chilton and Lisa M. Chilton, "Rebuilding the Public Service: Research the Origins of Public Perceptions of the Public Service in Children's Literature," *Review of Public Personnel Administration* 12 (1993): 72–78.

14. Terry L. Cooper, *An Ethic of Citizenship for Public Administration* (Englewood Cliffs, NJ: Prentice-Hall, 1991); Camilla Stivers, "Citizenship Ethics In Public Administration," in Terry L. Cooper, *Handbook of Administrative Ethics* (New York: Marcel Dekker, 2000): 583–602.

15. E.g., Richard T. Green, "Character Ethics and Public Administration," *International Journal of Public Administration* 17 (1994): 2137–2164; Larry Hubbell, "The Relevance of Heroic Myths to Public Servants," *American Review of Public Administration* 20 (1990): 139–154.

16. E.g., Alasdair MacIntyre, *After Virtue: A Study In Moral Theory*, 3rd ed. (Notre Dame, IN: University of Notre Dame Press, 2007); William D. Richardson, J. Michael Martinez, and Kerry R. Stewart, ed.s, *Ethics and Character: The Pursuit of Democratic Virtues* (Durham, NC: Carolina Academic Press, 1998).

17. Charlie D. Broad, *Five Types of Ethical Theory* (London: Routledge & Kegan, 1930): chapter 5; Tom L. Beauchamp, *Philosophical Ethics: An Introduction to Moral Philosophy*, 3rd ed. (New York: McGraw-Hill, 2001): 109.

18. Ralph Clark Chandler, "Deontological Dimensions of Administrative Ethics," in Terry L. Cooper, ed., *Handbook of Administrative Ethics,* 2nd ed. (New York: Marcel Dekker, 2000): 179–194.

19. A classic Judeo-Christian example of such "Natural Law" theories may be found in Russell Kirk, *The Roots of American Order* (Malibu, CA: Pepperdine University Press, 1974). An Islamic example may be found in Noel J. Coulson, *Conflicts and Tensions in Islamic Jurisprudence* (Chicago: University of Chicago Press, 1969).

20. W.D. Ross, *The Right and the Good* (Oxford, Eng.: Clarendon Press, 1930).

21. John Stuart Mill, *Utilitarianism* (London: Longmans, Green & Co., 1863): chapter 2.

22. Gerald M. Pops, "A Teleological Approach to Administrative Ethics," in Terry L. Cooper, ed., *Handbook of Administrative Ethics*, 2nd ed. (New York: Marcel Dekker, 2000), 195–206.

23. Guy B. Adams and Danny L. Balfour, *Unmasking Administrative Evil*, revised ed. (Armonk, NY: M.E. Sharpe, 2004).

24. Eugene P. Dvorin and Robert H. Simmons, *From Amoral to Humane Bureaucracy* (San Francisco, CA: Canfield Press, 1972).

25. Eugene P. Dvorin and Robert H. Simmons, *From Amoral to Humane Bureaucracy* (San Francisco, CA: Canfield Press, 1972): 19–26; Theodore J. Lowi, *The End of Liberalism: Ideology, Policy, and the Crisis of Public Authority* (New York: W.W. Norton, 1969): 85–92).

26. E.g., Allan Bloom, *The Closing of the American Mind: How Higher Education Has Failed Democracy and Impoverished the souls of Today's Students* (New York: Simon & Schuster, 1987); Richard B.

Brandt, *Ethical Theory* (Englewood Cliffs, NJ: Prentice-Hall, 1959): chapter 11, "Ethical Relativism"; John Ladd, ed., *Ethical Relativism* (Belmont, CA: Wadsworth, 1973).

27. E.g., Walter T. Stace, *The Concept of Morals* (New York: Macmillan, 1965): chapter 1, "Ethical Relativity and Ethical Absolutism."

28. Debra W. Stewart, Norman W. Sprinthall, and David M. Shafer, "Moral Development in Public Administration," in Terry L. Cooper, ed., *Handbook of Administrative Ethics* (New York: Marcel Dekker, 2000): 457–480.

29. Rushworth M. Kidder, "Universal Human Values: Finding an Ethical Common Ground," *Public Management* 77, no. 6 (1995): 4–9.

30. Terry Cooper, *The Responsible Administrator: An Approach to Ethics for the Administrative Role,* 4th ed. (San Francisco, CA: Jossey-Bass Publishers, 1998).

31. Debra W. Stewart, "Theoretical Foundations of Ethics in Public Administration: Approaches to Understanding Moral Action," *Administration and Society* 23, no. 3 (November 1991): 362.

32. John Rawls, *A Theory of Justice* (Cambridge, MA: Harvard University Press, 1971).

33. Debra W. Stewart, "Theoretical Foundations of Ethics in Public Administration: Approaches to Understanding Moral Action," *Administration and Society* 23, no. 3 (November 1991): 363.

34. This problem comes from Nicholas Henry, *Public Administration and Public Affairs*, 9th ed. (Upper Saddle River, NJ: Pearson, 2004): 440.

35. The majority of the discussion is drawn from two books by John Rohr. They include: *Ethics for Bureaucrats: An Essay on Law and Values,* 2d ed. (New York: Marcel Dekker, 1989); and *Public Service, Ethics and Constitutional Practice* (Lawrence, KS: University Press of Kansas, 1998).

36. Mark W. Huddleston and Joseph C. Sands, "Enforcing Administrative Ethics," *The Annals of the American Academy of Political and Social Science* 537 (January 1995): 139–150.

37. Rohr, *Ethics for Bureaucrats,* 68.

38. This thought is echoed by Waldo,103.

39. William D. Richardson and Lloyd G. Nigro, "The Constitution and Administrative Ethics," *Administration and Society* 23, no. 3 (November 1991): 285.

40. Ibid., 71.

41. Ibid., 75.

42. Stephen M. King, "Toward a New Administrative Ethic: An Understanding and Application of the Judeo-Christian Tradition to Administrative Issues." *Public Integrity* 2, no. 1 (Winter 2000): 17–28.

43. E.g., David J. Houston and Katherine E. Cartwright, "Spirituality and Public Service." *Public Administration Review* 67, no. 1 (January/February 2007): 88.

44. Jeffrey D. Greene, *Public Administration in the New Century: A Concise Introduction* (Belmont, CA: Thomson-Wadsworth, 2005), 369.

45. Dwight Waldo, *The Enterprise of Public Administration* (Novato, CA: Chandler and Sharp, 1988), 110.

46. Donald C. Menzel, "Spiritual Values in the PA Curriculum: Why or Why Not?" *Public Administration Times* (July 2005): 8.

47. Greene, 370.

48. Grenz, 211.

49. Karen Armstrong, *The Battle for God* (New York: Ballantine Books, 2000).

50. Alister E. McGrath, "In What Way Can Jesus Be a Moral Example for Christians?" *The Journal of Evangelical Theological Society* 34, no. 3 (September 1991): 289–98.

51. Lisa Sowle Cahill, "The New Testament and Ethics: Communities of Social Change," *Interpretation* 44 (October 1990): 383–95; and Stephen Charles Mott, "The Use of the New Testament, Part I," *Transformation* 1, no. 2 (April/June 1986): 21–26.

52. "Jesus and Public Administration," in *Handbook of Organization Theory and Management: The Philosophical Approach*, ed. Thomas D. Lynch and Todd J. Dicker (New York: Marcel Dekker, 1998), 57–68.

53. King, 21.

54. Willa Bruce, "Teaching Morality in Graduate Public Administration," paper prepared for presentation at the *Conference on Teaching Public Administration* (Tempe, AZ, February 4–5, 2001), 4, 5.

55. Stephen M. King, "A Proverbial Approach to Public Administration," *Public Voices* 7, no. 2 (2005): 28–40.

56. Harold F. Gortner, *Ethics for Public Managers* (New York: Greenwood, 1991), 19, 21.

57. Ibid., 20, 21; Waldo, 110, 111.

58. Melvin J. Dubnick and Barbara S. Romzek, *American Public Administration: Politics and the Management of Expectations* (New York: Macmillan, 1991), 76.

59. Henry, 436.

60. H. George Frederickson, "Accountability: The Word that ate Public Administration," *Public Administration Times* 28, no. 11 (November 2005): 11.

61. Debra W. Stewart, "Professionalism vs. Democracy: Friedrich vs. Finer Revisited." In *Public Administration in Action: Readings, Profiles, and Cases,* ed. Robert B. Denhardt and Barry R. Hammond (Pacific Grove, CA: Brooks Cole, 1992), 156.

62. Dubnick and Romzek, 77–82. Starling also describes a similar framework for public managers, p.180.

63. John A. Rohr, "An Address to the National Conference on Ethics in Public Administration," *Journal of Public Administration Research and Theory* 6, no. 4 (1996): 547–58.

64. Louis C. Gawthrop, "The Ethical Foundations of American Public Administration," *International Journal of Public Administration* 16, no. 2 (1993): 139–63; Brent Wall, "Assessing Ethics Theories from a Democratic Viewpoint," in *Ethical Frontiers in Public Management,* ed. James S. Bowman (San Francisco, CA: Jossey-Bass, 1991): 135–57; and Dwight Waldo, "Reflections on Public Morality," *Administration and Society* 6, no. 3 (1974): 267–82.

Chapter 12

1. Thomas L. Friedman, *The World is Flat: A Brief History of the 21st Century* (New York: Farrar, Straus and Giroux, 2005); *Hot, Flat, and Crowded: Why We Need a Green Revolution — And How It Can Renew America* (New York: Farrar, Straus and Giroux, 2008).

2. David Hazony, "David Hazony on *The World is Flat: A Brief History of the Twenty-First Century*," *Policy Review* (August/September 2005), www.printthis.clickability.com/pt/cpt?action=cpt&title= His+World+is+Flat&expire (accessed June 2007). Other reviews of Friedman's book include Clayton Jones, "Thomas Friedman Wants the Wired World to Let in the Other Half of Humanity," *The Christian Science Monitor*, 5 April 2005, www.csmonitor.com/20050405/p15s01-bogn.html (accessed June 2007); George Scialabba, "Zippie World!" *The Nation*, 13 June 2005, www.thenation.com/doc/20050613/ scialabba (accessed June 2007); Noel Malcolm, "Holy cow! We're shrinking," *Telegraph*, 5 August 2005, www.telegraph.co.uk/core/Content (accessed June 2007); Roberto J. Gonzalez, "Falling Flat: As the World's Boundaries Are Worn Smooth, Friedman Examines Changing Horizons," SFGate, 15 May 2005, www.sfgate.com/cgi-bin/article.cgi?file (accessed June 2007); and Michael Langan, "On the Level: Technology Has Created a Faster, Smaller, 'Flat' World," *Boston*, 3 April 2005, www.boston.com/ae/books/articles/2005/04/03/on_the_level?mode=PF (accessed June 2007).

3. James Q. Wilson, *Bureaucracy: What Government Agencies Do and Why They Do It* (New York: Basic Books, 1989), 376.

4. Louis C. Gawthrop, "The 1998 John Gaus Lecture: The Human Side of Public Administration," *PS: Political Science and Politics* 31, no. 4. (December 1998): 763–69.

5. Richard J. Stillman II, *The American Bureaucracy: The Core of Modern Government*, 3d ed. (Belmont, CA: Thomson-Wadsworth, 2004), 317.

6. In his "The Future of Public Administration: End of a Short Stay in the Sun? Or a New Day A-dawning?" *Public Administration Review* 56, no. 2, (March/April 1996): 139–48, Robert T. Golembiewski looks at public management as the future of public administration. John J. Kirlin and others have tried to focus on the "big questions" of public administration — obviously philosophical and theoretical in nature, but having distinct empirical implications. See his "Big Questions for a Significant Public Administration," *Public Administration Review* 61, no. 2, (March/April 2001): 140–43.

7. See Robert B. Denhardt and Joseph W. Grubbs, *Public Administration: An Action Orientation*, 4th ed. (Belmont, CA: Thomson-Wadsworth, 2003), 426–43; and Robert B. Denhardt, "The Future of Public Administration," *Public Administration and Management: An Interactive Journal* 4, no. 2 (1999): 279–92.

8. For an examination of public administration in a global context see Eric Welch and Wilson Wong, "Public Administration in a Global Context: Bridging the Gaps of Theory and Practice between Western and Non-Western Nations," *Public Administration Review* 58, no. 1 (January/February 1998): 40–49.

9. David Osborne and Peter Hutchinson, *The Price of Government: Getting the Results We Need in an Age of Permanent Fiscal Crisis* (New York: Basic Books, 2004).

10. See the following: Raymond W. Cox III, Susan J. Bush, and Betty N. Morgan, *Public Admin-*

istration in Theory and Practice (Englewood Cliffs, NJ: Prentice-Hall, 1994), 249–63; George J. Gordon and Michael E. Milakovich, *Public Administration in America*, 6th ed. (New York: St. Martin's Press, 1998), 455–83; David H. Rosenbloom and Robert S. Kravchuk, *Public Administration: Understanding Management, Politics, and Law in the Public Sector*, 6th ed. (Boston, MA: McGraw-Hill, 2005), 548–59; Melvin J. Dubnick and Barbara S. Romzek, *American Public Administration: Politics and the Management of Expectation* (New York: MacMillan, 1991), 379–91; H. George Frederickson, "The Repositioning of American Public Administration," *PS: Political Science and Politics* 32, no. 4 (December 1999): 701–11; and Carl E. Lutrin and Allen K. Settle, *American Public Administration: Concepts and Cases*, 3d ed. (Englewood Cliffs, NJ: Prentice-Hall, 1985), 470–92.

11. See Robert B. Reich, "Public Administration and Public Deliberation: An Interpretive Essay," *The Yale Law Journal* 94, no. 7 (1985): 1617–41.

12. See H. George Frederickson, "The Recovery of Civism in Public Administration," *Public Administration Review* 43, no. 6 (1982): 501–8.

13. See, for example, Richard C. Box, "Running Government Like a Business: Implications for Public Administration Theory and Practice," *American Review of Public Administration* 29, no. 1 (March 1999): 19–43; Richard C. Box and others, "New Public Management and Substantive Democracy," *Public Administration Review* 61, no. 5, (September/October 2001): 608–19; Robert B. Denhardt and Janet Vinzant Denhardt, "The New Public Service: Serving Rather than Steering," *Public Administration Review* 60, no. 6 (November/December 2000): 549–59; and Eran Vigoda, "From Responsiveness to Collaboration: Governance, Citizens, and the Next Generation of Public Administration," *Public Administration Review* 62, no. 5 (September/October 2002): 527–40.

14. Dubnick and Romzek, 388; Denhardt and Grubbs, 439; Rosenbloom and Kravchuk, 552; and David Schuman and Dick W. Olufs III, *Public Administration in the United States*, 2d ed. (Lexington, MA: D.C. Heath and Company, 1993), 506.

15. See Curtis Ventriss, "Toward a Public Philosophy of Public Administration: A Civic Perspective of the Public," *Public Administration Review* 49, no. 2 (March/April 1989): 173–79.

16. Box, "Running Government Like a Business"; Box and others, "New Public Management"; and Denhardt and Denhardt.

17. Stillman, 343.

18. Denhardt and Grubbs, 439.

Index

Tables are indicated with a **bold** T and figures are indicated by a **bold Fig** after the page number on which they appear. Book titles and case names are in *italic* font.